INTRODUCTION TO

# ECONOMICS

THE WEALTH AND POVERTY OF NATIONS

INTRODUCTION TO

# ECONOMICS

## THE WEALTH AND POVERTY OF NATIONS

James D. Gwartney
*Florida State University*

Richard L. Stroup
*Montana State University*

**The Dryden Press**
**Harcourt Brace College Publishers**
Fort Worth Philadelphia San Diego New York Orlando Austin San Antonio
Toronto Montreal London Sydney Tokyo

| | |
|---|---|
| Publisher | Liz Widdicombe |
| Acquisitions Editor | Rick Hammonds |
| Developmental Editor | Daryl Fox |
| Project Editor | Joan Harlan |
| Associate Project Editor | Matt Ball |
| Production Manager | Mandy Manzano |
| Art Director | Jeanette Barber |
| Copy Editor | Maggie Jarpey |
| Indexer | Sonsie Carbonara Conroy |
| Compositor | Clarinda Co. |
| Art Program | Tech Graphics |



ISBN: 0-03-098291-X

Library of Congress Catalog Card Number: 93-70946

Printed in the United States of America

3 4 5 6 7 8 9 0 1 2 032 9 8 7 6 5 4 3 2 1

The Dryden Press
Harcourt Brace College Publishers

*To our students,*
*who have helped us think*
*through many of these issues*
*and contributed to our*
*understanding of them.*

# THE DRYDEN PRESS SERIES IN ECONOMICS

Asch and Seneca
*Government and the Marketplace*
Second Edition

Baumol and Blinder
*Economics: Principles and Policy*
Sixth Edition (also available in micro and macro paperbacks)

Baumol, Panzar, and Willig
*Contestable Markets and the Theory of Industry Structure*
Revised Edition

Berch
*The Endless Day: The Political Economy of Women and Work*

Breit and Elzinga
*The Antitrust Casebook: Milestones in Economic Regulation*
Second Edition

Brue
*The Evolution of Economic Thought*
Fifth Edition

Demmert
*Economics: Understanding the Market Process*

Dolan and Lindsey
*Economics*
Seventh Edition (Also available in micro and macro paperbacks)

Eckert and Leftwich
*The Price System and Resource Allocation*
Tenth Edition

Edgmand, Moomaw, and Olson
*Economics and Contemporary Issues*
Second Edition

Friedman
*Milton Friedman Speaks* (Video)

Gardner
*Comparative Economic Systems*

Green
*Intermediate Macroeconomics*

Gwartney and Stroup
*Economics: Private and Public Choice*
Sixth Edition (Also available in micro and macro paperbacks)

Gwartney and Stroup
*Introduction to Economics: The Wealth and Poverty of Nations*

Heilbroner and Singer
*The Economic Transformation of America: 1600 to the Present*
Second Edition

Hirsch and Rufolo
*Public Finance and Expenditure in a Federal System*

Hirschey and Pappas
*Fundamentals of Managerial Economics*
Fourth Edition

Hirschey and Pappas
*Managerial Economics*
Seventh Edition

Hoerneman, Howard, Wilson, and Cole
*CAPER: Computer Assisted Program for Economic Review*

Hyman
*Public Finance: A Contemporary Application of Theory to Policy*
Fourth Edition

Kaufman
*The Economics of Labor Markets*
Fourth Edition

Keating and Wilson
*Fundamentals of Managerial Economics*

Keating and Wilson
*Managerial Economics*
Second Edition

Kennett and Lieberman
*The Road to Capitalism: The Economic Transformation of Eastern Europe and the Former Soviet Union*

Kidwell, Peterson, and Blackwell
*Financial Institutions, Markets, and Money*
Fifth Edition

Kohn
*Money, Banking, and Financial Markets*
Second Edition

Kreinin
*International Economics: A Policy Approach*
Sixth Edition

Link, Miller, and Bergman
*EconoGraphII: Interactive Software for Principles of Economics*

Lott and Ray
*Applied Econometrics with Data Sets*

Nicholson
*Intermediate Microeconomics and Its Application*
Sixth Edition

Nicholson
*Microeconomic Theory: Basic Principles and Extensions*
Fifth Edition

Ormiston
*Intermediate Microeconomics*

Puth
*American Economic History*
Third Edition

Ragan and Thomas
*Principles of Economics*
Second Edition (Also available in micro and macro paperbacks)

Ramanathan
*Introductory Econometrics with Applications*
Second Edition

Rukstad
*Corporate Decision Making in the World Economy: Company Case Studies*

Rukstad
*Macroeconomic Decision Making in the World Economy: Text and Cases*
Third Edition

Samuelson and Marks
*Managerial Economics*

Scarth
*Macroeconomics: An Introduction to Advanced Methods*
Third Edition

Thomas
*Economics: Principles and Applications*
(Also available in micro and macro paperbacks)

Wachtel
*Labor and the Economy*
Third Edition

Walton and Rockoff
*History of the American Economy*
Seventh Edition

Welch and Welch
*Economics: Theory and Practice*
Fourth Edition

Yarbrough and Yarbrough
*The World Economy: Trade and Finance*
Third Edition

## The Harcourt Brace College Outline Series

Emery
*Principles of Economics: Macroeconomics*

Emery
*Principles of Economics: Microeconomics*

Emery

# PREFACE

This book is designed to help students think seriously about the vital questions of economics: Why do people and nations prosper? When do markets work well? What can governments do to promote economic prosperity? It is easy for students of economics—perhaps distracted by new terminology, graphs, formulas, and the like—to lose sight of the central issues. Our objective is to keep that from happening.

The linkage between economic organization and the creation of wealth is the *central theme* of this book. Economics does not provide a precise recipe for material progress. It does, however, indicate several important ingredients—factors that contribute to the economic success of nations. We will highlight these sources of prosperity with the icon shown here and take the time to explain *why* they are important and *how* they contribute to economic progress.

Our central *objective* is to help the reader develop the economic way of thinking. This method of thinking is based on certain concepts that to a large degree are merely common sense, but when woven together in a logical manner, form a powerful tool of analysis. The economic way of thinking can help us better understand complex issues and differentiate between sound arguments and economic nonsense.

Three characteristics of this book will make it both interesting and user-friendly. *First, the text highlights the linkage between basic principles and economic progress.* We believe that most textbooks attempt to cover too many topics. As a result, they often fail to get across the importance of a relatively small number of factors that are central to the understanding of economic progress. Division of labor, mass-production methods, specialization and comparative advantage, capital formation, and improvements in technology provide the technical foundation of our modern living standards. The freedom to act in ways that result in gains from these sources, together with a mechanism that imposes the costs and confers the benefits on decision-makers, comprise the institutional basis for prosperity and growth. We explain why these factors are important sources of economic progress and analyze how the realization of gains from these sources is influenced by various economic policies and institutions. In addition, many of the exercises at the end of each chapter are designed to clarify the relationship between the basic concepts of economics and prosperity of nations.

*Second, we often use data from numerous countries to illustrate basic principles and the impacts of alternative policies* (see p. xxxi). The world is the laboratory of the economist. We can learn a great deal about economics by observing differences in economic outcomes across countries that have followed different economic paths. Nations around the world, particularly those of Latin America, Eastern Europe, and the former Soviet Union, are restructuring their political economy institutions and searching for policies that work. The global approach of this text will provide students with a greater appreciation for these events.

*Third, this text is a self-contained learning package.* Material that would normally be in a student workbook is incorporated into the text. Each chapter of the text includes learning exercises in the form of critical-analysis questions, a multiple-choice self-test, and problems. These exercises will increase student involvement and understanding. Answers for many of these questions are provided in Appendix A. This will make it easy for students to test their understanding of the material as they cover each chapter. Liberal use of examples and empirical data complement the analysis. This is a user-friendly text.

Our experience in writing and teaching principles of economics for more than two decades has made us painfully aware of an unpleasant fact: even good students can fail to understand the significance of many basic economic concepts (for example, comparative advantage, economies of scale, and gains from trade). It is one thing to know what a concept is and another to see why it is important. This text attempts to help students appreciate the significance of each concept by providing several examples and exercises, and, where possible, empirical evidence. Our approach reflects this strategy of showing why something is important as we explain it.

An introductory economics course cannot cover everything. This text focuses on a limited number of topics that are central to economic understanding and literacy. We have sought to cover these topics comprehensively and with clarity. We believe that an in-depth understanding of a few basic concepts is more important than surface knowledge of a wide range of topics. Our experience suggests that this approach will challenge students to think more seriously about the economic concepts and issues that will affect their lives long after the final exam is a faded memory.

## Organizational Features

We have employed several organizational features designed to make the presentation both more interesting and more understandable.

1. *Myths of Economics* In a series of boxed articles, commonly held fallacies of economic reasoning are dispelled. Each myth is followed by a concise explanation of why it is incorrect and each one is presented within a chapter containing closely related material.
2. *Chapter Focus Questions and Closing Summaries* Each chapter begins with several questions that summarize the focus of the chapter. A summary, which provides the student with a concise statement of the material (chapter learning objectives), appears at the end of each chapter. Reviewing the focus questions and chapter summaries will help the student better understand the material and integrate it into the broader economic picture.
3. *Key Terms* The terminology of economics is often confusing to introductory students. Key terms are introduced in the text in bold type; simultaneously, each term is defined in the margin opposite the first reference to the term. A glossary containing the key terms also appears at the end of the book.
4. *Study Guide* Each chapter concludes with a set of critical-analysis questions, a short multiple-choice self-test, and several problems designed to encourage student involvement and provide students with immediate feedback on their understanding of the material. Appendix A at the end of the text provides suggested answers for these exercises. These exercises illustrate the power of economics and will help students develop the economic way of thinking.

## Supplementary Materials

**TESTBANK** The accompanying testbank contains approximately 3,000 multiple-choice questions and 300 problem-and-analysis questions. The multiple-choice questions of each chapter are organized according to the major headings within the chapter. The testbank materials are also available on computer disk. The ExaMaster System of the computerized testbank version makes it easy to create tests, print scrambled versions of the same test, modify questions, and reproduce the graphic questions. The testbank contains a large number of graphical questions.

***INSTRUCTOR'S MANUAL*** The *Instructor's Manual* for the text was prepared by Professors Woody Studenmund and Robby Moore of Occidental College. The manual contains teaching tips, additional problems suitable for homework assignments, and suggested answers to critical-analysis questions that were not answered in Appendix A of the textbook.

**Color Transparencies** Color transparencies of the major exhibits of the book have been specially prepared for overhead projectors. They are available to adopters upon request.

**Video Packages** Following are video packages to supplement the text:

*Economics in Focus,* a video series, facilitates multi-level learning and critical thinking through its up-to-date coverage of current events in our society, while focusing on economic issues important to students and their understanding of the economy. Recent segments from *MacNeil/Lehrer News Hour* are updated quarterly.

These videos look at three major themes:

- *International Economic Scene* covers free trade, foreign policy, and other issues.
- *Economic Challenges and Problems* explores topics such as declining incomes, the budget deficit, and inflation.
- *The Political Economy* looks at the role of the government, free enterprise, and economic stabilization.

Each issue of *Economics in Focus* closes with a special feature story or one-to-one interview with a noted economist.

*Milton Friedman's Free to Choose* video series is available in ten half-hour videotapes. These videos update the earlier series, *Milton Friedman Speaks,* by including introductions by Arnold Schwarzenegger, George Schultz, Steve Allen, David Friedman, and Ronald Reagan.

**Laser Disks** This package contains a microeconomics disk and a macroeconomics disk. Each one focuses on the core principles and presents the information interactively. A brief 5–7 minute video from CBS begins each learning section. Related animated graphics follow. Once students understand the concepts, they are then challenged with critical-thinking questions. A printed *Media Instructor's Manual* explains how the laser disks coordinate with *Introduction to Economics: The Wealth and Poverty of Nations.*

## Acknowledgments

We would like to express our appreciation to Ed Bierhanzl, Mary Hirschfeld, Robby Moore, Russell Sobel, and Woody Studenmund for their preparation of supplementary materials accompanying the textbook and the general encouragement they have provided. We would also like to thank Valerie Nicholson Colvin for her assistance in the preparation of the manuscript and Jane Shaw Stroup and Amy Gwartney for their editorial assistance. Manuscript reviewers dramatically improved the quality of this text. They include Douglas Agbetsiafa, Indiana University—Southbend; David Hammes, University of Hawaii—Hilo; Bill Knight, Prince Georges Community College; Don Leet, California State University—Fresno; Brian Moehring, Ball State University; Kit Taylor, Bellevue Community College; Don Wells, University of Arizona; and Nora Wujcik, Central Virginia Community College.

We are also indebted to the excellent team of professionals at The Dryden Press: Rick Hammonds, senior acquisitions editor, Daryl Fox, senior developmental editor, Joan Harlan, senior project editor, Matt Ball, associate project editor, Jeanette Barber, art director, and Mandy Manzano, production manager.

James D. Gwartney
Richard L. Stroup

# A Note to Students

This text contains several features that we think will help you get the most from your study effort. Our past experience indicates that awareness of the following points will help you use the book more effectively.

- Each chapter begins with a series of focus questions that communicate the central issues of the chapter. Before you read the chapter, briefly think about the focus questions, why they are important, and how they relate to the material of prior chapters.
- The textbook is organized in the form of an outline. The headings within the text are the major points of the outline. The minor headings indicate the subpoints under the major headings. In addition, important subpoints within sections are often set off and numbered. Sometimes thumbnail sketches are used to help the reader better organize important points. Careful use of the headings and thumbnail sketches will help you better visualize the organization of the material.
- A summary appears at the end of each chapter. Use the summary as a checklist to determine whether or not you understand the major points of the chapter.
- Review of the exhibits will also provide you with a summary of each chapter. The accompanying legend briefly describes the content and analysis of each exhibit. After studying the chapter, briefly review the exhibits to ensure that you have mastered the central points.
- The key terms introduced in each chapter are defined in the margins. As you study the chapter, go over the marginal definition of each key term as it is introduced. Later, you may also find it useful to review the marginal definitions. If you have forgotten the meaning of a term introduced earlier, consult the glossary at the end of the book.
- The boxed features provide additional depth on various topics without disrupting the flow of the text. In general, the topics of

the boxed features have been chosen because of their relevance as an application of the theory and because of student interest in the topic. Reading the boxed features will supplement the text and enhance your understanding of important economic concepts.

- The study-guide material at the end of the chapter stresses the major points of the chapter and provides you with an opportunity to test your understanding of the material. Answers to most of the study-guide questions and exercises are provided in Appendix A.

# Contents in Brief

# Contents

# PART II MICROECONOMICS 95

## PART V THE WEALTH AND POVERTY OF NATIONS 513

# Comparative International Data on Economic Policy and Performance

# Comparative International Data on Economic Growth and Performance

# PART I

## THE ECONOMIC APPROACH AND THE MARKET PROCESS

CHAPTER

1

# THE ECONOMIC WAY OF THINKING

It [economics] is a method rather than a doctrine, an apparatus of the mind, a technique of thinking which helps its possessor to draw correct conclusions.

*J. M. Keynes, 1923*[1]

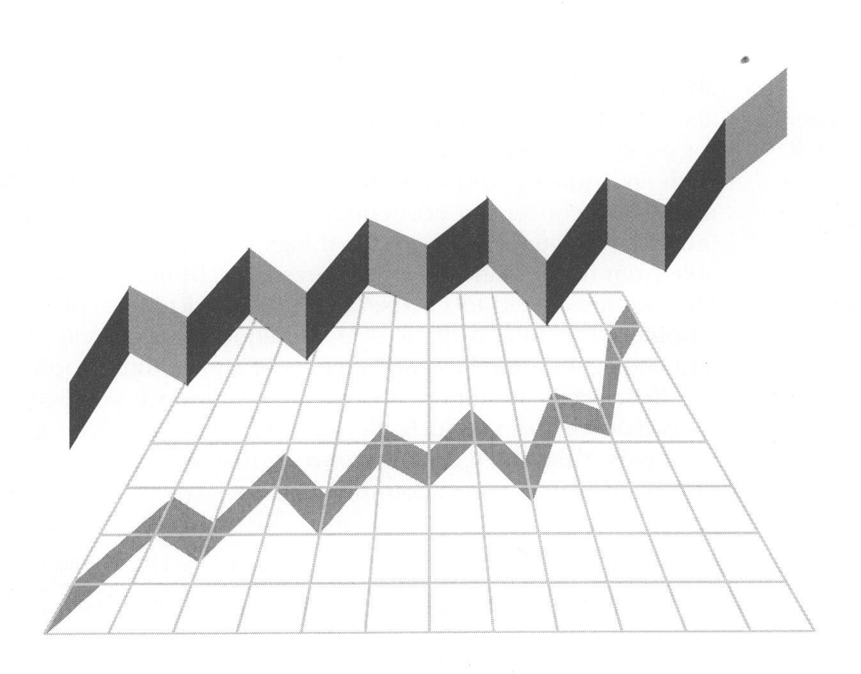

## CHAPTER FOCUS

- What is economics about? What are the basic ingredients of an economic problem?
- What is the economic way of thinking? What are the basic elements of this method of thinking?
- What limits our ability to produce? How can we expand our production possibilities?
- How do the income levels of nations vary? Do the poor nations remain poor, while the rich nations remain rich?

The study of economics is relevant for many different professions, since the "economic way of thinking" is a helpful tool in decision-making. Moreover, an understanding of economic events and policy alternatives is an asset to everyone living in this rapidly changing world of ours. While discussing the state of the economy in the former Soviet Union, a Russian woman recently told one of the authors, "We know what doesn't work. Now we are trying to figure out what will work." The goal of this book is to help provide those answers. Basic economic principles indicate that certain conditions are vitally important for economic progress. Throughout, we will focus on what these conditions are and explain why they are important.

## SCARCITY AND CHOICE

Would you like some new clothes, a nicer car, *and* a larger apartment? How about better grades *and* more time to watch television, go skiing *and* travel abroad? Most of us would like more of all of these **goods.** The human desire for goods is virtually unlimited. We cannot, however, have more of everything. Both individually and collectively we face a constraint called **scarcity,** the most basic concept in economics. Scarcity is the term used by economists to indicate that people's desire for things is far greater than what is freely available from nature. Since scarcity prevents us from having as much as we would like, we are forced to choose among a restricted set of potential alternatives. **Choice,** therefore, is the logical consequence of scarcity. These two—scarcity and choice—are the basic ingredients of an economic topic.

**good** Anything that people find desirable and therefore would like to have or consume.

**scarcity** Fundamental concept of economics which indicates that less of a good is freely available than consumers would like.

**choice** The act of selecting among alternatives.

**resource** An input used to produce economic goods. Land, labor, skills, natural resources, and capital are examples.

**Resources** are inputs that we use to produce goods. In essence, they are tools that we can use to battle scarcity. There are three general categories of resources. First, there are *human resources,* the knowledge, skill, and strength of human beings. Education, training, and experience can increase the future

[1]John Maynard Keynes (1883–1946) was an English economist whose writings during the 1920s and 1930s exerted an enormous impact on both economic theory and policy. Keynes established the terminology and the economic framework that are still widely used today when economists study problems of unemployment and inflation.

availability of human resources. Second, there are *physical resources,* things like tools, machines, and buildings that enhance our ability to produce goods. Economists often use the term **capital** when referring to these man-made resources. Third, there are *natural resources*—things like land, mineral deposits, oceans, and rivers. The ingenuity of humans is often required in order to transform these natural resources into useful productive inputs.

**capital** A man-made resource.

With the passage of time, the availability of resources can be expanded, but only at the expense of correct consumption. If we use more of today's resources to produce tools, machines, and factories, fewer resources will be available to produce consumption goods like food, clothing, and recreation. Economics is about trade-offs.

During the last 250 years, we have loosened the grip of scarcity a little. Think for a moment what life was like in 1750. People all over the world struggled 50, 60, and 70 hours a week to obtain the basic necessities of life—food, clothing, and shelter. Manual labor was the major source of energy. Animals provided the means of transportation. Tools and machines were primitive by today's standards. As the English philosopher Thomas Hobbes put it, life was "solitary, poor, nasty, brutish, and short."

Throughout much of South America, Africa, and Asia, economic conditions continue to be exceedingly difficult. In North America, Western Europe, Oceania, and Japan, however, substantial economic progress has been made. Of course, scarcity is still a fact of life in these areas, too; the desire for goods and services still far outstrips the ability of people to produce them. But from a material standpoint, life is now far less grueling. Petroleum, electricity, and nuclear power have replaced human and animal power as the major sources of energy. Automobiles, airplanes, and trains are now the major means of transportation. Subsistence levels of food, shelter, and clothing are taken for granted, and the typical family in these areas worries instead about financing summer vacations, obtaining videocassette recorders, and providing for the children's college education.

It is important to note that scarcity and poverty are not the same thing. Poverty implies some basic level of need, either in absolute or relative terms. Absence of poverty means that the basic level has been attained. In contrast, the absence of scarcity would imply that we have as much of all goods as we would like. Both individuals and countries may win the battle against poverty—people may achieve income levels that allow them to satisfy a basic level of need. But it is painfully obvious that we will not triumph over scarcity. Even in the wealthiest of countries, productive capabilities cannot keep pace with material desires. People always want more goods and services than they have.

## ECONOMIC WAY OF THINKING

One does not have to spend much time around economists to recognize that there is an "economic way of thinking." Admittedly, economists, like others, differ widely in their ideological views. A news commentator once remarked that "any half-dozen economists will normally come up with about six different policy prescriptions." Yet, in spite of their philosophical differences, there is a common ground in the approach of economists.

**economic theory** A set of definitions, postulates, and principles assembled in a manner that makes clear the "cause-and-effect" relationships of economic data.

That common ground is **economic theory,** developed from basic postulates of human behavior. Economic theory, like a road map or a guidebook, establishes reference points indicating what to look for, and how economic issues are interrelated. To a large degree, the basic economic principles are merely common sense. When applied consistently, however, these common-sense concepts can provide interesting and powerful insights. They are an aid to logical thinking and can help us focus on the central issues.

## Eight Guideposts to Economic Thinking

The economic way of thinking requires the incorporation of certain guidelines—some would say the building blocks of basic economic theory—into one's thought process. Once these guidelines are incorporated, we believe that economics can be a relatively easy subject to master. Students who have difficulty with economics have almost always failed to assimilate these principles. We will outline and discuss eight principles that characterize economic thinking and that are essential to the understanding of the economic approach.

**opportunity cost** The highest valued benefit that must be sacrificed (forgone) as the result of choosing an alternative.

**1. The use of scarce resources to produce a good is always costly.** The use of resources to produce one good diverts the resources away from the production of other goods that are also desired. The highest valued alternative that must be sacrificed is the **opportunity cost** of an option. For example, if you use one hour of your scarce time to study economics, you will have one hour less time to watch television, read magazines, sleep, work at a job, or study other subjects. The cost of the study time for other subjects may be the highest valued option that you will now have to forgo because of the additional time spent studying economics. Or perhaps time spent working at a job, or even time spent sleeping might be viewed as your highest valued option forgone. The cost of an action is always the highest valued option that must now be sacrificed because you chose the action.

If the residents of a community choose to build a new civic auditorium, the opportunity cost of the building is the highest valued option—perhaps a new hospital—that must now be forgone because the resources used to produce the auditorium are now unavailable for other uses. It is important to recognize that the "scarce resources have a cost" concept is true regardless of who pays for the good or service produced. In many countries, various kinds of schooling are provided free of charge to students. However, provision of the schooling is not free to the community. Buildings, books, and teachers' salaries must be paid for from tax revenues, which the taxpayer could have used for other goods and services. The scarce resources used to produce the schooling could have been used instead to produce more recreation, entertainment, housing, or other goods. The cost of the schooling is the highest valued option that must now be given up because the resources required for its production were instead used to produce the schooling.

By now the central point should be obvious. Economic thinking recognizes that the use of a scarce resource always involves a cost. The use of more resources to do one thing implies fewer resources with which to achieve other objectives.

**2. Decision-makers choose purposefully; therefore, they will economize.** Since resources are scarce, decision-makers seek to choose wisely and avoid wasting their valuable resources. Recognizing the restrictions imposed by the limited resources available to them (income, time, talent, and so on), they try to select the options that best advance their own personal objectives. In turn, the objectives or preferences of individuals are revealed by the choices they make. **Economizing behavior** results directly from purposeful decision-making. Economizing individuals will seek to accomplish an objective at the least possible cost to themselves. When choosing among things that yield equal benefit, an economizer will select the cheapest option. For example, if a pizza, lobster dinner, and a prime sirloin steak are expected to yield identical benefits, economizing behavior implies that the cheapest of the three alternatives, probably the pizza, will be chosen. Correspondingly, when choosing among alternatives of equal cost, economizing decision-makers will select the option that yields the greatest benefit. Purposeful decision-makers will not deliberately pay more for something than is necessary.

**economizing behavior** Decisions that are based on the objective of gaining a specific benefit at the least possible cost. A corollary of economizing behavior implies that when choosing among items of equal cost, individuals will choose the option that yields the greatest benefit.

Purposeful choosing implies that decision-makers have some basis for their evaluation of alternatives. Economists refer to this evaluation as **utility,** the benefit or satisfaction that an individual expects from the choice of a specific alternative. The utility of an alternative is highly subjective, often differing widely from person to person.

**utility** The benefit or satisfaction expected from a choice or course of action.

**3. Incentives matter—human choice is influenced in a predictable way by changes in economic incentives.** This guidepost to clear economic thinking might be called the basic postulate of all economics. As the personal benefits from choosing an option increase, other things constant, a person will be more likely to choose that option. In contrast, as the personal costs associated with the choice of an item increase, the individual will be less likely to choose that option. For a group, this basic economic postulate suggests that making an option more attractive will influence more people to choose it. In contrast, as the cost of a selection to the members of a group increases, fewer of them will make this selection.

This basic postulate of economics is a powerful tool because its application is so widespread. Incentives affect behavior in virtually all aspects of our lives, ranging from market decisions about what to buy to political choices at election time.

According to this basic postulate, how will consumers react if the price of beef increases (relative to other goods)? Since the higher beef prices make beef consumption more expensive, the basic postulate indicates that consumers will be less likely to choose it. The predicted result is a decline in the amount of beef consumed as the result of the increase in its price.

As another example of its broad application, let us apply this basic postulate of economics to the examination process. If a classroom instructor makes it more costly to cheat, students will be less likely to do so. There will be little cheating on a closely monitored, individualized, essay examination. Why? Because it is difficult (that is, costly) to cheat on such an exam. Suppose, however, that an instructor gives an objective "take-home" exam, basing students' course grades entirely on the results. More students will be likely to cheat because the benefits of doing so will be great and the risk (cost) minimal.

The "incentives matter" postulate is just as applicable to human behavior under socialism as under capitalism. For example, at one time in the former Soviet Union, the managers of glass plants were rewarded according to the

## MYTHS OF ECONOMICS

*"Economic analysis assumes people act only out of selfish motives. It rejects the humanitarian side of humankind."*

Probably because economics focuses on the efforts of individuals to satisfy material desires, many casual observers of the subject argue that its relevance hinges on the selfish nature of humankind. Some have even charged that economists, and the study of economics, encourage people to be materialistic rather than humanitarian.

This point of view stems from a basic misunderstanding of personal decision-making. Obviously, people act for a variety of reasons, some selfish and some humanitarian. The economist merely assumes that actions will be influenced by costs and benefits, as viewed by the decision-maker. As an activity becomes more costly, it is less likely that a decision-maker will choose it. As the activity becomes more attractive, it is more likely that it will be chosen.

The choices of both the humanitarian and the egocentric individual will be influenced by changes in personal costs and benefits. For example, both will be more likely to try to save the life of a small child in a three-foot swimming pool than in the rapid currents approaching Niagara Falls. Both will be more likely to give a needy person their hand-me-downs rather than their best clothes. Similarly, both will be more likely to support a policy that generates benefits for others (for example: farmers, the poor, or the elderly) when the personal cost of doing so is low. Incentives matter for both the humanitarian and the egocentric.

Observation would suggest that the right to control one's destiny is an "economic" good for most persons. Most of us would prefer to make our own choices rather than have someone else decide for us. But is this always greedy and selfish? If so, why do people often make choices in a way that is charitable toward others? After all, many people freely choose to give a portion of their wealth to the sick, the needy, the less fortunate, religious organizations, and charitable institutions. Economics does not imply that these choices are irrational. It does imply that if you make it more (less) costly to act charitably, fewer (more) persons will do so.

Economics deals with people as they are—not as we would like to remake them. Should people act more charitably? Perhaps so. But this is not the subject matter of economics.

tons of sheet glass produced. Not surprisingly, most plants produced sheet glass so thick that one could hardly see through it. The rules were changed so that the managers were rewarded according to the square meters of glass produced. Under the new rules, Soviet firms stretched their resources, producing very thin glass that was easily broken. Incentives matter in both capitalist and socialist countries.

**4. Economic thinking is marginal thinking.** Fundamental to economic reasoning and economizing behavior are the effects of decisions made to change the status quo. Economists refer to such decisions as **marginal.** Marginal choices always involve the effects of net additions to or subtractions *from the current conditions.* In fact, the word "additional" is often used as a substitute for marginal. For example, we might ask, "What is the marginal (or additional) cost of producing one more automobile?"

**marginal** Term used to describe the effects of a change, given the current situation. For example, the marginal cost is the cost of producing an additional unit of a product, given the producer's current facility and production rate.

Marginal decisions may involve large or small changes. The "one more unit" could be a new plant or a new stapler. It is marginal because it involves additional costs and additional benefits. *Given the current situation,* what marginal benefits (additional sales revenues, for example) can be expected from the plant, and what will be the marginal cost of constructing the facility? The answers to these questions will determine whether or not building the new plant is a good decision.

It is important to distinguish between "average" and "marginal." A manufacturer's current average cost of producing automobiles (total cost divided by total number of cars produced) may be $10,000, but the marginal cost of producing an additional automobile (or an additional 1,000 automobiles) might be much lower, say, $5,000 per car. Costs associated with research, testing, design, molds, heavy equipment, and similar factors of production must be incurred whether the manufacturer is going to produce 1,000 units, 10,000 units, or 100,000 units. Such costs will clearly contribute to the average cost of an automobile. However, since these activities have already been undertaken to produce the manufacturer's current output level, they may add little to the cost of producing *additional* units. Thus, the manufacturer's marginal cost may be substantially less than the average cost. When determining whether to expand or reduce the production of a good, the choice should be based on marginal costs, not the current average cost.

We often confront decisions involving a possible change from the current situation. The marginal benefits and marginal costs associated with the choice will determine the wisdom of our decisions. What happens at the margin is therefore an important element of the economic way of thinking.

**5. While information can help us make better choices, its acquisition is costly. Thus, we will almost always make choices based on limited knowledge.** Information that will help us make better choices is valuable. Like other resources, however, it is also scarce and therefore costly to acquire. As a result, individuals will economize on their search for information just as they economize on the use of other scarce resources. For example, when purchasing a pair of jeans, you may check price and evaluate quality at several different stores. At some point, though, you will decide that additional shopping—that is, acquisition of additional information—is simply not worth the trouble. You will make a choice based on the limited knowledge that you already possess.

The process is similar when individuals search for a place to eat, a new car, or a roommate. They will seek to acquire some information, but at some point, they will perceive that the expected benefit derived from still more information is simply not worth the cost. Limited knowledge and some uncertainty about the outcome characterize the decision-making process.

**6. Economic actions often generate secondary effects in addition to their immediate effects. Failure to consider these secondary effects is the most common source of economic error.** Frederic Bastiat, a nineteenth century French economist, stated that the difference between a good and a bad economist is that the bad economist considers only the immediate, visible effects, whereas the good economist is also aware of the **secondary effects,** effects that are indirectly related to the initial policy that can be seen or felt only with the passage of time.

**secondary effects**
Economic consequences of an initial economic change, even though they are not immediately identifiable. Secondary effects will be felt only with the passage of time.

Perhaps consideration of both immediate and secondary effects in areas outside of economics will help us grasp this point. For example, the immediate effect of an aspirin is a bitter taste in one's mouth. The indirect effect, which is not immediately observable, is relief from a headache. The immediate effect of drinking six cans of beer might be a warm, jolly feeling. The indirect effect, for many, would be a pounding headache the next morning.

In economics, the immediate, short-term effects that are highly visible are often quite different from the long-term effects. Changes in economic policy often alter the structure of incentives, which indirectly affect things like how much people work, earn, and invest, and care for things in the future. But the impact of the secondary effects is often observable only after the passage of time—and then only to those who know what to look for.

Consider the examples of tariffs, quotas, and other restrictions that limit imports. Proponents of such restrictions argue that they will increase employment; and, indeed, if for example, the supply of foreign-produced automobiles to the U.S. market were restricted, Americans would buy more American-made automobiles, increasing output and employment in the domestic auto industry. These are the immediate, easily identifiable effects. But consider the secondary effects. The restrictions will also reduce supply to the domestic market and increase the price of both foreign- and American-made automobiles. As a result of the higher prices, many auto consumers will pay more for automobiles and thus be forced to curtail their purchases of food, clothing, recreation, and literally thousands of other items. These reductions in spending will mean less output and employment in those areas. There will also be a secondary effect on foreigners. Since foreigners will sell fewer automobiles to Americans, they will acquire fewer dollars with which to buy American-made goods. U.S. exports, therefore, will fall as a result of the restrictions on automobile imports.

Once the secondary effects are considered, the net impact of the import restrictions on employment is no longer obvious. The restrictions will increase employment in the auto industry, but they will also reduce employment in other industries, particularly export industries. Primarily, they will reshuffle employment rather than increase it. As this example illustrates, consideration of the secondary effects is an important ingredient of the economic way of thinking.

**7. The value of a good or a service is subjective.** Preferences differ, sometimes dramatically, between individuals. How much is a ticket to see tonight's performance of the Bolshoi Ballet worth? Some would be willing to pay a very high price, while others might even be willing to pay to avoid the ballet if attendance were mandatory. Even for a given individual, circumstances can change from day to day. Alice, who usually would value the ballet ticket at $20, is invited to a party, and suddenly becomes uninterested in the ballet tonight. Now what is the ticket worth? If she knows a friend who would give her $5 for the ticket, it is worth at least that much. If she advertises on a bulletin board and gets $10 for it, a higher value is created. One thing is certain: the value of the ticket depends on many things, among them, who uses it and when.

Seldom will one individual know how others value an item. Consider how difficult it often is to know what would make a good gift, even for a close friend or family member! So, arranging trades, or otherwise moving items to higher-valued users and uses, is not a simple task. In fact, how society promotes such coordination in the behavior of individuals is a key subject in many of the chapters that follow.

**8. The test of a theory is its ability to predict. Economic thinking is *scientific thinking*.** The proof of the pudding is in the eating. The usefulness of

**scientific thinking** Development of theory from basic postulates and the testing of the implications of that theory as to their consistency with events in the real world. Good theories are consistent with and help explain real-world events. Theories that are inconsistent with the real world are invalid and must be rejected.

an economic theory is proved by its ability to predict the future consequences of economic action. Economists develop economic theory from **scientific thinking,** in which basic postulates are used to analyze how incentives will affect decision-makers and the analysis is then compared against events in the real world. If the events in the real world are consistent with a theory, we say that the theory has predictive value and is therefore valid.

If it is impossible to test the theoretical relationships of a discipline, the discipline does not qualify as a science. So, since economics deals with human beings, who can think and respond in a variety of ways, can economic theories really be tested? The answer to this question is yes, if, *on average,* human beings respond in predictable and consistent ways to changes in economic conditions. The economist believes that this is the case. Note that the economist is not saying that *all* individuals will respond in a specified manner. Economics usually does not seek to predict the behavior of a specific individual; instead, it focuses on the general behavior of a large number of individuals.

How can we test economic theory when controlled experiments with all the interactions of real life are not feasible? This is a problem, but economics is no different from astronomy in this respect. Astronomers must also deal with the world as it is. They cannot change the course of the stars or planets to see what impact the change would have on the gravitational pull of the earth.

So it is with economists, who cannot arbitrarily change the price of cars or unskilled labor services just to observe the effect on quantity purchased or level of employment. However, economic conditions (for example, prices, production costs, technology, transportation costs, and so on), like the location of the planets, do change from time to time. As actual conditions change, economic theory can be tested by comparing its predictions with real-world outcomes. Just as the universe is the laboratory of the astronomer, the real world is the laboratory of the economist.

## PRODUCTION POSSIBILITIES CURVE

**production possibilities curve** The maximum amount of two products that can be produced from a fixed set of resources, given the current technology and legal institutions.

Economists often use a simple conceptual tool called the **production possibilities curve,** which reveals the maximum amount of any two products that can be produced from a fixed set of resources, given the current level of technology and the legal institutions of the economy. Exhibit 1.1 presents the production possibilities curve for an economy producing only two goods: food and clothing. Our ability to produce goods is restricted by both our limited availability of resources and current technical knowledge. If an economy's resources are being used efficiently, it will be possible to achieve output combinations along the frontier of the curve (points like *S, A, B, C,* or *T*). However, output combinations outside the production possibilities curve will be unachievable, given our current supply of resources, technical knowledge and legal institutions.

Thus, the production possibilities curve illustrates that scarcity restricts our options. When the limited resources of an economy are used efficiently, we cannot have more of both goods. A larger output of one good can be achieved only by reducing the output of the other good. For example, if we want more food, we must reduce our output of clothing.

Sometimes output will fall below its potential—the economy will be at a point like *D,* inside the production possibilities curve. Why might this happen?

**EXHIBIT 1.1**

**The Concept of the Production Possibilities Curve for an Economy**

When an economy is using its limited resources efficiently, production of more clothing requires the economy to give up some other goods—food in this simple example. *With time,* a technological discovery or expansion of the economy's resource base could make it possible to produce more of both, shifting the production possibilities curve outward.

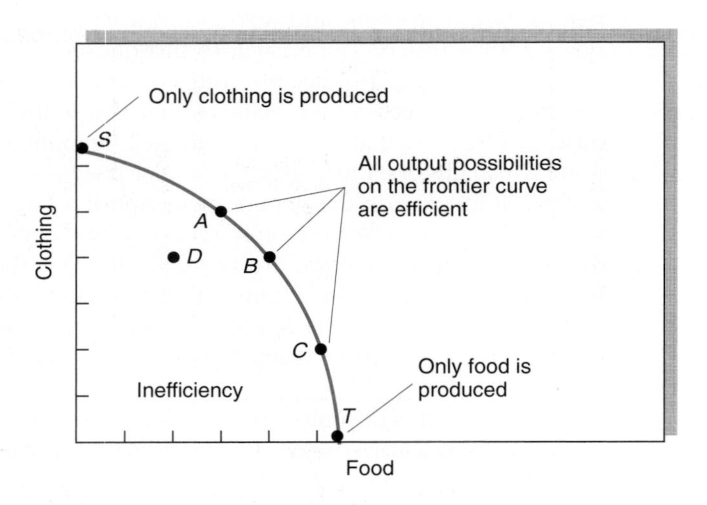


Because resources are being wasted and used inefficiently. A major function of economics is to help us figure out how to use scarce resources more efficiently, so we can achieve outputs along the production possibilities frontier. We will return to this problem again and again.

The production possibilities curve of Exhibit 1.1 is concave, or bowed out from the origin. Why? Resources are not equally well suited to produce food and clothing. Suppose this economy were using all of its resources to produce clothing. At that point ($S$), food production could be expanded by transferring those resources best suited for production of food (and least suitable for clothing production) from clothing to food production. Since the resources transferred are highly productive in food and not very productive in clothing, *in this range* the opportunity cost (clothing forgone) of additional food would be low. However, as successively larger amounts of food are produced (moving from $S$ to $A$ to $B$ and so on), the opportunity cost of food will rise. As more and more food is produced, additional food output can be achieved only by using resources that are less and less suitable for the production of food. Thus, as food output is expanded, successively larger amounts of clothing must be forgone per unit of additional food.

## Shifting Production Possibilities Curve Outward

Could an economy ever have more of all goods? Could the production possibilities curve be shifted outward? The answer is yes. There are three major methods: (1) increasing the resource base, (2) advancing in technology, and (3) improving economic organization.

**EXHIBIT 1.2**

**Investment and Production Possibilities in the Future**

Here we illustrate two economies that initially confront identical production possibilities curves *(RS)*. The economy illustrated on the left allocates a larger share of its output to investment ($I_a$, compared to $I_b$ for the economy on the right). As a result, the production possibilities of the high-investment economy will shift outward by a larger amount than will be true for the low-investment economy.

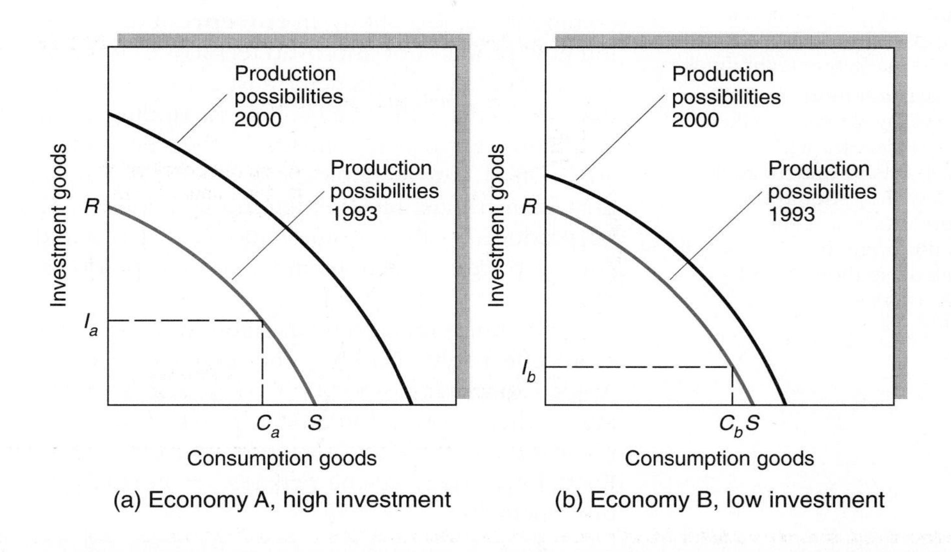


(a) Economy A, high investment

(b) Economy B, low investment

**INCREASING THE ECONOMY'S RESOURCE BASE** If we had more and better resources, we could produce a greater amount of all goods. Many resources are human-made. If we were willing to give up some current consumption, we could invest more of today's resources into the production of long-lasting physical structures, machines, education, and the development of human skills. This **capital formation** would provide us with better tools and skills in the future and thereby increase our ability to produce goods and services. Exhibit 1.2 illustrates the link between capital formation and the future production possibilities of an economy. The two economies illustrated start with the same production possibilities curve *(RS)*. However, since Economy A allocates more of its resources to investment than does Economy B, A's production possibilities curve shifts outward with the passage of time by a greater amount. The growth rate of A—the expansion rate of the economy's ability to produce goods—is enhanced by investment. Of course, more investment in machines and human skills will necessitate less current consumption.

**capital formation** The production of buildings, machinery, tools, and other equipment that will enhance the ability of future economic participants to produce. The term can also be applied to efforts to upgrade the knowledge and skill of workers and thereby increase their ability to produce in the future.

**technology** The body of skills and technological knowledge available at any given time. The level of technology establishes the relationship between inputs and the maximum output they can generate.

**ADVANCES IN TECHNOLOGY** Technology determines the maximum physical output obtainable from any particular set of resource inputs. New technology can make it possible to get more from our given base of resources.[2] An important

[2]Without modern technical knowledge, it would be impossible to produce the vast array of goods and services responsible for our standard of living. Thomas Sowell makes this point clear when he notes:

*The cavemen had the same natural resources at their disposal as we have today, and the difference between their standard of living and ours is a difference between the knowledge they could bring to bear on those resources and the knowledge used today. [Knowledge and Decisions* (New York: Basic Books, 1980), p. 47.]

**invention** The discovery of a new product or process, often facilitated by the knowledge of engineering and scientific relationships.

**innovation** The successful introduction and adoption of a new product or process; the economic application of inventions and marketing techniques.

**entrepreneur** A profit-seeking decision-maker who decides which projects to undertake and how they should be undertaken. A successful entrepreneur's actions will increase the value of resources.

form of technological change is **invention,** the use of science and engineering to discover new products or processes. Sending information instantly and cheaply by satellite, getting more oil from a well, and growing more corn from newly developed hybrid seed are all examples of technological advances resulting from inventions. Each one has pushed our production possibilities curve outward.

An economy can also benefit from technological change through **innovation,** the practical and effective adoption of new techniques. Such innovation is commonly carried out by an **entrepreneur**—one who seeks profit by introducing new products or improved techniques to satisfy consumers at a lower cost.[3] To prosper, an entrepreneur must convert and rearrange resources in a manner that will increase their value, thus expanding our production possibilities.

Henry Ford nicely illustrates the central role of the entrepreneur in the adoption of new technology. In the 1920s, Ford introduced assembly-line production methods into the automobile industry. Since more automobiles could be produced with the same amount of labor and materials, Ford was able to cut the price. His actions increased the production possibilities of the United States.

Sometimes entrepreneurs figure out ways to apply the inventions of others more effectively. This was the case with Steven Jobs, the co-founder of the Apple Computer Corporation. Jobs used the new computer technology to create smaller, more affordable computers and arranged for the "user friendly" software that made them so popular for personal and small-business use. Like Ford, Jobs expanded the nation's production possibilities by means of his entrepreneurship.

**IMPROVING ECONOMIC ORGANIZATION** The legal system of a country influences the ability of people to cooperate with each other and produce desired goods. Changes in legal institutions that promote social cooperation and enhance the incentive of people to produce will shift the production possibilities curve outward.

Historically, legal innovations have been an important source of economic progress. During the eighteenth century, a system of patents provided investors with a private property right to their ideas. About the same time, the recognition of the corporation as a legal entity reduced the cost of forming large firms that were often required for the mass production of manufactured goods. Both of these legal changes improved economic organization and thereby accelerated the growth of output (that is, shifted the production possibilities curve outward) in Europe and North America.

Sometimes countries may, perhaps as the result of ignorance or prejudice, adopt legal institutions that will reduce production possibilities. Laws that restrict or prohibit trade among various groups provide an illustration. For example, the laws of several southern states prohibited the employment of African Americans in certain occupations, and restricted other economic exchanges between blacks and whites for almost 100 years following the Civil War. This legislation was not only harmful to African Americans, it retarded progress and reduced the production possibilities of these states.

[3]This French-origin word literally means "one who undertakes." The entrepreneur is the person who is ultimately responsible. Of course, this responsibility may be shared with others (partners or stockholders, for example) or it may be partially delegated to technical experts. Nevertheless, the success or failure of the entrepreneur is dependent on the outcome of the choices he or she makes.

**EXHIBIT 1.3**

**Income per Capita of Selected Countries**

| | Per Capita Income (in 1985 dollars) | | |
|---|---|---|---|
| **Country** | **1960** | **1990** | **Growth Rate** |
| Ethiopia | $ 247 | $ 305 | 0.7 |
| Zaire | 373 | 321 | −0.5 |
| India | 613 | 830 | 1.0 |
| Ghana | 1,013 | 888 | −0.5 |
| Egypt | 530 | 1,738 | 4.0 |
| China | 727 | 2,427 | 4.1 |
| Argentina | 3,440 | 3,763 | 0.3 |
| Brazil | 1,380 | 4,225 | 3.8 |
| Mexico | 3,013 | 5,146 | 1.8 |
| Venezuela | 3,920 | 5,284 | 1.0 |
| South Korea | 916 | 5,891 | 6.4 |
| Spain | 2,693 | 8,008 | 3.7 |
| United Kingdom | 6,393 | 12,286 | 2.2 |
| France | 5,435 | 12,814 | 2.9 |
| Sweden | 6,417 | 13,072 | 2.4 |
| Australia | 7,263 | 13,161 | 2.0 |
| Japan | 2,612 | 13,395 | 5.6 |
| Germany[a] | 6,047 | 13,444 | 2.7 |
| Hong Kong | 2,307 | 13,629 | 6.1 |
| Switzerland | 9,265 | 16,782 | 2.0 |
| United States | 10,028 | 18,715 | 2.1 |

[a]Western Germany only.

**Source:** Derived from Robert Summer and Alan Heston, "The Penn World Table (Mark 5): An Expanded Set of International Comparisons, 1950–1988", *Quarterly Journal of Economics,* May 1991. These income comparisons are derived by the purchasing power parity method. The original 1988 data were updated to 1990 by the authors.

## PROSPERITY OF NATIONS

Our analysis of scarcity and production possibilities sheds light on why some nations grow and prosper, while others stagnate. In general, nations will tend to grow more rapidly when they allocate more of their resources toward investment, develop (and integrate) technological improvements more quickly, and adopt more efficient forms of economic organization. Failure to do these things will result in stagnation and regression. If a nation is going to grow and prosper, its economic institutions must encourage investment, technological improvements, and the efficient use of resources.

Historically, the economic record of nations is highly uneven. Exhibit 1.3 presents data on the income level in both 1960 and 1990 for several nations.[4]

[4]The income data of Exhibit 1.3 are derived by comparing the relative purchasing power of each currency in terms of a broad common bundle of goods and services. This purchasing power parity method is an outgrowth of nearly two decades of work on the United Nations International Comparison Program. Income comparisons based on this purchasing power parity method are widely believed to be more accurate than the more widely circulated estimates based on the value of foreign exchange rates.

The growth of income for the period is also indicated. Note the wide variation in the prosperity and income growth among nations. Measured in 1985 dollars, the 1990 per capita income in the United States was $18,715, more than 50 times the comparable figures for Ethiopia and Zaire. Furthermore, income was growing more rapidly in the United States.

As Exhibit 1.3 shows, some of the countries that were poor in 1960 are now relatively wealthy. Note the dramatic increase in the per capita income of South Korea, Japan, and Hong Kong since 1960. On the other hand, per capita income declined in both Zaire and Ghana between 1960 and 1990; Ethiopia, India, Argentina, and Venezuela experienced only modest increases in income during the period. Look at the income data for Ghana and South Korea. In 1960 the per capita income of these two countries was about the same—$1,013 in Ghana and $916 in South Korea. By 1990, however, the income level of South Korea was more than six times the figure for Ghana!

It is also interesting to compare the records of Argentina and Hong Kong. Argentina is a country rich in natural resources, lots of fertile land, and a highly literate population. Sixty years ago, Argentina was one of the ten wealthiest countries in the world. Its per capita income during the 1930s was approximately equal to that of Germany, France, and other wealthy Western European countries. The Argentine economy, however, has stagnated for six decades! Today, at least 40 countries have a higher per capita income than Argentina.

In contrast with Argentina, Hong Kong has few natural resources, little fertile soil, and no domestic sources of energy. As recently as 1960, the per capita income of Hong Kong was only $2,307, compared to $3,440 for Argentina. The situation is now reversed. In 1990 the per capita income of Hong Kong was $13,629, more than 3.5 times the figure for Argentina (see Exhibit 1.3).

Why have some countries like South Korea and Hong Kong prospered, while others like Ghana and Argentina stagnated? The basic principles of economics can help answer this question. Throughout this book, we will use these basic principles to investigate the wealth-creation process and analyze why some nations grow and others stagnate. The authors of this text believe that understanding why people and nations prosper is the most important benefit derived from the study of economics. The central message of this book is that countries with sound economic organization encouraging the creation of wealth will prosper; those without such policies will stagnate. This is true for both wealthy industrial countries and less-developed countries.

Economic prosperity, like the success of an athletic team, involves several ingredients. When one of these major ingredients is discussed in this text, it will be clearly labeled an "Important Source of Economic Prosperity" and the margin will show this icon:

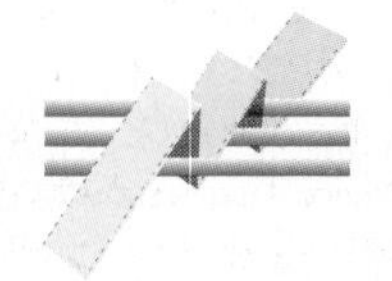

## LOOKING AHEAD

As we discuss the tools of economics and apply the economic way of thinking, we will analyze the major sources of progress in detail. The following chapter focuses on exchange, property rights, and the creation of wealth.

## CHAPTER SUMMARY

1. Economics is about scarcity and choice. Our desire for goods is virtually unlimited and far greater than the amount provided by nature. Therefore, goods are scarce; we cannot have as much as we would like. Choice is the logical consequence of scarcity. In the process of choosing among the alternatives that are available to us, we must forgo many desired items.
2. Our ability to produce desired goods has increased substantially during the last 250 years. In many parts of the world—particularly in North America, Western Europe, Oceania, and Japan—people are substantially wealthier than their ancestors were. Nonetheless, scarcity is still a fact of life throughout the world. Even in wealthy nations, the desire of people for goods is far greater than their productive capabilities.
3. Economics is a method of approach, a way of thinking. The economic way of thinking emphasizes the following:
   a. The use of resources to produce a good is always costly. The use of more resources to produce one good will force us to reduce our production of other goods.
   b. Individuals make decisions purposefully, always seeking to choose the option they expect to be most consistent with their personal goals. Purposeful decision-making leads to economizing behavior.
   c. Incentives matter. People will be more likely to choose an option as the benefits expected from that option increase. In contrast, higher costs will make an alternative less attractive, reducing the likelihood that it will be chosen.
   d. Marginal costs and marginal benefits (utility) are fundamental to economizing behavior. Economic reasoning focuses on the impact of marginal changes.
   e. Since information is scarce and costly to acquire, the choices of people will be based on limited knowledge.
   f. In addition to their initial impact, economic events often alter personal incentives in a manner that leads to important secondary effects that may be felt only with the passage of time.
   g. The value of a good or service is subjective and will differ according to the individual.
   h. The test of an economic theory is its ability to predict and to explain events in the real world.
4. The production possibilities curve illustrates the constraints imposed by the scarcity of resources. It purports to show the maximum combinations of any two products that can be produced with a fixed quantity of resources, assuming that the level of technology and the legal institutions of the economy are unchanged. When the resources of an economy are used

efficiently, it will be impossible to achieve current output rates beyond the economy's production possibilities frontier.

5. The production possibilities curve of an economy can be shifted outward by (a) current investment that expands the future resource base of the economy, (b) technological advancements, and (c) legal changes that improve economic organization.
6. Historically, nations have grown at different rates. Some nations have experienced prosperity and grown rapidly, while others have stagnated and regressed. Basic economic principles provide insight into the reasons. The primary purpose of this book is to explain the sources of economic prosperity and analyze the institutional arrangements that are capable of promoting it.

# *Study Guide*

# CHAPTER 1

## DEVELOPING THE ECONOMIC WAY OF THINKING

## CRITICAL-ANALYSIS QUESTIONS

1. Economic theory postulates that self-interest is a powerful motivation for action. Does this imply that people are selfish and greedy? Do self-interest and selfishness mean the same thing?

*2. "The government should provide goods such as health care, education, and highways because it can provide them free." True or false? Explain.

*3. "Individuals who economize are missing the point of life. Money is not so important that it should rule the way we live." Evaluate.

*4. Suppose that you were taking a college economics course. How would each of the following influence your study time for an examination next week?
   a. The knowledge that you need an A in the class to graduate.
   b. An announcement that the examination would not count toward your final grade.
   c. An unanticipated opportunity to spend the weekend at a beautiful beach (or ski resort, if you prefer) with your friends.
   d. An announcement that all students in the class are going to be given a grade of C, regardless of how well they do on the exam.

*5. Legislation was recently introduced in the United States that would have required commercial airlines to provide and parents to purchase a special safety seat for small children. Proponents of this legislation argue that it would save lives. Do you agree? Can you think of any "secondary effects" that might actually increase injuries and fatalities?

*6. The economic way of thinking stresses that good intentions lead to sound policy. True or false? Explain.

*Asterisk denotes critical-analysis questions for which answers are given in Appendix A.

## MULTIPLE-CHOICE SELF-TEST

1. In economics, the term "scarcity" refers to the fact that
   a. Everything really worthwhile costs money.
   b. Even in wealthy countries like the United States, some people are poor.
   c. No society is able to produce enough to satisfy fully the desires of people for goods and services.
   d. Sometimes shortages of a good arise when its price is set below the market equilibrium.

2. Opportunity cost is
   a. The cost incurred when one fails to take advantage of an opportunity.
   b. The cost incurred in order to increase the availability of attractive opportunities.
   c. The cost of the highest valued option forgone as the result of choosing an alternative.
   d. The drudgery and undesirable aspects of an option.

3. If you were deciding whether to purchase a second car, the economic way of thinking would lead you to compare

a. The total benefits expected from two cars with the cost of the two cars.
b. The additional benefits expected from a second car with the total cost of the two cars.
c. The dollar cost of the two cars with the potential income that the two cars will generate.
d. The additional benefits of the second car with its cost.

4. When economists say that an individual displays economizing behavior, they simply mean that the individual is
   a. Making a lot of money.
   b. Purchasing only those products that are cheap and of low quality.
   c. Learning how to run a business more effectively.
   d. Making choices so as to gain specific benefits at the least possible cost.

5. The economic way of thinking stresses that
   a. Changes in the personal costs and benefits will exert a predictable influence on the choices of human decision-makers.
   b. If one individual gains from an economic activity, then someone else must lose, and in the same proportion.
   c. If a good is provided free to an individual, its production will not consume valuable scarce resources.
   d. Good intentions lead to sound economic policy.

6. Since the test of a theory is its ability to predict, and since economics deals with human beings who can think and respond in a variety of ways, can economic theories really be tested?
   a. Yes, since, on the average, human beings will respond in a predictable way to changes in personal costs and benefits.
   b. Yes, since all individuals usually respond the same way.
   c. No, since individuals will seldom respond in a predictable way.
   d. No, since the general behavior of a large number of individuals cannot be predicted.

7. A production possibilities curve indicates that when resources are being used efficiently
   a. You can produce more of one good only if you lower its price.
   b. You can produce more of one good only if you produce more of another good.
   c. You can produce more of one good only if you produce less of another good.
   d. It will be impossible to expand total output in the future.

8. With time, w hich one of the following strategies would be most likely to result in an outward shift in the production possibilities curve of an economy?
   a. Passage of legislation reducing the length of the workweek to 30 hours.
   b. Institution of a tax policy encouraging capital investment at the expense of current consumption.
   c. Institution of a tax policy encouraging current consumption at the expense of capital investment.
   d. An increase in the marginal income tax rate, which would reduce the work effort of individuals.

9. Which of the following will be most likely to help a nation prosper and grow more rapidly?

a. A high rate of inflation.
b. High tax rates on personal income.
c. A high rate of capital investment.
d. High taxes on foreign-produced goods in order to protect the jobs in domestic industries that compete with foreigners.

10. Which of the following is true?
a. The countries that were poor in 1960 are still poor.
b. The per capita income of Argentina was substantially less than that of South Korea in both 1960 and 1990.
c. Cheap energy sources and abundant natural resources are necessary prerequisites for economic growth.
d. There is wide variation among nations in per capita income and rate of economic growth.

CHAPTER

# 2

# EXCHANGE, PROPERTY RIGHTS, AND THE CREATION OF WEALTH

Why do people do so much buying and selling? Presumably, they do not exchange just for the giddy fun of the activity. Instead, they swap in order to gain. . . . [A]fter the trade, the trader considers himself to be better off. In what sense? He feels himself to be better off, on balance, because he values more what he gets than what he gives up.

*William R. Allen*[1]

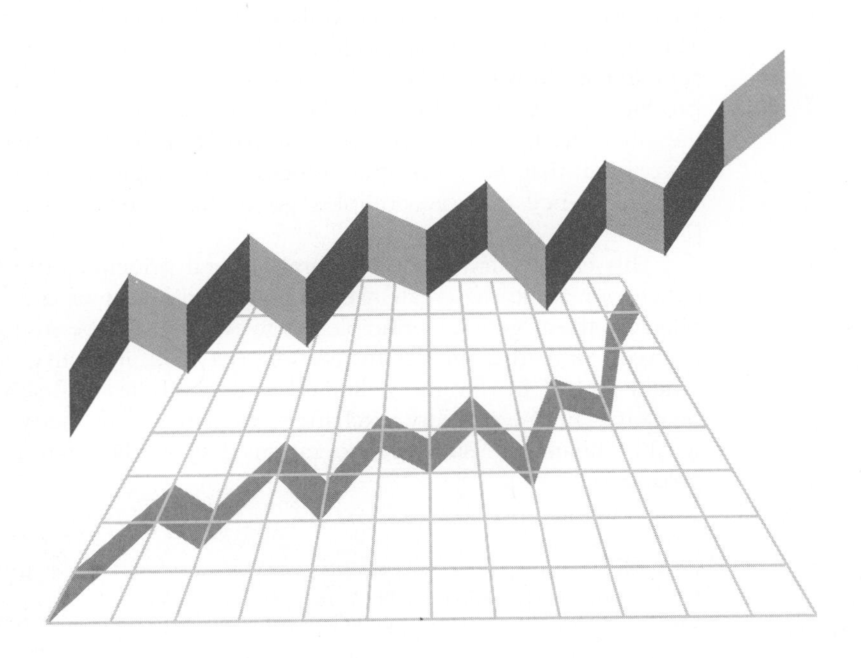

## CHAPTER FOCUS

- Why is exchange generally beneficial to both the buyer and the seller? Why does it enhance our ability to produce and create wealth?
- Why are transaction costs an obstacle to the creation of wealth? Are people who provide services that reduce transaction costs performing a productive function?
- How does private ownership influence the maintenance, use, and conservation of property? Does private ownership influence the incentive of people to cooperate with each other?
- How do trade restraints and poorly defined ownership rights influence our standard of living?
- What are the three economizing decisions that must be confronted by every economy?
- What are the two major methods of economic organization? How do they differ?

Our modern living standards reflect an almost incomprehensible amount of social cooperation among people. Consider this book. The paper probably came from trees produced by someone in Canada or South America. But the trees may have been cut with a chain saw produced in Japan, Hong Kong, or Germany. The various parts of the saw were produced with resources from literally dozens of countries, and the fuel to power the saw may have been extracted from oil wells in the Middle East, Norway, or Indonesia. The type of the book may well have been set with a computerized printer assembled in Taiwan, containing chips developed in California, and using ink produced in Kenya. Thus, this book incorporates the productive activities of literally thousands of people, most of whom have never met. So it is with most everything that we consume, ranging from simple items like an ordinary wooden pencil to more complex goods like watches, cameras, and automobiles.[2]

This chapter focuses on several general principles of production that enhance our ability to create wealth. The realization of the potential gains implied by these general principles, however, would be impossible without exchange. Similarly, the motivation to act and incentive to cooperate with others would be far more limited and much less effective without private property. Both voluntary exchange and private property are central to the wealth-enhancing, social cooperation that is the foundation of economic prosperity.

[1]William R. Allen, "Trade and Mutual Gain," *The Midnight Economist* (Los Angeles: Reason Foundation, 1992).

[2]See Leonard E. Read, "I, Pencil: My Family Tree," *Freeman,* December 1958, for an interesting account of the social cooperation and number of people involved in the production of a simple wooden pencil.

# IMPORTANT SOURCE OF PROSPERITY: GAINS FROM TRADE

Mutual gain is the foundation for voluntary exchange (see the chapter's opening quote). Trading partners agree to an exchange because both value what they receive more than what they give up. The motivation for exchange can be summed up this way: "If you give me this item that I want, I will give you this other thing that you want." Each trading partner expects to gain and usually does. If either thought he or she would lose, the exchange would not take place. Contrary to what some think, trade is a productive activity; it is productive precisely because it permits trading partners to get more of what they want.

There are three major sources of gains from trade. First, trade is productive because it tends to channel goods and services to those who value them most. Second, trade enhances our overall ability to produce since it makes it possible for each of us to specialize in those activities that we do best. Finally, trade is productive because it makes it possible for us to enlarge total output through the division of labor and adoption of mass production techniques. Let us consider each of these three sources of gains from trade in more detail.

## Trade Channels Goods to Those Who Value Them Most

Lay people often believe that material goods have value merely because they exist, or because it would take so much labor and natural resources to produce them.[3] This is a fallacious view. A particular item has value because somebody wants it and is willing to give up other things (for example, time, goods, or money) in order to get it. The preferences, knowledge, and goals of people vary widely. Thus, a good that is virtually worthless to one may be a precious gem to another. For example, a highly technical book on electronics that is of no value to an art collector may be worth hundreds of dollars to an engineer. Similarly, a painting that is unappreciated by an engineer may be an object of great wealth to an art collector. Goods have value only when they are in the hands of someone who values them.

Circumstances, time, and location influence the value of material items. Two physically identical items may differ substantially in value as the result of timing or location. The same air conditioner that sells for a premium price during a hot summer in Florida may be of little value in Alaska. Similarly, a color television in a department store is worth more than the same set in a warehouse or on a boat dock. By getting the TV set to a location where the customer can see, evaluate, and purchase it, the retailer has added value to the product even though the physical object itself is unchanged.

At the most basic level, trade provides us with gains by moving goods from people who value them less to people who value them more. For example, the seller of a used automobile who traded it to a buyer for $1,500 must have valued the car at less than $1,500, or otherwise she would not have sold it. On the other hand, the buyer places more than $1,500 of value on the car, or otherwise he would not have purchased it. Thus, the trade moved the good from someone who valued it less to someone who valued it more. The

[3]Economists refer to this as the "physical fallacy." See Thomas Sowell, *Knowledge and Decisions* (New York: Basic Books, 1980), pp. 67–72, for a detailed analysis of this fallacy.

exchange improved the welfare of both trading partners and enhanced the value of the automobile by channeling it to someone who has a greater appreciation for it. Thus, the trade was a positive-sum activity. It created value, even though it did not construct or develop anything new.

## Trade Permits Us to Expand Output through Specialization

Economizing means getting the most out of one's available resources. How can this be accomplished? When a product is produced by a high opportunity-cost supplier, the economy is giving up more than is necessary. In other words, it is not economizing. Economizing, or economic efficiency, requires that output always be generated by the producer who has the lowest opportunity cost.

A group of individuals, an entire economy, or a group of nations will be able to generate a larger output when each good is produced by the person (or firm) with the lowest opportunity cost. As a result, individuals, regions, and nations can gain by specializing in the production of goods they produce at a low cost, while trading for other desired goods for which they are a high opportunity-cost producer. Economists refer to this principle, initially developed in the early 1800s by the great English economist David Ricardo, as the **law of comparative advantage.**

**law of comparative advantage** A principle that states that individuals, firms, regions, or nations can gain by specializing in the production of goods that they produce cheaply (that is, at a low opportunity cost) and exchanging those goods for other desired goods for which they are high opportunity-cost producers.

In some ways the law of comparative advantage is merely commonsense. Obviously, more can be produced if productive tasks are conducted by the people who are most skilled at doing them. For example, suppose that it would take you two hours to type a paper and four hours to mow a lawn. In contrast, it would take your friend Alex eight hours to type the same paper, but only two hours to mow the lawn. Clearly, you are skilled at typing, but lousy at mowing lawns. The reverse is true for Alex.

Given your relative skills, you and Alex could achieve a larger output and gain from trade if you specialize in typing, while Alex specializes in mowing. For example, if Alex mows your yard in exchange for your typing a paper for him, you both would gain. It would take you four hours to mow the lawn, but only two hours to type the paper. Thus, when you trade a typed paper to Alex for a mowed lawn, you gain two hours (which could be used to do other things, including the typing of another paper). Similarly, it would take Alex eight hours to type his own paper, but only two hours to mow your lawn. Thus, Alex gains six hours of time for other things when he mows your lawn in exchange for your typing of his paper.

With trade, people can gain by specializing in those productive activities that they do best, while trading for those things that they do less well. For example, a farmer in Montana can specialize in the production of wheat (which can be produced at a low cost in Montana), and then trade the wheat for oranges, tomatoes, and other goods that can be produced more cheaply in areas farther to the south. At the same time, citrus and vegetable growers in Florida and California can specialize in the production of these products and trade them for other goods (like wheat) that are costly for them to grow.

It is easy to visualize the potential gains from specialization and trade when each trading partner is more skilled at the productive activity in which each specializes. However, it is important to recognize that the gains from trade are derived from differences between trading partners in *relative* costs, not absolute costs. Suppose that it not only takes Alex eight hours to type a paper, but also five hours to mow a yard. Since you can type a paper in two hours and mow a yard in four hours, you are faster at both typing and mowing than Alex. There is a tendency to think that your greater skill at both activities rules out the possibility of gains from specialization and exchange. This view is wrong. It is wrong because it is *comparative (relative) advantage* rather than absolute advantage that is the source of the gains from specialization and exchange.

Suppose that you and Alex are initially spending 20 hours per week at each of the tasks. In 20 hours, you can type 10 papers (one every two hours) or mow 5 lawns (one every 4 hours). On the other hand, Alex is able to type only 2.5 papers (one every 8 hours) or mow 4 lawns (one every 5 hours) during 20 hours of work. The following chart indicates the individual and aggregate outputs of the two of you.

| | Time Required for Task (in hours) | | Weekly Output—20 Hours on Each Task | |
|---|---|---|---|---|
| | **Type Paper** | **Mow Lawn** | **Papers Typed** | **Lawns Mowed** |
| Yours | 2 | 4 | 10 | 5 |
| Alex's | 8 | 5 | 2.5 | 4 |
| Total | — | — | 12.5 | 9 |

Prior to specializing, in aggregate you and Alex are able to type 12.5 papers and mow 9 lawns when you both work 20 hours per week at each task. With specialization in your respective area of comparative advantage, you both can do better—you can produce a larger output and derive mutual gains from trade. You are four times as good at typing as Alex, but only one-fourth (25 percent) better at mowing yards. Thus, your comparative advantage is in typing, while Alex's is in mowing. If you spend 28 hours per week typing and only 12 hours mowing, you can type 14 papers and mow 3 yards. When Alex spends all of his time mowing, he can mow 8 yards in a 40-hour workweek. As the chart below indicates, with specialization you and Alex can produce a total output of 14 typed papers and 11 mowed lawns.

| | Weekly Output after Specialization | | Potential Availability with Trade | |
|---|---|---|---|---|
| | **Papers Typed** | **Lawns Mowed** | **Papers Typed** | **Lawns Mowed** |
| Yours | 14 | 3 | 11 | 6 |
| Alex's | 0 | 8 | 3 | 5 |
| Total | 14 | 11 | 14 | 11 |

Comparison of these figures with the pre-specialization output data presented in the first chart shows that you and Alex have increased your total weekly output by 1.5 typed papers and 2 mowed yards.

As the result of the expansion in output, you and Alex can have more of both goods. For example, if Alex trades you 3 mowings for 3 typed papers, you would have 11 typed papers and 6 mowed yards (compared to 10 and 5 prior to the exchange). After specialization and exchange, Alex would end up with 3 typed papers and 5 mowed yards (compared to 2.5 and 4 before specialization and trade). Thus, specialization and exchange permits the trading partners to both enlarge total output and improve their mutual economic welfare.

Only comparative advantage is required for the realization of gains from specialization and trade. Since comparative advantage stems from one's proficiency in one area *relative* to proficiency in other areas, there will always be areas where individuals, regions, and nations have a comparative advantage. Even individuals who are good at several things will be extremely good at only a few things. They will have a comparative advantage only in the areas where they are extremely good. Similarly, even people with few skills will be less poor in some areas than others. Their comparative advantage lies in these areas.

Perhaps one additional illustration will help drive home the point that the gains from specialization and trade are dependent on comparative advantage rather than some absolute skill or time advantage. Consider the situation of an attorney who can type 120 words per minute. The attorney is trying to decide whether to hire a secretary, who types only 60 words per minute, to complete some legal documents. If the lawyer does the typing job, it will take 4 hours; if a secretary is hired, the typing job will take 8 hours. Thus, the lawyer has an absolute advantage in typing compared to the prospective employee. The attorney's time, though, is worth $50 per hour when working as a lawyer, whereas the typist's time is worth $5 per hour as a typist. Although a fast typist, the attorney is also a high opportunity-cost producer of typing service. If the lawyer types the documents, the job will cost $200, which is the opportunity cost of 4 hours (at $50 per hour) of lost time as a lawyer. Alternatively, if the typist is hired, the cost of having the documents typed is only $40 (8 hours of typing service at $5 per hour). The lawyer's comparative advantage thus lies in practicing law. The attorney will gain by hiring the typist and spending the additional time specializing in the practice of law.

## Trade Permits Us to Gain from Division of Labor and Mass Production

In the absence of exchange, productive activity would be limited to the individual household. Self-provision and small-scale production would be the rule. Voluntary exchange permits us to realize gains derived from the **division of labor** and the adoption of large-scale production methods. When we are able to break the production of a product into a series of specific operations and plan for large production runs, enormous increases in output per worker are often possible.

**division of labor** A method that breaks down the production of a commodity into a series of specific tasks, each performed by a different worker.

Adam Smith stressed the importance of gains from this source more than 200 years ago after observing the operation of a pin manufacturer:

> *One man draws out the wire, another straights it, a third cuts it, a fourth points it, a fifth grinds it at the top for receiving the head; to make the head requires two or three distinct operations; to put it on, is a peculiar business, to whiten the pins is another; it is even a trade by itself to put them into the paper; and the important business of making a pin is, in this manner, divided into about eighteen distinct operations, which, in some manufactories, are all performed by distinct hands.*[4]

[4]Adam Smith, *An Inquiry into the Nature and Causes of the Wealth of Nations,* 1776 (Cannon's edition, Chicago: University of Chicago Press, 1976), pp. 8–9.

When each worker specialized in a productive function, 10 workers were able to produce 48,000 pins per day, or 4,800 pins per worker. Without specialization and division of labor, Smith doubted an individual worker would have been able to produce even 20 pins per day.

The division of labor separates production tasks into a series of related operations. Each worker performs a single task, only one of perhaps hundreds of tasks necessary to produce the commodity. There are several reasons why the division of labor often leads to enormous gains in output per worker. First, specialization permits individuals to take advantage of their existing abilities and skills. (Put another way, specialization permits an economy to take advantage of the fact that individuals have different skills.) Productive assignments can be undertaken by those individuals who are able to accomplish them most efficiently. Second, a worker who specializes in just one task (or one narrow area) becomes more experienced and more skilled in that task with the passage of time. Most important, the division of labor lets us adopt complex, large-scale production techniques unthinkable for an individual household. As our knowledge of technology and the potential of machinery expands, capital-intensive production procedures and the division of labor permit us to attain living standards undreamed of just a few decades ago. Without exchange, however, these gains would be lost.

## TRANSACTION COSTS ARE A BARRIER TO GAINS FROM TRADE

Trade is productive because it enhances our ability to create wealth in that it directs goods toward those who value them most and permits us to expand aggregate output through specialization and mass production techniques. These gains are the source of the mutual benefits trading partners derive from exchange. However, while trade is productive, it is also costly. It takes time, effort, and other resources to search out trading possibilities, identify potential buyers (or sellers), evaluate the quality of a good, arrange for such legal protection as product warranties, negotiate the terms of the exchange and in some cases, transport the good to the desired location. Economists refer to these costs as **transaction costs.** Transaction costs limit our ability to gain from specialization, division of labor, and trade. Thus, they are an obstacle to the creation of wealth.

**transaction costs** The time, effort, and other resources needed to search out, negotiate, and consummate an exchange.

Since exchange is costly, we should not expect all potentially valuable trades to take place, any more than we should expect all potentially valuable goods to be produced or all potential A grades to be earned in economics. Reductions in transaction costs, however, permit us to realize more of the potential gains from trade. Therefore, provision of information and services that reduce the cost of trading and help trading partners make better choices is valuable. A specialist who provides buyers and sellers with services that reduce their transaction costs is commonly called a **middleman.**

**middleman** A person who buys and sells, or who arranges trades. A middleman provides services that reduce transaction costs.

Often, people believe that middlemen are unnecessary, that they increase the price of goods without providing benefits to either the buyer or the seller. Once we recognize that transaction costs are an obstacle to trade, it is easy to see the fallacy of this view. Since middlemen provide services that make exchange cheaper and more convenient, they increase the number of wealth-enhancing trades. In doing so, they themselves create value.

Let us consider a couple of examples of middlemen who create value by reducing transaction costs. The auto dealer provides services that make it cheaper for consumers to arrange transactions with automobile manufacturers. By keeping an inventory of autos and by hiring knowledgeable salespeople, the dealer helps the car shopper learn about the many cars offered and how each car looks, performs, and "feels." (Don't forget that preferences are subjective; they are not objectively known to others.) Car buyers also like to know that the local dealer will honor the warranty and provide parts and service for the car when they are needed. The automobile manufacturer, by using the dealer as a middleman, is able to concentrate on designing and making cars, leaving to middlemen—dealers—the task of marketing and servicing them in each community.

Grocers are another provider of middleman services. Each of us could deal with farmers and food processors directly, buy in large quantities, or perhaps shop through catalogs when choosing what we want. If we did, though, we would have to make long trips to deal with sellers, incur additional transportation costs, and maintain larger refrigerators and storage rooms for inventories. And it would be more difficult for us to squeeze the tomatoes and evaluate the quality of other food items. In a market setting, no one is required to use the services of a grocer or any other middleman. Some may want to form a consumer cooperative, purchase a warehouse to receive and display food, and operate with volunteer labor. In this manner, the middleman can be eliminated. Most people, however, prefer the services of the middleman. Thus, they "hire" a grocer and pay the usual markup for the services that he provides.

Real estate agents, publishers of the yellow pages in the telephone book and the classified ads in the newspaper, and merchants of all sorts are middlemen—specialists who provide potential traders with valuable information and often display, guarantee, and service items traded. For a fee, they reduce the transaction costs for both the shopper and the seller. Many traders find that the services of middlemen reduce the costs of exchange and thereby promote additional gain from specialization and trade.

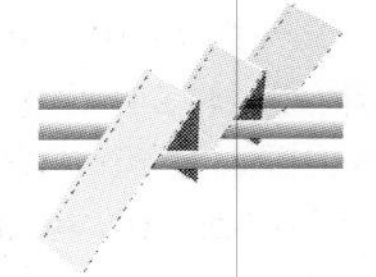

## Important Source of Prosperity: Private Ownership

*Whatever is produced or improved by a man's art or industry, ought, forever to be secure to him in order to give encouragement to such useful habits and accomplishments.*

David Hume

**private property rights** Property rights that are exclusively held by an owner, and that can be transferred to others at the owner's discretion.

With **private property rights,** owners are granted (1) the right of exclusive use (and benefit from that use); (2) legal protection against people who would use violence, theft, or fraud to take what does not belong to them; and (3) the right to transfer (sell) the property or the services of the property to others. Thus, exclusivity and transferability are central to private ownership.[5] Of course, all other property owners have identical rights. Therefore, no private

[5]It is important to note that, in addition to material things, our concept of property includes labor services, personal safety, money, ideas, inventions, scientific formulas, and so on. Our analysis of private ownership and explanation of why it is important applies equally to all of these things.

owner can use their property in a way that invades or alters the physical characteristics of property owned by others. For example, I cannot throw a hammer that I own through the screen of a computer that you own, because if I did, I would be violating your property right to your computer. Your property right to your computer restricts me and everyone else from the use of your computer without your permission. Similarly, my ownership of my hammer and other things that I own restricts you and everyone else from using them without my permission.

Clearly defined and enforced property rights are essential to the smooth operation of a market exchange economy. When people exchange goods or resources for money, they are really exchanging property rights. The amount buyers are willing to pay for the property right to a good (or resource) reveals their valuation of the good.

The strength of private property rights is dependent upon both ethical norms (for example, disapproval of stealing) and the degree of enforcement (and protection) provided by the government. Protection of the person and legitimately acquired property of each citizen is perhaps the most vital function of government.

Private ownership has sometimes been associated with selfishness on the part of owners. This is a mistaken view. In fact, private ownership would be more properly viewed as a means by which owners (including corporate and cooperative owners) are protected against the selfishness of others who would damage, abuse, or steal property that is not theirs.

From an economic viewpoint, private ownership is important because it provides people with a strong incentive to take care of things, to use them productively, and to plan for the future—activities that lead to economic progress. Human decision-makers must be motivated to carry out such productive activities. Let us consider how a system of well-defined, secure private ownership rights provides this motivation.

## Maintenance of Property

Private ownership encourages people to take care of things that they own. Private owners pay close heed to how their property is maintained and used because their property will decrease in value if it is damaged, abused, or poorly maintained. For example, if you own an automobile, you have a strong incentive to change the oil, see that the interior of the car is well kept, and have the car serviced regularly. Why? If you are careless in these areas, the car's value to both you and other potential future owners will decline. The market price of the car will fall, and you will bear the cost of this decline in value. Alternatively, if the car is well-maintained and kept in good running order, it will be of greater value to both you and others who might want to buy it from you. Your wise stewardship will be rewarded.

When property is owned by the government or owned in common by a large group of people, the incentive to take good care of it is weaker. For example when housing is owned by the government, there is no owner or small group of owners who will pay a dear price if the property is abused and poorly maintained. Therefore, it should not surprise us when we observe that compared to privately owned housing, government-owned housing is generally run down and poorly maintained in both capitalist counties like the United States and socialist counties like Russia and Poland. This laxity in care, maintenance, and repair simply reflects the incentive structure that accompanies government ownership of property. Private owners have a strong incentive to take good care of things because they both bear the cost of irresponsible use and reap the benefits of wise stewardship. In contrast, the incentive to take good care of things is much weaker in the case of property owned by governments.

## Development and Utilization of Resources

Private ownership provides people with an incentive to develop and utilize their resources in ways that are beneficial to others. Legally, private owners can do what they like with their assets, as long as they do not invade the property of others. The incentive structure emanating from private ownership, however, encourages owners to pay close heed to the *desires of others*. When individuals have a property right to their own labor services, and the right to make decisions concerning investments in education and training, they pay closer heed to what others value highly. Higher future earnings are the reward for developing and using skills demanded intensely by others.

Private owners of land, buildings, and other physical assets also have a strong incentive to heed the wishes of others. If they employ and develop their property in ways that others find attractive, the market value of the property will increase. In contrast, changes that are disapproved of by others—particularly customers or potential future buyers—will reduce the value of their property.

In essence, private ownership places people in a position where they can gain from changes that others like, but simultaneously owners must also bear the cost of modifications that others find unattractive. This is a vitally important characteristic of private ownership that is widely overlooked and misunderstood. Consider the situation of an apartment complex owner. The owner may not care anything about parking spaces, convenient laundry facilities, trees, or well kept ("green") open spaces accompanying the apartment complex. If consumers place a high value on these things, however, the owner has a strong incentive to provide them because they will enhance both earnings ("rents") and the market value of the apartments. An apartment owner who insisted on providing what he or she liked, rather than the things that consumers liked, would suffer a decline in earnings and the value of the capital asset (apartments).

The same forces are at work when houses are owned privately. Legally, private homeowners can make any modifications that they want. They can chop their house into small rooms, paint it a weird color, or cut down all the trees in the yard. However, if potential future buyers generally are likely to disapprove of these changes, the private homeowner has a strong incentive to refrain from them, since they would cause the value of the home to fall. On the other hand, if the homeowner makes changes favored by others, perhaps the construction of a deck or the planting of rosebushes and trees in the yard, the value of the property will rise. Therefore, while owners have the legal right "to do their own thing," their ownership also provides them with a strong incentive to heed the wishes of others—to make changes that others value highly relative to their costs (and refrain from changes that others dislike).

## Conserving for the Future

Private ownership encourages current resource owners to conserve for the future, since the current market value of property will reflect its expected future income. Suppose that several investors thought that the world was about to run out of oil and that therefore oil would be extremely valuable in the future. With private ownership, these conditions provide an opportunity for profit. People who believe that oil will be in short supply in the future can gain from conservation. If they are right, higher future oil prices will reward them with a handsome profit.

As long as private property is transferable, even current decision-makers who do not expect to personally reap the future harvest of an asset will have a strong incentive to take the preferences of future generations into account. Suppose a 60-year-old tree farmer is contemplating whether or not to plant Douglas fir trees that will not reach optimal cutting size for another 50 years. When ownership is transferable, the market value of the farmer's land will increase in anticipation of the future harvest as the trees grow and the expected day of harvest moves closer. Thus, the farmer will be able to sell the land and capture his contribution at any time, even though the actual harvest may not take place until well after his death.

Doomsday commentators who fear we are going to use up vital minerals, cut all the trees, or eliminate all the wilderness areas do not understand the conservation incentives accompanying private ownership. Should a resource become relatively more scarce in the future, its price will rise rapidly *when it is owned privately*. The expectation of higher future prices will induce individuals to cut back on their current use, preserve more of the resource for the future, and search more diligently for additional supplies of the resource (and good substitutes for it). As Dwight Lee, professor of economics at the University of Georgia, has stated, "No social institution does more to motivate current decision-makers to act as if they cared about the future than the institution of private property."[6]

## Accountability for Negligence

With private property rights, a negligent owner can be held accountable for damage to others through misuse of property. A car owner has a right to drive his car, but he has no right to drive it in a drunken or reckless way that injures others. A chemical company has control over the production of its products, but exactly for that reason, it is legally liable for damages if the production process or by-products injure or damage the health or property of others. Courts of law recognize and enforce the authority granted by ownership, but they also enforce the responsibility that goes with that authority. Property rights hold those with authority over the property (owners) accountable for any damages their actions impose on others.

For some natural resources it is difficult to assign ownership rights and hold violators responsible. If a property right is going to be legally enforceable, owners must be able to determine when a violation has occurred and to prove their case in a court. If Mr. Jones runs his car into Ms. Smith's vehicle, the case is often very simple, and the parties are likely to settle without going to a court of law. In other cases, however, it may be extremely difficult to prove that someone has invaded and damaged the property of another. For example, consider the case of Mr. Steele, the factory owner whose smoke fouls the air at Ms. Smith's home. Smith may have a right to clean air, which is

[6]Dwight Lee, "Patience Is a Market Virtue," *Reason*, January 1985, p. 44.

violated by Steele's smoke. To receive compensation, however, she must be able to demonstrate in court (1) the extent of the damage inflicted by the pollution, (2) that the pollutant in question actually caused the damage, and (3) that the pollutant came from Steele's plant. It may be very difficult, or even impossible for Smith to prove her contentions. When this is the case, Smith's property rights, even though they are defined, will be difficult for her to enforce. As we proceed, we will analyze these difficult cases in more detail and consider more fully potential alternatives to deal with them.

## TRADE RESTRAINTS AND POORLY DEFINED PROPERTY RIGHTS RETARD PROSPERITY

It is difficult to exaggerate the gains derived from specialization, division of labor, and exchange. These factors are the primary source of our modern standard of living. Can you imagine the difficulty involved in producing one's own housing, clothing, and food, to say nothing of radios, television sets, dishwashers, automobiles, and telephone services? Yet most families in North America, Western Europe, Japan, and Australia enjoy these conveniences. They are able to do so largely because their economies are organized in such a way that individuals can reap the benefits of the enormous increases in output—both in quantity and diversity—that accompany specialization, division of labor, and trade.

When people can trade with each other, they can specialize in the production and sale of goods and services that they can provide cheaply (that is, at a low opportunity cost). In turn, they can use the revenue from the sale of these goods to purchase those things that they could produce only at a high opportunity cost. No one will have to tell them to behave in this way. Pursuit of personal gain will encourage them to specialize and trade precisely in this manner. And in the process, they will also expand the aggregate output and improve the overall standard of living.

Obstacles that restrain trade retard our ability to expand output through specialization and mass production of goods. Sometimes these obstacles are physical restraints such as those imposed by bad roads, high transportation costs, and poor communications. In other instances, however, there are artificial obstacles that result from government policy. For example, tariffs, quotas, and restraints on the conversion of currencies restrain international trade. Similarly, price controls, restraints on entry into various businesses and occupations, and discriminatory taxes restrain trade among domestic citizens. In many countries, if you want to operate a business, you have to get permission from the government, show that you are qualified, prove that you have sufficient financing, charge a price set by the government and/or meet various other regulatory tests. Delays result because it takes time for all of this paperwork to be processed. Some officials may refuse your application unless you are willing to pay a bribe or make a contribution to their political coffers. The Peruvian economist Hernando De Soto found that in Lima, Peru, it took five full-time employees 289 days to meet the regulations required to legally open a small business producing garments. Furthermore, along the way, ten bribes were solicited, and on two occasions it was necessary to pay the bribes in order to get the permission to "legally" operate.[7] As if this is not enough, if you are a foreigner (or in many cases, if you are financed with foreign capital), you will be subject to an additional maze of regulations.

Needless to say, policies of this type stifle business competition, encourage political corruption, and drive decent people into the underground (or what De Soto calls the "informal" economy). Such artificially imposed restraints are like potholes in roads and blown up bridges. They retard both aggregate output and our realization of gains from trade and social cooperation. The higher the obstacles imposed by policies that restrain trade, the more the living standard of the citizenry will suffer.

Exchange is central to the social cooperation and the creation of wealth. The ability to provide a product or service that others are willing to purchase is powerful evidence that the activity is productive. On the other hand, policies that force traders to pass through various political roadblocks are generally counterproductive. They are equivalent to shooting oneself in the foot. If a country is going to realize its full potential, restrictions limiting trade and increasing the cost of doing business need to be kept to a minimum.

Poorly defined and enforced rights to property are also a major restraint on economic prosperity. When private property rights are well defined, individuals are both (1) able to gain from the positive things that they do for others (and for the society) and (2) held accountable for the damages that they do to the property of others. With private ownership, people will get ahead by producing things that others value highly relative to their costs. In essence, people help others in exchange for income. This organizational structure encourages wealth-creating activities. In contrast, when property rights are poorly defined and enforced or when one must get permission from the political authorities (rather than the owner) in order to use material assets, labor, or other resources, wealth creation is stifled. Predictably, people will spend more of their time and energy trying to take from others and soliciting favors from the political authorities. Output will fall short of its potential as the result of this diversion of resources.

## THREE QUESTIONS ALL NATIONS MUST ANSWER

Regardless of how the economy of a nation is organized, three basic questions must be answered:

1. What will be produced?
2. How will goods be produced?
3. For whom will goods be produced?

We cannot produce as many goods as we desire, so the first question is what goods should we produce and in what quantities? Should we produce more food and less clothing, more national defense and less personal consumption goods, or more for immediate consumption even though it will

[7]Hernando De Soto, *The Other Path: The Invisible Revolution in the Third World* (New York: Harper & Row, 1989).

mean less for future consumption? If we are using our resources efficiently, the choice to produce more of one commodity will reduce our ability to produce others. Every economy must decide what to produce among the possible combinations that could be generated from its resource base.

The second issue is how the goods will be produced. Usually, different combinations of productive resources can be used to produce a good. Education can be produced with less labor by the use of more television lectures, recording devices, and books. Wheat can be raised with less land and more fertilizer. Chairs can be constructed with more labor and fewer machines. What combinations of the alternative productive resources should be used to produce the goods of an economy?

The decision to produce is followed by the need to implement that decision. Resources must be organized and people must be motivated in order to transform the resources of an economy into a final output of goods and services. Economies may differ as to the combination of economic incentives, threats of force, and other types of competitive behavior that are permissible, but all still face the problem of how their limited resources can be used to produce goods.

Finally, every nation must address the issue of who will actually consume the available products. In economics, this is often referred to as the *distribution problem*. Property rights for resources, including labor skills, might be established and resource owners might be permitted to sell their services to the highest bidder. When this is the case, income generated from the sale of resources and their services would determine the amount of consumer goods each person would be able to afford. Alternatively, goods might be split on a strict per capita basis, with each person getting an equal share of the pie. Or they might be divided according to the relative political influence of citizens, with a larger share going to those who are more persuasive and skillful than others at organizing and obtaining political power. Finally, goods could be distributed according to need, with a dictator or an all-powerful, democratically elected legislature deciding the various "needs" of the citizens.

One thing is clear—these three questions are highly interrelated. How goods are distributed will exert considerable influence on the "voluntary" availability of labor services and other productive resources. The choice of what to produce will influence how resources are used. In reality, these three basic economic questions must be resolved simultaneously, and all economies, whatever their other differences, must somehow answer them. There are many ways to set up the institutions—the "rules of the game"—by which an economy makes these decisions. Each will result in a different set of answers to the universal questions.

## THE MARKET VERSUS GOVERNMENT PLANNING

**market mechanism** A method of organization that allows unregulated prices and the decentralized decisions of private property owners to resolve the basic economic problems of consumption, production, and distribution.

Two prominent ways to organize economic activity are through the market mechanism and collective decision-making. Let us briefly consider each of these methods. In an economy based on the **market mechanism,** the actions of participants are coordinated by voluntary agreements and market prices. Both goods and productive resources (including labor services) are owned privately. People are permitted to buy and sell ownership rights at mutually agreeable prices in unregulated markets. The role of government is limited to that of a referee—a neutral party enforcing the rules of the game. The government defines and protects private ownership rights, enforces contracts, and protects people from fraud. But the government is not an active player; the political process will not be used to modify market outcomes or favor some at the expense of others.

**collective decision-making** The method of organization that relies on public-sector decision-making (voting. political bargaining, lobbying, and so on). It can be used to resolve basic economic problems.

**socialism** A system of economic organization in which (a) the ownership and control of the basic means of production rest with the state and (b) resource allocation is determined by centralized planning rather than by market forces.

The major alternative to market organization is **collective decision-making,** the use of political organization and government planning to allocate resources. In some cases, the government may own the income-producing assets (machines, buildings, and land) and directly determine what goods they will be used to produce. This form of economic organization is referred to as **socialism.** Alternatively, the government may maintain private ownership in name, but use taxes, subsidies, and regulations to answer the basic economic questions. In both instances, political powers rather than market forces are used to direct the economy. In both cases, the decision to expand or contract the output of education, medical services, automobiles, electricity, steel, consumer durables, and thousands of other commodities is made by government officials and planning boards. This is not to say that the preferences of individuals are of no importance. If the government officials and central planners are influenced by the democratic process, they have to consider how their actions will influence their election prospects.

In most countries, a large number of decisions are made both through the decentralized pricing system and through public-sector decision-making. Both exert considerable influence on how we solve fundamental economic problems. Although the two arrangements are different, in each case the choices of individuals acting as decision-makers are important. Economics is about how people make decisions; the tools of economics can be applied to both market- and public-sector action. Constraints on the individual and incentives to pursue various types of activities will differ according to whether decisions are made in the public sector or in the marketplace. Still, people are people; changes in personal costs and benefits will influence their choices. In turn, the choices of political participants—voters, lobbyists, and politicians—will influence public policy and its economic consequences.

## LOOKING AHEAD

The next several chapters will focus on how the market mechanism works—the conditions necessary for it to work well and various situations where it does not work very well. Later we will also consider how the collective decision-making process works—how it allocates goods and resources. If we want to really understand the forces influencing the allocation of resources, we must apply the tools of economics to both market- and public-sector choices.

## CHAPTER SUMMARY

1. Trade is productive because it (a) channels each good toward the party that values it most, (b) directs producers into those areas where they have a comparative advantage, and (c) makes it possible for us to enlarge output through the division of labor and adoption of mass production

techniques. These gains from trade provide the foundation for economic prosperity.

2. Transaction costs are obstacles that retard the realization of gains from trade. Reductions in transaction costs make it possible for us to realize larger gains from trade, specialization, and social cooperation. People who provide trading partners with information and services that reduce their transaction costs and help them make better choices are producing a valuable good. Such specialists are commonly called middlemen.
3. When people exchange goods or resources for money, they are really exchanging property rights. Private ownership provides owners with (a) the right of exclusive use and benefit from that use (as long as their use does not invade or alter the property of others), (b) legal protection against invaders, and (c) the right to transfer (sell) their property to others.
4. From an economic viewpoint, private ownership is important because it encourages owners to (a) take care of things, (b) develop and utilize their resources productively, and (c) conserve for the future. Simultaneously, private ownership holds owners accountable if their actions impose physical damage on the property of others.
5. When governments impose obstacles that limit domestic and international trade, they reduce aggregate output and welfare. Such obstacles will reduce the living standard of the citizenry.
6. When property rights are poorly defined and enforced or when individuals must obtain permission from political authorities before they can use their resources, wealth creation will be stifled and output will fall short of its potential.
7. Every economy must answer three basic questions: (a) What will be produced? (b) How will goods be produced? (c) For whom will goods be produced? These three questions are highly interrelated.
8. There are two basic methods of making economic decisions: The market mechanism and public-sector decision-making. The decisions of individuals will influence the result in both cases. The tools of economics are general. They are applicable to choices that influence both market- and public-sector decisions.

# Study Guide

## CHAPTER 2

# DEVELOPING THE ECONOMIC WAY OF THINKING

## CRITICAL-ANALYSIS QUESTIONS

1. If Jones trades $2,000 to Smith for a used car, the items exchanged must be of equal value. True, false, or uncertain? Explain.

*2. "People in business get ahead by exploiting the needs of their consumers. The gains of business are at the expense of suffering imposed on their customers." Evaluate this statement from the producer of a prime-time television program.

3. In many states, the resale of tickets to sporting events at prices above the original purchase price ("ticket scalping") is prohibited. Who is helped and who is hurt by such prohibitions? Can you think of ways ticket owners who want to sell might get around the prohibition? Do you think it would be a good idea to extend the resale prohibition to other things—automobiles, books, works of art, or stock shares, for example? Why or why not?

*4. What forms of competition does a private property, market-directed economy authorize? What forms does it prohibit?

5. With regard to the use of resources, what is the objective of the entrepreneur? What is the major function of the middleman? Is the middleman an entrepreneur?

*6. Do private property rights permit owners to use their property selfishly to the detriment of others? Do private property rights protect owners against the selfishness of others? Explain.

7. "The rancher who owns his grazing land may over-graze it (let the cattle eat so much of the grass that erosion ruins the land) if he is desperate to make money now. Private ownership of land is dangerous." Evaluate.

8. The United States imposes tariffs (taxes) on textiles, automobiles, computer chips, and many other import products. Other trade restraints prohibit the importation of sugar and cheese products. How do these trade restraints affect the economic well-being of Americans?

*9. In the former Soviet Union, approximately 99 percent of the farm land was cultivated by either state-managed farms or cooperative farms operated by between 2,000 and 5,000 families. Private plots ranging up to one acre in size comprised about 1 percent of the land under cultivation. How would you expect the value of the output per acre on the private plots to compare with the output per acre on the government-owned and cooperative farms? Explain.

## MULTIPLE-CHOICE SELF-TEST

1. Does voluntary exchange create wealth (value)?
   a. No. Since exchange does not expand output, it cannot create wealth.
   b. No. If one person gains, the other party must lose an equal amount.

*Asterisk denotes critical-analysis questions for which answers are given in Appendix A.

c. Yes, if (and only if) the trade results in the creation of additional goods and services.
d. Yes, if the trade permits the parties to gain more of what they value.

2. When private ownership of a resource is clearly defined and enforced, the private owner
   a. Has little incentive to consider the wishes of others when deciding how to employ the resource.
   b. Has little incentive to take care of the resource.
   c. Has a strong incentive to care for and maintain the resource and consider seriously the wishes of others.
   d. Has a strong incentive to consume the resource during the current period rather than conserving it for possible use in the future.

3. Mary worked her way through law school as a typist. She is now making $85,000 per year as a lawyer. As the result of a heavy workload, she hires a typist at $18,000 per year. Mary discovers that she can type 50 percent faster than her new employee. Should Mary do her own typing?
   a. Yes, since Mary types faster than her new employee, she should do the typing.
   b. No, because if she did, she would have wasted her law school investment.
   c. Yes, because it will cost her less to do her own typing than to hire someone to do it.
   d. No, because when Mary spends time typing she is forgoing earnings as a lawyer; thus she is a high opportunity cost typist.

4. According to the law of comparative advantage,
   a. Individuals and nations gain when they specialize in the production of those goods which they consume.
   b. Individuals and nations gain when they specialize in the production of goods that they can produce at a high opportunity cost and exchange them for other desired goods that they can produce cheaply.
   c. The aggregate output of nations is maximized when trading partners specialize in the production of those items for which they are the low opportunity-cost producers.
   d. Gains from specialization and exchange are possible only in free-market economies.

5. Which of the following is an appropriate application of the law of comparative advantage?
   a. Countries with small endowments of labor relative to capital should specialize in the production of labor-intensive commodities.
   b. Since Mexican labor is cheaper than Canadian labor, trade between the countries results in exploitation of Canadian workers.
   c. Since workers in countries such as the United States utilize larger amounts of capital than workers in less developed nations, trade between capital-rich and capital-poor nations results in the exploitation of labor in the less developed countries.
   d. Countries that are low-cost producers of agricultural products should trade those products for goods that they can produce only at a high opportunity cost.

6. As the result of specialization and trade, according to the law of comparative advantage, total output
   a. Will decline because specialization is costly.
   b. Will rise, only when there is an accompanying decline in the total output of one's trading partners.
   c. Will rise if a nation is a net exporter, but will fall if the nation is a net importer of goods and services.
   d. Will increase, since resources will be better directed toward their highest valued uses.
7. What are three basic decisions that must be made by all economies?
   a. How much will be produced, when will it be produced, and how much will it cost?
   b. What will the price of each good be, who will produce each good, and who will consume each good?
   c. What will be produced, how will goods be produced, and for whom will goods be produced?
   d. How will the opportunity-cost principle be applied, how will the law of comparative advantage be utilized, and will the production possibilities constraint apply?
8. Even countries that rely primarily upon market forces to resolve the basic economic questions that confront all economies will usually rely on the collective decision-making process to
   a. Determine the prices of goods and resources.
   b. Allocate goods that are essential to life.
   c. Determine the distribution of income among citizens.
   d. Define and enforce private property rights and designate the acceptable forms of competitive economic behavior.
9. "The economic wealth of this country is primarily the result of the profit made by some individuals at the expense of others." The person who made this statement
   a. Has failed to comprehend that mutual gains result from specialization and exchange.
   b. Has failed to comprehend the fallacy of composition.
   c. Has failed to understand the significance of the production possibilities constraint.
   d. Has utilized the economic way of thinking. The statement is essentially correct.
10. Which of the following is most likely to promote the economic growth and prosperity of a country?
   a. A rapid increase in the general level of prices in the country.
   b. An increase in taxes on goods imported from other countries.
   c. A decline in transaction costs.
   d. Regulations that limit the ability of private owners to profit from the use of their property.

CHAPTER

# 3

# DEMAND AND SUPPLY

We might as reasonably dispute whether it is the upper or the under blade of a pair of scissors that cuts a piece of paper, as whether value is governed by utility [consumer demand] or cost of production [supply].

*Alfred Marshall*[1]

## CHAPTER FOCUS

- What is the law of demand? What does the demand curve for a good tell us about the consumer's valuation of the good?
- What is the law of supply? What does the supply curve for a good tell us about the opportunity cost of producing it?
- When will entrepreneurs earn profits and when will they experience losses? How will actions that generate profits and loss influence the wealth of a nation?
- What brings the choices of consumers and producers into harmony with each other?
- What is allocative efficiency? Do markets allocate goods efficiently?
- What goods will tend to be produced when the actions of consumers and producers are directed by market prices?

Consider the enormous challenge of coordinating the supply and demand of goods in a large city such as New York, Paris, or Tokyo. Literally millions of people in such a city have different skills, different preferences, and different economic goals. Some are highly educated, while others are illiterate. Some are virtually unable to start the day without a cup of coffee; others will go days without even a sip. Some prefer ham and eggs for breakfast, while others do just fine with tea and toast. Their views with regard to entertainment, vacations, clothing, and reading materials also vary dramatically.

How can the production and consumption activities of these people, with such varying skills and preferences, be coordinated in a sensible manner? How can they avoid producing too many (or too few) size 8 tennis shoes, belts with large buckles, economics textbooks, and so on? Every economy must deal with these coordination problems. In this chapter and the following one, we will analyze how a market-directed pricing system addresses such problems.

A market economy is a natural outgrowth of private property and exchange based on agreement and contracting. The economic role of government is limited to defining (and protecting) private property, enforcing contracts, protecting people from fraud, and similar activities that establish the rules of the game. In a market economy, no political official or planning board tells people what to do. But this does not mean that people are without direction. As we will see, markets provide people with direction and lead to economic order.

In the real world, of course, even economies that are strongly market-oriented, such as those of Hong Kong, Singapore, and the United States, use a combination of market and public-sector approaches to coordinate economic activities. Bear this in mind as we explore how a market pricing system

[1]Alfred Marshall, *Principles of Economics*, 8th ed. (London: Macmillan, 1920), p. 348.

functions, how it motivates people, and how it answers the basic questions of economics.

## CONSUMER CHOICE AND THE LAW OF DEMAND

Our desire for goods is far greater than the purchasing power of our income. Even rich consumers will be unable to purchase everything that they would like. Thus, all of us are forced to make choices.

Since we want to get as much satisfaction (value) as possible out of our limited income, we will make such choices purposefully. Predictably, we will choose those alternatives that we expect to enhance our welfare the most, relative to their cost. Prices will therefore influence our decisions. If the price of a desired good increases, we must give up more of other goods if we want to buy the now higher-priced commodity.[2]

According to the basic postulate of economics, an increase in the cost of an alternative reduces the likelihood that it will be chosen. This basic postulate implies that higher prices will discourage consumption. In contrast, lower prices, by reducing the opportunity cost of choosing a good, will stimulate the consumption of it. This inverse relationship between the price of a good and the amount of it that consumers are willing to buy is called the **law of demand.**

**law of demand** The principle that there is an inverse relationship between the price of a good and the amount of it buyers are willing to purchase.

Exhibit 3.1 illustrates the law of demand for Natasha, a consumer of oranges. When the price is 15 cents per orange, Natasha often has a glass of freshly squeezed orange juice for breakfast and sometimes has an orange with her lunch. At the 15 cent price, she consumes 24 oranges per month. A higher price will, according to the law of demand, induce Natasha to cut back on her consumption. When the price is 30 cents per orange, Natasha may consume only 16 per month, perhaps substituting apples, bananas, or other food products for the more expensive oranges. Should the price of oranges rise even higher, to 45 cents, for example, Natasha will economize still more on the more expensive oranges. Perhaps she will choose to have oranges only on special occasions and completely eliminate fresh-squeezed orange juice from her diet, dropping consumption to only 8 per month.

At this point, it is important to note two things about the law of demand. First, the inverse relationship between price and amount purchased by a consumer reflects the availability of substitute goods. When the price of a good increases, consumers turn to substitutes. When the price of oranges rose, Natasha turned to substitute food products like apples and bananas. To some extent, any good can be replaced by other goods. When the price of beef increases, consumers will turn to chicken, fish, and pork. Wood, aluminum, brick, and glass can often be substituted for steel. When gasoline prices rise, consumers will eliminate less essential travel, purchase smaller cars, use more mass-transit, and spend more time bicycling and walking. To summarize, when the price (and therefore the consumer's opportunity cost) of a good increases, people turn to substitute products and economize on their use of the

[2]When economists speak of an increase in the price of a good, they are assuming that the prices of other goods remain constant. Thus, the price of the good increases *relative* to the price of other goods.

**EXHIBIT 3.1**

**Law of Demand**

Here we illustrate the law of demand for Natasha—an individual consumer. When the price of oranges is 15 cents, Natasha consumes 24 oranges per month. When orange prices increase, Natasha cuts back on her consumption.

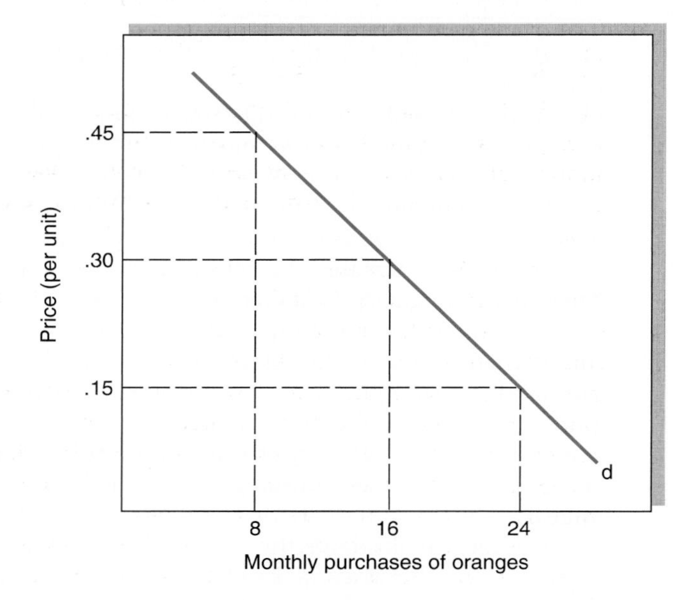


| P | Q |
|---|---|
| 45¢ | 8 |
| 30¢ | 16 |
| 15¢ | 24 |

more expensive good. Thus, the availability of substitutes provides the foundation for the law of demand.

**law of diminishing marginal utility** The principle that as the rate of consumption increases, the utility derived from consumption of additional units of a good will decline.

The law of demand might also be thought of as a reflection of the **law of diminishing marginal utility,** which states that as the rate of consumption increases, the utility derived from consumption of additional units of a good will decline. This law reflects the fact that when only a few units of a good are available, people will use the good to satisfy only their most urgent needs. At higher consumption rates, some of the good will be used to satisfy desires that are less urgent. For example, if you have only one quart of water per day available, you will probably use all of it for drinking purposes. If you have five gallons, you will be able to use some for cleaning or perhaps cooking as well. If you have 20 gallons, there will be enough to wash cars, clean floors, or water plants. As your consumption level increases, you allocate water and other goods to needs that are less and less urgent. As a result, the *marginal* (additional) *utility* derived from a good will decline as you consume more and more units of the good.

Consumer choices, like other decisions, are influenced by benefits and costs. A consumer will gain by purchasing more of a product as long as the benefit, that is, the marginal utility, derived from the consumption of an additional unit exceeds the cost of the unit (the expected marginal utility from other consumption alternatives that must now be given up). As consumption is expanded, however, the marginal utility of the good will decline, and eventually it will fall below the cost (price) of the good. Consumers will refrain from the purchase of such units. Of course, a decline in the price of a good will generally make it beneficial to purchase some additional units. However, as the additional units are consumed, the marginal utility of the good will decline, and once again it will eventually fall below even the lower price. Thus, the increase in consumption of a good will be a limited response.

## Market Demand Schedule

The market demand curve is merely the sum of the amounts demanded at various prices by all individuals in the market area. It is the horizontal sum of the individual demand curves. Since individual consumers purchase less at higher prices, the amount demanded in a market area is also inversely related to price.

Exhibit 3.2 illustrates the relationship between the individual and market demand curves for a hypothetical two-person market. Of course, real-world markets generally involve thousands (or even millions) of consumers. Nonetheless, the principle is precisely the same as for our simple two-person market. The individual demand of Alvin is added to that of Natasha to derive the market demand curve for oranges. When the price of oranges is 15 cents, Natasha and Alvin each consume 24 per month. The amount demanded in the two-person market is 48 oranges per month. If the price rises to 30 cents, Natasha purchases 16, and Alvin purchases 18. Thus, the quantity demanded in the market is 34 when the price of oranges is 30 cents. At a price of 45 cents, the market demand is 20 (8 purchased by Natasha and 12 by Alvin). The market demand is simply the horizontal sum of the individual demand

**EXHIBIT 3.2**

**Individual and Market Demand Curves**

The market demand curve is merely the horizontal sum of the individual demand curves. It will slope downward to the right just as the individual demand curves do.

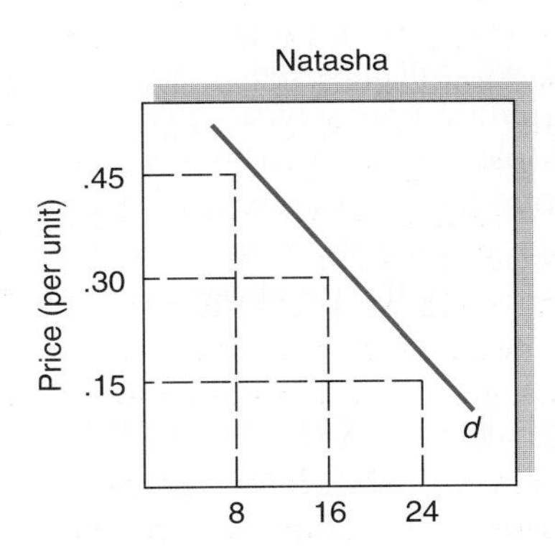


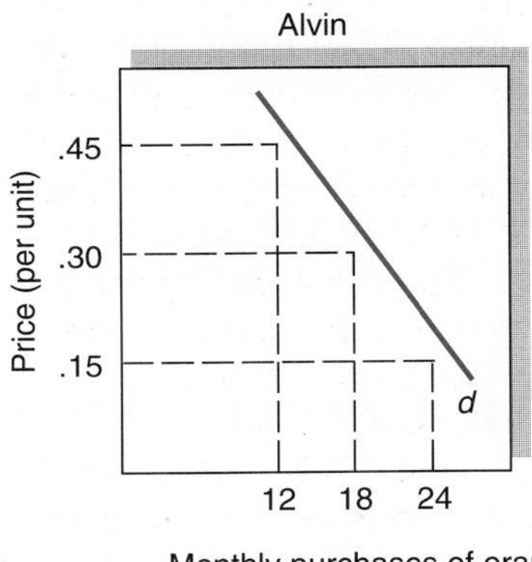


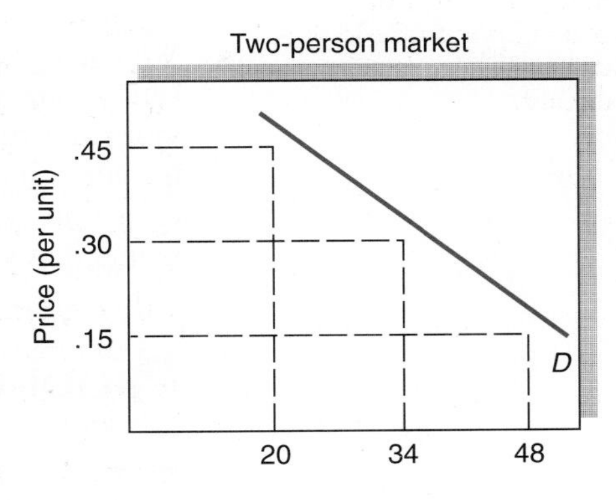


Monthly purchases of oranges

curves. Since individuals will buy less as the price increases, the amount demanded in the market will also decline as the price increases. So the market demand schedule is merely a reflection—an enlarged version—of the demand schedules for the individuals in the market.

The entire market demand schedule is not something that can be observed directly by government planners or decision-makers of a business firm. At any point in time, only the amount purchased at the current price is observed. Nonetheless, the choices of consumers reveal important information about their preferences—their valuation of goods. The height of the unseen demand curve indicates the maximum price that consumers are willing to pay for an additional unit of a product. If consumers value an additional unit of a product highly, they will be willing to pay a large amount (a high price) for it. Conversely, if their valuation of an additional unit of the good is low, they will be willing to pay only a small amount for it.

### Needs and Wants versus Demand

When discussing consumption decisions, noneconomists often speak of what they "need" or "want." For example, people sometimes say, "I need a new pair of shoes" when they already have a closetful back home. Two points should be recognized with regard to the relationship of demand to needs and wants. First, with regard to needs, there are no critical needs, minimum requirements, or absolute necessities in the sense that one must have some fixed amount of a good or service, regardless of its price. We live in a world of substitutes. There are alternative ways of satisfying needs. The amount of each good that it makes sense for us to consume cannot be determined by scientific study or the views of an outside expert. A vertical demand curve indicating that a fixed amount of a good is needed ("should be purchased") regardless of price is a myth.

Second, just because one wants a good, it does not follow that he or she should purchase it. Desires for goods are virtually unlimited. There are literally millions of goods and services that each of us would like to have more of. The authors want backyard tennis courts, a summer home in the mountains, and a vacation trip to Alaska, but we have not purchased any of them. Why? Because given the cost of these things and the constraints imposed by our finite income, there are other things that we value more highly than these items.

We live in a world of scarcity that restricts our consumption possibilities. We must choose to forgo many wants so that we will have the resources to satisfy our more urgent desires. Demand is important precisely because it provides information about the preferences of people—how much they value alternative scarce goods. After all, the choice to purchase a good reveals that the consumer values (needs or wants) that good more than the other needs and wants that must now remain unfulfilled as the result of the purchase.

## PRODUCER CHOICE AND THE LAW OF SUPPLY

How does the market process determine the amount of each good that will be produced? We cannot answer this question unless we understand the factors that influence the decision-making of those who supply goods. Producers of goods and services

1. Purchase and organize resources such as labor services, land, natural resources, and intermediate goods;
2. Transform and combine these factors of production into goods desired by households;
3. Sell the final products to consumers for a price.

Production involves the conversion of resources into commodities and services. In a market economy, producers have to pay the owners of scarce resources a price that is at least equal to what the resources could earn elsewhere. Stated another way, each resource employed has to be bid away from all other uses; its owner will have to be paid its opportunity cost. The sum of the amounts paid by the producers for each productive resource, including the cost of production coordination and management, will equal the product's opportunity cost. That cost represents the value of the things given up by society to produce the product.

The people of a nation will be better off if their resources are used to produce goods and services that are highly valued compared to the cost of the resources required for their production. At any given time, there is virtually an infinite number of potential business projects that might be undertaken. Some will increase the value of resources, thereby creating wealth and promoting economic progress. Others will reduce the value of resources and lead to economic regression.

**profit** An excess of sales revenue relative to the cost of production. The cost component includes the opportunity cost of all resources, including those owned by the firm. Therefore, profit accrues only when the value of the good produced is greater than the sum of the values of the individual resources utilized.

This is exactly what profits and losses generally do in a market setting. **Profit** is a residual "income reward" earned by decision-makers who produce a good or service that is valued more highly than the resources required for its production. It is what is left over after all costs have been paid. If an activity is to be profitable, the revenue derived from the sale of the product must exceed the cost of employing the resources that have been diverted from other uses to make the product. Profitable activities increase the value of resources. The good or service produced is valued more highly than the resources required for its production.

Suppose that it costs a chair manufacturer $50,000 per month to lease a building, rent the required machines, and purchase the labor, wood, cloth, and all other materials necessary to produce and market 1,000 chairs per month. The opportunity cost of producing the chairs is $50 per chair ($50,000 divided by 1,000 units of output). Suppose the manufacturer can sell the monthly output of chairs for an average price of $55 per chair. Under these circumstances, the actions of the manufacturer would create wealth. Consumers value the chairs more than they value the resources required for their production. The manufacturer's $5 profit per chair is a reward received for increasing the value of the resources.

**loss** Deficit of sales revenue relative to the cost of production, considering the opportunity costs of resources used. Losses are a penalty imposed on those who use resources in lower rather than higher valued uses as judged by buyers in the market.

In contrast, **losses** are a penalty imposed on businesses that reduce the value of resources. We live in a world characterized by imperfect information and dynamic change. Producers will sometimes make mistakes. The opportunity that looks so good when it is merely an idea may, when it is undertaken, turn out to be a business nightmare. Thus, producers will sometimes mistakenly use resources to produce goods and services that consumers value less than the opportunity costs of the resources used. Losses result, since the sales revenue derived from the project is insufficient to pay the opportunity cost of the resources. Business activities that generate losses destroy wealth, because the products generated are worth less than the resources it took to make them.

Losses are the market's way of bringing counterproductive activities to a halt. Sometimes losses will lead to the bankruptcy of producers. In other cases, producers will terminate production in order to minimize their losses. Losses are capable of disciplining even large producers. For example, International Business Machines (IBM) had to discontinue production in the mid-1980s of its small personal computer, the PC Jr, after experiencing several quarters of losses from the product. In the early 1990s, General Motors, one of the largest businesses in the world, was forced to scale back the size of its operations as the result of declining sales and economic losses.

## Central Role of the Entrepreneur

The entrepreneur plays a central role in the operation of a market economy, since it is his or her business to figure out which projects will, in fact, be profitable. The profitability of a project will be affected by the price consumers are willing to pay for it, the price per unit of resources required for production, and the cost of alternative production processes. Successful entrepreneurs must either be knowledgeable in each of these areas or obtain the advice of those who are.

To prosper, entrepreneurs must convert and rearrange resources in a manner that will increase their value. An individual who purchases 100 acres of raw land, puts in a street and sewage disposal system, divides the plot into one-acre lots, and sells them for 50 percent more than the opportunity cost of all resources used is clearly a successful entrepreneur. This entrepreneur "profits" because the value of the resources has been increased. Sometimes entrepreneurial activity is less complex. For example, a 15-year-old who purchases paint, brushes, and ladders and sells painting services to the neighbors is also seeking to profit by increasing the value of resources. In a market economy, profit is the reward to the entrepreneur who discovers and acts upon an opportunity to produce a good or service that is valued more highly than the resources required for its production.

## Supply Schedule

How will producer-entrepreneurs respond to a change in product price? Other things constant, a higher price will increase the producer's incentive to supply the good. New entrepreneurs, seeking personal gain, will enter the market and begin supplying the product. Established producers will expand the scale of their operations, leading to an additional expansion in output. In other words, higher prices obtainable for a product will induce producers to supply larger quantities of the product. The direct relationship between the price of a product and the quantity that producers are willing to supply is termed the **law of supply.**

**law of supply** The principle that there is a direct relationship between the price of a good and the amount of it offered for sale.

Exhibit 3.3 provides a graphic illustration of the law of supply. The supply schedule indicates the various quantities that producers are willing to supply at alternative prices per unit. Other things constant, producers will supply larger amounts at higher prices. Thus, the supply curve slopes upward to the right. Profit-seeking producers must cover their opportunity cost if they are going to continue to supply a good. Therefore, the height of the supply curve indicates not only the minimum price necessary to induce producers to supply a specific quantity, but also the opportunity cost of the resources used to supply the marginal unit of the good.

**EXHIBIT 3.3**

**Supply Curve**

As the per unit price of a product increases, *other things constant,* producers will increase the amount of the product supplied.

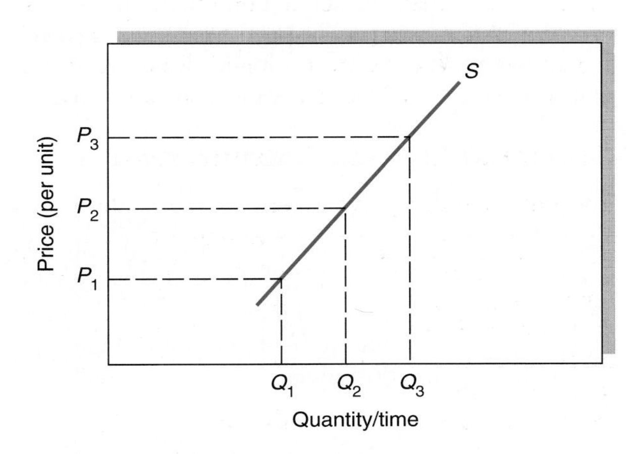


# MARKET COORDINATION OF SUPPLY AND DEMAND

**market** An abstract concept that encompasses the trading arrangements of buyers and sellers that underlie the forces of supply and demand.

**equilibrium** A state of balance between the conflicting market forces of supply and demand.

Consumer-buyers and producer-sellers make decisions independent of each other, but markets coordinate their choices and influence their actions. To the economist, a market is not a physical location. A **market** is an abstract concept that encompasses the forces generated by the buying and selling decisions of economic participants. A market may be defined in a narrow sense (for example, the market for razor blades, shoes, or bicycles). Alternatively, it may be useful to aggregate diverse goods into a single broad market, such as the market for "consumer goods." There is also a broad range of sophistication among markets. The New York, London, and Tokyo Stock Exchanges are highly computerized markets in which each weekday buyers and sellers, who never formally meet, exchange shares of corporate ownership worth billions of dollars. In contrast, the neighborhood market for child-care services is generally a highly informal market where buyers and sellers often agree to exchanges with a telephone call or as they pass in the street.

**Equilibrium** is a state in which conflicting forces are in perfect balance. When there is a balance—an equilibrium—the tendency for net change is absent. Before a market equilibrium can be attained, the decisions of consumers and producers must be coordinated. Their buying and selling activities must be brought into harmony with one another.

## Short-Run Market Equilibrium

The great English economist Alfred Marshall pioneered the development of supply and demand analysis. From the beginning, Marshall recognized that time

**short run** A time period of insufficient length to permit decision-makers to adjust fully to a change in market conditions. For example, in the short run, producers will have time to increase output by using more labor and raw materials, but they will not have time to expand the size of their plants or to install additional heavy equipment.

plays a role in the market process. He introduced the concept of the **short run,** a time period of such short duration that decision-makers do not have time to adjust fully to a change in market conditions. During the short run, producers are able to alter the amount of a good supplied only by using more (or less) labor and raw materials with their existing plant and heavy equipment. In the short run, there is insufficient time to build a new plant or to obtain new "made-to-order" heavy equipment for the producer's current facility.

In the short run, equilibrium will be present in a market when the quantity demanded by consumers is just equal to the quantity supplied by producers. The market price will tend to change in a manner that will bring these two forces into balance. If the price of a product is too high, the quantity supplied will exceed the quantity demanded. Producers will be unable to sell as much as they would like unless they reduce their price. Alternatively, if the price is too low, the quantity demanded will exceed the quantity supplied. Some consumers will be unable to get as much as they would like, unless they are willing to pay a higher price. Thus, there will be a tendency for price to move toward equilibrium—toward the single price that will bring the quantity demanded by consumers into balance with the quantity supplied by producers.

Exhibit 3.4 illustrates short-run supply and demand curves in the market for oranges. At a high price, 40 cents per orange, orange growers will plan to supply 600,000 bushels of oranges per month, whereas consumers will choose to purchase only 450,000 bushels. An excess supply of 150,000 bushels will result. Since production exceeds quantity sold at the 40-cent price, the inventories of growers will rise. In order to reduce their abnormally large inventories, some orange growers will cut their prices. The lower prices will make it less profitable to grow oranges. Some of the marginal orange growers will go out of business and others will reduce their current output. How much will the price of oranges decline? When price falls to 30 cents, the quantity supplied by growers and the quantity demanded by consumers will be in balance at 550,000 bushels per month. At this price the production plans of growers are in harmony with the purchasing plans of consumers.

What will happen if the price per orange is low—20 cents, for example? The amount demanded by consumers (650,000 bushels) will exceed the amount supplied by growers (500,000 bushels). An excess demand of 150,000 bushels will be present. At the 20-cent price, many consumers will be unable to find oranges for purchase. Rather than do without, some of these consumers would be willing to pay a higher price. Recognizing this fact, growers will raise their price. As the price increases to 30 cents, growers will expand their output and consumers will cut down on their consumption. At the 30-cent price, short-run equilibrium will be restored.

## Interrelation among Local, National, and International Markets

**price equalization principle** The tendency for markets, when trade restrictions are absent, to establish a uniform price for each good throughout the world (except for price differences due to transport costs and differential tax treatment of the good).

Local, national, and even international markets for tradeable commodities are highly interrelated. When there are no trade barriers (legal restrictions limiting exchange), transportable goods will tend to trade for the same price in all markets, except for price differences caused by transportation costs and taxes. This **price equalization principle** reflects the fact the any inequality in the price of a good, for reasons other than taxes and transport costs, creates a

**EXHIBIT 3.4**

**Supply and Demand**

The graph illustrates the supply and demand conditions for oranges listed in the table. When the price of oranges exceeds 30 cents, an excess supply is present, which places downward pressure on price. In contrast, when the price is less than 30 cents, an excess demand results, which causes the price to rise. Thus, the market price will tend toward 30 cents, the point at which supply and demand are in balance.

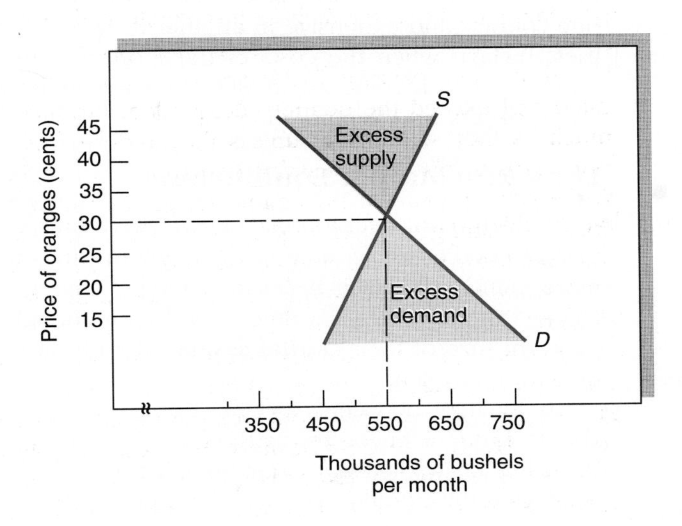


| Price per Orange (cents) | Quantity Supplied (thousand of bushels per month) | Quantity Demanded (thousand of bushels per month) | Condition in the Market | Direction of Pressure on Price |
|---|---|---|---|---|
| 45 | 625 | 400 | Excess supply | Downward |
| 40 | 600 | 450 | Excess supply | Downward |
| 35 | 575 | 500 | Excess supply | Downward |
| 30 | 550 | 550 | Balance | Equilibrium |
| 25 | 525 | 600 | Excess demand | Upward |
| 20 | 500 | 650 | Excess demand | Upward |
| 15 | 475 | 700 | Excess demand | Upward |

profit opportunity for entrepreneurs. One could profit by buying the good in the market where its price is low and selling it in the high-price market. But the additional buying will push the good's price upward in the low-price market, and the additional supply will drive its price down in the high-price market. Therefore, as entrepreneurs act on the opportunity for profit, they tend to equalize the price of each good across all markets—except for price differences reflecting transport costs and taxation among markets.

The price equalization principle explains why if it cost 5 cents to transport oranges from Florida to New York, oranges will not sell for 30 cents in Florida and 50 cents in New York. If such a price differential did prevail, entrepreneurs would buy the oranges at the cheap Florida price and ship them to New York for resale. But their actions would drive the price up in Florida while decreasing the New York price. Eventually the price differential between the two locations would be reduced to only the cost of transportation (assuming similar tax treatment between the states).

The principle is just as applicable to international markets. It explains why the price of a good, transportable at a relatively low cost, will not be cheap in one country and expensive in another if there is free trade between the countries. In fact, when the costs of transportation are low, the presence of substantial price differences between two markets is clear evidence of substantial trade barriers or differences in taxation.

## Long-Run Market Equilibrium

**long run** A time period of sufficient length to enable decision-makers to adjust fully to a market change. For example, in the long run, producers will have time to alter their utilization of all productive factors, including the heavy equipment and physical structure of their plants.

**capital assets** Long-lasting assets like buildings, machinery, and durable resources that are used to produce goods and services.

In the **long run,** decision-makers will have time to adjust fully to a change in market conditions by altering their output, not only using their current plant more intensively but if necessary, even changing the size of their production facility. The long run is a time period long enough to permit producers to expand the size of their **capital assets**—the physical structure and heavy equipment of their plant.

A balance between amount supplied and amount demanded will bring about market equilibrium in the short run. For equilibrium in the long run, however, an additional condition must be present: The opportunity cost of producing the product must also be equal to the market price.

If the market price of a good is greater than the opportunity cost of producing it, suppliers will gain from an expansion in production. Profit-seeking entrepreneurs will be attracted to the industry. Investment capital will flow into the industry, and output (supply) will expand until the additional supply lowers the market price sufficiently to eliminate the profits.[3] In contrast, if the market price is less than the good's opportunity cost of production, suppliers will lose money if they continue to produce the good. The losses will drive producers from the market, and capital will flow away from the industry. Eventually the decline in supply and shrinkage in the capital assets employed in the industry will push prices upward and eliminate the losses.

**rate-of-return equalization principle** The tendency for capital investment in each market to move toward a uniform, or normal, rate of return. An abnormally high return in a market will attract additional investment, which will drive returns down. Conversely, an abnormally low return will result in investment flight from the market, which will eventually lead to the restoration of normal returns.

In a market economy, characterized by freedom of entry and exit, there will be a tendency for the *after-tax* rate of return on investment to move toward a uniform rate, the competitive or normal-profit return. Neither abnormally high nor abnormally low after-tax returns will persist for long periods of time. This tendency for returns on investment capital to move toward a uniform, normal rate is sometimes referred to as the **rate-of-return equalization principle.**

It is easy to see why there is a tendency for abnormal investment returns—that is, both profits and losses—to be eliminated with the passage of time in a competitive environment. Suppose the after-tax investment return on

[3]Bear in mind that economists use the opportunity cost concept for *all* factors of production, including those owned by the producers. Therefore, the owners are receiving a return equal to the opportunity cost of their investment capital even when profits are zero. Zero profits mean that the capital owners are being paid precisely their opportunity cost, precisely what they could earn if their resources were employed in the highest valued alternative that must be forgone as the result of current use. Far from indicating that a firm is about to go out of business, zero economic profits imply that each factor of production, including the capital owned by the firm and the managerial skills of the owner-entrepreneur, is earning the market rate of return.

capital is abnormally high in the retail clothing industry and abnormally low in the publishing industry. The high return in retail clothing will attract additional investors (rival suppliers). Supply in the clothing industry will expand, causing both prices and returns on investment to decline. Eventually, normal returns will be restored in the clothing industry. Conversely, the abnormally low return in the publishing industry will cause investment flight and a reduction in supply. This shrinkage of the capital base and decline in supply in the publishing industry will lead to higher prices until eventually the remaining firms in the industry can once again earn normal returns.

The rate-of-return equalization principle explains why it will be very difficult for public policy to alter the market returns to any activity over the long term. Suppose the government tries to enhance the returns of farmers (or small business operators, or any other group). For example, it might provide low-cost loans, tax breaks, and subsidies in other forms. Such a policy might initially increase the returns in farming, but it will fail to do so in the long run. If the subsidies increase the returns in farming, capital will flow into the industry, driving commodity prices down (or production costs up) until normal returns are restored. In the long run, the subsidies do not enhance the profitability of investment in farming.

Conversely, consider what will happen if the government imposes higher taxes or discriminatory regulations on an industry. Returns in the industry may temporarily fall below normal. But if they do, capital flight and reductions in supply will push prices upward and eventually restore normal returns.

## MARKET COORDINATION AND ALLOCATIVE EFFICIENCY

If we are going to get the most from our productive efforts, we must allocate resources efficiently. Two conditions are required for allocative efficiency to exist:

*Condition 1: All economic activities that generate more benefits than costs to the participants must be undertaken.* Such actions result in gain—improvement in the well-being of at least some individuals without creating reductions in the welfare of others. Failure to undertake such activities means that potential gain has been forgone.

*Condition 2: No economic activity that is more costly than the benefits it generates should be undertaken.* When an action results in greater costs than benefits, somebody must be harmed. The benefits that accrue to those who gain are insufficient to compensate for the losses imposed on others. Therefore, when all persons are considered, the net impact of such an action is counterproductive.

Violating either of these conditions means allocative inefficiency, which retards the prosperity of nations.

It is informative to view demand, supply, and long-run equilibrium in regard to allocative efficiency. The *market demand curve* for a commodity, bicycles, for example, reveals the number of units that consumers are willing to purchase at various prices. It also reveals the consumers' valuation for various amounts of the good. Each point on a demand curve indicates that a consumer would be willing to pay the amount indicated by the height of the demand curve for that unit. Thus, the height of the demand curve at each quantity indicates the value that a specific consumer—the one willing to buy at that price—places on the unit.

Similarly, the *supply curve* indicates the number of units that producers are willing to supply at various prices. The height of the supply curve at each quantity indicates the producer's opportunity cost of supplying that unit.

Whenever the consumer's valuation of additional units of a good exceeds the producer's opportunity cost, producing and selling more of the good will generate mutual gain. Pursuit of this potential gain will motivate both the consumer and the producer. Directed by market prices, they will tend to produce output levels of each good that are consistent with allocative efficiency.

When only the consumer and producer are affected by production and exchange, an efficient output rate will be present when a market is in long-run equilibrium. Exhibit 3.5 illustrates why this is true. Suppliers of a good, bicycles in this example, will produce additional units as long as the market price exceeds the production cost. Similarly, consumers will gain from the purchase of additional units as long as their benefits, revealed by the height of the demand curve, exceed the market price. Market forces will result in an equilibrium output level of $Q$: All units for which the benefits to consumers exceed the costs to suppliers will be produced. Condition 1 is met; all potential gains from exchange (the area *abc*) between consumers and producers are fully

**EXHIBIT 3.5**

**Long-Run Equilibrium and Allocative Efficiency**

When a market is in long-run equilibrium, the opportunity cost of producing the last unit ($Q$) will just equal the value of the unit to the consumer. All potential mutual gains from production and exchange are realized. The difference between the amount consumers would be willing to pay (the height of the demand curve) and the market price represents the surplus (net gain) to consumers. The difference between the market price and the opportunity cost (the height of the supply curve) represents the surplus (net gain) of producers, including the suppliers of resources.

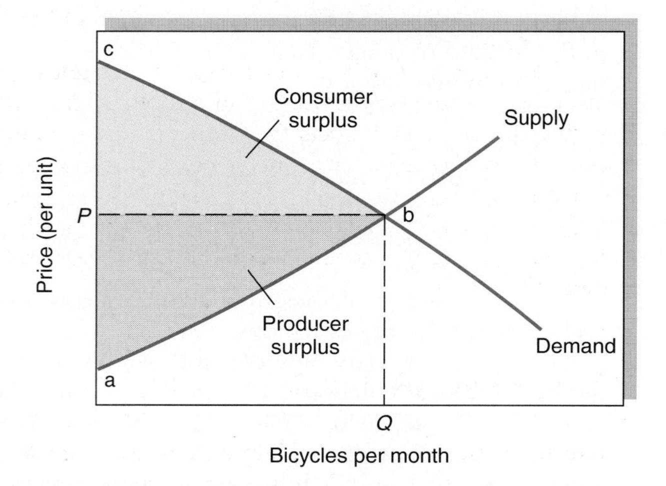

realized. Production beyond $Q$, however, will be inefficient. If more than $Q$ bicycles are produced, Condition 2 is violated; consumers value the additional units less than their cost. In long-run equilibrium, suppliers will find it unprofitable to produce units beyond $Q$ because the cost of the additional units will exceed revenues. Consumers and producers alike will thus be guided by the pricing system to output level $Q$, the output consistent with allocative efficiency.

**consumer surplus** The difference between the maximum amount a consumer would be willing to pay for a unit of a good and the payment that is actually made.

**producer surplus** The difference between the price producers receive for a good and the amount that would be necessary to induce producers (including resource owners) to supply each unit of the good.

The difference between the amount that consumers would be willing to pay and the amount they actually pay for a good is called **consumer surplus.** As Exhibit 3.5 illustrates, it is measured by the area under the demand curve but above the market price. Previously, we indicated that voluntary exchange was advantageous to buyer and seller alike. Consumer surplus is a measure of the net gain to the buyer/consumer.

The difference between the market price and the opportunity cost as measured by the height of the supply curve is called **producer surplus.** This is a measure of the gains that accrue to resource suppliers from the production and exchange of the good.

## How Markets Determine What Should Be Produced

Exhibit 3.5 illustrates how a market economy determines what goods will be produced. A market economy will tend to direct resources toward the production of a good as long as consumers value the additional units more than their opportunity cost. When the price that consumers are willing to pay for a good exceeds the opportunity cost of producing additional units, producers can gain by supplying the units.

Remember, because of scarcity, no society can produce as much as it would like. Scarcity forces all of us to make choices, since the resources used to produce one commodity are consequently not available to produce a different commodity. The price consumers are willing to pay for a specific good is a measure of how much they value it. The most highly valued of the foregone opportunities when a good is produced constitutes the good's opportunity costs of production.

The demand for a product can be thought of as the voice of consumers instructing firms to produce it. On the other hand, the opportunity cost of supplying the product reflects the desire of consumers for other goods that must now be foregone because the necessary resources have been employed producing the first item. Perhaps most significantly, markets will tend to direct entrepreneurs and resource owners toward the production of goods that are valued more than the other things that must now be given up as the result of their production.

## Looking Ahead

The concept of market equilibrium is essential to an understanding of economics. The real world, however, is characterized by dynamic changes that continually disrupt equilibrium between the forces of supply and demand in markets. The following chapter considers the major factors underlying changing market conditions.

## CHAPTER SUMMARY

1. Since our desire for goods is far greater than the purchasing power of our income, we are unable to consume as much as we would like. We have to make choices about what to consume and what to forgo. Prices influence those choices. Consumers will choose to purchase a good only if its value is greater than its opportunity cost (other things that must now be given up).
2. The law of demand holds that there is an inverse relationship between price and the amount of a good purchased. A rise in price will cause consumers to purchase less because they now have a greater incentive to use substitutes. On the other hand, a reduction in price will induce consumers to buy more, since they will substitute the cheaper good for other commodities.
3. The law of demand reflects the law of diminishing marginal utility, which states that the marginal utility (or value) of a good will tend to decline as more and more units of the good are consumed.
4. The market demand curve reflects the demand of individuals. It is simply the horizontal sum of the demand curves of individuals in that particular market.
5. We live in a world of substitutes. There is no critical need or fixed amount of any good that will be purchased regardless of price. Some substitute is always available. Also, wants and demand are fundamentally different. Our wants are unlimited and can never be satisfied. Demand is important precisely because it provides information about the intensity of wants—how much a consumer values a good relative to other things that must be given up if the good is purchased.
6. In a market economy, producers have to bid resources away from their alternative uses. The sum of the amounts paid by producers for each productive resource, including the cost of production coordination and management, constitutes the opportunity cost of producing a good. If the value of the good produced exceeds the opportunity costs, the producer-entrepreneur will earn a profit and increase the wealth of the nation.
7. Sometimes business entrepreneurs make mistakes and undertake the production of output that consumers value less than the opportunity cost of the resources used. When this happens, the producer-entrepreneur experiences losses, and the wealth of the nation declines.
8. Wealth is created by activities that convert and rearrange resources in a manner that increases their value. Profit is a reward to entrepreneurs who increase the value of resources, while losses are a penalty imposed on those who reduce the value of resources.
9. The law of supply states that there is a direct relationship between the price of a product and the amount supplied. Other things constant, an increase in the price of a product will induce established firms to expand

their output and new firms to enter the market. The quantity supplied will expand.

10. Market prices will bring the conflicting forces of supply and demand into balance. If the quantity supplied to the market by producers exceeds the quantity demanded by consumers, price will decline until the excess supply is eliminated. On the other hand, if the quantity demanded by consumers exceeds the quantity supplied by producers, price will rise until the excess demand is eliminated.
11. If there are no restrictions on the movement of a good, the good will tend to sell for the same price in all markets, except for price differences resulting from differences in transport costs and taxes among markets. This price equalization principle applies to local regional, national, and global markets.
12. When a market is in long-run equilibrium, supply and demand will be in balance, and the producer's opportunity cost will equal the market price. If the opportunity cost of supplying the good is less than the market price, profits will accrue. However, competition will tend to erode profit (abnormally high returns). The profits will attract additional suppliers, cause lower prices, and push the market toward a long-run equilibrium. On the other hand, if the opportunity cost of producing a good exceeds the market price, suppliers will experience losses. The losses will induce producers to leave the market, causing price to rise until long-run equilibrium is restored.
13. If we are going to make the most of our resources, they must be allocated efficiently. Two conditions are necessary for allocative efficiency: (a) all activities that produce more benefits than costs for the individuals of the economy must be undertaken, and (b) no activity that generates more costs than benefits can be undertaken. When a competitive market is in long-run equilibrium, the outcome is consistent with allocative efficiency.
14. The demand for a product indicates the value consumers place on various amounts of the good. The opportunity cost of supplying additional units of the product indicates the value that consumers place on other things that will have to be forgone if the good is produced. Markets will tend to direct producer-entrepreneurs to supply goods that consumers value most relative to their costs of production.

# Study Guide

## CHAPTER 3

# Developing the Economic Way of Thinking

## CRITICAL-ANALYSIS QUESTIONS

*1. "Economics is unable to explain the value of goods in a sensible manner. A quart of water is much cheaper than a quart of oil. Yet water is essential to both animal and plant life. Without it, we could not survive. How can oil be more valuable than water? Yet economics says that it is." Analyze the fallacy in this statement.

2. Most systems of medical insurance substantially reduce the costs to users of physician services and hospitalization. Some reduce these costs to zero. How does this method of payment affect the consumption levels of medical services? Might this method of organization result in "too much" consumption of medical services? Discuss.

3. How many of the following "goods" do you think conform to the general law of supply: (a) gasoline, (b) cheating on exams, (c) political favors from legislators, (d) the services of heart specialists, (e) children, (f) legal divorces, (g) the services of a minister? Explain your answer in each case.

4. "Production should be for people and not for profit."
   a. If production is profitable, are people helped or hurt? Explain.
   b. Are people helped more if production results in a loss than if it leads to profit?
   c. Is there a conflict between production for people and production for profit?

5. Explain how markets decide what goods should be produced. Do you think this is a good set of criteria? Why or why not?

6. In centrally planned socialist economies, the prices of many goods are fixed below market equilibrium levels by the government. Do you think keeping the price of certain goods cheap is beneficial to people? Why or why not?

## MULTIPLE-CHOICE SELF-TEST

1. The law of demand refers to
   a. The decrease in price that can be expected as more and more units of a product are demanded.
   b. The increase in price that results from an increase in demand for a good of limited supply.
   c. The inverse relationship between the price of a good and the quantity of the good demanded by purchasers.
   d. The increase in the quantity of a good available when the price of the good increases.

2. The concept of "demand" is different from the "needs" and "desires" of a person in that
   a. Needs and desires take into consideration the opportunity costs of consuming each item, while demand does not.

*Asterisk denotes critical-analysis questions for which answers are given in Appendix A.

b. A person's needs and desires are virtually unlimited, while individual demand is constrained by income, prices, and time.
c. The demand for a "need" is vertical, while the demand for a "desire" is horizontal.
d. This is a trick question, since "demand" and "need" are essentially the same thing.

3. According to the law of supply,
   a. More of a good is supplied as the prices of the resources required to produce it rise.
   b. There is a direct relationship between the price of a good and the amount that buyers choose to purchase.
   c. There is a direct relationship between the price of a good and the amount offered for sale by suppliers.
   d. There is an inverse relationship between the price of a good and the amount purchased by suppliers.
4. In order to be economically successful, the entrepreneur must
   a. Obtain the financial assistance of the government.
   b. Manage the firm efficiently, since efficient management is the sole route to economic profit.
   c. Use personal financial capital to avoid interest payments that would drive up the costs of the firm.
   d. Transform or rearrange resources so as to increase their market value.
5. When a market is in long-run equilibrium,
   a. The quantity demanded by buyers equals the quantity supplied by sellers.
   b. The opportunity cost of producing a good is equal to the market price of the good.
   c. The gains of buyers will be exactly offset by the losses of sellers in the market.
   d. Both "a" and "b" are true.
6. When there is an excess supply of a product in a market,
   a. Price tends to fall.
   b. Price tends to rise.
   c. Price is below equilibrium.
   d. Producers will have a strong incentive to expand output.
7. The height of the demand curve for good A represents
   a. The minimum price at which units of A could be produced without a loss to the seller.
   b. The maximum amount the consumer of each unit of A is willing to pay for the unit.
   c. The price at which the consumer's valuation of A is just equal to the producer's opportunity cost of providing A.
   d. The price at which producers are willing to supply the product.
8. When only the buyer and seller are affected by production and exchange of a good, competitive markets will generally
   a. Drive prices down to a level below cost and allocate too many resources to the production of a good.
   b. Lead to inefficient methods of production.

c. Direct suppliers to produce and consumers to purchase all units that are valued more highly than the resources used in their production.
d. Result in too little output of the good unless the government subsidizes the production of the good.

9. In a market economy, entrepreneurs are motivated to increase the supply of a product if the opportunity for profit is present. Profit opportunities will exist if
   a. The price consumers are willing to pay for the product indicates that they value it less than the opportunity cost of producing it.
   b. The government imposes a price ceiling below the market equilibrium price.
   c. The price consumers are willing to pay for the product indicates that they value it more than the cost of producing it.
   d. The producer has a good reputation and advertises regularly.
10. Market prices generally promote social cooperation because they
   a. Clarify the options available to people and encourage individuals to help others in exchange for income.
   b. Encourage government officials to levy taxes in order to provide people with the necessities of life.
   c. Eliminate the plague of scarcity by allowing prices to rise.
   d. Reward only altruistic actions whereby people seek to help others without the expectation of personal gain.

## PROBLEMS

1. The following table presents hypothetical weekly demand and supply schedules for tomatoes in a local market.

| Price (per pound) | Quantity Demanded (in thousands of pounds) | Quantity Supplied (in thousands of pounds) |
|---|---|---|
| $ .25 | 200 | 0 |
| .50 | 150 | 0 |
| .75 | 110 | 40 |
| 1.00 | 75 | 75 |
| 1.25 | 40 | 90 |
| 1.50 | 20 | 120 |
| 1.75 | 0 | 150 |

   a. Construct a graph of the supply and demand schedule.
   b. What is the market equilibrium price for tomatoes?
   c. If the price of tomatoes were 75 cents, how would the amount demanded by consumers compare with the amount supplied by producers? What would happen?
   d. If the price were $1.50, what would happen?
   e. Indicate the consumer surplus and producer surplus at the equilibrium price on your graph.

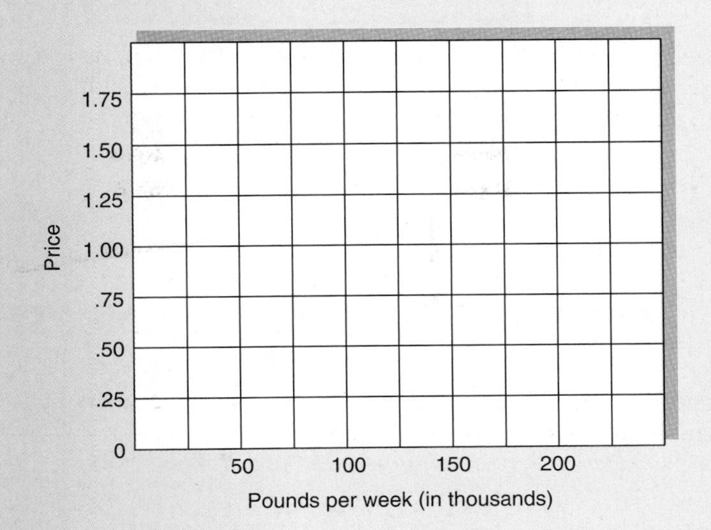


2. Susan owns and operates a dressmaker's shop. She leases sewing machines, purchases materials, rents space, and employs five workers to produce the dresses. Current output is 500 dresses per month. The following table indicates the resources that she uses when making the dresses and the costs of those resources.

| Resources | Cost (per month) |
|---|---|
| Employee compensation (5 workers) | $5,000 |
| Sewing machines (leased) | $3,000 |
| Cloth, thread and other materials (for 500 dresses) | $2,500 |
| Utilities | $1,000 |
| Rent (for shop) | $ 700 |
| Susan's managerial services | $2,000 |

Notice that costs include $2,000 for Susan's managerial services. If she were not operating the shop, she could earn $2,000 working for another firm.

a. Is the $2,000 for managerial services really a cost of producing the dresses? Why or why not?
b. Indicate the total cost of producing the 500 dresses. What is the cost per dress?
c. Susan currently sells all 500 dresses to a retailer for $30 each. What are her monthly sales revenues?
d. How large is Susan's profit or loss? Is Susan's dressmaking a productive activity? Explain.

CHAPTER

4

# DYNAMIC CHANGE AND THE MARKET PROCESS

I am convinced that if it [the market system] were the result of deliberate human design, and if the people guided by the price changes understood that their decisions have significance far beyond their immediate aim, this mechanism would have been acclaimed as one of the greatest triumphs of the human mind.

*Nobel laureate Friedrich Hayek*[1]

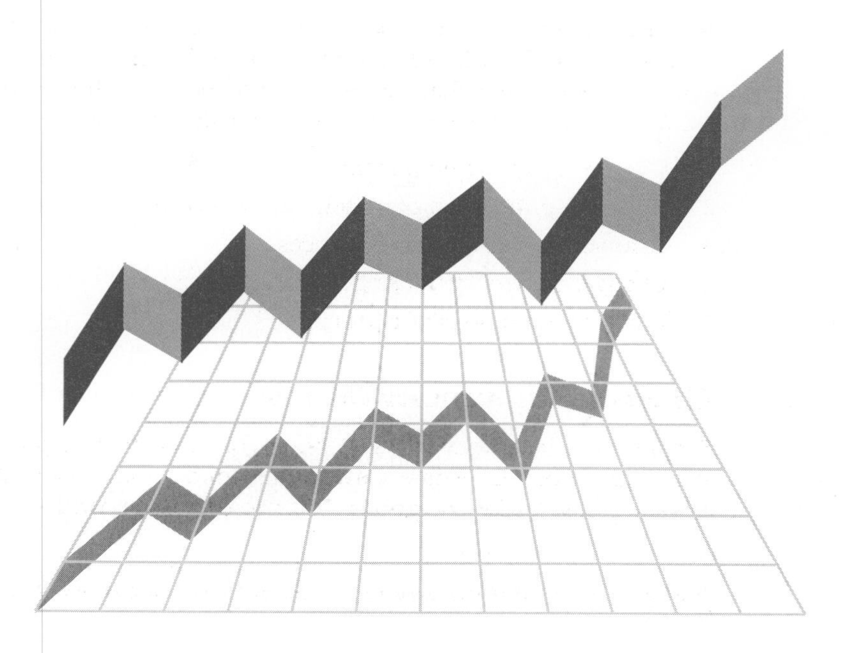

## CHAPTER FOCUS

- Why might the demand curve for a product shift? How will a change in demand affect the market price and output?
- Why might the supply curve for a product shift? How will a change in supply affect the market price and output?
- What is elasticity? How does time influence the elasticity of demand and supply? What role does time play in the market adjustment process?
- What happens when governments fix the price of a product above the market level? Below the market level?
- What is the invisible hand principle? Why are waiting lines, "sold out" signs, and huge inventories seldom observed in market economies?

We live in a changing world. New products are continually being introduced. Some are relatively unimportant, while others may transform our lives. New information may cause consumers to modify their choices, and changes in technology may alter costs of production. Preferences, incomes, and the scarcity of resources are constantly changing. This chapter analyzes how markets adjust and coordinate the actions of buyers and sellers in this dynamic world of ours.

# CHANGES IN MARKET DEMAND

The demand curve for a product isolates the impact of a change in the price on the amount purchased, assuming that other factors are held constant. Of course, factors other than price will influence the choices of consumers and the market demand. Let us consider five major factors:

1. Changes in consumer income.
2. Changes in the price of closely related goods.
3. Changes in consumer preferences.
4. Changes in expectations about future prices.
5. Changes in number of consumers.

### Changes in Consumer Income

Expansion in income makes it possible for consumers to purchase more goods at current prices. Consumers usually respond by increasing their purchases of a wide cross section of goods. Therefore, the demand for most products is

[1]Friedrich Hayek, "The Use of Knowledge in Society," *American Economic Review 35* (September 1945): 519–530.

positively related to income. As a result, the demand curve for most products shifts outward as the income of consumers increases. Conversely, a reduction in income generally causes the demand for a product to shift inward (to the left).

## Changes in the Price of Closely Related Goods

**substitutes** Products that are related such that an increase in the price of one will cause an increase in demand for the other (for example, butter and margarine, or Chevrolets and Fords).

Changes in the prices of closely related products also influence the choices of consumers. The related goods may be either substitutes or complements. When two products perform similar functions or fulfill similar needs, they are **substitutes.** There is a direct relationship between the price of a product and the demand for its close substitutes. For example, butter and margarine are substitutes. If the price of butter were to rise, many consumers would substitute margarine for the more expensive butter. The demand curve for margarine would increase (shift to the right) as a result. On the other hand, the demand for a good will decrease (shift to the left), if the price of a substitute good should fall. For example, lower coffee prices will reduce the demand for substitutes like tea and cocoa. A substitute relationship exists between beef and pork, pencils and pens, apples and oranges, and so forth.

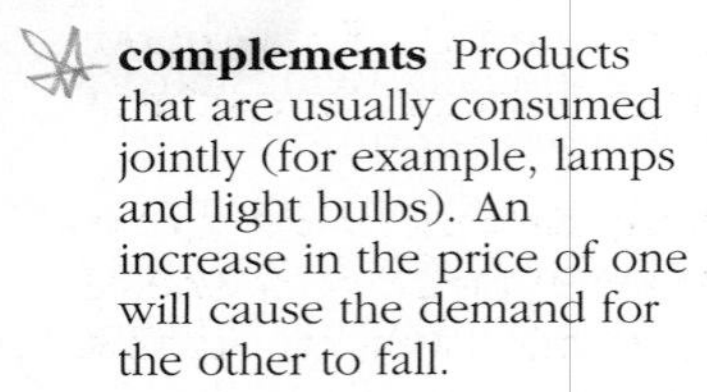

**complements** Products that are usually consumed jointly (for example, lamps and light bulbs). An increase in the price of one will cause the demand for the other to fall.

Other closely related products are consumed jointly. Goods that "go together," so to speak, are called **complements.** Coffee and cream are examples, as are bacon and eggs or film and cameras. With complements, there is an inverse relationship between the price of one and the demand for the other. For example, as the experiences of the 1970s illustrate quite well, higher gasoline prices cause the demand for large automobiles to decline. Gasoline and large automobiles are complementary. Similarly, lower prices for videocassette players during the 1980s increased the demand for videocassettes.

## Changes in Consumer Preferences

With time and additional information, the tastes and preferences of people change. The goods that people want tomorrow may differ from those that they prefer today. In the 1970s Americans consumed large amounts of beef, pork, and other goods containing substantial saturated fats that tend to increase cholesterol levels. New information linking diets of this type to heart disease and other medical problems caused many Americans to alter their eating habits. Therefore, during the 1980s the demand for chicken, vegetables, and salads increased sharply. Similarly, there was an increase in demand for goods like olive oil, canola oil, and yogurt that were thought to be better for your health. In contrast, the demand for red meats, whole milk, butter, and ice cream declined or increased only sluggishly during the 1980s. Thus, changes in preferences influenced the demand for goods.

## Changes in Expectations about Future Prices

When consumers expect the future price of a product to rise (fall), their current demand for it will expand (decline). "Buy now, before the price goes even higher" becomes the order of the day. For example, if you think that the price of automobiles is going to rise by 20 percent next month, this will increase your incentive to buy now, before the price increases. In contrast, if you think that the price of a product is going to decline, you will demand less now, as you attempt to delay your purchases until the price drops.

### Number of Consumers

The demand for a product is directly related to the number of consumers in the market. Changes in population and its composition can have a large influence on the demand for various products. There were a large number of people born in the United States during the 15 years (1946–1960) following the Second World War. As this baby boom generation increased the number of consumers in the 15–24 age group during the 1970s, the demand for jeans (a good purchased often by young Americans) increased sharply. The situation reversed during the 1980s, however. As the number of Americans in the 15–24 group fell by more than 5 million during the 1980s, fewer jeans were demanded. The sales of jeans fell from 500 million pairs in 1980 to less than 400 million pairs in 1989.

## CHANGE IN QUANTITY DEMANDED VERSUS CHANGE IN DEMAND

An economist constructing a demand curve for a product assumes that the five factors just discussed are held constant. Thus, a specific demand curve isolates the impact of a change in price on the quantity demanded of the good. Changes in any of the five factors will cause a change in demand, a shift of the entire demand schedule.

Failure to distinguish between a change in *quantity demanded* due to the change in price and a change in *demand*, a shift in the entire curve is one of the most common mistakes made by introductory economics students. Exhibit 4.1 clearly demonstrates the difference between the two. (Also review the accompanying "Thumbnail Sketch.") Exhibit 4.1a illustrates a change in *quantity*

### THUMBNAIL SKETCH

**Change in Quantity Demanded versus Change in Demand**

As Exhibit 4.1a illustrates, this factor will cause an increase in *quantity demanded:*

1. A decline in the current price of the good.

As Exhibit 4.1b illustrates, these factors will cause an increase in *demand* (a shift of the entire curve to the right):

1. An increase in consumer income (true for most goods).
2a. An increase in the price of substitutes.
2b. A decrease in the price of complements.
3. A change in consumer preferences (consumers prefer more of the good).
4. An increase in the expected future price of the good.
5. An increase in the number of consumers.

**EXHIBIT 4.1**

**Change in Quantity Demanded versus Change in Demand**

Frame a illustrates a change in *quantity demanded,* a movement along the demand curve $D_1$. A change in quantity demanded is brought about by a change in the price of the good. Frame b illustrates a change in *demand,* a shift in the entire curve from $D_1$ to $D_2$. A change in any one of the following factors will cause a change in demand: (1) consumer income, (2) price of a related good, (3) consumer preferences, (4) expectation about the future price of the good, or (5) the number of buyers.

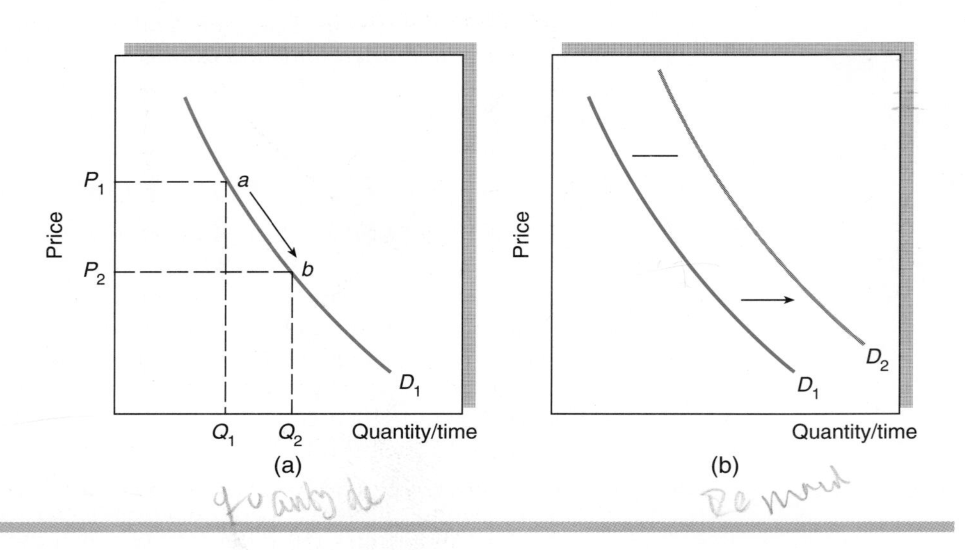


*demanded.* As the price of the good declines from $P_1$ to $P_2$, the quantity demanded increases from $Q_1$ to $Q_2$ (a movement from *a* to *b* along the same demand curve, $D_1$). The change in the price of the product causes a change in quantity demanded (but not demand). Exhibit 4.1b illustrates a change in *demand,* a shift in the entire curve as the result of a change in income, the price of a related good, consumer preferences, the expected future price, or the number of buyers. Changes that will increase the amount purchased (at each price) by consumers will shift the demand curve to the right (from $D_1$ to $D_2$). In contrast, changes that would reduce the amount purchased at each price would reduce demand (shift the curve to the left).

## Market Adjustment to a Change in Demand

How will a market adjust to a change in demand conditions? Using bicycles as an example, Exhibit 4.2 illustrates how the market for a product will react to an increase in demand. Initially, the market for bicycles reflected the demand $D_1$ and supply *S*. Given the initial market conditions, the equilibrium price of bicycles was $P_1$. Now suppose that consumer incomes increase or that people suddenly decide that they want to exercise more or engage in more recreational activities. As a result, the demand for bicycles increases from $D_1$ to $D_2$. This increase in demand will disrupt the initial equilibrium. After the increase in demand, consumers will want to purchase a larger quantity of bicycles than producers are willing to supply at the initial price ($P_1$). This excess demand

**EXHIBIT 4.2**

**Market Adjustment to an Increase in Demand**

Initially the market for bicycles reflected demand $D_1$ and supply $S$. Suppose that there is an increase in demand for bicycles (shift from $D_1$ to $D_2$), perhaps as the result of an increase in income or an exercise craze. The higher level of demand would increase both the equilibrium price (from $P_1$ to $P_2$) and the quantity supplied (from $Q_1$ to $Q_2$) in the market for bicycles.

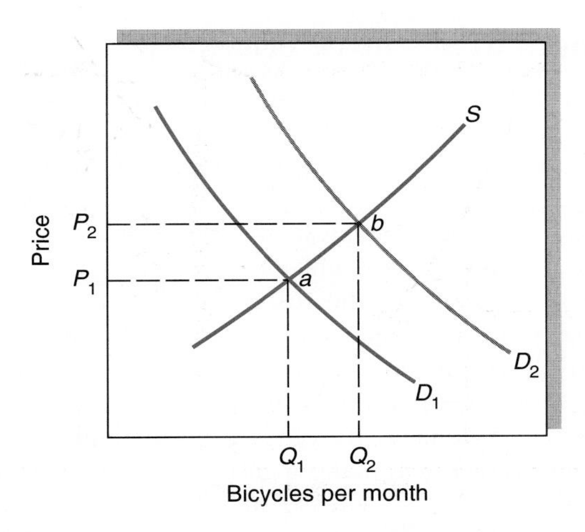


will push the price of bicycles up to $P_2$. At the higher price, producers are willing to supply a larger quantity ($Q_2$ rather than $Q_1$). The higher price will also moderate the increase in purchases by consumers. At the price of $P_2$, the quantity demanded by consumers will again be brought into balance with the quantity supplied by producers. The pricing system responded to the increase in demand by providing (1) producers with a stronger incentive to supply more bicycles and (2) consumers with more incentive to search for substitutes and moderate their additional purchases.

When the demand for a product declines, the adjustment process will provide buyers and sellers with just the opposite signals. A decline in demand (a shift to the left) will lead to lower prices. In turn, the lower prices will reduce the incentive of producers to supply the goods and moderate the decline in purchases by consumers.

## CHANGES IN MARKET SUPPLY

The supply curve reflects the impact of price on the choices of producers. Other things constant, the supply curve indicates the amount of a good that producers are willing to supply at alternative prices. As with demand, it is important to note the differences between (1) a change in quantity supplied and (2) a change in supply. A change in *quantity supplied* is a movement along the same curve in response to a change in price (see Exhibit 4.2, movement from *a* to *b*). A change in *supply* indicates a shift in the entire supply curve.

What factors would cause a shift in the entire supply curve? We previously indicated that a profit-seeking entrepreneur will undertake to produce a good only if the selling price of the good is expected to exceed the good's opportunity cost. Factors that increase the producer's opportunity cost of a good will discourage production and thereby decrease supply (shift the entire curve to the left). Conversely, changes that decrease the opportunity cost of supplying the good will increase supply (shift the entire curve to the right). Let us consider a number of important factors that will shift the supply curve.

## Changes in Resource Prices

Resource and product markets are closely linked. Firms demand labor, machines, and other resources because they contribute to the production of goods and services. In turn, individuals supply resources in order to earn income.

How will an increase in the price of a resource affect product markets? Higher resource prices will increase the opportunity cost of producing consumer goods that use the resource. The higher costs will reduce supply and increase price in the product market. Exhibit 4.3 illustrates this point. Aluminum alloys are an important resource used in the production of bicycle frames. Suppose that aluminum prices increase sharply, perhaps as the result of a stronger demand by other users or higher refinement costs. The higher aluminum prices will make it more expensive to produce bicycles. As the exhibit illustrates, this increase in the opportunity cost of producing bicycles

**EXHIBIT 4.3**

**Impact of Higher Resource Prices on Supply**

Aluminum alloys are often utilized in the production of bicycle frames. Therefore, an increase in aluminum prices would increase the opportunity cost of producing bicycles and thereby reduce the supply of bicycles (shift from $S_1$ to $S_2$). This reduction in supply would push bicycle prices upward (to $P_2$) and lead to a reduction in the equilibrium quantity (to $Q_2$).

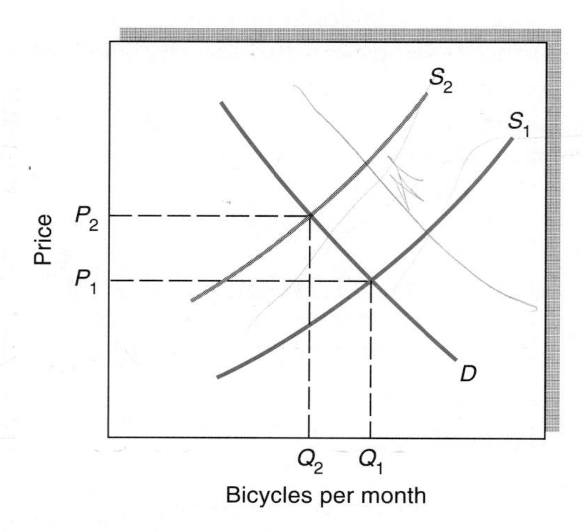

will cause the supply curve in the bicycle market to shift to the left. At any given price, the quantity of bicycles that producers are willing to supply will decline as the result of the higher aluminum prices (and therefore higher production costs for bicycles). The reduction in the supply of bicycles will push the price of bicycles upward from $P_1$ to $P_2$ and lead to a new smaller equilibrium quantity ($Q_2$).

Of course, lower resource prices would exert the opposite effect in the product market. A reduction in resource prices will reduce costs and expand the supply (shift the entire curve to the right) of consumer goods using the lower-priced resources. The increase in supply will lead to a lower price in the product market.

## Changes in Technology

Technological improvements—the discovery of new, lower-cost production techniques—will reduce the opportunity cost of production and increase supply (shift the supply curve to the right) in the product market. Exhibit 4.4 uses the market for videocassette recorders (VCRs) to illustrate the impact of a technological improvement. In 1981 VCRs sold for approximately $1,200, and American consumers purchased only 2 million units at that price. Between 1981 and 1987, improvements in technology substantially reduced the opportunity cost of producing VCRs. The reduction in costs made it more attractive for entrepreneurs to produce the product. Established firms expanded output. New firms began production, further contributing to the expansion of supply.

**EXHIBIT 4.4**

**Improved Technology and Shift in the Supply Curve**

In 1981, VCRs sold for approximately $1,200 (in 1987 dollars) and American consumers purchased approximately 2 million units. As the result of improved technology, production costs declined sharply during the next six years, shifting the supply curve to the right (from $S_{81}$ to $S_{87}$). Prices declined, inducing consumers to purchase a larger quantity.

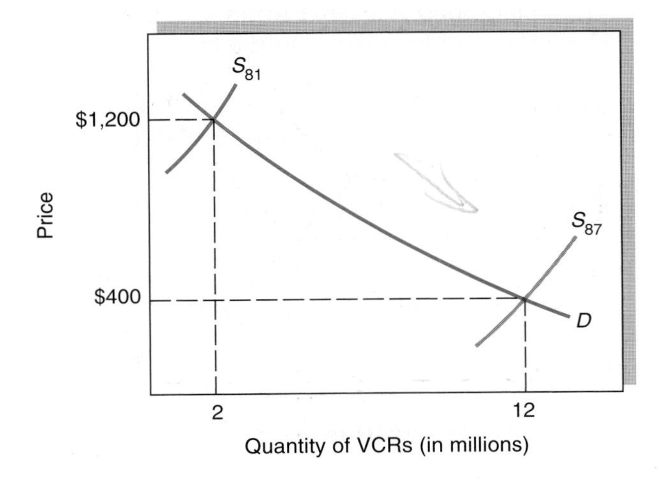

The supply curve shifted to the right (shift from $S_{81}$ to $S_{87}$). As the supply increased due to the lower production costs, the market price of VCRs declined sharply. By 1987 the price had plunged to only $400. At the $400 price, suppliers were willing to produce and consumers were willing to purchase approximately 12 million VCRs, six times the equilibrium quantity of 1981. This decline in the market price reflected the improved technology and brought the choices of buyers and sellers into harmony with each other.

### Natural Disasters and Political Disruptions

Natural disasters and changing political conditions may also alter supply, sometimes dramatically. For example, in 1986 a drought hit Brazil, destroying a substantial portion of that year's coffee crop. War and political unrest in Iran exerted a major impact on the supply of oil in the late 1970s, as did the invasion of Kuwait by Iraq in 1990.

When a natural disaster or political upheaval reduces the supply of a product, the market price of the good will increase. At the higher price, consumers who can switch to substitutes and cut back on their usage of the product without undue hardship will do so. The higher price will also increase the incentive of alternative suppliers of the good (and substitutes for it) to expand their output. This combination of forces will bring the choices of decision-makers into harmony, albeit at a higher price.

### Changes in Taxes

If they are going to continue supplying a good, producers must cover all of their opportunity costs, including the costs of taxes. If the taxes on a product increase, the opportunity cost of providing the good will rise. Like other increases in costs, the higher taxes will reduce supply and increase the market equilibrium price. Of course, a reduction in taxes will have the opposite effect. If the taxes imposed on the producers of a product decline, supply will increase and the equilibrium price of the good will decline.

The accompanying "Thumbnail Sketch" summarizes the major factors affecting both quantity supplied and supply. As we noted, an increase in the price of a good will lead to an increase in quantity supplied (a movement along the supply curve). On the other hand, an increase in supply (a shift in the entire curve to the right) will result from lower resource prices, improvements in technology, more favorable weather and/or political conditions in areas where the good is produced, and lower taxes.

## Concept of Elasticity

How responsive will consumers be to a change in the price of a good? How many more units will producers supply if the price of a good increases? Economists have developed a concept—*elasticity*—that they use when discussing the responsiveness of consumers and producers to changes in price.

### Elasticity of Demand

The term elasticity means responsiveness. If consumers are highly responsive to a change in price—for example, if the amount purchased by consumers de-

## THUMBNAIL SKETCH

### Change in Quantity Supplied versus Change in Supply

This factor will cause an increase in *quantity supplied:*

1. An increase in the current price of the good.

These factors will cause an increase in *supply* (a shift in the entire curve to the right as illustrated by Exhibit 4.4):

1. A decline in the price of resources used to produce the good.
2. An improvement in technology.
3. Favorable weather and improvements in political conditions that influence the supply of the good.
4. A reduction in taxes imposed on the good (and producers of the good).

clines sharply in response to a price increase—demand is said to be elastic. In contrast, if a substantial increase in price results only in a small reduction in quantity demanded, the demand is inelastic. An inelastic demand curve indicates inflexibility or little consumer response to variation in price.

**price elasticity of demand** The percent change in the quantity of a product demanded divided by the percent change in the price causing the change in quantity. Price elasticity of demand indicates the degree of consumer response to variation in price.

**Price elasticity of demand** is defined as

$$\frac{\text{Percent change in quantity demanded}}{\text{Percent change in price}}$$

This ratio is called the *elasticity coefficient.*[2] It permits us to make a precise distinction between elastic and inelastic. When the elasticity coefficient is greater than 1 (ignoring the sign), demand is elastic. When it is less than 1, demand is inelastic. *Unitary elasticity* is the term used to denote a price elasticity of 1. Although the sign of the coefficient for price elasticity of demand is often ignored, it is always negative, since a change in price causes the quantity demanded to change in the opposite direction.

The primary determinant of demand elasticity is the availability of substitutes. When there are attractive substitutes available for a product, demand will be elastic, because when the price of the product rises, consumers switch to the substitute products. For example, if the price of Chevrolets increases, many consumers will switch to Fords, Hondas, Volkswagens, and other cars.

[2]This formula provides an estimate for the elasticity *at a point* on the demand curve. One can also calculate the *arc* elasticity between two points on the demand curve. The formula for arc elasticity is

$$[(q_0 - q_1)/(q_0 + q_1)] \div [(P_0 - P_1)/(P_0 + P_1)]$$

where the subscripts 0 and 1 refer to the respective prices and amounts demanded at two alternative points on a specific demand curve. The arc elasticity is really the point elasticity at the midpoint of a line between the two points on the curve. In most cases, the point elasticity and arc elasticity coefficients will be quite similar.

Similarly, if the price of beef increases, consumers will substitute chicken, fish, pork, and other food products for the more expensive beef.

When good substitutes are unavailable, the demand for a product tends to be inelastic. Medical services are an example. When we are sick, most of us find witch doctors, faith healers, palm readers, and cod-liver oil to be highly imperfect substitutes for a physician. Not surprisingly, the demand for physician services is inelastic.

Exhibit 4.5 provides a graphic illustration for both elastic and inelastic demand curves. In Exhibit 4.5a the demand curve for ballpoints is elastic, because there are good substitutes—for example, pencils and felt-tip pens—for ballpoint pens. Therefore, when the price of the pens increases by 50 percent (from $1.00 to $1.50), the quantity purchased declines sharply from 100,000 to only 25,000, a 75 percent reduction. The price elasticity coefficient will equal 1.5 (75 percent divided by 50 percent). The fact that it is greater than 1 also confirms that the demand for ballpoint pens is elastic over the price range illustrated.

Exhibit 4.5b illustrates the demand curve for cigarettes. Since most consumers do not find other products to be a good substitute, the demand for cigarettes is highly inelastic. In the case of cigarettes, a 50 percent increase in price leads to only a 10 percent reduction in quantity demanded. Thus, the price elasticity coefficient is 0.2 (10 percent divided by 50 percent), substantially less than 1.

**EXHIBIT 4.5**

**Inelastic and Elastic Demand**

Using ballpoint pens as an example, frame a illustrates an elastic demand curve. As the price of ballpoint pens rose by 50 percent (from $1.00 to $1.50), the quantity sold plunged by 75 percent (from 100,000 to 25,000). The percent reduction in quantity is larger than the percent increase in price. Thus, the demand for the pens is elastic.

Using cigarettes as an example, frame b illustrates a demand curve that is relatively inelastic. A 50 percent increase in the price of cigarettes results in only a 10 percent reduction in the number sold. Reflecting the inelasticity of demand, the percent reduction in quantity is smaller than the percent increase in price.

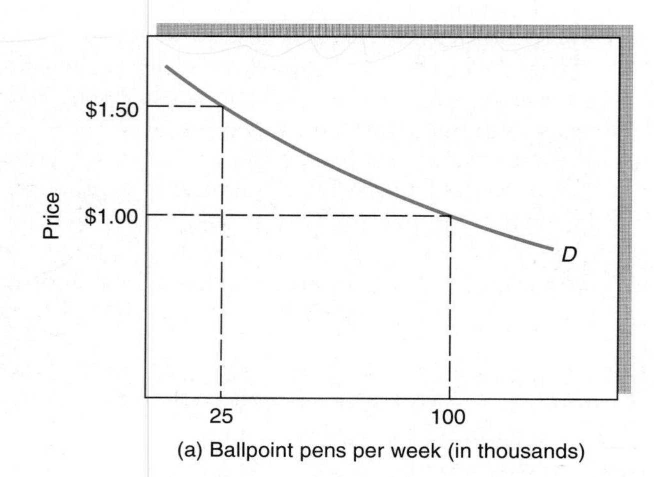

(a) Ballpoint pens per week (in thousands)

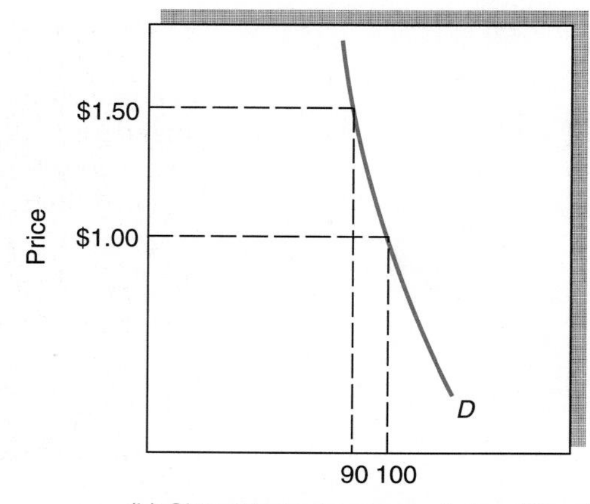

(b) Cigarette packs per week (in millions)

## Elasticity of Demand and Total Expenditures

The price elasticity of demand shows us the relationship between a change in price and the resulting change in total expenditures on the product. When demand is inelastic, the percent change in unit sales is less than the percent change in price. Since quantity demanded changes by a smaller amount than price, the change in price will exert a larger impact on total expenditures than will the change in quantity demanded. Therefore, total expenditures will change in the same direction as price when demand is inelastic.

Look what happened to the total expenditures on cigarettes as their price rose in Exhibit 4.5b. At the $1.00 price, consumers spent $100 million per week ($1.00 multiplied by the 100 million packs purchased) on cigarettes. As the price rose to $1.50, the total expenditures by consumers rose to $135 million per week ($1.50 multiplied by 90 million packs). The higher cigarette prices increased the total expenditures because the demand for cigarettes was inelastic.

When demand is elastic, on the other hand, quantity demanded is more responsive to a change in price. The percent decline in quantity demanded will exceed the percent increase in price. The loss of sales will exert a greater influence on total expenditures than the rise in price. Therefore, a price increase will reduce total expenditures when the demand for a product is elastic.

The demand for ballpoint pens in Exhibit 4.5a illustrates this point. At the $1.00 price, the total expenditures on the pens was $100,000 per week. An increase in the price to $1.50 per pen would result in total expenditures of only $37,500 ($1.50 multiplied by 25,000). Since the demand for the pens is elastic, the increase in price reduced the total expenditures on product.

The accompanying "Thumbnail Sketch" summarizes the relationship between changes in price and total expenditures for demand curves of varying elasticity. When demand is inelastic, like the demand for cigarettes illustrated in Exhibit 4.5b, a change in price will cause total expenditures to change in the same direction. If demand is elastic, like that for ballpoint pens illustrated in Exhibit 4.5a, price and total expenditures will change in opposite directions. For unitary elasticity, total expenditures will remain constant as price changes.

### THUMBNAIL SKETCH

**Demand Elasticity, Change in Price, and Change in Total Expenditures**

| Price Elasticity of Demand | Numerical Elasticity Coefficient[a] | Impact of Change in Price on Total Expenditures (and Sales Revenues) |
|---|---|---|
| Elastic | 1 to ∞ | Price and total expenditures change in opposite directions. |
| Unitary | 1 | Total expenditures remain constant as price changes. |
| Inelastic | 0 to 1 | Price and total expenditures change in the same direction. |

[a]The sign of the elasticity coefficient is negative.

## Elasticity of Supply

**price elasticity of supply** The percent change in quantity supplied, divided by the percent change in price that causes that change in quantity supplied.

The **price elasticity of supply** is equal to

$$\frac{\text{Percent change in quantity supplied}}{\text{Percent change in price}}$$

If the amount supplied is highly responsive to a change in price, the supply curve (in this price range) is elastic. When supply is elastic, the percent change in quantity will be larger than the percent change in the price that caused the change in quantity supplied. Therefore, the elasticity coefficient of supply will be greater than 1.

Conversely, if the amount supplied by producers is not very responsive to a change in price, supply is said to be inelastic. When supply is inelastic, the percent change in quantity supplied will be smaller than the percent increase in price causing the change in amount supplied. For example, if there was only a 10 percent increase in quantity supplied as the result of a 30 percent increase in price, supply over this price range would be inelastic. When supply is inelastic, the value of the elasticity coefficient of supply will be less than 1.

# TIME AND THE RESPONSE TO PRICE CHANGES

As changing market conditions alter the price of a product, both consumers and producers will respond. However, their response will not be instantaneous, and it may change over time. In general, when the price of a product increases, consumers will reduce their consumption by a larger amount in the long run than in the short run. Thus, the demand for most products will be more elastic in the long run than in the short run.

Using gasoline as an example, Exhibit 4.6 illustrates the role of time in the adjustment of a market to a decline in supply. During the late 1970s, political turmoil in Iran—an important oil producer—caused a reduction in supply and a sharply higher price in the market for gasoline. Adjusted for inflation, gasoline prices rose by more than 50 percent between 1978 and 1980. Initially, consumers responded to the higher prices by cutting out some unnecessary trips and leisure driving. Some drove more slowly in order to get better gasoline mileage. As the result of these adjustments, consumers were able to reduce their consumption of gasoline, but only by a small amount (from 7.4 million to 7.0 million barrels per day). Since the demand for gasoline in the short run was highly inelastic, the reduction in supply (shift from $S_1$ to $S_2$) pushed the price of gasoline up sharply (from 70 cents to $1.20).

Given time, however, consumers were able to make another adjustment that influenced their consumption of gasoline. As larger cars that used a lot of gasoline wore out, new car purchases shifted toward smaller cars with better gas mileage. Therefore, the long-run demand for gasoline was more elastic. By late 1981, the consumption of gasoline had declined to 6.6 million barrels per day, and there was downward pressure on prices.

This adjustment process for gasoline was a typical one. The consumption response to a price change will usually be less in the short run than over a longer period of time. As a result, an unexpected reduction in the supply of a

**EXHIBIT 4.6**

**Time, Elasticity of Demand, and Adjustment to a Reduction in Supply**

Here we illustrate the adjustment of a market to an unanticipated reduction in supply, such as occurred in the market for gasoline during 1978–1982. Initially, the price of gasoline was 70 cents (equilibrium *a*). Supply declined (shifted from $S_1$ to $S_2$) as the result of military conflict and political unrest in the Middle East. In the short run, prices rose sharply to $1.20, and consumption declined by only a small amount (equilibrium moved from *a* to *b*). In the long run, however, the demand for gasoline was more elastic. As a result, in the long run the price increase was more moderate (equilibrium moved from *b* to *c*).

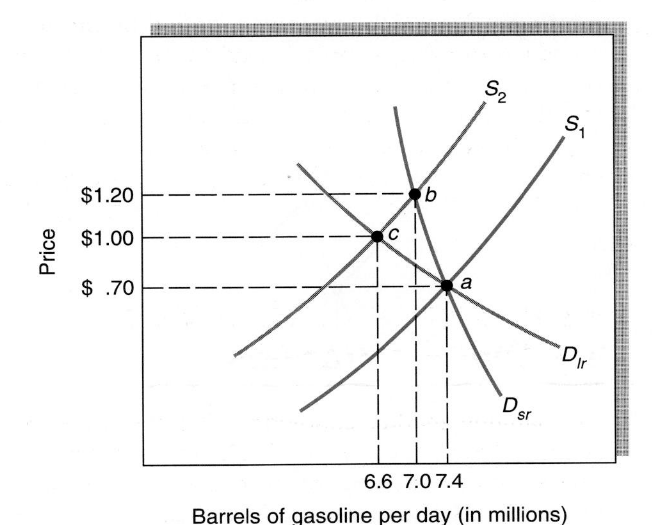


product will generally push price up more in the short run than in the long run. Similarly, the output response of producers to a price increase tends to be larger in the long run than in the short run. Thus, the market supply curve is usually more elastic in the long run than in the short run.

Using athletic shoes as an example, Exhibit 4.7 illustrates how supply elasticity influences the adjustment of a market to an unanticipated increase in demand. How will manufacturers of athletic shoes know that the demand for their product has increased? Initially, they will observe larger orders for the shoes as retailers seek to replenish their inventories, which have been drawn down by strong sales. At first, a manufacturer may be unsure whether the increase in orders is a random, temporary phenomenon or a lasting change. As orders continue at an unusually high level, more and more producers will be convinced that the strong demand is going to be long-lasting. As this happens, producers will both raise their price and expand their output. The higher prices will improve profitability and encourage producers to supply more athletic shoes. A rapid increase in output, however, will be costly. In order to expand output quickly, producers will often have to resort to overtime payments, air shipments of raw materials, and/or the employment of less experienced workers as they try to squeeze more output from their current facilities.

**EXHIBIT 4.7**

**Time, Elasticity of Supply, and Adjustment to an Increase in Demand**

It takes time for producers to respond to an increase in price. Therefore, supply is generally more elastic in the long run than in the short run. If the market for athletic shoes was initially in equilibrium at $P_1$ and $Q_1$, an unexpected increase in demand would push the price of the shoes up sharply to price $P_2$ (moving from *a* to *b*). Given more time, however, producers will expand output by a larger amount in response to higher prices. The long-run supply curve will be more elastic than the short-run curve ($S_{lr}$ rather than $S_{sr}$). The more elastic supply will place downward pressure on price (moving from *b* to *c*) with the passage of time.

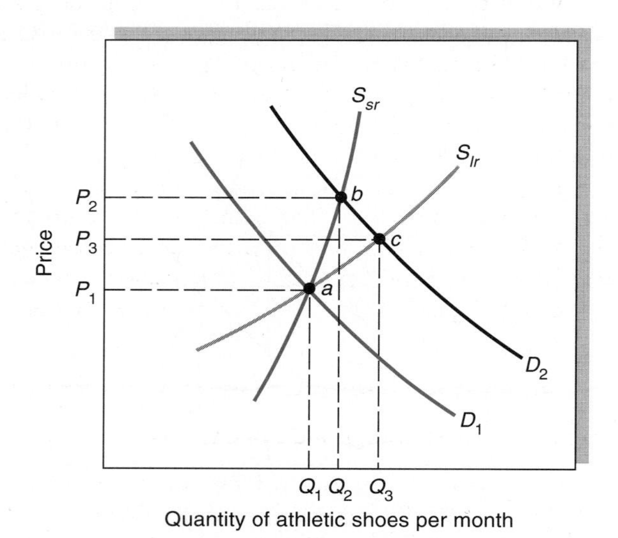


Since it is costly to expand output quickly, the higher market price ($P_2$) will lead to only a modest increase in output ($Q_2$) in the short run.

With the passage of time, however, the higher prices will elicit a larger expansion in output. The market supply will be more elastic in the long run ($S_{lr}$ rather than $S_{sr}$). Therefore in the long run, the price increase will be more moderate ($P_3$ rather than $P_2$). Time plays an important role in the adjustment process of markets.

## REPEALING THE LAWS OF SUPPLY AND DEMAND

Buyers often believe that prices are too high, and sellers that they are too low. Unhappy with prices established by market forces, individuals and organized interest groups may seek to have prices set by legislative action. Fixing prices looks like a simple solution, and countries around the world have tried it. However, fixing prices is more complex than it appears and often produces unintended consequences.

**price ceiling** A legally established maximum price that sellers may charge.

**shortage** A condition in which the amount of a good offered by sellers is less than the amount demanded by buyers at the existing price. An increase in price will eliminate the shortage.

Buyers seeking lower prices are sometimes able to persuade political officials to approve a **price ceiling** on various products. Exhibit 4.8a illustrates the impact of a price ceiling that fixes the price of a product below its equilibrium level. Of course, the price ceiling does result in a lower price than market forces would produce, at least in the short run. However, that is not the end of the story. At the below-equilibrium price, producers will be unwilling to supply as much as consumers would like to purchase. A **shortage** ($Q_D - Q_S$, Exhibit 4.8a) of the goods will result; that is, the quantity demanded by consumers will exceed the quantity supplied by producers *at the existing price.* Normally, competing buyers would bid up the price. Fixing the price will prevent that, but it will not eliminate the competition for the good.

When price is prevented from allocating the good to those most willing to pay, nonprice factors will play a greater role in determining who will receive the limited quantity of the good. As a result, price ceilings invariably have unintended secondary effects. (Remember, the consideration of the secondary effects is an important element of the economic way of thinking). Four of these unintended side effects are particularly important.

1. *Black markets will develop.* Frustrated by the shortage of the product, some buyers will offer sellers illegal side payments to obtain the good.

2. *The below-equilibrium price reduces the incentive of sellers to expand the future supply of the good.* Fewer resources will flow into the production of the good. Higher profits will be available elsewhere. With the passage of time,

**Exhibit 4.8**

**Impact of Price Ceilings and Price Floors**

Frame a illustrates the impact of a price ceiling. When price is fixed below the equilibrium level, shortages will develop. Frame b illustrates the effects of a price floor. If price is fixed above its equilibrium level, then a surplus will result. When ceilings and floors prevent prices from bringing about a market equilibrium, nonprice factors will play a more important role in the allocation of the good.

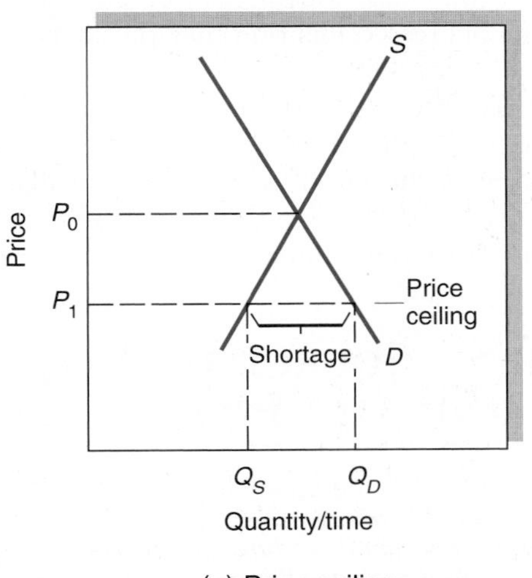


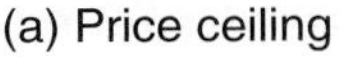

(a) Price ceiling

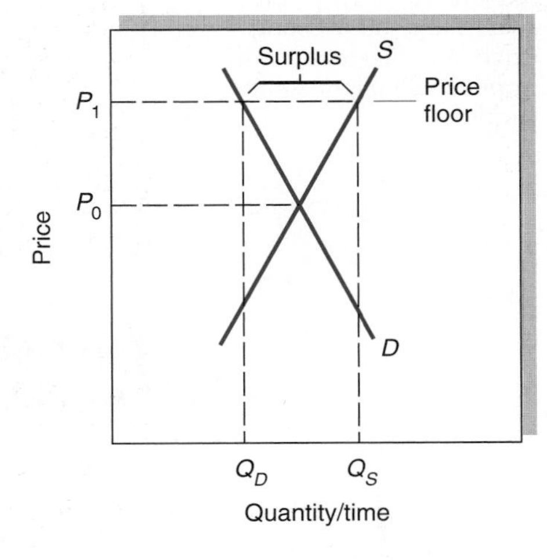


(b) Price floor

the shortage conditions will worsen as suppliers direct resources away from production of this commodity and into other areas.

3. *The quality of the product will deteriorate.* In the real world, there are two ways that sellers can raise price. Obviously, they can raise the money price of the good, holding quality constant. But they also have another option. Sellers can hold the money price constant and allow the quality of the good to diminish. Confronting a price ceiling, sellers will rely on this latter method of raising prices. They will use less durable inputs, cut maintenance, and reduce quality in other ways. Rather than do without the good, some buyers will accept the lower-quality product. It is not easy to repeal the laws of supply and demand.

4. *There will be an increase in discrimination.* Since there is an excess demand for the good, sellers are in a position to pick and choose among buyers. Predictably, they will tend to favor friends, persons with influence, and those with life-styles and skin colors like their own. When price is not allowed to play its allocative role, these nonprice discriminating factors will be more important.

Rent controls are one of the most widely used price ceilings. Rent controls that have been imposed in England, Sweden, New York City, and other places provide us with a test of our theory. And just as our theory predicts, we observe housing shortages, black markets, a deterioration in the quality of housing, and complaints of discrimination when these price ceilings are imposed. Observing these factors, the Swedish economist Assar Lindbeck remarked that rent controls "appear to be the most efficient technique presently known to destroy a city—except for bombing."[3]

**price floor** A legally established minimum price that buyers must pay for a good or resource.

**surplus** A condition in which the amount of a good that sellers are willing to offer is greater than the amount that buyers will purchase at the existing price. A sufficient decline in price will eliminate the surplus.

Exhibit 4.8b illustrates a case of a **price floor,** which fixes the price of a good or resource above its equilibrium level. At the higher price, sellers will want to bring a larger amount to the market, while buyers will choose to buy less of the good. A **surplus** ($Q_S - Q_D$) will result. Agricultural price supports and minimum wage legislation are examples of price floors. Predictably, nonprice factors will again play a larger role in the allocation process. Buyers can now be more selective, since sellers want to sell more than buyers, in aggregate, desire to purchase. Buyers can be expected to seek out sellers willing to offer them favors (discounts on other products, easier credit, or better service, for example). Some sellers may be unable to market their product or service. Unsold merchandise and underutilized resources will result.

Note that a surplus does not mean the good is no longer scarce. People still want more of the good than is freely available from nature, even though they desire less, *at the current price,* than sellers desire to bring to the market. A decline in price would eliminate the surplus but not the scarcity of the item.

## IMPORTANT SOURCE OF PROSPERITY: MARKET PRICES AND THE INVISIBLE HAND PRINCIPLE

> *Every individual is continually exerting himself to find out the most advantageous employment for whatever capital he can command. It is his own advantage, indeed, and not that of the society which he has in view. But the study of his own advantage naturally, or rather necessarily, leads him to prefer that*

[3]Assar Lindbeck, *The Political Economy of the New Left, 1970* (New York: Harper & Row, 1972), p. 39.

> *employment which is most advantageous to society. . . . He intends only his own gain, and he is in this, as in many other cases, led by an invisible hand to promote an end which was not part of his intention. By pursuing his own interest he frequently promotes that of society more effectually than when he really intends to promote it.*
>
> Adam Smith[4]

**invisible hand principle**
The tendency of market prices to direct individuals pursuing their own interests into productive activities that also promote the economic well-being of the society.

As Adam Smith noted more than two centuries ago, the remarkable thing about an economy based on private property and freedom of contract is that market prices will bring the actions of self-interested individuals into harmony with the general prosperity of a community or nation. The entrepreneur "intends only his own gain" but he is directed by the "invisible hand" of market prices to "promote an end [economic prosperity] which was not part of his intention." Let us take a closer look at how this **invisible hand principle** operates as market prices communicate information, coordinate actions, and motivate self-interested individuals to help others even as they help themselves.

## Communicating Information to Decision-Makers

Communication of information is one of the most important functions of a market price. We cannot directly observe the preferences of consumers, how highly they value bicycles relative to attic fans, television sets relative to oriental rugs, or automobiles relative to swimming pools. But product prices and quantities sold communicate up-to-date information about consumers' valuation of additional units of these and numerous other commodities. Similarly, we cannot turn to an engineering equation in order to calculate the opportunity cost of alternative commodities. But resource prices tell the business decision-maker the relative importance others place on production factors (skill categories of labor, natural resources, and machinery, for example). With this information, in addition to knowledge of the relationship between potential input combinations and the output of a product, producers can make reliable estimates of their opportunity costs.

Without the information provided by market prices, it would be impossible for decision-makers to determine how intensively a good is desired relative to its opportunity costs—that is, relative to the value of other things that might be produced with the resources required to produce the good. Markets collect and register bits and pieces of information about consumer preferences, costs, and matters related to timing, location, and circumstances and tabulate this information into a single summary statistic—the market price. This statistic reflects information on the relative scarcity of both products and resources; it provides producers with everything they need to know in order to bring their actions into harmony with the actions and preferences of others.

When weather conditions, consumer preferences, technology, political revolution, or natural disasters alter the relative scarcity of a product or resource, market prices communicate this information to decision-makers. Direct knowledge of why conditions were altered is not necessary. A change in the market price provides sufficient information to determine whether an item has become more or less scarce.

[4]Adam Smith, *An Inquiry into the Nature and Causes of the Wealth of Nations* (New York: Modern Library, 1937), p. 423.

## Coordinating Actions of Market Participants

Market prices coordinate the choices of buyers and sellers, bringing their decisions into line with each other. If producers are currently supplying a larger amount than consumers are willing to purchase at the current price, then the excess supply will lead to falling prices, which discourage production and encourage consumption and thereby eliminate the excess supply. Alternatively, if consumers want to buy more than producers are willing to supply at the current price, then the excess demand will lead to price increases. The price rise will encourage consumers to economize on their uses of the good and encourage suppliers to produce more of it. Eventually, these forces will eliminate the excess demand and bring the choices of market participants into harmony.

Prices also direct entrepreneurs to undertake the production projects that are demanded most intensely (relative to their cost) by consumers. Entrepreneurial activity is guided by the signal lights of profits and losses. If consumers really want more of a good—for example, luxury apartments—the intensity of their demand will lead to a market price that exceeds the opportunity cost of constructing the apartments. A profitable opportunity will be created. Entrepreneurs will soon discover this opportunity for gain, undertake construction, and thereby expand the availability of the apartments. In contrast, if consumers want less of a good—large cars, for example—the opportunity cost of supplying such cars will exceed the sales revenue from their production. Entrepreneurs who undertake such unprofitable production will be penalized by losses.

An understanding of the importance of the entrepreneur also sheds light on the market adjustment process. Since entrepreneurs, like the rest of us, have imperfect knowledge, they will not be able to instantaneously identify profitable opportunities and the disequilibrium conditions that accompany them. With the passage of time, however, information about a profitable opportunity will become more widely disseminated. More and more producers will move to supply a good that is intensely desired by consumers relative to its cost. Of course, as entrepreneurs expand supply, they will eventually eliminate the profit.

The move toward equilibrium will typically be a groping process. With time, successful entrepreneurial activity will be more clearly identified. Successful production and marketing methods will be copied by others. Learning-by-doing and trial-and-error will help producers sort out attractive projects from "losers." The process, though, will never quite be complete. By the time entrepreneurs discover one intensely desired product (or a new, more efficient production technique), change will have occurred elsewhere, creating other unrealized profitable opportunities. The wheels of dynamic change never stop.

## Motivating the Economic Players

As many leaders of centrally planned economies have discovered, people must be motivated to act before production plans can be realized. One of the major advantages of the pricing system is its ability to motivate people. Market prices establish a reward-penalty (profit-loss) structure that induces the participants to work, cooperate with others, use efficient production methods, supply goods that are intensely desired by others, and invest for the future.

No government agency needs to tell business decision-makers to use resources wisely and thereby minimize the cost of producing their product. The pursuit of profit will encourage them to economize, and if they do not they will be unable to compete successfully with more cost-effective rivals. No control authority has to force the farmer to raise wheat, the construction firm to build houses, or the furniture manufacturer to produce chairs. When the market prices of these and literally millions of other products indicate that consumers value them as much or more than their production costs, producers seeking personal gain will supply them.

Similarly, no one has to tell resource suppliers to invest in and develop productive resources. Why are many young people willing to undertake the necessary work, stress, late hours of study, and financial cost to acquire a medical or law degree, a doctoral degree in economics or physics, or a master's degree in business administration? Why do others seek to master a skill requiring an apprentice program? Why do individuals save to buy businesses, machines, and other capital assets? Although many factors undoubtedly influence one's decision to acquire skills and capital assets, the expectation of financial reward is an important stimulus. Without this stimulus, the motivation to work, create, develop skills, and supply capital assets to those productive activities most desired by others would be weakened.

## Prices and Market Order

How is it that grocery stores in thousands of different locations have approximately the right amount of milk, bread, vegetables, and other goods—an amount sufficiently large that the goods are nearly always available but not so large that spoilage and waste are a problem? How is it that refrigerators, automobiles, and VCRs, produced at diverse places around the world, are supplied to local markets in approximately the same amount that they are demanded by consumers? Why are long waiting lines and "sold out until next week" signs that are commonplace in centrally planned economies almost completely absent in market economies? In each case, the answer is that the invisible hand of market prices directs self-interested individuals into cooperative action and brings their choices into harmony.

The market process works so automatically that it is little understood and seldom appreciated. Perhaps an illustration will help the reader grasp the forces at work. In many ways, markets direct people in the same manner that open and congested lanes direct drivers on a busy freeway. No central planning authority assigns lanes and directs traffic on a freeway. Nonetheless, order and mutual cooperation generally result. Typically, drivers will switch from congested lanes to open lanes because they want to get where they are going faster. In so doing, they promote the social interest as they adjust their actions to mesh better with the choices of others.

Like the freeway driving, market success is often dependent upon one's ability to act upon opportunities. Like the degree of traffic in a lane, profits and losses provide market participants with information concerning the advantages and disadvantages of alternative economic activities. Losses indicate that an economic activity is congested, and as a result, producers are unable to cover their costs. Successful market participants will shift away from such activities. The most mobile resources will be moved to other, more valuable uses. Conversely, profits are indicative of an open lane, the opportunity to experience gain if one shifts into an activity where price is currently high relative to costs. As producers and resource suppliers shift away from activities characterized by congestion and into those characterized by the opportunity for gain (profit), they smooth out economic activity and enhance its flow. Order is the result, even though central authority is absent. This order in the absence of central planning is precisely what Adam Smith was referring to more than 200 years ago when he spoke of the "invisible hand" of market coordination.

### Qualifications

In this chapter, we have focused on the operation of a market economy. The efficiency of market organization is dependent on (1) competitive markets and (2) well-defined private property rights. Competition, the great regulator, can protect both buyer and seller. The presence (or possible entry) of independent alternative suppliers protects the consumer against a seller who seeks to charge prices substantially above the cost of production. The existence of alternative resource suppliers protects the producer against a supplier who might otherwise be tempted to withhold a vital resource unless granted exorbitant compensation. The existence of alternative employment opportunities protects the employee from the power of any single employer. Competition can equalize the bargaining power between buyers and sellers.

Understanding the information, coordination, and motivation results of the market mechanism helps us see all the more clearly the importance of property rights, the things actually traded in markets. Although property rights are often thought to increase selfish behavior, they are actually an arrangement to (1) force resource users—including those who own them—to bear fully the opportunity cost of their actions and (2) prohibit persons from engaging in destructive forms of competition. When property rights are well-defined, secure, and tradeable, suppliers of goods and services will be required to pay resource owners the opportunity cost of each resource employed. They will not be permitted to seize and use scarce resources without compensating the owner, that is, without bidding the resources away from alternative users.

Similarly, secure property rights eliminate the use of violence as a competitive weapon. A producer you do not buy from (or work for) will not be permitted to burn down your house. Nor will a competitive resource supplier whose prices you undercut be permitted to slash your automobile tires or threaten you with bodily injury.

Lack of competition and poorly defined property rights will alter the operation of a market economy. As we proceed, we will investigate each of these problems in detail.

## LOOKING AHEAD

As we have indicated, costs influence market supply. Entrepreneurs generally use business firms when organizing production. The following chapter focuses on the relationship between the output of firms and the cost of supplying products.

# CHAPTER SUMMARY

1. It is important to distinguish between a change in *quantity demanded* and a change in *demand*. The first is a movement along the demand curve due to a change in price, the latter a shift in the entire curve.
2. The following factors will cause an increase in demand: (a) an increase in consumer income, (b) an increase in the price of substitutes (or a decline in the price of complements), (c) an increase in the desire of consumers for the good, (d) an increase in the expected future price of the good, and (e) an increase in the size (number of consumers) of the market. If these factors changed in the opposite direction, the demand for the product would decline.
3. An increase (decrease) in demand for a product will cause both the equilibrium price and quantity to increase (decrease).
4. It is also important to distinguish between a change in *quantity supplied* (a movement along a supply curve) and a change in *supply* (a shift in the supply curve). An increase in price will lead to an increase in quantity supplied. The following factors will lead to an increase in supply: (a) lower resource prices, (b) improvements in technology, (c) an improvement in weather or political conditions in areas where the good is produced, and (d) lower taxes on the good (or the producers of the good).
5. An increase (decrease) in the supply of a product will reduce (increase) the market price and lead to a larger (smaller) equilibrium level of output.
6. Price elasticity of demand indicates the responsiveness of the amount purchased to a change in price. When the amount purchased by consumers is highly responsive to a change in price, demand is elastic. Conversely, if a substantial change in price results in only a small change in quantity demanded, demand is inelastic. When there are good substitutes available for a product, the demand for the good will tend to be more elastic.
7. The concept of elasticity also applies to supply. When the percent change in the quantity supplied by producers is greater than the percent change in price, supply is elastic.
8. With time, both consumers and producers will be able to respond more fully to a change in price. Therefore, both demand and supply will tend to be more elastic in the long run than in the short run.
9. When there is an unexpected reduction in supply, the immediate increase in price (when demand is more inelastic) is generally larger than the price increase over the longer term (when demand tends to be more elastic). Similarly, an unexpected increase in demand will generally lead to a larger price increase in the short run (when supply is more inelastic) than will emerge in the long run (when supply will be more elastic).
10. When a price is fixed below the market equilibrium, buyers will want to purchase more than sellers are willing to supply. A shortage will result. Nonprice factors such as waiting lines, quality deterioration, and illegal (black market) transactions will play a more important role in the allocation process. When a price is fixed above the market equilibrium level, sellers will want to supply a larger amount than buyers are willing to purchase at the current price. A surplus will result.

11. When competition is present and property rights are securely defined, market prices will generally direct self-interested individuals into productive activities. Even self-interested individuals will be willing to do things that are highly valued by others because such actions lead to high incomes (and profits). In the process, the highly valued productive activities will promote the general welfare. Economists refer to this phenomenon as the invisible hand principle.
12. The information provided by prices instructs entrepreneurs as to (a) how to use scarce resources and (b) which products are intensely desired (relative to their opportunity cost) by consumers. Market prices establish a reward-penalty system that motivates people to work efficiently, invest for the future, supply intensely desired goods, economize on the use of scarce resources, and use efficient production methods. The efficiency of the system is dependent on (a) competitive market conditions and (b) securely defined private property rights.

# *Study Guide*

## CHAPTER 4

# DEVELOPING THE ECONOMIC WAY OF THINKING

## CRITICAL-ANALYSIS QUESTIONS

*1. How would substantially lower gasoline prices affect (a) the demand for large cars, (b) the demand for small cars, (c) the demand for hotels in popular vacation areas, (d) the incentive to experiment and develop electric-powered cars, and (e) the demand for gasoline? (Be careful when answering e.)

2. "As the price of pineapple rises, the demand of consumers will begin to decline. Economists estimate that a 10 percent increase in pineapple prices will cause the demand for pineapples to decline by 20 percent." Indicate two errors in this statement.

*3. A severe drought in major agricultural areas of the United States during the summer of 1988 sharply reduced the 1988 output of wheat, corn, soybeans, and hay. Indicate the expected impact of the drought on the following:
   a. Prices of feed grains and hay during the summer of 1988.
   b. Price of cattle during the summer and fall of 1988.
   c. Price of cattle during the summer and fall of 1989.

4. Indicate how each of the following would influence the supply and market price of ice cream.
   a. A sharp decline in the price of raw milk.
   b. An increase in the price of sugar.
   c. An increase in the price of yogurt.
   d. A decline the price of strawberries and bananas, goods that are often used as toppings with ice cream.
   e. An increase in consumer income.

5. "Economists claim that when the price of something goes up, producers bring more of it to the market. But the last year in which the price was really high for oranges, there were not nearly as many oranges as usual. The economists are wrong!" How would an economist respond?

6. Indicate whether the demand for the following goods is likely to be elastic or inelastic: tomatoes, electricity, apples, gasoline, Chevrolet automobiles, and fresh green beans. In each case, briefly explain your answer.

*7. Indicate whether the following statements are true or false.
   a. If a 10 percent increase in the price of a good leads to a 25 percent reduction in amount purchased, demand for the product is elastic.
   b. If a 10 percent increase in price leads to a 25 percent increase in the quantity supplied, supply is elastic.
   c. If an increase in the price of a product leads to an increase in consumer expenditures on the product, demand is elastic.

8. If there is a surplus of a good, does this mean that the good is not scarce? Indicate what the supply and demand curves would look like for a good that is not scarce.

9. What is the "invisible hand principle"? Does it indicate that "good intentions" are necessary if one's actions are going to be beneficial to others? Why or why not?

*Asterisk denotes critical-analysis questions for which answers are given in Appendix A.

*10. "The future of our industrial strength cannot be left to chance. Somebody has to develop notions about which industries are winners and which are losers." Is this statement by a newspaper columnist true? Who is the "somebody"?

11. Suppose that a construction boom leads to an unexpected increase in demand for plywood. What will happen to the price of plywood in the short run? What will happen in the long run? Explain.

12. How will each of the following influence the price and quantity traded of apples?
    a. An increase in the demand for apples.
    b. A decrease in the supply of apples.
    c. An increase in demand for oranges, a substitute for apples.
    d. An increase in demand for apple jelly, a product made with apples.
    e. The imposition of a below-market price ceiling on apples.

*13. When the price of a commodity (for example, rental housing or campus parking) is below equilibrium, then waiting in line rather than monetary payments will play a greater role in the allocation of the good. What is a major disadvantage of rationing by waiting in line rather than price. (Hint: How do the alternative methods affect future supply?)

## MULTIPLE-CHOICE SELF-TEST

1. Which one of the following would be most likely to cause the demand for firewood to increase?
   a. A decrease in the price of firewood.
   b. A decrease in the price of electricity, a substitute product.
   c. An increase in the price of fuel oil, a substitute product.
   d. A reduction in the price of chain saws that are used to cut firewood.

2. Which of the following would be most likely to cause the price of wheat to decline?
   a. An increase in the costs of production of corn, a substitute for wheat.
   b. A decrease in the price of soybeans, a substitute for wheat.
   c. An increase in the price of fertilizer, a factor of production used to produce wheat.
   d. A sandwich craze among Americans, causing them to increase their demand for whole wheat bread.

3. Which of the following would be most likely to cause the supply curve for Nintendo video games to shift to the left?
   a. An increase in the price of Nintendo video games.
   b. An increase in the price of computer chips used to make Nintendo games.
   c. A decrease in the demand for Nintendo games.
   d. An increase in the demand for Nintendo games.

4. "As the price of gasoline rose, consumer demand declined. In addition, the quantity demanded of compact cars increased, causing their price to rise." This statement
   a. Is essentially correct.
   b. Contains one error: the quantity demanded, not the consumer demand (for gasoline), declined.

c. Contains two errors: demand and quantity demanded are confused twice.
d. Contains two errors: higher gasoline prices would cause demand to increase (rather than decline) and the quantity demanded of the compact cars would decline (rather than increase).

5. When a price ceiling is imposed below the equilibrium price of a commodity,
   a. Supply and demand will adjust downward to the new equilibrium.
   b. The problems of scarcity and high prices are solved.
   c. Shortages occur.
   d. Surpluses become a problem.
6. If a 40 percent reduction in the price of airline tickets between Chicago and New York leads to a 16 percent increase in the quantity of tickets purchased, the price elasticity of demand for the tickets is minus
   a. 0.20
   b. 0.40
   c. 0.50
   d. 2.50
7. Suppose that consumers in the United States are the primary purchasers of bananas produced in Guatemala and that the demand for bananas in the U.S. market is inelastic. If adverse weather conditions reduce the size of their crop by 25 percent, Guatemalan banana exporters would
   a. Experience no change in their total revenue from banana exports.
   b. Experience a decline in total revenue even though the price of bananas would increase.
   c. Experience an increase in total revenue even though they sold a smaller quantity.
   d. Experience losses that would cause them to reduce their acres planted next year.
8. The invisible hand principle stresses
   a. That benevolence is a powerful motivator that encourages individuals to engage in productive economic activity.
   b. The tendency of the competitive market process to direct self-interested individuals into activities that enhance the economic welfare of society.
   c. The potential of government regulation as a means of bringing the self-interest of individuals into harmony with the economic welfare of society.
   d. The tendency of self-interested individuals to promote the economic welfare of society under several alternative forms of economic organization.
9. In 1975 a pocket calculator cost more than $50. By 1985 a calculator of the same quality cost less than $10. Which of the following explanations is most consistent with these facts?
   a. An increase in the demand for calculators forced down their price.
   b. A change in technology caused the supply of calculators to increase, depressing the price of calculators.
   c. As the population grew, fewer expensive calculators were needed, causing their price to fall.
   d. Intense competition in the calculator industry caused the supply curve for calculators to shift to the left, depressing price.
10. If the demand for a product is elastic, a technological improvement that increases the supply of the product will

a. Lower the price, and the total consumer expenditures on the product will fall.
b. Raise the price, and the total consumer expenditures on the product will fall.
c. Raise the price, and the total consumer expenditures on the product will rise.
d. Lower the price, and the total consumer expenditures on the product will rise.

## PROBLEMS

1. The estimated demand schedule for milk in a market area is present in the accompanying table.

| Price of Milk | Gallons Purchased (in millions) | Consumer Expenditures on Milk |
|---|---|---|
| $1.50 | 125 | ____ |
| 1.60 | 110 | ____ |
| 1.70 | 100 | ____ |
| 1.80 | 94 | ____ |
| 1.90 | 90 | ____ |
| 2.00 | 86 | ____ |
| 2.10 | 83 | ____ |

a. Fill in the total expenditure schedule. Based on the relationship between a change in price and change in total expenditure, is the demand for milk elastic or inelastic for a price increase from $1.70 to $1.80? From $1.80 to $1.90? From $1.90 to $2.00?
b. Calculate the price elasticity of demand for a price increase from $1.70 to $1.80. From $1.80 to $1.90. From $1.90 to $2.00. In each case, indicate whether the price elasticity coefficient implies that demand is elastic or inelastic. Are your answers to Problems 1a and 1b consistent?

2. The accompanying table presents data on the effect of a change in the price of gasoline on the consumption of gasoline, automobile tires, and air travel.

| Price of Gasoline (per gallon) | Consumption of Gasoline (millions of gallons per day) | Consumption of Auto Tires (millions per year) | Consumption of Air Travel Passenger Miles (millions per week) |
|---|---|---|---|
| $1.00 | 7.0 | 50 | 75 |
| 1.20 | 6.6 | 48 | 78 |
| 1.40 | 6.2 | 45 | 84 |
| 1.60 | 5.8 | 41 | 88 |
| 1.80 | 5.0 | 35 | 95 |

a. Is the demand for gasoline elastic or inelastic between the prices of $1.20 and $1.40? Between the prices of $1.60 and $1.80?
b. Which of the following goods are substitutes for each other: gasoline and automobile tires or gasoline and air travel? Which are complements? Explain how you can tell from the data.

3. Information on the demand and supply schedules for apples is presented in the accompanying table.

| Quantity Demanded (thousands of bushels) | Price per Bushel | Quantity Supplied (thousands of bushels) |
|---|---|---|
| 200 | $3.00 | 90 |
| 180 | 3.25 | 110 |
| 165 | 3.50 | 130 |
| 155 | 3.75 | 155 |
| 145 | 4.00 | 180 |
| 130 | 4.25 | 210 |
| 110 | 4.50 | 250 |

a. Construct a graph of the demand and supply schedules for apples. What is the equilibrium price and quantity?
b. If a $3.25 price ceiling were imposed on apples, how many bushels would consumers want to purchase at that price? How many bushels would producers be willing to supply? How would the price ceiling influence the quantity of apples produced and traded? Given the quantity supplied by producers at the $3.25 price, how much value would consumers place on the marginal bushel of apples produced? Would consumers and producers gain if more apples were produced?
c. Suppose that a price floor of $4.25 per bushel were imposed. How many bushels would producers be willing to supply at the $4.25 price? How many would consumers want to purchase? How many units would be traded if the price were fixed at $4.25? What would the government have to do to maintain the $4.25 price floor?

# PART II

## MICROECONOMICS

CHAPTER

5

# The Firm and Costs of Production

Opportunity cost is the value of the best alternative that must be sacrificed in order to engage in an activity. This is the only relevant cost in economic analysis because it is based on the very nature of the science—the formulation of principles for maximum satisfaction of human wants and scarce resources. The supply curve of any commodity or service consequently reflects opportunity costs which are determined indirectly by consumers clamoring for a myriad of goods.

*Colberg, Forbush, and Whitaker*[1]

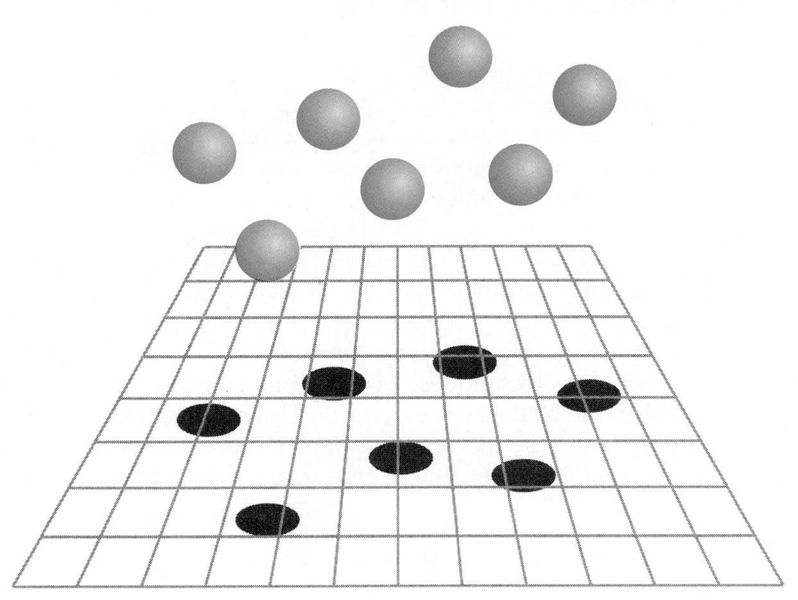

## CHAPTER FOCUS

- Why are business firms used by societies everywhere to organize production?
- How are firms organized in market economies? What internal information and incentive problems must they solve?
- What are explicit and implicit costs, and what role do they play in guiding the behavior of a firm?
- How does economic profit differ from accounting profit? What is the role of profit for a firm, and for an industry?
- How do short-run costs differ from long-run costs for a firm?
- What factors can shift a firm's cost curves?

In previous chapters we showed how demand and supply interact to determine the production rate and the market price of a good, and how a market responds to change. In this chapter, we focus on the firm. Why are firms formed? How do costs discipline firms in their use of resources? Why do economists view a firm's costs differently than accountants? How does the speed of adjustment, or the passage of time, affect a firm's response to cost changes? In answering these questions, we show more fully how firms are affected by costs, and how we can expect them to react to changes. This provides a more complete look at the relationship between costs and market supply.

## ORGANIZATION OF THE BUSINESS FIRM

The business firm is an entity designed to organize raw materials, labor, and machines with the goal of producing goods and/or services. Firms (1) purchase or hire productive resources from households and other firms, (2) transform them into goods and services, and (3) sell the transformed products or services to consumers.

Economies may differ in the amount of freedom they allow business decision-makers. They may also differ in the incentive structure used to stimulate and guide business activity. Nevertheless, every society relies on business firms to organize resources and transform them into products. In Western economies, most business firms choose their own prices, output levels, and productive techniques. In socialist countries, government policy often establishes the selling price and constrains the actions of business firms in various other ways. The central position of the business firm as the organized productive unit, however, is universal to capitalist and socialist economies alike.

[1]Marshall R. Colberg, Dascomb R. Forbush, and Gilbert R. Whitaker, *Business Economics* (Homewood, IL: Irwin, 1980), p. 12.

## Incentives, Cooperation, and the Nature of the Firm[2]

Most firms are privately owned in capitalist countries. The owners, who may or may not act as entrepreneurs, are the individuals who risk their wealth on the success of the business. If the firm is successful and makes profits, these financial gains go to the owners. Conversely, if the firm suffers losses, the owners must bear the consequences. Because the owners gain (or lose) what remains after the revenue of the firm is used to pay the costs, they are called **residual claimants.**

**residual claimant** Individual who personally receives the excess, if any, of revenues over costs. Residual claimants gain if the firm's costs are reduced and if revenues are increased.

In a market economy, the property right of owners to the residual income of the firm plays a very important role: it provides owners with a strong incentive to organize and structure their business in a manner that will keep their cost of producing output low. The wealth of these residual claimants is directly influenced by the success or failure of the firm. Thus, they have a strong incentive to see that resources under their direction are used efficiently.

There are two ways of organizing productive activity: contracting and **team production,** in which workers are hired by a firm to work together under the supervision of the owner, or the owner's representative. Most business firms use both contracting and team production.

**team production** Employees hired by a firm to work together under the supervision of the owner or the owner's representative.

In principle, any production could be accomplished by contracts among individuals. For example, a builder might have a house built by contracting with one person to pour the concrete for the floor, another to construct the wooden part of the house, a third to install the roofing, a fourth to do the electrical wiring, and so on. No employees would have to be involved in such a project. More commonly though, goods and services are produced with some combination of contracting and the use of team production by employees of a firm.

Why do firms use team production? If contracting alone is used to produce something, the producer must, for each project, (1) determine what is required to produce the desired result in the best way, given the circumstances and the current technology and prices, (2) search out reliable suppliers, and (3) negotiate and enforce the contracts. The entrepreneur who wants to produce by this method must have specialized knowledge in a variety of areas and must devote a great deal of time and effort to the planning and contracting processes. Not many people have the expertise or the time to take care of all these tasks by themselves except on a small scale.

Accordingly, a builder is likely to hire knowledgeable, experienced workers to plan, to purchase materials, and to build structures such as a house. The firm itself will then contract with others to obtain materials and specialized labor services.

A firm, then, is a business organization that may use team production to reduce many of the transaction costs associated with contracting. Team production, however, raises another set of problems. Team members—that is, the employees working for the firm—must be monitored and provided with an incentive system that discourages **shirking,** that is working at less than a normal rate of productivity. Taking long work breaks, paying more attention to their own convenience than to results, and wasting time when diligence is called for are examples of shirking. A worker will shirk more when the costs

**shirking** Working at less than a normal rate of productivity, thus reducing output. Shirking is more likely when workers are not monitored and the cost of their lower output falls on others.

[2]A classic article on this topic is Ronald Coase, "The Nature of the Firm," *Economica,* (1937), pp. 386–405. See also Armen Alchian and Harold Demsetz, "Production, Information Costs, and Economic Organization," *American Economic Review,* (Dec. 1972), pp. 777–795.

of doing so are shifted to other team members, including the owners of the firm. Hired managers, even including those at the top, must be monitored and provided with the incentive to avoid shirking.

When team production is utilized, the problem of imperfect monitoring and imperfect incentives is always present. It is part of a larger class of problems called **principal-agent problems.** Any person who has taken a car to an auto mechanic has experienced such problems. The mechanic wants to get the job done quickly and to make as much money on it as possible. The car owner wants to get the job done quickly also, but in a way that permanently fixes the problem, at as low a cost as possible. Since the mechanic typically knows far more about the job than the customer, it is hard for the customer to monitor his work. There is a possibility, therefore, that the mechanic may charge a large amount for a "quick fix" that will not last.

**principal-agent problem** The incentive problem arising when the purchaser of services (the principal) lacks full information about the circumstances faced by the seller (the agent) and thus cannot know how well the agent performs the purchased services. The agent may to some extent work toward objectives other than those sought by the principal paying for the service.

The owner of a firm is in a similar situation. It is often difficult to monitor the performance of individual employees and provide them with an incentive structure that will encourage high productivity. Nonetheless, the success of the firm is crucially dependent upon how these problems are resolved. If a firm is going to keep costs low, it must discover and use an incentive structure that motivates workers and discourages shirking.

## Structuring the Firm

How do owners share the risks and liabilities of the firm? How do they participate in the making of decisions? Each firm is organized in one of three ways: a proprietorship, a partnership, or a corporation.

**proprietorship** A business firm owned by an individual who possesses the ownership right to the firm's profits and is personally liable for the firm's debts.

**partnership** A business firm owned by two or more individuals who possess ownership rights to the firm's profits and are personally liable for the debts of the firm.

**corporation** A business firm owned by shareholders who possess ownership rights to the firm's profits, but whose liability is limited to the amount of their investment in the firm.

A **proprietorship** is a business firm owned by a single individual. He or she has full authority to make decisions and is personally liable for all debts and other liabilities of the firm. In the United States, about 70 percent of all firms are proprietorships. Since most proprietorships are small, they produce only about 6 percent of total output.

A **partnership** consists of two or more persons who are co-owners of a business firm. They share the decision-making authority (in a manner they arrange among themselves) and, like proprietors, each partner is fully liable for business debts incurred by the firm. In the United States, partnerships account for 10 percent of the total number of firms and approximately 4 percent of the total output.

The third, very important form of business organization is the **corporation.** In the United States, while corporations comprise only 20 percent of the business firms, they account for about 90 percent of all business receipts. Three factors account for the popularity of the corporate form for business.

First, stockholders own the firm and any profits belong to them, but their liability is limited to what they have explicitly invested in the firm. Those who loan money to the firm must recognize that the owners are not personally accountable for the debt. In a corporation, the assets of the firm, but not the personal assets of its owners, can be called upon to settle a debt owed by the firm.

Second, because the personal liability of the corporate owners (stockholders) is limited, the corporation can attract investments from more individuals, including many—often a great majority—who do not participate in management and can rest easily without closely monitoring the operation of the firm, since only their limited investment is at stake. Under the corporate structure, production, marketing, and other business decisions are typically made by a management team employed by the owners.

Third, shares of corporate stock can be easily traded, often in organized stock markets. A share owner who disapproves of the direction the corporation is taking, or who wants out for personal reasons, can easily bail out by selling the stock.

This market for ownership and control of a corporation has an important impact on the information received by corporate managers, and on their personal reputations regarding the decisions they make while they are in control. If many stockholders choose to sell, the stock price will fall relative to that of other firms in the same market, sending an immediate message to management. Similarly, if investors like a new strategy adopted by management, their purchase of stock will drive the price up. This, too, will send a message to management.

In a market economy, no one is told whom to hire, what resources to employ, or how to organize a business. These decisions are left to business owners and agents that they employ. However, the property right of owners to the residual income of the firm (including profits) provides them with a strong incentive to figure out how output can be produced at a low cost. Other things constant, lower cost will increase the residual income and wealth of the owners.

A market economy does not mandate the structure of the business firm. Any form of business organization is permissible. Proprietorships, partnerships, corporations, employee-owned firms, consumer cooperatives, or any other form of business organization may be utilized. If an organizational structure is going to succeed, however, it must be cost effective. If a structure of business organization, such as a proprietorship or employee-owned corporation, is able to achieve low per unit cost in a market, it will tend to survive. Correspondingly, a business structure that results in high per unit cost will have difficulty surviving in a market.

## ECONOMIC FUNCTION OF COSTS

Consumers would like to have more economic goods, but resources to produce them are scarce. Using resources to make one commodity takes resources from the production of others that also are desired. Thus, the desire for more of one good must be balanced against the desire for the other goods that could be produced instead with the same resources. Every economic system has to make these balancing judgments. Some are made in the political arena by means of the budget process. Congress (or the central committee, or the dictator) decides which goods will be produced. Taxes and agency budgets are set accordingly.

In a market economy, this balancing function is usually performed by consumer demand and producer costs. The demand for a product can be thought of as the voice of consumers instructing firms to produce a good. In order to produce the good, however, producers must bid resources away from their alternative uses—primarily the production of other goods. As they do so, they incur costs. These costs of production represent the voice of consumers saying that *other goods* that could be produced with the resources are also desired.

Thus costs play a vitally important function: they help us balance our desire for more of a good against our desire for more of *other* goods that could be produced instead. If we do not consider these costs, we will end up using scarce resources to produce the wrong things—goods that we do not value as much as other things that we might have produced.

## CALCULATING ECONOMIC COSTS AND PROFITS

Business firms, regardless of their size, are primarily concerned with profit. What is profit? It is the firm's total revenue, minus the sum of its costs. But to state profit correctly, it is imperative that costs be measured properly. Most people, including some who are in business, think of costs as the amount paid for raw materials, labor, machines, and similar inputs. However, this concept of cost, which stems from accounting procedures, may fail to include some of the firm's real costs. Consequently, profit is misstated and unwise decisions may result.

The key to understanding the economist's concept of profit is our old friend, opportunity cost. The firm incurs a cost whenever it uses a resource, thereby requiring the resource owner to forgo the highest valued alternative. These costs may either be explicit or implicit. **Explicit costs** result when the firm makes a monetary payment to resource owners. Money wages, interest, and rental payments are a measure of what the firm gives up to employ the services of labor and capital resources. Firms may also incur **implicit costs**—costs associated with the use of resources owned by the firm. Since implicit costs do not involve a direct money or contractual payment, they are sometimes excluded from accounting statements. For example, the owners of small proprietorships often supply labor services to their businesses. There is an opportunity cost associated with the use of this resource; other opportunities have to be given up because of the time spent by the owner in the operation of the business. The highest valued alternative forgone is the opportunity cost of the labor service provided by the owner. The **total cost** of production is the sum of the explicit and implicit costs of using all of the resources involved in the production process.

**explicit costs** Money paid by a firm to purchase the services of productive resources.

**implicit costs** The opportunity costs associated with a firm's use of resources that it owns. These costs do *not* involve a direct money payment. Examples include wage income and interest forgone by the owner of a firm who also provides labor services and equity capital to the firm.

**total cost** The costs, both explicit and implicit, of all the resources used by the firm. Total cost includes an imputed normal rate of return for the firm's equity capital.

Accounting statements generally omit the implicit cost of equity capital—the cost of funds supplied by owners. If a firm borrows financial capital from a bank or other private source, it will have to pay interest. Accountants properly record this interest expense as a cost. In contrast, when the firm acquires financial capital through the issuance of stock, accountants make no allowance for the cost of this financial capital. Regardless of whether it is acquired by borrowing or stock (equity capital), the use of financial capital involves an opportunity cost. Persons who supply equity capital to a firm expect to earn a normal rate of return—a return comparable to what they could earn if they chose other investment opportunities (including bonds). If they do not earn this normal rate of return, investors will not continue to supply financial capital to the business.

When calculating costs, economists use the normal return on financial capital as a basis for determining the implicit **opportunity cost of equity capital.** If the normal rate of return on financial capital is 10 percent, equity investors will refuse funds to firms unable to earn a 10 percent rate of return on capital assets. As a result, earning the normal rate of return—that is, covering the opportunity cost of all of its capital—is vital to the survival of a business firm.

**opportunity cost of equity capital** The implicit rate of return that must be earned by equity investors in order to induce them to continue supplying financial capital to the firm.

## ACCOUNTING PROFIT AND ECONOMIC PROFIT

**economic profit** The difference between the firm's total revenues and total costs.

Since economists seek to measure the opportunities lost due to the production of a good or service, they include both explicit and implicit costs in total cost. **Economic profit** is equal to total revenues minus total costs, including both the explicit and implicit cost components. Economic profits will be present only if the earnings of a business are in excess of the opportunity cost of using the assets owned by the firm. Economic losses result when the earnings of the firm are insufficient to cover explicit and implicit costs. When the firm's revenues are just equal to its costs, both explicit and implicit, economic profits will be zero.

Remember that zero economic profits do not imply that the firm is about to go out of business. On the contrary, they indicate that the owners are receiving exactly the market (normal) rate of return on their investment (assets owned by the firm).

**accounting profits** The sales revenues minus the expenses of a firm over a designated time period, usually one year. Accounting profits typically make allowances for changes in the firm's inventories and depreciation of its assets. No allowance is made, however, for the opportunity cost of the equity capital of the firm's owners, or other implicit costs.

Since accounting procedures often omit implicit costs, such as those associated with owner-provided capital and labor services, the accounting costs of the firm generally understate the opportunity costs of production. This understatement of cost leads to an overstatement of economic profits. Therefore, the **accounting profits** of a firm are generally greater than the firm's economic profits (see "Applications in Economics" box on p. 104). When the omission of the costs of owner-provided services is unimportant, as is the case for most large corporations, accounting profits approximate the returns to the firm's equity capital. High accounting profits (measured as a rate of return on a firm's assets), relative to the average for other firms, suggest that a firm is earning an economic profit. Correspondingly, a low rate of accounting profit implies economic losses.

## COSTS IN THE SHORT RUN AND THE LONG RUN

**short run (in production)** A time period so short that a firm is unable to vary some of its factors of production. The firm's plant size typically cannot be altered in the short run.

A firm cannot instantaneously adjust its output. Time plays an important role in the production process. All of a firm's resources can be expanded or contracted over time, but for specialized or heavy equipment, expanding or contracting availability quickly may be very expensive or even impossible. Economists often speak of the **short run** as a time period so short that the firm is unable to alter its present plant size. In the short run, the firm is "stuck" with its existing plant and heavy equipment. They are "fixed" for a given time period. The firm can alter output, however, by applying larger or smaller amounts of variable resources, such as labor and raw materials. The firm's existing plant capacity can thus be used more or less intensively in the short run.

In sum, we can say that the short run is that period of time during which at least one factor of production, usually the size of the firm's plant, cannot be varied. How long is the short run? The length varies from industry to industry. In some industries, substantial changes in plant size can be accomplished in a few months. In other industries, particularly those that use assembly lines and mass production techniques (for example, aircraft and automobiles), the short run might be a year or even several years.

**long run (in production)** A time period long enough to allow the firm to vary all factors of production.

The **long run** is a time period of sufficient length to allow a firm the opportunity to alter its plant size and capacity and all other factors of production.

## APPLICATIONS IN ECONOMICS

### Economic and Accounting Cost—A Hypothetical Example

The revenue-cost statement for a corner grocery store owned and operated by Terry Smith is presented here.

Terry works full-time as the manager, chief cashier, and janitor. He has $30,000 worth of refrigeration and other equipment invested in the store. Last year Terry's total sales were $85,000; suppliers and employees were paid $50,000. His revenues exceeded explicit costs by $35,000. Did Terry make a profit last year? The accounting statement for the store will probably show a net profit of $35,000. However, if Terry did not have a $30,000 personal investment in equipment, these funds could be collecting 10 percent interest. Thus, Terry is forgoing $3,000 of interest each year. Similarly, if the building that Terry owns were not being used as a grocery store, it could be rented to someone else for $500 per month. Rental income thus forgone is $6,000 per year. In addition, since Terry is tied up working in the grocery store, a $28,000 managerial position with the local A&P is forgone. Considering the interest, rental, and salary income that Terry had to forgo in order to operate the grocery store last year, his implicit costs were $37,000. The total costs were $87,000. The total revenue of Terry's grocery store was less than the opportunity cost of the resources utilized. Terry incurred an economic loss of $2,000, despite the accounting profit of $35,000.

| | |
|---|---|
| **Total revenue** | **$85,000** |
| Sales (groceries) | |
| **Total (explicit costs)** | |
| Groceries, wholesale | $38,000 |
| Utilities | 2,000 |
| Taxes | 3,000 |
| Advertising | 1,000 |
| Labor services (employees) | 6,000 |
| **Total (explicit) costs** | $50,000 |
| **Net (accounting) profit** | $35,000 |
| **Additional (implicit) costs** | |
| Interest (personal investment) | $ 3,000 |
| Rent (Terry's building) | 6,000 |
| Salary (Terry's labor) | 28,000 |
| **Total implicit costs** | $37,000 |
| **Total explicit and implicit costs** | **$87,000** |
| Economic profit **(total revenue minus explicit and implicit costs)** | **–$2,000** |

All resources of the firm are variable in the long run. At the industry level, new firms may be established and enter the industry, while other firms dissolve and leave the industry over the long run.

Perhaps an example will help to clarify the distinction between the short- and long-run time periods. If a battery manufacturer hired 200 additional workers and ordered more raw materials to squeeze a larger output from the existing plant, this would be a short-run adjustment. In contrast, if the manufacturer built an additional plant (or expanded the size of its current facility) and installed additional heavy equipment, this would be a long-run adjustment.

## Output and Costs in the Short Run

We have emphasized that in the short run some of a firm's factors of production, such as the size of the plant, will be fixed. Other productive resources will be variable. In the short run, then, we can break the firm's costs into these two categories—fixed and variable. Examining how each category of costs behaves, and seeing that behavior graphically, will help us to understand how decision-makers determine the profit-maximizing level of output for a firm.

**fixed costs** Costs that do not vary with output. However, fixed costs will be incurred as long as a firm continues in business and the assets have alternative uses.

**average fixed cost** Fixed cost divided by the number of units produced. It always declines as output increases.

**Fixed costs** will remain unchanged even though output is altered. For example, a firm's insurance premiums, its property taxes, and, most significantly, the opportunity cost of using its fixed assets will be present whether the firm produces a large or a small rate of output. Fixed costs will be present at all levels of output, including zero. They can be avoided only if the firm goes out of business.

What will happen to **average fixed cost** (AFC) as output expands? Remember that the firm's fixed cost will be the same whether output is 100 or 1,000. The average fixed cost is simply fixed cost divided by output. As output increases, AFC declines, since the fixed cost will be spread over more and more units (see Exhibit 5.1a).

**variable costs** Costs that vary with the rate of output. Examples include wages paid to workers and payments for raw materials.

**average variable cost** The total variable cost divided by the number of units produced.

**Variable costs** are those costs that vary with output. For example, additional output can usually be produced by hiring more workers and expending additional funds on raw materials. Variable costs involve expenditures on these and other variable inputs. At any given level of output, the firm's **average variable cost** (AVC) is the total variable cost divided by output.

**average total cost** Total cost divided by the number of units produced. It is sometimes called per unit cost.

We have noted that total cost includes explicit and implicit costs. The total cost of producing a good is also the sum of the fixed and variable costs at each output level. At zero output, total cost will equal fixed cost. As output expands from zero, variable cost and fixed cost must be added to obtain total cost. **Average total cost** (ATC), sometimes referred to as *unit cost,* can be found by dividing total cost by the total number of units produced. ATC is also equal to the sum of the average fixed and average variable costs. It indicates the amount per unit of output that must be gained in revenue if total cost is to be covered.

## EXHIBIT 5.1

**General Characteristics of Short-Run Cost Curves**

Average fixed costs (a) will be high for small rates of output, but they will always decline as output expands. Marginal cost (b) will rise sharply as the plant's production capacity $q$ is approached. ATC will be a U-shaped curve *(c),* since AFC will be high for small rates of output and MC will be high as the plant's production capacity is approached.

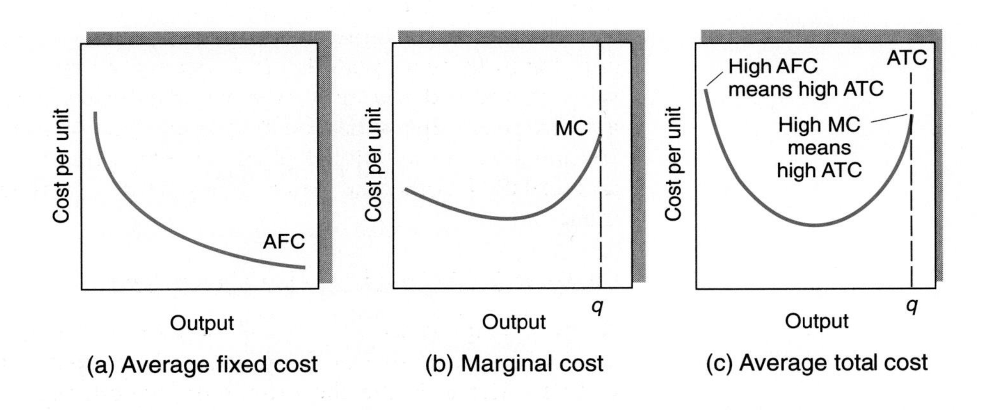

**marginal cost** The change in total cost required to produce an additional unit of output.

The economic way of thinking emphasizes the importance of what happens "at the margin." How much does it cost to produce an additional unit? **Marginal cost** (MC) is the change in total cost that results from the production of one additional unit. The profit-conscious decision-maker recognizes MC as the addition to cost that must be covered by additional revenue if producing the marginal unit is to be profitable. In the short run, as illustrated by Exhibit 5.1b, MC will generally decline if output is increased, then eventually reach a minimum, and then increase. The rising MC curve simply reflects the fact that it becomes increasingly difficult to squeeze additional output from a plant as the facility's maximum capacity (the dotted line of Exhibit 5.1b) is approached. The "Thumbnail Sketch" summarizes the interrelationships among a firm's various costs.

As a firm alters its rate of output in the short run, how will unit cost be affected? First, let us look at this question intuitively. In the short run, the firm can vary output by using its fixed plant size more (or less) intensively. As Exhibit 5.1 illustrates, there are two extreme situations that will result in a high unit cost of output. First, when the output rate of a plant is small relative to its capacity, it is obviously being underutilized. Under these circumstances, AFC will be high, making ATC high also. To operate a large plant substantially below its designed production capacity is costly and inefficient. At the other extreme, operating a plant well above its designed capacity is also costly. An overutilized plant will mean congestion, time spent by workers waiting for machines, and similar costly delays. As output approaches the maximum capacity of a plant, overutilization will lead to high MC and therefore to high ATC.

**law of diminishing returns** The postulate that as more and more units of a variable resource are combined with a fixed amount of other resources, employment of *additional* units of the variable resource will eventually increase output only at a decreasing rate. Once diminishing returns are reached, it will take successively larger amounts of the variable factor to expand output by one unit.

Thus, the ATC curve will be U-shaped, as pictured in Exhibit 5.1c. ATC will be high for both an underutilized plant (because AFC is high) and an overutilized plant (because MC is high).

The upward-sloping MC curve as the firm tries to produce more and more output from its fixed size of plant is a reflection of a long-established economic law, the **law of diminishing returns,** which states that as more and more units of a variable factor are applied to a fixed amount of other resources, output will eventually increase by smaller and smaller amounts. The law of diminishing returns is as famous in economics as the law of gravity is in physics. The law is based on common sense. Have you ever noticed that as you apply a single resource more intensively, the resource eventually

## THUMBNAIL SKETCH

### Relationships among a Firm's Costs

1. Total cost includes both explicit and implicit costs.
2. Total cost = fixed cost + variable cost.
3. Marginal cost = change in total cost per additional unit of output.
4. Average total cost = total cost ÷ output.
5. Average fixed cost = fixed cost ÷ output.
6. Average variable cost = variable cost ÷ output.
7. Average total cost = average fixed cost + average variable cost.

tends to accomplish less and less? Consider a farmer who applies fertilizer more and more intensively to an acre of land (a fixed factor). At some point, the application of additional 100-pound units of fertilizer will expand the wheat yield by successively smaller amounts.

So when a firm tries to use more variable factors (resources like labor and materials) in order to increase the output from its fixed size of plant and amount of heavy equipment, it eventually experiences diminishing returns. Output expands by smaller and smaller amounts as employment of the variable resources is increased by a specific amount. Thus, it takes more and more of the variable resources to generate each additional unit of output. Employing the successively larger amounts of the variable resources pushes MC upward. Eventually MC exceeds average variable costs (AVC) and ATC, causing these costs also to rise. A U-shaped short-run ATC curve results.

It is easy to see why ATC will rise when MC exceeds ATC. What happens when an above-average student is added to a class? The class average goes up. What happens if a unit of above-average cost is added to output? ATC rises. The firm's MC curve therefore crosses the ATC curve at the ATC's lowest point. For output rates beyond the minimum ATC, above average marginal costs cause ATC to increase.

Exhibit 5.2 numerically illustrates the implications of diminishing returns and rising marginal costs. Here, we assume that Royal Roller Blades, Inc., combines units of a variable input with a fixed factor to produce units of output (pairs of blades). Columns 2, 3, and 4 indicate how total cost schedules vary as output is expanded. Total fixed costs, representing the opportunity

**EXHIBIT 5.2**

**Numerical Short-Run Cost Schedules of Royal Roller Blades, Inc.**

| | Total Cost Data (per Day) | | | Average/Marginal Cost Data (per Day) | | | |
|---|---|---|---|---|---|---|---|
| (1) Output per Day | (2) Total Fixed Cost | (3) Total Variable Cost | (4) Total Cost, (2) + (3) | (5) Average Fixed Cost, (2) ÷ (1) | (6) Average Variable Cost, (3) ÷ (1) | (7) Average Total Cost, (4) ÷ (1) | (8) Marginal Cost, Δ(4) ÷ Δ(1) |
| 0 | $50 | $ 0 | $ 50 | — | — | — | — |
| 1 | 50 | 15 | 65 | $50.00 | $15.00 | $65.00 | $15 |
| 2 | 50 | 25 | 75 | 25.00 | 12.50 | 37.50 | 10 |
| 3 | 50 | 34 | 84 | 16.67 | 11.33 | 28.00 | 9 |
| 4 | 50 | 42 | 92 | 12.50 | 10.50 | 23.00 | 8 |
| 5 | 50 | 52 | 102 | 10.00 | 10.40 | 20.40 | 10 |
| 6 | 50 | 64 | 114 | 8.33 | 10.67 | 19.00 | 12 |
| 7 | 50 | 79 | 129 | 7.14 | 11.29 | 18.43 | 15 |
| 8 | 50 | 98 | 148 | 6.25 | 12.25 | 18.50 | 19 |
| 9 | 50 | 122 | 172 | 5.56 | 13.56 | 19.11 | 24 |
| 10 | 50 | 152 | 202 | 5.00 | 15.20 | 20.20 | 30 |
| 11 | 50 | 202 | 252 | 4.55 | 18.36 | 22.91 | 50 |

cost of the fixed factors of production, are $50 per day. For the first four units of output, total variable costs increase at a *decreasing rate*. Why? In this range, there are increasing returns to the variable input. Beginning with the fifth unit of output, however, diminishing marginal returns are present. From this point on, total variable costs and total costs increase by successively larger amounts as output is expanded.

Columns 5 through 8 of Exhibit 5.2 reveal the general pattern of the average and marginal cost schedules. For small output rates, the average total cost of producing roller blades is high, primarily because of high average fixed cost. Initially, marginal costs are less than average total costs. When diminishing returns set in for output rates beginning with five units, however, marginal costs rise. Beginning with the sixth unit of output, marginal costs exceed average variable cost, causing average variable costs to rise. Beginning with the eighth unit of output, marginal costs exceed average total costs, causing them also to rise. Average total costs thus reach a minimum at seven units of output.

Observe the data of Exhibit 5.2 carefully to ensure that you fully understand the relationships among the various cost curves. Note that when marginal costs are less than average variable and average total costs, the latter two will decline as output expands. Correspondingly, when marginal cost exceeds average variable costs and average total costs, it will pull each of them up. Thus, marginal cost will intersect both the AVC curve and the ATC curve at the point of their minimum values.

## Output and Costs in the Long Run

The short-run analysis relates costs to output for a specific size of plant. Firms, though, are not committed forever to their existing plant. In the long run, a firm may alter its plant size and all other factors of production. All resources used by the firm are variable in the long run.

How will the firm's choice of plant size affect production costs? Exhibit 5.3 illustrates the short-run average total cost (ATC) curves for three plant sizes, ranging from small to large. If these three plant sizes were the only possible choices, which one would be best? The answer depends on the rate of output the firm expects to produce. The smallest plant would have the lowest cost if an output rate of less than $q_1$ were produced. The medium-sized plant would provide the least-cost method of producing output rates between $q_1$ and $q_2$. For any output level greater than $q_2$, the largest plant would be the most cost-efficient.

The long-run ATC curve shows the minimum average cost of producing each output level when the firm is free to choose among all possible plant sizes. It can best be thought of as a "planning curve," because it reflects the expected per unit cost of producing alternative rates of output while plants are still in the blueprint stage.

Exhibit 5.3 illustrates the long-run ATC curve when only three plant sizes are possible. The planning curve *ABCD* is mapped out. Given sufficient time, of course, firms can usually choose among many plants of various sizes. Exhibit 5.4 presents the long-run planning curve under these circumstances. Note that it is a smooth planning curve. Each short-run ATC curve will be tangent to the long-run planning curve.[3]

[3]The tangency, though, will occur at the least-cost output level for the short run only when the long-run curve is parallel to the $x$-axis, as in $q_n$, Exhibit 5.4.

**EXHIBIT 5.3**

**Long-Run Average Cost**

The short-run average cost curves are shown for three alternative plant sizes. If these three were the only possible plant sizes, the long-run average total cost curve would be *ABCD*.

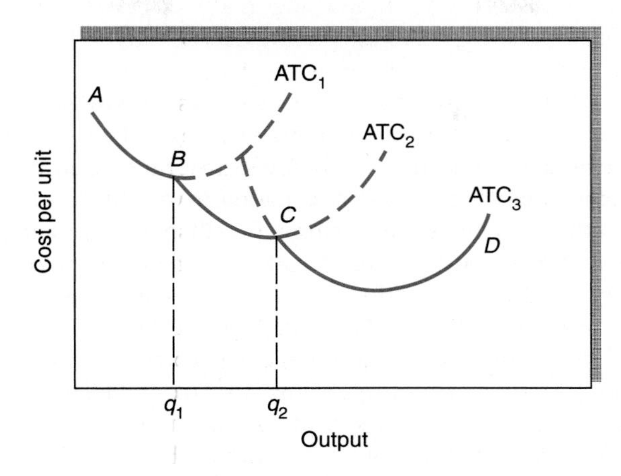


**EXHIBIT 5.4**

**Planning Curve**

When many alternative plant sizes are possible, the long-run average total cost curve *LRATC* is mapped out.

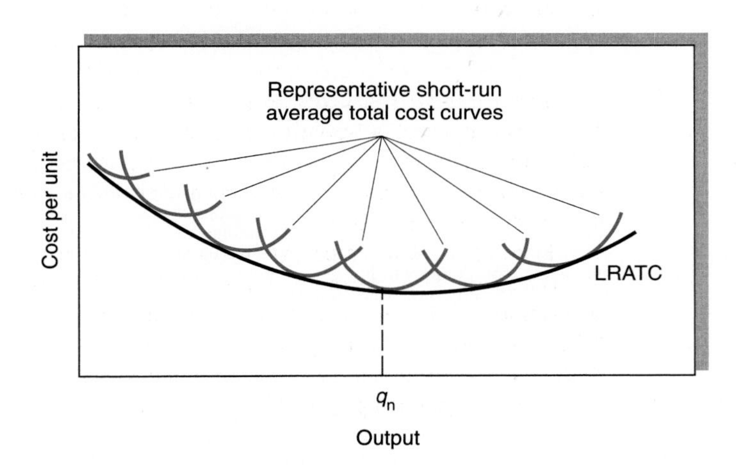

It is important to keep in mind that no single plant size could produce the alternative output rates at the costs indicated by the planning curve (LRATC). Each of the planning curve options is available before a plant size is chosen and the plant is built, but while the firm can plan for the long run, choosing among many options, it can only *operate* in the short run. The LRATC curve outlines the possibilities available in the planning stage, indicating the expected average costs of production for each of a large number of plants, which differ in size.

**SIZE OF FIRM AND UNIT COST IN THE LONG RUN** Do larger firms have lower minimum unit costs than smaller ones? The answer to this question depends on which industries are being considered. There is a sound basis, though, for expecting some initial reductions in per-unit cost from large-scale production methods. Why? Large firms typically produce a large total volume of output.[4] Volume of output denotes the total number of units of a product that the firm expects to produce.[5] There are three major reasons why planning a larger volume generally reduces, at least initially, unit costs: (1) mass production, (2) specialization, and (3) improvements in production as a result of experience, and "learning by doing." Let us consider each of these factors.

Mass production techniques usually are economical only when large volumes of output are planned, since they tend to involve large development and setup costs. Once the production methods are established, though, marginal costs are low. Thus, the use of molds, dies, and assembly-line production methods reduce the per-unit cost of automobiles only when the planned volume is in the millions. High volume methods, although cheaper to use for high rates of output and high volumes, will typically be far more costly if utilized for low volumes of production.

Large-scale operation also permits specialized use of labor and machines. Adam Smith noted 200 years ago that the output of a pin factory is much greater when one worker draws the wire, another straightens it, a third cuts it, a fourth grinds the point, a fifth makes the head of the pin, and so on.[6] In economics, the whole can sometimes be greater than the sum of the parts. Specialization provides the opportunity for people to become exceptionally proficient at performing small but essential functions. When each of them acts as a specialist, more is produced than if each made the final product from start to finish.

[4]Throughout this section, we assume that firms with larger plants necessarily plan a larger volume of output than do their smaller counterparts. Reality approximates these conditions. Firms choose large plants because they are planning to produce a large volume.

[5]Note the distinction between rate and volume of output. *Rate* of output is the number of units produced during a specific period (for example, the next six months). *Volume* is the total number of units produced during all time periods. For example, Boeing might produce two 767 airplanes per month (rate of output) while planning to produce a volume of two hundred 767s during the expected life of the model. Increasing the rate (reducing the time period during which a given output is produced) tends to raise costs, whereas increasing the volume (total amount produced) tends to lower costs. For additional information on production and costs, see Armen Alchian, "Costs," in *International Encyclopedia of the Social Sciences* (New York: Macmillan, 1968), pp. 404–415; and Jack Hirshleifer, "The Firm's Cost Function: A Successful Reconstruction," *Journal of Business* (July 1962), pp. 235–255.

[6]Smith went on to state, "I have seen a small manufactory of this kind where ten men only were employed, and where some of them consequently performed two or three distinct operations. Those ten persons, therefore, could make among them upwards of forty-eight thousand pins in a day. But if they had all wrought separately and independently, and without any of them having been educated to this peculiar business, they certainly could not each of them have made twenty, perhaps not one pin in a day," (Adam Smith, *An Inquiry into the Nature and Causes of the Wealth of Nations,* 1776 [Cannan's edition, Chicago: University of Chicago Press, 1976], pp. 8–9) .

Workers and managers in a firm that has made more units have probably learned more from their experience than their counterparts in smaller firms that have produced less output. Improvements in the production process result. Baseball players improve by playing, and musicians improve by performing. Similarly, workers and management improve their skills as they "practice" productive techniques. This factor of "learning by doing" has been found to be tremendously important in the aircraft and automobile industries, among others.

**economies of scale**
Reductions in the firm's per unit costs that are associated with the use of large plants to produce a large volume of output.

**ECONOMIES AND DISECONOMIES OF SCALE** Economic theory suggests that compared to smaller firms, larger firms have lower unit costs. When unit costs decline as output expands, **economies of scale** are present over the initial range of outputs. The long-run average total cost curve is falling.

Are diseconomies of scale possible—that is, are there ever situations in which the long-run average total costs are greater for larger firms than they are for smaller ones? The economic justification for diseconomies of scale is less obvious (and less tenable) than that for economies of scale. However, as a firm gets bigger and bigger, bureaucratic inefficiencies may result. Code-book procedures tend to replace managerial genius. Motivating the work force and carrying out managerial directives are also more complex when the firm is larger. Principal-agent problems grow as there are more employees and more levels of monitoring to be done. Coordinating more people and conveying information to them is more difficult. These factors combine to cause rising long-run average total costs in some, though certainly not all, industries.

Exhibit 5.5 outlines three different long-run average total cost (LRATC) curves that describe real-world conditions in differing situations. In Exhibit 5.5a, both economies and diseconomies of scale are present. Higher per unit costs will result if the firm chooses a plant size other than the one that minimizes the cost of producing output $q$. If each firm in an industry faces the same cost conditions, we can generalize and say that any plants that are larger or smaller than this ideal size will experience higher unit costs. A very narrow range of plant sizes would be possible in industries with the LRATC depicted by Exhibit 5.5a. Some lines of retail sales and agriculture might approximate these conditions.

**constant returns to scale**
Unit costs are constant as the scale of the firm is altered. Neither economies nor diseconomies of scale are present.

Exhibit 5.5b demonstrates the general shape of the LRATC that economists believe is present in most industries. Initially, economies of scale exist, but once a minimum efficient scale is reached, wide variation in firm size is possible. Firms smaller than the minimum efficient size would have higher per unit costs, but firms larger than that would not gain a cost advantage. **Constant returns to scale** are present for a broad range of output rates (between $q_1$ and $q_2$). This situation is consistent with real-world conditions in many industries. For example, small firms can be as efficient as larger ones in such industries as apparel, lumber, shoes, publishing, and in many lines of retailing.

Exhibit 5.5c indicates that economies of scale exist for all relevant output levels. The larger the firm size, the lower the per unit cost is. The LRATC in the local telephone service industry may approximate the curve of Exhibit 5.5c.

## SHIFTS IN COST CURVES

In outlining the general shapes of a firm's cost curves in both the long run and short run, we assumed that certain other factors remained constant, not

**EXHIBIT 5.5**

**Three Different Types of Long-Run Average Cost Curves**

Frame a indicates that for output levels less than $q$, economies of scale are present. Immediately beyond $q$, diseconomies of scale dominate. Frame b indicates that economies of scale are important until some minimum output level, $q_1$, is attained. Once the minimum has been attained, there is a wide range of output levels ($q_1$ to $q_2$) that are consistent with the minimum ATC for the industry. Frame c indicates that economies of scale exist for all relevant output levels. As we will see later, this type of long-run ATC curve has important implications for the structure of the industry.

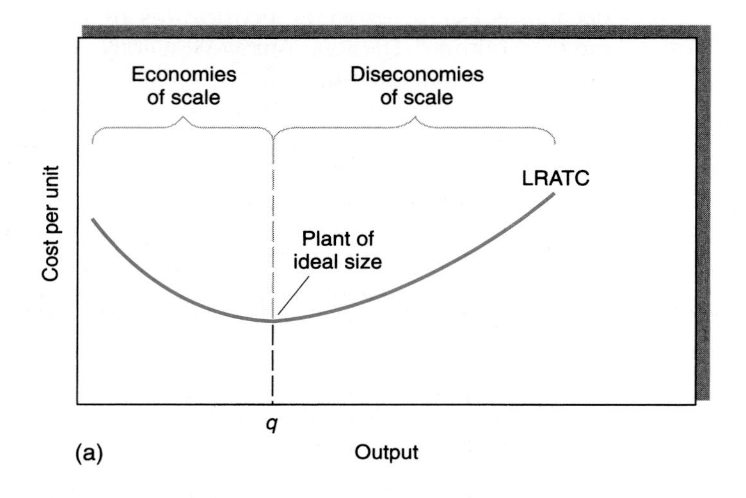


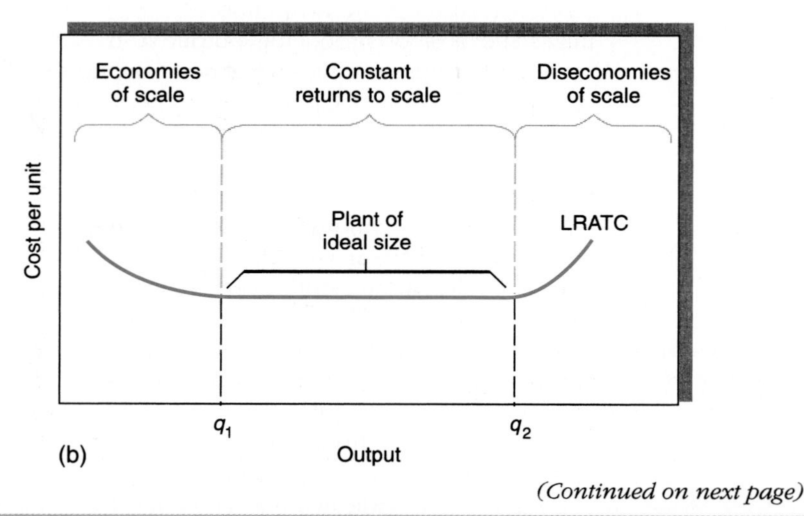


*(Continued on next page)*

changing with the firm's output. What are those other factors, and how will they affect production costs?

1. *Prices of resources.* If the prices of resources used should rise, the firm's cost curves will shift upward, as Exhibit 5.6 illustrates. For example, what happens to the cost of producing automobiles when the price of steel

**EXHIBIT 5.5** **Three Different Types of Long-Run Average Cost Curves, (*continued*)**

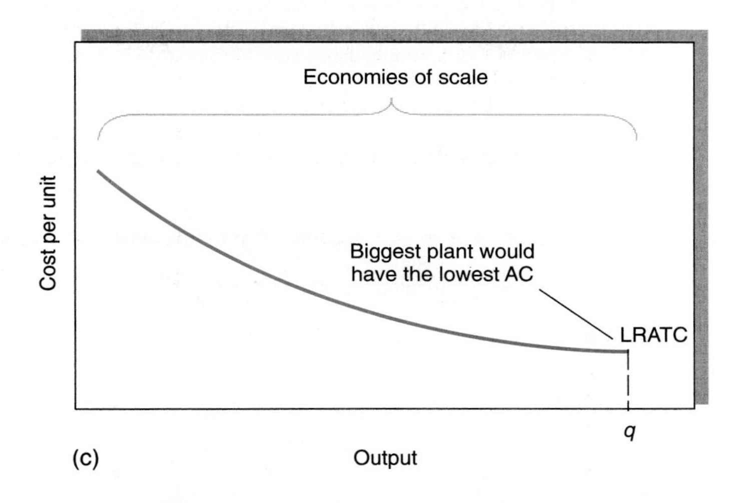


**EXHIBIT 5.6** **Higher Resource Prices and Cost**

An increase in resource prices will cause the firm's cost curves to shift upward.

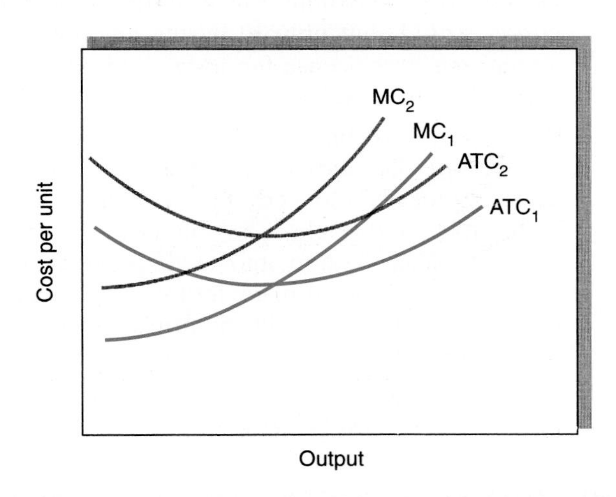


rises? The cost of producing automobiles also rises. Conversely, lower resource prices will result in cost reductions, or a shift downward.

2. *Taxes.* Taxes are a component of a firm's cost. Suppose that an excise tax of 20 cents were levied on each gallon of gasoline sold by a service station. What would happen to the seller's costs? They would increase, just

**EXHIBIT 5.7**

**Technological Improvements and the Cost of Microcomputers**

In the mid-1970s, scientists figured out how to make more powerful computer chips at a lower cost. This technological improvement reduced the cost of producing microcomputers. As a result, both the ATC and MC curves of microcomputer manufacturers shifted downward.

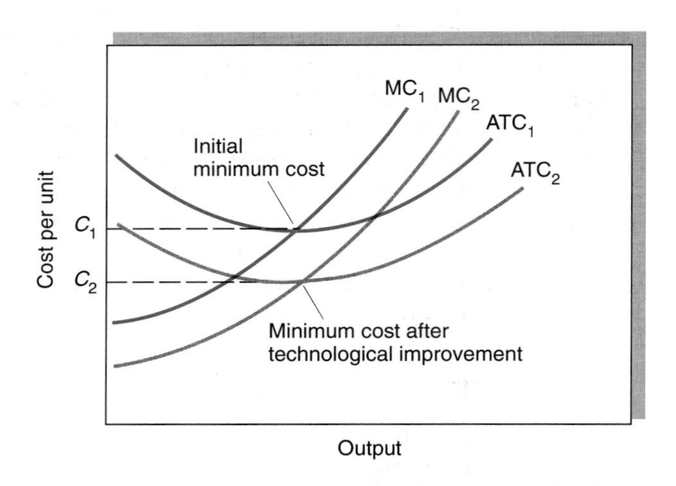


as they did in Exhibit 5.6. The firm's average total and marginal cost curves would shift upward by the amount of the tax. If the tax were an annual business license fee instead, the average total cost would rise, but variable costs would not.

3. *Technology.* Technological improvements often make it possible to produce a specific output with fewer resources. For example, the printing press drastically reduced the number of labor-hours required to print newspapers and books. The spinning wheel reduced the labor-hours necessary to make cotton into cloth. More recently, computers and robots have reduced costs in many industries. As Exhibit 5.7 shows, a technological improvement will shift the firm's cost curves downward, reflecting the reduction in the amount of resources used to produce alternative levels of output.

## COST AND THE ECONOMIC WAY OF THINKING

When analyzing the firm's costs, economists often present a highly mechanical—some would say unrealistic—view. The role of personal choice tends to be glossed over.

It is important to keep in mind that costs are incurred when choices are made. When business decision-makers choose to purchase raw materials, hire new employees, or renew the lease on a plant, they incur costs. All these decisions, like other choices, must be made under conditions of uncertainty. Of course, past experience acts as a useful guide, giving the decision-maker a good idea of the costs that will be associated with alternative decisions.

Opportunity costs are usually "expected costs"—they represent the highest valued option which the decision-maker expects to give up as the result of a choice. Think for a moment of what the cost curves developed in this chapter really mean. The firm's short-run marginal cost curve represents the opportunity cost of expanding output, *given the firm's current plant size.* The firm's long-run average total cost curve represents the opportunity cost per unit of output associated with varying plant sizes and rates of output, *given that the alternative plants are still on the drawing boards.* Opportunity costs look forward, reflecting expectations—often based on the past record—as to what will be forgone as a result of current decisions. At decision time, neither the short-run marginal cost nor the long-run average total cost can be determined from accounting records. Accounting costs look backward. They yield valuable information about historical costs.

## Sunk Costs

**sunk costs** Costs that have already been incurred as a result of past decisions. They are sometimes referred to as historical costs.

Historical costs associated with past decisions—economists call them **sunk costs**—should exert no direct influence on current choices. The outcome of past choices will provide knowledge relevant to current decisions, but the specific costs themselves are no longer relevant. Past choices cannot be reversed; money that has been spent is gone for good. Current choices should be based on the costs and benefits expected in relation to *current* market conditions. (See the "Myths of Economics" box.)

## Cost and Supply

Economists are interested in cost because they seek to explain the supply decisions of firms. A strictly profit-maximizing firm will compare the expected revenues derived from a decision or a course of action with the expected costs. If the expected revenues exceed costs, the course of action will be chosen because it will expand profits (or reduce losses).

In the short run, when making supply decisions, the marginal cost of producing additional units is the relevant cost consideration. A profit-maximizing decision-maker will compare the expected marginal costs with the expected additional revenue from larger sales. If the latter exceeds the former, output (the quantity supplied) will be expanded.

Whereas marginal costs are central to the choice of short-run output, the expected average total cost is vital to a firm's long-run supply decision. *Before entry into an industry,* a profit-maximizing decision-maker will compare the expected market price with the expected long-run average total cost. Profit-seeking potential entrants will supply the product if, and only if, they expect the market price to exceed their long-run average total cost. Similarly, existing firms will continue to supply a product only if they expect that the market price will enable them at least to cover their long-run average total cost.

## MYTHS OF ECONOMICS

***"A good business decision-maker will never sell a product for less than its production costs."***

This statement contains a grain of truth. A profit-seeking entrepreneur would not *undertake* a project knowing that the costs could not be covered. However, this view fails to emphasize (1) the time dimension of the production process and (2) the uncertainty associated with business decisions. The production process takes time. Raw materials must be purchased, employees hired, and plants equipped. Retailers must contract with suppliers. As these decisions are made, costs result. Many of the firm's costs of production are incurred long before the product is ready for marketing.

Even a good business decision-maker is not always able to predict the future correctly. Market conditions may change in an unexpected manner. At the time the product is ready for sale, buyers may be unwilling to pay a price that will cover the seller's past costs of production. These past costs, however, are now sunk costs and no longer relevant. Current decisions must be made on the basis of current cost and revenue considerations.

Should a grocer refuse to sell oranges that are about to spoil because their wholesale cost cannot be covered? The grocer's current opportunity cost of selling the oranges may be nearly zero. The alternative may be to throw them in the garbage next week. Almost any price, even one far below past costs, would be better than letting the oranges spoil.

Consider another example. Suppose a couple who own a house plan to relocate temporarily. Should they refuse to rent their house for $400 (if this is the best offer available) because their monthly house payment is $600? Of course not. The house payment will go on, regardless of whether they rent the house. If the homeowners can cover their opportunity costs (perhaps wear and tear plus a $60 monthly fee for a property management service), they will gain by renting rather than leaving the house vacant.

Past mistakes provide useful lessons for the future, but they cannot be reversed. Bygones are bygones, even if they resulted in business loss. Only current revenue and cost considerations are relevant to current decisions about prices, output, and amount supplied. There is no need to fret over spilt milk, burnt toast, or yesterday's business losses.

## Technology, Mass Production, and Costs

As noted, technological improvements and learning from prior experience often lead to lower costs. In fact, a pattern often develops as goods are introduced, marketed, and modified. When a new product is initially introduced, it is often so expensive that only a few consumers can afford it. As producers experiment with alternative production methods and product modifications, however, they are often able to offer it at a significantly lower price. Mass production, technological modifications, market penetration, and learning from experience are the keys to success during this phase. Entrepreneurs who reduce costs and bring a product within the budget constraint of the mass of consumers often reap enormous gains. As they do so, however, they improve the standard of living for many other people.

We have seen many products go through this cycle. When ballpoint pens were initially introduced in the 1940s, their unit cost of production was approximately $60. Not many people could afford one at that price. Over time, however, modifications were made and producers learned how to produce them more cheaply. By 1960 the pens were available for less than $1, and almost everyone in America had at least one. The automobile, microwave oven, calculator, microcomputer, and video cassette recorder, among numerous other products, have gone through this same dynamic cycle. Initially, they were expensive and affordable to only a few. With time, however, producers learned more about how to produce them. Eventually, technological improvements, modifications, and large-scale production methods resulted in substantial reductions in per-unit costs. Such dynamic cost reductions are a driving force underlying economic progress.

## LOOKING AHEAD

In this chapter, we outlined several basic principles that affect the costs of business firms. We will use these basic principles when we analyze the price and output decisions of firms under alternative market conditions in the chapters that follow.

## CHAPTER SUMMARY

1. The business firm is used to organize productive resources and transform them into goods and services. There are three major business structures—proprietorships, partnerships, and corporations. Proprietorships are the most numerous, but far more business activity is conducted through corporations.
2. In a market economy, business owners have a property right to the residual income of the business firm. This property right provides them with a strong incentive to organize and structure their business in a manner that will minimize the cost of producing any given level of output.
3. The demand for a product indicates the intensity of consumers' desires for the item. The (opportunity) cost of producing the item indicates the desire of consumers for other goods that must now be given up to provide the necessary resources for production of the item. In a market economy, these two forces—demand and costs of production—balance the desire of consumers for more of a good against the reality of scarce resources and the desire of consumers for other goods that must be forgone as more of any one specific item is supplied.
4. Economists employ the opportunity-cost concept when figuring a firm's costs. Therefore, total cost includes not only explicit (money) costs but also implicit costs associated with the use of productive resources owned by the firm.
5. Since accounting procedures generally omit the opportunity cost of the firm's equity capital and sometimes (in the case of owner-operated firms) omit the cost of owner-provided services, accounting costs understate the opportunity cost of producing a good. As a result of these omissions, the accounting profits of a firm are generally larger than the firm's economic profits.

6. Economic profit (loss) results when a firm's sales revenues exceed (are less than) its total costs, both explicit and implicit. Firms that are making the market rate of return on their assets will therefore make zero economic profit. Firms that transform resources into products of greater value than the opportunity cost of the resources used will make an economic profit. On the other hand, if the opportunity cost of the resources used exceeds the value of the product, losses will result.
7. The firm's short-run average total cost curve will tend to be U-shaped. When output is small (relative to plant size), average fixed cost (and therefore ATC) will be high. As output expands, however, AFC (and ATC) will fall. As the firm attempts to produce a larger and larger rate of output using its fixed plant size, diminishing returns will eventually set in, and marginal cost will rise as the plant's maximum capacity is approached. Eventually, marginal costs will exceed average total costs, causing the latter to rise also. Thus, the firm's short-run ATC will be high for both small output rates (because AFC is high) and large output rates (because of diminishing returns and rising MC).
8. The ability to plan a larger volume of output often leads to cost reductions. These cost reductions associated with the scale of one's operation result from (a) a greater opportunity to employ mass production methods, (b) specialized use of resources, and (c) learning by doing.
9. The LRATC reflects the costs of production for plants of various sizes. When economies of scale are present (that is, when larger plants have lower per-unit costs of production), LRATC will decline. When constant returns to scale are experienced, LRATC will be constant. A rising LRATC is also possible. Bureaucratic decision-making and other diseconomies of scale may in some cases cause LRATC to rise.
10. In analyzing the general shapes of a firm's cost curves, we assumed that the following factors remained constant: (a) resource prices, (b) technology, and (c) taxes. Changes in any of these factors would cause the cost curves of a firm to shift.
11. In any analysis of business decision-making, it is important to keep the opportunity-cost principle in mind. Economists are interested in costs primarily because costs affect the decisions of suppliers. Short-run marginal costs represent the supplier's opportunity cost of producing additional units *with the existing plant facilities of the firm.* The long-run average total cost represents the opportunity cost of supplying alternative rates of output, *given sufficient time to vary all factors, including plant size.*
12. Sunk costs are costs that have already been incurred. They should not exert a *direct* influence on current business choices. However, they may provide a source of information useful in making current decisions.

# *Study Guide*

## CHAPTER 5

# DEVELOPING THE ECONOMIC WAY OF THINKING

## CRITICAL-ANALYSIS QUESTIONS

*1. What is economic profit? How might it differ from accounting profit? Explain why firms that are making zero economic profit are likely to continue in business.

*2. Which of the following do you think reflect sound economic thinking? Explain your answer.
   a. "I paid $200 for this economics course. Therefore, I'm going to attend the lectures even if they are useless and boring."
   b. "Since we own rather than rent, housing doesn't cost us anything."
   c. "I own 100 shares of stock that I can't afford to sell until the price goes up enough for me to get back at least my original investment."
   d. "It costs to produce private education, whereas public schooling is free."

3. Explain the factors that cause a firm's short-run average total costs to decline initially, but eventually to increase as the rate of output rises.

*4. Is profit maximization consistent with the self-interest of corporate owners? Is it consistent with the self-interest of corporate managers? Is there a conflict between the self-interest of owners and of managers?

5. "The American steel industry cannot compete with Korean and Japanese steel producers. These countries built modern, efficient mills that made use of the latest technology. In contrast, American mills are older and less efficient. Our costs are higher because we are stuck with old facilities." Analyze this view critically.

6. Why do economists consider normal returns to capital as a cost? How does economic profit differ from normal returns (or "normal profit")?

7. What are implicit costs? Do implicit costs contribute to the opportunity cost of production? Should an implicit cost be counted as cost? Give three examples of implicit costs. Does the firm's accounting statement take implicit costs into account? Why or why not?

*8. Consider a machine purchased one year ago for $12,000. The machine is being depreciated $4,000 per year over a three-year period. Its current market value is $5,000, and the expected market value of the machine one year from now is $3,000. If the interest rate is 10 percent, what is the expected cost of holding the machine during the next year?

*9. Investors seeking to take over a firm often bid a positive price for the business even though it is currently experiencing losses. Why would anyone ever bid a positive price for a firm operating at a loss?

*10. The following story, which may or may not be true, has for many years been told in certain economics classes: "Years ago a visitor to China, strolling along a barge canal, saw a group of men rowing a cargo barge along the canal. He was appalled to see a man with a whip walking alongside the barge, watching the crew and lashing out with the whip anytime a crewmember would appear to slacken his efforts. The visitor exclaimed his disgust at this sight to a local Chinese companion. The companion smiled. He explained that crews like this hired themselves out to get rowing jobs done, and in fact often themselves paid such a man with a

*Asterisk denotes critical-analysis questions for which answers are given in Appendix A.

whip." What was the purpose of the man with the whip? Why were the crewmembers willing to pay him?

11. "If it were not for the law of diminishing returns, it would be possible to raise all of the world's foodstuff on an acre of the world's most fertile land." Is this statement true? Why is less fertile land used for agriculture in the real world?

## MULTIPLE-CHOICE SELF-TEST

1. Which of the following provides the strongest evidence that the corporate form of business structure is relatively cost-efficient in many industries?
   a. The ability of the corporate business structure to compete effectively in most industries with proprietorships, partnerships, consumer cooperatives, employee-owned firms, and other forms of business structure.
   b. The fact that nearly three out of every four business firms in the United States are individual proprietorships.
   c. The fact that economic theory indicates corporate managers have some leeway to pursue their own interest at the expense of greedy capitalists.
   d. The ability of some corporate managers to achieve high salaries even though the firms they are directing are not earning economic profit.
2. The owners of a business firm
   a. Are paid the market rate of return for resources they supply to the firm.
   b. Are residual income claimants.
   c. Have little incentive to monitor shirking on the part of employees.
   d. Have little incentive to provide the employees of their firm with an incentive system that encourages operational efficiency.
3. The difference between the firm's total revenues and total costs when all explicit and implicit costs are included is the firm's
   a. Economic profit.
   b. Accounting profit.
   c. Opportunity cost of capital.
   d. Long-run average total cost.
4. According to the income statement of Joe's Clothing Store, total revenue was $67,000 and total cost was $48,000. However, Joe worked full time in his store without a salary and invested $30,000 to buy and stock merchandise. Given this information, can we conclude that the economic profit of Joe's Clothing Store is $19,000?
   a. Yes, the last sentence is true, given the information supplied.
   b. No. The interest income forgone on this investment should be subtracted from $19,000 in order to correctly calculate Joe's profit.
   c. No. The opportunity cost of Joe's labor services should be subtracted from $19,000 in order to correctly calculate Joe's profit.
   d. No. Both the interest income forgone and the opportunity cost of Joe's labor services should be subtracted from $19,000 in order to correctly calculate Joe's profit.
5. Accounting costs are often unsatisfactory from the economist's point of view because
   a. Accounting costs fail to make an allowance for depreciation—the wearing out of capital assets during a period.

b. Accountants attempt to minimize costs in order to make profits look good.
c. Accounting costs often fail to include the opportunity cost of resources owned by the firm.
d. Accounting procedures are designed to overstate costs in order to minimize business tax liability.

6. Average fixed costs
   a. Will remain unchanged as the rate of output expands.
   b. Are equal to total costs minus variable costs.
   c. Are defined as the change in total costs divided by the change in output.
   d. Will always decline as the rate of output increases.
7. Which of the following is always true of the relationship between average total costs and marginal costs?
   a. Average total costs are increasing when marginal costs are increasing.
   b. Marginal costs are increasing when average total costs are higher than marginal costs.
   c. Average total costs are increasing when marginal costs are higher than average total costs.
   d. Average total costs are constant when marginal costs are constant.
8. Which of the following explains most accurately why the firm's short-run marginal cost curve will eventually rise?
   a. As more of the variable factor is used, its price will eventually rise.
   b. When diminishing marginal returns set in, it will take larger and larger quantities of the variable resources to produce an additional unit of output.
   c. As the variable factor is used more intensely, its marginal product will rise, causing an increase in marginal costs.
   d. As the size of the firm increases, the operational efficiency of the firm declines, causing an increase in marginal costs.
9. When a plant is still in the blueprint stage, the expected per unit cost of producing alternative rates of output is reflected by the firm's
   a. Short-run marginal cost curve.
   b. Short-run total cost curve.
   c. Long-run variable cost curve.
   d. Long-run average total cost curve.
10. Which of the following would be most likely to cause the average total cost curve of a firm producing steel bolts to shift from $ATC_1$ to $ATC_2$? Refer to the following figure:

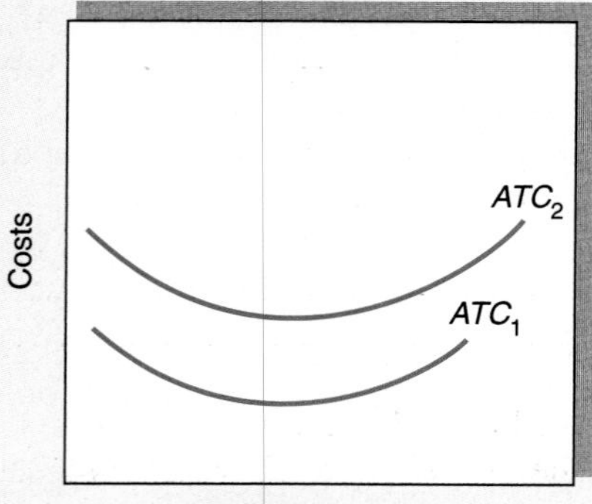

a. An increase in demand for steel bolts.
b. An increase in the market price of steel bolts.
c. Diminishing returns for the variable factors used to produce steel bolts.
d. An increase in the price of steel.

## PROBLEMS

1. Draw a U-shaped short-run average total cost curve for a firm. Construct the accompanying marginal cost and average variable cost curves.

2. **Income Statement: Sam's Shirt Shop**

| Revenues | | Costs | |
|---|---|---|---|
| Sales | $95,000 | Wholesale clothing | $50,000 |
| Inventory adjustment | 2,000 | Store rental | 2,000 |
| | | Labor | 15,000 |
| | | Utilities and insurance | 1,000 |
| Total revenues | $97,000 | Total costs | $68,000 |

The annual income statement of Sam's Shirt Shop for 1993 is presented here. Sam worked full time in the store and invested $100,000 to purchase some equipment and stock the store with merchandise. He recently turned down an offer of a salaried position paying $30,000 per year to manage another clothing store. He did not pay himself a salary during the year. According to the income statement,

a. What were Sam's accounting profits?
b. What major items did he exclude from his costs?
c. Assuming that the market rate of interest was 10 percent, recalculate Sam's total costs.
d. What was the economic profit or loss of Sam's Shirt Shop in 1993?

3. **Costs and Output: Jaynie's Furniture Store**

| Output (per week) | Total Cost | Total Fixed Cost | Total Variable Cost | Average Total Cost | Average Variable Cost | Marginal Cost |
|---|---|---|---|---|---|---|
| 1 | $100 | $50 | | | | |
| 2 | 140 | | | | | |
| 3 | 177 | | | | | |
| 4 | 216 | | | | | |
| 5 | 265 | | | | | |
| 6 | 324 | | | | | |
| 7 | 399 | | | | | |
| 8 | 496 | | | | | |

Jaynie owns a small shop and produces dining room sets. The accompanying chart presents data on her expected total cost per set at various output levels.

a. Complete the chart.
b. At what output level is Jaynie's average total cost at a minimum?
c. Graph the firm's average total cost, average variable cost, and marginal cost curves.

4. The data necessary to evaluate the cost of owning and operating two alternative automobiles are presented in the accompanying table.

| | Auto A | Auto B |
|---|---|---|
| Purchase price | $5,000 | $4,000 |
| Annual fee for insurance and license | 200 | 100 |
| Operating cost per mile including gas, oil, and maintenance | 0.15 | 0.14 |
| Resale value one year from now | 4,000 | 2,800 |

a. Assuming that the market rate of interest is 10 percent, calculate the average cost per mile of owning the automobile one year and driving it 10,000 miles for both Auto A and Auto B. Which is cheaper?
b. If the automobiles were driven 20,000 miles during the year, their respective resale values would be $3,700 for A and $2,200 for B. Which would be cheaper to purchase, own, and drive 20,000 miles during the year? Explain.
c. What happens to the average total cost per mile as the miles driven per year increase? Explain.

5. Draw a graph for the average fixed cost, average variable cost, average total cost, and marginal cost data of Exhibit 5.2.
a. At what output rate per day was AVC at its minimum?
b. At what output rate was ATC (unit cost) at a minimum?
c. Why was the unit cost high at an output rate like 2? Why was it high at an output rate like 11?
d. What happens to average fixed cost as output increases?

CHAPTER

6

# PRICE TAKERS AND THE COMPETITIVE PROCESS

Competition means decentralized planning by many separate persons.

*Friedrich A. von Hayek*[1]

Competition is conducive to the continuous improvements of industrial efficiency. It leads some producers to eliminate wastes and cut costs so that they may undersell others. It compels others to adopt similar measures in order that they may survive. It weeds out those whose costs remain high and thus operates to concentrate production in the hands of those whose costs are low.

*Clair Wilcox*[2]

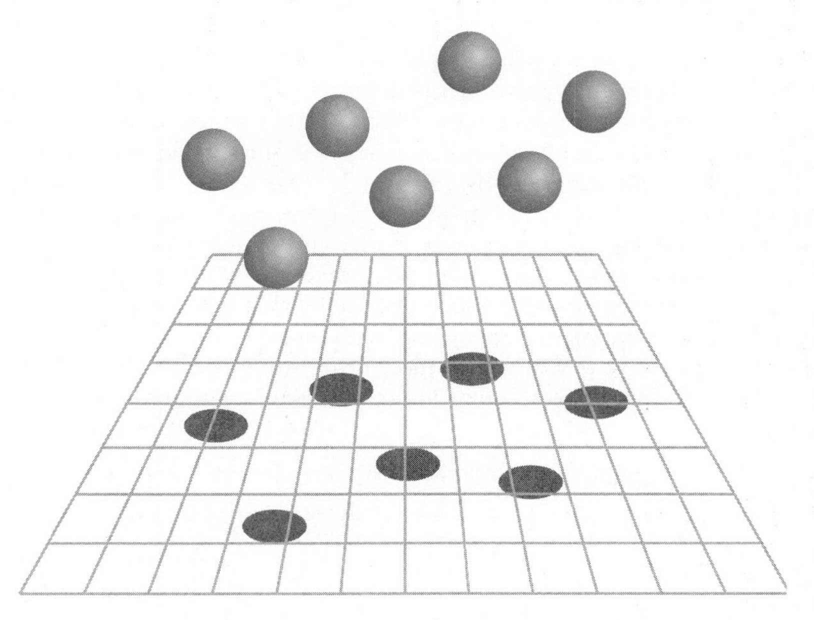

## CHAPTER FOCUS

- What is the difference between firms that are price takers and those that are price searchers?
- What determines the output of a price taker?
- How do price takers change their output when price changes in the short run? In the long run?
- What is the role of time in determining the elasticity of supply?
- What must firms do in order to make profits? How do profits and losses influence the supply and market price of a product?
- How does competition influence the incentive of self-interested producers to supply goods that consumers want at an economical cost?

In the previous chapters we saw how firms make production decisions, and how costs affect those decisions. In this and the next two chapters, we take a closer look at how the product prices and profit levels that emerge from market trading will influence production. How much will be produced in a given market? What determines the profitability of firms, and how does the level of profit influence market supply over time? When goods and services are allocated by markets, will resources be allocated efficiently? Is there any reason to believe that there will be a linkage between market allocation and economic prosperity? These are the major questions that we will address in the next several chapters.

# PRICE TAKERS AND PRICE SEARCHERS

**price takers** Sellers who must take the market price in order to sell their product. Because each price taker's output is small relative to the total market, price takers can sell all of their output at the market price, but are unable to sell any of their output at a price higher than the market price. Thus, they face a horizontal demand curve.

This chapter will focus on markets where the firms are **price takers:** they simply take the price that is determined in the market. In a price-taker market, the firms all produce identical products (for example, wheat, eggs, or regular unleaded gasoline) and each seller is small relative to the total market. Thus, the output supplied by any single firm exerts little or no effect on the market price. Each firm can sell all of its output at the market price, but it is unable to sell any of its output at a price higher than the market price. When a firm is a price taker, there is no price decision to be made. Price takers will merely attempt to choose the output level that will maximize profit, given their costs and the price determined by the market.

In the real world, most firms are not price takers. Firms are usually able to increase their price, at least a little, without losing all of their customers.

[1]F. A. Hayek, "The Use of Knowledge in Society," *American Economic Review* 35 (September 1945): 519–550.
[2]Clair Wilcox, *Competition and Monopoly in American Industry,* Monograph no. 21, Temporary National Economic Committee, Investigation of Concentration of Economic Power, 76th Congress, 3d session (Washington, DC: U.S. Government Printing Office, 1940).

Similarly, they will be able to increase the number of units sold if they reduce their price. For example, if Nike increased the price of its athletic shoes by 10 percent, the number of shoes sold would decline (although it would not fall to zero). Firms like Nike are **price searchers:** they can choose what price they will charge for their product, but the quantity that they are able to sell is very much related to their price. As price searchers seek maximum profit, they must not only decide how much to produce, but also what price to charge. We will examine markets where the firms are price searchers in the following two chapters.

**price searcher** A firm that faces a downward-sloping demand curve for its product. The amount that the firm is able to sell is inversely related to the price that it charges.

If most real-world firms are price searchers rather than price takers, why take the time to analyze the latter? There are several reasons to do so. First, although most firms are not price takers, some are, and they are in several important markets, particularly markets for agricultural goods. Second, the price-taker model helps clarify the relationship between the decision-making of individual firms and market supply in both price taker and price searcher markets.

Finally, and perhaps most importantly, markets where firms are price takers enhance our knowledge of **competition as a dynamic process.** In fact, economists generally refer to markets where firms are price takers as "purely competitive" markets. Unfortunately, this terminology is confusing. It conceals the fact that there also is often an intense rivalry—that is, a strong competitiveness—among firms that are price searchers. In fact, price searchers generally use a broad array of competitive weapons—for example, quality of product, style, convenient location, advertising, and price—all in an effort to attract consumers. Thus, competition as a dynamic process applies to both price takers and price searchers. Understanding how the competitive process works when firms are price takers will also contribute to our understanding of the process as it applies to many price searchers.

**competition as a dynamic process** A term that denotes rivalry or competitiveness between or among parties (for example, producers or input suppliers), each of which seeks to deliver a better deal to buyers when quality, price, and product information are all considered. Competing implies a lack of collusion among sellers.

## MARKETS WHEN FIRMS ARE PRICE TAKERS

Consider the situation of Les Parrot, a Texas cattle rancher. As Parrot consults the financial pages of the local newspaper, he finds that the current market price of quality steers is 88 cents per pound. Even if his ranch is quite large, there is little that Parrot can do to change the market price of beef cattle. After all, there are tens of thousands of farmers who raise cattle. Thus, Parrot supplies only a small portion of the total cattle market. The amount that he sells will exert little or no impact on the market price of cattle. Parrot is a price taker.

The firms in a market will be price takers when the following four conditions are met:

1. All of the firms in the market are producing an identical product (for example, beef cattle of a given grade).
2. There are a large number of firms in the market.
3. Each firm supplies only a very small portion of the total amount supplied to the market.
4. There are no barriers limiting the entry or exit of firms in the market.

When these conditions are met, the firms in the market must accept the market price. This is why they are called price takers. Exhibit 6.1 illustrates the relationship between the market forces (frame b) and the demand curve facing

**EXHIBIT 6.1**

**Price Taker's Demand Curve**

The market forces of supply and demand determine price (frame b). The individual price taker has no control over price. Thus, the demand for the product of the firm is perfectly elastic (frame a).

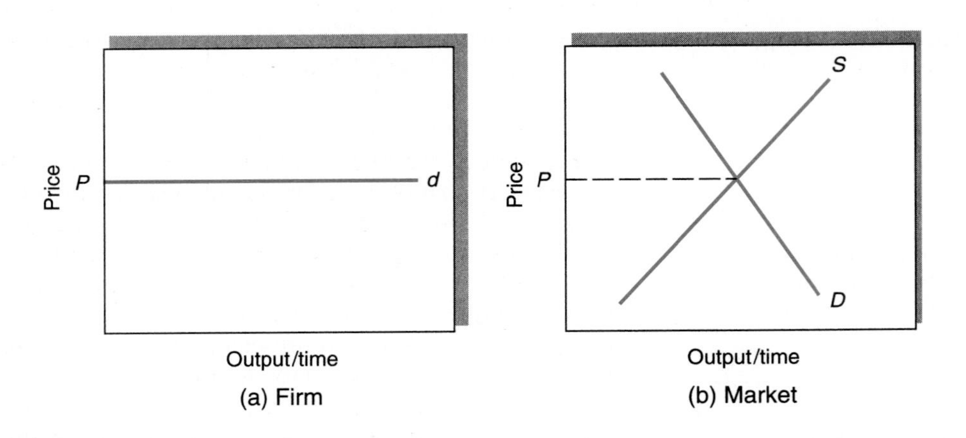


the price taking firm (frame a). If the firm sets a price above the market level, consumers will simply buy from other sellers. Why pay the higher price when the identical good is available elsewhere at a lower price? For example, if the price of wheat were \$3 per bushel, a farmer would be unable to find buyers for wheat at \$3.50 per bushel. A firm could lower its price, but since it is small relative to the total market, the firm can already sell as much as it wants at the market price. A price reduction would merely reduce revenues. A firm that is a price taker thus confronts a perfectly elastic demand for its product.

## Output in the Short Run

The firm's output decision is based on comparison of benefits with costs. If a firm produces at all, it will continue expanding output as long as the benefits (additional revenues) from the production of the additional units exceed their marginal costs.

How will changes in output influence the firm's costs? In the last chapter, we discovered that the firm's short-run marginal costs will *eventually* increase as the firm expands its output by working its fixed plant facilities more intensively. The law of diminishing marginal returns assures us that this will be the case. Eventually, both the firm's short-run marginal and average total cost curves will turn upward.

**marginal revenue** The incremental change in total revenue derived from the sale of one additional unit of a product.

What about the benefits or additional revenues from output expansion? **Marginal revenue** (MR) is the change in the firm's total revenue per unit of output. It is the additional revenue derived from the sale of an additional unit of output. Mathematically,

$$\text{MR} = \frac{\text{Change in total revenue}}{\text{Change in output}}$$

Since the price taker sells all units at the same price, its marginal revenue will be equal to the market price.

In the short run, the price taker will expand output until marginal revenue (its price) is just equal to marginal cost. This decision-making rule will maximize the firm's profits (or minimize its losses).

Exhibit 6.2 helps explain why. Since the firm can sell as many units as it would like at the market price, the sale of one additional unit will increase revenue by the price of the product. Does the firm gain by producing an extra unit? The answer is yes, as long as the marginal revenue (price, for the price taker) is greater than or equal to the marginal cost of that unit. Profit is simply the difference between total revenue and total cost. Profit will increase as long as production and sale of a unit add more to revenue than to cost. As long as marginal revenue exceeds marginal cost, the firm will gain from an expansion in output. However, as the firm produces a larger and larger quantity from its fixed size of plant, marginal costs will eventually rise and exceed price and marginal revenue. When production of an additional unit adds more to cost than it adds to revenue, profit will be reduced if the unit is produced. Thus, the profit of the price taker is at a maximum when $P = \text{MR} = \text{MC}$. In Exhibit 6.2, this occurs at output level $q$.

A profit-maximizing firm with the cost curves indicated by Exhibit 6.2 would produce exactly $q$. The total revenue of the firm would be the sales price $P$ multiplied by output sold $q$. Geometrically, the firm's total revenues would be *POqB*. The firm's total cost would be found by multiplying the average total cost by the output level. Geometrically, total costs are represented by *COqA*. The firm's total revenues exceed total costs, and the firm is making short-run economic profit (the shaded area).

In the real world, of course, decisions are not made by entrepreneurs who sit around drawing demand and marginal cost curves. Many have not even

**EXHIBIT 6.2**

**Profit Maximization and the Price Taker**

The price taker would maximize profits by producing the output level $q$ where $P = \text{MC}$.

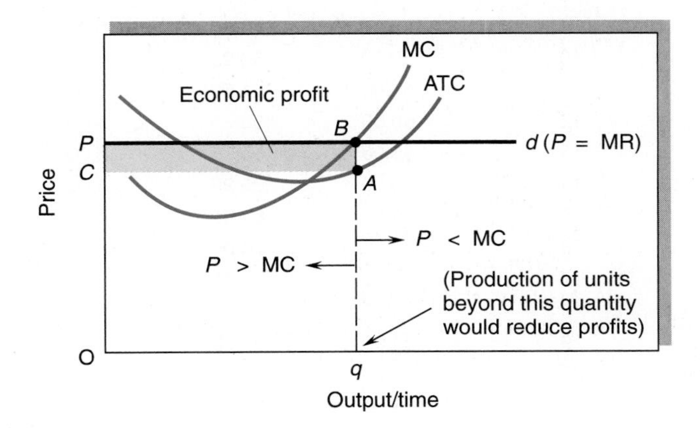

heard of these concepts. A business decision-maker who has never heard of the $P$ = MC rule for profit maximization, however, probably has another rule that yields approximately the same outcome. For example, the rule might be to produce those units, and only those units, that add more to revenue than to cost. This ensures maximum profit (or minimum loss). It also takes the firm to the point at which $P$ = MC. Why? To stop short of that point would mean not producing some profitable units—units that would add more to revenue than to cost. Similarly, the decision-maker would not go beyond that point because production of such units would add more to costs than to revenues. This commonsense rule thus leads to the same outcome as our model, even when the decision-maker knows none of the technical jargon of economics. No wonder economics is sometimes thought of as "organized common sense."

## Profit Maximizing —A Numeric Example

Exhibit 6.3 uses numeric data to illustrate profit-maximizing decision-making for a firm that is a price taker. The firm's short-run total and marginal cost schedules have the general characteristics we discussed in the previous chap-

**EXHIBIT 6.3** **Profit Maximization of a Price-Taker Firm—A Numeric Illustration**

| (1) Output (per Day) | (2) Total Revenue | (3) Total Cost | (4) Marginal Revenue | (5) Marginal Cost | (6) Profit (TR – TC) |
|---|---|---|---|---|---|
| 0 | $ 0.00 | $ 25.00 | $0.00 | $ 0.00 | $–25.00 |
| 1 | 5.00 | 29.80 | 5.00 | 4.80 | –24.80 |
| 2 | 10.00 | 33.75 | 5.00 | 3.95 | –23.75 |
| 3 | 15.00 | 37.25 | 5.00 | 3.50 | –22.25 |
| 4 | 20.00 | 40.25 | 5.00 | 3.00 | –20.25 |
| 5 | 25.00 | 42.75 | 5.00 | 2.50 | –17.75 |
| 6 | 30.00 | 44.75 | 5.00 | 2.00 | –14.75 |
| 7 | 35.00 | 46.50 | 5.00 | 1.75 | –11.50 |
| 8 | 40.00 | 48.00 | 5.00 | 1.50 | – 8.00 |
| 9 | 45.00 | 49.25 | 5.00 | 1.25 | – 4.25 |
| 10 | 50.00 | 50.25 | 5.00 | 1.00 | – 0.25 |
| 11 | 55.00 | 51.50 | 5.00 | 1.25 | 3.50 |
| 12 | 60.00 | 53.25 | 5.00 | 1.75 | 6.75 |
| 13 | 65.00 | 55.75 | 5.00 | 2.50 | 9.25 |
| 14 | 70.00 | 59.25 | 5.00 | 3.50 | 10.75 |
| 15 | 75.00 | 64.00 | 5.00 | 4.75 | 11.00 |
| 16 | 80.00 | 70.00 | 5.00 | 6.00 | 10.00 |
| 17 | 85.00 | 77.25 | 5.00 | 7.25 | 7.75 |
| 18 | 90.00 | 85.50 | 5.00 | 8.25 | 4.50 |
| 19 | 95.00 | 95.00 | 5.00 | 9.50 | 0.00 |
| 20 | 100.00 | 108.00 | 5.00 | 13.00 | – 8.00 |
| 21 | 105.00 | 125.00 | 5.00 | 17.00 | –20.00 |

ter. Since the firm confronts a market price of $5 per unit, its marginal revenue is $5. Total revenue thus *increases* by $5 per additional unit of output. The firm maximizes its profit when it supplies an output of 15 units.

There are two ways of viewing this profit-maximizing output rate. First, we could examine the difference between total revenue and total cost, identifying the output rate at which this difference is greatest. Column 6, the profit data, provides this information. For small output rates (less than 11), the firm would actually experience losses. But at 15 units of output, an $11 profit is earned ($75 total revenue minus $64 total cost). Inspection of the profit column indicates that it is impossible to earn a profit larger than $11 at any other rate of output.

Exhibit 6.4a presents the total revenue and total cost approach in graph form. (However, the curves are drawn smoothly, as though output could be increased in any amounts including tiny amounts, not just in whole-unit increments as shown in Exhibit 6.3.) Profits will be maximized when the total revenue line exceeds the total cost curve by the largest vertical amount. That takes place, of course, at 15 units of output.

The marginal approach also can be used to determine the profit-maximizing rate of output for the competitive firm. Remember, as long as price (marginal revenue) exceeds marginal cost, production and sale of additional units will add to the firm's profit (or reduce its losses). Inspection of columns 4 and 5 of Exhibit 6.3 indicates that MR is greater than MC for the first 15 units of output. Production of these units will expand the firm's profit. In contrast, the production of each unit beyond 15 adds more to cost than to revenue. Profit will therefore decline if output is expanded beyond 15 units. Given the firm's cost and revenue schedule, the profit-maximizing manager will choose to produce 15, and only 15, units per day.

Exhibit 6.4b graphically illustrates the marginal approach. Note here that the output rate (15 units) at which the marginal cost and marginal revenue curves intersect coincides with the output rate in Exhibit 6.4a at which the total revenue curve exceeds the total cost curve by the largest amount.

## Losses and Going Out of Business

Suppose changes take place in the market that depress the price below a firm's average total cost. How will a profit-maximizing (or loss-minimizing) firm respond to this situation? The answer to this question depends on both the firm's current sales revenues relative to its *variable cost* and its expectations about the future. The firm has three options—it can (1) continue to operate in the short run, (2) shut down temporarily, or (3) go out of business.

If the firm anticipates that the lower market price is temporary, it may want to continue operating in the short run as long as it is able to cover its variable cost.[3] Exhibit 6.5 illustrates why. The firm shown in this exhibit

[3]In thinking about this issue, we must keep in mind the opportunity-cost concept. The firm's fixed costs are *opportunity costs* that do not vary with the level of output. They can be avoided if, and only if, the firm goes out of business. Following this course releases the fixed-cost resources to their best alternative use, and thus eliminates the fixed costs. Fixed costs are *not* (as some economics texts have stated) the depreciated value of the firm's fixed assets. Such accounting measures may have little to do with the firm's opportunity cost of those fixed assets. To specify fixed costs, we need to know (1) how much the firm's fixed assets would bring if they were sold or rented to others and (2) any other costs, such as operating license fees and debts, which could be avoided if the firm declared bankruptcy and/or went out of business. Since fixed costs can be avoided if the firm goes out of business, the firm should not operate even in the short run if it does not expect conditions to improve. See Marshall Colberg and James King, "Theory of Production Abandonment," *Revista Internazionale di Scienze Economiche e Commerciali* 20 (1973): 961–1072.

**EXHIBIT 6.4**

**Profit Maximization—Total and Marginal Approaches**

Using the data of Exhibit 6.3, here we provide two alternative ways of viewing profit maximization. As frame a illustrates, the profits of a price taker are maximized at the output level at which total revenue exceeds total cost by the maximum amount. Frame b demonstrates that the maximum-profit output can also be identified by comparing marginal revenue and marginal cost.

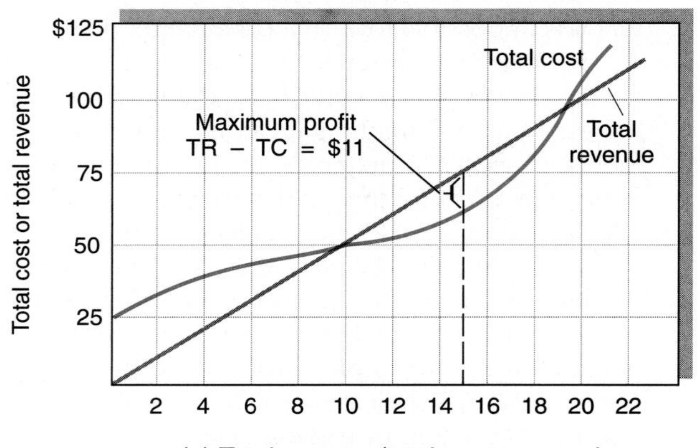


(a) Total revenue/total cost approach

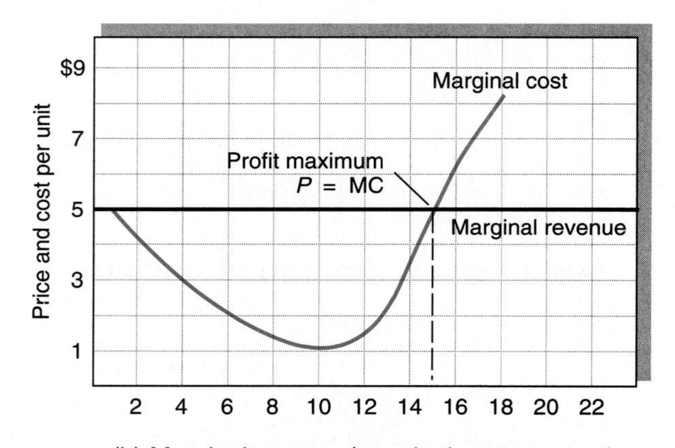


(b) Marginal revenue/marginal cost approach

would minimize its loss at output level $q$, where $P = \text{MC}$. At $q$, total revenues ($OqBP_1$) are, however, less than total costs ($OqAC$). The firm confronts short-run economic losses. Even if it shuts down completely, it will still incur fixed costs, *unless it goes out of business.* If the firm anticipates that the market price will increase enough that it will be able to cover its average total costs in the future, it may not want to sell out. It may choose to produce $q$ units in the short run, even though losses are incurred. At price $P_1$, production of output $q$ is clearly more advantageous than shutting down, because the firm is able to cover its variable costs and pay some of its fixed costs. If it were

**EXHIBIT 6.5**

**Operating with Short-Run Losses**

A firm making losses will operate in the short run if it can cover its variable costs now and also expects price to be high enough in the future to cover all its costs.

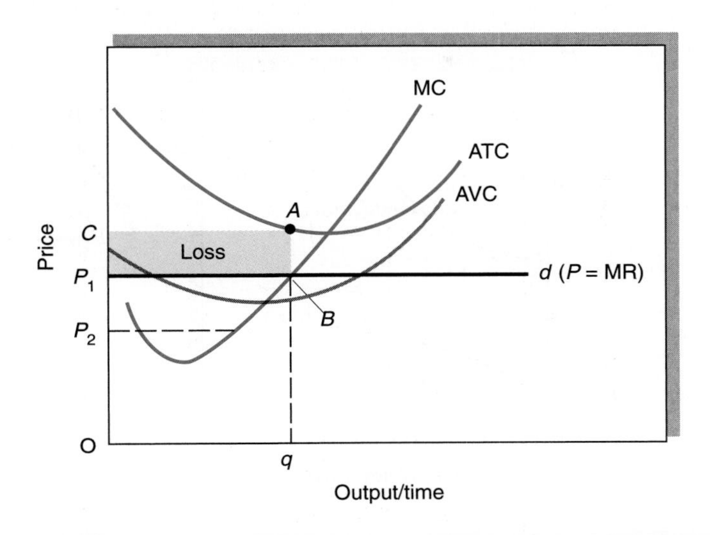


to shut down, *but not sell out,* the firm would lose the entire amount of its fixed cost.

What if the market price declines below the firm's average variable cost (for example, $P_2$)? Under these circumstances, a temporary **shutdown** is preferable to short-run operation. If the firm continues to operate in the short run, operating losses merely supplement losses resulting from the firm's fixed costs. Therefore, even if the firm expects the market price to increase, enabling it to survive and prosper in the future, it will shut down in the short run when the market price falls below its average variable cost.

**shutdown** A temporary halt in the operation of a business. The firm does *not* sell its assets. Its variable cost will be eliminated, but fixed costs will continue. The shutdown firm anticipates a return to operation in the future.

**going out of business** The sale of a firm's assets and its permanent exit from the market. By going out of business, a firm is able to avoid fixed cost, which would continue during a shutdown.

The firm's third option is **going out of business** immediately. After all, even the losses resulting from the firm's fixed costs (remember that if they are costs of doing business, they must be avoidable by not doing business) can be avoided if the firm sells out. If market conditions are not expected to change for the better, then going out of business is the preferred option.

## Firm's Short-Run Supply Curve

The price taker that intends to stay in business will maximize profits (or minimize losses) when it produces the output level at which $P$ = MC and variable costs are covered. Therefore, the portion of the firm's short-run marginal cost curve that lies above its average variable cost is the short-run supply curve of the firm.

Exhibit 6.6 illustrates that as the market price increases, the firm will expand output along its MC curve. If the market price were less than $P_1$, the firm would shut down immediately because it would be unable to cover even its variable costs. If the market price is $P_1$, however, a price equal to the firm's

**EXHIBIT 6.6**

**Supply Curve for Firm and Market**

(a) As the market price increases, the firm will expand ouptut along its marginal cost curve. (b) When resource prices are constant, the short-run market supply is merely the sum of the amounts supplied by all the firms in the market area.

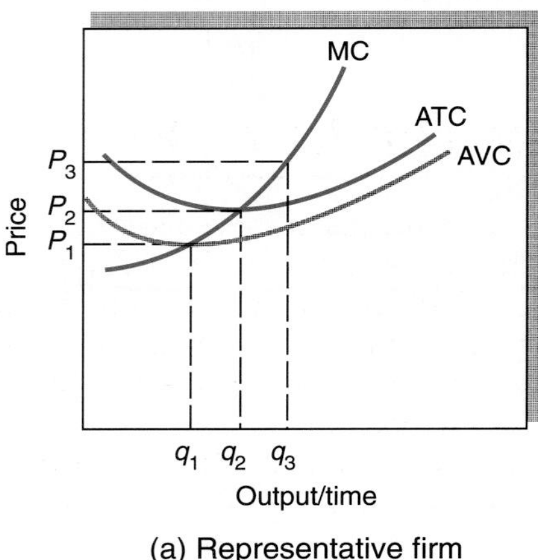

(a) Representative firm

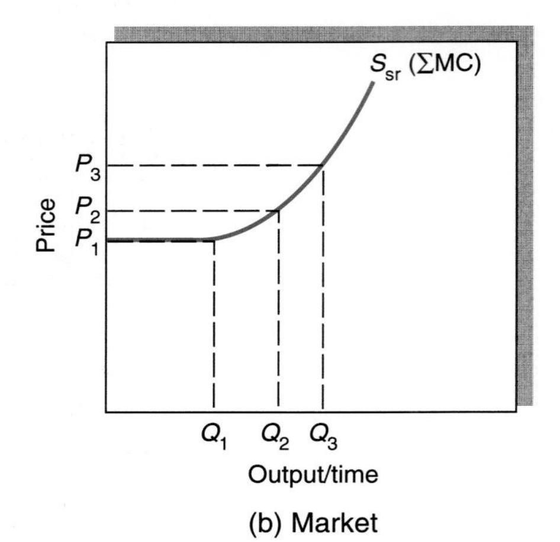

(b) Market

average variable cost, the firm may supply output $q_1$ *in the short run*. Economic losses will result, but the firm would incur similar losses if it shut down completely. As the market price increases to $P_2$, the firm will happily expand output along its MC curve to $q_2$. At $P_2$, price is also equal to average total costs. The firm is making a "normal rate of return," or zero economic profits. Higher prices will result in a still larger short-run output. The firm will supply $q_3$ units at market price $P_3$. At this price, economic profits will result. At still higher prices, output will be expanded even more. As long as price exceeds average variable cost, higher prices will cause the firm to expand output along its MC curve, which therefore becomes the firm's short-run supply curve.

## Short-Run Market Supply Curve

The short-run market supply curve corresponds to the total amount supplied by all of the firms in the industry. When the firms are price takers, the short-run market supply curve is the horizontal summation of the marginal cost curves (above the level of average variable cost) for all firms in the industry. Since individual firms will supply a larger amount at a higher price, the short-run market supply curve will slope upward to the right.

Exhibit 6.6 illustrates this relationship. As the price of the product rises from $P_1$ to $P_2$ to $P_3$, the individual firms expand their output along their marginal cost curves. Since the individual firms supply a larger output as the market price increases, the total amount supplied to the market also expands.

Our construction of the short-run market supply curve assumes that the prices of the resources used by the industry are constant. When the entire industry (rather than just a single firm) expands output, resource prices may rise.

If so, the short-run market supply curve (reflecting the higher prices of purchased inputs) will be slightly more inelastic (steeper) than the sum of the supply curves of the individual firms.

The short-run market supply curve, together with the demand curve for the industry's product, will determine the market price. At the short-run equilibrium market price, each of the firms will have expanded output until marginal costs have risen to the market price. They will have no desire to change output, *given their current size of plant.*

## SUPPLY IN THE LONG RUN

In the long run, firms can alter their plant size. New firms can enter the industry, and existing firms can exit. If the industry is profitable, resources will be drawn into the market, encouraging existing firms to expand and new firms to enter. Both of these changes will increase short-run supply, putting downward pressure on the market price. Conversely, when the firms in the industry are suffering losses, they will tend to contract, and entry by new firms will be unlikely. Losses will lead to a reduction in the quantity of capital and other resources committed to the industry. Supply will decline, placing upward pressure on the market price.

In general, then, the level of profit within an industry determines whether resources are drawn into the industry or are taken from it. So long as positive economic profits prevail, additional resources are attracted into the industry and there is downward pressure on the market price. Whenever economic losses prevail, resources tend to leave the industry and there is upward pressure on price. Only when economic profit is zero (the return on assets is normal), is there no incentive to move resources into or out of the market.

### Response to Increased Demand

The summed response of all firms to the level of profit in an industry provides a dynamic market response to any change in industry demand. When demand increases in a market, price rises and the firms expand output along their short-run marginal cost curves. More output is forthcoming due to the increase in the market price. The higher price leads to larger profits for price takers, as all the units they sell, not just the higher-cost additional units, sell at the higher price. With time, however, the higher profits will attract additional resources—new firms will enter and old firms will expand—into the industry. This increase in supply will eventually place downward pressure on price. The entry of new resources will continue until prices have fallen low enough to eliminate positive economic profits and firms can just cover their full costs of doing business.

Does price fall all the way to its previous level after the industry adjusts to the new, higher level of demand? That depends on what happens to the price of inputs. If the increase in the industry's demand for those inputs is small enough that input prices do not rise, then in the long run, cost conditions will be unchanged. When this is the case, the market price of the industry output will return to its previous level. More resources will be present in the expanded industry, but both the firm's per unit cost and the market price will return to their prior levels.

In most markets, however, an expansion in total output will cause the production costs of firms to rise. As the output of an industry increases, demand for resources used by the industry expands. This usually results in higher resource prices, which cause the firm's cost curves to shift upward. For example, an increase in demand for housing places upward pressure on the prices of lumber, roofing, window frames, and construction labor, causing the cost of housing to rise. Similarly, an increase in demand (and market output) for beef may cause the prices of feed grains, hay, and grazing land to rise. Thus, the production costs of beef rise as more of it is produced.

Exhibit 6.7 illustrates why higher resource prices and rising costs will cause the long-run market supply to slope upward to the right. Consider a market that was initially in long-run equilibrium at price $P_1$ and quantity $Q_1$. Given their initial average total cost ($ATC_1$) and marginal cost ($MC_1$), the firms in the market are just able to cover their costs at the $P_1$ price. As the market demand increases (from $D_1$ to $D_2$), the market price initially jumps to $P_2$. At this higher price, the firms will happily expand output along their original marginal cost curve ($MC_1$). In the short run, firms in the industry will make economic profit at the $P_2$ price. In the long run, though, the profits will attract new firms into the industry, market supply will increase (shift from $S_1$ to $S_2$), and the market output will expand (to $Q_2$). As the *industry* expands, however, the firms will bid up the prices of the resources used intensely by the industry.

**EXHIBIT 6.7**

**Increased Costs and Long-Run Supply Curve**

Most often, higher factor prices will cause costs to rise as the market output increases. When this is true, the long-run supply curve ($S_{lr}$, frame b) will slope upward to the right.

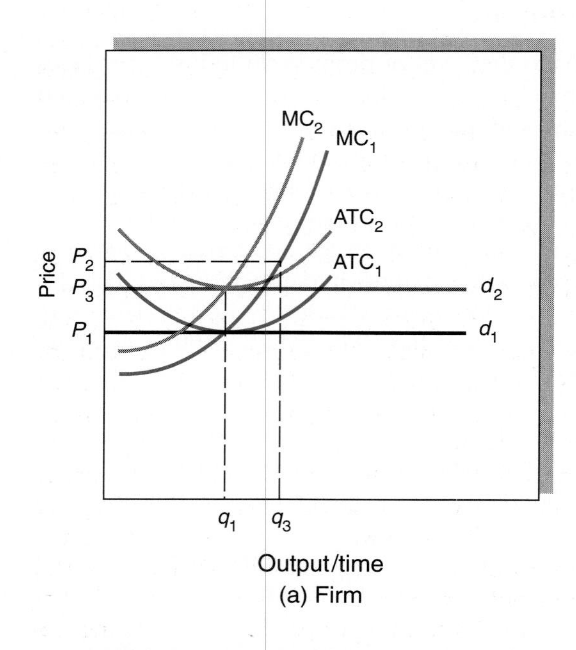

(a) Firm

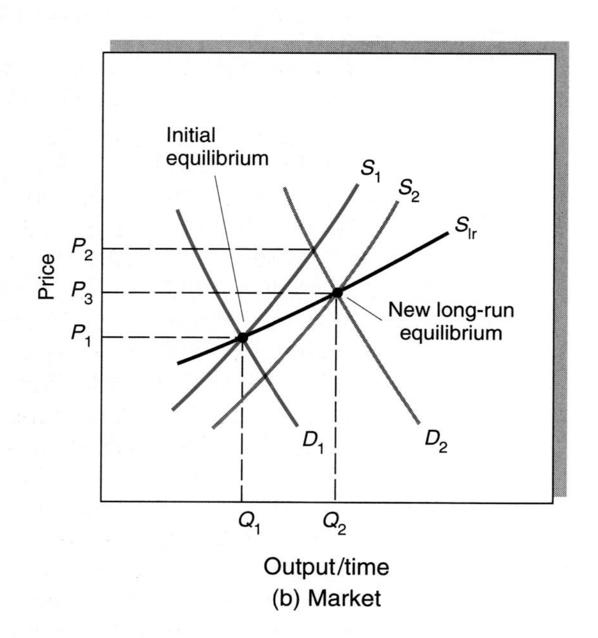

(b) Market

How will the higher resource prices affect the firm's cost curves? Both the average and marginal cost curves rise (shift to $ATC_2$ and $MC_2$). This increase in production cost necessitates a higher long-run price ($P_3$) than the price ($P_1$) that was initially present in the industry. Therefore, when an expansion in demand leads to higher resource prices and an increase in the per-unit costs of firms, the long-run market supply curve for the product will be upward-sloping. Under the circumstances, the larger output will be produced only at a higher price.

## Response to Decreased Demand

The response by an industry of price takers to a decrease in demand is just the reverse of what we described for an increase. Profits that are temporarily low because of a lower market price in the short run lead to the exit of firms and resources from the industry. The exit continues until the level of profit has returned to normal. The resulting long-run product price will decline if resource prices fall as the result of the smaller output of the product and accompanying weak demand for resources. If resource prices are unchanged, then in the long run the market price for the product will return to its previous level despite the smaller level of output.

## Supply Elasticity and the Role of Time

It takes time for firms to adjust to a change in the price of a product. In the short run, firms are stuck with the existing size of their plant. If price increases in the short run, they can expand output only by utilizing their existing plant more intensely. Thus, their output response will be limited. In the long run, however, they will have time to build new plants. This will allow them to expand output by a larger amount in response to an increase in price. Thus, the market supply curve will be more elastic in the long run than in the short run.

The short- and long-run distinction offers a convenient two-stage analysis, but in the real world there are many intermediate production "runs." Some factors that could not be easily varied in a one-week time period can be varied over a two-week period. Expansion of other factors might require a month, and still others, six months. To be more precise, the cost penalty for quicker availability is greater for some production factors than for others. In any case, a faster expansion usually means that greater cost penalties are necessary to provide for an earlier availability of productive factors.

When a firm has a longer time period to plan output and adjust all of its productive inputs to the desired utilization levels, it will be able to produce any specific rate of output at a lower cost. Because it is less costly to expand output slowly in response to a demand increase, the expansion of output by firms will increase with time, as long as price exceeds cost. Therefore, the elasticity of the market supply curve will be greater when more time is allowed for firms to adjust output.

Exhibit 6.8 illustrates the impact of time on the response by producers to an increase in price resulting from an expansion in demand. When the price of a product increases from $P_1$ to $P_2$, the *immediate* supply response of the firms is small because it is costly to expand output hastily. After one week, firms are willing to expand output only from $Q_1$ to $Q_2$. After one month, because of cost reductions made possible by the longer production planning period, firms are willing to offer $Q_3$ units at the price $P_2$. After three months, the

**EXHIBIT 6.8**

**Time and Elasticity of Supply**

The elasticity of the market supply curve usually increases as more time is allowed for adjustment to a change in price.

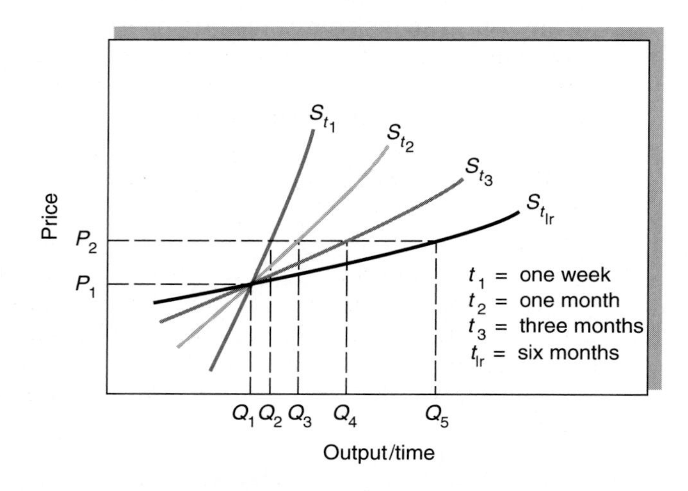


rate of output expands to $Q_4$. In the long run, when it is possible to adjust all inputs to the desired utilization levels (after a six-month time period, for example), firms are willing to supply $Q_5$ units of output at the market price of $P_2$. The supply curve for products is typically more elastic over a longer time period than for a shorter period.

## ROLE OF PROFITS AND LOSSES

The price-taker model highlights the role of profits and losses: they are signals sent to producers by consumers. Economic profits will be largest in those areas in which consumer wants at the margin are greatest *relative to costs of production.* Profit-seeking entrepreneurs will guide additional resources into these areas. Supply will increase, driving prices down and eliminating the profits. Free entry and the competitive process will protect the consumer from arbitrarily high prices. In the long run, competitive prices will reflect costs of production.

Economic profits result because a firm or entrepreneur increases the value of resources. Business firms purchase resources and use them to produce a product or service that is sold to consumers. Costs are incurred as the business pays workers and other resource owners for their services. If the sales of the business firm exceed the costs of employing all of the resources required to produce the firm's output, then the firm will make a profit. In essence, profit is a reward that business owners will earn if they produce a good that consumers value more (as measured by their willingness to pay) than the resources required for the good's production (as measured by the cost of bidding the resources away from their alternative employment possibilities).

For example, suppose that it costs a shirt manufacturer $20,000 per month to lease a building, rent the required machines, and purchase the labor, cloth, buttons, and other materials necessary to produce and market 1,000 shirts per month. If the manufacturer sells the 1,000 shirts for $22 each, its actions create wealth. Consumers value the shirts more than they value the resources required for their production. The manufacturer's $2 profit per shirt is a reward received for increasing the value of the resources.

In contrast, losses are a penalty imposed on businesses that reduce the value of resources. The value of the resources used up by such unsuccessful firms exceeds the price consumers are willing to pay for their product. Losses and bankruptcies are the market's way of bringing such wasteful activities to a halt.

We live in a world of changing tastes and technology, imperfect knowledge, and uncertainty. Business decision-makers cannot be sure of either future market prices or costs of production. Their decisions must be based on expectations. Nonetheless, the reward-penalty structure of a market economy is clear. Firms that produce efficiently and anticipate correctly the products and services for which future demand will be most urgent (relative to production cost) will make economic profits. Those that are inefficient and allocate resources incorrectly into areas of weak future demand will be penalized with losses.

A look at the market for videotape rental business provides a vivid illustration of the role played by profits and losses when entry barriers are low.[4] In 1982 videotape rental stores, were new, and there were only an estimated 5,000 stores in the United States. They could charge $5 and more per 24-hour rental. The availability of rentals and the falling prices of home video players meant that profits could at times reach 80 percent of rental revenues. More importantly, *expected* profits were very high. This optimism led to the rapid entry of many new stores, which increased competition and forced prices down. By 1990 there were about 25,000 stores. Prices had fallen dramatically. Even new releases were typically renting for $1.99, and most videos rented for even less. At times, video rental supply expanded faster than the demand for rentals, and some of the firms had to leave the business. Even for those who were efficient and stayed in the business, profits were slim. Consumers, however, benefited tremendously from the highly competitive nature of the video rental business.

## PRICE TAKERS, COMPETITION, AND PROSPERITY

Our analysis indicates that market forces provide price takers with a strong incentive to use resources wisely. Each firm will have a strong tendency to produce its output as cheaply as possible. Given the quality of output needed for the market, the price taker can maximize profits only by minimizing the cost of production—using the least valued set of resources needed to produce the desired output.

Firms have a strong incentive to produce goods that are valued more highly than the resources required for their production. Thus, resources are

[4]The facts in this example are taken from Tim Tregarthen, "Supply, Demand, and Videotape," *The Margin* 6 (September–October, 1990): 29.

drawn to those uses where they are most productive, as judged by the consumers' willingness to pay for the various goods produced. The ability of firms freely to expand or contract their businesses, and to enter or exit the market, means that resources that could be more valuable elsewhere will not be trapped unproductively in a particular industry. Resource owners can move them to where they are most highly valued in production.

The price-taker model highlights the more general importance of the competitive process. As the chapter opening quotation from Professor Wilcox indicates, competition places pressure on producers to operate efficiently and to avoid waste. It weeds out the inefficient—those who fail to provide consumers with quality goods at low prices. Competition also keeps producers on their toes in other areas. The production techniques and product offerings that lead to success today will not necessarily pass the competitive market test tomorrow. Producers who survive in a competitive environment cannot be complacent. They must be forward-looking and innovative. They must be willing to experiment and quick to adopt improved methods.

In competitive markets, business firms must serve the interests of consumers. As Adam Smith noted more than 200 years ago, competition harnesses personal self-interest and puts it to work, elevating our standard of living and directing our resources toward the production of those goods that we desire most intensely relative to their cost. Smith stated:

> *It is not from the benevolence of the butcher, the brewer, or the baker, that we expect our dinner, but from their regard to their own self-interest. We address ourselves, not to their humanity but to their self-love, and never talk to them of our own necessities, but of their advantages.*[5]

In a competitive environment, even self-interested individuals and profit-seeking business firms have a strong incentive to serve the interests of others and supply products that are valued more highly than the resources required for their production. This is the path to greater income and larger profits. Paradoxical as it may seem, personal self-interest—a characteristic many view as less than admirable—is a powerful source of economic progress when it is directed by competition.

## Looking Ahead

In the real world, consumers often seek variety in product design, style, durability, service, and location. As a result, most firms are price searchers rather than price takers. In addition, barriers to entry sometimes limit competition. In the next two chapters, we will examine markets where the firms are price searchers and will consider the importance of entry barriers into such markets.

## Chapter Summary

1. Firms producing identical products in markets where they have to accept the market price are called price takers. A price taker confronts a perfectly

[5]Adam Smith, *An Inquiry into the Nature and Causes of the Wealth of Nations* (1776; Cannan's ed., Chicago: University of Chicago Press, 1976), p. 18.

elastic demand for its product. Firms that are able to raise their price without losing all of their customers (and lower their price in order to sell more units) are called price searchers.

2. A price taker will maximize profit by expanding output as long as the additional output adds more to revenues than to costs. Therefore, the profit-maximizing price taker will produce the output level at which marginal revenue (and price) equals marginal cost.
3. The firm's short-run marginal cost curve (above its average variable cost) is its supply curve. The short run *market* supply curve is the horizontal summation of the marginal cost curves (when MC is above AVC) for all firms in the industry.
4. If a firm is covering its average variable cost and anticipates that the price is only temporarily below average total cost, it may operate in the short run even though it is experiencing a loss. However, even if it anticipates more favorable market conditions in the future, loss minimization will require the firm to shut down if it is unable to cover its average variable cost. If the firm does not anticipate that it will be able to cover its average total cost even in the long run, loss minimization requires that it immediately go out of business (even if it is covering its average *variable* cost) so that it can at least avoid its fixed cost.
5. When price exceeds average total cost, a firm will make economic profits. When there are no entry barriers, profits will attract new firms into the industry and stimulate the existing firms to expand. The market supply will increase, pushing price down to the level of average total cost. Firms will be unable to make long-run economic profits.
6. Losses exist when the market price is less than the firm's average total cost. They will cause firms either to leave the industry or to reduce the scale of their operations. Market supply will decline, pushing the market price upward until the firms remaining in the industry are able to earn normal (that is, zero economic) profits.
7. As the output of an industry expands, marginal costs will increase in the short run, causing the short-run market supply curve to slope upward to the right. If the prices of resources purchased by the industry remain unchanged, as the market output is expanded, the long-run supply curve will be perfectly elastic. However, as the output of an industry expands, rising factor prices will normally cause the firm's costs to increase. Therefore, the long-run market supply curve for most products will slope upward to the right.
8. In the short run, "fixed" resources like the size of the firm's plant will limit the ability of firms to expand output quickly. In the long run, the firms in a market will have time to alter the size of their plants and other resources that are fixed in the short run. As a result, the market supply curve will generally be more elastic as more time is allowed for firms to adjust their fixed factors in response to a price change.
9. Firms will earn economic profit if they produce a product that they can sell for more than the cost of the resources required for its production. In essence, profit is a reward derived from actions that increase the value of resources. Conversely, losses are a penalty imposed on those who reduce the value of resources.

10. Firms that produce efficiently and anticipate correctly the goods for which the future demand will be most urgent, relative to costs of production, will make profits. Firms that produce inefficiently and that incorrectly use resources to produce goods for which future demand turns out to be weak will be penalized with losses. Over time, entry and exit of resources and firms will eliminate economic profits and losses.
11. The competitive process places producers under strong pressure to operate efficiently and heed the views of consumers. As Adam Smith recognized long ago, self-interest is a strong motivator of human beings. If it is bridled by competition, self-interest leads producers to search for and undertake wealth-creating activities.

# *Study Guide*

## CHAPTER 6

# Developing the Economic Way of Thinking

## CRITICAL-ANALYSIS QUESTIONS

* 1. Farmers are often heard to complain about the high cost of machinery, labor, and fertilizer, suggesting that these costs drive down their profit rate. Does it follow that if, for example, the price of fertilizer fell by 10 percent, farming (a highly competitive industry with low barriers to entry) would be more profitable? Explain.

* 2. If the firms in a price-taker market are making short-run profits, what will happen to the market price in the long run? Explain.

3. "In a price-taker market, if a business operator produces efficiently—that is, if the cost of producing the good is minimized—the operator will be able to make at least a normal profit." True or false?

4. Suppose that the government of a large city levies a 5 percent sales tax on hotel rooms. How will the tax affect (a) prices of hotel rooms, (b) the profits of hotel owners, and (c) gross (including the tax) expenditures on hotel rooms?

* 5. Within the framework of the price-taker model, how will an unanticipated increase in demand for a product affect each of the following in a market that was initially in long-run equilibrium?
   a. The short-run market price of the product.
   b. Industry output in the short run.
   c. Profitability in the short run.
   d. The long-run market price in the industry.
   e. Industry output in the long run.
   f. Profitability in the long run.

* 6. Suppose that the development of a new drought-resistant hybrid seed corn leads to a 50 percent increase in the average yield per acre without increasing the cost to the farmers who use the new technology. If the producers in the corn production industry are price takers, what will happen to the following:
   a. The price of corn.
   b. The profitability of corn farmers who quickly adopt the new technology.
   c. The profitability of corn farmers who are slow to adopt the new technology.
   d. The price of soybeans, a substitute product for corn.

7. "When the firms in the industry are just able to cover their cost of production, economic profit is zero. Therefore, if there is a reduction in demand causing prices to go down even a little bit, all of the firms in the industry will be driven out of business." True or false? Explain.

8. Why does the short-run market supply curve for a product slope upward to the right? Why does the long-run market supply curve generally slope upward to the right? Why is the long-run market supply curve generally more elastic than the short-run supply curve?

9. How does competition among firms affect the incentive of each firm to (a) operate efficiently (produce at a low per unit cost) and (b) produce goods that consumers want? What happens to firms that fail to do these two things?

*Asterisk denotes critical-analysis questions for which answers are given in Appendix A.

10. Will firms in a price-taker market be able to earn profits in the long run? Why or why not? What are the major determinants of profitability for a firm? Discuss.

## MULTIPLE-CHOICE SELF-TEST

1. Which one of the following is a price-taker?
   a. A star baseball player.
   b. A respected heart surgeon.
   c. A local ice cream shop owner.
   d. An Indiana cattle farmer (beef producer).
2. The short-run market supply curve in a price-taker market is equal to
   a. The horizontal sum of the individual firm's MC curves above AVC.
   b. The horizontal sum of the individual firm's AVC curves above marginal revenue.
   c. The horizontal sum of the individual firm's MC curves above ATC.
   d. The horizontal sum of the individual firm's MC curves between AVC and ATC.
3. The horizontal demand curve facing an individual firm in a price-taker market is
   a. A violation of the law of demand.
   b. A reflection of the firm's small size relative to the total market.
   c. Maintained only with the help of high barriers to entry.
   d. A reflection of the firm's price searching ability.
4. In the short run, a price taker will maximize its profit if output is expanded until
   a. Marginal costs exceed average total costs.
   b. The profit margin (that is, the difference between price and average cost per unit) is maximized.
   c. Per unit production cost of the firm is minimized.
   d. Marginal costs rise to equal marginal revenue.
5. The textile industry is composed of a large number of small firms. In recent years, firms in the industry have suffered economic losses, and many sellers have left the industry. With time, economic theory suggests losses will
   a. Cause the demand curve to shift to the right so that price will rise to the level of production cost.
   b. Cause the remaining firms to collude so that they can produce more efficiently.
   c. Cause the market supply to decline and the price of textiles to rise.
   d. Cause firms in the textile industry to expand their output in the long run.
6. As market price increases, in the short run a price taker will expand output along its
   a. Market demand curve.
   b. Average total cost curve.
   c. Average variable cost curve.
   d. Marginal cost curve.

7. Suppose that there are 1,000 identical firms producing a product in an industry with low barriers to entry. In the short run, the total revenues of each firm exceed total costs. What will happen in the long run?
   a. Nothing will happen, because each firm is already maximizing its profits.
   b. Many firms will enter the market, and each firm will eventually operate at a loss.
   c. Additional firms will enter the market, and price will be driven down to the point where each firm will be making just enough to stay in business.
   d. Additional firms will enter the market, but the price will remain the same because the existing firms will not allow price to decrease.
8. The long-run supply curve for a product differs from the short-run supply curve in that the long-run supply curve is usually
   a. Vertical.
   b. More inelastic.
   c. More elastic.
   d. Of unitary elasticity.
9. When a firm is unable to earn enough revenue from the sale of its products to pay its workers and suppliers of capital, it suffers losses. Economic thinking suggests that such a firm
   a. Should be subsidized, if its products have value.
   b. Is probably facing unfair competition.
   c. Is receiving a market signal that wages and the price of capital are higher than they should be.
   d. Is receiving a market signal that consumers value other items more than this firm's output, relative to its costs.
10. The dynamic process of competition
   a. Is hindered by the self-interest of business decision-makers.
   b. Provides self-interested sellers with a strong incentive to produce goods that consumers value highly relative to their costs.
   c. Conflicts with the interest of consumers by causing business firms to pursue profit rather than the public interest.
   d. Will permit business decision-makers to earn long-run economic profit unless they are regulated by government officials.

## PROBLEMS

1. The accompanying table presents the expected cost and revenue data for the Tucker Tomato Farm. The Tuckers produce tomatoes in a greenhouse and sell them wholesale in a purely competitive market.
   a. Fill in the firm's marginal cost, average variable cost, average total cost, and profit schedules.
   b. If the Tuckers are profit maximizers, how many tomatoes should they produce when the market price is $500 per ton? Indicate their profits.
   c. Indicate the firm's output level and maximum profit if the market price of tomatoes increases to $550 per ton.
   d. How many units would the Tucker Tomato Farm produce if the price of tomatoes declined to $450?
   e. Indicate the firm's profits. Should the firm continue in business? Explain.

**Cost and Revenue Schedules—Tucker Tomato Farm, Inc.**

| Output (Tons per Month) | Total Cost | Price per Ton | Marginal Cost | Average Variable Cost | Average Total Cost | Profits (Monthly) |
|---|---|---|---|---|---|---|
| 0 | $1000 | $500 | ____ | ____ | ____ | ____ |
| 1 | 1200 | 500 | ____ | ____ | ____ | ____ |
| 2 | 1350 | 500 | ____ | ____ | ____ | ____ |
| 3 | 1550 | 500 | ____ | ____ | ____ | ____ |
| 4 | 1900 | 500 | ____ | ____ | ____ | ____ |
| 5 | 2300 | 500 | ____ | ____ | ____ | ____ |
| 6 | 2750 | 500 | ____ | ____ | ____ | ____ |
| 7 | 3250 | 500 | ____ | ____ | ____ | ____ |
| 8 | 3800 | 500 | ____ | ____ | ____ | ____ |
| 9 | 4400 | 500 | ____ | ____ | ____ | ____ |
| 10 | 5150 | 500 | ____ | ____ | ____ | ____ |

2. The student government of a major university arranges a monthly campuswide "flea market" sale where talented students can sell products they produce in their leisure time. Mary brings her handmade wallets to sell at the flea market. Since there are several other suppliers, Mary has no control over the market price. Mary's estimated cost and output data are presented in the table below.
   a. Fill in the missing cost information.
   b. If Mary were a profit maximizer, how many wallets should she produce monthly if the market price was $20? Indicate her economic profit (or loss).
   c. Indicate what Mary's monthly output and maximum profit would be if the price rose to $25.

| Monthly Output | Total Cost | Average Total Cost | Average Fixed Cost | Average Variable Cost | Marginal Cost |
|---|---|---|---|---|---|
| 1 | $ 25 | ____ | 0 | ____ | ____ |
| 2 | 50 | ____ | ____ | ____ | ____ |
| 3 | 69 | ____ | ____ | ____ | ____ |
| 4 | 84 | ____ | ____ | ____ | ____ |
| 5 | 100 | ____ | ____ | ____ | ____ |
| 6 | 119 | ____ | ____ | ____ | ____ |
| 7 | 140 | ____ | ____ | ____ | ____ |
| 8 | 168 | ____ | ____ | ____ | ____ |

3. José Gonzales operates a construction firm, Gonzales' Construction Company, Inc., that specializes in the production of small frame houses. José's expected cost schedule is presented in the accompanying table.
   a. Complete the chart indicating José's FC, VC, ATC, AFC, AVC, and MC.
   b. The current market price for houses of the quality produced by Gonzales' Construction is $29,500. Assume José wants to maximize profits. How many houses should he produce per month? What is his profit (or loss)?

c. Suppose that there is population growth in the area, causing the demand for housing to expand. The market price of houses increases to $32,000. Indicate José's new profit-maximizing monthly output and profit (or loss).
d. Indicate José's output and maximum profit (or minimum loss) if the market price were to fall to $25,000; to $21,000. Should he continue in business at the latter price? Explain.

**Cost Schedules—Gonzales Construction Co.**

| Housing Units per Month | Total Cost per Month | Fixed Cost (FC) | Variable Cost (VC) | Average Total Cost (ATC) | Average Fixed Cost (AFC) | Average Variable Cost (AVC) | Marginal Cost (MC) |
|---|---|---|---|---|---|---|---|
| 0 | $ 40,000 | ______ | ______ | ______ | ______ | ______ | ______ |
| 1 | 60,000 | ______ | ______ | ______ | ______ | ______ | ______ |
| 2 | 80,000 | ______ | ______ | ______ | ______ | ______ | ______ |
| 3 | 100,000 | ______ | ______ | ______ | ______ | ______ | ______ |
| 4 | 120,000 | ______ | ______ | ______ | ______ | ______ | ______ |
| 5 | 142,000 | ______ | ______ | ______ | ______ | ______ | ______ |
| 6 | 168,000 | ______ | ______ | ______ | ______ | ______ | ______ |
| 7 | 198,000 | ______ | ______ | ______ | ______ | ______ | ______ |
| 8 | 232,000 | ______ | ______ | ______ | ______ | ______ | ______ |
| 9 | 270,000 | ______ | ______ | ______ | ______ | ______ | ______ |
| 10 | 315,000 | ______ | ______ | ______ | ______ | ______ | ______ |

CHAPTER

# 7

# MARKETS WHEN FIRMS ARE PRICE SEARCHERS AND ENTRY BARRIERS ARE LOW

Differences in tastes, desires, incomes and locations of buyers, and differences in the uses which they wish to make of commodities all indicate the need for variety and the necessity of substituting for the concept of a "competitive ideal," an ideal involving both monopoly and competition.

*Edward H. Chamberlin*[1]

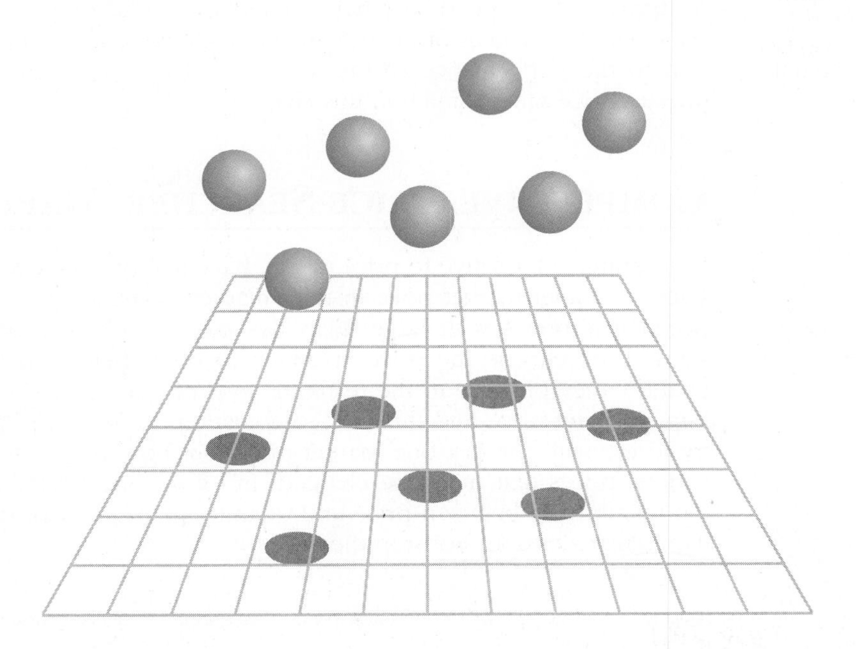

## CHAPTER FOCUS

- Why do firms engage in competitive advertising and price cutting?
- How do price searchers act when entry barriers are low? How do consumers fare in such markets?
- What do entrepreneurs do? Why is the important role of the entrepreneur left out of economic models?
- How can competition be encouraged when there is room for only one or a few competitors?
- Why do some economists criticize price-searcher behavior when entry barriers are low, while others like the results?
- Why is competition critical to a prosperous, innovative economy?

In the previous chapter we learned that *price takers* make no pricing decisions, but simply accept, or take, the price determined in the market. They adjust their output until the cost of producing another unit would just exceed that market price. *Price searchers* have a more complex set of decisions to make in their search for profit. In this chapter we consider the choices facing price searchers in markets where entry barriers are low, encouraging firms searching for new profit opportunities to enter the market or expand their production. We will refer to such markets as **competitive price-searcher markets.**

**competitive price-searcher market** A market where the firms have a downward-sloping demand curve and it is relatively easy for them to enter into and exit from the market.

Why do firms engage in competitive advertising and price cutting? How do firms that are price searchers choose price and output combinations? Are the business practices of price searchers inefficient? How important is competition to the performance of the economy? These are some of the important questions we will examine in this chapter.

# COMPETITIVE PRICE-SEARCHER MARKETS

Price searchers, relative to price takers, have a very complex problem to solve. There is no set market price in their market. Instead, sellers must choose between low prices with large quantities sold, and higher prices with smaller sales. They choose the price at which to offer their output, then adjust the quantity they produce to the resulting level of sales. In trying to find the profit-maximizing price and quantity combination, therefore, price searchers must try to estimate not just one market price, but how buyers will respond to the various prices that might be charged. In effect, price searchers must estimate the relationship between price and quantity demanded for their product. And the complexity does not stop there.

[1]Edward H. Chamberlin, *The Theory of Monopolistic Competition* (Cambridge: Harvard University Press, 1948), p. 214.

Demand is not simply a given for a price searcher. The firm, by changing product quality, location, and service (among many other factors), and by advertising, can alter the demand for its products. It can increase demand by drawing customers from rivals if it can convince consumers that its products provide more value. When an airline adopts a more generous frequent-flier program or a soap manufacturer provides "cents-off" coupons, each is trying to make its product a little more attractive than competitors' to potential customers. The precise effects of such decisions cannot easily be predicted, but they can make the difference between profit and loss for the firm. In the real world, most firms occupy this complex and risky territory of the price searcher.

When entry barriers are low, sellers face competition both from firms that are already producing in the market and from new firms entering the market. If profits are present, firms can expect that new entrants will be attracted to the market. In this respect, competition restrains both price takers and price searchers when they operate in markets with low entry barriers. However, there is a major difference for the price searchers in that the products supplied by the alternative sellers in a market are not identical. They differ from one another in design, dependability, location, ease of purchase, or any of a multitude of other factors. It is this availability of **differentiated products** that distinguishes a competitive price-searcher's market.

**differentiated products**
Products distinguished from similar products by such characteristics as quality, design, location, and method of promotion.

Product differentiation explains why a firm in a price-searcher market can raise its price without losing all of its customers to rivals. Since some consumers are willing to pay more in order to get the distinctive product, the firm in a price searcher market will face a downward-sloping demand curve. Rival firms, however, supply products that are quite similar to that supplied by the price searcher, so if the firm raises its price too much, many of its consumers will switch to the substitutes. In other words, the demand curve faced by the firm in a competitive price-searcher market will be highly elastic, because good substitutes for its output are readily available from other suppliers.

## PRICE AND OUTPUT IN COMPETITIVE PRICE-SEARCHER MARKETS

How does a price searcher decide what price to charge and what level of output to produce? As the price searcher reduces price in order to expand output and sales, there will be two conflicting influences on total revenue. As Exhibit 7.1 illustrates, the increase in sales (from $q_1$ to $q_2$) due to the lower price will, by itself, add to the revenue of the price searcher. The price reduction, however, also applies to units that *would otherwise have been sold at a higher price* ($P_1$, rather than the lower price, $P_2$). This factor by itself will cause a reduction in total revenue. As price is reduced in order to sell additional units, these two conflicting forces will result in marginal revenue—that is, change in total revenue—that is less than the sales price of the additional units. Since the price of units that could have been sold at the higher price must also be reduced, the price searcher's marginal revenue will be less than price. As Exhibit 7.1 shows, the marginal revenue curve of the price searcher will always lie below the firm's demand curve.[2]

[2]For a straight-line demand curve, the marginal revenue curve will bisect any line parallel to the $x$-axis. For example, the MR curve will divide the line $P_2F$ into two equal parts, $P_2E$ and $EF$.

**EXHIBIT 7.1**

**Marginal Revenue of Price Searcher**

When a firm faces a downward-sloping demand curve, a price reduction that increases sales will exert two conflicting influences on total revenue. First, total revenue will rise because of an increase in the number of units sold (from $q_1$ to $q_2$). However, revenue losses from the lower price ($P_2$) on units that could have been sold at a higher price ($P_1$) will at least partially offset the additional revenues from increased sales. Therefore, the marginal revenue curve will lie inside the firm's demand curve.

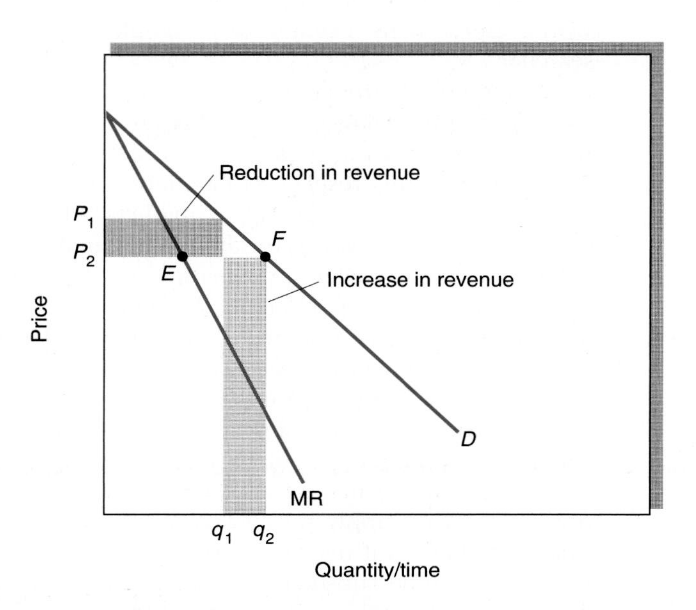


Any firm can increase profits by expanding output as long as marginal revenue exceeds marginal cost. Therefore, a price searcher will lower price and expand output until marginal revenue is equal to marginal cost.

Exhibit 7.2 illustrates the profit-maximizing price and output. The price searcher will increase profit by expanding output to *q,* where marginal revenue is equal to marginal cost and price *P* can be charged. Beyond *q,* the price reduction required for the sale of additional output would reduce the firm's profit. For any output level less than *q* (for example, *R*), a price reduction and sales expansion will add more to total revenues than to total costs. At output *R,* marginal revenues exceed marginal costs. Thus, profits will be greater if price is reduced so output can be expanded. On the other hand, if output exceeds *q* (for example, *S*), sale of additional units beyond *q* will add more to costs (MC) than to revenues (MR). The firm will therefore gain by raising the price to *P,* even though the price rise will result in the loss of customers. Profits will be maximized by charging price *P* and producing the output level *q,* where MC = MR.

The firm pictured in Exhibit 7.2 is making an economic profit. Total revenues *PAqO* exceed the firm's total costs *CBqO* at the profit-maximizing output level. Since barriers to entry are low, profits will attract rival competitors. If

**EXHIBIT 7.2**

**The Price Searcher's Price and Output**

A price searcher maximizes profits by producing output *q*, for which MR = MC, and charging price *P*. The firm is making economic profits. What impact will they have, if this is a typical firm?

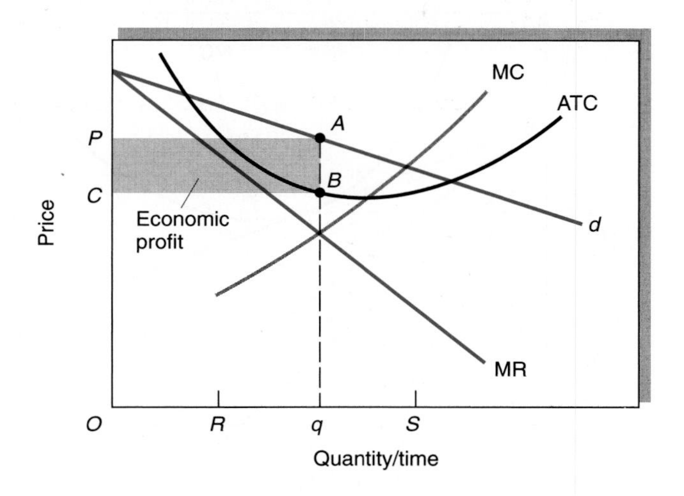


this is a typical firm, other firms will enter the market and attempt to produce a similar product (or service).

What impact will the entry of new rivals have on the demand for the products of the firms already in the market? These new rivals will draw customers away from existing firms. As long as new entrants expect to make economic profits, additional competitors will be attracted to the market. This pressure will continue until the competition among rivals has shifted the demand curve of the typical price searcher inward far enough to eliminate economic profits. In the long run, as illustrated by Exhibit 7.3, a price searcher in a market with low entry barriers will just be able to cover its production costs. It will produce to the MR = MC output level, but for the typical firm, the entry of new competition will force the price down to the average per-unit cost.

If losses exist in an industry, some of the existing firms in the industry will go out of business over a period of time. As firms leave, some of their previous customers will buy from other firms. The demand curve facing the remaining firms in the industry will be shifted outward by this process until the economic losses are eliminated and the long-run, zero-profit equilibrium illustrated by Exhibit 7.3 is restored.

Whenever firms can freely enter and exit a market, profits and losses play an important role in determining the size of the industry. Economic profits will attract new competitors to the market. The increased availability of the product (and similar products) will drive the price down until the profits are eliminated. Conversely, economic losses will cause competitors to exit from the market. The decline in the availability of the product (supply)

EXHIBIT 7.3

**Competitive Price Searcher and Long-Run Normal Profit**

Since entry and exit are free, competition will eventually drive prices for the representative price searcher down to the level of average total cost.

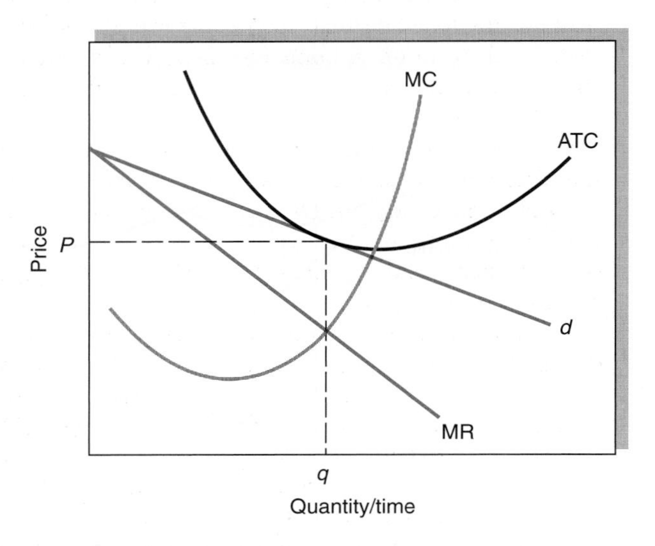


will allow the price to rise until firms are once again able to cover their average total costs.

In the short run, a price searcher may make either economic profits or losses, depending on market conditions. After long-run adjustments have been made, however, only a normal profit (that is, zero economic profit) will be possible because of the competitive conditions caused by freedom of entry. As we will see in the following section, price adjustments are sometimes made even before entry occurs, in order to prevent that entry.

## CONTESTABLE MARKETS AND THE COMPETITIVE PROCESS

Markets with few sellers are sometimes more competitive than they seem. Consider the case of the airline route between Salt Lake City, Utah, and Albuquerque, New Mexico. Only two airlines serve this route directly, since it has so little traffic. Further, there would seem to be high barriers to entry, since it takes multimillion-dollar airplanes to compete, as well as facilities for reservations, ticketing, baggage handling and so on. The two airlines are well aware of the rivalry (with or without competition) between them, and they both charge a similar price. One might expect the price to be high, perhaps close to the monopoly level. But there is reason to believe that the two airlines, much as they would like to collude and drive up the price, will not be able to do so, as long as other airlines are free to enter this market.

**contestable market** A market in which the costs of entry and exit are low, so a firm risks little by entering. Efficient production and zero economic profits should prevail in a contestable market. A market can be contestable even if capital requirements are high.

To compete on an airline route may require millions of dollars in equipment, but if there is no problem with renting access to airport facilities, then the barriers to entry are much lower than equipment costs suggest. The Salt Lake City–Albuquerque market, for example, can be entered simply by shifting aircraft, personnel, and equipment from other locations. The aircraft can even be rented or leased. By the same token, if a new entrant (or an established firm) wants to leave that market, nearly all the invested capital values can be recovered, through shifting the aircraft and other capital equipment to other routes, or leasing them to other firms. An airline route then, in the absence of legal barriers, is a classic case of a **contestable market:** the costs of entry and exit are low, so a firm risks little by entering.[3] If entry is later judged to be a mistake, exit is relatively easy because large components of the capital costs are not sunk costs, but they are instead recoverable. Entry into a contestable market may require the use of large amounts of capital, but so long as the capital is recoverable, and not a sunk cost, the large capital requirement is not a high barrier to entry.

In a contestable market, potential competition, as well as actual entry, can discipline firms selling in the market. When entry and exit are not expensive, even a single seller in a market faces the serious prospect of competition. Contestable markets yield two important results: (1) prices will not for long be higher than the level necessary to achieve zero economic profits, and (2) least-cost production will occur. The reason is that both inefficiency and prices above costs present a profitable opportunity to new entrants. Potential competitors who see an opportunity for economic profit can be expected to enter and drive the price down to the level of per unit costs.

These results do have a policy implication: if policymakers are concerned that a market is not sufficiently competitive, they should consider what might be done to make the market in question contestable. Much of the enthusiasm of economists for deregulation can be traced to the fact that regulation often is the primary restraint to entry. Many economists believe that deregulation permitting new entry can make many markets contestable, achieving lower prices and more efficiency than can direct regulation of producers. We will have more to say about this in the next chapter.

Our model of price and output for price-searcher markets with low entry barriers is, of course, a very much simplified view of the real world. The market process is complex, and competition is an ongoing, dynamic process. It is important to recognize that since this ongoing competitive process is at work, the experience of a specific market participant may differ considerably from that of the "typical firm" being discussed. We turn now to a brief discussion of the important variable not found in economic models: entrepreneurship.

## THE LEFT-OUT VARIABLE: ENTREPRENEURSHIP

To help us understand facts and make predictions, a scientific model must simplify what it describes, and draw attention to the most important relationships. Economic models are no exception. Our model of decision-making in business firms is designed to highlight the decision-making elements common

[3]The classic article on this topic is William J. Baumol's "Contestable Markets: An Uprising in the Theory of Industry Structure," *American Economic Review* 72 (March 1982), pp. 1–15.

to all firms, and it performs this job quite well. But it leaves out some important steps in the decision-making process of real-world firms. Typically, a great many judgments are needed before the process we describe can even begin.

Would profits increase if prices were raised, or would lower prices lead to larger profits? Real-world decision-makers cannot go into the back room and look at their demand-cost diagram to answer these questions. They must search for clues, experiment with actual price changes, and interpret what they see, often using a great deal of "seat-of-the-pants" judgment. The successful entrepreneur will search and find (or at least approximate) the profit-maximizing price—the MR = MC price-and-output combination that our model shows so simply.

For real-world entrepreneurs, the problem of uncertainty goes well beyond setting the profit-maximizing price and output. How can an entrepreneur decide whether demand and cost conditions will make entry into a price-searcher market profitable? How large should the plant be? How should production be organized? How much variety, and what combination of qualities should be built into the firm's product or service? What location will be best? What forms of advertising will be most effective? These questions and many more require entrepreneurial judgment. Entrepreneurial judgment is necessary when there is no decision rule that can be applied using only information that is freely available. For this reason, the entrepreneurial function has not been put into economic models. There simply is no way to model such judgmental decisions. All we can do is note their importance and recognize that our models are limited by the fact that they are missing this critical element of successful business decision-making.

## The Entrepreneur: A Job Description

If we cannot put entrepreneurship into our models, what can we say about its function? One way to answer this question is to consider a generalized job description for an entrepreneurial position. An investor who lacks the desire, or perhaps the skill, to be an entrepreneur, but nonetheless wants to be in business, may well seek someone to act as the business entrepreneur, while the investor provides some of the capital. A newspaper ad to find such a person (while perhaps not the usual way for the investor to search) might read as follows:

> **Wanted: Entrepreneur.** Must have many qualities. Must be: (1) Alert to new business opportunities and to new problems before they become obvious. (2) Willing to back judgments with investments of hard work and creative effort before others recognize correctness of judgments. (3) Able to make correct decisions and to convince others of their validity, so as to attract additional financial backing. (4) Able to recognize own inevitable mistakes and to back away from incorrect decisions without wasting additional resources. Exciting, exhausting, high-risk position. Pay will be very good for success, and very poor for failure.

Entrepreneurship is not for the faint-hearted or the lazy. Entrepreneurs are at the center of the action in the real world, even if they do not have a place in most economic models.[4]

[4]For a more complete overview of entrepreneurship, and references on the topic, see Mark Crosson, "Entrepreneurship," in *The New Palgrave: A Dictionary of Economics,* edited by John Eatwell, et al., (New York: Stockton Press, 1987), pp. 151–153.

# An Evaluation of Competitive Price-Searcher Markets

As we saw earlier, determination of price and output for price searchers is in some ways very similar to that for price takers. Also, since the long-run equilibrium conditions in price-taker markets are consistent with ideal economic efficiency, it is useful to compare and contrast them with conditions in price-searcher markets when entry barriers are low. There are both similarities and differences.

Neither price takers nor price searchers in markets with low entry barriers will be able to earn long-run economic profit. In the long run, competition will drive the price of competing firms down to the level of average total cost. In each case, entrepreneurs have a strong incentive to manage and operate their businesses efficiently. Inefficient operation will lead to losses and forced exit from the market. Price takers and competitive price searchers alike will be motivated to develop and adopt new cost-reducing procedures and techniques because lower costs will mean higher short-run profits (or at least smaller losses).

The response to changing demand conditions of price takers and price searchers in markets with low entry barriers is similar. In both cases, an increase in market demand leads to higher prices, short-run profits, and the entry of additional firms. With the entry of new producers, and the concurrent expansion of existing firms, the market supply will increase, lowering the demand each firm faces. The process will continue until the market price falls to the level of average total cost, squeezing out all economic profit. Similarly, a reduction in demand will lead to lower prices and short-run losses, causing output to fall and some firms to exit. The remaining firms can raise prices until short-run losses are eliminated. Profits and losses will direct the activities of firms in markets with low entry barriers.

As Exhibit 7.4 illustrates, while the price taker confronts a horizontal demand curve, the demand curve faced by a price searcher is downward-sloping. This is important because it means that the marginal revenue of the price searcher will be less than, rather than equal to, price. So, when the profit-maximizing price searcher expands output until MR = MC, price will still exceed marginal cost (Exhibit 7.4b). In contrast, the price charged by a profit-maximizing price taker will equal marginal cost (Exhibit 7.4a). In addition, when a price searcher is in long-run equilibrium, the firm's output rate will be less than the rate that would minimize average total cost. The price searcher would have a lower per unit cost (97 cents rather than $1) if a larger output were produced.

## Allocative Efficiency for Price-Searcher Markets with Low Entry Barriers

The efficiency of price searchers in markets with low entry barriers has been the subject of debate among economists for years. At one time, the dominant view seemed to be that allocative inefficiency results because price searchers fail to operate at an output level that minimizes their long-run average total cost. As a result of the proliferation in the number of firms, the sales of each competitor fall short of their least-cost capacity level. The potential social gain

**EXHIBIT 7.4**

**Comparing Price Taker and Price Searcher**

Here we illustrate the long-run equilibrium conditions of a price taker and a price searcher when entry barriers are low. In both cases, price is equal to average total cost, and economic profit is zero. However, since the price searcher confronts a downward-sloping demand curve for its product, its profit-maximizing price exceeds marginal cost, and output is not large enough to minimize average total cost when the market is in long-run equilibrium. *For identical cost conditions,* the price of the product in a price searcher market will be slightly higher than in a price taker market. This slightly higher price is considered by some to be indicative of inefficiency, while others perceive it to be the premium a society pays for variety and convenience (product differentiation).

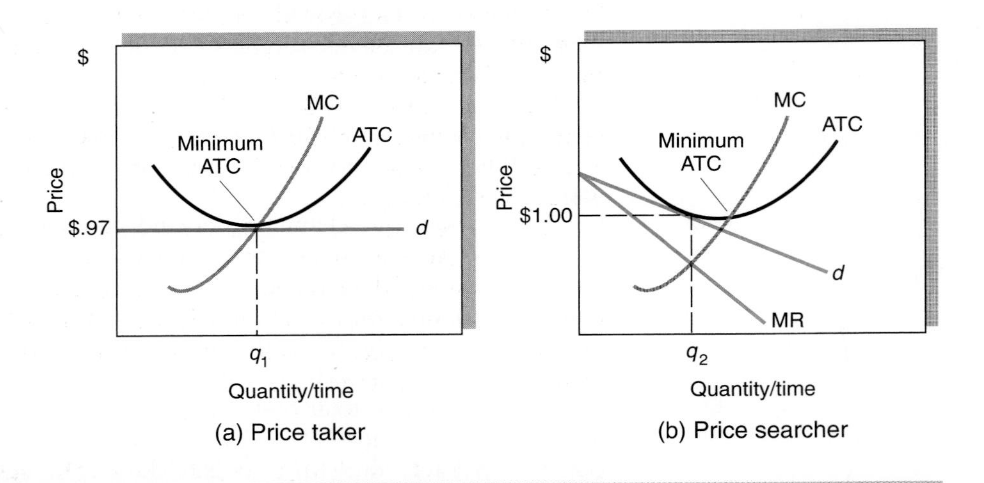


(a) Price taker (b) Price searcher

associated with the expansion of production to the P = MC output rate is therefore lost. The advocates of this view argue that if there were fewer producers, each would be able to operate at the minimum-cost output rate. They see inefficiency resulting from costly duplication—too many producers each operating below their minimum-cost output capacity. The location of two or more filling stations, restaurants, grocery stores, or similar establishments operating side by side are given as examples of the economic waste generated by price-searcher markets.

In addition, the various price searchers' efforts to inform and convince consumers that their differentiated products are better than others also brings criticism. Their competitive advertising campaigns are charged with being self-defeating and wasteful. Firms have an incentive, critics say, to use advertising to promote artificial distinctions between similar products, and firms that do not engage in such advertising can expect their sales to decline. Advertising, though, results in higher prices for consumers and thus is costly from society's point of view.

In recent years, this traditional view has been seriously challenged. Many economists now believe that it is mechanistic and fails to take into account the significance of dynamic competition. Most important, the traditional view assumes that consumers place no value on the wider variety of qualities and styles that result. Prices might very well be slightly lower if there were fewer gasoline stations, if they were located farther apart, and if they offered a more limited variety of service and credit plan options. Similarly, the prices of groceries might very well be slightly lower if there were fewer supermarkets, each a bit more congested and located less conveniently for some customers. However, since customers value product diversity as well as lower prices, some argue that consumers are served quite well by price-searcher markets. According to this view, the higher prices (and costs) are simply the premium consumers pay for variety and convenience.

When consumers receive utility from differentiated products, one cannot conclude that uniform products with a lower price, but less variety from which to select, would be preferable to products of greater diversity with somewhat higher prices. In fact, consumers often do pay more for various unique products, rather than all flocking to a single, cheaper version of the product in cases where that cheaper version exists.

The defenders of product diversity also deny that price-searcher markets lead to excessive, wasteful advertising. They point out that advertising often reduces the consumer's search time and provides valuable information about prices, new products, and new firms entering the market. If advertising results in higher prices with no compensating benefits, consumers can turn to cheaper, nonadvertised products. After all, consumers are under no obligation to purchase advertised products. In fact, some price searchers use higher-quality service and lower prices to compete with rivals who advertise heavily. When consumers really prefer lower prices and less advertising, firms offering that combination do quite well.

## A Special Case: Price Discrimination

Thus far, we have assumed that all sellers of a product will charge each customer the same price. Sometimes, though, price searchers can increase their revenues (and profits) by charging different prices to different groups of consumers. Businesses such as hotels, fast-food restaurants, and drug stores often charge senior citizens less than other customers; students and children are often given discounts at movie theaters and athletic events. Sometimes bars and sports teams charge women lower prices than men. This practice is called **price discrimination.** To gain from this practice, price searchers must be able to do two things: (1) identify and separate at least two groups who have differing elasticities of demand, and (2) prevent those who buy at the low price from reselling to customers who are charged a high price. A seller who meets these two conditions can gain by charging some buyers a higher price. But price discrimination can also increase market efficiency, lower the price available to buyers whose demands are elastic, and sometimes even allow production where none would otherwise occur.

**price discrimination** A practice whereby a seller charges different consumers different prices for the same product or service.

Why do sellers charge different prices to their customers? Profits can be increased when (1) groups with the most inelastic demand are charged high prices and (2) groups with a more elastic demand are charged lower prices. The pricing of airline tickets illustrates this point. The airline industry has found that the demand of business fliers is substantially more inelastic than the demand of vacationers, students, and other travelers. Thus, airlines usually charge high fares to persons who are unwilling to stay over a weekend, who spend only a day or two at their destination, and who make reservations a short time before their flight. These high fares fall primarily on business travelers who are less sensitive to price. In contrast, discount fares are offered to fliers willing to make reservations well in advance, travel during off-peak hours, and stay at their destinations over a weekend before returning home. Such travelers are likely to be vacationers and students, who are highly sensitive to price.

Exhibit 7.5 illustrates the logic of this policy. Panel (a) shows what would happen if a single price were charged to all customers. Given the demand, the profit-maximizing firm expands output to 100, where MR equals MC. The profit-maximizing price on coast-to-coast flights is $400, which generates $40,000 of revenue per flight. Since the marginal cost per passenger is $100, this provides the airline with net operating revenue of $30,000 with which to cover other costs.

However, as Exhibit 7.5(b) shows, although the market demand schedule is unchanged, the airline can do even better if it uses price discrimination. When it charges business travelers $600, most of these passengers continue to travel since their demand is highly inelastic. On the other hand, a $100 price

**EXHIBIT 7.5**

**Price Discrimination**

As panel a illustrates, a $400 ticket price will maximize profits on coast-to-coast flights *if an airline charges a single price*. However, the airline can do still better if it raises the price to $600 for passengers (business travelers) with a highly inelastic demand and *reduces* the price to $300 for travelers (for example, students and vacationers) with a more elastic demand. When sellers can segment their market, they can gain by (a) charging a higher price to consumers with a less elastic demand and (b) offering discounts to customers whose demand is more elastic.

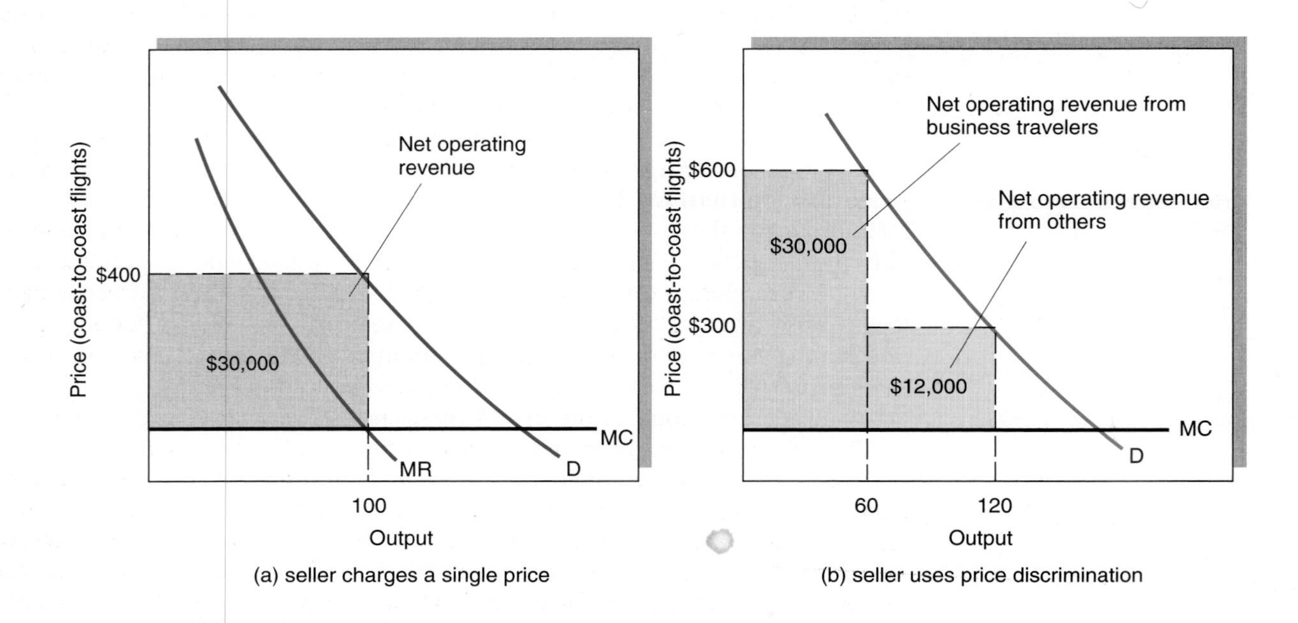

(a) seller charges a single price

(b) seller uses price discrimination

cut generates substantial additional ticket sales from vacationers, students, and others whose demands are more elastic. Therefore, with price discrimination, the airline can sell 60 tickets (primarily to business travelers) at $600 and 60 additional tickets to others at $300. Total revenue jumps to $54,000 and leaves the airline with $42,000 ($54,000 minus 120 times the $100 marginal cost per passenger) of revenue in excess of variable cost. Compared to the single price outcome (Exhibit 7.5a), the price discrimination strategy expands profit by $12,000.

When sellers can segment their market (at a low cost) into groups with differing price elasticities of demand, price discrimination can increase profits. *For each group,* the seller will maximize profit by equating marginal cost and marginal revenue. This rule will lead to higher prices for groups with the most inelastic demand and lower prices for the groups with the most elastic demand. Compared to the single-price situation, price discrimination increases profitability because a higher price increases the net revenue from groups with an inelastic demand, while a lower price increases the net revenue from price-sensitive customers. With price discrimination, the number of units sold also increases (compare Exhibit 7.5a with 7.5b) because the discounts provided to price-sensitive groups increase the quantity sold more than the higher prices charged the less price-sensitive groups reduce sales.

Sometimes price discrimination is subtle. Colleges engage in price discrimination by charging a high standard tuition to get additional revenue from high-income students with a more inelastic demand, while providing low-income students with scholarships based on need (tuition "discounts"). The partial tuition scholarships given to students whose parents are less wealthy enables the college to attract students who have a more elastic demand. Low-income students thus are not priced out of their market by the high standard tuition.

How do buyers fare when a seller can price discriminate? Some buyers pay more than they would if a single intermediate price were offered. They purchase fewer units, and they are worse off. In contrast, those for whom the price discrimination process lowers the price are better off. Of course, with some products, such as airline transportation, a single buyer might be better off with some purchases and worse off with others.

On balance, however, we can expect that output will be greater with price discrimination than it would be with a single price. The market is not as understocked as it would have been in the absence of the price discrimination. Thus, from an allocative standpoint, price discrimination gets high marks; it reduces the allocative inefficiency due to price being set above marginal cost. Some of the gains that would accrue to consumers with an inelastic demand are transferred to the price searcher as increased revenue, but additional gains from trade are created by the increased output of goods which would be lost if the price searcher did not (or could not) price discriminate.

In some markets, there is an additional gain emanating from price discrimination: production may occur that would be lost if only a single price were charged. With price discrimination, some otherwise unprofitable firms may be able to generate enough additional revenue to operate successfully in the marketplace. For example, some small towns in Montana might not provide enough revenue at a single price to enable a local physician to cover her opportunity costs. However, if she is able to discriminate on the basis of income, charging higher-income patients more than normal rates and lower-income patients less, the resulting revenues from practice in the small town may enable the physician to stay in the community. In this case, all residents of the town may be better off as the result of the price discrimination, since it provides them with access to a local physician. After all, even those being charged the highest prices are not disadvantaged if the price discrimination keeps the physician in town. They are just as able to seek physician services elsewhere as they would have been in the absence of the price-discriminating local doctor. With or without price discrimination, access to competing sellers (or buyers) protects market participants from unfair treatment.

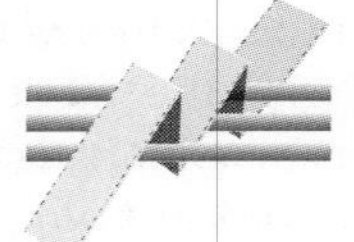

## IMPORTANT SOURCE OF PROSPERITY: COMPETITION AMONG FIRMS

When barriers to entry are low, businesses must compete for the loyalty of customers. This is true for price takers and price searchers alike, for small-scale or large-scale firms, in local, regional, national, or even global markets. There are three major reasons why firms operating in a competitive environment will be a force promoting economic progress.

1 Competition places pressure on producers to operate efficiently and cater to the preferences of customers.
2. Competition provides firms with a strong incentive to develop improved products and discover lower-cost methods of production.
3. Competition causes firms to discover the type of business structure and size that can best keep the per unit costs of production low.

### Efficient Operation and Consumer Satisfaction

First, competition weeds out the inefficient. Firms that fail to provide consumers with quality goods at competitive prices will experience losses and eventually be driven out of business. Successful competitors have to outperform rival firms. They may do so through a variety of methods—quality of product, style, service, convenience of location, advertising, and price—but they must consistently offer consumers as much or more value than they can get elsewhere.

What keeps McDonald's, General Motors, or any other business firm from raising prices, selling shoddy products, and providing lousy service? Competition does. If McDonald's fails to provide an attractively priced sandwich with a smile, people will turn to Burger King, Wendy's, Dairy Queen, and other rivals. Similarly, as recent experience has shown, even a firm as large as General Motors will lose customers to Ford, Honda, Toyota, Chrysler, Volkswagen, Mazda, and other automobile manufacturers if it fails to please the customer as much as rival suppliers.

### Incentive for Innovation

When markets are competitive, suppliers have a strong incentive to be innovative. A supplier who figures out how to produce a good more efficiently or who develops a new improved product gains an advantage over rivals. Such producers will earn larger profits.

Think of the new products that have been introduced during the last 50 years: microwave ovens, videocassette recorders, color television sets, personal computers, solar heating units, compact disk players, photocopying machines, non-wrinkle clothes, fast-food restaurants, and coronary artery bypass devices come to mind. New improved products are constantly upgrading the way that we live and work.

Since no one knows precisely what products consumers will want next or which production techniques will minimize per unit costs, competition is necessary to motivate an attempt to discover the answers. Is that new visionary idea the greatest thing since the development of the fast-food chain? Or is it simply another dream that will soon turn to vapor? Entrepreneurs need only win the support of investors willing to finance the potentially successful new product or production technology. Competition demands that a firm make such discoveries before its rivals do. Yet, at the same time, competition holds entrepreneurs and the investors who support them accountable; their ideas must face a "reality check" imposed by consumers. Consumers must value the innovative idea enough to cover its cost. When competition is present, consumers are the ultimate judge and jury of business innovation and performance.

Since today's successful product may not pass tomorrow's competitive test, businesses in a competitive market must be good at anticipating, identifying, and quickly adopting improved ideas, whether their own or others'. Again, the ongoing, dynamic characteristic of competition must continually be considered.

## Appropriate Structure and Size

Competition also demands that a firm discover the type and size of business structure that best keeps the per unit cost of its product or service low. Unlike other economic systems, a market economy does not mandate or limit the types of firms that are permitted to compete. Any form of business organization is permissible. An owner-operated firm, partnership, corporation, employee-owned firm, consumer cooperative, commune, or any other form of business is free to enter the market. In order to be successful, however, a business structure must be cost-effective. A form of business organization that results in high per-unit cost will be driven from a competitive market.

The same is true for the size of a firm. For some products, a business must be quite large to take full advantage of economies of scale. When per unit costs decline as output increases, small businesses tend to have higher production costs (and therefore higher prices) than their larger counterparts. When this is the case, consumers interested in maximum value for their money will tend to buy from the lower-priced larger firm. Consequently, most small firms will eventually be driven from the market. Larger firms, generally organized as corporations, tend to survive in such markets. The auto and airplane manufacturing industries are examples.

In other instances, small firms, often organized as individual proprietorships or partnerships, will be more cost-effective. When personalized service and individualized products are valued highly by consumers, it may be difficult for large firms to compete. Under these circumstances, mostly small firms will survive. For example, this is generally true for law and medical practices, printing shops, and hair-styling salons. A market economy permits cost considerations and the interaction between producers and consumers to determine the type and size of firm in each market.

When large-scale enterprises have lower costs, it will be particularly important that nations do not either limit competition from foreign suppliers or prevent domestic firms from selling abroad. This point is vitally important for small countries. For example, since the domestic market of a country like South Korea is small, a Korean automobile manufacturer would have extremely high costs per unit if it could not sell automobiles abroad. Similarly, domestic consumers in small countries would have to pay an exceedingly high price for automobiles if they were prohibited from buying from large-scale, lower-cost foreign producers.

In essence, competition harnesses personal self-interest—an undeniably powerful motivator—and puts it to work elevating our standard of living. Rival firms struggle for the dollar votes of consumers. When entry barriers are low, attracting buyers means providing them with at least as good a deal as is available elsewhere. In order to earn a profit, businesses have to figure out better ways of doing things and supply goods that consumers value highly relative to their cost. As they do so, they create wealth and increase the value of resources. Thus, paradoxical as it may seem, competition uses a human characteristic that many perceive of as less than admirable—self-interest—to achieve economic progress and promote the general welfare, an outcome that almost all of us consider highly desirable.

## LOOKING AHEAD

In this chapter we have analyzed the choices facing price searchers, and their behavior when barriers to entry are low. Next, we will see how barriers to entry might be formed, how price searchers react, and how the results differ when entry barriers are high rather than low.

## CHAPTER SUMMARY

1. The economic model of the price taker, while quite useful, does not explain rivalrous business behavior, such as competitive advertising, "cents-off" coupons, and airline frequent-flier programs. Economists use the model of the price-searcher market with low barriers to entry to explain such rivalrous behavior.
2. The distinguishing characteristic of the price-searcher market with low barriers to entry is product differentiation. Each price searcher in such a market faces a gently downward-sloping demand curve. Price searchers use product quality, style, convenience of location, advertising, and price as competitive weapons. Since all rivals within the market are free to duplicate another's products (or services), the demand for the product of any one firm is highly elastic.

3. A profit-maximizing firm will expand output as long as marginal revenue exceeds marginal cost. Thus, a price searcher will lower its price so that output can be expanded until MR = MC. The price charged by the profit-maximizing price searcher will be greater than its marginal cost.
4. If firms in a price-searcher market with low barriers to entry are making economic profits, rival firms will be induced to enter the market. They will expand the supply of the product (and similar products), enticing some customers away from established firms. The demand curve faced by an individual firm will fall (shift inward) until the profits have been eliminated.
5. Economic losses will cause price searchers to exit from the market. The demand for the products of each remaining firm will rise (shift outward) until the losses have been eliminated.
6. When barriers to entry are low, firms in a market will make only normal profits in the long run. In the short run, they may make either economic profits or losses, depending on market conditions.
7. Competition can come from potential as well as actual rivals. If entry and exit are not expensive, and if there are no legal barriers to entry, the theory of contestable markets indicates that competitive results may occur even if only one or a few firms are actually in the market.
8. Although standard economic models do not include the judgments made under uncertainty by entrepreneurs, economists generally recognize that the world is not so simple as our models indicate, and that entrepreneurial judgments are, in fact, important.
9. Traditional economic theory has emphasized that price-searcher markets with low barriers to entry are inefficient because (a) price exceeds marginal cost at the profit-maximizing output level; (b) long-run average cost is not minimized; and (c) excessive advertising is sometimes encouraged. However, other economists have argued more recently that this criticism is misdirected. According to the newer view, when barriers to entry are low, price searchers have an incentive to (a) produce efficiently; (b) undertake production if and only if their actions will increase the value of resources used; and (c) be innovative in offering new product options.
10. When a price searcher can (a) identify groups of customers that have different price elasticities of demand and (b) prevent customers from retrading the product, price discrimination may emerge. The seller may be able to gain by charging higher prices to groups with a more inelastic demand and lower prices to those with a more elastic demand. The practice generally leads to a larger output and more gains from trade than would otherwise occur.
11. When barriers to entry are low, competition is an important disciplinary force in a market. In a competitive environment, even profit-seeking business firms have a strong incentive to (a) operate efficiently and cater to the preferences of consumers, (b) improve products and discover lower-cost methods of production, and (c) discover the type of business structure and size of firm that can best keep the per unit cost of a product or service low. These factors are important elements of economic progress.

# *Study Guide*

## CHAPTER 7

## DEVELOPING THE ECONOMIC WAY OF THINKING

## CRITICAL-ANALYSIS QUESTIONS

1. Street-corner vendors using pushcarts have sometimes engaged in price wars at popular locations within Washington, D.C. Explain why a strategy of cutting price below cost in order to drive out other vendors from a given location would not make sense if there were no legal barriers to entry.

*2. Suppose that a group of investors wants to start a business operated out of a popular Utah ski area, and the group is considering either building a new hotel complex or starting a new local airline serving that market. Each new business would require about the same amount of capital and personnel hiring. The group believes each to have the same profit potential. Which is the safer (less likely to result in a substantial capital loss) investment? Why? Is there an offsetting advantage to the other investment?

*3. What determines the *variety* of styles, designs, and sizes of different products? Why do you think there are only a few different varieties of toothpicks but lots of different types of napkins on the market?

*4. How would the imposition of a fixed, per unit tax of $2,000 on new automobiles affect the average *quality* of automobiles, if the proceeds of the tax were used to subsidize a government-operated lottery?

5. What is the primary function of the entrepreneur? Some economists have charged that the major market-structure models of economic theory assume away the function of the entrepreneur. In what sense is this true? Is the function of the entrepreneur important? Discuss.

6. Is quality and style competition as important as price competition? Would you like to live in a country where government regulation restricted the use of quality and style competition? Why or why not? Do you think you would get more or less for your consumer dollar if quality and style competition were restricted? Discuss.

*7. Suppose that a price searcher is currently charging a price that maximizes the firm's total revenue. Will this price also maximize the firm's profit? Why or why not? Explain.

8. "Competition protects buyers against price gouging by sellers. It does nothing to protect sellers." Comment.

9. "Really tough competition is deadly to innovation. Producers have no profits to plow back into innovation." Evaluate. (Hint: Investments are made in search of future profit.)

10. "In a market where competition is fierce, as in the airline industry in 1993, quality is sure to suffer, as producers fight to cut costs in order to stay alive." Discuss.

*11. "When competition is really severe, only the big firms survive. The little guy has no chance." True or false? Explain.

12. "Cutthroat competition pits the buyer against the seller. Greed controls both, and no one can win." Evaluate.

*Asterisk denotes critical-analysis questions for which answers are given in Appendix A.

13. Is price discrimination harmful to the economy? How does price discrimination affect the total amount of gains from exchange? Explain. Why do colleges often charge students different prices, based on their family income?

## MULTIPLE-CHOICE SELF-TEST

1. Which of the following statements best describes the price, output, and profit of a price searcher operating in a market with low barriers to entry?
   a. Price will equal marginal cost at the short-run, profit-maximizing level of output; economic profit will be zero in the long run.
   b. Price will always equal average total cost in the short run; in the long run, either profits or losses may result.
   c. Price will be less than marginal cost at the short-run, profit-maximizing level of output; in the long run, firms may make either profits or losses.
   d. Price exceeds marginal cost at the short-run, profit-maximizing level of output; in the long run, firms will earn only normal profits (zero economic profit).
2. Which of the following statements best describes the competitiveness among price searchers in a market with low barriers to entry?
   a. The firms use advertising competitively, but there is little price or quality competition.
   b. The firms are rivals, using quality, location, advertising, and price as weapons to gain the favor of consumers.
   c. There is little competitiveness among price searcher firms, except on the basis of price.
   d. There is little competitiveness among the firms in price-searcher markets.
3. When the products offered by firms are differentiated, each firm in the market will
   a. Face a demand curve that slopes downward to the right.
   b. Face a supply curve that slopes downward to the right.
   c. Be able to earn economic profit.
   d. Face a perfectly elastic demand curve.
4. A long-run normal rate of return (zero economic profit) results in competitive price-searcher markets because
   a. With low barriers to entry, competition between rival firms will force prices down to the level of average production costs.
   b. Barriers to entry into such markets are high.
   c. Government legislation will induce firms to moderate their price demands.
   d. Cutthroat competition will cause some firms to incur losses, but, simultaneously, high barriers to entry will increase the profitability of the remaining firms in the industry.
5. If a price searcher had a level of output where marginal cost was $25 and marginal revenue $42, it would be well advised to
   a. Reduce output in order to lower costs.
   b. Increase the price of its product in order to raise the firm's per unit profit.

c. Decrease the price of its product in order to expand sales.
d. Reduce both price and output.

6. A successful entrepreneur must be able to
   a. Quickly identify areas where the current demand for a good is strong relative to the opportunity cost of producing the good.
   b. Figure out how to produce a good at a low cost compared to rival firms in the market.
   c. Recognize mistakes that inevitably occur and back away from incorrect decisions quickly, without wasting additional resources.
   d. All of the above are correct.
7. A characteristic that is common among price searchers but not price takers is
   a. Advertising.
   b. Low barriers to entry.
   c. Economic profit.
   d. Accounting profit.
8. If a firm faces a downward-sloping demand curve, which of the following will consistently be true?
   a. The firm could increase profits, if it decreased its price.
   b. The firm could increase profits, if it raised its price.
   c. The firm's marginal revenue from additional sales will exceed the sales price.
   d. The firm's marginal revenue from additional sales will be less than the sales price.
9. Which of the following is true?
   a. A price-discriminating seller will charge consumers with an elastic demand a higher price than consumers with an inelastic demand.
   b. When sellers use price discrimination, they will generally produce a larger output than if they charged only a single price to consumers.
   c. Price discrimination always harms consumers and helps sellers.
   d. A seller must be the only seller in the market in order to gain from price discrimination.
10. The driving factor that forces producers to operate efficiently and supply consumers with the goods they desire most intensely, relative to costs, is
   a. Monopoly power.
   b. Competition.
   c. Fear of government regulation.
   d. Labor unions.

## PROBLEMS

1. The graph below shows the short-run demand and cost situation for a price searcher in a market with low barriers to entry.
   a. What level of output will maximize the firm's profit level?
   b. What price will the firm charge?
   c. How much revenue will the firm receive in this situation? How much is total cost? Total profit?
   d. How will this situation change with the passage of time?

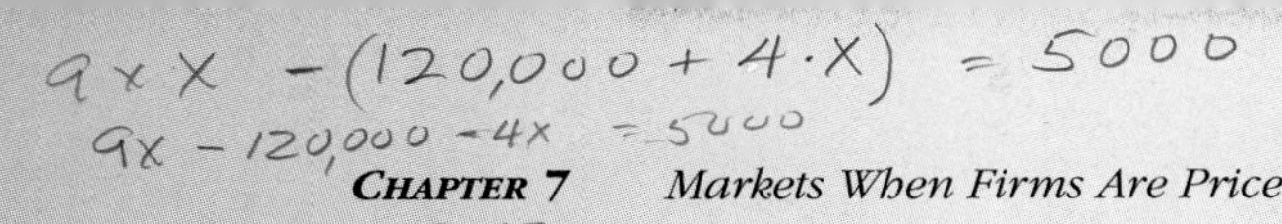



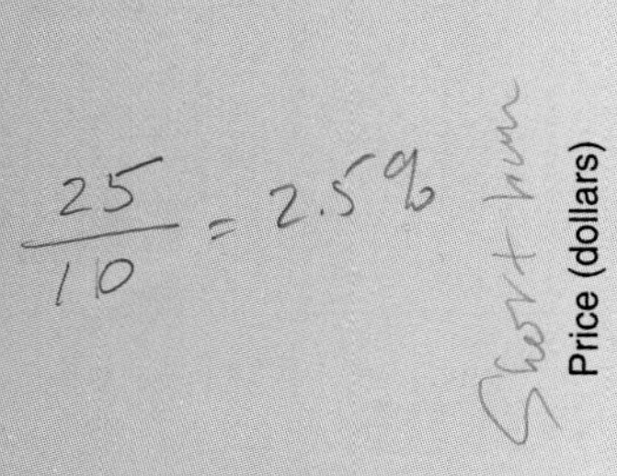

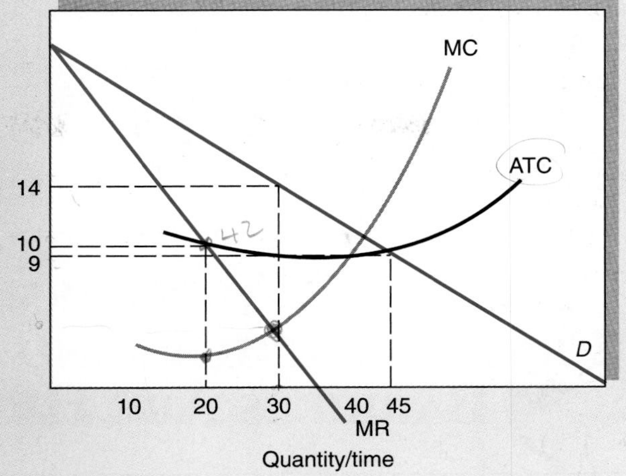


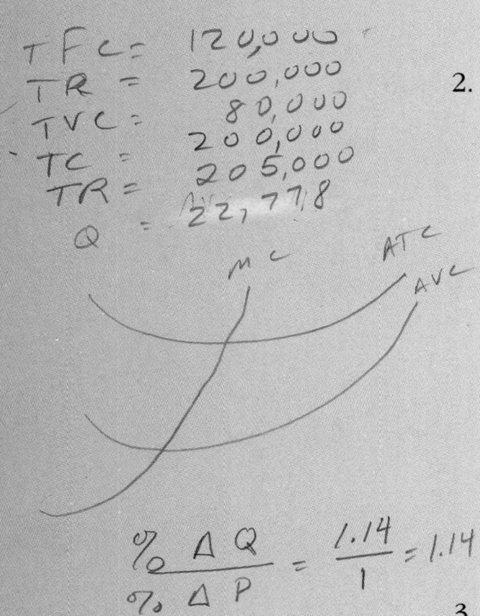

2. Johnson Tricycle Manufacturers currently sells 20,000 tricycles per month at a price of $10 each. The firm's fixed costs are currently 60 percent of sales revenues. At the current level of production, the firm's average variable cost per tricycle is $4. The firm is just covering its total cost. The sales manager argues that a reduction in the price of tricycles to $9 would enable the firm to earn a monthly profit of $5,000 as the result of increased sales. Since the firm has ample capacity, the necessary expansion in output could be accomplished without any increase in the average variable cost of tricycles.
   a. Does the sales manager's argument make sense? Explain.
   b. How much would sales have to increase in order for the firm to earn a monthly profit of $5,000? (Hint: Remember that fixed costs will not vary with output.)
   c. What price elasticity of demand is necessary for the sales manager's prediction to be realized?

3. Write an essay on competition. Be sure to deal with the following issues.
   a. What is meant by competition? What makes a market competitive?
   b. Is competition a necessary condition for markets to work well?
   c. Can competition protect the consumer from high prices?
   d. Is competition sometimes destructive or counterproductive?
   e. Are there alternative forms of economic organization that will work as well as competition?

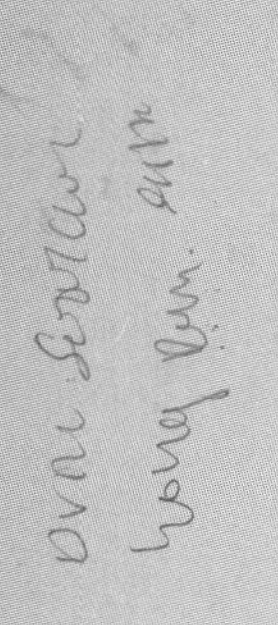

CHAPTER

8

# MARKETS WHEN FIRMS ARE PRICE SEARCHERS AND ENTRY BARRIERS ARE HIGH

If there are economies of scale throughout the region of possible industry outputs, only one or a few firms may be able to exist in the industry.

*George Stigler*[1]

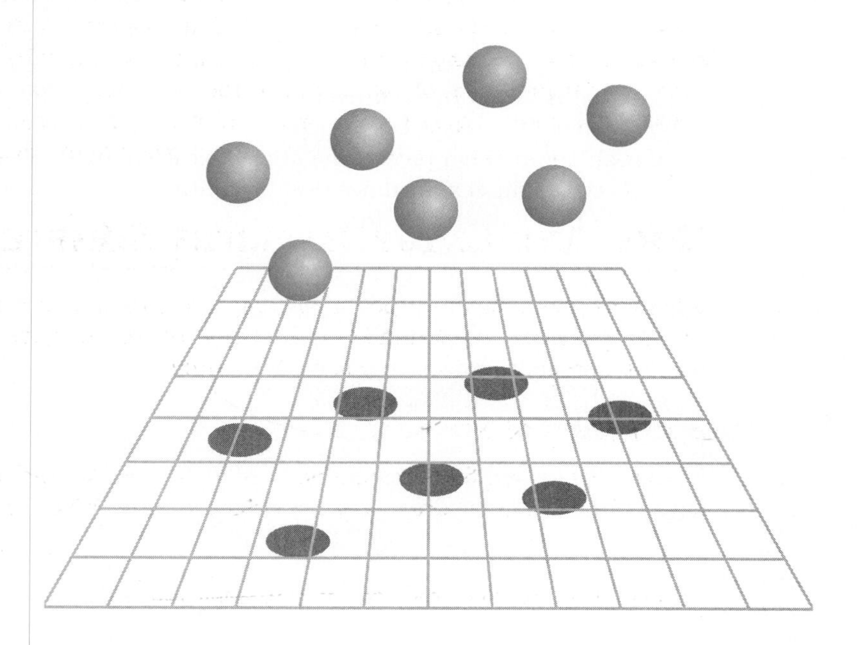

## Chapter Focus

- What are the barriers to entry that protect some firms against competition from potential market entrants?
- What is a monopoly? Does it guarantee the ability to make a profit?
- What is an oligopoly? When are oligopolists likely to collude? Why is it impossible for economics to construct a general theory of output and price for an oligopolist?
- Why are economists critical of high barriers to entry?
- What policy alternatives do economists suggest can reduce the problems associated with high barriers to entry?
- What do we know about the extent to which the U.S. economy is uncompetitive due to high barriers to entry?

In the previous two chapters, we analyzed the way firms behave in competitive markets, characterized by low barriers to entry. We now turn to an examination of firm behavior when potential competitors face high barriers to entry. In this case there will be fewer sellers of a product, and the sellers will exert more control over price and output. Even when buyers can choose from only a few suppliers of a good, though—or even, in the extreme case, only one supplier—sellers are not completely free from competitive pressures. They still must compete with sellers of *other* goods and services for the dollar votes of consumers.

However, high-entry barriers and few—or no—direct rivals do influence both decision-making within the firm and the operation of the market. This chapter focuses on how firms in this situation decide what price to charge, what special problems of strategy arise for them, how they allocate resources toward their most highly valued uses, and whether government regulation, or other policy alternatives, can promote further gains from trade in such markets.

# Why Are Entry Barriers Sometimes High?

What makes it difficult for potential competitors to enter a market? Four factors are of particular importance: economies of scale, government licensing, patents, and control over an essential resource.

### Economies of Scale

In some industries, firms experience declining average total costs over the full range of output that consumers are willing to buy. When this is the case, the

[1] George J. Stigler, *The Theory of Price* (New York: Macmillan, 1987), p. 204.

larger firm will always have lower unit costs. Since smaller firms have higher per unit costs, it will be difficult for them to enter the market, build a reputation, and compete effectively with larger firms. Under these circumstances, a single firm will tend to emerge from the competitive process in the industry, and the cost advantage resulting from its size will provide the firm with protection from potential rivals.

## Government Licensing

Legal barriers are the oldest and most effective method of protecting a business firm from potential competitors. Kings once granted exclusive business rights to favored citizens or groups. Today, governments continue to establish barriers, restricting the right to buy and sell goods. To compete in certain parts of the communications industry in the United States (for example, to operate a radio or television station), one must obtain a government franchise. Local governments generally grant exclusive franchises to public utilities in most areas of the United States.

*Licensing,* a process by which one obtains permission from the government to enter a specific occupation or business, often limits entry. In many states, a person must obtain a license before operating a liquor store, barbershop, taxicab, funeral home, or drugstore. Sometimes these licenses cost little and are designed to ensure certain minimum standards. In other cases, they are expensive and designed primarily to limit competition.

## Patents

Most countries have established patent laws designed to provide inventors with a property right to their inventions. Patent laws grant the owner the exclusive legal right to the commercial use of a newly invented product or process for a limited period of time, 17 years in the United States. Once a patent is granted, other persons are prevented from producing the product or using the procedure unless they obtain permission from the patent holder. Costs, as well as benefits, accompany a patent system. As we will soon illustrate, the barrier to entry created by the grant of a patent generally leads to higher prices for consumers of already existing products. On the positive side, however, patents increase the potential returns to inventive activity, thus encouraging scientific research and technological improvements. Without patents, the pace of technological development would be slowed.

## Control over Essential Resource

If a single firm has sole control over a resource essential for entry into an industry, it can eliminate potential competitors. An example often cited is the Aluminum Company of America, which before the Second World War controlled the known supply of bauxite conveniently available to American firms. Without this critical raw material, potential competitors could not produce aluminum. With time, however, other supplies of bauxite were found, and this source of monopoly was lost to the company.

New technology, mineral exploration, and other ways to exploit profitable price situations are always sought. Over time, they are usually found. Barriers to entry are often temporary. Nevertheless, they do exist. We now move on to see what happens when, at least temporarily, there is a barrier to entry high enough to limit the market to only one seller.

# Price and Output in the Case of Monopoly

**monopoly** A market structure characterized by (1) a single seller of a well-defined product for which there are no good substitutes and (2) high barriers to the entry of any other firms into the market for that product.

We begin with the extreme case, where there is only one seller in the market. The word *monopoly,* derived from two Greek words, means "single seller." We will define **monopoly** as a market characterized by (1) high barriers to entry and (2) a single seller of a well-defined product for which there are no good substitutes. Even this definition is ambiguous, because "high barriers" and "good substitutes" are both relative terms. Are the barriers to entry into the automobile or steel industries high? Many observers would argue that they are. After all, it would take a great deal of financial capital to compete successfully in these industries.

However, there are no *legal* restraints that prevent an entrepreneur from producing automobiles or steel. If price is well above cost, so that substantial profits are being made, it should not be difficult to find the necessary investment capital. After all, even a tiny portion of the investors who make up the capital market would be enough to finance a full-scale steel plant, for example, if profits were expected. And profit, it seems, draws investment capital the way honey draws bears. Perhaps access to financial capital is not in itself such a high barrier to entry. On the other hand, economies of scale may be critical in producing autos and steel. Barriers to entry are like expected profits: In both cases, assessing their size requires subjective judgments and provides only uncertain results.

"Good substitutes" is also a subjective term. There is always some substitutability among products, even those produced by a single seller. Is a letter a good substitute for telephone communication? For some purposes—correspondence between law firms, for example—a letter delivered by mail is a very good substitute. In other cases, when the speed of communication and immediacy of response are important, telephone communication has a tremendous advantage over letter writing. Are there any good substitutes for electricity? Most of the known substitutes for electric lighting (candles, oil lamps, and battery lights, for example) are inferior to electric lights in most uses. Natural gas, fuel oil, and wood, though, are often excellent substitutes for electric heating.

Monopoly, then, is always a matter of degree. Only a small fraction of all markets are served by only one seller. Nevertheless, there are two reasons why it is important to understand how such markets work. First, the monopoly model will help us understand markets in which there are few sellers and little active rivalry. When there are only two or three producers in a market, rather than competing with each other, they may seek to collude and thus together behave like a monopoly. Second, in a few important industries there is by law often only a single producer in each market. Local telephone and electricity services are examples. The monopoly model will illuminate the operation of such markets.

## A Hypothetical Monopoly

Suppose you invent, patent, and produce a microwave device that locks the hammer of any firearm in the immediate area. This fabulous invention can be used to immobilize potential robbers or hijackers. Since you own the exclusive patent right to the device, you are not concerned about a competitive supplier in the foreseeable future. Although other products are competitive with your invention, they are poor substitutes. In short, you are a monopolist.

What price should you charge for your product? To maximize profit, you will want to expand output as long as marginal revenue exceeds marginal cost. As with any firm, price taker or price searcher, once the quantity is reached at which marginal revenue equals marginal cost, additional sales will reduce profits. Since the marginal revenue curve lies below the demand curve for a price searcher, price will exceed marginal cost when profit is maximized. The price at which the chosen output level can be sold is given by the height of the demand curve.

Exhibit 8.1 provides a graphic illustration of profit maximization for a price searcher—in this case a monopolist. The firm will continue to expand output as long as marginal revenue exceeds marginal cost. Therefore, output will be expanded to *Q*, where MR = MC. The monopolist will be able to sell the profit-maximizing output *Q* for a price indicated by the height of the demand curve. At any output less than *Q*, the benefits (marginal revenue) of producing the *additional* units will exceed their costs. The monopolist will gain by reducing price and expanding output. For any output greater than *Q*, the monopolist's costs of producing additional units will be greater than the benefits (marginal revenue). Production of such units would reduce profits.

Exhibit 8.1 also depicts the profits of a monopolist. At output *Q*, the monopolist would charge price *P*. Price times the number of units sold yields the firm's total revenue *(PAQO)*. The firm's total cost would be *CBQO*, the average per unit cost multiplied by the number of units sold. The firm's profits are merely total revenue less total cost, the shaded area of Exhibit 8.1.

**EXHIBIT 8.1**

**Short-Run Price and Output of Monopolist**

The monopolist will reduce price and expand output as long as MR exceeds MC. Output *Q* will result. When price exceeds average total cost at any output level, profit will accrue at that output level.

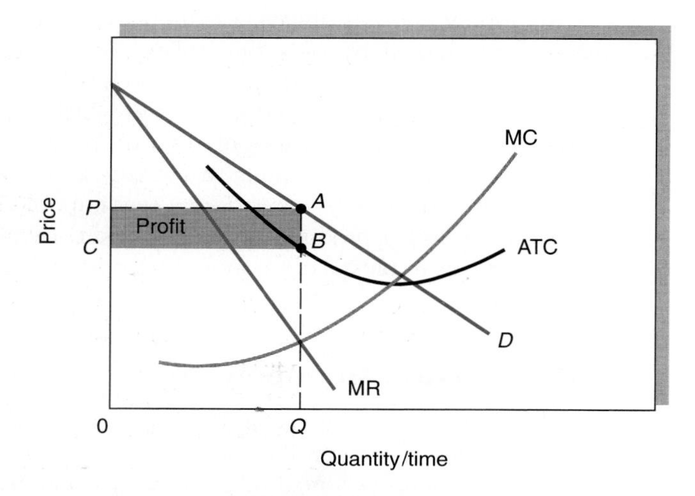

Exhibit 8.2 provides a numeric illustration of profit-maximizing decision-making. At low output rates, marginal revenue exceeds marginal cost. The monopolist will continue expanding output as long as MR is greater than MC. Thus, an output rate of eight units per day will be chosen. Given the demand for the product, the monopolist can sell eight units at a price of $17.25 each. Total revenue will be $138, compared to a total cost of $108.50. The monopolist will make a profit of $29.50. The profit rate will be smaller at all other output rates. For example, if the monopolist reduces the price to $16 in order to sell nine units per day, revenue will increase by $6. However, the marginal cost of producing the ninth unit is $6.25. Since the cost of producing the ninth unit is greater than the revenue it brings in, profits will decline.

When high barriers to entry are present, they will insulate the monopolist from direct competition with rival firms producing a similar product. In markets with high entry barriers, monopoly profits will not attract—at least not quickly—rivals who will expand supply, cut prices, and spoil the seller's market. Protected by high entry barriers, therefore, a monopolist may be able to continue earning a profit, even in the long run. Does this mean that monopolists can charge as high a price as they want? Monopolists are often accused of price gouging. In evaluating this charge however, it is important to recognize that, like other sellers, monopolists will seek to maximize *profit*, not *price*. Consumers will buy less as price increases. Thus, a higher price is not always best for monopolists. Exhibit 8.2 illustrates this point. What would happen to the profit of the monopolist if price were increased from $17.25 to $18.50? At

**EXHIBIT 8.2** **Profit Maximization for Monopolist**

| Rate of Output (per Day) (1) | Price (per Unit) (2) | Total Revenue (1) × (2) (3) | Total Cost (per Day) (4) | Profit (3) – (4) (5) | Marginal Cost (6) | Marginal Revenue (7) |
|---|---|---|---|---|---|---|
| 0 | — | — | $ 50.00 | $-50.00 | — | — |
| 1 | $25.00 | $ 25.00 | 60.00 | -35.00 | $10.00 | $25.00 |
| 2 | 24.00 | 48.00 | 69.00 | -21.00 | 9.00 | 23.00 |
| 3 | 23.00 | 69.00 | 77.00 | -8.00 | 8.00 | 21.00 |
| 4 | 22.00 | 88.00 | 84.00 | 4.00 | 7.00 | 19.00 |
| 5 | 21.00 | 105.00 | 90.50 | 14.50 | 6.50 | 17.00 |
| 6 | 19.75 | 118.50 | 96.75 | 21.75 | 6.25 | 13.50 |
| 7 | 18.50 | 129.50 | 102.75 | 26.75 | 6.00 | 11.00 |
| 8 | 17.25 | 138.00 | 108.50 | 29.50 | 5.75 | 8.50 |
| 9 | 16.00 | 144.00 | 114.75 | 29.25 | 6.25 | 6.00 |
| 10 | 14.75 | 147.50 | 121.25 | 26.25 | 6.50 | 3.50 |
| 11 | 13.50 | 148.50 | 128.00 | 20.50 | 6.75 | 1.00 |
| 12 | 12.25 | 147.00 | 135.00 | 12.00 | 7.00 | –1.50 |
| 13 | 11.00 | 143.00 | 142.25 | .75 | 7.25 | –4.00 |

the higher price, only seven units would be sold, and total revenue would equal $129.50. The cost of producing seven units would be $102.75. Thus, when price is $18.50 and output seven units, profit is only $26.75, less than could be attained at the lower price ($17.25) and larger output (eight units). The highest price is not always the best price for the monopolist. Sometimes a price reduction will increase the firm's total revenue more than its total cost.

Will a monopolist always be able to make an economic profit? The profitability of a monopolist is limited by the demand for the product that it produces. In some cases, a monopolist—even one protected by high barriers to entry—may be unable to sell for a profit. For example, there are thousands of clever, patented items that are never produced because demand-cost conditions are not favorable. Exhibit 8.3 illustrates this possibility. When the average total cost curve of a monopolist is above its demand curve at every level of output, economic losses will result. Even a monopolist will not want to operate under these conditions. If a monopolist were operating in this market, it would produce output $Q$ (at which MR = MC) and charge price $P$, *operating in the short run* as long as variable cost could be covered. If the loss-producing conditions persisted, however, the monopolist would discontinue production.

Until now, we have proceeded as if monopolists always knew exactly what their revenue and cost curves looked like. Of course, this is not true in the real world. Like other price searchers, a monopolist cannot be sure of the demand conditions for a product. Demand curves frequently shift, and choices must be made without the benefit of perfect knowledge. The monopolist, as a price searcher, tries to find the price at which profit will be maximized. How

**EXHIBIT 8.3**

**Short-Run Losses of Monopolist**

Even a monopolist will incur short-run losses if the average total cost curve lies above the demand curve.

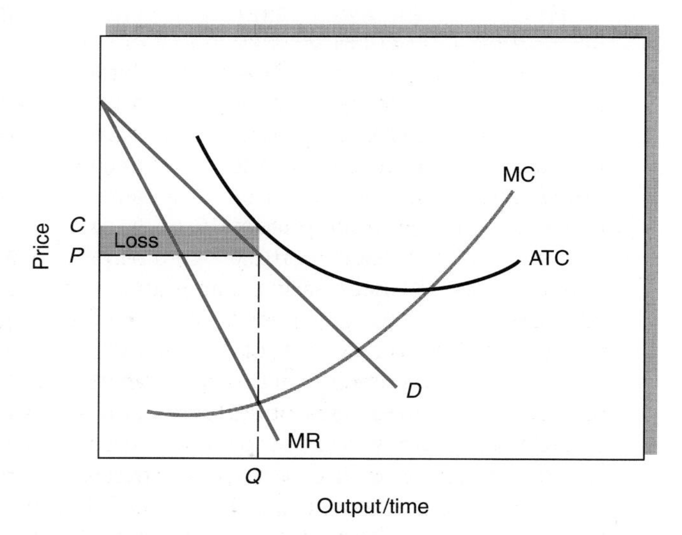

many sales will be lost if the price is raised? How many sales will be added if the price is lowered? Trial and error are often necessary to learn the answers. A firm that is a price searcher will price its product on the basis of what it *expects* to happen if the price is changed. The revenue and cost data illustrated in Exhibits 8.1, 8.2, and 8.3 might be thought of as representing *expected* revenues and costs associated with various output levels. To complicate matters further in real life, quality changes of various sorts can be undertaken by the monopolist searching for additional profits. Buyer reactions to potential quality changes, and resulting revenue shifts, are an additional variable in the decision-making process of a price searcher–monopolist.

A monopolist, like other business decision-makers, seldom calculates what we have called demand, marginal revenue, and cost curves. Even so, the same questions are asked: Would a lower price add more to revenue than to cost? Would a higher price decrease revenue more than cost? The profit-maximizing price is usually just approximated. However, the monopolist who is maximizing profits acts *as if* MR and MC had been calculated, so our model of monopoly shows what a profit-maximizing monopolist is trying to do.

It is difficult for a monopolistic firm to predict the demand conditions it will face, and thus consumer response to alternative prices (and quality changes). But life is even more complex for the next class of price searchers we consider: large firms with few rivals in a market protected by high barriers to entry.

## PRICE AND OUTPUT IN THE CASE OF OLIGOPOLY

**oligopoly** A market situation in which a small number of sellers comprise the entire industry. It is competition among the few.

*Oligopoly* means "few sellers." When there are only a few firms that are large relative to the market, the firms are said to comprise an **oligopoly.** In the United States, the great majority of output in such industries as automobiles, steel, cigarettes, and aircraft is produced by five or fewer dominant firms. In addition to a small number of producers, there are several other characteristics that oligopolistic industries have in common.

Since the number of sellers in an oligopolistic market is small, the activities of one firm are likely to be noticed by the others. How will those rivals react? Decision-making in each firm is more complex because each firm must take the potential reactions of rivals into account whenever it makes price and output decisions. The decisions of one seller often influence the price of products, the output, and the profits of rival firms.

In an oligopolistic industry, large-scale production (relative to the total market) is usually necessary to attain a low per-unit cost. When economies of scale are significant, only a small number of the large-scale, cost-efficient firms will be required to meet the total market demand for the product.

Using the automobile industry as an example, Exhibit 8.4 illustrates the importance of economies of scale as a source of oligopoly. It has been estimated that each firm must produce approximately 1 million automobiles annually before its per unit cost of production is minimized. However, when the selling price of automobiles is barely sufficient for firms to cover their costs, the total quantity demanded from these producers is only 6 million. To minimize costs, then, each firm must produce at least one-sixth (1 million of the 6

**EXHIBIT 8.4**

**Economies of Scale and Oligopoly**

Oligopoly exists in the automobile industry because firms do not fully realize the cost reductions from large-scale output until they produce approximately one-sixth of the total market.

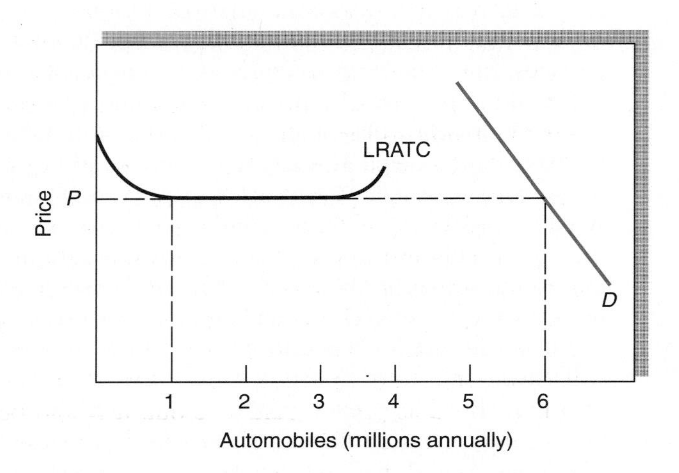


million) of the output demanded. In other words, the industry can support no more than five or six domestic firms of cost-efficient size.

Economies of scale are probably the most significant entry barrier protecting firms in an oligopolistic industry.[2] A potential competitor may be unable to start out small and gradually grow to the optimal size, since it must gain a large share of the market before it can minimize per unit cost. The manufacture of refrigerators and diesel engines, as well as automobile production, seems to fall into this category. Other factors, including patent rights, control over an essential resource, and government-imposed entry restraints may also prevent new competitors from entering profitable oligopolistic industries.

The products of sellers in an oligopolistic industry may be either similar or differentiated. When firms produce identical products, such as milk or gasoline, there is less opportunity for nonprice competition. On the other hand, rival firms producing differentiated products are more likely to use style, quality, and advertising as competitive weapons.

Unlike a monopolist or a price taker, an oligopolist cannot determine the product price that will deliver maximum profit simply by estimating market demand and cost conditions. A key factor in determining the demand facing an oligopolistic firm is the pricing behavior of close rivals. Thus, an oligopolist must predict not only how consumers will react to options, but also how rival firms (that is, the rest of the industry) will react to alternative price (and

[2]Economies of scale will not be a barrier to entry in the industry, of course, if resources can be freely moved into and out of the industry at a low cost. Such resource mobility would render the market contestable, as we learned in Chapter 7, removing scale economies as a barrier to entry in this special case.

quality) adjustments that it is considering. Each oligopolist confronts this complex problem, and since economics cannot specify the reaction of each to the action of the others, it is impossible to determine the precise price and output policy that will emerge in oligopolistic industries. Economics does, however, indicate a potential range of prices, and the factors that will determine whether prices in the industry will be high or low relative to costs of production.

Consider an oligopolistic industry in which seven or eight rival firms produce the entire market output. Substantial economies of scale are present. The firms produce identical products and have similar costs of production. Exhibit 8.5 depicts the market demand conditions and long-run costs of production of the individual firms for such an industry.

What price will prevail? We can answer this question for two extreme cases. First, suppose that each firm sets its price independently of the other firms. There is no collusion, and each competitive firm acts independently, seeking to maximize profits by offering consumers a better deal than its rivals. Under these conditions, the market price would be driven down to $P_c$. Firms would be just able to cover their per unit costs of production. What would happen if a single firm raised its price? Its customers would switch to rival firms, which would now expand to accommodate the new customers. The firm that raised its price would lose out. It would be self-defeating for any one firm to raise its price if the other firms did not raise theirs.

What would happen if supply conditions were such that the market price was above $P_c$? Since the demand curve faced by each individual firm

**EXHIBIT 8.5**

**Range of Price and Output under Oligopoly**

If oligopolists competed with one another, price-cutting would drive price down to $P_c$. In contrast, perfect cooperation among firms would lead to a higher price $P_m$ and a smaller output ($Q_m$ rather than $Q_c$). The shaded area shows profit if firms collude. Demand here is the market demand.

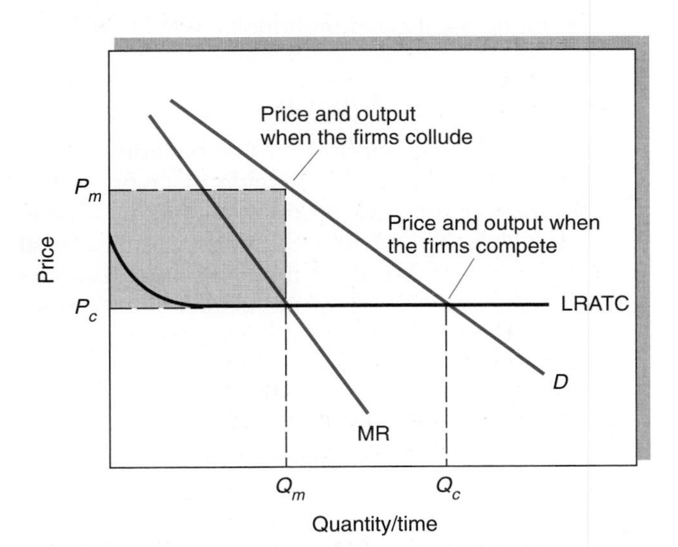

is relatively elastic, rival sellers would have a strong incentive to reduce their price. Any firm that reduced its price slightly, by 1 or 2 percent, for example, would gain numerous customers. The price-cutting firm would attract some new buyers to the market, but more importantly, that firm would also lure many buyers away from rival firms charging higher prices. Total profit would expand as the price-cutter gained a larger share of the total market. But what would happen if all firms attempted to undercut their rivals? Price would be driven down to $P_c$, and the economic profit of the firms would be eliminated.

When rival oligopolists compete (pricewise) with one another, they drive the market price down to the level of costs of production. They do not always compete, however. There is a strong incentive for oligopolists to collude, raise price, and restrict output.

**cartel** An organization of sellers designed to coordinate supply decisions so that the joint profits of the members will be maximized. A cartel will seek to create a monopoly in the market.

Suppose the oligopolists, recognizing their interdependence, acted cooperatively to maximize their joint profit. They might form a **cartel,** such as the Organization of Petroleum Exporting Countries (OPEC), to accomplish this objective. Alternatively, they might collude without the aid of a formal organization. Under federal antitrust laws in the United States, collusive action to raise price and expand the joint profit of the firms would, of course, be illegal. Nevertheless, let us see what would happen if oligopolists followed this course. Exhibit 8.5 shows the marginal revenue curve that would accompany the market demand $D$ for the product. Under perfect cooperation, the oligopolists would refuse to produce units for which marginal revenue was less than marginal cost. Thus, they would restrict joint output to $Q_m$ where MR = MC. Market price would rise to $P_m$. With collusion, substantial joint profits (the shaded area of Exhibit 8.5) could thus be attained. The case of perfect cooperation would be identical with the outcome under monopoly.

In the real world, however, the outcome is likely to fall between the extremes of price competition and perfect cooperation. Oligopolists generally recognize their interdependence and try to avoid vigorous price competition, which would drive price down to the level of per unit costs. But there are also obstacles to collusion, which is why prices in oligopolistic industries do not rise to the monopolistic level. Oligopolistic prices are typically above marginal cost but below those a monopolist would set.

## Obstacles to Collusion

**collusion** Agreement among firms to avoid various competitive practices, particularly price reductions. It may involve either formal agreements or merely tacit recognition that competitive practices will be self-defeating in the long run. Tacit collusion is difficult to detect. In the United States, antitrust laws prohibit collusion and conspiracies to restrain trade.

**Collusion** is the opposite of competition. It involves cooperative actions by sellers to turn the terms of trade in favor of the group, and against buyers. Since oligopolists can profit by colluding to restrict output and raise price, economic theory suggests that they will have a strong incentive to do so. To accomplish this, however, the firms must also agree on production quotas for each firm, or a division of the market so that production is limited to the level that will be purchased at the chosen cartel price.

Each individual oligopolist, though, also has an incentive to cheat on collusive agreements. Exhibit 8.6 will help us understand why. An undetected price cut will enable a firm to attract (1) customers who would not buy from any firm at the higher price *and* (2) those who would normally buy from other firms. The demand facing the oligopolistic firm will thus be considerably more elastic than the industry demand curve. As Exhibit 8.6 shows, the price $P_i$ that maximizes the industry's profits will be higher than the price $P_f$ that is best for each individual oligopolist. If a firm can find a way to undercut the

**EXHIBIT 8.6**

**Gaining from Cheating**

The industry demand ($D_i$) and marginal revenue curves are shown in frame b. The joint profits of oligopolists would be maximized at $Q_i$, where $MR_i = MC$. Price $P_i$ would be best for the industry as a whole. However, the demand curve ($d_f$) facing each firm (frame a, drawn under the assumption that no other firms cheat) would be much more elastic than $D_i$. Given the greater elasticity of its demand curve, an individual firm would maximize its profit by cutting its price to $P_f$ and expanding output to $q_f$, where $MR_f = MC$. Thus, individual oligopolists could gain by secretly shaving price and cheating on the collusive agreement.

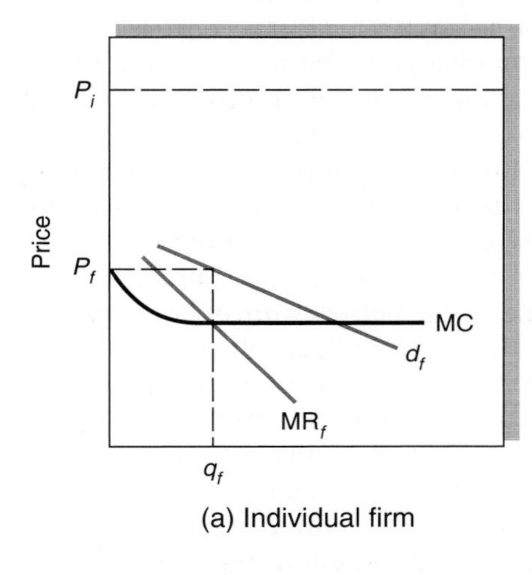

(a) Individual firm

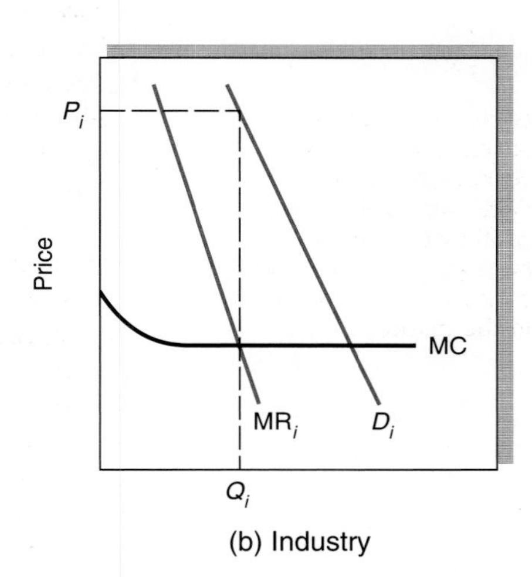

(b) Industry

price set by the collusive agreement, while other sellers maintain the higher price, expanded sales, beyond the level agreed upon by the cartel, will more than make up for the reduction in per unit profit margin.

In oligopolistic industries, there are two conflicting tendencies. An oligopolistic firm has a strong incentive to cooperate with its rivals so that joint profit can be maximized. However, it also has a strong incentive to cheat secretly on any collusive agreement in order to increase its share of the joint profit. Oligopolistic agreements therefore tend to be unstable. This instability exists whether the cooperative behavior is formal, as in the case of a cartel, or informal.

There are certain situations in which it is difficult for oligopolists to collude. Five major obstacles can limit collusive behavior, as follows.

1. *When the number of oligopolists is larger, effective collusion is less likely.* Other things constant, as the number of major firms in an industry increases, it becomes more costly for the oligopolists to communicate, negotiate, and enforce agreements among themselves. In addition, the greater the number of firms, the more likely it is that the objectives of individual firms will conflict with those of the industry. Each firm will want a bigger slice of the pie. Opinions about the best collusive price arrangement will differ because marginal costs, unused plant capacity, and estimates of market demand elasticity are likely to differ among firms. Aggressive, less mature firms may want to expand

their share of total output. These conflicting interests contribute to the breakdown of collusive agreements.

2. *When it is difficult to detect and eliminate price cuts, collusion is less attractive.* Unless a firm has a way of policing the pricing activities of its rivals, it may be the "sucker" in a collusive agreement. Firms that secretly cut prices may gain a larger share of the market, while others maintain their higher prices and lose customers and profits. Price-cutting can sometimes be accomplished in ways that are difficult for the other firms to identify. For example, a firm might provide better credit terms, faster delivery, and other related services "free" to improve slightly the package offered to the buyer.

When firms sell a differentiated product, improvements in quality and style can be used as competitive weapons. "Price cuts" like this are particularly attractive to an oligopolist because they cannot be easily and quickly duplicated by rivals. Competitors can quickly match a reduction in money price, but it will take time for them to match an improvement in quality. When firms can freely use improvements in quality to gain a larger share of the market, collusive agreements on price are of limited value. When cheating (price-cutting) is profitable and difficult for rivals to police, it is a good bet that oligopolistic rivals will be induced to cheat.

3. *Low entry barriers are an obstacle to collusion.* Unless potential rivals can be excluded, oligopolists will be unable to make unusually large profits. Successful collusion will merely attract competitors into the industry, which will eliminate the profits. Even with collusion, long-run profits will not be possible unless entry into the industry can be blocked.

Local markets are sometimes dominated by a few firms. For example, many communities have only a small number of ready-mix concrete producers, bowling alleys, accounting firms, and furniture stores. In the absence of government restrictions, however, entry barriers into these markets are often low. The threat of potential rivals reduces the gains from collusive behavior under these conditions.

4. *Unstable demand conditions are an obstacle to collusion.* Demand instability tends to increase the honest differences of opinion among oligopolists about what is best for the industry. One firm may want to expand because it anticipates a sharp increase in future demand, while a more pessimistic rival may want to hold the line on existing industrial capacity. Greater differences in expectations about future demand create greater conflict among oligopolistic firms. Successful collusion is more likely when demand is relatively stable.

5. *Vigorous antitrust action increases the cost of collusion.* Under existing antitrust laws, collusive behavior is prohibited. Secret agreements are, of course, possible. Simple informal cooperation might be conducted without discussions or collusive agreements. However, like other illegal behavior, all such agreements are not legally enforceable by any firm. Vigorous antitrust action can discourage firms from making such illegal agreements. As the threat of getting caught increases, participants will be less likely to attempt collusive behavior.

**market power** The ability of a firm that is not a pure monopolist to earn unusually large profits, indicating that it has some monopoly power. Because the firm has a few (or weak) competitors, it has a degree of freedom from the discipline of vigorous competition.

Uncertainty and imprecision characterize the theory of oligopoly. We know that firms will gain if they can successfully agree to restrict output and raise price. However, collusion is fraught with conflicts and difficulties. In some industries, these difficulties are so great that the **market power** of the oligopolists is relatively small. In other industries, oligopolistic cooperation, although not perfect, may raise prices significantly, indicating a higher degree of market power, which is, in effect, a degree of monopoly power. Analysis of the costs and benefits of collusive behavior, while it does not yield precise predictions on oligopoly pricing, at least allows us to determine when discipline by competitive pressures is more likely to exist for an oligopolist.

## DEFECTS OF MARKETS WITH HIGH ENTRY BARRIERS

> *Monopolists, by keeping the market constantly understocked, by never fully supplying the effectual demand, sell their commodities much above the natural price, and raise their emoluments, whether they consist of wages or profit, greatly above their natural rate.*
>
> Adam Smith[3]

What types of problems arise when competition is restricted by barriers to entry—a protected monopoly comprising the extreme case? Can public policy improve resource allocation in markets having high entry barriers?

From Adam Smith's time to the present, economists have generally considered monopoly a necessary evil at best. Markets with only a few sellers, protected against new entrants by high barriers to entry, have been deemed only slightly better. Open competition, unfettered by high barriers to entry, has been recognized as a key form of market discipline restraining the behavior of producers. There are four major reasons for this view.

1. *Reduced competition limits the options available to consumers.* If you do not like the food at a local restaurant, you can go to another restaurant. If you do not like the wares of a local department store, you can buy good substitutes from other retailers. The competition of rivals, both existing and potential, protects the consumer from the arbitrary behavior of any seller. But consider your alternatives if you do not like the local telephone service. The entry of competitors is typically forbidden in that market. What can you do when the service is bad? You can complain to the company or your legislative representative, but you have no option other than sacrificing your phone service if your complaints are ignored. This lack of options reduces the ability of consumers to discipline sellers in a market with high barriers to entry. When consumers must take what the seller offers or do without, their ability to discipline sellers is greatly reduced.

2. *Reduced competition results in allocative inefficiency.* Allocative efficiency requires that additional units be produced when they are valued more highly than what it costs to produce them. When barriers to entry are low, production of each good will be expanded until its price is driven down to the level of per unit costs. With high barriers to entry, however, this will not generally be the case. A monopolist or cartel that does not have to worry about rivals entering the market can often gain by restricting output and raising price. That is, output may not be produced even though consumers value it more than its costs of production. Prices may exceed not only marginal costs, but also average total cost for a long period of time when entry barriers into a market are high. As Adam Smith noted more than 200 years ago, monopolists

[3]Adam Smith, *An Inquiry into the Nature and Causes of the Wealth of Nations* (1776; Cannan's ed., Chicago: University of Chicago Press, 1976), p. 69.

(and cartels) will understock the market and charge a higher price than would prevail if the producers were disciplined by independent rivals and the threat of new entrants.

3. *When barriers to entry are high, consumers are less able to direct producers to serve their interests.* With low barriers to entry, producers have little choice but to serve the interests of consumers. Producers that do not operate efficiently will lose out to lower-cost rivals. Firms that fail to produce goods that consumers value highly relative to their costs will experience losses. Thus, if producers want to make profits when entry barriers are low, they will have to provide consumers what they want at an attractive price.

When entry barriers are high, and rivals are few or none, the discipline of close competition will be absent. Even though losses will induce exit from the market when costs are high relative to demand, the ability of profits and losses to discipline firms is weakened. Firms that are inefficient may nonetheless earn a satisfactory profit, protected from potential new competitors. Their benefits are enjoyed at the consumer's expense.

4. *Government grants of high barriers to entry will encourage rent seeking; resources will be wasted by firms attempting to secure and maintain grants of market protection.* Grants of special favor by the government will lead to costly activities seeking those favors. Economists refer to such activities as rent seeking. When government licenses or other grants of entry barriers increase profitability and provide protection from the rigors of market competition, people will expend scarce resources in an attempt to secure and maintain these monopoly grants. From an efficiency standpoint, such rent-seeking activities are wasteful; they consume valuable resources without contributing to output. In aggregate, output is reduced as the result of these wasteful activities. Inefficiency emanating from this source will supplement the welfare losses resulting from the allocative inefficiency.

By way of illustration, suppose the government issues a license providing a seller with the exclusive right to sell liquor in a specific market. If this grant of monopoly power permits the licensee to earn monopoly profit, potential suppliers will expend resources trying to convince government officials that they should be granted the license. The potential monopolists will lobby government officials, make political contributions, hire representatives to do consulting studies, and undertake other actions designed to convince politicians and their appointees that they can best "serve the public interest" as a monopoly supplier. Any firm that expects its rent-seeking activities to be successful will be willing to spend up to the present value of the future expected monopoly profits, if necessary, to obtain the monopoly protection. Other suppliers, of course, may also be willing to invest in rent-seeking activities. When several suppliers believe they can win, the total expenditures of all firms on rent-seeking activities may actually consume resources worth more than the economic profit expected from the monopoly enterprise.

## POLICY ALTERNATIVES WHEN ENTRY BARRIERS ARE HIGH

What government policies might be used to counteract the problems that result from high barriers to entry? Economists suggest four policy options:

1. Force a restructuring of the existing firms in the market to provide more competitors.
2. Reduce tariffs and other artificial barriers that restrain trade.
3. Regulate the price and output of firms in the market.
4. Supply the market with goods produced by a government firm.

Each of these policies is used by governments either to reduce entry barriers or to counteract their negative results. We will briefly discuss each in turn.

## Restructure Existing Firms

The most serious problems raised by a monopoly would be avoided if the monopolist faced the threat of rivals producing the same product or even close substitutes. The presence of competitors would prevent independent firms from restricting output and raising prices.

Why not break up the monopoly into several rival units, substituting competition for monopoly? If it were not for economies of scale, this might be a very good strategy. If economies of scale are important, however, larger firms will have a lower per unit cost than smaller rivals. Sometimes economies of scale can be so important that the per unit cost of production will be lowest when the entire output of the industry is produced by a few firms (an oligopoly) or even a single firm (a monopoly). In the latter case, without government intervention, the "natural" tendency will then be toward monopoly—a **natural monopoly**—in which a single firm, large enough to have the lowest attainable cost in this situation, produces the entire output demanded in the market. When natural monopoly (or oligopoly) exists, the problems associated with high barriers to entry will be present. Under these circumstances, however, imposing a "competitive" market structure is not an attractive alternative. Splitting up the large firm(s) into several competing firms will be costly and difficult to maintain due to the constant pressure on each firm in the industry to grow or merge in order to achieve lower per unit costs and gain a competitive advantage over its smaller (and therefore higher-cost) rivals.

**natural monopoly** A market situation in which the average costs of production continually decline with increased output. Therefore, average costs of production will be lowest when a single large firm produces the entire output demanded.

## Reduce Artificial Barriers to Trade

A second strategy, which works to take advantage of economies of scale, is to reduce tariffs, quotas, exchange rate controls, bureaucratic regulations on importers or exporters, and other types of trade restraints that increase transaction costs and reduce the gains from exchange. Reducing trade barriers may increase the competitiveness of markets that would otherwise be dominated by a small number of domestic producers. This strategy is particularly important for small nations. Opening domestic markets to free trade means that both domestic producers and consumers can gain from reductions in per unit costs that often accompany large-scale production, marketing, and distribution. Domestic producers can operate on a larger scale and therefore achieve lower per unit costs than would be possible if they were solely dependent on their domestic market. For example, textile manufacturers in Hong Kong, Taiwan, and South Korea would have much higher per unit costs if they were unable to sell abroad. With international trade, however, textile firms in these countries are able to produce (and sell) large outputs and compete quite effectively in the world market.

Open trade, free of artificial barriers, also benefits domestic consumers by permitting them to purchase from large-scale producers abroad. The aircraft industry provides a vivid illustration. Given the huge designing and engineering costs of this industry, the domestic market of almost all countries would be substantially less than the quantity required to achieve low per unit costs of jet planes. With international trade, however, consumers around the world are able to purchase planes economically from a large-scale producer such as Boeing or McDonnell Douglas. The same principle applies to small markets within a nation. Allowing consumers to fill prescriptions for drugs or contact lenses by mail, for example, allows even rural buyers access to economical suppliers that carry large and varied inventories of goods in large markets.

By promoting competition in small markets and allowing consumers to purchase a wide variety of goods at economical prices, trade keeps local and domestic producers on their toes. It forces them to improve the quality of their products and keep costs low. The experience of the auto industry in the United States is consistent with the view. In the 1960s three large domestic producers dominated the U.S. automobile manufacturing market. As the cost of transporting automobiles declined, U.S. auto producers faced stiff competition from abroad, particularly from Japanese firms. Responding to the increased competition, U.S. auto manufacturers worked hard to improve the quality of their vehicles. As a result, the reliability of the automobiles and light trucks available to American consumers—including those vehicles produced by domestic manufacturers—is almost certainly higher than would have been the case in the absence of competition from abroad.

Trade restraints are like a blockade that a government imposes on its own people. Just as a blockade imposed by an enemy will harm a nation, so too will a self-imposed blockade in the form of trade restrictions. However, the many benefits of free trade are spread widely among participants of the economy. In contrast, the barriers to trade that harm the economy in general, and consumers in particular, confer concentrated benefits on a much smaller number of owners and workers in protected firms. The few individuals protected by a specific trade barrier will often organize politically and resist its removal. Consumers, who would be the main beneficiaries of reducing such barriers, are so numerous and the benefits are spread so widely and thinly among them, that organizing them politically is seldom possible. Political pressure is often stronger on the side of keeping the high barriers to entry that protect favored firms at the expense of the economy as a whole. Free trade makes excellent economic sense, but it does not always make good political sense for elected officials.

## Regulate the Protected Producer

Can government regulation improve the allocative efficiency of a monopoly or an oligopoly? In theory, the answer to this question is clearly yes. Government regulation can force the price searcher to reduce its price. At the lower government-imposed price ceiling, the firm will voluntarily produce a larger output.

Exhibit 8.7 illustrates why ideal government price regulation, in the case of a monopolist, would improve resource allocation. The profit-maximizing monopolist sets price at $P_0$ and produces output $Q_0$, where MR = MC. Consumers, however, would value additional units more than the opportunity cost. There are steps that the regulatory agency can take to improve resource allocation in the presence of a monopoly or oligopoly.

**EXHIBIT 8.7**

**Regulation of Monopolist**

If unregulated, a profit-maximizing monopolist with the costs indicated here would produce $Q_0$ units and charge $P_0$. If a regulatory agency forced the monopolist to reduce price to $P_1$, the monopolist would expand output to $Q_1$. Ideally, we would like output to be expanded to $Q_2$, where $P = MC$, but regulatory agencies usually do not attempt to keep prices as low as $P_2$. Can you explain why?

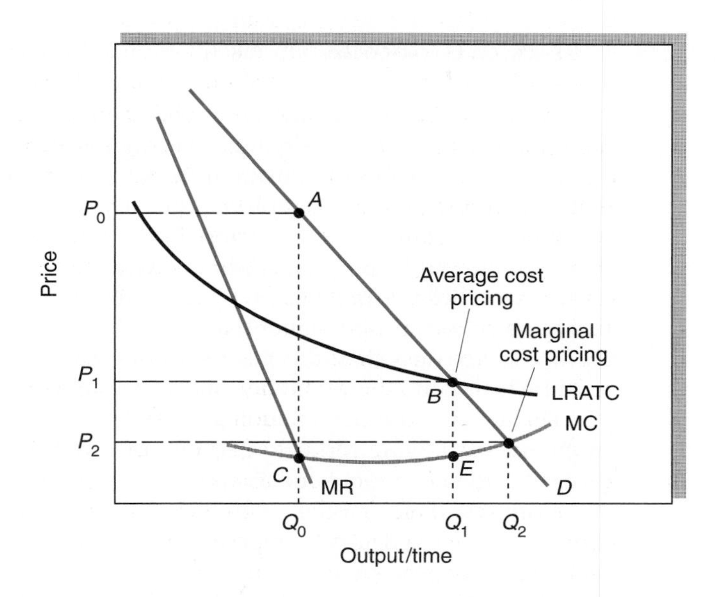


1. *Average cost pricing.* If a regulatory agency forces the firm in Exhibit 8.7 to reduce price to $P_1$, at which the ATC curve intersects with the market (and firm) demand curve, the firm will expand output to $Q_1$. Since it cannot charge a price above $P_1$, it cannot increase revenues by selling a smaller output at a higher price. Once the price ceiling is instituted, the firm can increase revenues by $P_1$, and by only $P_1$, for each unit it sells. The regulated firm's MR is constant at $P_1$ for all units sold until output is increased to $Q_1$. Since the firm's MC is less than $P_1$ (and therefore less than MR), the profit-maximizing regulated firm shown here will expand output from $Q_0$ to $Q_1$. The benefits from the consumption of these units ($ABQ_1Q_0$) clearly exceed their costs ($CEQ_1Q_0$). Social welfare has improved as a result of the regulatory action (we will ignore the impact on the distribution of income). At that output level, revenues are sufficient to cover costs. The firm is making zero economic profit (or "normal" accounting profit).

2. *Marginal cost pricing.* Ideally, since even at the $Q_1$ output level, marginal cost is still less than price, additional welfare gains are possible if output is increased to $Q_2$. However, if a regulatory agency forced the monopolist to reduce price to $P_2$ (so that price would equal marginal cost at the output level $Q_2$), economic losses would result. Even a monopolist, unless subsidized, would not undertake production if the regulatory agency set the price at $P_2$ or any price below $P_1$. Usually, problems associated with determining and allocating the necessary subsidy would make this option unfeasible.

Even though government regulation of monopoly seems capable of improving market results, as in the preceding average cost pricing example, economic analysis suggests that regulation will usually not be an ideal solution. Why? The lack of incentive to produce at a low cost is important. Information is another factor. Together, the lack of incentives and information form a serious problem for regulators who would act on behalf of citizens to control monopoly. Let us look at the various factors that make this such a difficult task.

**LACK OF INFORMATION** In discussing ideal regulation, we assumed that we knew what the firm's ATC, MC, and demand curves looked like. In reality, of course, this would not be the case. The firms themselves have difficulty knowing their costs, and especially their demand curves, with any precision.

Because estimates of demand and marginal costs are difficult to obtain, regulatory agencies usually use profits (or rate of return) as a gauge to determine whether the regulated price is too high or too low. The regulatory agency, guarding the public interest, seeks to impose a "fair" or "normal" rate of return on the firm. If the firm is making profits (that is, an abnormally high rate of return), the price must be higher than $P_1$ and should be lowered. If the firm is incurring losses (less than the fair or normal rate of return), the regulated price must be less than $P_1$, and the firm should be allowed to increase price.

The actual existence of profits, though, is not easily identified. Accounting profit, even allowing for a normal rate of profit, is not the same as economic profit. In addition, regulated firms have a strong incentive to adopt reporting techniques and accounting methods that conceal profits. This will make it difficult for a regulatory agency to identify and impose the price consistent with allocative efficiency.

**COST SHIFTING** As long as demand is sufficient, the owners of the regulated firm can expect the long-run rate of profit to be essentially fixed, regardless of whether efficient management reduces costs or inefficient management allows costs to increase. If costs decrease, the "fair return" rule imposed by the regulatory agency will force a price reduction; if costs increase, the "fair return" rule will allow a price increase. Thus, the owners of the regulated firm have less incentive to be concerned about costs than the owners of unregulated firms. Managers, therefore, will have a freer hand to pursue personal objectives. They will be more likely to fly first-class, entertain lavishly on an expense account, give their relatives and friends good jobs, grant unwarranted wage increases, and in general make decisions that yield personal benefits and increase company costs. Since monopoly means that buyers do not have a close substitute to turn to, consumers will bear the burden of managerial inefficiency. Normally, wasteful activities would be policed by the owners, but since the firm's rate of return is set by the regulatory agency, the owners have little incentive to be concerned.

**SPECIAL-INTEREST INFLUENCE** The difficulties of government regulation discussed thus far are practical limitations that a regulatory agency would confront in seeking to perform its duties efficiently. But, in the political arena, regulatory authorities cannot necessarily be expected to pursue only efficiency. Regulated firms have a strong incentive to see that "friendly," "reasonable" people serve as regulators, and they will invest political and economic resources to this end.

Just as rent-seeking activities designed to gain monopoly privileges can be expected, so can activities to influence regulatory decisions.

Consumer interests, in contrast to those of industry, are widely dispersed and disorganized. Ordinarily, consumers cannot be expected to invest time, resources, votes, and political contributions to ensure that a particular regulatory commission represents their views. The firms that are regulated can, however, be expected to make such investments. Even though the initial stimulus for a regulating agency might come from consumer interests, economic theory suggests that such agencies will eventually reflect the views of the business and labor interests they are supposed to regulate.

## Supply Market with Government Production

Government-operated firms—socialized firms such as the U.S. Post Office, the Tennessee Valley Authority, and many local public utilities—present an alternative to both private monopoly and regulation. However, both theory and experience indicate that socialized firms will fail to counteract fully the problems that stem from high barriers to entry. The same perverse managerial incentives—incentives to ignore efficiency and pursue personal or professional objectives at the firm's expense—that regulated firms confront also tend to plague the government-operated firm. And since the "owners" of a socialized firm (voters) are typically uninformed about how well a socialized firm is run, or how it might be run better, they are unable to police management inefficiency. This is especially true when the firm has no direct competitors against which the firm's performance can be easily compared. Voters tend to be ignorant, quite rationally, about matters on which, as individuals, they have no decisive vote. This is in sharp contrast with individual stockholders in a firm, each of whom can personally either "bail out" (sell his or her stock) upon learning about approaching trouble from the firm's decisions or buy more stock upon seeing promising management initiatives.

Government-operated firms do not confront an environment that rewards efficient management and reductions in cost. Unlike investors in the private sector, no small group of voters normally is in a position to gain substantial wealth by taking over the socialized firm and improving its management. Even more than with monopoly or oligopoly in the private sector, customers of the socialized monopoly (voter-taxpayers) cannot easily switch their business to other sellers. Even those voter-taxpayers who do not consume the product often have to pay taxes to support the socialized firm. The end result is that when the government operates a business—particularly one with monopoly power—there is typically less consumer and investor scrutiny, less reward for efficiency, and less penalty for inefficiency. Higher costs are an expected result.

Government ownership, like unregulated monopoly and government regulation, is a less than ideal solution. Thus, it should not be surprising that those who denounce monopoly in, for instance, the telephone industry seldom point to a government-operated monopoly—such as the post office—as an example of how an industry should be run.

## Pulling It Together

The policy implications that can legitimately be drawn from an analysis of high barriers to entry are less than fully satisfying. We may not like the reduction in competition or its effects, but economic analysis suggests important qualifications to the "solutions" usually put forth.

Most of the policy alternatives are not terribly attractive. Economies of scale reduce the benefits from breaking up existing firms to provide additional competitors. Since smaller firms have higher per unit costs, restructuring the industry to increase the number of firms may be costly and difficult to maintain. Government measures such as tariff reductions and removal of entry barriers into markets are perhaps the surest recommendation for increasing competition in a market. Such policies, however, will certainly face political opposition, primarily from owners and workers in protected industries.

We have pointed out that regulation is a less than ideal solution. Regulators do not possess the information necessary to impose an efficient outcome, and they may be susceptible to manipulation by industrial and labor interests. Moreover, since public-sector managers are likely to pursue political objectives at the expense of economic efficiency, public ownership is also a less than ideal solution. Thus, economic theory indicates that there are no ideal solutions when substantial economies of scale are present. Choices must be made among alternatives, all of which are imperfect.

## How Competitive Are Markets in the Real World?

How much of our economy is competitive? The question is difficult to answer for any nation with a large market sector. In a very real sense, every firm competes with every other firm for the consumer's additional dollar of spending. Competition is everywhere; the seller of compact discs, for example, competes with the bookstore and the local restaurant for our entertainment budgets.

As we have discussed, even within an industry, competition is multidimensional. Dynamic innovation, entrepreneurship, and product-quality competition may be important even in highly concentrated industries. Product-quality competition may also account for strong rivalry even among a limited number of competitors. Moreover, in a firm as big as General Motors, even the rivalry among divisions (Buick versus Oldsmobile, for example) may be intense. Direct price competition within the firm is presumably controlled, but competition involving quality remains. Leaders in each division compete for recognition and advancement, and each is judged by monthly sales and profit figures. Thus, competitive forces are not entirely absent even when output in an industry is supplied by only a few firms.

Economist William G. Shepherd has examined the structure of the U.S. economy in depth, and uses four categories to classify the structure of various industries. He has also looked at how much of the U.S. national income is produced by firms in each category, and how those percentages have changed over time. As Exhibit 8.8 shows, he finds that firms in competitive industries have produced a rising share of national income, while monopolies have produced a falling share. The intermediate categories have also declined in importance. Shepherd attributes the sharp increase in competition from 1958 to 1980 to antitrust policy, increased import competition, and reduced regulatory barriers to competition. Other economists also point to reductions in transportation costs as a factor contributing to the increase in competition.

**Exhibit 8.8** **Increasing Competitiveness of U.S. Economy, 1939–1980**

This chart presents the findings of a study by William G. Shepherd, an industrial economist from the University of Michigan. Shepherd found that the share of national income produced by the competitive sectors of the U.S. economy has been rising for several decades, while the share produced in less competitive markets has been falling. The "single dominant firm" here is one with more than a 50 percent market share, the protection of high barriers to entry, and the ability to control pricing and to influence innovation. A "tight oligopoly" means that the largest four firms together have at least a 60 percent market share of the industry output or that the industry is dominated by government-regulated firms with the ability to strongly influence the regulated prices.

| Market Structure Category | Percentage Shares of National Income Produced in Each Category | | |
|---|---|---|---|
| | 1939 | 1958 | 1980 |
| 1. Pure monopoly | 6.2 | 3.1 | 2.5 |
| 2. Single dominant firm | 5.0 | 5.0 | 2.8 |
| 3. Tight oligopoly | 36.4 | 35.6 | 18.0 |
| 4. Effectively competitive firm | 52.4 | 56.3 | 76.7 |
| Total | 100.0 | 100.0 | 100.0 |

**Source:** William G. Shepherd, "Causes of Increased Competition in the U.S. Economy, 1939–1980," *Review of Economics and Statistics,* November 1982, p. 618.

Another sign of a large degree of competitiveness in the U.S. economy is the fact that the firms comprising the largest 100 or 200 corporations are different from one another and are constantly changing. As successful management and the vagaries of business fortune exert their influences, some firms are pushed out of the top group and others enter. Following the fate of various firms over time is not easy, since mergers occur and names change, but historical research indicates that of the largest 100 manufacturing corporations in 1909, only 36 remained on the list in 1948. Of the 50 largest in 1947, only 25 remained on the list in 1972, and 5 failed to make even the top 200. Of the firms on the *Fortune* 500 list in 1980, only about half were able to make the list in 1990. With time, in an economy as competitive as that in the United States, even giants tumble and fall, as technology, leadership, and consumer preferences change.

## Looking Ahead

The last several chapters have focused on product markets. Business firms must acquire resources in order to produce the products that they supply. Households generally supply these resources—the labor, financial capital, materials, and entrepreneurship required to produce goods and services. The next two chapters will focus on the operation of resource markets.

## CHAPTER SUMMARY

1. In a market with few sellers of a product and high barriers to entry, the sellers, though not completely free from competitive pressures, will exert more control over price and output.
2. The four major barriers to entry into a market are economies of scale, government licensing, patents, and control of an essential resource.
3. A monopoly is characterized by (a) high barriers to entry and (b) a single seller of a well-defined product for which there are no good substitutes.
4. Analysis of pure monopoly is important for two reasons. First, the monopoly model will help us understand the operation of markets dominated by a few firms. Second, in a few important industries, such as local telephone services and utilities, there is often only a single producer in a market area. The monopoly model will help us understand these markets.
5. The monopolist's demand curve is the market demand curve. As a price searcher, a profit-maximizing monopolist will lower price and expand output as long as marginal revenue exceeds marginal cost. At the maximum-profit output, MR will equal MC. The monopolist will charge the price on its demand curve corresponding to that rate of sales.
6. If losses occur in the long run, a monopolist will go out of business. If profit results, high barriers to entry will shield a monopolist from competitive pressures. Therefore, monopolists can sometimes earn long-run economic profits.
7. An oligopolistic market is characterized by high barriers to entry, including substantial economies of scale that result in only a small number of interdependent firms in the industry.
8. There is no general theory of price, output, and equilibrium for oligopolistic markets. If rival oligopolists acted totally independently of their competitors, they would drive price down to the level of cost of production. Alternatively, if they used collusion to obtain perfect cooperation, price would rise to the level that a monopolist would charge. The actual outcome will generally fall between these two extremes.
9. Collusion is the opposite of competition. Oligopolists have a strong incentive to collude and raise their prices. However, the interests of individual firms will conflict with those of the industry as a whole. Since the demand curve faced by individual firms is far more elastic than the industry demand curve, each firm could gain by cutting its price (or raising product quality) by a small amount so that it could attract customers from rivals. If several firms tried to do this, however, the collusive agreement would break down.
10. Oligopolistic firms are less likely to collude successfully against the interests of consumers if (a) the number of rival firms is large; (b) it is costly to prohibit competitors from offering secret price cuts (or quality improvements) to customers; (c) entry barriers are low; (d) market demand conditions tend to be unstable; and/or (e) the threat of antitrust action is present.
11. Economists are critical of markets with high barriers to entry because (a) the ability of consumers to discipline producers is weakened; (b) the un-

regulated monopolist or oligopolist can often gain by restricting output and raising price; (c) profits are less able to stimulate new entry, which would expand the supply of the product until price declined to the level of average production costs; and (d) legal barriers to entry will encourage firms to "invest" resources seeking additional protective barriers and the maintenance of existing ones.

12. Economies of scale can produce an oligopoly or a natural monopoly. A natural monopoly exists when long-run average total costs continue to decline as firm size increases, over the entire range of market demand. Thus, a larger firm always has lower costs. When natural monopoly is present, costs of production will be lowest when a single firm generates the entire output of the industry.
13. Economists suggest four kinds of policy alternatives to reduce the problems stemming from high barriers to entry: (a) breaking up firms in the industry into additional, more competitive firms—an option that is not attractive when economies of scale are important; (b) reduction of artificial barriers to trade, such as tariffs and import restrictions—an economically sound option that will generate strong political opposition from owners and workers in protected industries; (c) government regulation of firms—an option hampered by regulators' incomplete ability to control aspects of quality and their lack of knowledge about the firm's cost curves and market demand conditions, and by consumers' frequent inability to neutralize political pressure on regulators by firms; and finally (d) provision of output by government firms, which is also made unattractive by the inability of voters and consumers to properly monitor and discipline government-owned firms.
14. Competitive forces are widespread, even having influence in markets with high barriers to entry. An increasing proportion of the U.S. economy has become competitive over the past several decades, probably because of rising import competition, antitrust policy, and deregulation.

# *Study Guide*

**CHAPTER**

# 8

## Developing the Economic Way of Thinking

## CRITICAL-ANALYSIS QUESTIONS

*1. "Barriers to entry are crucial to the existence of long-run profits, but they cannot guarantee the existence of profits." Evaluate.

2. "Monopoly is good for producers but bad for consumers. The gains of the former offset the losses of the latter. On balance, there is no reason to think that monopoly is bad for the economy." Evaluate.

*3. Do monopolists charge the highest prices for which they can sell their products? Do they maximize their average profit per sale? Are monopolistic firms always profitable? Why or why not?

4. The retail liquor industry is potentially a competitive industry. However, the liquor retailers of a southern state organized a trade association that sets prices for all firms. For all practical purposes, the trade association transformed a competitive industry into a monopoly. Compare the price and output policy for a purely competitive industry with the policy that would be established by a profit-maximizing monopolist or trade association. Who benefits and who is hurt by the formation of the monopoly?

5. Does economic theory indicate that a monopoly forced by an ideal regulatory agency to set prices according to either marginal or average cost would be more efficient than an unregulated monopoly? Explain. Does economic theory suggest that a regulatory agency will in fact follow a proper regulation policy? What are some of the factors that complicate the regulatory function?

6. Is a monopolist subject to any competitive pressures? Explain. Would an unregulated monopolist have an incentive to operate and produce efficiently? If so, why?

*7. If tariff and quota barriers for foreign imports are lifted, making imports easier to obtain, does this strengthen or weaken the case for strict antitrust legislation and enforcement?

*8. Why is oligopolistic collusion more difficult when there is product variation than when the products of all firms are identical?

9. In large cities, taxi fares are often set above the market equilibrium rate. Sometimes the number of licenses is limited in order to maintain the above-market price. Other times licenses are automatically granted to anyone wanting to operate a taxi. When taxi fares are set above market equilibrium, compare and contrast resource allocation under the restricted license system (assume the licenses are tradable) and the free-entry system. In which case will it be easier for customers to get a taxi? In which case will the amount of capital required to enter the taxi business be greater?

10. Which of the following are monopolists: (a) your local newspaper, (b) the Boston Celtics, (c) General Motors, (d) the U.S. Postal Service, (e) Jay Leno, (f) the American Medical Association? Is the definition of an industry or market area important in the determination of a seller's monopoly position? Explain.

*11. Historically, the real cost of transporting both goods and people has declined substantially. What impact does a reduction in transportation cost have on

*Asterisk denotes critical-analysis questions for which the answers are given in Appendix A.

the market power of individual producers? Do you think the U.S. economy is more or less competitive today than it was 100 years ago? Explain.

## MULTIPLE-CHOICE SELF-TEST

1. Firms that are price searchers
   a. Will eventually find and charge the highest price at which consumers will purchase any units.
   b. Face inelastic demand curves for their products.
   c. Do not confront rival sellers the way price takers do.
   d. Face a downward-sloping demand curve.
2. Which of the following statements is true of a monopolist?
   a. A monopolist will maximize profit when price is reduced and output expanded until MR = MC.
   b. A monopolist will always be able to earn economic profit.
   c. A profit-maximizing monopolist will supply a larger output than the amount consistent with the ideal static efficiency conditions for an economy.
   d. A monopolist has no incentive to produce efficiently, because higher costs can always be passed along to consumers in the form of higher prices.
3. Which of the following are sources of economic inefficiency that arise under monopoly?
   a. Monopoly reduces the ability of consumers to discipline the seller of a product.
   b. A monopolist will fail to expand output to the level where the consumer's valuation of the marginal unit is equal to the producer's cost of producing the unit.
   c. Since legally protected monopolists can often earn economic profit, government protection of monopoly producers will encourage rent-seeking activities.
   d. All of the above are sources of inefficiency arising from monopoly.
4. Suppose the Department of Agriculture organizes the orange growers of Florida and California into a monopoly cartel. Economic theory suggests that, relative to the competitive situation, the price of oranges would
   a. Rise, and output would expand.
   b. Rise if demand were inelastic and decline if demand were elastic.
   c. Rise, and output would decline.
   d. Decline in the short run but increase with the passage of time.
5. "Monopolists do not worry about efficient production and cost-saving, since they can just pass along any increase in costs to their consumers." Which of the following is true about this statement?
   a. The statement is false, because price increases will mean fewer sales and lower costs will mean higher profits (or smaller losses).
   b. The statement is true, and it is the primary reason why economists believe that monopolies result in economic inefficiency.
   c. This statement is false, because the monopolist is a price taker.
   d. Monopolists will worry about keeping costs down only if they are motivated by social considerations rather than profit.

6. Which of the following factors has helped increase the competitiveness of the U.S. economy in recent decades?
   a. Increases in tariffs and other trade restrictions.
   b. An expansion in the relative size of the manufacturing sector.
   c. Reductions in transportation costs and increased competition from foreign producers.
   d. Increased government regulation of the transportation industry.
7. Which of the following conditions is most important if a firm is going to earn long-run economic profits?
   a. An inelastic market demand for the product.
   b. A small number of firms, even though competitors are free to enter the industry.
   c. A differentiated product.
   d. Restrictions that limit entry of potential competitors into the industry.
8. An oligopolistic firm
   a. Will take into account the potential response of its rivals when business decisions are made.
   b. Is likely to be formed when the minimum cost output is only a small portion of the market output.
   c. Is likely to be formed when barriers to entry are low.
   d. Will seldom use product quality as a competitive weapon.
9. Which of the following is an obstacle that would reduce the likelihood of effective collusion among oligopolists?
   a. A small number of firms.
   b. High barriers to entry.
   c. Production of a homogenous product.
   d. Instability in the market demand for the product.
10. The demand curve facing an individual oligopolistic firm will be
   a. Considerably more elastic than the industry demand curve.
   b. Identical to the industry demand curve.
   c. Considerably more inelastic than the industry demand curve.
   d. Perfectly elastic at the market price.

## PROBLEMS

1. Suppose that you produce and sell dining tables in a localized market. Past experience permits you to estimate your demand and marginal cost schedules. This information is presented in the accompanying table.

| Price | Quantity Demanded (per week) | Marginal Cost | Total Revenue | Marginal Revenue | Fixed Cost | Total Cost |
|---|---|---|---|---|---|---|
| $60 | 1 | $50 | ______ | ______ | $40 | ______ |
| 55 | 2 | 20 | ______ | ______ | ______ | ______ |
| 50 | 3 | 24 | ______ | ______ | ______ | ______ |
| 45 | 4 | 29 | ______ | ______ | ______ | ______ |
| 40 | 5 | 35 | ______ | ______ | ______ | ______ |
| 35 | 6 | 45 | ______ | ______ | ______ | ______ |

a. Fill in the missing revenue and cost schedules.
b. Assuming you are currently charging $55 per dining table set, what should you do if you want to maximize profits?
c. Given your demand and cost estimates, what price should you charge if you want to maximize weekly profit? What output should you produce? What is your maximum weekly profit?

2. The diagram below shows demand and long-run cost conditions in an industry.
a. Explain why the industry is likely to be monopolized.
b. Indicate the price that a profit-maximizing monopolist would charge, and label it *P*.
c. Indicate the monopolist's output level, and label it *Q*.
d. Indicate the maximum profits of the monopolist.
e. Will the profits attract competitors to the industry? Why or why not? Explain.

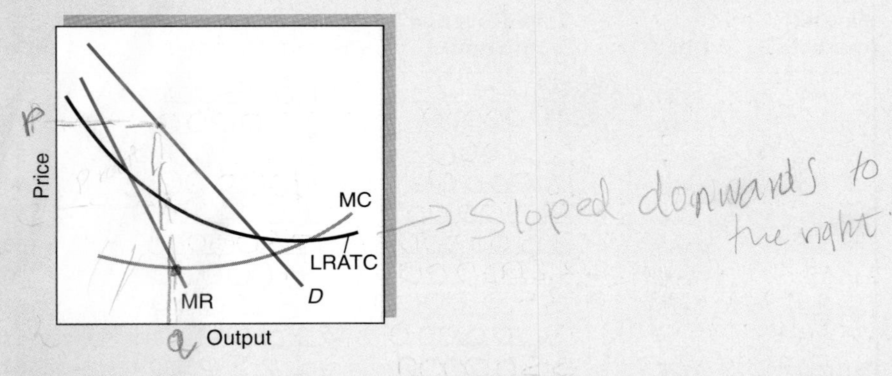


3. Sociable Corporation (SC) produces and sells gizmos in an oligopolistic market comprised of only a very few firms. The accompanying table presents two different demand schedules for SC. The first one shows how SC's quantity demanded varies when the industry price varies, and the second one shows how SC's quantity demanded varies when only SC's price varies. Assume throughout that SC's marginal cost is constant at $10 per gizmo and that fixed costs are zero.

| Demand When Industry Price Varies | | | | Demand When Only SC's Price Varies | | | |
|---|---|---|---|---|---|---|---|
| Quantity | Price | Total Revenue | Marginal Revenue | Quantity | Price | Total Revenue | Marginal Revenue |
| 1 | $130 | $130 | $130 | 1 | $100 | $100 | $100 |
| 2 | 110 | 220 | 90 | 2 | 90 | 180 | 80 |
| 3 | 90 | ____ | ____ | 3 | 80 | ____ | ____ |
| 4 | 70 | ____ | ____ | 4 | 70 | ____ | ____ |
| 5 | 50 | ____ | ____ | 5 | 60 | ____ | ____ |
| 6 | 30 | ____ | ____ | 6 | 50 | ____ | ____ |
| 7 | 10 | ____ | ____ | 7 | 40 | ____ | ____ |
| 8 | 0 | ____ | ____ | 8 | 30 | ____ | ____ |
| 9 | 0 | ____ | ____ | 9 | 20 | ____ | ____ |
| 10 | 0 | 0 | 0 | 10 | 10 | ____ | ____ |

a. Fill in the missing information (Hint: Remember that marginal revenue can be negative as well as positive.)

b. Suppose the industry could engage in successful collusion. What price would SC want the industry to set? Calculate SC's profits at this price. Explain your answer.

c. Suppose the industry has established the collusively determined price of part b above and that SC believes it could "cheat" on the agreement and not be detected. Assuming that sales of gizmos must be in whole units, what quantity would SC decide to sell? What price would it charge? Compare SC's new profit level to the level it achieved in part b.

d. If each firm in the industry believes what SC believes, could each firm increase its profits the way SC believes it can? Explain.

| Output (market) | Price | Total Revenue (market) | Total Revenue (each firm) | Average Total Cost (firm) |
|---|---|---|---|---|
| 1,000 | $750 | | | $200 |
| 2,000 | 500 | | | 170 |
| 3,000 | 450 | | | 150 |
| 4,000 | 400 | | | 150 |
| 8,000 | 300 | | | 150 |
| 12,000 | 250 | | | 150 |
| 16,000 | 200 | | | 150 |
| 20,000 | 175 | | | 150 |
| 24,000 | 150 | | | 150 |
| 28,000 | 125 | | | 150 |
| 32,000 | 100 | | | 150 |

4. Currently there are four rival firms in the typewriter industry. Assume that the four firms are of identical size, produce similar products (consumers think they are homogeneous), and have identical cost schedules. The cost schedule for a firm along with the market demand schedule is presented in the accompanying table.

a. Fill in the missing information.

b. What price would prevail if there were no collusion and each firm sought to offer the consumer a better deal than that available from rivals (as long as the firm's opportunity cost of production was covered)? How many units would be sold in the market? How many would each firm sell?

c. If each firm produced one-fourth of the total market, what market price would prevail when each firm supplied 1,000 units? 2,000 units? 3,000 units?

d. Which of the listed prices would prevail if the firms acted cooperatively (so as to maximize their joint profit)? What is the maximum joint profit of the firms?

e. Given the demand and cost conditions in this oligopolistic industry, what outcome would be most likely to prevail in the real world? Explain.

CHAPTER

# 9

# RESOURCE MARKETS

It is . . . necessary to attach price tags to the various factors of production . . . in order to guide those who have the day-to-day decisions to make as to what is plentiful and what is scarce.

*James Meade*[1]

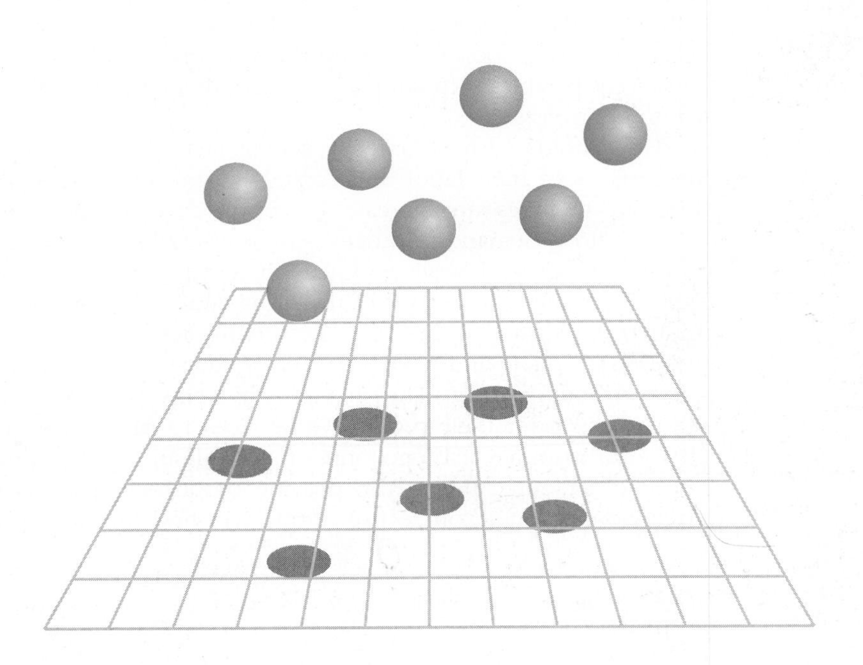

## CHAPTER FOCUS

- Why is the quantity demanded of a productive resource inversely related to its price? Why is the quantity supplied directly related to its price?
- What major factors influence the price of a resource?
- Why do the earnings of people differ?
- Why are wages higher in the United States than they are in India or China? Why are the wages of Americans higher today than they were 50 years ago?
- Does automation destroy jobs? Does it harm workers?
- Do minimum-wage laws help low-skill workers?

**resource markets** Markets in which business firms demand factors of production (for example, labor, capital, and natural resources) from household suppliers. The resources are then used to produce goods and services. These markets are sometimes called *factor markets*.

In previous chapters we focused on the demand and supply conditions in product markets. In product markets, consumers purchase goods and services that are produced by business firms. We now turn to an analysis of **resource markets,** or, as they are sometimes called, *factor markets,* where households are sellers (they supply resources to business firms in exchange for income) and business firms are purchasers (they demand resources in order to produce consumer goods and services).

Exhibit 9.1 illustrates the relationship between resource and product markets. As we have already discussed, households utilize their limited incomes to demand (buy) goods and services in product markets. In turn, business firms incur costs as they bid resources away from their alternative uses and utilize them to produce a good or service. The forces of demand and supply in product markets (top loop of the exhibit) combine to determine the market prices and direct producers to supply those goods that are most highly valued relative to their costs.

Households earn income by selling factors of production—for example, the services of their labor and capital—to business firms. Their offers to sell (hire out) their resources create the supply curve in resource markets. In turn, business firms demand resources from households because they are needed to produce goods and services. Prices in resource markets (bottom loop of exhibit) coordinate the actions of the firms demanding factors of production and the households supplying them. Resource prices influence the actions of both resource suppliers and resource-using producers and provide them with information about scarcity. The income payments provide individuals with the incentive to offer their productive services to producers. An increase in the price of a resource will encourage potential suppliers to provide more of the resource. Resource prices also provide profit-seeking firms with an incentive to economize on resource use. Firms will find that it is profitable to hire a

[1]James E. Meade, "Economic Efficiency and Distributional Justice," in *Contemporary Issues in Economics,* ed. Robert W. Crandall and Richard S. Eckaus (Boston: Little, Brown, 1972), p. 319.

**EXHIBIT 9.1**

**Market for Resources**

Until now, we have focused on product markets, where households demand goods and services that are supplied by firms (upper loop). We now turn to resource markets, where firms demand factors of production—human capital (for example, skills and knowledge of workers) and physical capital (for example, machines, buildings, and land) that are supplied by households in exchange for income (bottom loop). In resource markets, firms are buyers and households are sellers, just the reverse of the case for product markets.

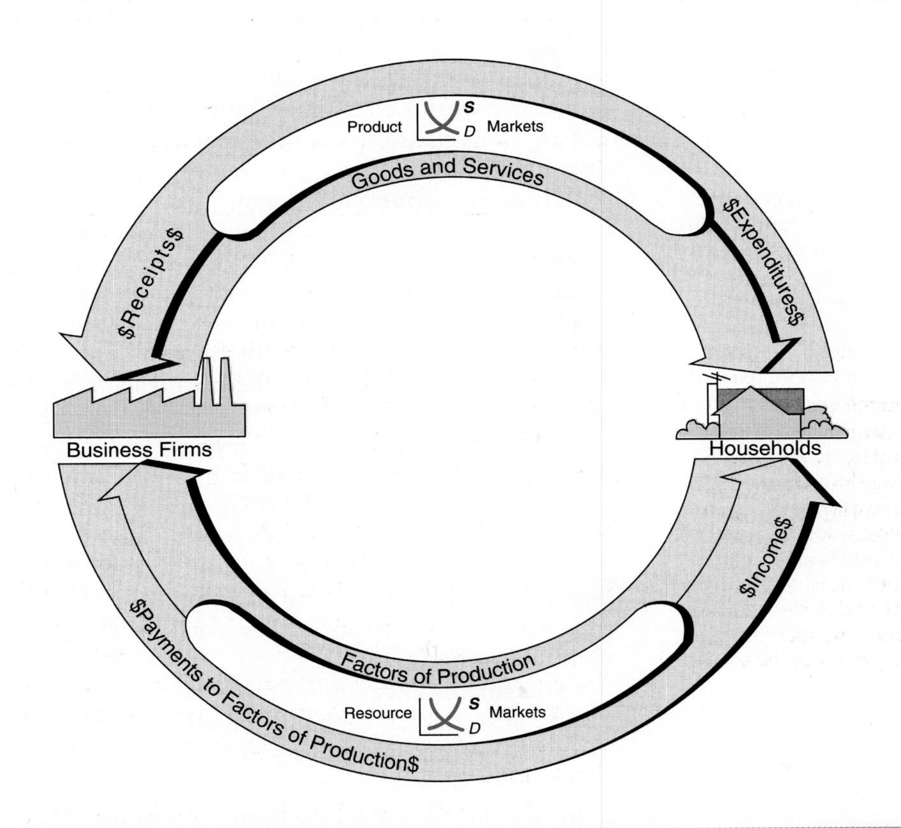


resource if, and only if, the resource adds more to the firm's revenue than to its cost. Thus, an increase in resource prices will encourage firms to cut back on their use of the resource.

**nonhuman resources**
The durable, nonhuman inputs that can be used to produce both current and future output. Machines, buildings, land, and raw materials are examples. Investment can increase the supply of nonhuman resources. Economists often use the term *physical capital* when referring to nonhuman resources.

## HUMAN AND NONHUMAN RESOURCES

Broadly speaking, there are two different types of productive inputs—nonhuman and human resources. **Nonhuman resources** are further broken down into the categories of physical capital, land, and natural resources. Investment involves the use of resources to produce other resources that can then be utilized to expand future output. For example, if a nation is willing to use more of its resources to produce machines and buildings, upgrade the quality of land, and discover more natural resources, such investments will expand the future supply of nonhuman resources. In turn, the larger stock of nonhuman capital will help the nation expand its future output.

Investment can sometimes expand output by means other than direct production of a good. For example, Robinson Crusoe found he could catch more fish by taking some time off from hand-fishing to build a net. Even though his initial investment in the net reduced his current catch, once the net was completed, he was able to more than make up for his earlier loss of output.

It is important to remember that investment is costly; it involves the current sacrifice of consumer goods that might otherwise have been produced if less investment had been undertaken. Therefore, investment projects will increase the wealth of a nation only when the benefits of the larger future output are more valuable than the reduction in current output as the result of the investment.

**human resources** The abilities, skills, and health of human beings that can contribute to the production of both current and future output. Investment in training and education can increase the supply of human resources.

**investment in human capital** Expenditures on training, education, and skill development designed to increase the productivity of an individual.

**Human resources** are comprised of the skills and knowledge of workers. Laypersons sometimes act as if these resources are strictly the result of inheritance or happenstance. This is not the case. Investment in such things as education, training, health, and skill-building experience can increase worker productivity and thereby the availability of human resources. Economists refer to such activities as **investment in human capital.**

Decisions to invest in human capital involve all the basic ingredients of other investment decisions. Consider the decision of whether to go to college. For most people, it is partly an investment decision. As many of you are acutely aware, investment in a college education requires the sacrifice of current earnings as well as payment for direct expenses such as tuition and books. The investment is expected to lead to a better job, considering both monetary and nonmonetary factors, and other benefits associated with a college education. The rational investor will weigh the current costs against the expected future benefits. College will be chosen only if the latter are greater than the former.

Human resources differ from nonhuman resources in two important respects. First, human capital is embodied in the individual. Choices concerning the use of human resources are vitally affected by working conditions, location, job prestige, and similar nonmonetary factors. Although monetary factors influence human capital decisions, individuals have some leeway in trading off money income for better working conditions. Second, human resources cannot be bought and sold in nonslave societies. However, the *services* of human resources are bought and sold daily. Individuals have the right to quit, to sell their labor services to another employer, or to use them in an alternative manner in a nonslave society.

In competitive markets, the prices of resources, like the prices of products, are determined by supply and demand. Let us now turn to an analysis of how market forces determine the prices of both human and nonhuman resources.

## DEMAND FOR RESOURCES

**derived demand** Demand for an item based on the demand for products the item helps to produce. Thus, the demand for resources is a derived demand.

The demand for a resource is a **derived demand,** meaning it exists because there is a demand for a consumer good that the resource can help to produce. For example, the demand for the services of a carpenter is derived from demand of consumers for houses, cabinets, and other goods that carpenters help produce. Similarly, the demands for the services of cooks, waitresses, and waiters are derived from the demand of consumers for food at restaurants and other eating establishments.

## Downward-Sloping Demand Curve

There are two major reasons why the quantity demanded of a resource will decline as its price increases (relative to other prices). In other words, there are two reasons for the downward slope of the demand curve. First, there is the *substitution-in-production effect.* When the price of a resource goes up, cost-conscious firms will turn to lower-cost substitutes and cut back on their use of the more expensive resource. Thus, the presence of substitute resources ensures an inverse relationship between the price of a resource and the quantity demanded. For example, if the price of copper tubing increases, construction firms and plumbers will substitute plastic PVC pipe for the more expensive tubing. Similarly, if the price of bricks increases, builders will substitute wood, concrete blocks, aluminum, and other siding materials for the more expensive bricks. Of course, the degree to which firms will be able to reduce their use of a more expensive resource will vary. If good substitutes in production are available, making it relatively easy to conserve on the use of a more expensive resource, then this substitution effect ensures that not only will the quantity demanded be inversely related to price, but also the demand for the resource will be highly elastic.

The second reason for the downward slope of the demand curve is that when the price of a resource increases, both the per unit production cost and price of the finished product will rise. In turn, the higher product price will cause consumers to purchase less of the product and producers to demand fewer resources, including less of the resource that rose in price. Economists refer to this as the *substitution-in-consumption effect.* The relationship between the price of steel and the consumption of automobiles illustrates it well: An increase in the price of steel will make it more expensive to produce automobiles. As steel prices push up both the production cost and prices of autos, consumers will reduce their automobile purchases. This, in turn, will reduce the quantity of steel demanded by the automobile manufacturers.

Other things constant, the more elastic the demand for the product, the more elastic the demand for the resource. This relationship stems from the derived nature of resource demand. An increase in the price of a product for which the demand is highly elastic will cause a sharp reduction in the sales of the good. There will accordingly be a relatively sharp decline in the demand for the resources used to produce the good.

## Time and the Demand for Resources

It will take time for producers to adjust fully to a change in the price of a resource. Typically, a producer will be unable to alter a production process or the design of a product immediately to conserve on the use of a more expensive input or to use more efficiently an input whose price has declined. Similarly, consumers may be unable to alter their consumption patterns immediately in response to price changes. Thus, the short-run demand for resources is typically less elastic than the demand in the long run.

Using steel as an example, Exhibit 9.2 illustrates the relationship between time and the change in the quantity demanded of a resource. Initially, higher steel prices may lead to only a small reduction in usage. If the high price of

**EXHIBIT 9.2**

**Time and the Demand Elasticity of Resources**

An increase in the price of steel will lead to a much larger reduction in amount demanded in the long run than in the short run. That is, the demand for resources will be more inelastic in the short run.

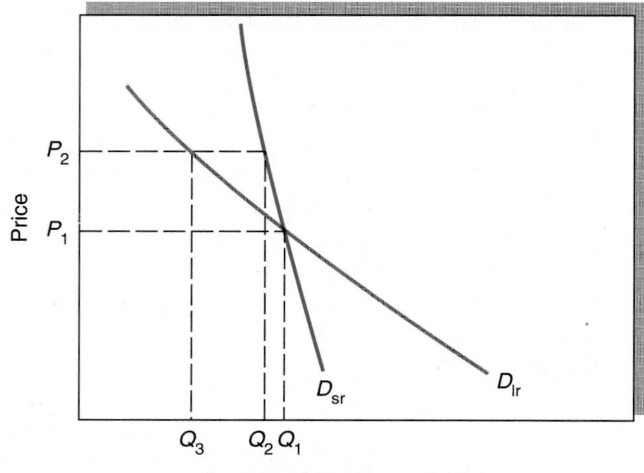


steel persists, however, automobile manufacturers will alter their designs, moving toward lighter-weight cars that require less steel. Architectural firms will design buildings that permit more substitution of plastics, wood, aluminum, glass, and other resources for steel. Products made with steel will increase in price, which will encourage consumers to find more and more ways to cut back on their use. These and numerous similar adjustments will help conserve on the use of the more expensive steel. It will take time, however, for decision-makers to carry out many of these adjustments. Therefore, the demand for steel, like that for most other resources, will be more inelastic in the short run ($D_{sr}$) than in the long run ($D_{lr}$).

## Strength of Demand for a Resource

The intensity of demand for any resource is directly related to (1) the price of the consumer good the resource is helping to produce and (2) the productivity of the resource (how much output increases as the result of employing the resource). An increase in the demand for and price of a product that a resource helps to produce will increase the value of the resource to employers. Therefore, when the demand for a consumer good increases, the demand for the resources required to produce the good will also increase (the demand curve will shift to the right).

**marginal product** The change in total output that results from the employment of one additional unit of a factor of production—one workday of skilled labor, for example.

An increase in the productivity of a resource will increase its value to employers as well. Several factors combine to determine the productivity of a resource. First, the **marginal product** of any resource will depend on the amount of other resources with which it is working. For example, additional capital will generally increase the productivity of labor. Thus, someone with a lawn mower can mow more grass than the same person with a pair of shears. A student working with a textbook, class notes, and tutor can learn more economics than the same student without these tools. The quantity and quality of the tools (resources) with which we work significantly affects our productivity.

Second, technological advances can improve the productivity of resources, including labor. Advances in the computer industry illustrate this point. Working with computer technology, an accountant and a data-entry person can maintain business records and create bookkeeping reports that previously would have required 10 to 15 workers. Improvements in word processing equipment have vastly increased the productivity of typists, journalists, lawyers, and writers. Similarly, computers have substantially increased the productivity of typesetters, telephone operators, quality-control technicians, and workers in many other occupations.

Third, improvements in the quality (skill level) of a resource will increase productivity and therefore the demand for the resource. As workers obtain valuable new knowledge and/or upgrade their skills, they enhance their productivity. In essence, such workers move into a different skill category, where demand is greater.

A profit-maximizing firm will demand (employ) a resource only if the employment adds more to the firm's revenues than to its costs. The additions to the firm's revenues will be directly related to the marginal product of the resource and the price of the consumer good the resource helps to produce. Consequently, there will be a strong demand for a resource that contributes substantially—that is, its marginal product is high—to the production of a good that is highly valued by consumers. In contrast, the demand will be weak for resources that are relatively unproductive—that is, those that fail to add much to the output of goods that consumers value highly.

## SUPPLY OF RESOURCES

Employers will hire a resource only if they can gain from doing so. Resource suppliers will apply the same basic principle. They will supply their services to an employer only if they perceive that the benefits of doing so exceed their costs (other things they could do with their time or resources). Thus, in order to attract factors of production, employers must offer resource owners at least as good a deal as they can get elsewhere. For example, if an employer does not offer a potential employee a package of income payments and working conditions that is as good or better than the employee can get elsewhere, the employer will be unable to attract the employee. Resource owners will supply their services to those who offer them the best deal, all factors considered.

Other things constant, an increase in the price of a specific resource (for example, steel or craft labor) will cause the owner to supply more of the resource. In contrast, some resource suppliers will shift into other activities when the price of a resource falls. Thus, the supply curve for a specific resource will slope upward to the right.

As in the case of demand, the supply response in resource markets may vary between the short run and long run. There is insufficient time in the short run to alter the availability of a resource through investment in human and physical capital.

When a resource can be easily and quickly transferred to other resource supply categories, its supply curve will be more elastic. For example, agricultural land can usually be used to produce a variety of products. Therefore, if higher wheat prices pushed up the value of land to grow wheat, many landowners could easily use more of their land to produce wheat rather than corn or oats. Thus, the supply of wheat acreage is fairly elastic. Similarly, building space can usually be quickly converted from one use to another. Trucks can typically be modified rather easily to haul one product rather than another. In these instances, the supply response to an increase in resource price will be substantial.

In many cases, however, it will be necessary to undertake investments in order to increase the supply of a resource significantly. Sometimes investment can increase the availability of a resource fairly quickly. For example, it does not take very long to train additional over-the-road truck drivers. Thus, in the absence of barriers to entry, the quantity of truck drivers supplied will expand rapidly in response to higher wages. However, the gestation period between expansion in investment and an increase in quantity supplied is substantially longer for some resources. It takes a long time to train physicians, dentists, lawyers, and pharmacists. Higher earnings in these occupations may have only a small impact on their current availability. Similarly, it will take a substantial amount of time to build a new steel mill or automobile manufacturing plant. Thus, the supply of these resources will be quite inelastic in the short run.

When it takes a substantial period of time to expand the availability of a resource through investment, the supply of the resource will be much more elastic in the long run than in the short run. Using engineering services as an example, Exhibit 9.3 shows that an increase in the price of engineering services (the wage rate of engineers) will result in some immediate increase in quantity supplied. Persons currently employed as engineers may choose to work more hours. In addition, the higher wage may induce workers with engineering skills currently employed in mathematics, physics, or similar fields to switch to engineering. While these adjustments are important, they may fail to substantially increase the quantity supplied in the short run. With time, however, the more attractive earning opportunities in engineering will raise the level of investment in human capital in this area. More students will enter engineering programs. Since it takes time to acquire an engineering degree, several years may pass before the additional newly acquired engineering degrees exert a major impact on supply. Nevertheless, the expanded human capital investments will eventually exert important effects. Thus, in the long run, the quantity of engineering services may be quite elastic, even though supply is highly inelastic in the short run.

## SUPPLY, DEMAND, AND RESOURCE PRICES

The theories of supply and demand for resources are all we need to develop the theory of resource pricing in competitive markets. When factor prices are free to vary, resource prices will bring the choices of buyers and sellers into line with each other. Continuing with our example of engineers, Exhibit 9.4 illustrates how the forces of supply and demand push the market price toward equilibrium, where quantity demanded and quantity supplied are equal. Equilibrium is achieved when the price (wage) of engineering services is $P_1$.

**EXHIBIT 9.3**

**Time and the Elasticity of Supply for Resources**

The supply of engineering services (and other resources that require a substantial period of time between current investment and expansion in the future quantity supplied) will be far more inelastic in the short run than in the long run.

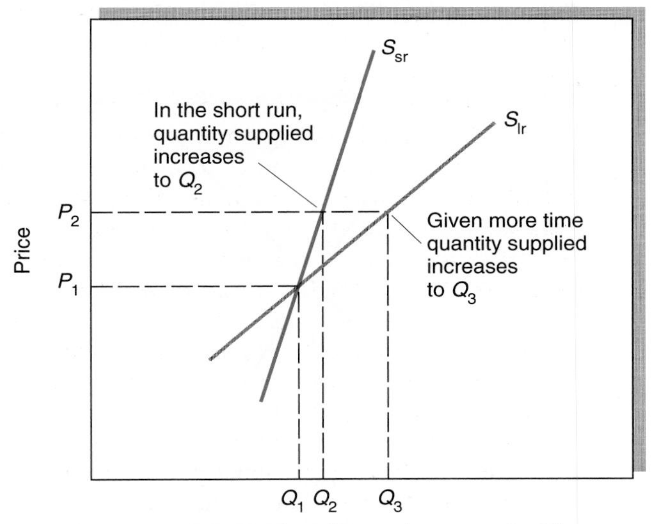


Given the market conditions illustrated by the exhibit, excess supply is present if the price of engineering services exceeds $P_1$. Some resource owners are unable to sell their services at the above-equilibrium price. Responding to this situation, they will cut their price (wage) and thereby push the market toward equilibrium. In contrast, if the resource price is less than $P_1$, excess demand is present. Employers are unable to obtain the desired amount of engineering services at a below-equilibrium resource price. Rather than doing without the resource, employers will bid the price up to $P_1$ and thereby eliminate the excess demand.

How will a resource market adjust to an unexpected change in market conditions? As is true for product markets, adjustments to changes do not take place instantaneously in resource markets. Our analysis of short-run and long-run responses makes the nature of the adjustment process clear. Suppose there is an unanticipated increase in demand for a resource. As Exhibit 9.5 illustrates, an increase in market demand (from $D_1$ to $D_2$) initially leads to a sharp rise in the price of the resource (from $P_1$ to $P_2$), particularly if the short-run supply is quite inelastic. However, at the higher price, the quantity of the resource supplied will expand with time. If it is a natural resource, individuals and firms will put forth a greater effort to discover and develop the now more valuable productive factor. If it is physical capital (for example a building or machine), current suppliers will have greater incentive to work intensively to expand production. New suppliers will be drawn into the market. Higher

EXHIBIT 9.4

**Equilibrium in Resource Market**

The market demand for a resource, such as engineering services, is a downward-sloping curve reflecting the declining marginal product of the resource. The market supply slopes upward, since higher resource prices (wage rates) will induce individuals to supply more of the resource. Resource price $P_1$ brings the choices of buyers and sellers into harmony. At the equilibrium price ($P_1$), the quantity demanded will just equal the quantity supplied.

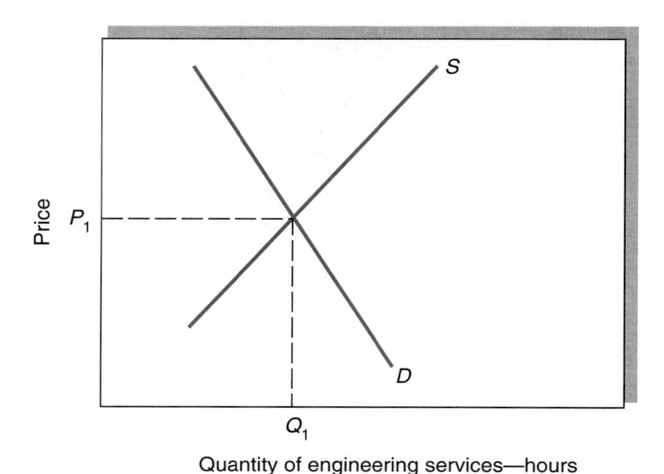


prices for human capital resources will also lead to an expansion in the quantity supplied. With time, more people will acquire the training, education, and experience necessary to supply the service that now commands a higher price. The expansion of the supply will eventually moderate the price rise. Because of these forces, as the exhibit illustrates, the long-run price increase will be less than the short-run increase.

The market adjustment to an unexpected reduction in demand for a resource is symmetrical. A reduction in demand will cause the price of the resource to fall further in the short run than over a longer period of time. At the lower price, some resource suppliers will use their talents in other areas. The incentive for potential new suppliers to offer the resource will be reduced by the fall in price. With time, the quantity of the resource supplied will decline, making the long-run decline in price more moderate. Those with the poorest alternatives (that is, the lowest opportunity cost) will continue to provide the resource at the lower prices. Those with better alternatives will move to other areas.

## WHY EARNINGS DIFFER

The major source of income for most people is earnings derived from labor services. These earnings differ substantially. A lawyer or doctor may earn 10

**EXHIBIT 9.5**

**Adjusting to Dynamic Change**

An increase in demand for a resource will typically cause price to rise more in the short run than in the long run. Can you explain why?

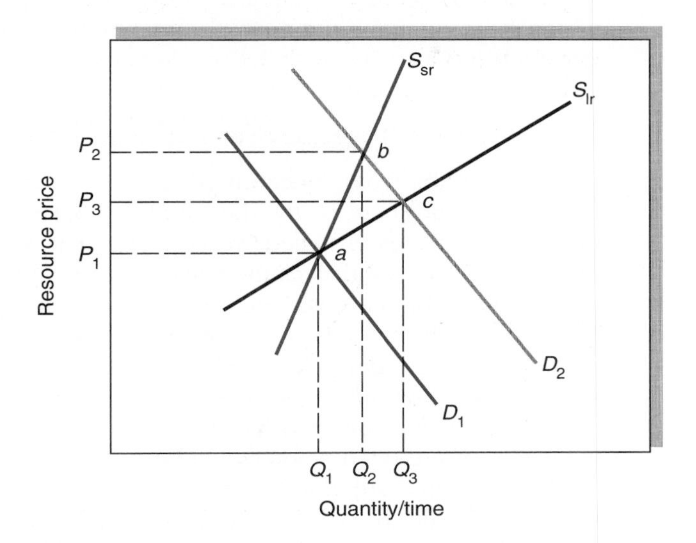


times as much as a carpenter and 20 times as much as an unskilled worker. What factors account for such large differentials in earnings among workers?

Let us begin our analysis of this topic with a thought experiment. Suppose that (1) all individuals are exactly the same (they have the same skill level and preferences), (2) all jobs are equally attractive, and (3) workers can easily shift from one job to another. If these three conditions were present, the earnings of all employees in a competitive economy would be equal. If, given these conditions, higher wages existed in any area of the economy, the supply of workers to that area would expand until the wage differential was eliminated. Similarly, low wages in any area would cause workers to exit until wages in that area returned to parity. Obviously, however, these three conditions are not present in the real world, and in that fact lies the explanation for why earnings among individuals vary.

## Differences in Workers

**WORKER PRODUCTIVITY AND SPECIALIZED SKILLS** The demand for employees who are highly productive—those with a higher marginal product—will be greater than the demand for those who are less productive. Persons who can operate a machine more skillfully, hit a baseball more consistently, or sell life insurance policies with greater regularity will have a higher marginal product than their less skillful counterparts. Because they are more productive, their services will command a higher wage from employers.

Worker productivity is the result of a combination of factors, including native ability, parental training, hard work, and investment in human capital. The link between higher productivity and higher earnings provides individuals with the incentive to invest in themselves and thereby upgrade their knowledge and skills. If additional worker productivity did not lead to higher earnings, individuals would have little incentive to incur the direct and indirect cost of productivity-enhancing educational and training programs.

Exhibit 9.6 illustrates the impact of worker productivity and the cost of investment in human capital on the wages of skilled and unskilled workers. Since the productivity of skilled workers exceeds the productivity of unskilled workers, the demand for skilled workers ($D_s$) exceeds the demand for unskilled workers ($D_u$). The vertical distance between the two demand curves reflects the higher marginal product of skilled workers relative to the unskilled workers (Exhibit 9.6a). Since investments in human capital (for example, education or training) are costly, the supply of skilled workers ($S_s$) will be smaller than the supply of unskilled workers ($S_u$). The vertical distance between the two supply curves indicates the wage differential that is necessary to compensate workers for the costs incurred in the acquisition of their skills (Exhibit 9.6b). As Exhibit 9.6c illustrates, wages are determined by demand *relative* to supply. Since the demand for skilled workers is large, while their supply is small, the equilibrium wage of skilled workers will be high ($20 per hour). In contrast, since the supply of unskilled workers is large relative to the demand, the wages of unskilled workers will be substantially lower ($5 per hour).

Some people are able to command high earnings because they have developed specialized skills that are possessed by few other people. If their skills are highly valued by consumers, and if the skills of others are not considered a good substitute, these people are able to earn exceedingly high salaries. Star

**EXHIBIT 9.6**

**The Demand, Supply, and Wage Rates of Skilled and Unskilled Workers**

The productivity (and therefore MP) of skilled workers is greater than that of unskilled workers. Therefore, as frame a illustrates, the demand for skilled workers ($D_s$) will exceed the demand for unskilled workers ($D_u$). Education and training generally enhance skills. Since upgrading skills through investments in human capital is costly, the supply of skilled workers ($S_s$) is smaller than the supply of unskilled workers (frame b). As frame c illustrates, the wages of skilled workers are high relative to those of unskilled workers because of the strong demand and small supply of skilled workers relative to unskilled workers.

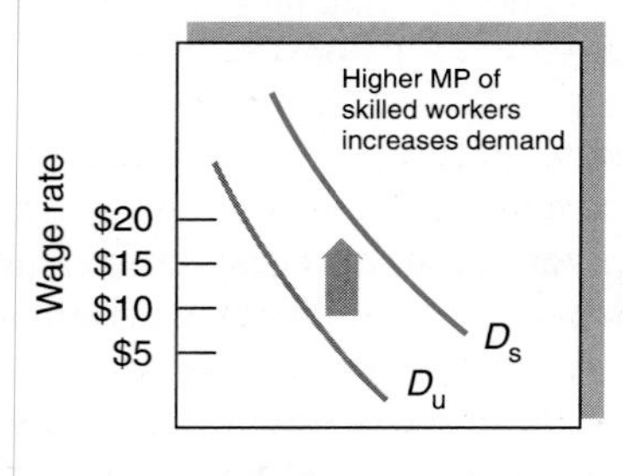


(a) Demand for skilled and unskilled labor

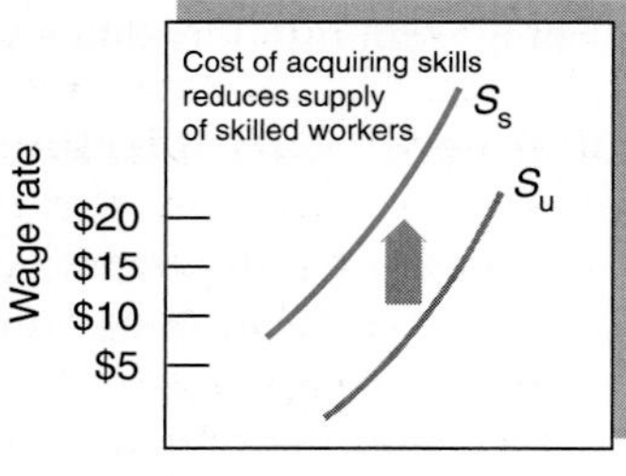


(b) Supply of skilled and unskilled labor

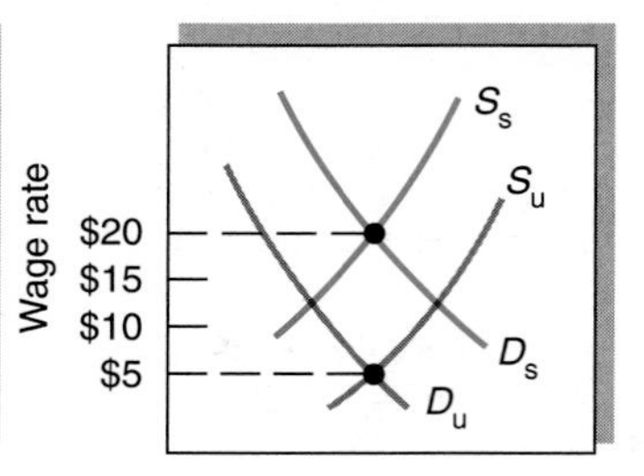


(c) Wages of skilled and unskilled labor

athletes like Michael Jordan and entertainers like Bill Cosby are examples. Similarly, the specialized skills of heart surgeons, trial lawyers, engineers, and successful business entrepreneurs are able to command a high wage because their supply is small relative to the demand.

Other things constant, a skilled specialist will always command a higher wage than one with less skill. High skill, however, will not guarantee a high wage. For example, expert harness makers and blacksmiths typically command low wages today, no matter how highly skilled they are—because demand is low even for the services of experts in these areas.

**WORKER PREFERENCES** Worker preferences are a very important source of earnings differentials that are sometimes overlooked. People have different objectives in life. Some want to make a great deal of money. Many are willing to work long hours, undergo agonizing training and many years of education, and sacrifice social and family life to make money. Others may be "workaholics" because they enjoy their jobs. Still others may be satisfied with just enough money to get by, preferring to spend more time with their family, the Boy Scouts, television, or the local tavern keeper.

Economics does not indicate that one set of worker preferences is more desirable than another, any more than it suggests that people should eat more spinach and less pastrami. Economics does indicate, however, that these factors contribute to differences in wages and earnings. Other things constant, persons who are more highly motivated by monetary objectives will be more likely to do the things necessary to command higher wage rates.

**employment discrimination** Unequal treatment of persons on the basis of their race, gender, or religion, which restricts their employment and earnings opportunities compared to others of similar productivity. Employment discrimination may stem from the prejudices of employers, consumers, or fellow employees.

**WORKERS' RACE AND GENDER DIFFERENCES** **Employment discrimination** on the basis of race or gender contributes to earnings differences among individuals. Such discrimination may directly limit the earnings opportunities of minorities and women by treating them in a manner different from similarly productive whites or men. Nonemployment discrimination may also be a factor in earnings differentials, limiting the opportunities of minority groups and women to acquire human capital (for example, quality education or specialized training) that would enhance both their productivity and earnings.

## Differences in Jobs

**nonpecuniary job characteristics** Working conditions, prestige, variety, location, employee freedom and responsibilities, and other nonwage characteristics of a job that influence how employees evaluate the job.

**compensating wage differentials** Wage differences that compensate workers for risk, unpleasant working conditions, and other undesirable nonpecuniary aspects of a job.

When individuals evaluate employment alternatives, they consider working conditions as well as wage rates. Is a job dangerous? Does it offer the opportunity to acquire the experience and training that will enhance future earnings? Is the work strenuous and nerve-racking? Are the working hours, job location, and means of transportation convenient? These factors are what economists call **nonpecuniary job characteristics.** People will accept jobs with unpleasant working conditions if the wages are high enough (compared to jobs with better working conditions for which the workers are qualified) to compensate for the undesirable nonpecuniary job characteristics. Since the higher wages, in essence, compensate workers for the unpleasant nonpecuniary attributes of a job, economists refer to wage differences stemming from this source as **compensating wage differentials.** There are numerous examples of compensating wage differences. Because of the dangers involved, aerial window washers (those who hang from windows 20 stories up) earn higher wages than other window washers. Sales jobs involving a great deal of out-of-town travel typically pay more than similar jobs without such inconvenience. Coal miners and sewer workers accept these physically demanding jobs because they generally pay more than the alternatives available to low-skill workers. Compensating factors even influence the earnings of economists. When economists work for colleges or universities, they generally enjoy a more independent work environment and stimulating intellectual climate than when they are employed in the business sector. Unsurprisingly, the earnings of economists in academia are typically lower than those of economists in business.

### Immobility of Labor

It is costly to move to a new location or train for a new occupation in order to obtain a job. Such movements do not take place instantaneously. In the real world, labor, like other resources, does not possess perfect mobility. Some wage differentials thus result from an incomplete adjustment to change.

Since the demand for labor resources is a derived demand, it is affected by changes in product markets. An expansion in the demand for a product causes a rise in the demand for specialized labor to produce the product. Since resources are often highly immobile (that is, the supply is inelastic) in the short run, the expansion in demand may cause the wages of the specialized laborers to rise sharply. This is what happened in the oil-drilling industry in the late 1970s. An expansion in demand triggered a rapid increase in the earnings of petroleum engineers, oil rig operators, and other specialized personnel. Falling oil prices triggered the opposite effect in the mid-1980s. The demand and employment opportunities of specialized resources declined substantially as output in the oil industry fell during 1985–1986. Demand shifts in the product market favor those in expanding industries but work against those in contracting industries.

Institutional barriers may also limit the movement of labor. Licensing requirements limit the mobility of labor into many occupations—medicine, taxicab driving, architecture, and mortuary science among them. Unions may also follow policies that limit labor mobility and alter the free-market forces of supply and demand. These restrictions on labor mobility will influence the size of wage differentials among workers.

### Summary of Wage Differentials

As the "Thumbnail Sketch" shows, some wage differentials play an important allocative role, compensating people for (1) human capital investments that increase their productivity or (2) unfavorable working conditions. Other wage differentials reflect, at least partially, locational preferences or the desires of individuals for higher money income rather than nonmonetary benefits. Still other differentials, such as those related to discrimination and occupational restrictions, are unrelated to worker preferences and are not required to promote efficient production.

## PRODUCTIVITY AND EARNINGS

Productivity and earnings are closely linked. Production provides the source of earnings. Workers who produce more will tend to earn more. In fact, differences in labor productivity—the value of the output produced per worker—

## THUMBNAIL SKETCH

### Sources of Earnings Differentials

**Differences in workers:**

1. Productivity and specialized skills (reflect native ability, parental training, and investment in human capital).
2. Worker preferences (tradeoff between money earnings and other things).
3. Race and gender discrimination.

**Differences in jobs:**

1. Location of job.
2. Working conditions (for example, job safety, likelihood of temporary layoffs, comfort of work environment, and opportunity for training).

**Immobility of resources:**

1. Temporary disequilibrium resulting from dynamic change.
2. Institutional restrictions (for example, occupational licensing and union-imposed restraints).

are the major source of variations in real earnings per capita between nations and between time periods.

Real earnings are vastly greater in the United States than they are in India or China, because the output per worker is much greater here, approximately 20 times greater. As a result, the average U.S. worker also earns approximately 20 times as much as the average worker in India or China. If U.S. workers did not produce more, they would not be able to earn more. They are able to produce more because they are better educated, work with more productive machines, and benefit from more efficient economic organization than the average person in such countries as India or China.

Not surprisingly, growth of productivity and growth of real earnings are also closely linked. The growth of earnings is dependent upon the growth of real output. The average earnings per worker in the United States approximately doubled between 1950 and 1990. Growth of productivity provided the source for this earnings growth. The output of goods and services per worker in 1990 was approximately twice the output of the average U.S. worker in 1950.

**automation** A production technique that reduces the amount of labor required to produce a good or service. It is beneficial to adopt the new labor-saving technology only if it reduces the cost of production.

As we have previously stressed, the productivity of workers is influenced not only by their investments in skill development, but also by the equipment with which they work. Some believe that **automation**—the use of machines and improvements in technology—adversely affects workers (see the "Myths of Economics" box). In fact, just the opposite is true. Better machinery and technology make it possible for workers both to produce more and earn more. For example, a farmer can produce far more with a modern tractor and related equipment than he could produce with a horse and plow or even the agricultural equipment of two or three decades ago. Similarly, an accountant can prepare far more tax returns and accounting statements with a microcomputer than with a pencil, paper, and calculator. Machines help us produce more and, by doing so, they help us earn more.

## MYTHS OF ECONOMICS

*"Automation is the major cause of unemployment. If we keep allowing machines to replace people, we are going to run out of jobs."*

Machines are substituted for people if, and only if, the machines reduce costs of production. Why has the automatic elevator replaced the operator, the tractor replaced the horse, and the power shovel replaced the ditch digger? Because each is a cheaper method of accomplishing a task.

The fallacy that automation causes unemployment stems from a failure to recognize the secondary effects. Employment may decline in a specific industry as the result of automation. However, lower per unit costs in that industry will lead to either (1) additional spending and jobs in other industries or (2) additional output and employment in the specific industry as consumers buy more of the now cheaper good.

Perhaps an example will help illustrate the secondary effects of automation. Consider the impact of economical word processing equipment. The output of typists on computers is often three or four times higher than on typewriters. Their employment has declined—this is the visible effect. But there has also been a less visible secondary effect on the composition of employment. An improvement in word processing has reduced the prices of numerous goods and services, allowing people to spend more of their income on other things. This additional spending on other goods has generated additional demand and employment in these areas.

If the demand is elastic for the products that can be produced more cheaply and supplied at a lower price, a cost-saving invention can even generate an increase in employment *in the industry affected by the invention.* This was essentially what happened in the automobile industry when Henry Ford's mass production techniques reduced the cost (and price) of cars. When the price of automobiles fell 50 percent, consumers bought three times as many cars. Even though the worker-hours per car decreased by 25 percent between 1920 and 1930, employment in the industry increased from 250,000 to 380,000 during the period, an increase of approximately 50 percent.

Of course, technological advances that release labor resources may well harm specific individuals or groups. Home appliances such as automatic washers and dryers, dishwashers, and microwave ovens reduced the job opportunities of maids. Computer technology has also reduced the demand for telephone operators and bookkeepers. In the future, videotaped lectures may even reduce the job opportunities available to college professors. Thus, the earnings opportunities of specific persons may, at least temporarily, be adversely affected by cost-reducing automated methods. It is understandable why groups directly affected fear and oppose automation.

Focusing on jobs alone, though, can lead to a fundamental misunderstanding about the importance of machines, automation, and technological improvements. The real impact of cost-reducing machines and technological improvements is an increase in production. Technological advances make it possible for us to produce as much with fewer resources, thereby releasing valuable resources so that production (and consumption) can be expanded in other areas. Other tasks can be accomplished with the newly available resources.

Since there is a direct link between improved technology and productivity per worker, automation exerts a positive influence on economic welfare from the viewpoint of society as a whole. In aggregate, running out of jobs is not a problem. Jobs represent obstacles, tasks that must be accomplished if we desire to loosen the bonds of scarcity. As long as our ability to produce goods and services falls short of our consumption desires, there will be jobs. A society running out of jobs would be in an enviable position: it would be nearing the impossible goal—victory over scarcity.

Without high productivity per worker, there can be no high wages per worker. Similarly, without growth in the production of goods and services valued by consumers, there can be no growth in the real income of a nation. Production provides the source of income.

## ECONOMICS OF MINIMUM WAGE

**minimum-wage legislation** Legislation requiring that all workers in specified industries be paid at least the stated minimum hourly rate of pay.

Several countries have **minimum-wage legislation** that establishes a price floor, forcing employers to pay their workers at least a minimum wage. As of 1993, the minimum wage in the U.S. was $4.25. The minimum wage is intended to help low-skill workers. There is good reason to question, however, whether it actually does so.

Economic theory indicates that the quantity demanded of labor, particularly a specific skill category of labor, will be inversely related to its wage rate. If a higher minimum wage increases the wage rates of unskilled workers above the level that would be established by market forces, the quantity of unskilled workers employed will fall. The minimum wage will price the services of the least productive (and therefore lowest-wage) workers out of the market.

Exhibit 9.7 provides a graphic illustration of the direct effect of a $4.25 minimum wage on the employment opportunities of a group of low-skill

**EXHIBIT 9.7**

**Employment and Minimum Wage**

If the market wage of a group of employees were $3.50 per hour, a $4.25-per-hour minimum wage would increase the earnings of persons who were able to maintain employment and reduce the employment of others ($E_0$ to $E_1$), pushing them onto the unemployment rolls or into less-preferred jobs.

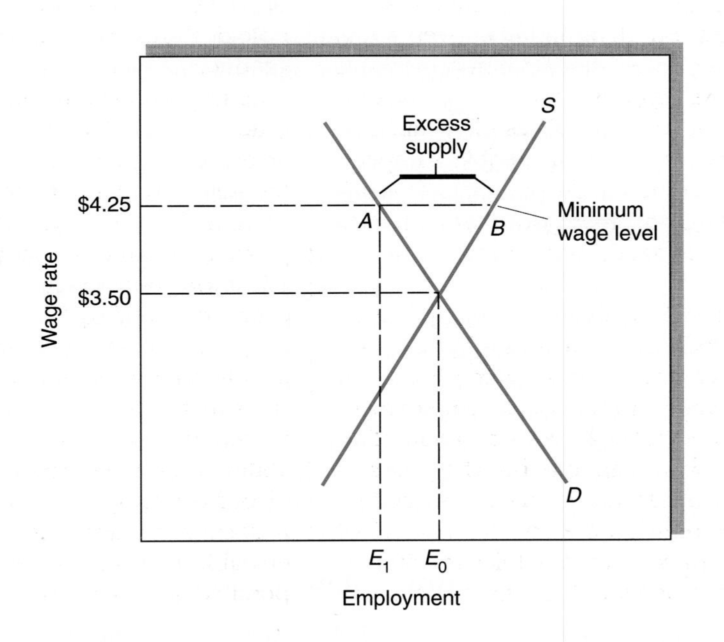

workers. Without a minimum wage, the supply of and demand for these low-skill workers would be in balance at a wage rate of $3.50. The $4.25 minimum wage makes the low-skill labor service more expensive. Employers will substitute machines and high-skill workers (whose wages have not been raised by the minimum) for the now more expensive low-productivity employees. Jobs in which low-skill employees are unable to produce enough to cover their employment costs will be eliminated. As a result, the employment level of low-skill workers will decline.

Of course, some low-skill workers will be able to maintain their jobs, but others will be driven into sectors not covered by the legislation (self-employment, for example) or onto the unemployment and welfare rolls. Workers who retain their jobs will gain. The most adverse effects will fall on those workers who are already most disadvantaged—those whose market earnings are lowest relative to the minimum wage—because it will be so costly to bring their wages up to the minimum.

The direct results of minimum-wage legislation are clearly mixed. Some workers, most likely the better qualified among those whose previous wages were near the minimum, will enjoy higher wages. Others, particularly those with the lowest prelegislation wage rates and skill levels, will be unable to find work. They will be pushed into the ranks of the unemployed or out of the labor force.

## Indirect Effects of Minimum Wage

When analyzing the effects of the minimum wage, the secondary effects must not be ignored. The money wage is only one dimension of an employment transaction. The imposition of the minimum wage will almost certainly lead to changes in other aspects of labor/service exchanges involving low-skill workers. When a minimum rate pushes wages of low-skill workers above the market level, employers will have no trouble hiring workers. Therefore, they have little incentive to offer workers training, convenient working hours, continuous employment, fringe benefits, and other nonwage components of the total compensation package. Predictably, the training opportunities and working conditions available to low-skill workers will be adversely affected by the minimum wage.

Of the nonwage elements adversely affected by minimum wage legislation, the decline in training opportunities is particularly important. Many inexperienced workers face a dilemma: they cannot find a job without experience (or skills), but they cannot obtain experience without a job. This is particularly true for younger workers. Employment experience obtained at an early age, even on seemingly menial tasks, can help one acquire work habits (for example, promptness and self-confidence), skills, and attitudes that will enhance one's value to employers in the future. Since minimum-wage legislation prohibits the payment of even a temporarily low wage, it substantially limits the employer's ability to offer employment to inexperienced workers. In effect, the minimum wage acts as an institutional barrier limiting the on-the-job training opportunities available to low-skill workers.

## Are Minimum-Wage Workers Poor?

Perhaps surprising to some, more than half of the minimum-wage workers in the United States are members of a family with an income *above* the median.

Most (two-thirds) minimum-wage employees work only part time. Approximately 40 percent are teenagers. In recent years, less than 10 percent of the workers earning the minimum wage were heads of households with an income below the poverty level. The typical minimum-wage worker is a spouse or a teenage member of a household with an income well above the poverty level. Therefore, even if the adverse impact of a higher minimum wage on both employment and nonwage forms of compensation is ignored, a higher minimum wage would exert little positive impact on the economic status of the poor.

## LOOKING AHEAD

As this chapter suggests, the growth of income of both individuals and nations is influenced by investment. The following chapter analyzes the investment choices of individuals and considers how differences in public policy affect these choices, and thereby the wealth of nations.

## CHAPTER SUMMARY

1. Resource markets coordinate the actions of business firms that demand productive resources and households that supply them. There are two broad classes of productive resources––nonhuman capital and human capital. Both are durable in the sense that they will last into the future, thereby enhancing future productive capabilities. Both yield income to their owners. Investment can expand the future supply of both.
2. The demand for resources is derived from demand for products that the resources help to produce. The quantity of a resource demanded is inversely related to its price. There are two reasons why less of a resource will be used if its price increases. First, producers will substitute other resources for the now more expensive input (substitution in production). Second, the higher resource price will lead to higher prices for products that the resource helps to make, inducing consumers to reduce their purchases of those goods (substitution in consumption).
3. The short-run market demand curve will be more inelastic than the long-run curve. It will take time for producers to adjust their production process to use more of the resources that are now cheaper and less of the ones that are more expensive.
4. The intensity of the demand for a resource will be directly related to the productivity of the resource and the prices of the goods it helps to produce. The demand will be strong for resources that contribute substantially (the marginal product of the resource is high) to the production of goods that are highly valued by consumers.
5. An increase in the price of a resource will increase the incentive of potential suppliers to provide the resource. Thus, there will be a direct relationship between resource price and the quantity of the resource supplied. In the long run, investment can expand the availability of a resource. Since it takes time to undertake investment, the supply of resources will generally be more elastic in the long run than the short run.

6. In market economies, the prices of resources are determined by supply and demand. The demand for a resource will reflect its productivity and the demand for the goods it helps to produce. The supply of resources will reflect the human and physical capital investment decisions of individuals and firms.
7. Changes in resource prices will influence the decisions of users and suppliers alike. Higher resource prices give users a greater incentive to turn to substitutes and suppliers a greater incentive to provide more of the resource. Since these adjustments take time, when the demand for a resource expands, the price will usually rise more in the short run than in the long run. Similarly, when there is a fall in resource demand, price will generally decline more in the short run than in the long run.
8. There are three major sources of wage differentials among individuals: differences in workers, differences in jobs, and degree of labor mobility. Individual workers differ with respect to productivity (skills, human capital, motivation, native ability, and so on), specialized skills, employment preferences, race, and gender. These factors influence either the demand for or the supply of labor. In addition, differences in nonpecuniary job characteristics, changes in product markets, and institutional restrictions that limit labor mobility contribute to variations in wages among workers.
9. Productivity is the ultimate source of high earnings. Workers in the United States, Canada, Japan, and other industrial countries earn high wages because their output per hour is high as the result of (a) worker knowledge and skills (human capital) and (b) the use of modern machinery (physical capital).
10. Automated methods of production will be adopted only if they reduce costs. Although automation might reduce expenditures and employment in a specific industry, the lower cost of production will increase real income, causing demand in other industries to expand. These secondary effects will cause employment to rise in other industries. Improved technology expands our ability to produce. It is production of goods that people value, not the number of jobs, that determines our economic well-being.
11. Minimum-wage legislation increases the earnings of some low-skill workers, but others are forced to accept inferior employment opportunities, join the ranks of the unemployed, or drop out of the labor force. The training opportunities and working conditions of low-skill workers can also be adversely affected by minimum-wage legislation.

# *Study Guide*

## CHAPTER 9

# DEVELOPING THE ECONOMIC WAY OF THINKING

# CRITICAL-ANALYSIS QUESTIONS

1. "The demand for resources is a derived demand." What is meant by that statement? Why is the employment of a resource inversely related to its price?
2. Suppose that lawn service operators always use one worker with one mower to produce output. The resources are always used in the same proportion; there is no substitutability between labor and capital. Under these circumstances, would a change in wages influence employment? Explain.

*3. "The earnings of engineers, doctors, and lawyers are high because lots of education is necessary to practice in these fields." Evaluate this statement.

4. Other things constant, what impact will a highly elastic demand for a product have on the elasticity of demand for the resources used to produce the product? Explain.
5. What are the major reasons for the differences in earnings among individuals? Why are wages in some occupations higher than in others? How do wage differentials influence the allocation of resources? How important is this function? Explain.

*6. Why are real wages in the United States higher than in other countries? Is the labor force itself responsible for the higher wages of U.S. workers? Explain.

7. If Jones has a skill that is highly valued, she will be able to achieve high market earnings. In contrast, Smith may work just as hard or even harder, and still earn only a low income.
   a. Does hard work necessarily lead to a high income?
   b. Why are the incomes of some workers high and others low?
   c. Do you think the market system of wage determination is fair? Why or why not?
   d. Can you think of a more equitable system? If so, explain why it is more equitable.

*8. People who have invested heavily in human capital (for example, lawyers, doctors, and even college professors) generally have higher wages, but they also generally work more hours than other workers. Can you explain why?

9. What are the major factors that would normally explain earnings differences between (a) a lawyer and a minister, (b) an accountant and an elementary school teacher, (c) a business executive and a social worker, (d) a country lawyer and a Wall Street lawyer, (e) an experienced, skilled craftsperson and a 20-year-old high school dropout, and (f) an upper-story and a ground-floor window washer?

*10. "If individuals had identical abilities and opportunities, earnings would be equal." True or false?

*11. Are productivity gains the major source of higher wages? If so, how does one account for the rising real wages of barbers, who by and large have

*Asterisk denotes critical-analysis questions for which answers are given in Appendix A.

used the same technique for half a century? (Hint: Do not forget opportunity cost and supply.)

*12. Other things being constant, how will the following factors influence hourly earnings?
   a. The employee must work the midnight to 8:00 A.M. shift.
   b. The job involves broken intervals (work 3 hours, off 2 hours, work 3 additional hours, and so on) of employment during the day.
   c. The employer provides low-cost child care services on the premises.
   d. The job is widely viewed as prestigious.
   e. The job requires employees to move often from city to city.
   f. The job requires substantial amounts of out-of-town travel.

*13. "Jobs are the key to economic progress. Unless we create more jobs, our standard of living will fall." True or false? Explain.

*14. Consider two occupations (A and B) that employ persons with the same skill and ability. When employed, workers in the two occupations work the same number of hours *per day*. In occupation A, employment is stable throughout the year, while employment in B is characterized by seasonal layoffs. In which occupation will the *hourly* wage rate be highest? Why? In which occupation will the *annual* wage rate be highest? Why?

## MULTIPLE-CHOICE SELF-TEST

1. An increase in the price of a resource would cause
   a. Producers to substitute other inputs for the resource that increased in price.
   b. Consumers to substitute other products for goods that increase in price as the result of the higher resource price.
   c. Both a and b are true.
   d. Neither a nor b is true.
2. When economists use the term *human capital,* they imply that
   a. People invest time and resources improving their abilities so they can expand their future income.
   b. All productive resources require the use of human ingenuity.
   c. Human beings should be viewed as productive machines rather than citizens with inalienable rights.
   d. Human resources can be bought and sold just as physical assets are.
3. An unexpected increase in the demand for the services of chemists will lead to
   a. An increase in their earnings and an expansion in the future supply of chemists.
   b. A decline in the incentive of college students to study chemistry.
   c. A reduction in the current earnings of chemists, followed by a reduction in the future supply of chemists.
   d. An increase in wages and a decline in the number of chemists employed.
4. If a construction boom leads to an increase in the price of lumber, how will the higher lumber prices influence the wood furniture market? (Lumber is used to produce wood furniture).

a. The demand for wood furniture will decline and furniture prices will fall.
b. There will be a shortage of wood furniture.
c. There will be a surplus of wood furniture.
d. The supply of wood furniture will decline and furniture prices will increase.

5. Wages in the United States are higher than those in India primarily because
   a. The weather is better in the United States.
   b. A larger proportion of the labor force is unionized in the United States.
   c. Less capital per employee is required in the United States.
   d. The human and physical capital of U.S. workers exceeds that of their Indian counterparts.
6. Which of the following best explains why productive workers are able to command high wages in the marketplace?
   a. The bargaining power of labor unions.
   b. The presence of minimum-wage legislation.
   c. Wage and price controls that reflect the political power of labor organizations.
   d. Competition among employers for the services of workers.
7. If positions A and B required identical levels of skill, *other things constant,* which one of the following would be most likely to elevate the hourly wage rate of position A relative to position B?
   a. The workplace of position A is air-conditioned, whereas the workplace of B is in the hot sun.
   b. The employees in position A are paid only if they work; the employees in position B are provided several days of sick leave and paid holidays.
   c. The work environment of position A is safe; employees in position B are required to come in contact with a chemical that is widely viewed as potentially dangerous.
   d. Position A provides steady employment; employees holding position B are often laid off.
8. Which of the following would cause the demand for computer programmers to increase?
   a. A decrease in the productivity of computer programmers.
   b. An increase in the demand for products that computer programmers help to make.
   c. An increase in the wages of computer programmers due to legislative action (that is, the establishment of a price floor for computer programmers).
   d. A reduction in the price of a competitive input that can be substituted for computer programmers.
9. The fallacy that automation causes unemployment and reduces living standards stems from a failure to recognize
   a. That some people would rather collect unemployment compensation than work.
   b. That it takes a lot of labor to build a machine.
   c. The secondary effects—the fact that cost-effective automation releases resources so that production in other areas can be expanded.
   d. The primary effects—the fact that machines do not replace workers, they merely encourage them to work harder in order to keep their current jobs.

10. Which of the following would be the most likely result of an increase in the legal minimum wage?
   a. The job opportunities available to low-skill, inexperienced workers would decline, causing the employment rate of such workers to decline.
   b. The rate of unemployment among low-skill, inexperienced workers would decline.
   c. The demand for low-skill workers would increase, as employers adjusted to the higher minimum wage.
   d. Fewer employment opportunities would become available to high-skill workers, who might be replaced by low-skill workers.

## PROBLEMS

| Quantity Demanded per Month | Price | Quantity Supplied per Month |
|---|---|---|
| 0 | $600 | 6000 |
| 1000 | 500 | 5000 |
| 2000 | 400 | 4000 |
| 3000 | 300 | 3000 |
| 4000 | 200 | 2000 |
| 5000 | 100 | 1000 |
| 6000 | 0 | 0 |

1. The accompanying table is a hypothetical, demand-supply schedule for a standard microcomputer in a competitive industry.
   a. What will be the equilibrium quantity and price in this market?
   b. Suppose that a new labor-saving technology is developed, resulting in an increase of 2,000 in quantity supplied at every price. What will happen to the equilibrium quantity and price of the microcomputers?
   c. The new technology reduces the quantity of labor used *per computer* by 20 percent. What will happen to total employment in the industry? (Original employment was 10,000 workers.)
   d. "If we continue to allow machines to replace workers, we will run out of jobs. Automation is the major cause of unemployment." True or false? Explain.
2. Consider the following hypothetical information about productivity in Canada and Brazil:

**Labor Output per Week**

| | Tons of Steel | Bushels of Wheat | Autos |
|---|---|---|---|
| Canada | 10 | 5000 | 1 |
| Brazil | 5 | 500 | 1/5 |

a. If wages depend on productivity, how high would Canadian wages be, compared to Brazilian wages, if both countries produced
   i. Only steel? ______________________
   ii. Only wheat? ______________________
   iii. Only autos? ______________________
b. Suppose that the actual wage rate per week is $800 in Canada and $160 in Brazil. Assuming that other input costs are the same in both countries for each of these goods, indicate below which country is the low-cost producer of
   i. Steel ______________________
   ii. Wheat ______________________
   iii. Autos ______________________
c. Based on your answers to parts a and b, decide whether the following is true or false: "High-paid Canadian workers can't compete with cheap foreign labor." Explain.

3. The text describes the following determinants of earnings differentials:
   a. Nonhomogeneous labor
      A1: Worker productivity and specialized skills
      A2: Workers' preferences
      A3: Race and gender
   b. Nonhomogeneous jobs
      B1: Location of jobs
      B2: Nonpecuniary job characteristics
   c. Immobility of labor
      C1: Temporary disequilibrium
      C2: Institutional restrictions

   Indicate the main reason from the preceding list for each of the following wage differentials:

   _____ a. Urban wages are higher than rural wages.
   _____ b. Police officers in metropolitan areas with high violent crime rates earn higher wages than police officers elsewhere.
   _____ c. White basketball players receive about 20 percent higher salaries than equally talented black basketball players.
   _____ d. The salaries of elementary and secondary school teachers are generally lower than for other workers with similar amounts of schooling.
   _____ e. College graduates with degrees in engineering generally earn more than graduates with degrees in sociology or history.
   _____ f. Nurses that work special-duty assignments with patients that are critically ill are generally paid higher wage rates than other nurses.

CHAPTER

# 10

# INVESTMENT, CAPITAL FORMATION, AND THE WEALTH OF NATIONS

To produce capital, people must forgo the opportunity to produce goods for current consumption. People can choose whether to spend their time picking apples or planting apple trees. In the first case there are more apples today; in the second, more apples tomorrow.

*Steven Landsburg*[1]

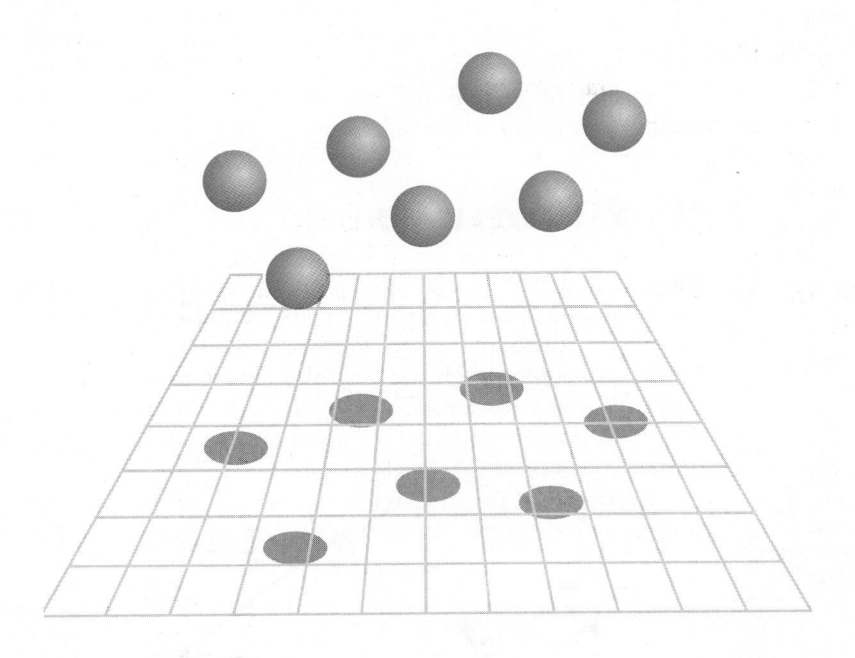

## CHAPTER FOCUS

- Why do people invest? Why are capital resources often used to produce consumer goods?
- Why are investors willing to pay interest to acquire loanable funds? Why are lenders willing to loan funds?
- What is the interest rate? How is the nominal interest rate influenced by the inflation rate and the riskiness of a loan?
- Why is the interest rate so important when evaluating costs and revenues across time periods?
- When is an investment profitable? How do profitable and unprofitable investments influence the wealth of nations?
- How important are investment and the efficient use of capital to the wealth of a nation?

In the previous chapter we noted that the income of both individuals and nations is closely related to their productivity—their ability to supply goods and services that are highly valued by others. In turn, productivity is influenced by investment choices. Consider choices such as whether to construct an office building, purchase a harvesting machine, or go to law school. The returns derived from investments such as these are generally spread over several years (or even decades). In some cases, the costs of investments may also be incurred over a lengthy time period. How can people compare the benefits and costs of an activity when they are spread across lengthy periods of time? What factors determine whether an investment project should be undertaken? How can investment funds be channelled toward projects that will increase the wealth of people and nations? This chapter will address such questions and related issues.

## WHY PEOPLE UNDERTAKE INVESTMENTS

**capital** Resources that enhance our ability to produce output in the future.

**investment** The purchase, construction, or development of capital resources including both nonhuman capital and human capital. Investments increase the supply of capital.

**Capital** is a term used by economists to describe long-lasting resources that are valued because they can help us produce goods and services in the future. As we previously discussed, there are two broad categories of capital: (1) nonhuman resources such as buildings, machines, tools, and natural resources, and (2) human resources, that is, the knowledge and skills of people. In contrast with goods produced for current consumption, capital resources enhance our ability to produce goods for future consumption.

**Investment** is the purchase, construction, or development of a capital resource. For example, when a road construction firm purchases a grader, it is

[1]Steven E. Landsburg, *Price Theory and Applications* (Fort Worth: The Dryden Press, 1992), p. 581.

**saving** Current income that is not spent on consumption goods.

making an investment because it is purchasing a resource that will expand the firm's future output. When economists refer to **saving,** they mean income that is not spent on consumption goods or services.

Investment and saving are closely linked. In fact, the two words describe different aspects of the capital-formation process. Saving applies to the nonconsumption of income, while investment applies to the use of the unconsumed income to produce a capital resource. Sometimes saving and investment are conducted by the same person, as when a farmer saves current income (refrains from spending it on consumption goods) in order to purchase a new tractor (as an investment for producing future output).

It is important to recognize that saving is required for investment. Someone must save—refrain from consumption—in order to provide the resources for investment. When investors finance a project with their own funds, they are also saving (refraining from current consumption). Investors, however, do not always use their own funds to finance investments. Sometimes they will borrow funds from others. When this is the case, it is the lender, rather than the investor that is doing the saving.

The alternative use of resources also highlights the linkage between investment and saving. Resources used to produce capital will be unavailable for the direct production of consumption goods. If we invest more—if we use more of our resources to produce capital resources today, fewer current resources will be available to produce consumption goods. Thus, if we invest more, we will have to reduce our current consumption.

Why would anyone want to delay consumption in order to undertake an investment? Consumption is the ultimate objective of all production. However, we can sometimes magnify our production of consumption goods by first using resources to produce capital resources and then applying these resources to the production of the desired consumer goods. Therefore, the use of capital to produce consumption goods makes sense only when the capital enhances our total production of consumption goods.

Perhaps a simple illustration will help clarify the major considerations involved in the use of capital to produce consumption goods. Suppose that Robinson Crusoe could catch fish by either (a) combining his labor with natural resources (direct production) or (b) constructing a net and eventually combining his labor with this capital resource (indirect production). Let us assume that Crusoe could catch 2 fish per day by hand-fishing, but could catch 3 fish per day if he constructed and used a net that would last for 310 days. Suppose it would take Crusoe 55 days to build the net. The opportunity cost of constructing the net would be 110 fish (2 per day for each of the 55 days Crusoe spent building the net). As the accompanying chart indicates, if Crusoe invested in the capital resource (the net), his output during the next year (including the 55 days required to build the net) would be 930 fish (3 per day for 310 days). Alternatively, hand-fishing during the year would lead to an output of only 730 (2 fish per day for 365 days).

| | Number of Fish Caught | |
|---|---|---|
| | **Without Net** | **With Net** |
| Per Day | 2 | 3 |
| Annual | 730 | 930 |

Crusoe's investment in the net will enhance his productivity. With the net, his total output during the year will increase by 200 fish. In the short term, however, investing in the net will impose a sacrifice. During the 55 days it takes to construct the net, Crusoe's production of consumption goods will decline.

How can Crusoe or any other investor know if the value of the larger future output is worth the short-term cost? Most of us have a preference for goods now rather than later. For example, if you are typical, you would prefer a sleek new sports car now rather than the same car 10 years from now. On average, individuals possess a **positive rate of time preference.** By this we mean that people subjectively value goods obtained in the immediate or near future (including the present) more highly than goods obtained in the distant future.

**positive rate of time preference** The desire of consumers for goods now rather than in the future.

When only Crusoe is involved, the attractiveness of the investment in the fishing net is dependent upon his time preference. If he places a high value on a couple of fish per day during the next 55 days, as indeed he may if he is on the verge of starvation, the cost of the investment may well exceed the value of the larger future output. If Crusoe could find someone who would loan him fish while he built the net, however, this would open up an additional option. In this case, the attractiveness of the investment would be influenced by the price of borrowing fish, or more broadly, on the interest rate.

## INTEREST RATES

When making decisions across time periods, the interest rate is of central importance because it links the future to the present. The interest rate allows individuals to place a current evaluation on future income and costs. In essence, the interest rate is the price of earlier availability; it is the premium that must be paid if you want to acquire goods now rather than later. From the lender's viewpoint, interest is a reward for waiting—a return received if you are willing to delay possible expenditures into the future.

In a modern economy, people often borrow funds in order to finance current investments and consumption. Because of this, the interest rate is often defined as the price of loanable funds. This definition is proper. But we should remember that it is the earlier availability of goods and services purchased, not the money itself, that is desired by the borrower.

### Determination of Interest Rates

Interest rates are determined by the demand for and supply of loanable funds. Investors demand funds in order to finance capital assets that they believe will increase output and generate profit. Simultaneously, consumers demand loanable funds because they have a positive rate of time preference; they prefer earlier availability.

The demand of investors for loanable funds stems from the productivity of capital. Investors are willing to borrow in order to finance the use of capital in production because they expect that an expansion in future output will provide them with the resources to repay both the principal and interest on the loan. Our prior example of Robinson Crusoe illustrates this point. Remember, Crusoe could increase his output by 200 fish this year if he could take off 55 days to build a net. Crusoe's fish production, however, would decline (by 2 fish per day) while he was constructing the net. Suppose a fishing crew from a neighboring island visited Crusoe and offered to lend him 110 fish so that he could undertake the capital investment project (building the net). If Crusoe could borrow the 110 fish (the principal) in exchange for, say, 165 fish *a year later* (110 to repay the principal and 55 as interest on the loan), the investment project would be highly profitable. Crusoe could repay the funds borrowed, plus the 50 percent interest rate, and still have 145 additional fish (the 200 additional fish caught minus the 55 fish paid in interest).

Crusoe's demand for loanable fish—and more generally, the demand of investors for loanable funds—stems directly from the productivity of the capital investment. Crusoe can gain by borrowing to finance the construction of a fishing net only because the net enables him to expand his total output during the year. Similarly, investors can gain by borrowing funds to undertake investment projects only when the capital assets purchased permit them to expand output (or reduce costs).

As Exhibit 10.1 illustrates, the interest rate brings the choices of investors and consumers wanting to borrow funds into harmony with the choices of lenders willing to supply funds. Higher interest rates make it more costly for investors to undertake capital spending projects and for consumers to buy now rather than later. Both investors and consumers will curtail their borrowing as the interest rate rises. Investors will borrow less because some investment projects that would be profitable at a low interest rate will be unprofitable at higher rates. Similarly, rather than pay the high interest premium,

**EXHIBIT 10.1**

**Determination of Interest Rates**

The demand for loanable funds stems from consumers' desire for earlier availability and the productivity of capital. As the interest rate rises, current goods become more expensive in comparison with future goods. Therefore, borrowers will reduce the amount of loanable funds demanded. On the other hand, higher interest rates will stimulate lenders to supply additional funds to the market.

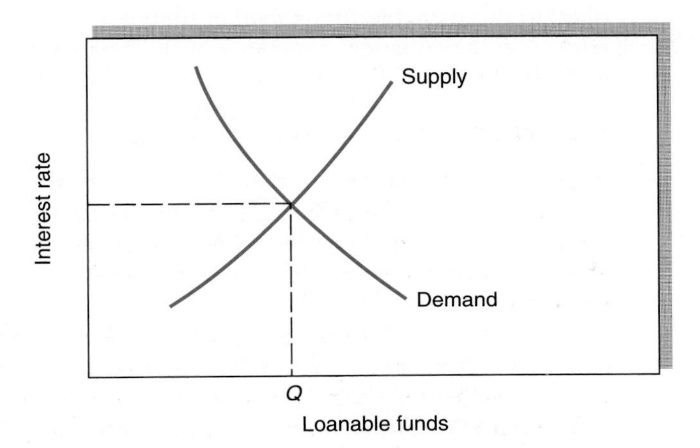

some consumers will reduce their current consumption when the rates increase. Therefore, the amount of funds demanded by borrowers is inversely related to the interest rate.

The interest rate also provides a reward to persons (lenders) willing to reduce their current consumption in order to provide loanable funds to others. If some individuals are going to borrow in order to undertake an investment project (or consume more than their current income), others must curtail their current consumption by an equal amount. In essence, the interest rate provides lenders with the incentive to reduce their current consumption so that borrowers can either invest or consume beyond their current income. Higher interest rates provide persons willing to save (willing to supply loanable funds) with *more future* goods in exchange for the sacrifice of current consumption. Even though people have a positive rate of time preference, they will give up current consumption to supply funds to the loanable funds market if the price is right—that is, if the interest rate is attractive enough. Therefore as the interest rate rises, the quantity of funds supplied to the loanable funds market expands.

As Exhibit 10.1 illustrates, the interest rate will bring the quantity of funds demanded into balance with the quantity supplied. At the equilibrium interest rate, the quantity of funds borrowers demand for investment and consumption now (rather than later) will just equal the quantity of funds lenders save. So the interest rate brings the choices of borrowers and lenders into harmony.

## Money Rate versus Real Rate of Interest

**money rate of interest** The rate of interest in monetary terms that borrowers pay for borrowed funds. During periods when borrowers and lenders expect inflation, the money rate of interest exceeds the real rate of interest.

**inflationary premium** A component of the money interest rate that reflects compensation to the lender for the expected decrease, due to inflation, in the purchasing power of the principal and interest during the course of the loan. It is determined by the expected rate of future inflation.

**real rate of interest** The money rate of interest minus the expected rate of inflation. The real rate of interest indicates the interest premium, in terms of real goods and services, that one must pay for earlier availability.

We have emphasized that the interest rate is a premium paid by borrowers for earlier availability and a reward received by lenders compensating them for delaying consumption. However, during a period of inflation—a general increase in prices—the nominal or **money rate of interest** is a misleading indicator of how much borrowers are paying and lenders are receiving. Inflation reduces the purchasing power of a loan's principal. When the principal is repaid in the future, it will not purchase as much as it would have when the funds were initially loaned.

Recognizing the decline in the purchasing power of the dollars with which they will be repaid, lenders will therefore reduce the amount of money supplied to the loanable funds market unless they are compensated for the anticipated rate of inflation. Simultaneously, once borrowers become fully aware that they will be paying back their loans with dollars of less purchasing power, they will be willing to pay this **inflationary premium,** an additional amount that reflects the expected rate of future price increases. If borrowers and lenders fully anticipate a 5 percent rate of inflation, for example, they will be just as willing to agree on a 10 percent interest rate as they were to agree on a 5 percent interest rate when both anticipated stable prices. Borrowers will agree so that they can purchase goods and services before they become even more expensive in the future.

Compared to the situation when the general price level is stable, the supply of loanable funds will decline (the curve will shift to the left) and the demand will increase (the curve will shift to the right) once decision-makers anticipate future inflation. The money interest rate thus rises, overstating the "true" cost of borrowing and yield from lending. This true cost is the **real rate of interest,** which is equal to the money rate of interest minus the inflationary premium. It reflects the real burden to borrowers and payoff to lenders in terms of command over goods and services.

To clarify the distinction between the money and real rates of interest, suppose a person borrows $1,000 for one year at an 8 percent interest rate. After a year, the borrower must pay the lender $1,080—the $1,000 principal plus the 8 percent interest. Now, suppose during the year prices rose 8 percent as the result of inflation. Because of this, the $1,080 repayment after a year commands exactly the same purchasing power as the original $1,000 did when it was loaned. In effect, the borrower pays back exactly the same amount of purchasing power as was borrowed. The lender receives nothing for making the purchasing power available to the borrower. In this case, the effective real interest rate was zero.

Lenders are unlikely to continue making funds available at such bargain rates. When they anticipate the 8 percent inflation rate, lenders will demand (and borrowers will agree to) a higher money interest rate, 16 percent, for example, to compensate for the decline in the purchasing power of the dollar. Under these circumstances, the 16 percent money rate of interest reflects both an 8 percent real interest rate and an inflationary premium of 8 percent.

Our analysis indicates that high rates of inflation will push up the money rate of interest. The real world is consistent with this view. Money interest rates rose to historical highs in the United States as inflation soared to double-digit rates during the 1970s. Cross-country comparisons also illustrate the linkage between inflation and high interest rates. The lowest money interest rates in the world are found in Germany and Switzerland, and in recent years Japan. All are countries with low rates of inflation. In contrast, the highest money interest rates are observed in Brazil, Argentina, Israel, and other countries with high rates of inflation.

## Interest Rates and Risk

We have proceeded as though there was only a single interest rate present in the loanable funds market. In the real world, of course, there are many interest rates. There is the mortgage rate, the prime interest rate (the rate charged to business firms with strong credit ratings), the consumer loan rate, and the credit card rate, to name only a few.

Interest rates in the loanable funds market will differ primarily as the result of differences in the risk associated with the loan. It is riskier to loan funds to an unemployed worker than to a well-established business with substantial assets. Similarly, extending an unsecured loan like that accompanying purchases on a credit card is riskier than extending a loan that is secured by an asset, such as a mortgage loan on a house. The risk also increases with the duration of the loan. The longer the time period, the more likely that the financial standing of the borrower will deteriorate substantially or that market conditions will change dramatically. The greater the risk that the borrower will be unable to repay the loan, the higher the interest rate will be.

As Exhibit 10.2 illustrates, the money rate of interest on a loan has three components. The pure interest component is the real price one must pay for earlier availability. The inflationary premium component reflects the expectation that the loan will be repaid with dollars of less purchasing power as the result of inflation. The third component—the *risk premium*—reflects the risk imposed on the lender by the possibility that the borrower may be unable to

**EXHIBIT 10.2**

**Three Components of the Money Interest Rate**

The money interest rate reflects a pure interest return, an inflationary premium, and a risk premium. When decision-makers expect a high rate of inflation during the period in which the loan is outstanding, the inflationary premium will be substantial. Similarly, the risk premium will be large when the probability of default by the borrower is substantial.

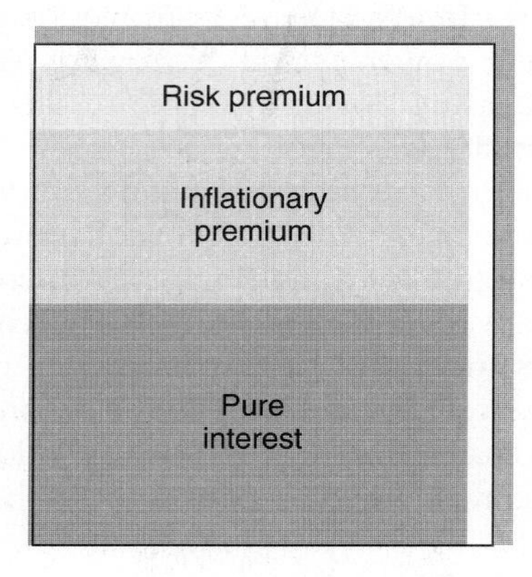


repay the loan. The risk premium, therefore, is directly related to the probability of default by the borrower.

## VALUE OF FUTURE INCOME (AND COSTS)

If you deposited $100 today in a savings account earning 6 percent interest, you would have $106 one year from now. Therefore, the *present value* of $100 a year from now is equal to the amount that you would have to invest today in order to have that amount at that time. The interest rate allows us to make this calculation. The interest rate connects the value of dollars (and capital assets) today with the value of dollars (and expected receipts) in the future. It is used to discount the value of a dollar in the future so that its present worth can be determined today.

**present value** The current worth of future income after it is discounted to reflect the fact that revenues in the future are valued less highly than revenues now.

The **present value** (PV) of a payment received one year from now can be expressed as follows:

$$PV = \frac{\text{receipts one year from now}}{1 + \text{interest rate}}$$

If the interest rate is 6 percent, the current value of the $100 to be received one year from now is

$$PV = \frac{\$100}{1.06} = \$94.34$$

If you placed $94.34 in a savings account yielding 6 percent interest, during the year the account would earn $5.66 interest (6 percent of $94.34) and therefore grow to $100 one year from now. Thus, the present value of $100 a year from now is $94.34.

**discounting** The procedure used to calculate the present value of future income. The present value of future income is inversely related to both the interest rate and the amount of time that passes before the funds are received.

Economists use the term **discounting** to describe this procedure of reducing the value of a dollar to be received in the future to its present worth. Clearly, the value of a dollar in the future is inversely related to the interest rate. For example, if the interest rate were 10 percent, the present value of $100 received one year from now would be only $90.91 (100 divided by 1.10).

The present value of $100 received two years from now is

$$\text{PV} = \frac{\$100}{(1 + \text{interest rate})^2}$$

If the interest rate were 6 percent, $100 received two years from now would be equal to $89 today ($100 divided by $1.06^2$ ). In other words, $89 invested today would yield $100 two years from now.

The present value procedure can be used to determine the current value of any future income stream. If *R* represents receipts received at the end of various years in the future (indicated by the subscript) and *i* represents the interest rate, the present value of the future income stream[2] is

$$\text{PV} = \frac{R_1}{(1+i)} + \frac{R_2}{(1+i)^2} + \ldots + \frac{R_n}{(1+i)^n}$$

Exhibit 10.3 shows the present value of $100 received at various times in the future at several different discount rates. The chart clearly illustrates two points. First, the present value of income received at a date in the future declines with the interest rate. The present value of the $100 received one year from now, when discounted at a 4 percent interest rate, is $96.15, compared to $98.04 when a 2 percent discount rate is applied. Second, the present value of the $100 also declines as the date of its receipt is set farther into the future. If the applicable discount rate is 6 percent, the present value of $100 received one year from now is $94.34, compared to $89 if the $100 is received two years from now. If the $100 is received five years from now, its current worth is only $74.43. So the present value of a future dollar payment is inversely related to both the interest rate and how far in the future the payment will be received.

## PRESENT VALUE, PROFITABILITY, AND INVESTMENT

Investment decisions involve an up-front cost of acquiring a machine, skill, or other asset that is expected to generate additional output and revenue in the future. How can an investor know if the expected future revenues will be sufficient to cover the costs? The discounting procedure helps provide the

[2]For a specific annual income stream in perpetuity, the present value is equal simply to *R/i*, where *R* is the annual revenue stream and *i* the interest rate. For example, if the interest rate is 10 percent, the PV of a $100 annual income stream in perpetuity is equal to $100/.10, or $1,000.

**EXHIBIT 10.3**

**Present Value of $100**

The columns indicate the present value of $100 to be received a designated number of years in the future for alternative interest rates. For example, at a discount rate of 2 percent, the present value of $100 to be received five years from now is $90.57. Note that the present value of the $100 declines as either the interest rate or the number of years in the future increases.

| | Present Value of $100 to Be Received a Designated Number of Years in the Future for Alternative Interest Rates | | | | | |
|---|---|---|---|---|---|---|
| **Years in Future** | **2%** | **4%** | **6%** | **8%** | **12%** | **20%** |
| 1 | 98.04 | 96.15 | 94.34 | 92.59 | 89.29 | 83.33 |
| 2 | 96.12 | 92.46 | 89.00 | 85.73 | 79.72 | 69.44 |
| 3 | 94.23 | 88.90 | 83.96 | 79.38 | 71.18 | 57.87 |
| 4 | 92.39 | 85.48 | 79.21 | 73.50 | 63.55 | 48.23 |
| 5 | 90.57 | 82.19 | 74.73 | 68.06 | 56.74 | 40.19 |
| 6 | 88.80 | 79.03 | 70.50 | 63.02 | 50.66 | 33.49 |
| 7 | 87.06 | 75.99 | 66.51 | 58.35 | 45.23 | 27.08 |
| 8 | 85.35 | 73.07 | 62.74 | 54.03 | 40.39 | 23.26 |
| 9 | 83.68 | 70.26 | 59.19 | 50.02 | 36.06 | 19.38 |
| 10 | 82.03 | 67.56 | 55.84 | 46.32 | 32.20 | 16.15 |
| 15 | 74.30 | 55.53 | 41.73 | 31.52 | 18.27 | 6.49 |
| 20 | 67.30 | 45.64 | 31.18 | 21.45 | 10.37 | 2.61 |
| 30 | 55.21 | 30.83 | 17.41 | 9.94 | 3.34 | 0.42 |
| 50 | 37.15 | 14.07 | 5.43 | 2.13 | 0.35 | 0.01 |

answer, since it permits the investor to place both the costs and the expected future revenues of an investment project *into present-value terms*. If the present value of the revenue derived from the investment exceeds the present value of the cost, it makes sense to undertake the investment. If revenues and costs of such an investment turn out as expected, the investor will reap economic profit. In turn, profitable investments will increase the value of resources, and thereby create wealth.

On the other hand, if the cost of the project exceeds the discounted value of the future receipts, losses will result. The losses indicate the resources used to undertake the investment were more valuable than the future revenues generated by the investment. Thus, investments that result in losses reduce the value of resources and thereby diminish wealth. Such investments are counterproductive.

Suppose a truck rental firm is contemplating the purchase of a new $40,000 truck. Past experience indicates that after the operational and maintenance expenses have been covered, the firm can rent out the truck for $12,000 per year (received at the end of each year) for the next four years, the expected life of the vehicle.[3] Since the firm can borrow and lend funds at an interest rate of 8

[3]For the sake of simplicity, we assume that the truck has no scrap value at the end of four years.

**EXHIBIT 10.4**

**Discounted Present Value of $12,000 of Truck Rental for Four Years (Interest Rate = 8 percent)**

| Year (1) | Expected Future Income (Received at Year-end) (2) | Discounted Value (8 Percent Rate) (3) | Present Value of Income (4) |
|---|---|---|---|
| 1 | $12,000 | 0.926 | $11,112 |
| 2 | 12,000 | 0.857 | 10,284 |
| 3 | 12,000 | 0.794 | 9,528 |
| 4 | 12,000 | 0.735 | 8,820 |
| | | | $39,744 |

percent, we will discount the future expected income at an 8 percent rate. Exhibit 10.4 illustrates the calculation. Column 4 shows how much $12,000, available at year-end for each of the next four years, is worth today. In total, the present value of the expected rental receipts is $39,744—less than the purchase price of the truck. Therefore, the project should not be undertaken.

The decision to accept or reject a prospective project is highly sensitive to the interest rate. If the interest rate in our example had been 6 percent, the present value of the future rental income would have been $41,580.[4] Since it pays to purchase a capital good whenever the present value of the income generated exceeds the purchase price of the capital good, the project would have been profitable at the lower interest rate.

## Expected Future Earnings and Asset Values

The present value of the expected revenue minus cost of an investment reveals whether the project should be undertaken. However, *once an investment project has been completed,* the present value of the expected future net earnings will determine the market value of the asset. If the present value of the expected net earnings rises (falls), so too will the value of the asset.

The value of an asset is equal to the present value of the expected net revenues that can be earned by the asset. If the asset is expected to generate an annual net income each year in the future, its value would be equal to

$$\text{Asset value} = \frac{\text{annual net income from the asset}}{\text{interest rate}}$$

[4]The derivation of this figure is shown in the following tabulation:

| *Year* | *Expected Future Income (dollars)* | *Discounted Value per Dollar (6% rate)* | *Present Value of Income (dollars)* |
|---|---|---|---|
| 1 | 12,000 | 0.943 | 11,316 |
| 2 | 12,000 | 0.890 | 10,680 |
| 3 | 12,000 | 0.840 | 10,080 |
| 4 | 12,000 | 0.792 | 9,504 |
| | | | 41,580 |

How much would a tract of land that was expected to generate $1,000 of rental income net of costs each year indefinitely in the future be worth? If the market interest rate were 10 percent, investors would be willing to pay $10,000 for the land. When purchased at this price, the land would provide an investor with the 10 percent market rate of return. Correspondingly, if an asset generated $2,500 of net earnings annually and the market interest rate were 10 percent, the asset would be worth $25,000. There is a direct relationship between the expected future earnings of an asset and the asset's market value.

Clearly, investors have a strong incentive to search for and undertake profitable projects. Such investments will both increase their personal wealth and that of the nation. Identifying profitable opportunities, however, is not easy. We live in a changing world characterized by uncertainty and imperfect information. Among virtually an infinite number of investment projects, there is no guarantee that one's project of choice will succeed.

Some people are very good at identifying profitable opportunities that have gone unnoticed by others. An economist might say that they possess the quality of entrepreneurial alertness. Successful entrepreneurs are people who are able to introduce new products that are highly valued relative to their costs, discover lower-cost production methods, and develop better marketing techniques. Originality, quickness to act, and imagination are important aspects of entrepreneurship and successful investing.

Some entrepreneurial investors are particularly good at (1) identifying a business that is poorly operated, (2) purchasing the business at a depressed price, (3) improving the operational efficiency of the firm, and (4) then reselling the business at a handsome profit. Suppose that a poorly run business currently has net earnings of $1 million per year. What is the market value of the business? If the firm is expected to continue earning $1 million per year, the market value of the firm would be $10 million if the interest rate is 10 percent. Suppose that an alert entrepreneur buys the business for $10 million, hires new management, and improves the operational efficiency of the firm. As the result of these changes, the annual net earnings of the firm increase to $2 million per year. Now how much is the firm worth? If the $2 million annual earnings are expected to continue into the future, the net present value of the firm would rise to $20 million. Thus, the entrepreneur who improved the performance of the firm would be able to sell the firm for a very substantial profit.

In a competitive environment, there is a strong incentive for business managers and asset owners to use the resources under their control efficiently. If they do not, the value of the assets will decline, and the business will be vulnerable to a takeover by alert entrepreneurs capable of operating the firm more efficiently and using the assets more profitably.

## Investing in Human Capital

In principle, investments in human capital—a choice about continuing in school, for example—involve all of the ingredients of other investment decisions. Since the returns and some of the costs normally accrue in the future, the discounting procedure helps one to assess the present value of expected costs and revenues associated with a human capital investment.

**EXHIBIT 10.5**

**Investing in Human Capital**

Here we illustrate the human capital investment decision confronting Susan, an 18-year-old who just finished high school. If Susan goes to college and majors in business administration, she will incur the direct cost ($C_d$) of the college education (tuition, books, transportation, and so on) plus the opportunity cost ($C_o$) of earnings forgone while in college. However, with a business degree, she can expect higher future earnings ($B$) during her career. If the discounted present value of the additional future earnings exceeds the discounted value of the direct and indirect cost of a college education, the business degree will be a profitable investment for Susan.

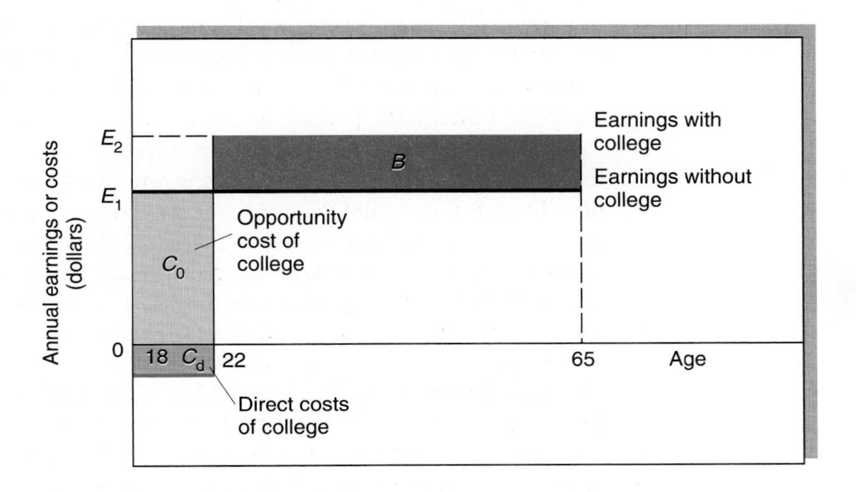


Exhibit 10.5 illustrates the potential human capital decision confronting Susan, an 18-year-old high school graduate contemplating the pursuit of a bachelor's degree in business administration. Just as an investment in a truck would involve a cost in order to generate a future income, so too does a degree in business administration. If Susan does not go to college, she will be able to begin work immediately at annual earnings of $E_1$. Alternatively, if she goes to college, she will incur direct costs ($C_d$) in the form of tuition, books, transportation, and related expenses. She will also bear the opportunity cost ($C_o$) of lower earnings while in college. However, the study of business will expand Susan's knowledge and skills, and thereby enable her to earn a higher future income ($E_2$ rather than $E_1$).

Will the higher future income be worth the cost? To answer this question, Susan must discount each year's *additional* income stemming from completion of the business degree and compare that with the discounted value of the cost, including the opportunity cost of earnings lost during the period of study. If the discounted present value of the additional future income exceeds the discounted present value of the cost, acquiring the degree is a worthwhile human capital investment.

Of course, nonmonetary considerations may also be important, particularly for human capital investment decisions, since human capital is embodied in the individual. For example, Susan's preferences might be such that she would really prefer working as a college graduate in the business world (rather than in the jobs available to high school graduates) even if she did not make more money. Thus, the nonmonetary attractiveness of business may induce her to pursue the business degree even if the monetary rate of return is low (or even negative).

Although nonmonetary factors are more important in human capital decision-making, opportunity cost and the pursuit of profit guide human capital investors just as they guide physical capital investors. As with choosing to purchase a new machine, choosing a human capital investment project (obtaining a law degree, for example) involves cost, the possibility of profit, and uncertainty. In both instances, the expected return will influence the investor. Giving due consideration to nonmonetary factors, physical and human capital investors will both seek to undertake only those projects that they anticipate will yield benefits in excess of costs.

Both interest and profit perform important allocative functions. Interest induces people to give up current consumption, a sacrifice that is a necessary ingredient for capital formation. Economic profit provides both human and physical capital decision-makers with the incentive to (1) undertake investments yielding an uncertain return and (2) discover and develop beneficial and productive investment opportunities.

## FUNCTION OF CAPITAL MARKET

If a nation is going to realize its potential, it must have a mechanism capable of attracting savings and channeling them into investment projects that create wealth. In a market economy, the capital market performs this function. This highly diverse market includes markets for stocks, real estate, and businesses, as well as the loanable funds market. Financial institutions such as banks, insurance companies, brokerage firms, and mutual funds play important roles.

The capital market brings together people who are willing to save with those willing to invest. Some people save and supply funds to the capital market in exchange for a fixed rate of return. People who purchase bonds and maintain savings deposits are examples. Other people supply funds in exchange for an uncertain return linked to the success or failure of a business or investment project. Stockholders and partnership investors fall into this category. Still others supply funds to the capital market when they use their own funds to purchase a business or acquire additional schooling.

The key attribute of the capital market is its ability to direct funds toward wealth-creating projects. When investment in a capital asset generates additional output (and revenue) that is valued more highly than the value of the resources required for its production, the investment will create wealth. When property rights are securely defined and enforced, wealth-creating investments will also be profitable.

Therefore, the capital market provides investors with a strong incentive to evaluate potential projects carefully and search for profitable projects. Investors ranging from stockholders to partnership investors to small business owners will pursue profitable ventures because such investments will increase their personal wealth. However, there will also be a strong tendency for profitable investments to increase not only the wealth of the investor, but also the wealth of the nation.

Of course, in an uncertain world private investors will sometimes make mistakes, undertaking projects that prove unprofitable. If investors were unwilling to take such chances, many new ideas would go untested and many worthwhile but risky projects would not be undertaken. Mistaken investments are a necessary price paid for fruitful innovations in new technologies and products. The capital market will at least assure that the mistakes are self-correcting. Losses will signal investors to terminate unprofitable and unproductive projects.

Without a private capital market, it is virtually impossible to attract funds and consistently channel them into wealth-creating projects. When investment funds are allocated by the government rather than the market, an entirely different set of criteria comes into play. Political clout replaces market return as the basis for allocating the funds. Investment funds will often be channeled to political supporters and to projects that benefit individuals and groups with political clout. When politics replaces the market mechanism, investment projects that reduce wealth rather than enhance it become more likely.

The experience of Eastern Europe and the former Soviet Union illustrates this point. The investment rates of these countries were among the highest in the world. The central planners of these countries allocated approximately one-third of the national output to investment. But even these high rates of investment did little to improve the standard of living. Political rather than economic considerations determined which investment projects would be undertaken. Therefore, investment funds were often wasted on political boondoggles and high-visibility projects favored by important political leaders.

## IMPORTANT SOURCE OF ECONOMIC PROSPERITY: INVESTMENT AND EFFICIENT USE OF CAPITAL

Economic analysis indicates that production and income are closely linked. Investment is an important potential source of productivity and income growth. Countries that invest more and channel more of their investments into productive projects today will tend to have a higher income tomorrow.

Investments in both physical and human capital enhance productivity. Farmers with modern tractors and plows (physical capital) can plant, cultivate, and raise more corn than farmers working with a horse and plow or a hoe. Similarly, a secretary working with word-processing equipment can type more letters than an equally skilled secretary working with a traditional typewriter. Likewise, training, education, and other investments in human capital that improve the skills of workers will enhance productivity, too. Such investment in both physical and human capital, allocated in an efficient manner, is one of the most important sources of productivity and income growth.

## INVESTMENTS IN PHYSICAL CAPITAL AND ECONOMIC GROWTH: A CROSS-COUNTRY COMPARISON

Exhibit 10.6 compares the growth rates during the 1980s of the 10 countries that invested the largest share of their total output with the growth rate of the 10 countries with the lowest investment rates. A diverse set of countries are included in the group with a high investment rate. Some (Singapore, Hong Kong, Switzerland, and Norway) are small countries. Others (Japan and Indonesia) are quite large. Seven Asian and three European nations are included in the group. Several (Japan, Switzerland, and Norway) in the high-investment group are

**EXHIBIT 10.6** **Annual Growth Rate of Domestic Output for Countries with Highest and Lowest Investment Rates**

| Country | Investment as Share of Economy, 1980–1990 | Average Annual Growth Rate of Output per Capita, 1980–1990 |
|---|---|---|
| *Highest Investment Rates* | | |
| Singapore | 41.5 | 4.2 |
| Japan | 30.2 | 3.5 |
| South Korea | 29.9 | 8.6 |
| Malaysia | 29.6 | 2.6 |
| Switzerland | 26.8 | 1.6 |
| Hong Kong | 26.5 | 5.7 |
| Portugal | 26.4 | 2.1 |
| Thailand | 26.4 | 5.8 |
| Norway | 26.0 | 2.5 |
| Indonesia | 26.0 | 3.7 |
| Average Growth Rate | | **4.0** |
| *Lowest Investment Rates* | | |
| Ghana | 8.6 | –0.4 |
| Uganda | 10.0 | 0.3 |
| Central Africa Repub. | 10.8 | –1.2 |
| Uruguay | 11.3 | –0.3 |
| Bolivia | 12.2 | –2.6 |
| Sierra Leone | 12.7 | –0.9 |
| Haiti | 13.2 | –2.5 |
| Guatemala | 13.3 | –2.1 |
| Argentina | 13.5 | –1.7 |
| Niger | 13.8 | –4.6 |
| Average Growth Rate | | **–1.6** |

**Source:** Derived from the World Bank *World Development Report* (annual).

high-income industrial nations, while several others (South Korea, Malaysia, Thailand, and Indonesia) are relatively poor. All of the high-investment countries experienced growth during the 1980s. The average annual growth of real output per capita in the high investment group ranged from a low of 1.6 percent in Switzerland to a high of 8.6 percent in South Korea. The average growth rate of per capita output in the ten high-investment countries was 4 percent.

Now look at the economic record of the 10 low-investment countries. Only one (Uganda) of the 10 low-investment countries experienced an increase in per capita output during the 1980–1990 period. On average, annual output in the 10 low-investment countries *declined* by 1.6 percent. None was able to achieve a growth rate even close to that of a high-investment country.

Just as economic theory predicts, the countries with a high investment rate tended to grow rapidly. In contrast, those with a low investment rate stagnated and often regressed.

Many countries impose a ceiling on the nominal interest rate in the loanable funds market and couple this policy with an inflationary monetary policy. Suppose that a country is following a monetary policy that has resulted in a 20 percent rate of inflation. In a market setting, the nominal interest rate would rise to reflect the high rate of inflation. If the money interest rate were 22 percent, for example, lenders would earn a modest 2 percent real return on their savings. Exhibit 10.7 illustrates what happens when an inflationary policy is

**EXHIBIT 10.7**

**How an Interest Rate Ceiling Coupled with Inflationary Monetary Policy Destroys the Loanable Funds Market**

Here we illustrate the impact of a 10 percent interest rate ceiling in a country that is experiencing a 20 percent rate of inflation. If it were not for the interest rate ceiling, the nominal interest rate would be 22 percent and lenders would earn a modest 2 percent real return. With the interest rate ceiling, however, the real interest rate is minus 10 percent! Lenders lose purchasing power if they supply funds to the loanable funds market. Such policies remove the incentive to save and virtually destroy the financial capital market.

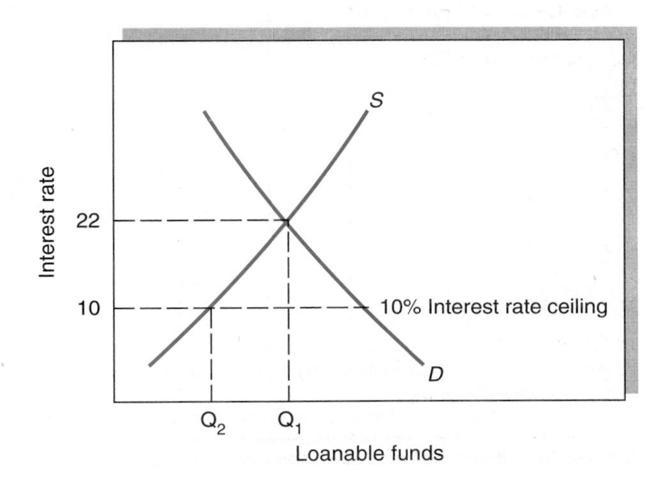

coupled with a ceiling on the nominal interest rate. When the government fixes the nominal interest rate below equilibrium, 10 percent in our example, people who save are stuck with a negative real return. When such a policy is present, there is little or no incentive for people to supply funds to the domestic loanable funds market. The quantity of loanable funds supplied to the domestic market will decline sharply (from $Q_1$ to $Q_2$). Domestic financial investors will seek positive returns abroad. Foreign investors will completely shun the country. Such policies destroy the domestic capital market.

Predictably, the savings and investment rate will be low in countries that follow policies that lead to negative real interest rates! The level of investment in such countries may not even be sufficient to replace the machines and structures that wear out during the period. Under these circumstances, the growth of income will stagnate or even regress.

Exhibit 10.8 provides data on real interest rates, investment, and the growth of output for 10 countries that followed such policies throughout much of the 1980s. The real interest rate in each of these countries was at least 10 percent negative during both 1983–1985 and 1988–1990. With a couple of exceptions, the investment rate of these countries was quite low. In fact, 5 of these countries (Ghana, Uganda, Bolivia, Sierra Leone, and Argentina) rank among the 10 countries with the lowest investment rates in the world (see Exhibit 10.6).

**EXHIBIT 10.8**

**Changes in Output for Countries with Persistent Negative Real Interest Rates**

| Country | Average Real Interest Rate[a] | | Investment as Share of Economy 1980–1990 | Average Annual Growth Rate of Output per Capita 1980–1990 |
|---|---|---|---|---|
| | 1983–1985 | 1988–1990 | | |
| Argentina | −163 | −1179 | 13.5 | −1.7 |
| Bolivia | −4240 | n/a | 12.2 | −2.6 |
| Peru | −101 | n/a | 19.6 | −2.6 |
| Uganda | −74 | −65 | 10.0 | 0.3 |
| Zambia | −16 | −77 | 15.3 | −2.8 |
| Ghana | −46 | −15 | 8.6 | −0.4 |
| Somalia | −35 | −69 | 25.3 | −0.7 |
| Sierra Leone | −37 | −41 | 12.7 | −0.9 |
| Ecuador | −19 | −21 | 21.3 | −0.4 |
| Tanzania | −21 | −12 | 19.1 | −0.3 |
| Average Growth Rate | | | | **−1.2** |

[a]The real interest rate for each country is equal to the country's nominal deposit interest rate minus the inflation rate of the country.

**Source:** The data on the change in per capita income are from the World Bank, *World Development Report 1992* (Tables 2 and 26). The deposit interest rate data are from the International Monetary Fund, *International Financial Statistics Yearbook* (various issues).

All of these countries fixed the nominal interest rate while following an inflationary monetary policy. Thus, they destroyed the mechanism that would normally provide potential private investors with loanable funds and channel those funds toward wealth-creating projects. Lacking a mechanism to perform this vitally important function, these countries regressed during the 1980s. On average, the output per capita of the 10 countries declined at a 1.2 percent annual rate. Only one (Uganda) of the 10 was able to achieve any positive growth in per capita output. Capital formation and its efficient allocation are important sources of economic growth. Countries that destroy their capital markets will pay a severe price for their folly.

## LOOKING AHEAD

As the last two chapters have stressed, investment in physical and human capital will influence the wealth and income of both individuals and nations. Differences among individuals in these factors will also contribute to income inequality. The following chapter will focus on the sources and measurement of income inequality.

## CHAPTER SUMMARY

1. We can often produce more consumption goods by first using our resources to produce physical and human capital resources and then by using the capital resources to produce the desired consumption goods. Resources used to produce capital goods will be unavailable for the direct production of consumption goods. Therefore, someone must save—refrain from current consumption—in order to release the resources required for investment.
2. People have a positive rate of time preference; they generally value present consumption more highly than future consumption.
3. In decisions made across time periods, the interest rate is of central importance because it allows individuals to place a current evaluation on future revenues and costs. The demand for loanable funds stems from the productivity of capital resources and the positive rate of time preference of consumers.
4. The interest rate is the price of earlier availability. Interest provides lenders with an incentive to curtail current consumption and to supply loanable funds to others. The market interest rate will bring the quantity of funds demanded by borrowers (to undertake current investments and to consume beyond their current income) into balance with the supply of funds provided by lenders willing to forgo current consumption in exchange for the interest premium.
5. During inflationary times, the money rate of interest incorporates an inflationary premium reflecting the expected future increase in the price level. Under these circumstances, the money rate of interest exceeds the real rate of interest.

6. The money rate of interest on a specific loan reflects three basic factors—the pure interest rate, an inflationary premium, and a risk premium that is directly related to the probability of default by the borrower.
7. Since a dollar in the future is valued less than a dollar today, the value of future receipts must be discounted to calculate their current worth. The discounting procedure can be used to calculate the present value of an expected net income stream from a potential investment project. If the present value of the expected revenues exceeds the present value of the expected costs, the project will be profitable when things turn out as expected.
8. The present value of expected future net earnings will determine the market value of *existing* assets. An increase (decline) in the expected future earnings derived from an asset will increase (reduce) the market value of the asset.
9. If a nation is to grow and prosper, it must have a mechanism that will attract savings and channel them into investment projects that create wealth. The capital market performs this function in a market economy. When the value of the output (and revenue) derived from an investment exceeds its costs (the value of the resources required for the production of the capital resource), the investment will be productive. When property rights are defined and securely enforced, productive investments will also be profitable. Then, the profit motive will prompt private investors to search for and undertake productive investments.
10. Investment in both physical and human capital is an important source of productivity growth. The economies of countries that invest more and channel their investment funds into more productive projects generally grow more rapidly.
11. The empirical evidence confirms the importance of investment. Per capita output has grown rapidly in countries like Singapore, Japan, and South Korea that have high rates of investment. In contrast, per capita output has usually declined in countries with low investment rates.

*Study Guide*

**CHAPTER**

# 10

## Developing the Economic Way of Thinking

## CRITICAL-ANALYSIS QUESTIONS

*1. How would the following changes influence the rate of interest in the United States?
   a. An increase in the positive time preference of lenders.
   b. An increase in the positive time preference of borrowers.
   c. An increase in domestic inflation.
   d. Increased uncertainty about a nuclear war.
   e. Improved investment opportunities in Europe.

2. "Any return to capital above the pure interest yield is unnecessary. The pure interest yield is sufficient to provide capitalists with the earnings necessary to replace their assets and to compensate for their sacrifice of current consumption. Any return above that is pure gravy; it is excess profit." Do you agree with this view? Why or why not?

3. How are human and physical capital investment decisions similar? How do they differ? What determines the profitability of a physical capital investment? Do human capital investors make profits? If so, what is the source of profit? Explain.

*4. A lender made the following statement to a borrower, "You are borrowing $1,000, which is to be repaid in 12 monthly installments of $100 each. Your total interest charge is $200, which means your interest rate is 20 percent." Is the effective interest rate on the loan really 20 percent? Explain.

5. Suppose U.S. investors are considering the construction of bicycle factories in two different countries, one in Europe and the other in Africa. Projected costs and revenues are at first identical, but the chance of guerrilla warfare (and possible destruction of the factory) is suddenly perceived in the African nation. In which country will the price of bicycles (and the current rate of return to bicycle factories) probably rise? Will the investors be better off in the country with the higher rate of return? Why or why not?

6. In a market economy, investors have a strong incentive to undertake profitable investments. What makes an investment profitable? Do profitable investments create wealth? Why or why not? Do all investments create wealth? Discuss.

*7. Over long periods of time, the rate of return of an average investment in the stock market has exceeded the return on high-quality bonds. Is the higher return on stocks surprising? Why or why not?

8. The interest rates charged on outstanding credit card balances are generally higher than the interest rate that banks charge customers with a good credit rating. Why do you think the credit card rate is so high? Should the government impose an interest rate ceiling of, say, 4 percent, above the prime lending rate (the rate banks charge customers with a good credit rating) on credit card loans? If it did, who would be hurt and who would be helped? Discuss.

*9. If the money rate of interest on a low-risk government bond is 10 percent and the inflation rate for the last several years has been steady at 4 percent, what is the estimated real rate of interest?

*Asterisk denotes critical-analysis questions for which answers are given in Appendix A.

10. Will low interest rates encourage investment? If the current interest rate in a country is 15 percent, would the investment rate be higher if the government imposed a ceiling reducing the rate of interest in the loanable funds market to 8 percent? Why or why not?

11. The data presented in Exhibit 10.6 indicates that countries investing more of their total output grow more rapidly. Explain in your own words why this is true. Do you think the government should adopt policies designed to increase the saving and investment rates of citizens? Why or why not? Discuss.

*12. Alicia's philosophy of life is summed up by the proverb: "A penny saved is a penny earned." She plans and saves for the future. In contrast, Mike's view is: "Life is uncertain, eat dessert first." Mike wants as much as possible now.
   a. Who has the highest rate of time preference?
   b. Do people like Alicia benefit from people like Mike?
   c. Do people like Mike benefit from the presence of people like Alicia? Explain.

*13. Some countries with very low incomes per capita are unable to save very much. Are people in these countries helped or hurt by people in high-income countries with much higher rates of saving?

## MULTIPLE-CHOICE SELF-TEST

1. If a person undertakes an investment,
   a. The person must reduce current consumption.
   b. The person must borrow funds.
   c. Someone must reduce current consumption, but it does not necessarily have to be the person undertaking the investment.
   d. Someone must borrow funds, but it does not necessarily have to be the person undertaking the investment.

2. When economists say that people possess a "positive rate of time preference," they mean that people
   a. Are shortsighted and irrational.
   b. Value goods during the current time period more highly than the same goods in the future.
   c. Prefer to save rather than consume.
   d. Value goods in the future more highly than the same goods during the current time period.

3. Which of the following is true?
   a. When people make decisions involving income and cost across time periods, the interest rate is highly important because it links the future to the present.
   b. During an extended period of inflation, the money rate of interest will generally be less than the real rate of interest. F
   c. When economists say that people have a positive rate of time preference, they mean that consumers are optimistic that the future will be better than the past. F
   d. An increase in the interest rate will make current consumption cheaper and future goods more expensive. F

4. The interest rate
   a. Is the price of earlier availability.
   b. Provides a reward to persons willing to reduce their current consumption in order to provide loanable funds to others.
   c. Allows individuals to place a current evaluation on future income and costs.
   d. All of the above are true.
5. The real rate of interest is
   a. The rate that a low-risk borrower must pay for money.
   b. The money rate of interest minus the inflationary premium.
   c. The yield that one can expect to receive on loanable funds without taking any significant risk.
   d. The risk component associated with the ownership of real assets.
6. If a company rented a certain machine for two years, its revenues would rise by $1,000 per year (to be received at the end of each year) for the next two years. To rent the machine, the company would have to pay $1,900 immediately. Which of the following statements about this project is true?
   a. The project should be undertaken, since revenues exceed costs.
   b. The project should not be undertaken, since it would lower the firm's accounting profits during the first year.
   c. The project would not affect the firm's profitability.
   d. Without information on the interest rate for purposes of discounting, one cannot tell if the project should be undertaken.
7. The present value of $1,000 to be received in the future will be highest in which of the following situations?
   a. The interest rate is high, and the period of time before the $1,000 is to be received is long.
   b. The interest rate is high, and the period of time before the $1,000 is to be received is short.
   c. The interest rate is low, and the period of time before the $1,000 is to be received is long.
   d. The interest rate is low, and the period of time before the $1,000 is to be received is short.
8. If the interest rate were 10 percent and an investment project was expected to yield net revenue of $5,000 per year (to be received at year-end) for each of the next three years, profit-maximizing decision-makers would undertake the investment *only* as long as its cost was less than
   a. $12,434.
   b. $13,363.
   c. $13,636.
   d. $15,000.
9. When an investment is profitable, it will
   a. Yield a rate of return that is greater than the interest rate.
   b. Provide revenues that are greater than costs when measured in present-value terms.
   c. Increase the value of resources.
   d. All of the above.

10. Other things constant, the real output of countries will tend to grow more rapidly when they
   a. Use interest rate controls to keep interest rates low.
   b. Follow policies that result in high money interest rates.
   c. Keep out foreign investment
   d. Invest a larger share of their total output.

## PROBLEMS

1. Suppose you are contemplating the purchase of a minicomputer at a cost of $1,000. The expected lifetime of the asset is three years. You expect to lease the asset to a business for $400 annually (payable at the end of each year) for three years. If you can borrow (and lend) money at an interest rate of 8 percent, will the investment be a profitable undertaking? Is the project profitable at an interest rate of 12 percent? Provide calculations in support of your answer.
2. According to a news item, the owner of a lottery ticket paying $3 million over 20 years is offering to sell the ticket for $1.2 million cash *now*. "Who knows?" the ticket owner explained, "We might not even be here in 20 years, and I do not want to leave it to the dinosaurs."
   a. Assuming that the ticket pays $150,000 per year at the end of each year for the next 20 years, what is the present value of the ticket if the appropriate rate for discounting the future income is thought to be 10 percent?
   b. Assuming the discount rate is in the 10 percent range, is the offer price of $1.2 million reasonable?
   c. Can you think of any disadvantages of buying the lottery earnings rather than a bond?
3. Suppose you decide to rent an apartment for 5 years. Further suppose that the owner offers to let you use an old refrigerator for free and promises to keep the refrigerator repaired for all 5 years. You also have the option of buying a new energy efficient refrigerator (with a 5-year free maintenance agreement) for $700. The new refrigerator will reduce your electric bill by $150 per year and will have a market value of $200 after 5 years. If necessary, you can borrow money from your bank at an 8 percent rate of interest. Which option should you choose?
4. Suppose that you are considering whether or not to enroll in a summer computer training program which costs $2,500. In addition, if you take the program, you will have to give up $1,500 of earnings from your summer job. You figure that the program will increase your earnings by $500 per year for each of the next 10 years. Beyond that, it is not expected to affect your earnings. If you take the program, you will have to borrow the funds at an 8 percent rate of interest. From strictly a monetary viewpoint, should you enroll in the program?

CHAPTER

# 11

# Income Inequality and Poverty

All animals are equal, but some animals are more equal than others.

*George Orwell*[1]

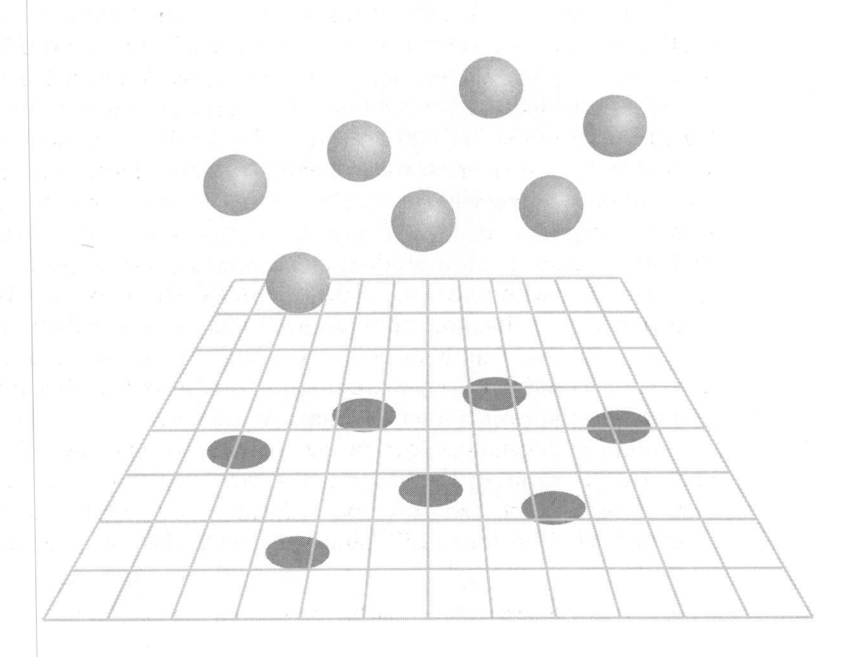

## CHAPTER FOCUS

- How much income inequality is there in a market economy such as the United States? What are the major factors that influence the distribution of income?
- Why has income inequality increased in recent years in the United States?
- How does the degree of income inequality in the United States compare with that of other countries?
- How much income mobility is there in the United States—do the rich remain rich while the poor remain poor?
- What are the characteristics of the poor? Have they changed in recent decades?
- Have income transfers reduced the poverty rate?

In a market economy, people have a strong incentive to produce goods and generate income. As we have explained, the personal income of market participants is determined by their productivity: those who use their human and physical resources to produce a lot of things that are highly valued by others will therefore have very high incomes. The close link between personal prosperity and productivity provides market participants with a strong incentive to work, use their resources productively, and find better ways to do things.

With markets, there is no central distributing agency that carves up the economic pie and allocates slices to various individuals. Rather, the income of each individual is received from others in exchange for productive services or as a gift. In a market economy, returns to work effort are by far the largest contributor to income—more than 80 percent of national income in the United States, for example, comes in return for work performed. But people differ with regard to their productive abilities, opportunities, preferences, and intestinal fortitude. Some will be able to hit a baseball, perform a rock concert, design a computer, or operate a restaurant so effectively that people will pay millions to consume the product or service that they supply. There will be others, however, with disabilities and few skills who may be unable even to support themselves. Income from physical capital is less than 20 percent of total income. Like the capability for work, however, ownership of physical capital and income derived from it are unequally distributed. When markets are used to allocate resources, income inequality will result.

There is substantial income variation in all societies. Substituting politics and central planning for markets will not eliminate economic inequality. Efforts to reduce income differences, in fact, will reduce the productive incentives provided by those differences. Nonetheless, most of us are troubled by

[1]George Orwell, *Animal Farm* (New York: Harcourt Brace & Co., 1946), p. 112.

the extremes of inequality—extravagant luxury on the one hand and grinding poverty on the other. How much inequality is there in a market economy, such as the United States? In a market economy, do the same families continually enjoy high incomes, while those in poverty are unable to escape that condition? How have income-transfer programs designed to reduce poverty influenced the distribution of income and the welfare of the poor? This chapter focuses on these questions and related issues.

## INCOME INEQUALITY IN A MARKET ECONOMY

Money income is only one component of economic well-being. Such factors as leisure, noncash transfer benefits, the nonpecuniary advantages and disadvantages of a job, and the expected stability of future income are also determinants of economic welfare. Nevertheless, since money income represents command over market goods and services, it is highly significant. Moreover, it is readily observable. Consequently, it is the most widely used measure of economic well-being and the degree of inequality prevailing in society.

Exhibit 11.1 indicates for one (largely) market economy, the United States, the share of *before-tax* annual money income received by *quintile*—that is, each fifth of families, ranked from the lowest to the highest. If there were total equality of annual income, each quintile of the population would have

**EXHIBIT 11.1**

**Inequality in the Money Income of Families—Selected Years 1935–1991**

| | Percentage of Aggregate Money Income Received by: | | | | |
|---|---|---|---|---|---|
| **Before Taxes** | **Lowest 20 Percent of Recipients** | **Second Quintile** | **Third Quintile** | **Fourth Quintile** | **Top 20 Percent of Recipients** |
| 1935–1936 | 4.1 | 9.2 | 14.1 | 20.9 | 51.7 |
| 1950 | 4.5 | 12.0 | 17.4 | 23.4 | 42.7 |
| 1960 | 4.8 | 12.2 | 17.8 | 24.0 | 41.3 |
| 1970 | 5.4 | 12.2 | 17.6 | 23.8 | 40.9 |
| 1980 | 5.2 | 11.5 | 17.5 | 24.3 | 41.5 |
| 1985 | 4.7 | 10.9 | 16.8 | 24.1 | 43.5 |
| 1990 | 4.6 | 10.8 | 16.6 | 23.8 | 44.3 |
| 1991 | 4.5 | 10.7 | 16.6 | 24.1 | 44.2 |
| **After Taxes and Transfers** | | | | | |
| 1990 | 6.5 | 11.2 | 16.1 | 23.2 | 43.0 |

**Source:** Bureau of the Census, *Current Population Reports,* Series P-60, No. 167, Table 10, and No. 180, Table B-7, and *Economic Report of the President, 1992* (Washington, DC: U.S. Government Printing Office, 1992), Table 4-2.

received 20 percent of the aggregate income. Clearly that was not the case. In 1991 the bottom 20 percent of family income recipients received 4.5 percent of the total before-tax money income. At the other end of the spectrum, the 20 percent of families with the highest annual incomes received 44.2 percent of the total money income in 1991. The top quintile of income recipients thus received almost ten times as much before-tax money income as the bottom quintile.

As Exhibit 11.1 illustrates, the United States experienced a substantial reduction in income inequality between the mid-1930s and 1970s. In 1970 the top quintile of recipients received 40.9 percent of the aggregate money income, down from 51.7 percent in the mid-1930s. Simultaneously, the income shares of the other quintile groupings increased during the 1935–1970 period.

Since 1970 income inequality has increased. The income share of the lowest quintile of income recipients in 1991 was well below the 1970 figure. Simultaneously, the income share received by the top quintile of earners rose between 1970 and 1991.

## A Closer Look at Income Inequality

How meaningful are the data of Exhibit 11.1? If all families were similar except in the amount of income received, the use of annual income data as an index of inequality would be far more defensible. However, this is not the case. The aggregate data lump together (1) small and large families, (2) prime-age earners and elderly retirees, (3) multi-earner families and families without any current earners, and (4) husband-wife families and single-parent families. Even if individual incomes over a lifetime were exactly equal, these factors would result in substantial inequality of annual income.

Consider how just one factor, age, affects income as people move through different phases of life. Typically, the annual income of young people is low, particularly if they are going to school or acquiring training. After completing their formal education and acquiring work experience, however, individuals move into their prime working years. During this phase of life, annual income is generally quite high, particularly for families where both the husband and wife work. Finally, there is the retirement phase, characterized by less work, more leisure, and a lower income. Even individuals who are quite well off tend to experience a current income that is well below the average for the entire population during this phase of life.

Exhibit 11.2 illustrates how low- and high-income recipients differ with regard to several important factors—including age, education, family status, and time worked—that underlie the distributional data of Exhibit 11.1. In contrast with those in lower income brackets, the typical family in the top quintile is headed by a person with far more education, often in the prime working-age phase of life, whose income is supplemented with the earnings of other family members, particularly a working spouse. Persons with little education, nonworking retirees, younger workers (under age 25), and single-parent families are much more likely to be found among families in the bottom quintile of income recipients.

Note that Exhibit 11.2 shows a striking difference in work time between low- and high- income families in 1991. No doubt, much of this difference reflects factors such as family size, age, working wives, and the incidence of husband-wife families. On a per-family basis, high-income families provide far

EXHIBIT 11.2

**The Differing Characteristics of High and Low-Income Families, 1991.**

| | Bottom 20 Percent of Income Recipients | Top 20 Percent of Income Recipients |
|---|---|---|
| Mean years of schooling (household head) | 10.5 | 14.7 |
| Age of household head (percent distribution) | | |
| Under 35 | 36 | 13 |
| 35-64 | 40 | 78 |
| 65 and over | 24 | 9 |
| Family status | | |
| Married-couple family (percent of total) | 50 | 94 |
| Single-parent family (percent of total) | 50 | 6 |
| Persons per family | 2.99 | 3.37 |
| Earners per family | .80 | 2.26 |
| Percent of married-couple families in which wife works | 2.8 | 7.9 |
| Percent of total weeks worked supplied by group | 7 | 32 |

**Source:** U.S. Department of Commerce, *Money Income of Households, Families, and Persons in the United States: 1991* (Washington, DC: U.S. Government Printing Office, 1992).

more workers, more full-time workers, and more weeks worked, than low-income families. According to the data for 1991, the number of weeks worked by members of high-income families was 4.6 times the number worked by members of low-income families. The high-income families earned almost 10 times as much income as the low-income families. This implies that the *earnings per week worked* of family members in the top-income quintile were only slightly greater than twice the *earnings per week worked* of individuals in the bottom-income quintile. Clearly, then, differences in the amount of time worked were a major factor contributing to the income inequality of Exhibit 11.1.

Except for the last row, the income data of Exhibit 11.1 are for money income before taxes and noncash transfers. Low-income households are the primary beneficiaries of noncash transfer programs that provide people with food (food stamps), health care, and housing. Correspondingly, under a system of progressive taxation, taxes take a larger share of income as one's income increases. After taxes and transfers, the bottom quintile of income recipients received 6.5 percent of the aggregate income in 1990, compared to 43 percent for the top quintile of earners. Thus, the top quintile received approximately 6.6 times the annual income of the bottom 20 percent of recipients after taxes and transfers (including noncash transfers), compared with almost 10 times the amount of their income prior to taxes and noncash transfers.

## Why Has Income Inequality Increased?

Exhibit 11.1 indicates that there has been an increase in income inequality in the United States during the last couple of decades. Why has the gap between the rich and the poor been growing? The answer to this question is a point of controversy among social scientists. No single factor can fully explain the recent changes. Research in this area, however, indicates that at least three factors have contributed substantially to the shift toward greater income inequality during the last two decades:

1. Increased proportions of single-parent and dual-earner families.
2. Increased earnings differentials across educational groupings.
3. Reduced marginal tax rates, giving high-income Americans greater incentive to earn rather than engage in tax-shelter activities.

Let's consider each of these factors. First, the nature of the family and the allocation of work responsibilities within the family have changed dramatically in recent decades. In 1991 slightly more than one-fifth (22 percent) of all families were headed by a single parent, approximately double the figure of the mid-1960s. Simultaneously, the labor force participation rate of married women has approximately doubled during the last 25 years, increasing the number of dual-earner families.

Since we now have more single-parent families and more dual-earner families, income inequality is greater. Perhaps an example will illustrate why. Consider two hypothetical families, the Smiths and the Browns. In 1973 both were middle-income families with two children and one market worker earning $30,000 (in 1993 dollars). Now consider their 1993 counterparts. The Smiths of 1993 are divorced and one of them, probably Mrs. Smith, is trying to work part-time and take care of the two children. The probability is very high that the single-parent Smith family of 1993 will be in the low, rather than middle, income category. They may well be in the bottom quintile of the income distribution. In contrast, the Browns of 1993 both work outside the home and each earns $30,000 annually. Given their dual incomes, the Browns are now in the high, rather than middle, income category. Indeed, as Exhibit 11.2 indicates, most high-income families (79 percent) achieve that status because both husband and wife are in the labor force.

Even if there were no changes in earnings between skilled and less-skilled workers, the recent changes within the family would enhance income inequality among families and households. More single-parent families like the Smiths increase the number of families with low incomes, while more dual-earner families like the Browns increase the number of high-income families. Thus both trends promote income inequality.

A second factor contributing to income inequality is the widening of earnings differentials across educational groupings in recent years. Throughout the 1950s and 1960s, guidance counselors told high school students that a college education was essential for economic success. For a long time, it appeared that they were wrong. As Exhibit 11.3 shows, in 1974 the annual earnings of men who graduated from college were only 27 percent higher than the earnings of male high school graduates, hardly a huge payoff for the time and cost of a college degree. Since then, however, things have changed dramatically. By 1991 the earnings premium of college graduates relative to high school

**EXHIBIT 11.3**

**Earnings Differential According to Educational Attainment, 1974–1991**

| | Percent by Which the Median Income of College Graduates Exceeds That of High School Graduates | |
|---|---|---|
| **YEAR** | **Males** | **Females** |
| 1974 | 27 | 54 |
| 1980 | 35 | 63 |
| 1984 | 49 | 74 |
| 1990 | 57 | 75 |
| 1991 | 60 | 77 |

**Source:** U.S. Commerce Department, Current Population Reports, Series P-60, No. 167, *Trends in Income, by Selected Characteristics: 1947 to 1988,* Table 50, and *Money Income of Households, Families, and Persons in the United States: 1990,* Table 29. The data for college graduates are for persons with a bachelor's degree *only,* while the data for high school graduates are for persons with *only* 12 years of schooling.

grads had risen to 60 percent, more than twice the premium of 1974. Similarly, the earnings of women college graduates increased sharply over women with only a high school education during the same period.

Why have the earnings of persons with more education (and skill) risen relative to those with less education (and skill)? Deregulation of the transport industry and the waning power of unions may have reduced the number of high-wage, blue-collar jobs available to workers with less education. No doubt, international competition has also played an important role here. Increasingly, American workers compete in a global economy. Recent innovations and cost reductions in both communications and transportation provide firms with greater flexibility with regard to location. Firms producing goods that require substantial amounts of low-skill labor are now better able to move to places such as Korea, Taiwan, and Mexico, where low-skill labor is cheaper. As firms using lots of low-skill labor move overseas, both the demand for and earnings of Americans with few skills and little education will decline. In an international setting, the United States will be far more attractive to firms requiring substantial amounts of high-skill, well-educated workers. Thus, the globalization of our economy, as it makes better and cheaper goods available to workers and other consumers, also tends to widen the earnings differences across educational and skill categories in the United States.

**marginal tax rate** The amount of one's additional (marginal) earnings that must be paid explicitly in taxes or implicitly in the form of a reduction in the level of one's income supplement. Since it establishes the fraction of an additional dollar earned that an individual is permitted to keep, it is an important determinant of the incentive to work.

Finally, a third factor increasing income inequality was the reduction during the 1980s of **marginal tax rates**—that is, the amount of additional earnings that had to be paid in taxes. The observed incomes of high-income Americans increased partially because they had more incentive to earn and less incentive to engage in tax-shelter activities. Prior to 1981, high-income Americans confronted top marginal tax rates of up to 70 percent (50 percent on earnings). Such high rates encouraged them to undertake investments and structure their business affairs in a manner that sheltered much of their income from the Internal Revenue Service. Business decisions were based more on convenience, reduced financial risk, greater pleasure for owners, and lower tax bills, and less on increasing productivity and profits. The taxable incomes of the top quintile of earners expanded sharply when the top marginal tax rates were reduced to the 30 percent range during the 1980s. Some of this increase in income reflected greater work effort and concentration on raising productivity and profits due to the increased incentive to earn. Much of it, however, merely reflected a reduction in tax-shelter activities. The flip side of the reduction in tax-shelter activities accompanying the lower marginal tax rates of the 1980s was an increase in the *visible* income of the rich. As the earnings of the rich became more readily observable, so, too, did income inequality.

## INCOME INEQUALITY AROUND THE WORLD

How does income inequality in the United States compare with that in other nations? Exhibit 11.4 presents a summary of household income data compiled by the World Bank. These data indicate that the degree of income inequality in the United States exceeds that of most other large industrial economies. Among the developed nations, income appears to be most equally distributed in Japan, Sweden, Italy, and Germany (prior to unification). In light of their relatively homogeneous populations—that is, uniformity with respect to race and ethnicity—and welfare-state policies (except for Japan), the lesser degree of inequality in these countries is not surprising. Among the developed countries for which data are available, only Australia has a similar amount of income inequality as the United States.

The share of income going to the wealthy is usually greater in less developed countries. According to the World Bank study, the top 20 percent of income recipients received 62.6 percent of the aggregate income in Brazil, 59 percent in Botswana, 54.5 percent in Costa Rica, and 53 percent in Colombia. Among the developing nations of Exhibit 11.4, only Indonesia, Taiwan, and Ghana were marked by a degree of inequality similar to that of developed countries.

The data of Exhibit 11.4 are not adjusted for either differences across countries in size of households or the demographic composition of the population. In addition, procedures used to make the estimates and the reliability of the data vary across countries. Thus, these data should be interpreted with a degree of caution.

## INCOME MOBILITY—DO THE POOR STAY POOR AND THE RICH STAY RICH?

The distribution of annual income is like a snapshot. It presents a picture at a moment in time. However, since the picture does not reveal the degree of movement across income groupings, it may be misleading. Consider two countries with identical distributions of annual income.[2] In both cases, the annual income of the top quintile of income recipients is eight times greater than the bottom quintile. Now, suppose that in the first country—we will refer to it

[2]The authors are indebted to Mark Lilla, from whose work this illustrative example was drawn. See Mark Lilla, "Why the 'Income Distribution' Is So Misleading," *The Public Interest* 77 (Fall 1984), pp. 63–76.

**EXHIBIT 11.4** **Income Inequality around the World**

| Country | Year | Percentage Share of Household Income Received by: | | |
|---|---|---|---|---|
| | | Bottom 20 percent | Middle Three Quintiles | Top 20 percent |
| **Developing Nations** | | | | |
| Indonesia | 1987 | 8.8 | 49.9 | 41.3 |
| Taiwan | 1990 | 7.9 | 53.9 | 38.2 |
| Ghana | 1988–1989 | 7.1 | 49.2 | 43.7 |
| Jamaica | 1988 | 5.4 | 45.4 | 49.2 |
| Cote d'Ivoire | 1986–1987 | 5.0 | 42.3 | 52.7 |
| Venezuela | 1987 | 4.7 | 44.7 | 50.6 |
| Malaysia | 1987 | 4.6 | 44.2 | 51.2 |
| Colombia | 1988 | 4.0 | 43.0 | 53.0 |
| Costa Rica | 1986 | 3.3 | 42.2 | 54.5 |
| Botswana | 1985–1986 | 2.5 | 38.5 | 59.0 |
| Brazil | 1983 | 2.4 | 35.0 | 62.6 |
| **Developed Nations** | | | | |
| Japan | 1979 | 8.7 | 53.8 | 37.5 |
| Sweden | 1981 | 7.4 | 50.9 | 41.9 |
| Italy | 1986 | 6.8 | 52.2 | 41.0 |
| Germany | 1984 | 6.8 | 54.1 | 40.2 |
| New Zealand | 1985–1986 | 5.7 | 53.5 | 40.8 |
| Canada | 1987 | 5.7 | 54.1 | 40.2 |
| United States | 1985 | 4.7 | 53.4 | 41.9 |
| Australia | 1985 | 4.4 | 53.4 | 42.2 |

**Source:** The World Bank, *World Development Report, 1992,* Table 30; *Statistical Yearbook of the Republic of China,* 1991, Table 61; and Peter Saunders, Helen Stott, and Garry Hobbes, "Income Inequality in Australia and New Zealand: International Comparisons and Recent Trends," *Review of Income and Wealth,* March 1991, pp. 63–79.

**income mobility**
Movement of individuals and families either up or down income distribution rankings when comparisons are made at two different points in time. When substantial income mobility is present, one's current position will not be a very good indicator as to what one's position will be a few years in the future.

as Static—the same people are at the top of the income distribution year after year. Similarly, the poor people of Static remain poor year after year. Static is characterized by an absence of **income mobility.** In contrast, earners in the second country, which we will call Dynamic, are constantly changing places. Indeed, during every five-year period, each family spends one year in the upper-income quintile, one year in each of the three middle-income quintiles, and one year in the bottom-income quintile. In Dynamic, no one is rich for more than one year (out of each five) and no one is poor for more than a year. Obviously, the degree of economic inequality in Static is vastly different from that in Dynamic. You would not know it, though, by looking at their annual income distributions. In fact, the annual income distributions in the two countries are identical.

The contrast between Static and Dynamic indicates why it is important to consider income mobility when addressing the issue of economic inequality. Isabel V. Sawhill and Mark Condon, at the Urban Institute, studied the income mobility between 1977 and 1986 for families headed by a person 25 to 54 years old. Exhibit 11.5 summarizes their major findings. After grouping families by their income in 1977, the table then shows the relative income position of the families nine years later. For example, the first row indicates the relative income position in 1986 of families who were in the top quintile of income recipients in 1977. Surprisingly, only 50 percent of the Americans who were best off (the top quintile) in 1977 were able to retain the same position nine years later. Almost 30 percent of the top earners in 1977 fell to the bottom three quintiles of the 1986 income distribution. The bottom row of Exhibit 11.5 tracks the experience of families in the lowest-income quintile in 1977. A little more than half (53 percent) of the families in the bottom-income quintile in 1977 remained there in 1986. On the other hand, 22 percent of the families at the bottom in 1977 were able to move into one of the top three income quintiles by 1986.

As the data of Exhibit 11.5 illustrate, many of the people in the highest income category during the initial year fell to middle and lower income categories during the latter year. Similarly, many of the people initially in the lowest income category were able to move up to middle and even high income categories in subsequent years. This indicates that many of the families in the top quintile moved up to this status because they had a particularly good year. On the other hand, many of those in the bottom quintile are there temporarily

**EXHIBIT 11.5** **Income Mobility—Family Income Ranking, 1977 and 1986**

| | Income Status in 1986 | | | | |
|---|---|---|---|---|---|
| Income Status in 1977 | Top-Paid Quintile | Next-Highest Paid Quintile | Middle Quintile | Next-Lowest Paid Quintile | Lowest-Paid Quintile |
| Top-Paid Quintile | 50.0 | 20.5 | 12.5 | 11.0 | 6.0 |
| Next-Highest-Paid Quintile | 25.0 | 34.0 | 21.5 | 14.5 | 5.0 |
| Middle Quintile | 13.0 | 24.0 | 29.5 | 19.0 | 14.5 |
| Next-Lowest-Paid Quintile | 8.5 | 14.5 | 25.5 | 30.0 | 21.5 |
| Lowest-Paid Quintile | 4.0 | 7.0 | 11.0 | 25.0 | 53.0 |

**Note:** Sample limited to adults, ages 25–54 in 1977.

**Source:** Isabel V. Sawhill and Mark Condon, "Is U.S. Income Inequality Really Growing?" *Policy Bites* (Washington, DC: Urban Institute, U.S. Department of the Treasury), June 1992.

because things went poorly during the year—perhaps a family member lost a job or suffered a business setback. Thus, the degree of income inequality among families and individuals over a longer time period—a decade, for example—is less than the income inequality during any given year.

Sawhill and Cordon were also able to calculate the changes in the income of the families that started out in each quintile. As Exhibit 11.6 shows, the average real income (that is, income adjusted for inflation) of families in every quintile increased between 1977 and 1986. Those starting in the bottom quintile, however, had much greater income increases than those starting in any of the higher income brackets. In nine years, their incomes, corrected for inflation, rose by 77 percent. By contrast, the incomes of those starting in the highest income quintile rose by only 5 percent. On average, families who were in any quintile in 1977 other than the top quintile had larger percentage income increases than families of any quintile above them.

We noted earlier that since 1970, income inequality has slowly increased in the United States. Those in the highest quintile have received a gradually larger share of national income, and those in the lowest quintile gradually less. These "static" income data suggest that "the rich are getting richer while the poor are getting (relatively) poorer."

The static income data, however, conceal the dynamics of the situation. As Exhibit 11.6 illustrates, low-income families have experienced substantial income gains—more rapid than those of the rich—in recent years. Many of those with incomes in the lowest quintiles have moved up the income ladder into middle and upper income quintiles. As they exit from lower brackets, however, they are replaced by a new group of youthful, inexperienced families with low incomes. Thus, the income inequality during any given year does not change very much, even though the income gains of the poor, on average, are substantially greater than those of the rich.

**EXHIBIT 11.6**

**Income Mobility: How 1977 Quintiles Fared in 1986**

| | Average Family Income (in 1991 dollars) | | |
|---|---|---|---|
| **Income Status in 1977** | **1977 Quintile Members in 1977** | **1977 Quintile Members in 1986** | **Percent Gain** |
| Top-Paid Quintile | $92,531 | $97,140 | 5% |
| Next-Highest-Paid Quintile | 57,486 | 63,314 | 10 |
| Middle-Quintile | 43,297 | 51,796 | 20 |
| Next-Lowest-Paid Quintile | 31,340 | 43,041 | 37 |
| Lowest-Paid Quintile | 15,873 | 27,998 | 77 |
| All Families | $48,101 | $56,658 | 18 |

**Note:** Sample limited to adults, ages 25–54 in 1977.

**Source:** Isabel V. Sawhill and Mark Condon, "Is U.S. Income Inequality Really Growing?" *Policy Bites* (Washington DC: Urban Institute, U.S. Department of the Treasury), June 1992.

Both economic thinking and the empirical data indicate that drawing conclusions from *annual* income data must be done with care. The annual data camouflage the fact that many high-income earners had much lower incomes just a few years earlier. Similarly, many with low current incomes have attained significantly higher incomes previously (and others can be expected to do so in the future). Changes in family incomes through time indicate that the inequalities observed at a point in time are substantially reduced over time as individuals and families exchange relative economic positions.

## POVERTY IN THE UNITED STATES

In an affluent society such as the United States, income inequality and poverty are related issues. Poverty could be defined in strictly relative terms—the bottom one-fifth of all income recipients, for example. However, this definition would not be very helpful, since that would mean that no increase in wealth could change the number of those in poverty.

**poverty threshold income level** The level of money income below which a family is considered to be poor. It differs according to family characteristics (for example, number of family members) and is adjusted when consumer prices change.

Since consumption survey data indicated that low- and middle-income families spent about one-third of their income on food in the 1960s, when poverty was initially defined, the U.S. government established the **poverty threshold income level** at three times the cost of an economical, nutritionally adequate food plan. The poverty threshold income level varies according to family size, because the food costs vary by family size and composition. It is adjusted annually to account for rising prices. When determining a person's or family's income, the *official poverty rate,* the percentage of people or families below the poverty threshold income level, considers only money income. Income received in the form of *noncash* benefits such as food stamps, medical care, and housing subsidies is completely ignored.

How many people are poor? According to the official definition of poverty, there were 35.7 million persons, and 7.7 million poor families in 1991. As Exhibit 11.7 indicates, 14.2 percent of the population and 11.5 percent of the families were officially classified as poor in that year. During the 1950s and 1960s, the poverty rate declined substantially. By 1970 it was 10.1 percent, down from 18.1 percent in 1960 and 32.0 percent in 1947. During the 1970s, the overall poverty rate changed little. Since then, it has risen. To understand why, it is useful to examine the composition of the poverty population.

In recent years, the composition of the poverty population has changed substantially. In 1959 elderly persons and the working poor formed the core of the poverty population. Twenty-two percent of the poor families were headed by an elderly person in 1959. Most poor people (70 percent) worked at least part of the year. By 1991 the picture had changed dramatically. Only 9 percent of the poor families were headed by an elderly person, and nearly half (46 percent) of the poor households were headed by a person 18 to 64 years of age *who did not work at all during the year.* Today, the issue of poverty is interrelated with that of family instability. In recent years, there has been a substantial growth in the proportion of single-parent families—particularly female-headed families—and an accompanying decline in the proportion of husband-wife families. Since the poverty rate of female-headed families (35.6 percent) is several times higher than the rate for husband-wife families (6.0 percent), an increase in family instability tends to push the poverty rate upward. In 1991 more than half (54 percent) of the poor families were headed

**EXHIBIT 11.7**

**The Poverty Rate of Persons and Families in the United States 1947–1991**

| | Poverty Rate (percent) | |
|---|---|---|
| **Year** | **Persons** | **Families** |
| 1947 | n.a. | 32.0 |
| 1960 | 22.2 | 18.1 |
| 1970 | 12.6 | 10.1 |
| 1980 | 13.0 | 10.3 |
| 1985 | 14.0 | 11.4 |
| 1987 | 13.4 | 10.7 |
| 1989 | 12.8 | 10.3 |
| 1990 | 13.5 | 10.7 |
| 1991 | 14.2 | 11.5 |

**Source:** Bureau of the Census, *Money Income and Poverty Status in the United States: 1989,* Tables 18 and 21, and *Economic Report of the President, 1964* (Washington, DC: U.S. Government Printing Office, 1964), Table 7, and *Economic Report of the President, 1993,* Table B-28.

by a female, compared with only 23 percent in 1959. Given the exceedingly high poverty rate of female-headed families, the overall poverty rate is unlikely to decline as long as the proportion of female-headed families continues to increase.

## Transfer Payments and the Poverty Rate

In the mid-1960s, it was widely believed that an increase in income transfers directed toward the poor would substantially reduce, if not eliminate, the incidence of poverty. The 1964 *Economic Report of the President* (p. 77) presented the dominant view:

> Conquest of poverty is well within our power. About $11 billion [approximately $44 billion measured in 1990 dollars] a year would bring all poor families up to the $3,000 income level we have taken to be the minimum for a decent life. The majority of the nation could simply tax themselves enough to provide the necessary income supplements to their less fortunate citizens. The burden—one-fifth of the annual defense budget, less than 2 percent of GNP—would certainly not be intolerable.

**means-tested income transfers** Transfers that are limited to persons or families with an income below a certain cutoff point. Eligibility is thus dependent on low-income status.

This view became popular, and income-transfer programs for the poor grew rapidly. Measured in constant dollars, **means-tested income transfers** tripled, rising to more than $91 billion (measured in 1990 dollars) in 1975—more than twice the expenditure level that some thought would be sufficient to virtually eliminate poverty in the United States. *As a proportion of personal income,* transfers directed toward the poor (for example, Aid to Families with Dependent Children, food stamps, and Medicaid) doubled during the 1965–1975 period. Since 1975 the percent of aggregate income allocated to transfers has been maintained at the higher level.

**EXHIBIT 11.8**

**The Poverty Rate, 1947–1991**

The official poverty rate of families declined sharply during the 1950s and 1960s, changed little during the 1970s, and rose during the early 1980s. The shaded area of the bars indicates the additional reduction in the poverty rate when noncash benefits are counted as income. In 1991 the poverty rate adjusted for noncash benefits was 8.8 percent.

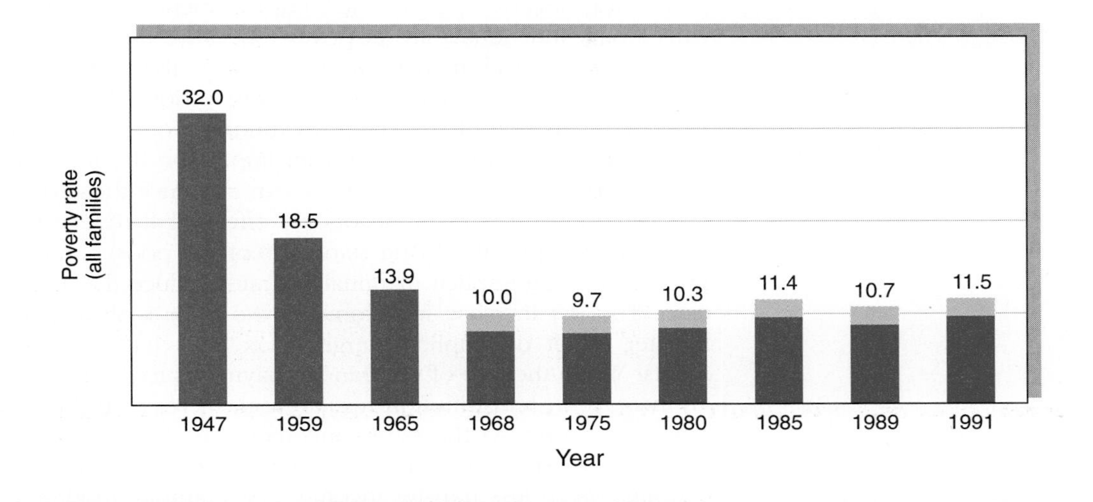


Did the expansion in government income transfers reduce the poverty rate as the 1964 *Economic Report of the President* anticipated? Antipoverty programs provide both cash and noncash benefits. Exhibit 11.8 shows the poverty rate with and without the benefits of noncash transfer programs counted as income. Continuing the trend of the post–Second World War era, the official poverty rate fell throughout the 1960s. During the 1970s, however, the rate leveled off. By 1980 it was 10.3 percent, virtually unchanged from the 1968 rate. By 1991, as we reported earlier, the rate had drifted up to 11.5 percent. The record for the nonelderly was even more disappointing. In 1991, almost three decades after President Lyndon Johnson declared "war on poverty" in the United States, the official poverty rate of nonelderly families was 12.5 percent, compared to 9.0 percent in 1968 (and 10.9 percent in 1965). Even after adjustment for the noncash benefits, the 1991 poverty rate of the nonelderly was approximately the same as it was in the 1960s prior to the increase in expenditures accompanying the War on Poverty programs.

## Factors Limiting Effectiveness of Transfer Programs

Why weren't the income-transfer programs more effective? Clearly, a slowdown in economic growth has retarded progress against poverty. While the employment rate has increased during the last 15 years, real wages have stagnated. The real wages of workers with few skills and little education have actually declined in recent years. Social changes have also slowed progress against poverty. The divorce rate, proportion of births to unwed mothers, and the incidence of female-headed households have all increased significantly in recent years, pushing the poverty rate upward.

Nonetheless, the results achieved have been disappointing. After all, per capita income adjusted for inflation in the United States was more than 50 percent greater in 1991 than 1965. Why didn't this growth of income significantly reduce the poverty rate? Many economists believe that the secondary effects accompanying transfer programs provide part of the answer. While government transfers improve the living standards of many poor people, the programs also severely penalize self-improvement efforts by low-income Americans. Some individuals are in poverty because they are victims of debilitating disease, or physical, mental, or emotional disability. For others, however, periods of poverty reflect factors such as loss of job, change in family status, premature termination of schooling (or training), or choice of a high-risk lifestyle. For them, personal choices exert an impact on the incidence and duration of poverty. Transfer programs, in turn, can influence those decisions.

There are three major secondary effects that reduce the ability of transfer programs to uplift the living standards of the poor, particularly the marginally poor. First, high implicit marginal tax rates reduce the incentive of the poor to earn. The net increase in income of the poor is thus much smaller than the transfer. What do implicit marginal tax rates have to do with transfer payments? When the size of the transfer payments to the poor is linked to income, an increase in redistribution results in an increase in this implicit marginal tax rate of the poor. As the poor's incomes rise, they qualify for fewer programs, and the size of their transfer income is reduced. For the poor, then, higher earnings mean less transfer income. For example, food stamp benefits are reduced by $30 for each $100 of monthly earnings up to monthly earnings of $800 for a family of four. The implicit marginal tax rates for some programs are even higher.

The problem is much greater, of course, when the potential benefits from multiple programs are considered. For a family that is eligible for several antipoverty transfer programs at one time, an increase in earned income will reduce benefits and thereby substantially reduce the *net* increase in income derived from work. In extreme cases, higher earnings may even reduce the individual's net income once the accompanying loss of transfer benefits is considered. These high implicit marginal tax rates reduce the incentive of low income recipients to work and earn. As a result, some portion of the transfer benefits is merely replacement income; that is, it simply replaces income the recipient would have earned in the absence of the transfer. Thus, the net income of recipients increases by less than the amount of the transfer.

When the poor opt out of the labor force because of the high implicit marginal tax rates, declining skills further limit their ability to escape poverty. This is another secondary negative effect. Individuals who do not use their skills for extended periods of time will find it difficult to compete with otherwise similar individuals with continuous labor force participation. The long-term consequences of an incentive structure that encourages nonwork is even more destructive than the short-term effects. As marginal poor people opt for nonwork, their work record deteriorates. With the passage of time, they become less and less able to support themselves.

Finally, some economists believe that transfer programs may encourage individuals to engage in behavior that can lead to poverty. By partially ensuring against various adversities that often accompany certain choices, the transfer programs reduce the opportunity cost of births by single mothers, marital dissolution, abandonment of children by fathers, dependence on drugs or alcohol, and dropping out of school or the labor force. Indirectly, antipoverty transfer programs, as currently structured, subsidize and thereby encourage choices that often lead to low-income status. This is not the intent of the transfers, but it is nonetheless a secondary effect.

In the short run, this secondary effect is probably not very important. Over the longer term, however, the unintended negative consequences may be substantial. In addition, government antipoverty transfers crowd out private charitable efforts by families, individuals, churches, and civic organizations. When taxes are levied to do more, private individuals and groups will predictably adjust and do less. This too erodes the effectiveness of the programs.

Consideration of all these secondary effects makes it easier to understand why increased spending on transfer programs has failed to reduce the poverty rate as much most people expected.

## The Impact of Transfers—A General Analysis

Since this chapter focuses on the distribution of income and incidence of poverty, our analysis has centered on antipoverty income transfers. Most income transfers, however, are not directed toward the poor. By far, the Social Security program is the largest income-transfer program in the United States. In essence, it is an intergenerational income-transfer program. Taxes are collected from the current generation of workers and, for the most part, paid out to retirees and other beneficiaries. Other transfer programs levy taxes in order to provide income and subsidies to farmers, unemployed workers, small businesses, firms that export goods, and other groups. Still other subsidies are designed to benefit specific regions, industries, or occupations.

When considering the effects of these transfers, it is important to keep two points in mind. *First, when funds are taxed away from some in order to provide benefits to others, resources will tend to move away from production and toward plunderous activities (and defensive activities against plunder).* The quantity of resources directed toward lobbying, political campaigns, and the various forms of "favor seeking" from the government will be directly in proportion to the ease with which the political process can be used for personal (or interest group) gain at the expense of others. When a government becomes heavily involved in income-transfer activities, people will spend more time organizing and lobbying politicians and less time producing goods and services. Resources that would otherwise be used to create wealth and generate income are wasted fighting over slices of a smaller economic pie.

*Second, competition for transfers will erode most of the long-term gain of the intended beneficiaries.* While transfers can generate short-term gains for a group, their ability to bestow favors on a class of recipients in a manner that will *permanently* improve their well-being is severely limited.[3] This point merely reflects the competitive process; competition erodes abnormally high returns. In a world of scarce resources, governments must establish a criterion for the receipt of income transfers and other political favors. If they did not do so, the transfers would bust the budget. Generally, the government will

[3]See James Gwartney and Richard Stroup, "Transfers, Equality, and the Limits of Public Policy," *Cato Journal* (Spring–Summer 1986), for a detailed analysis of this issue.

require a transfer recipient to own something, do something, or be something. However, once a criterion is established, people will modify their behavior to qualify for the "free" money or other government favors. As individuals "invest" resources attempting to meet the criterion—that is, as they compete for the subsidy—they erode much of the gain. Predictably, the *net* gain of the recipients will be substantially less than the amount of the income transfer or subsidy.

Perhaps a thought experiment will help illustrate this general point. Suppose the U.S. government decided to give away a $50 bill between 9 a.m. and 5 p.m. to persons willing to wait in line at the teller windows of the U.S. Treasury. Long lines would emerge. How long? How much time would people be willing to take from their leisure and their productive activities? A person whose time was worth $5 per hour would be willing to spend up to 10 hours waiting in line for the $50. Enormous amounts of time would be wasted. Moreover, the competition among potential recipients would guarantee that the *net* gains of each would be quite small, considering the time they spent in line.

When beneficiaries have to do something (for example, wait in line, fill out forms, lobby government officials, take an exam, endure delays, or contribute to selected political campaigns) in order to qualify for a transfer, a great deal of their potential gain will be lost as they seek to meet the qualifying criteria. Similarly, when beneficiaries have to own something (for example, land with an acreage allotment to grow wheat or a license to operate a taxicab or sell a product to foreigners) in order to get a subsidy, people will bid up the price of the asset needed to qualify for the subsidy until the higher asset price captures the value of the subsidy. In each case, the potential beneficiaries will compete to meet the criteria until they dissipate much of the *net* value of the transfer. As a result, the recipient's *net gain* will generally be substantially less than the amount of the transfer payment.

The relative ineffectiveness of antipoverty transfer programs reflects a more general point: once a transfer program is institutionalized, competition and market adjustments will erode much of its value to the recipients. Thus, the net benefits that accrue to the intended beneficiaries will be substantially less than the amount of the transfer. Of course, unanticipated changes in transfer programs can generate temporary gains or losses for various groups. Over the longer term, though, transfer programs will be largely ineffective as a means of improving the economic status of the recipients.

## INCOME INEQUALITY AND FAIRNESS—CONCLUDING THOUGHTS

Throughout this chapter, we have presented descriptive data on income inequality and poverty. These data focus our attention on outcomes. When considering the significance of these data, two additional points should be kept in mind. First, economics does not indicate that one pattern of outcomes (distribution of income) is superior to another. Such a conclusion would involve interpersonal comparisons among individuals—the value judgment that some people (or groups) are more deserving than others. Modern economists are unwilling to make such comparisons.

Second, some would argue that the *pattern* of economic outcomes is not nearly so important as the *process* that generates the outcomes. According to this view, the fairness of the outcome should be judged by the fairness of the process, rather than the pattern of the income distribution. For example, suppose that an athlete, rock star, or business entrepreneur was able to provide a product or service that 5 million people per year were willing to pay for at a price large enough to generate a net income of one dollar per buyer for the individual. As a result, this individual would have an annual income of $5 million, which would result in a substantial amount of income inequality. But the income inequality merely reflects voluntary exchanges between responsible individuals. Individual consumers gain as a result of the purchases that generate the income. What is unfair about this situation? Those who stress the importance of the process would generally conclude that since the process was fair, so, too, was the outcome.

## LOOKING AHEAD

Thus far, we have focused on narrowly defined markets, decision-making of firms, and incomes of individuals. We are now ready the consider more highly aggregated markets and how economic policy affects an economy's overall level of output, prices, and employment. The following chapter focuses on the meaning and construction of several important indicators that economists utilize to measure the performance level of an economy.

## CHAPTER SUMMARY

1. In 1991 the annual income data before taxes and transfers indicate that the bottom 20 percent of families received 4.5 percent of the aggregate income, while the top 20 percent received just under 45 percent of the total income.
2. During the 1940s there was a substantial reduction in income inequality in the United States, and this trend continued, though at a slower rate, throughout the 1950s and 1960s. The earlier trend has reversed, however. Since 1970, there has been an increase in income inequality.
3. A substantial percentage of the inequality in the annual income distribution reflects differences in age, education, family status, number of earners in the family, and time worked. Young, inexperienced workers, students, and retirees are overrepresented among those with low incomes. Persons in their prime working years are overrepresented among high-income recipients. Persons with high incomes have substantially more years of schooling. Married-couple families with multi-earners are overrepresented among the high-income recipients, while single-parent families with few earners make up a large share of the low-income recipients.
4. Differences in time worked accounted for much of the inequality of annual income. While the income of families in the top earnings quintile was almost 10 times the income of families in the bottom quintile in 1991, the number of weeks worked by members of the top quintile of families was 4.6 times the weeks worked by those in the bottom quintile. Thus, the before-tax income per week worked of the top earners was only about twice the income per week worked of the low-income families.

5. No single factor can explain the shift toward greater measured income inequality during the 1970s and 1980s in the United States. However, the following three factors contributed to this shift: (a) an increasing number of single-parent and dual-earner families, (b) an increase in the earnings of persons with more education relative to those with less education, and (c) reduced tax-shelter activities due to the sharp reduction in marginal tax rates during the 1980s.
6. Among the advanced industrial nations, the degree of income inequality is smallest in Japan, Sweden, Italy, and Germany and greatest in Australia and the United States. In general, income is distributed more equally in the advanced industrial countries than in less developed nations.
7. In interpreting the significance of the annual income distribution, it is important to recognize that the annual data camouflage the movement of persons up and down the distribution over time. Many persons with middle and high current income had substantially lower incomes just a few years earlier. Similarly, many low-income recipients have attained significantly higher incomes in the past (and many will do so again in the future).
8. According to the official data, more than 11 percent of the families in the United States were poor in 1991. Those living in poverty were generally younger, less educated, less likely to be working, and more likely to be living in families headed by a single parent than those who were not poor.
9. During the 1965–1975 period, transfer payments—including means-tested transfers—increased quite rapidly in both real dollars and as a share of personal income. As income transfers expanded, the poverty rate of the elderly continued to decline. However, beginning in the late 1960s, the poverty rate began to rise. Even after adjustment for in-kind food, housing, and medical benefits, the poverty rate of working-age Americans has been rising gradually since the late 1960s.
10. When considering the impact of current income-transfer programs on the poverty status of working-age persons, it is important to recognize the following points:
    a. When the transfer benefits of low-income families decline with income, the incentive of the poor to earn personal income is reduced. Thus, means-tested transfers tend to increase the net income of the poor by less than the amount of the transfer.
    b. When high marginal tax rates accompanying transfers induce the poor to opt out of the labor force, their skills depreciate, further limiting their ability to escape poverty.
    c. The effectiveness of transfers may also be limited because programs designed to protect against adversity tend to encourage choices that actually increase the occurrence of the adversity.
11. When governments become more heavily involved in tax-transfer activities, they discourage production and encourage plunder. The ability of government transfers to improve the long-term economic status of the intended beneficiaries is limited. As markets adjust and people modify their behavior to qualify for transfers, the net gains derived by the transfer recipients will decline.

# Study Guide

## CHAPTER 11

# Developing the Economic Way of Thinking

## CRITICAL-ANALYSIS QUESTIONS

1. Do you think the current distribution of income in the United States is too unequal? Why or why not? What criteria do you think should be used to judge the fairness of the distribution of income?

*2. Is annual money income a good measure of economic status? Is a family with a $50,000 annual income able to purchase twice the quantity of goods and services as a family with $25,000 of annual income? Is the standard of living of the $50,000 family twice as high as the $25,000 family? Discuss.

3. What is income mobility? If there is substantial income mobility in a society, how does this influence the importance of income-distribution data?

*4. Consider a table in which the family income of parents is grouped by quintiles down the rows and the family income of their offspring is grouped by quintiles across the columns. If there were no intergenerational mobility in this country, what pattern of numbers would be present in the table? If the nation had attained complete equality of opportunity, what pattern of numbers would emerge? Explain.

5. Do individuals have a property right to income they acquire from market transactions? Is it a proper function of government to tax some people in order to provide benefits to others? Why or why not? Should there be any constitutional limitations on the use of the political process to take income from some in order to provide benefits to others? Discuss.

*6. Since income transfers to the poor typically increase the marginal tax rate confronted by the poor, does a $1,000 additional transfer payment necessarily cause the income of poor recipients to rise by $1,000? Why or why not?

*7. Sue is a single parent with two children considering a job at $800 per month ($5 per hour). She is currently drawing monthly cash benefits of $300, plus food stamp benefits of $100, and Medicaid benefits valued at $80. If she accepts the job, she will be liable for employment taxes of $56 per month and lose all transfer benefits. What is Sue's implicit marginal tax rate for this job?

8. Some argue that taxes exert little effect on people's incentive to earn income. In considering this issue, suppose you were required to pay a tax rate of 50 percent on all money income you earn while in school. Would this affect your employment? How might you minimize the personal effects of such a tax?

*9. Transfer payments targeted to the poor make up only a small portion of the total government income transfers. Large income transfers are targeted toward the elderly, farmers, and the unemployed, regardless of their economic condition. Why do you think this is so? Does an expansion in the size of tax-transfer activities reduce income inequality?

10. "Welfare is a classic case of conflicting goals. Low welfare payments continue to leave people in poverty, but high welfare payments attract people

*Asterisk denotes critical-analysis questions for which the answers are given in Appendix A.

to welfare rolls, reduce work incentives, and cause higher rates of unemployment" (quoted from *There Is No Free Lunch Newsletter*). Evaluate. (Hint: apply the opportunity-cost concept.)

11. "Means-tested transfer payments reduce the current poverty rate. However, they also create an incentive structure that discourages self-provision and self-improvement. Thus, they tend to increase the future poverty rate. Welfare programs essentially purchase a lower poverty rate today in exchange for a higher poverty rate in the future." Evaluate.

## MULTIPLE-CHOICE SELF-TEST

1. Imagine two cities, Engelgrad and Legreeville, where the high-, middle-, and low-income recipients in one city have annual incomes identical to their counterparts' incomes in the other city. In the city of Engelgrad, the poorest families one year almost always end up as the richest families the next year and become middle-income families the year after that. In the city of Legreeville, however, the poor remain poor and the rich remain rich. Which of the following is true about the two cities?
   a. Annual data on the distribution of income will indicate that the degree of income inequality in the two cities is identical.
   b. The degree of lifetime income inequality in the two cities is identical.
   c. The income mobility for the two cities is identical.
   d. The distribution of annual income is more unequal in Legreeville than Engelgrad.
2. International comparisons of income inequality indicate that the degree of inequality in annual income is greatest in
   a. More developed countries.
   b. Less developed countries.
   c. Countries with a homogeneous population.
   d. The United States.
3. Compared to high-income families, a larger proportion of low-income families are
   a. Headed by a person under age 35.
   b. Headed by an elderly person.
   c. Single-parent families.
   d. All of the above are true.
4. Which of the following would tend to increase the degree of income inequality among families?
   a. A decline in the unemployment rate of low-skill workers.
   b. An increase in the proportion of both single-parent and dual-earner families.
   c. A reduction in the earnings differential between college graduates and high school graduates.
   d. A reduction in the earnings differential between high school graduates and high school dropouts.
5. The data on the distribution of income among individuals and families in the United States indicate that

a. The power of labor unions and corporations is the major determinant of income inequality.
b. The rich stay rich and the poor stay poor from one generation to another.
c. Substantial inequality in annual income emanates from differences in education, age, hours worked, and family size.
d. Members of poor families work substantially more hours per year than members of high-income families.

6. Which of the following is an accurate statement with regard to income statistics?
a. Current annual income is an accurate indicator of relative economic status over a longer period of time such as a decade or lifetime.
b. Recent studies indicate that one's relative income position also generally determines the relative income position of one's children and grandchildren.
c. Income inequalities observed at a point in time are significantly reduced over time as individuals and families move up and down the income ladder.
d. Even though annual income data camouflage the fact, high-income earners generally maintain their status year after year, while those with low current incomes tend to stay poor year after year.

7. When determining whether an income places a family or individual in poverty, the *official poverty rate* excludes
a. Money income derived from sources other than labor.
b. Money income received from transfer programs.
c. Noncash benefits derived from programs supplying recipients with food, housing, and medical benefits.
d. Noncash benefits provided to the nonelderly, but it counts these benefits when they are supplied to the elderly.

8. Which of the following limits the ability of the current system of transfer programs to increase the incomes of the able-bodied poor?
a. The high implicit marginal tax rates that accompany the current-income transfer programs reduce the incentive of the poor to earn.
b. The transfer programs encourage the poor to marry and form dual-earner families.
c. The transfer programs tend to increase the wage rates that employers must pay for low-skill labor.
d. The transfer programs reduce the likelihood of single-parent families.

9. Jane is a single parent with two children considering a job at $1,200 per month ($7.50 per hour). She is currently drawing monthly cash benefits of $300, plus monthly food stamps of $100, and Medicaid benefits valued at $100 per month. If she accepts the job, she will be liable for payroll taxes of $100 per month and lose all of her transfer benefits. How large is Jane's *implicit marginal tax rate* associated with acceptance of the job?
a. 25 percent.
b. 50 percent.
c. 55 percent.
d. 60 percent.

10. The marginal tax rate can be an important determinant of the incentive to earn income because it establishes the

a. Total tax liability of a taxpayer.
b. Fraction of an additional dollar earned that the individual is permitted to keep for personal use.
c. Fraction of one's *total* income that must be paid in taxes.
d. Degree of inequality that exists between the rich (the top 20 percent of the income recipients) and the poor (the bottom 20 percent of the income recipients).

## PROBLEMS

1. Lucy Fong is an orthodontist. Hillary Schmidt is a part-time clerk in a small store, where she earns $7.00 per hour. Hillary would like Dr. Fong to straighten the teeth of Brenda Schmidt, Hillary's daughter, and she is willing to work an extra part-time job (at the same pay) to meet this expense, even though it is not a medical necessity. Dr. Fong would be willing to take on this extra work if she were paid $700 after taxes.
   a. In the absence of taxes, how many hours does Hillary have to work in order to pay for her daughter's treatment?
   b. If Dr. Fong was in the 50 percent tax bracket, and Hillary received transfer payments (for example, food stamps, housing subsidies, AFDC) that put her in the 65 percent *implicit* tax bracket, how many hours must Hillary work to provide Dr. Fong the same after tax $700 in exchange for the treatment? (Hint: Hours × $7.00 × 0.35 × 0.5 = $700.)
   c. If Dr. Fong paid no taxes, but Hillary was in the 65 percent implicit tax bracket, how many hours must Hillary work to earn the $700?
   d. If Dr. Fong paid 70 percent of her income in taxes, and Hillary paid none at all, how many hours would Hillary have to work for Dr. Fong to take home $700?
   e. Considering your answer to part d, would you say that high taxes on productive, highly paid people hurt low-income people?
   f. Considering your answer to part c, would you say that taxes on productive lower-paid people hurt higher-income recipients?
   g. Would Hillary (and Brenda) Schmidt be better off without the transfer program that puts Hillary in the implicit 65 percent tax bracket? Discuss.
2. Robert Reckman is currently unemployed and qualifies for unemployment compensation of $138.00 per week. He has been offered a new job paying $200.00 per week, subject to income taxes of 33 percent and social security taxes of 7 percent.
   a. From society's point of view, is it desirable that Reckman accept the job? Why?
   b. Is it to Reckman's financial advantage to accept the job? Why?
   c. Calculate Reckman's marginal tax rate (including both explicit and implicit taxes) if he accepted the job.
   d. If Reckman's unemployment benefits had been subject to an income tax of 20 percent, would it have been in his financial interest to accept the job? Why?
3. The more income mobility there is, the less serious the poverty problem.
   a. The accompanying table presents income mobility information for the United States between 1980 and 1984.

| Family Income Position, 1980 | Family Income Position, 1984 | | |
|---|---|---|---|
| | **Top 20%** | **Middle 60%** | **Bottom 20%** |
| Top 20% | 62% | 36% | 2% |
| Middle 60% | 12 | 77 | 11 |
| Bottom 20% | 1 | 34 | 65 |

Which occurs more frequently, falling from the top, or rising from the bottom?

b. Consider the country of Static discussed in the text. Complete the table below to reflect the complete absence of income mobility in Static:

| Family Income Position, 1980 | Family Income Position, 1984 | | |
|---|---|---|---|
| | **Top 20%** | **Middle 60%** | **Bottom 20%** |
| Top 20% | ______ | ______ | ______ |
| Middle 60% | ______ | ______ | ______ |
| Bottom 20% | ______ | ______ | ______ |

c. Now consider the country of Dynamic discussed in the text. Complete the table below to reflect perfect income mobility:

| Family Income Position, 1980 | Family Income Position, 1984 | | |
|---|---|---|---|
| | **Top 20%** | **Middle 60%** | **Bottom 20%** |
| Top 20% | ______ | ______ | ______ |
| Middle 60% | ______ | ______ | ______ |
| Bottom 20% | ______ | ______ | ______ |

# PART III

## MACROECONOMICS

CHAPTER

# 12

# OUTPUT, INFLATION, AND EMPLOYMENT

It has been said that figures rule the world; maybe. I am quite sure that it is figures which show us whether it is being ruled well or badly.

*Johann Wolfgang Goethe, 1830*

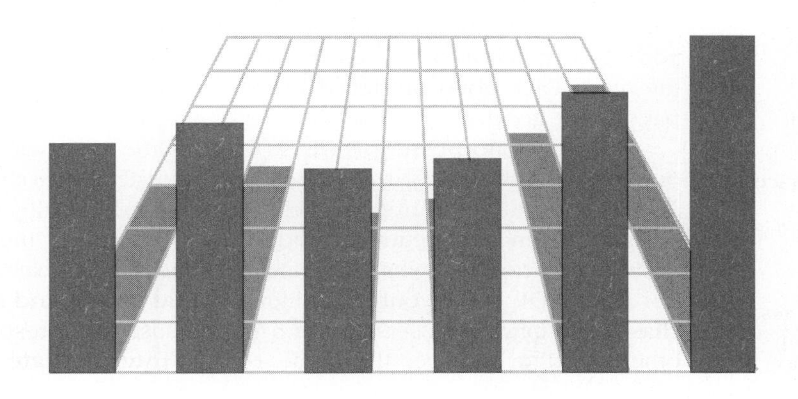

## CHAPTER FOCUS

- How is output measured? What is GDP, and how is it calculated?
- What is the difference between real and nominal GDP? Why is it important to adjust income and output data for changes in prices?
- How is inflation measured? What are some of its side effects?
- What is the business cycle? How do fluctuations in business activity affect the labor market?
- What is the source of unemployment? Does unemployment indicate that resources are being used inefficiently?
- What do economists mean by full employment? How is full employment related to the natural rate of unemployment?

This chapter focuses on various indicators that reflect the overall performance of an economy. We will explain how the output of an economy is measured and how it is affected by inflation. Finally, we will analyze the cyclical nature of economic activity and consider its impact on the labor market.

# HOW IS OUTPUT MEASURED?

In elementary school, most of us were told that you cannot add apples and oranges. However, this is precisely the nature of the problem we confront when we seek to measure output. Somehow, we must add together the production of apples, oranges, shoes, roast beef sandwiches, television sets, automobiles, medical services, and literally thousands of other items.

The diverse goods produced in our modern world have only one thing in common: someone pays a price for them. Therefore, to measure output, we must weight units of each good according to their purchase price. If a consumer pays $10,000 for a new automobile and $10 for a nice meal, production of the automobile adds 1,000 times as much to output as production of the meal. Similarly, production of a television set that is purchased for $500 will add 1/20 as much to output as the new automobile and 50 times the amount of the meal. Each good produced increases output by the amount the consumer pay for the good.

**gross domestic product (GDP)** The total market value of all final goods and services produced domestically during a specific period, usually a year.

**final goods and services** Goods and services purchased by their ultimate users.

**intermediate goods** Goods purchased for resale or for use in producing another good or service.

The **gross domestic product (GDP)** is the most widely used measure of output. It is the sum of the market value of all final goods and services produced domestically during a specific time period, usually a year. Since GDP is designed to measure current production, it is not just the sum of all transactions. Let us consider what GDP includes and what it excludes.

First, GDP counts only the value of **final goods and services,** those purchased by their final users. When a good is used as a resource to produce another good or service, the value of this **intermediate good** is embodied within the price of the final good or service. Double-counting would result if we added both the price of the intermediate good and the price of the final-user good to GDP. Instead, the value of the intermediate good (resource) is reflected in the price of the final-user good it helps to produce. For example, when a wholesale distributor sells steak to a restaurant, the final purchase price paid by the patron of the restaurant for a steak dinner will reflect the cost of the meat. GDP would be overstated if we included both the sale price of the intermediate good (the steak sold by the wholesaler to the restaurant) and the final purchase price of the steak dinner.

Exhibit 12.1 will help clarify the accounting methods for GDP. Before the final good, bread, is in the hands of the consumer, it goes through several intermediate stages of production. The farmer produces a pound of wheat and sells it to the miller for 30 cents. The miller grinds the wheat into flour and sells it to the baker for 65 cents. The miller's actions have added 35 cents to the value of the wheat. The baker combines the flour with other ingredients,

**EXHIBIT 12.1**

**GDP and Stages of Production**

Most goods go through several stages of production. This chart illustrates both the market value of a loaf of bread as it passes through the various stages of production (column 1) and the amount added to the bread by each intermediate producer (column 2). GDP counts only the market value of the final product. Of course, the amount added by each intermediate producer (column 2) sums to the market value of the final product.

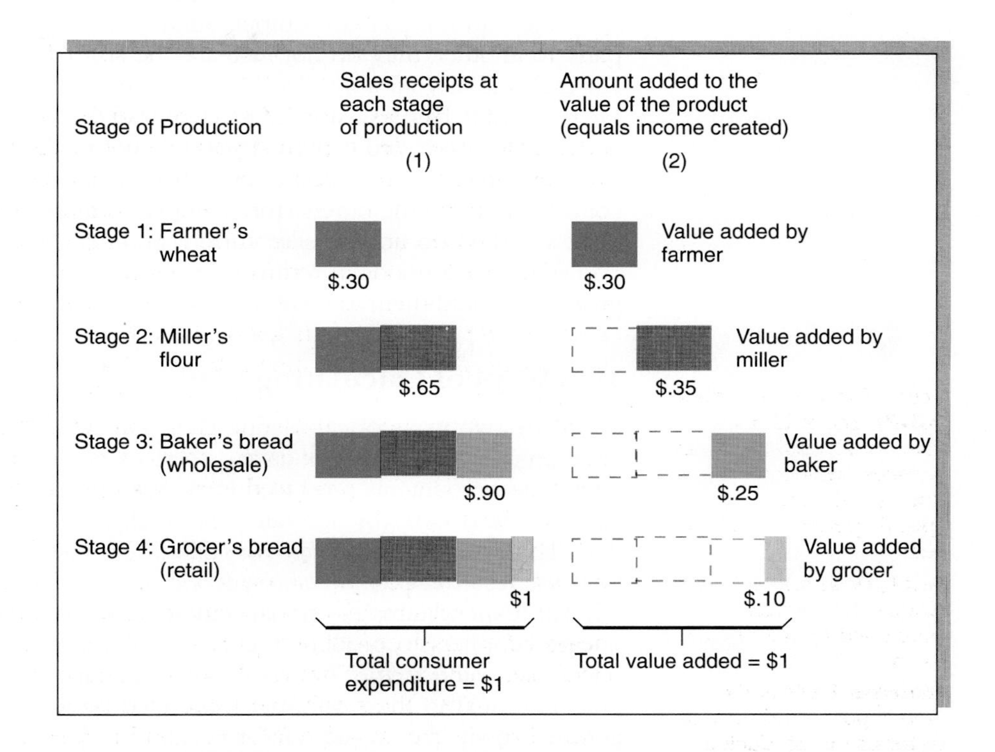

makes a loaf of bread, and sells it to the grocer for 90 cents. The baker has added 25 cents to the value of the bread. The grocer stocks the bread on the grocery shelves and provides a convenient location for consumers to shop. The grocer sells the loaf of bread for $1, adding 10 cents to the value of the final product. Only the market value of the final product—the $1 for the loaf of bread—is added to GDP.

As this exhibit illustrates, the price of the final good reflects the *value added* at each stage of production. The 30 cents added by the farmer, the 35 cents by the miller, the 25 cents by the baker, and the 10 cents by the grocer sum to the $1 purchase price. Thus, GDP reflects both the value of the final goods and services produced and the value added—that is, the amount of income created—at each stage of production.

Since GDP is a measure of current production, exchanges of goods produced during earlier time periods and ownership rights to financial assets are excluded. For example, the purchase of a used automobile produced last year will not enhance current GDP, nor will the sale of a home constructed five years ago. Production of these goods was counted at the time they were produced. Neither will the purchase or sale of stocks, bonds, or other financial assets add to GDP. These transactions merely transfer ownership of previously produced goods or financial assets from one party to another. They do not involve current production of additional goods. Therefore, they are not included in GDP. (Note: if a sales commission is involved in the exchange of a used good or the ownership right to a financial asset, the commission does represent the provision of a service during the current period, so the commission, but not the sales price, is included in GDP.)

Income transfers, whether private or public-sector, are also excluded, since they do not increase output. Such transfers merely shift wealth from one party to another, they do not increase the size of the aggregate economic pie. For example, if your aunt sends you $100 to help pay for your college expenses, your aunt has less wealth and you have more, but the transaction adds nothing to current production. Thus, it is not included in GDP. Similarly, when the government taxes income away from some citizens in order to make income transfers to the others (for example, farmers, or the elderly, or the poor), these transfers do not increase current output. The recipients of such transfers do not produce goods in return for the transfers. Therefore, it would be inappropriate to add them to GDP.

## Two Ways of Calculating GDP

There are two ways of calculating GDP. One way is to sum the total expenditures on the "final user" goods and services produced during a period. National income accountants refer to this method as the *expenditure approach*. GDP can also be derived by summing the total costs incurred as the result of producing the goods and services supplied during the period—a method referred to as the *resource cost–income approach*.

The expenditures on goods and services provide the wherewithal for inducing suppliers to produce the output. From an accounting viewpoint, total payments to the factors of production, including the producer's profit or loss, must be equal to the sales price generated by the good. This is true for each good or service produced, and it is also true for the aggregate economy. This is a fundamental accounting identity. The equation is

Dollar flow of expenditures on final goods = GDP = dollar flow of the producer's cost on final goods

Thus, GDP obtained by adding the dollar value of final goods and services purchased will equal GDP obtained by adding the total of all "cost" items, including the producer's profits, associated with the production of final goods. Exhibit 12.2 summarizes the components of GDP for both the expenditure approach and resource cost approach.

**EXPENDITURE APPROACH** There are four components of GDP when it is calculated by the expenditure approach: (1) consumption purchases, (2) gross private domestic investment, (3) government purchases, and (4) net exports. **Consumption** purchases include household expenditures on both durable goods like automobiles and appliances and non-durable goods and services like food, clothing, fuel, medical services, and recreation. Consumption purchases are nearly always the largest component of GDP.

**consumption** Household spending on consumer goods and services during the current period. Consumption is a flow concept.

**investment** The flow of expenditures on durable assets (fixed investment) plus the addition to inventories (inventory investment) during a period. These expenditures enhance our ability to provide consumer benefits in the future.

**Investment** purchases are expenditures on long-lasting goods that are used to produce goods for future consumption. Unlike food or medical services, investment goods are not immediately "used." A house, for example, is an investment good because it will provide a stream of services long into the future. Business plants and equipment are investment goods for the same reason. Changes in business inventories are also classified as investment goods, since they too will provide future consumer benefits. When business firms have more goods and services at the end of the year than they had at the beginning of the year, investment in inventories will be positive.

Government purchases include both investment and consumption goods produced and purchased by governments during the period. Current government expenditures on national defense, highways, and dams for flood control projects would be included in this category. So too, would government

**EXHIBIT 12.2**

**The Two Ways of Measuring GDP**

There are two methods of calculating GDP. It can be calculated either by summing the expenditures on the final-user goods and services of each sector (left, below) or by summing the costs associated with the production of these goods and services (right, below).

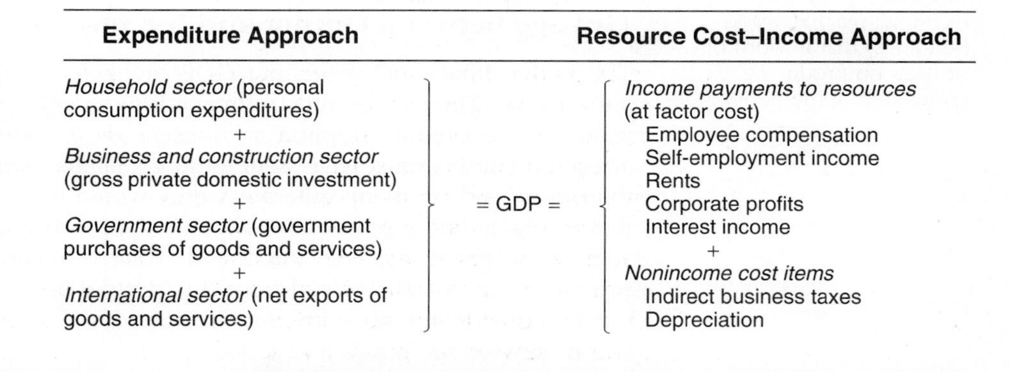

| Expenditure Approach | | Resource Cost–Income Approach |
|---|---|---|
| *Household sector* (personal consumption expenditures)<br>+<br>*Business and construction sector* (gross private domestic investment)<br>+<br>*Government sector* (government purchases of goods and services)<br>+<br>*International sector* (net exports of goods and services) | = GDP = | *Income payments to resources* (at factor cost)<br>Employee compensation<br>Self-employment income<br>Rents<br>Corporate profits<br>Interest income<br>+<br>*Nonincome cost items*<br>Indirect business taxes<br>Depreciation |

expenditures on police protection, schools, and the administration of a judicial system. Since transfer payments add to government spending but do not involve the production of goods and services, government purchases will be less than total government expenditures.

**exports** Goods and services produced domestically but sold to foreigners.

**imports** Goods and services produced by foreigners but purchased by domestic consumers, investors, and governments.

**net exports** Exports minus imports.

**Exports** are domestically produced goods and services sold to foreigners. **Imports** are foreign-produced goods and services purchased domestically. We want GDP to measure only domestic production. Therefore, when measuring GDP by the expenditure approach, we must (1) add exports (goods produced domestically that were sold to foreigners) and (2) subtract imports (goods produced abroad that were purchased by domestic residents). For national accounting purposes, we can combine these two factors into a single entry, **net exports,** where net exports is equal to exports minus imports.

**RESOURCE COST–INCOME APPROACH** Exhibit 12.2 (right side) indicates the components of GDP when it is calculated by summing the cost of the output produced during the period. Production of goods involves human work and ingenuity. Therefore, payments to the workers—both the compensation of employees and the income of self-employed proprietors—who provide labor services and undertake the risks of organizing their own businesses, are major components of GDP under the resource cost–income approach. Machines, buildings, land, and other physical assets also contribute to the production process. Rents, corporate profits, and interest income are payments to persons who provide either physical resources or the financial resources with which to purchase physical assets. *Rents* are returns to resource owners who permit others to use their assets during the time period. *Corporate profits* are compensation earned by stockholders, who bear the risk of the business undertaking and who provide financial resources with which the firm purchases resources. *Interest* is a payment to parties who extend loans to producers.

**indirect business taxes** Taxes that increase the business firm's costs of production and therefore the prices charged to consumers. Examples would include sales, excise, and property taxes.

**depreciation** The estimated amount of physical capital (for example, machines and buildings) that is worn out or used up producing goods during the period.

Not all cost components of GDP result in an income payment to a resource supplier. There are two major indirect costs. **Indirect business taxes** boost the market price of goods when GDP is calculated by the expenditure approach. Similarly, when looked at from the factor-cost viewpoint, indirect taxes are a cost of supplying the goods to the purchasers. **Depreciation,** the wear and tear on the machines, buildings, and other physical assets used to produce goods, is also an indirect cost of production. Unless producers are able to cover the cost of the machinery and other physical capital used to produce a good, they will not continue to supply these capital assets.

## Linkage between Output and Income

The two methods of calculating GDP highlight the linkage between output and income. The expenditure approach indicates that GDP is a measure of the value of the output supplied to households, businesses, and governments. These purchasers must have valued the goods and services at least as much as the prices paid for them; otherwise, they would not have purchased them. Alternatively, as the resource cost–income approach highlights, GDP is also the sum of the payments, both direct and indirect, to the resource suppliers who produced the goods. Viewed from this perspective, GDP is a measure of the income (including the entrepreneur's residual income) generated by those who produced the goods and services.

In essence, output and income are opposite sides of the same coin. When a good is produced and sold, the purchase price is a measure of the output produced. But the income received by the resource suppliers, including that of entrepreneurs, must also sum to the purchase price. It is an accounting identity.

Consider the following example. Suppose that a construction company hires workers and purchases other resources, such as lumber, nails, and bricks to build a home. When the home is sold to a buyer, the sales price is a measure of output. Simultaneously, the sum of the payments to the workers, suppliers of the other resources, and the residual income received by the construction company (which may be either positive or negative) is a measure of income. Both the output and income add up to the sales price of the good, which represents the value of what was produced.

The link between output and income reveals the real source of economic progress. People and nations that produce more goods and services valued by purchasers will also generate more income for resource suppliers. Thus, growth in the production of goods and services valued by people provides the source for income growth and improvements in our living standards.

## ADJUSTING FOR INFLATION

**nominal values** Values expressed in current dollars. Also called *money values.*

**real values** Values that have been adjusted for the effects of inflation.

It is important to distinguish between real and nominal economic values. **Nominal values** (or *money values,* as they are often called) are expressed in current dollars. Over time, nominal values reflect both (1) changes in the real size of an economic variable and (2) inflation—a change in the general level of prices. In contrast, **real values** eliminate the impact of changes in the price level, leaving only the real changes in the size of an economic variable. Whenever economists use the term "real" (for example, "real GDP" and "real income"), this means that the data have been adjusted for the effects of inflation. When comparing data at different points in time, it is nearly always the real changes that are of most interest.

### Inflation, Nominal GDP, and Real GDP

**inflation** A general increase in the level of prices and therefore a decline in the purchasing power of the money.

**price index** Measures the cost of purchasing a given bundle of goods at a point in time relative to the cost of the same goods during a prior base year, which is assigned a value of 100.

**Inflation** is a general increase in the level of prices and therefore a decline in the purchasing power of the money. How can we determine whether prices, in general, are rising or falling? Economists use a **price index,** which measures the cost of purchasing a given bundle of goods at a point in time relative to the cost of purchasing the same bundle of goods during a prior base year. The base year is assigned a value of 100. If prices are higher during the current period (that is, if the cost of purchasing the given bundle of goods has risen), the value of the price index during the current period will exceed 100. For example, if the cost of purchasing the typical bundle of goods consumed by households increases by 10 percent during a year, the price index will also increase by 10 percent. This 10 percent change in the price index is a measure of inflation during the year.

Price index data allow us to separate real changes in output from nominal changes that merely reflect price increases. Exhibit 12.3 illustrates this point. Between 1987 and 1992, the nominal GDP of the United States increased from

**EXHIBIT 12.3**

**Changes in Prices and the Real GDP of the United States, 1987–1992**

Between 1987 and 1992, nominal GDP increased by 31.1 percent. But, when the 1992 GDP is deflated to account for price increases, real GDP increased by only 8.4 percent.

| | Nominal GDP (billions of dollars) | Price Index (GDP deflator, 1987 = 100) | Real GDP (billions of 1987 dollars) |
|---|---|---|---|
| 1987 | $4,540 | 100.0 | $4,540 |
| 1992 | 5,951 | 120.9 | 4,922 |
| Percent Increase | 31.1 | 20.9 | 8.4 |

**Source:** U.S. Department of Commerce.

**GDP deflator** The price index that measures changes in the cost of all goods included in GDP.

$4,540 billion to $5,951 billion, an increase of 31.1 percent. However, a large portion of this increase in nominal GDP reflected inflation rather than an increase in real output. The **GDP deflator,** the price index that measures changes in the cost of all goods included in GDP, increased from 100 in the 1987 base year to 120.9 in 1992. This indicates that prices rose by 20.9 percent between 1987 and 1992. To determine the real GDP for 1992 in terms of 1987 dollars, we deflate the 1992 nominal GDP for the rise in prices:

$$\text{Real GDP}_{92} = \text{nominal GDP}_{92} \times \frac{\text{GDP deflator}_{87}}{\text{GDP deflator}_{92}}$$

Because prices were rising, the latter ratio is less than 1. In terms of 1987 dollars, the real GDP in 1992 was $4,922 billion, only 8.4 percent more than in 1987. So, although money GDP expanded by 31.1 percent, real GDP increased by only 8.4 percent.

A change in money GDP tells us nothing about what is happening to the rate of real production unless we also know what is happening to prices. Money GDP could double while production actually declines if prices more than double. On the other hand, money GDP could remain constant while real GDP increases if prices fall during a time period. Data for both money GDP and price changes are essential for a meaningful comparison of real output between two time periods.

**consumer price index (CPI)** An indicator of the general level of prices. It attempts to compare the cost of purchasing the market basket bought by a typical consumer during a specific period with the cost of purchasing the same market basket during an earlier period.

Of course, inflation will also influence the nominal values of incomes and wage rates. When adjusting personal income and wage data for the effects of inflation, it is most appropriate to use the **consumer price index (CPI),** which measures the change in the cost of purchasing the bundle of goods consumed by the typical household. In contrast with the GDP deflator, which includes prices of goods and services purchased by businesses and governments, the CPI includes only goods and services purchased by households. As the cost of purchasing the typical bundle of goods bought by households increases, the CPI increases by the same proportion. For example, if the cost of purchasing the typical combination actually consumed by households during the base period increases by 5 percent during a year, the CPI would also increase by 5 percent.

Just as was true for GDP data, the ratio of the price index in Period 1 divided by the price index in Period 2 should be used to deflate nominal income and nominal wage data and thereby convert them to real values (measured in Period 1 dollars). This ratio ($CPI_1 \div CPI_2$) will be less than 1 if there has been a general increase in prices of consumer goods. Thus, multiplication by the ratio will reduce the nominal values and thereby eliminate the nominal increases that reflect merely the change in the general level of prices.

## Variations in Inflation Rates

The rate of inflation varies widely among countries. As Exhibit 12.4 illustrates, the annual inflation rate in the United States, Japan, Singapore, and Thailand was generally less than 5 percent during the period of 1986–1990. Moreover, it varied within a relatively small range and seldom changed by more than 1 or 2 percent from year to year. In contrast, the inflation rates of Venezuela, Turkey, Mexico, Brazil, and Argentina were substantially higher, and the year-to-year changes in the rate were much larger. For example, the inflation rate in Venezuela jumped from 11.5 percent in 1986 to 28.4 percent in 1987 and 84.3 percent in 1989, before receding to 40.8 percent in 1990. In Argentina, the inflation rose from 90 percent in 1986 to 342.7 percent in 1988 and 3079.2 percent in 1989. This latter figure indicates that the general level of prices in Argentina in 1989 was more than 30 times the level of just one year earlier!

**unanticipated inflation**
An increase in the general level of prices that was not expected by most decision-makers.

It is important to distinguish between unanticipated and anticipated inflation. **Unanticipated inflation** is an increase in the price level that comes as a surprise, at least to most individuals. The actual inflation rate may either

**EXHIBIT 12.4**

**Inflation Rate of Various Countries, 1986–1990**

| | Rate of Inflation | | | | |
|---|---|---|---|---|---|
| **Country** | **1986** | **1987** | **1988** | **1989** | **1990** |
| Japan | 0.6 | 0.1 | 0.7 | 2.3 | 3.1 |
| Singapore | –1.4 | 0.5 | 1.5 | 2.4 | 3.5 |
| United States | 1.9 | 3.7 | 4.0 | 4.3 | 5.4 |
| Thailand | 1.8 | 2.6 | 3.8 | 5.4 | 5.9 |
| Venezuela | 11.5 | 28.4 | 29.5 | 84.3 | 40.8 |
| Turkey | 34.6 | 38.8 | 75.4 | 63.3 | 60.3 |
| Mexico | 86.2 | 131.8 | 114.2 | 20.0 | 26.7 |
| Brazil | 145.0 | 229.8 | 682.8 | 1286.9 | 2928.4 |
| Argentina | 90.0 | 131.6 | 342.7 | 3079.2 | 2311.3 |

**Source:** International Monetary Fund, *International Financial Statistics,* April 1992. The consumer price index was used to measure the inflation rate of each country.

exceed or fall short of the inflation rate expected by most people. For example, suppose that, based on the recent past, most people anticipate an inflation rate of 4 percent. If that rate ensues, it will not disrupt the economy, since it was planned for. However, if the actual inflation turns out to be 10 percent, for example, it will catch people off guard. In this instance, the actual inflation rate exceeds the expected rate. Conversely, if the actual inflation rate had been zero, when 4 percent inflation was widely anticipated, the stable price level would also have caught people by surprise. In this instance, an over-estimate of inflation would result.

High rates of inflation are almost always associated with wide year-to-year swings in the inflation rate. When the rate of inflation is high and variable, as in Venezuela, Turkey, Mexico, Brazil, and Argentina during 1986–1990, it will be virtually impossible for decision-makers to anticipate the future path of inflation with any degree of accuracy. Decision-making and planning for the future will be extremely difficult under these circumstances.

**anticipated inflation** An increase in the general level of prices that is expected by economic decision-makers based on their evaluation of past experience and current conditions.

**Anticipated inflation** is a change in the price level that is widely expected by decision-makers. For example, if individuals expect prices to rise 5 percent annually, the occurrence of 5 percent inflation merely fulfills their expectations. In contrast with unanticipated inflation, decision-makers are neither surprised nor caught off guard by inflation rates that they anticipate. Decision-makers are generally able to anticipate slow steady rates of inflation, such as those present in the United States, Japan, Singapore, and Thailand during 1986–1990, with a high degree of accuracy.

## Effects of Inflation

At first glance, it might appear that inflation consistently helps debtors relative to creditors. This is true when the inflation is unanticipated (or underestimated), since it erodes the purchasing power of the principal and interest repayment of borrowed funds. Thus, in terms of command over goods and services, debtors give up less (and lenders receive less repayment) than each anticipated at the time they agreed to the loan.

However, debtors will not gain when the inflation rate is anticipated. When inflation persists, its primary impact is on nominal interest rates. When decision-makers come to anticipate the inflation, lenders will demand and borrowers will grant higher interest rates on loans because both parties expect the value of the dollar to depreciate. A borrower and a lender might agree to a 5 percent interest rate if they anticipate stable prices during the course of the loan. However, if both expected prices to rise 10 percent annually, they would instead agree to a 15 percent interest rate. The higher interest rate would compensate the lender for the expected decline in the purchasing power of the dollar during the course of the loan.

When borrowers and lenders accurately anticipate an inflation rate, even high rates of inflation fail to systematically redistribute income from debtors to lenders. Debtors gain at the expense of lenders only if the actual rate of inflation exceeds the rate expected at the time the terms of the transaction are established.

Laypersons have a tendency to think that inflation is "robbing us of the purchasing power of our paycheck." This view, however, is largely illusionary. Wages are also prices. A general inflation will increase wages as well as other prices. Thus, while inflation reduces the purchasing power of a paycheck *of a given size,* it also tends to increase the size of the paychecks.

It is important to note that an increase in the relative price of a good is not the same thing as inflation. Suppose that the price of oil increases from $20 to $30 per barrel. As a result, oil is now more expensive relative to all other goods. The higher oil prices will increase the cost of living and reduce the income level of people (and oil-importing countries) that buy oil. As the result of the oil price increase, purchasers of oil will now have to give up more of other goods in order to acquire a barrel of oil (or products made with oil). In contrast, inflation is a *general* increase in the nominal prices of goods and resources. Basically, it is a general increase in the price of goods relative to money. Goods are more expensive in terms of money. This explains why we often define inflation as a decline in the purchasing power of money.

# INSTABILITY IN REAL GDP

Historically, economic growth has been uneven. Even in countries that have achieved rapid economic growth, periods of economic expansion have traditionally been followed by economic slowdown and contraction. During the slowdown, real GDP grows at a slower rate, if at all. During the expansion phase, real GDP grows rapidly. Economists refer to these fluctuations in economic conditions as **business cycles,** meaning periods of up-and-down motion in aggregate measures of current economic output and income.

**business cycle**
Fluctuations in the general level of economic activity as measured by such variables as the rate of unemployment and changes in real GNP.

Exhibit 12.5 illustrates a hypothetical business cycle. When most businesses are operating at capacity level and real GDP is growing rapidly, a business *peak* or *boom* is present. A business peak is characterized by high levels of

**EXHIBIT 12.5**

**Business Cycle**

In the past, ups and downs have characterized aggregate business activity. Despite these fluctuations, an upward trend in real GNP is usually observed in most countries.

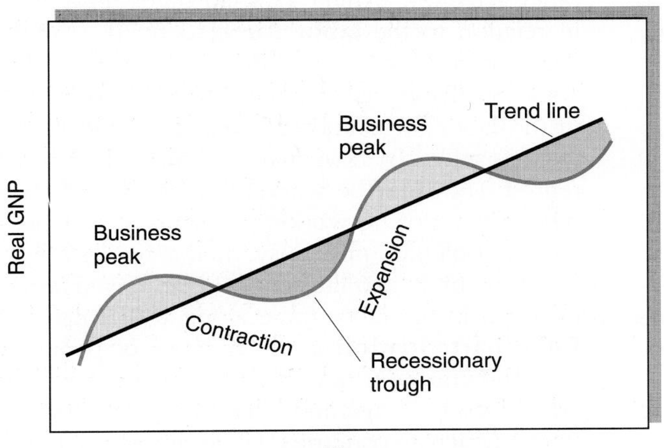

economic activity and real GDP compared with the recent past and near future. As aggregate business conditions slow, the economy begins the contraction or recessionary phase of a business cycle. During the contraction, the sales of most businesses fall, real GDP grows at a slow rate or perhaps declines, and unemployment in the aggregate labor market increases.

The bottom of the contraction phase is referred to as the *recessionary trough*. After the downturn reaches bottom, and economic conditions begin to improve, the economy enters an expansionary stage. Here business sales rise, GDP grows rapidly, and the rate of unemployment declines. The expansion eventually blossoms into another business peak. The peak, however, peters out and turns into a contraction, beginning the cycle anew.

**recession** A downturn in economic activity characterized by declining real GDP and rising unemployment. In an effort to be more precise, many economists define a recession as two consecutive quarters in which there is a decline in real GDP.

**depression** A prolonged and very severe recession.

The term **recession** is widely used to describe conditions during the contraction and recessionary trough phases of the business cycle—that is, a period during which real GDP declines. Many economists specify that a recession means a decline for two or more successive quarters. When a recession is prolonged and characterized by a sharp decline in economic activity, it is called a **depression.**

The hypothetical business cycle of Exhibit 12.5 indicates steady and smooth movement from business peak to recessionary trough and back again to the peak. In the real world, cycles are not nearly so regular or predictable. Sometimes the expansionary phase may last only a year or two, while at other times it will last four, five, or six years or even longer. Similarly, the depth and length of recessions varies substantially. Despite their lack of predictability, economic ups and downs are observable. As we proceed, we will analyze the causes of this cyclical behavior and consider alternative strategies to reduce the magnitude of economic fluctuations and promote more stable economic growth.

## Economic Fluctuations and the Labor Market

**labor force** The portion of the population 16 years of age and over who are either employed or unemployed.

Fluctuations in real GDP influence the demand for labor and employment. In our modern world, people are busy with jobs, household work, school, and other activities. Exhibit 12.6 illustrates how economists classify these activities in relation to the **labor force,** defined as that portion of the population 16 years and over who are either working or seeking work. The non-institutional adult population is grouped into the two broad categories of (1) persons not in the labor force and (2) persons in the labor force. There are a variety of reasons why a person may not currently be in the labor force. They may be retired. They may be working in their own household or attending school. Still others may not be working as a result of illness or disability. While many of these people are quite busy, their activities are outside the market labor force.

**rate of labor force participation** The number of persons 16 years of age or over who are either employed or actively seeking employment as a percentage of the total noninstitutional population 16 years of age and over.

As Exhibit 12.6 illustrates, unemployed workers who are seeking work are included in the labor force along with employed workers. The **rate of labor force participation** is the number of persons in the labor force (including both the employed and the unemployed) as a percentage of the total population 16 years of age and over. The rate of labor force participation varies substantially across countries. For example, in 1990 the rate of labor force participation rate was 67 percent in Canada and 66 percent in the United States, but only 55 percent in Germany and 47 percent in Italy. The percent of married

**EXHIBIT 12.6**

**Population, Employment, and Unemployment, 1990**

The accompanying diagram illustrates the alternative participation status categories for the adult population.

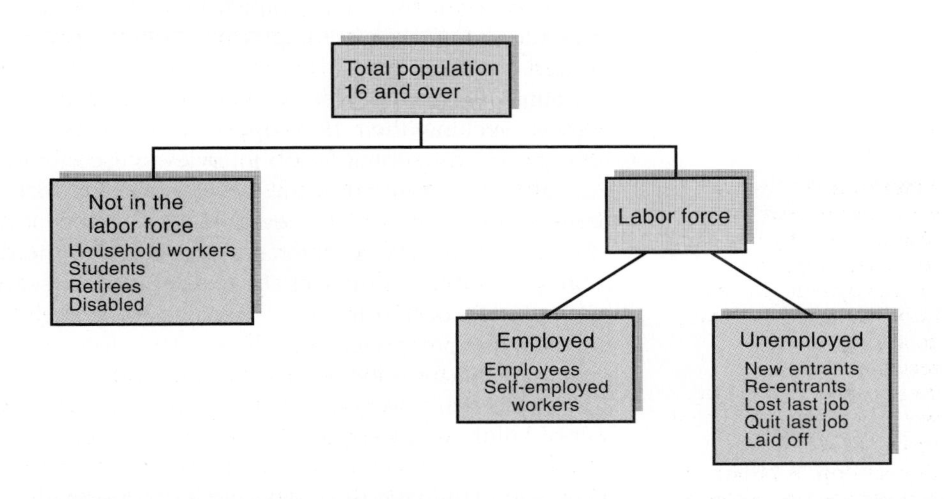


**rate of unemployment** The percent of persons in the labor force who are not employed. Mathematically, it is equal to

$$\frac{\text{Number of persons unemployed}}{\text{Number in the labor force}} \times 100$$

**unemployed** The term used to describe a person, not currently employed, who is either (1) actively seeking employment or (2) waiting to begin or return to a job.

women in the labor force is generally smaller in countries like Italy and Germany that have a low rate of labor force participation.

The **rate of unemployment** is a key barometer of conditions in the aggregate labor market. This notwithstanding, the term is often misunderstood. At the most basic level, it is important to note that *unemployment* is different from *not working*. As we have already indicated, there are several reasons why a person may not currently be working. In order to be classified as **unemployed,** a person must be both not working and available and looking for work (or waiting to return to or begin a job.) The rate of unemployment is the number of persons unemployed expressed as a percentage of the labor force. Working through Problem 4 (in the Study Guide) will enhance your understanding of these basic labor force concepts by illustrating variations in these rates among the major industrial countries.

## Reasons for Unemployment

In a dynamic world where information is imperfect and people are free to choose among jobs, some unemployment is inevitable. As new products are introduced and new technologies developed, some firms are expanding while others are contracting. Still other firms may be going out of business. This process results in the creation of new jobs and the disappearance of old ones. Similarly, at any point in time potential workers are switching from school (or nonwork) into the labor force, while others are retiring or taking a leave from the labor force. As long as workers are mobile—as long as they can voluntarily quit and search for better opportunities in a changing world, switching from one job to another and reallocating work responsibilities within the family—some unemployment will be present.

The basic cause of this unemployment that results from dynamic change is imperfect information. In the real world, information is scarce. Both employers and employees search for it to help them make better choices. Employers looking for a new worker want to find the "best available" worker to fill their opening. It is costly to hire workers who perform poorly. It is sometimes even costly to terminate their employment. So, employers search—they expend time and resources screening applicants and choose only those who have the desired qualifications.

Similarly, unemployed workers seeking a job search among potential alternatives, seeking their best option. They make telephone calls, respond to newspaper ads, submit to job interviews, use employment services, and so on. Pursuit of personal gain—the landing of a job that is more attractive than the current options of which they are aware—motivates job seekers to engage in job search activities. Additional search leads to the discovery of higher-paying, more preferable alternatives. However, as a job searcher finds out about more potential job opportunities, it becomes less likely that additional search will uncover a more preferable option. Therefore, as Exhibit 12.7 illustrates, the marginal gain from job search declines with time spent searching. The primary cost of job search is generally the opportunity cost of wages forgone as the result of failure to accept one's best current alternative. This cost will increase as additional search leads to the discovery of better alternatives not accepted. Thus, the marginal cost of job search will rise with time spent searching.

**EXHIBIT 12.7**

**Benefits and Costs of Job Search**

The marginal gain from job search generally declines with time spent searching for a job, because it becomes less likely that additional search will lead to a better position. Conversely, the marginal cost of additional search rises with search time, primarily because still more search means forgoing wages on more attractive jobs discovered by prior search. When the job seeker perceives that the marginal gain from additional search no longer exceeds the marginal cost, the best option discovered by the search process will be accepted.

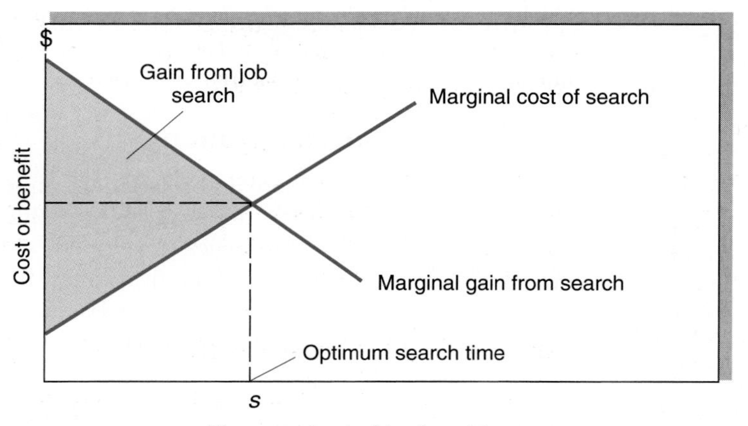

The rational job seeker will search for employment as long as the expected marginal gain from the search exceeds the expected marginal cost of the search. Eventually, as the marginal gains decline and marginal costs rise, the job seekers will conclude that additional search is not worth the cost. The best alternative resulting from the search process will be accepted. However, this process takes time, and during this time the job searchers will experience unemployment.

It is important to note that even though unemployment is a side effect, there is a positive side to the job search process. (See the "Myths of Economics" box.) Job search generally leads to a better match between the skills and preferences of workers and the requirements of jobs. When employees are working on jobs that fit their skills better, their productivity and incomes will be higher. If a job seeker were to search less than the optimal amount (point *s* in Exhibit 12.7), potential gains (from the achievement of a better job) in excess of the marginal search costs would be forgone. Similarly, job search beyond the optimal level is simply not worth the cost.

**cyclical unemployment** Unemployment due to recessionary business conditions and inadequate aggregate demand for labor.

While some unemployment is perfectly consistent with economic efficiency, abnormally high rates are generally the result of unexpected reductions in the demand for goods and services. Economists refer to unemployment emanating from this source as **cyclical unemployment.** In a world of imperfect information, adjustments to *unexpected* declines in demand will be painful. When the demand for labor declines generally, workers will at first not know whether they are being laid off because of a specific shift in demand away from their previous employer or because of a general decline in aggregate demand. Similarly, they will not be sure whether their current bleak employment prospects are temporary or long-term. Workers will search for employment, hoping to find a job at or near their old wage rate. If their situation was merely the result of shifts among employers in demand, or, if the downturn is brief, terminated workers will soon find new employment similar to their old jobs. When there is a general decline in demand, however, most workers' search efforts will be fruitless. Their duration of unemployment will be abnormally long.

With time, the unemployed workers will lower their expectations and be willing to take some cut in wages. However, when the reduction in aggregate demand is substantial, the adjustment process may be lengthy, and a substantial increase in the unemployment rate is the expected result. As we proceed, we will investigate potential sources of cyclical unemployment and consider policy alternatives to reduce it.

**full employment** The level of employment that results from the efficient use of the labor force after allowance is made for the normal (natural) rate of unemployment due to information cost, dynamic changes, and the structural conditions of the economy. For the United States, full employment is thought to exist when between 94 and 95 percent of the labor force is employed.

Output and employment are closely linked over the business cycle. A rapid increase in output such as occurs during a strong business expansion generally requires an increase in employment. As a result, output and employment tend to be positively related. Conversely, output and unemployment are inversely related—the unemployment rate generally increases when the economy dips into a recession.

## The Concept of Full Employment

As we have already discussed, given their imperfect information, employees will search for the most attractive positions they can find and employers will search for workers that best fit their job openings. Thus, some unemployment is inevitable. Economists define **full employment** as the level of employment

## MYTHS OF ECONOMICS

***"Unemployed resources would not exist if the economy were operating efficiently."***

Nobody likes unemployment. Certainly, extended unemployment can be a very painful experience. Not all unemployment, however, reflects waste and inefficiency. If the resources of an economy are going to be used effectively, individuals must end up working on jobs that fit their knowledge, skills, and preferences. Similarly, firms must employ workers who are well suited for their jobs. Waste will result if, for example, a person with outstanding skills as an engineer or computer specialist ends up working as an unskilled laborer. Similarly, inefficiency will generally result if someone is employed in a job for which he or she has inadequate skills.

Prospective employees searching for the right job need information on job requirements and availability, wage rates, work environment, and so on. This information is scarce and is generally acquired by "shopping"—searching for employment. Often, this shopping is easier (cheaper) if the job seeker is unemployed. Thus, job seekers usually do not take just any available job. They search, all the while acquiring valuable information, because they believe searching will lead to a preferred job opportunity.

Similarly, employers shop when they are seeking labor services. They, too, acquire information about available workers that will help them select employees whose skills and preferences match with the demands of the job. Improvement in the match between employees and jobs will lead to an expansion in real output and higher wage rates. Thus, job search can yield a return (in excess of its cost) to both the individual and to society. Such job search, even though it often involves unemployment, is a natural part of an efficiently operating labor market.

Perhaps thinking about the housing market will help the reader better understand why search time can be both beneficial and productive. As with the employment market, the housing market is characterized by dynamic change. New housing structures are brought into the market; older structures depreciate and wear out. Families move from one community to another. Within the same community, renters move among housing accommodations as they seek the housing quality, price, and location that best fit their preferences and budget. As in the employment market, information is imperfect. So, renters shop among the available accommodations, seeking the most for their housing expenditures. Similarly, landlords search among renters, seeking to rent their accommodations to those who value them most highly. *Frictional unemployment* of houses is inevitable, but does it indicate inefficiency? No. It results from people's attempts to acquire information that will eventually promote an efficient match between housing units and renters.

Some unemployment, particularly cyclical unemployment, is indicative of inefficiency. However, the shopping of job seekers while they are unemployed provides valuable information to both workers and employers and often leads to a more efficient match of applicants with job openings than would be possible otherwise.

---

**natural rate of unemployment** The long-run average unemployment rate due to frictional and structural conditions of labor markets. This rate is affected both by dynamic change and by public policy. It is sustainable into the future.

that results when the rate of unemployment is normal. Full employment incorporates the idea that at a given time there is some **natural rate of unemployment** in a dynamic exchange economy. This natural rate of unemployment arises from employees and employers shopping in a world characterized by both (1) dynamic change and (2) imperfect (scarce) information concerning job opportunities and the availability of potential workers. The natural rate of unemployment is neither a temporary high nor an artificial low. Rather, it is a normal, or average, rate that is both achievable and sustainable into the future.

Economists sometimes refer to it as the unemployment rate accompanying the economy's "maximum sustainable rate of output."

The natural rate of unemployment, though, is not immutably fixed. It is influenced both by the structure of the labor force and by changes in public policy. For example, youthful workers experience more unemployment because they change jobs and move in and out of the labor force often, so the natural rate of unemployment increases when youthful workers comprise a larger proportion of the work force. This is precisely what happened in the United States during the 1965–1980 period. The natural rate of unemployment in the United States rose during this period as youthful workers became a larger share of the labor force when the high influx of persons born during the 15 years following the Second World War entered the labor force.

Public policies also affect the natural rate of unemployment. Policies that (1) encourage workers to reject job offers and continue to search for employment, (2) prohibit employers from offering wage rates that would induce them to employ (and train) low-skill workers, and (3) reduce the employer's opportunity cost of using layoffs to adjust rates of production, will all increase the natural rate of unemployment. With regard to these points, most economists believe that increases in the legislated minimum wage and higher unemployment benefits push the natural rate of unemployment upward.

Without detracting from the importance of full employment (maximum sustainable employment), we must not overlook another vital point. Employment is a means to an end. We use employment to produce desired goods and services. Full employment is an empty concept if it means employment at unproductive jobs. The meaningful goal of full employment is productive employment—employment that will generate goods and services desired by consumers at the lowest possible cost.

## LOOKING AHEAD

A stable economic environment is crucial to the efficient operation of an economy. Abrupt changes in the general level of prices and overall demand make it extremely difficult for individuals and businesses to make sensible plans. Political leaders are generally vocal in their support of price stability, growth of output, and a high level of employment. They often choose policies, however, that conflict with these objectives. As we proceed, we will analyze what types of policies governments should follow if they want to promote economic stability and prosperity.

## CHAPTER SUMMARY

1. The gross domestic product (GDP) is the most widely used measure of the market value of the goods and services produced domestically during a time period, usually a year.
2. GDP counts only the value of final-user goods. Double-counting would result if the price of intermediate goods were added every time they went through a stage of production. Since GDP is a measure of current production, exchanges of ownership rights and goods produced during earlier

time periods are omitted. Income transfers are also omitted since they do not add to current production.

3. There are two methods of calculating GDP: (a) the expenditure approach and (b) the resource cost–income approach. When calculated by the expenditure approach, GDP is equal to the sum of consumption purchases, gross private domestic investment, government purchases, and net exports. Alternatively, GDP can also be calculated by summing the costs of the goods and services produced during the period. The costs include both the direct income of resource suppliers (employee compensation, self-employment income, rents, interest, and corporate profits) and the indirect cost of indirect business taxes and depreciation.
4. The two alternative methods of measuring GDP illustrate that output and income are closely linked. Production of goods and services that people value provides the source of the income received by resource suppliers. The growth of real output is the source of growth in real income.
5. It is important to distinguish between real and nominal values. Changes in nominal values reflect changes in the general level of prices, as well as changes in real quantities. In contrast, data measured in real terms have been adjusted to eliminate the impact of changes in the price level. Since economics focuses primarily on real changes, economists generally use real data to measure output, income, and other variables influenced by the level of prices.
6. Inflation is a general increase in the level of prices and therefore a decline in the purchasing power of money. Price indexes are used to measure changes in the level of prices and the rate of inflation. They compare the cost of purchasing a typical bundle of goods in the current period with the cost of purchasing the same bundle during an earlier base year. As the cost of purchasing the typical bundle increases, the price index will rise, indicating that there has been a general increase in the level of prices. The GDP deflator and the consumer price index (CPI) are two widely used price indexes.
7. GDP may increase because of an increase in either output or prices. The GDP deflator—a price index based on the typical bundle of goods included in GDP—can be used to convert nominal GDP to real GDP. Measured in Period 1 dollars,

$$\text{Real GDP}_2 = \text{nominal GDP}_2 \times \frac{\text{GDP deflator}_1}{\text{GDP deflator}_2}$$

8. It is important to distinguish between unanticipated and anticipated inflation. When inflation is unanticipated, it changes the intended terms of trade for transactions involving long-term contracts and commitments. When it is anticipated, however, the nominal terms of long-term agreements will reflect the expected rate of inflation.
9. Historically, the growth of GDP has been uneven. Economic booms characterized by rapid growth have been followed by periods of recession and declining real GDP. Economists refer to this uneven pattern as the business cycle.

10. In a world of dynamic change and imperfect information, some unemployment will be present as employees shop for jobs and employers search for quality employees. Even though unemployment is a side effect, the job-search process typically leads to higher real incomes and an improvement in the match between the skills of employees and requirements of jobs. However, some unemployment may also result from unexpected reductions in demand. Reducing unemployment from this source—economists refer to it as cyclical unemployment—is a primary concern of macroeconomics.

# Study Guide

CHAPTER

12

## DEVELOPING THE ECONOMIC WAY OF THINKING

## CRITICAL-ANALYSIS QUESTIONS

1. What is the distinction between all market transactions and final-good transactions? Which is a better measure of the economy's rate of production? Why? What is the relationship between final-good transactions and the sum of the value added of producers?

*2. How much does each of the following contribute to GDP?
   a. Jones pays a repair shop $1,000 to have the engine of her automobile rebuilt.
   b. Jones spends $200 on parts and pays a mechanic $400 to rebuild the engine of her automobile.
   c. Jones spends $200 on parts and rebuilds the engine of her automobile herself.
   d. Jones sells her four-year-old automobile for $5,000 and buys Smith's two-year-old model for $10,000.
   e. Jones sell her four-year-old automobile for $5,000 and buys a new car for $10,000.

3. Explain why the rate of growth of GDP in current dollars is often a misleading indicator of changes in real output.

4. If a nation's gross investment exceeds its depreciation during the year, what has happened to the nation's stock of capital during the year? How will this affect future output? Is it possible for the net investment (gross investment minus depreciation) of a nation to be negative? Explain. What would negative net investment during a year imply about the nation's capital stock and future production potential?

*5. Indicate how each of the following will affect this year's GDP:
   a. You suffer $10,000 of damage when you wreck your automobile.
   b. You pay $300 for this month's rental of your apartment.
   c. You are paid $300 for computer services provided to a client.
   d. You receive a $300 cash gift from your parents.
   e. You get a raise from $4 to $5 per hour and simultaneously decide to reduce your hours worked from 20 to 16 per week.

*6. "As the inflation proceeds and the real value of the currency fluctuates widely from month to month, all permanent relations between debtors and lenders, which form the ultimate foundation of capitalism, become so utterly disordered as to be almost meaningless; and the process of wealth-getting degenerates into a gamble and a lottery." Do you agree with this view of a well-known economist? Why or why not? How high do you think the inflation rate would have to climb before these effects would become pronounced? Do you see any evidence in support of this view in your country?

*7. Classify each of the following as employed, unemployed, or not in the labor force:
   a. Brown, who is not working but is available for work, applied for a job at XYZ Company and is awaiting the result of her application.

*Asterisks denote critical-analysis questions for which answers are given in Appendix A.

b. Smith is vacationing in Europe during a layoff at a General Motors plant due to a model changeover, but he expects to be recalled in a couple of weeks.
c. Green was laid off as a carpenter when a construction project was completed. He is looking for work but has been unable to find anything except an $8-per-hour job, which he turned down.
d. West works 50 to 60 hours per week as a homemaker for her family of nine.
e. Carson, a 17-year-old, works 6 hours per week as a route person for the local newspaper.
f. Johnson works 3 hours in the mornings at a clinic and for the last two weeks has spent the afternoons looking for a full-time job.

*8. Is the natural rate of unemployment fixed? How are the following related to each other?
a. Actual rate of unemployment.
b. Natural rate of unemployment.
c. Cyclical unemployment.

*9. Explain why even an efficiently functioning economic system will have some unemployed resources.

10. What is full employment? How are full employment and the natural rate of unemployment related? Indicate several factors that would cause the natural rate of unemployment to change. Is the actual rate of unemployment currently greater than or less than the natural rate of unemployment? Explain?

## MULTIPLE-CHOICE SELF-TEST

1. Which one of the following transactions would be included in the calculation of GDP?
   a. Allen's purchase of a used picture frame at a neighborhood garage sale.
   b. Ritch's purchase of $500 of the common stock of Quick-Gro, Inc.
   c. Doe's donation of $300 to his town's junior college scholarship fund.
   d. Brown's $500 repair bill to fix the front end of her car damaged in a recent accident.
2. Gross domestic product is the sum of the purchase price of
   a. All goods and services exchanged during the current period.
   b. All final goods and services produced domestically during the current period.
   c. All goods and services produced during the period minus the allowance for the depreciation of productive assets during the period.
   d. All goods and services produced during the period minus the estimated depreciation cost arising from production during the period.
3. When economists speak of changes in GDP measured in constant dollars, they mean that
   a. Money GDP is constant.
   b. The price level is constant.
   c. A price index has been used to adjust money GDP for the effects of inflation.

d. The growth rate of money GDP has been adjusted for changes in population.

4. If nominal GDP increased by 10 percent during a year while real GDP increased by only 5 percent, then
   a. The price level must have risen by approximately 10 percent compared to the prior year.
   b. The price level must have risen by approximately 5 percent compared to the prior year.
   c. The price level must have fallen by approximately 10 percent compared to the prior year.
   d. The price level must have risen by approximately 15 percent compared to the prior year.
5. The value of money
   a. Remains constant during periods of deflation.
   b. Varies inversely with the general level of prices.
   c. Varies directly with the general level of prices.
   d. Varies indirectly with the level of output.
6. When inflation is fully anticipated, debtors do *not* systematically gain at the expense of creditors because
   a. Debtors will overextend themselves in the money market and find their holdings no longer liquid.
   b. The federal government will reimburse creditors through tax breaks.
   c. The market rate of interest that borrowers will have to pay and that lenders will be able to obtain will rise to reflect the expected annual rate of inflation.
   d. The market value of financial assets such as bonds, savings deposits, and insurance policies will be unaffected by the rate of inflation.
7. The total population (age 16 and over) of Lebos is 400 million. Of this total, 20 million are unemployed and 230 million currently hold jobs. What are the rates of unemployment and labor force participation of Lebos?
   a. The rate of unemployment is 8 percent and the rate of labor force participation is 62.5 percent.
   b. The rate of unemployment is 8 percent and the rate of labor force participation is 92 percent.
   c. The rate of unemployment is 8.7 percent and the rate of labor force participation is 62.5 percent.
   d. The rate of unemployment is 5 percent and the rate of labor force participation is 57.5 percent.
8. Economists use the phrase "business cycle" to refer to the pattern of fluctuations in
   a. The general level of prices as measured by the consumer price index.
   b. Interest rates as measured by the prime bank-loan rate.
   c. The money supply.
   d. Aggregate measures of current economic output and real income.
9. The natural rate of unemployment
   a. Increases sharply during a recession but declines significantly during a business expansion.
   b. Is the unemployment rate accompanying the economy's maximum sustainable rate of output.

c. Is generally less than the unemployment rate associated with the economy's full employment rate of unemployment.
d. Is present when the economy is operating at approximately 94 percent of its potential capacity.

10. Suppose that Jim works a 40-hour-per-week job at a steel mill and his daughter Susan works a 15-hour-per-week job at McDonald's. From the viewpoint of the employment statistics,
    a. Jim is counted as a full worker and Susan as a half-worker.
    b. Jim is considered employed, and Susan is considered unemployed.
    c. Jim is considered employed, and Susan is considered half-unemployed.
    d. Both Jim and Susan are considered employed.

## PROBLEMS

1. Consider an economy with the following data:

| | Nominal GDP (in billions) | GDP Deflator |
|---|---|---|
| 1992 | $100 | 150 |
| 1993 | $120 | 225 |

   a. What was the 1993 GDP in 1992 dollars?
   b. What was the rate of change in real GDP between 1992 and 1993?
   c. What was the 1993 inflation rate?

2. Use the following data to calculate (a) the labor force participation rate and (b) the rate of unemployment: population = 10,000; labor force = 6,000; not currently working = 4,500; employed full-time = 4,000; employed part-time = 1,500; and unemployed = 500.

3. Fill in the blanks in the following table:

| Year | Nominal GDP (in billions) | GDP Deflator (1987= 100) | Real GDP (billions of 1987 dollars) |
|---|---|---|---|
| 1960 | $ 513.4 | 26.0 | $a.____ |
| 1970 | 1,010.7 | 35.1 | b.____ |
| 1975 | 1,585.9 | c.____ | 3,221.7 |
| 1980 | d.____ | 71.7 | 3,776.3 |
| 1985 | 4,038.7 | e.____ | 4,279.8 |
| 1990 | 5,513.8 | 112.9 | f.____ |

4. The accompanying table presents the population and labor force data for several countries.

| Country | Population: 16 years and over (in millions) | No. of Employed (in millions) | No. of Unemployed (in millions) | Rate of Labor Force Participation (percent) | Rate of Unemployment (percent) |
|---|---|---|---|---|---|
| United States | 188.0 | 117.9 | 6.87 | | |
| Canada | 20.4 | 12.6 | 1.11 | | |
| Japan | 101.9 | 62.4 | 1.34 | | |
| Germany | 54.6 | 28.5 | 1.53 | | |
| France | 44.1 | 22.2 | 2.22 | | |
| United Kingdom | 45.0 | 26.8 | 1.99 | | |
| Italy | 50.1 | 21.4 | 2.35 | | |

a. Calculate the number of people in the labor force for the United States, Canada, and Japan in 1990.
b. Calculate the 1990 rate of labor force participation for each country. Indicate this rate in the space provided. Which country had the highest rate of labor force participation? Which country had the lowest?
c. Calculate the rate of unemployment in 1990 for each country and place it in the space provided. Which country had the highest rate of unemployment? Which had the lowest?

5. The accompanying chart presents 1991 data from the national income accounts of the United States.

| | (in billions) | | (in billions) |
|---|---|---|---|
| Personal consumption | $3888 | Corporate profits | $346 |
| Employee compensation | 3391 | Interest income | 450 |
| Rents | 26 | Exports | 598 |
| Government purchases | 1091 | Gross private investment | 721 |
| Imports | 620 | Indirect business taxes | 471 |
| Depreciation | 626 | Self-employment income | 368 |

a. Indicate the various components of GDP when it is derived by the expenditure approach. Calculate GDP using the expenditure approach.
b. Indicate the various components of GDP when it is derived by the resource cost–income approach. Calculate GDP using the resource cost–income approach.

CHAPTER

# 13

# AGGREGATE DEMAND, AGGREGATE SUPPLY, AND OUTPUT

Macroeconomics is interesting . . . because it is challenging to reduce the complicated details of the economy to manageable essentials. Those essentials lie in the interactions among the goods, labor, and assets [loanable funds] markets of the economy.

*Rudiger Dornbusch and Stanley Fischer*[1]

## CHAPTER FOCUS

- What are the major markets that coordinate macroeconomic activities?
- What are aggregate demand and aggregate supply?
- What determines the equilibrium level of GDP in the short run? In the long run?
- What is the relationship between long-run equilibrium and full employment?
- What factors will cause shifts in aggregate demand? Shifts in aggregate supply?
- How will the goods and services market adjust to changes in aggregate demand? Changes in aggregate supply?
- Does a market economy have a self-correcting mechanism that will lead it to full employment? If so, how well does the mechanism work?

Why was the inflation rate so high during the 1970s? What about the large budget deficits of the 1980s and 1990s—are they leading us toward economic destruction? What is the cause of economic instability? Could anything like the massive unemployment of the Great Depression recur?

These are important questions, and we will address them. Before we can do so sensibly, however, we must develop a model—a road map, if you like—to help us better understand the interrelationships among macroeconomic markets and thus how policy alternatives can affect its operation.

Macroeconomic policy is usually divided into two components: fiscal policy and monetary policy. **Fiscal policy** entails the use of the government's taxation, spending, and debt-management policies. In the United States, fiscal policy is conducted by Congress and the president. It is thus a reflection of the collective decision-making process. **Monetary policy** encompasses actions that alter the money supply. The direction of monetary policy is determined by a nation's central bank, the Federal Reserve System in the United States. Ideally, both monetary and fiscal policy should be used to promote business stability, high employment, the growth of output, and a stable price level.

**fiscal policy** The use of government taxation and expenditure policies for the purpose of achieving macroeconomic goals.

**monetary policy** The deliberate control of the money supply, and in some cases credit conditions, for the purpose of achieving macroeconomic goals.

Initially, as we develop our basic macroeconomic model, we will assume that monetary and fiscal policy are unchanged. Stated another way, we will proceed as if the government's tax and spending policies were unaffected by economic circumstances. Similarly, we will assume that policymakers maintain a constant **money supply**—that they follow policies that keep the amount of cash in our billfolds and deposits in our checking accounts constant. Of course, changes in government expenditures, taxes, and the money supply are potentially important. We will investigate their impact in detail in subsequent

**money supply** The supply of currency, checking account funds, and traveler's checks. These items are counted as money since they are used as the means of payment for purchases.

[1]Rudiger Dornbusch and Stanley Fischer, *Macroeconomics* (New York: McGraw-Hill, 1978).

**resource market** A highly aggregated market encompassing all resources (labor, physical capital, land, and entrepreneurship) that contribute to the production of current output. The labor market forms the largest component of this market.

chapters. For now, though, things will go more smoothly if we simply assume that policymakers are holding government expenditures, taxes, and the supply of money constant.

# KEY MACROECONOMIC MARKETS

Exhibit 13.1 provides a visual illustration of the organization and interrelationships among the key markets of a simple macroeconomic model. The bottom loop of this circular-flow diagram depicts the **resource market,** a highly

**EXHIBIT 13.1**

**Three Key Markets and the Circular Flow of Income**

A circular flow of income is coordinated by three key markets. First, the resource market (bottom loop) coordinates the actions of businesses demanding resources and households supplying them in exchange for income. Second, the loanable funds market (lower center) coordinates the saving choices of households and the borrowing decisions of businesses and governments. Finally, households, investors, governments, and foreigners (net exports) purchase products supplied by the business sector. These exchanges are coordinated in the goods and services market (top loop).

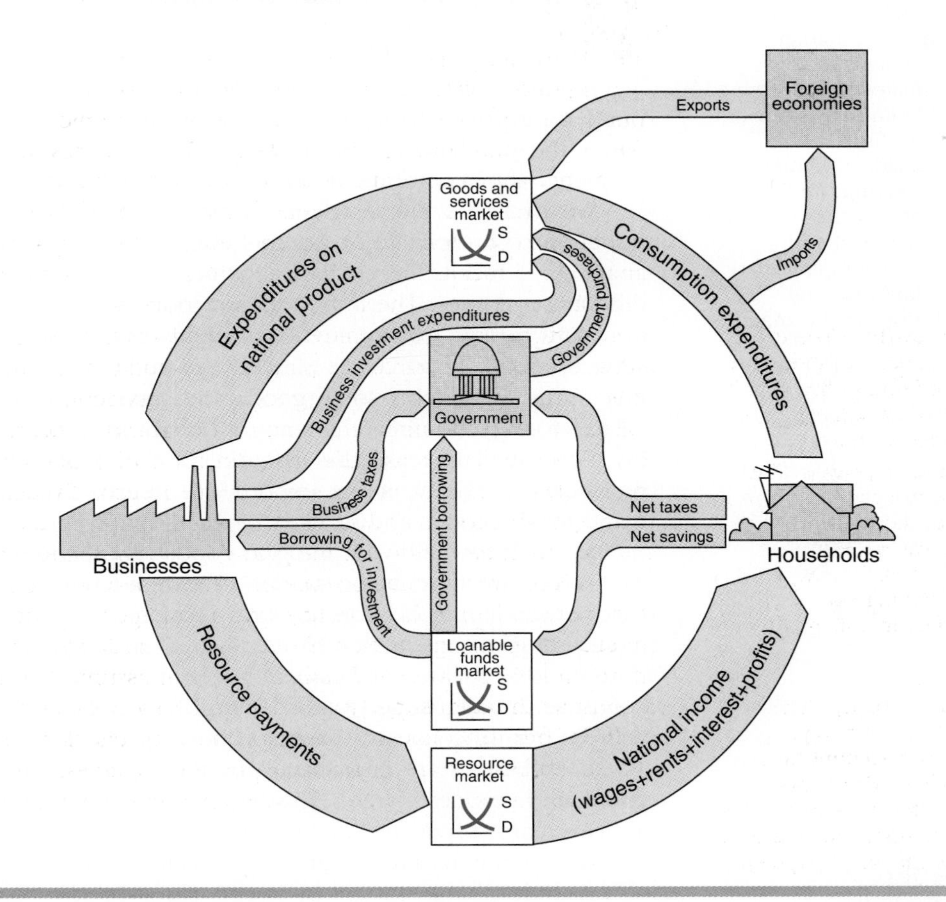

aggregated market that includes the markets for labor services, natural resources, and physical capital. In the resource market, business firms demand resources because of their contribution to the production of goods and services. In turn, households supply resources in exchange for income. The forces of demand and supply determine prices in the resource market. As we have previously discussed, the demand for resources is a derived demand, meaning that it is directly linked to the demand for goods and services.

**goods and services market** A highly aggregate market encompassing all final-user goods and services during a period. The market counts all items that enter into GDP. Thus, real output in this market is equal to real GDP.

**saving** Disposable income that is not spent on consumption. Saving is a "flow" concept. Thus, it is generally measured in terms of an annual rate.

**loanable funds market** A general term used to describe the market arrangements that coordinate the borrowing and lending decisions of business firms and households. Commercial banks, savings and loan associations, the stock and bond markets, and insurance companies are important financial institutions in this market.

The **goods and services market** comprises the top loop of the circular-flow diagram. Businesses supply goods and services in exchange for sales revenue. Households spend much of their income on consumer goods and housing. These expenditures contribute substantially to the demand for goods and services. As Exhibit 13.1 illustrates, however, there are also two indirect routes by which funds can flow from the household to the business sector. First, the net savings of households can flow through the loanable funds market to (1) business firms purchasing investment goods and (2) governments purchasing public services. **Saving** is that portion of one's disposable income that is not spent on consumption. It is income not consumed. Net saving by the household sector supplies funds to the **loanable funds market.** In turn, businesses borrow loanable funds to finance investment expenditures. In addition, governments often finance their expenditures by borrowing. When the borrowed funds are spent on investment goods and government purchases, they return to the circular flow. The price of loanable funds is the interest rate. The actions of borrowers and lenders are coordinated by the interest rate in the loanable funds market.

Second, some of the income of households is taxed in order to transfer purchasing power to governments. In turn, as these revenues are used to finance the purchase (or production) of goods and services provided by governments, they contribute to the demand in the goods and services market.

We live in a world where instant communications and shrinking transportation costs facilitate exchange between trading partners thousands of miles apart. As a result, the exchange partners of modern economies often live in different countries. The import-export loop of Exhibit 13.1 depicts this interaction with foreign economies. Households will import some of the goods and services that they purchase. Similarly, in addition to their domestic sales, business firms will export some goods and services. Net exports are the amount sold to foreigners minus the amount bought from them. If net exports are positive, they will increase the demand for the goods and services of domestic producers. Similarly, if net exports are negative, they will decrease the demand for the goods and services of domestic producers.

As the arrows flowing into the goods and services market (top loop) indicate, there are four major sources of expenditures in this market: (1) household expenditures on consumption (and new housing), (2) business investment, (3) government purchases, and (4) net exports. These expenditures of households, business investors, governments, and foreigners (net exports) comprise the aggregate (total) demand for goods and services. Purchasing resources from the household sector, business firms supply goods and services. These exchanges are coordinated by the forces of supply and demand in the goods and services market. This highly aggregated market includes items such as ice cream, pizza, hairstyling, movie tickets, television sets, and dishwashers—goods purchased primarily by consumers. The goods and services market also includes things bought by businesses such as tools, machines, and factory buildings. Finally, items such as highways, fire protection, and national defense, which are usually purchased by governments, are also part of the goods and services market.

As we noted in the previous chapter, there are two ways of measuring gross domestic product (GDP), the aggregate output of an economy. First, GDP can be measured by adding up the expenditures of consumers, investors, governments, and foreigners (net exports) on goods and services produced during the year. This method is equivalent to measuring the flow of output as it moves through the top loop—the goods and services market—of the circular-flow diagram. Alternatively, GDP can be measured by summing the income payments, both direct and indirect—received by the resource suppliers who produced the goods and services. This method uses the bottom loop—the resource market—to measure the flow of output.

## AGGREGATE DEMAND AND AGGREGATE SUPPLY

What goes on in the aggregate goods and services market is vital to the health of an economy. Indeed, if we could keep our eye on just one market in an economy, we would choose the goods and services market, since it exerts a vital impact on our economic opportunity and standard of living. It is important to note that the *quantity* and *price* variables in this highly aggregated market differ from their counterparts in the market for a specific good. The quantity variable in the aggregate goods and services market is real GDP—the flow of goods and services produced and purchased during a period. The price variable in the goods and services market represents the average price of goods and services purchased during the period. In essence, it is the economy's price level, as measured by a general price index (for example, the GDP deflator).

### Aggregate Demand

Just as the concepts of demand and supply enhance our understanding of markets for specific goods, they also contribute to our understanding of a highly aggregated market such as that for goods and services. The purchases of consumers, investors, governments, and foreigners comprise the nation's demand for goods and services. The **aggregate demand curve** indicates the various quantities of goods and services that purchasers are willing to buy at different price levels. As Exhibit 13.2 illustrates, the aggregate demand curve (*AD*) is a downward-sloping schedule, indicating that as the price level declines, people are willing to purchase more and more output. Alternatively, the quantity of goods and services purchased declines as the price level rises.

**aggregate demand curve**
A downward-sloping curve indicating an inverse relationship between the price level and the quantity of goods and services that households, business firms, governments and foreigners (net exports) are willing to purchase during a period.

The explanation of the downward-sloping aggregate demand schedule differs from that for a specific commodity. The inverse relationship between price and the amount demanded of a specific commodity, TV sets, for example, reflects the fact that consumers turn to substitutes when a price increase makes a good more expensive. This relative price change will not be present when there is a change in the price of all goods. Instead, the inverse relationship between the price level and aggregate amount demanded reflects the impact of the fixed quantity of money. As the *level* of prices declines, the purchasing power of the fixed quantity of money increases. For example, if you

EXHIBIT 13.2

**Aggregate Demand Curve**

As illustrated here, the quantity of goods and services purchased will increase (to $Y_2$) as the price level declines (to $P_2$). Given a fixed quantity of money, a reduction in the level of prices will increase the wealth of people holding the fixed quantity of money balances. At the lower price level, the demand for money may also decline, causing a reduction in interest rates. Both of these factors will increase the quantity of goods and services purchased at the lower price level.

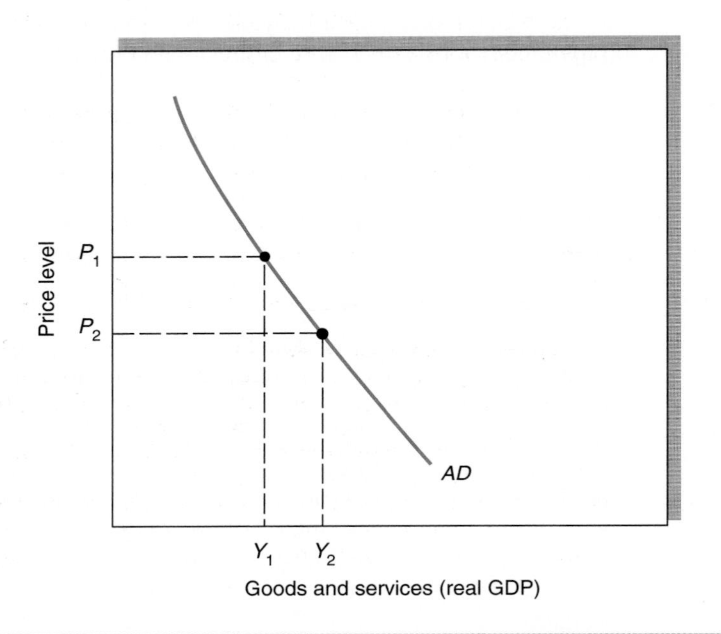


have $2,000 in your bank account, your wealth would increase if there was a 25 percent reduction in the price of goods and services. At the lower price level, your $2,000 will buy more goods and services. Other people are in an identical position. As the price level declines, the purchasing power of their money balances also increases. This increase in wealth derived from the expansion in the purchasing power of the fixed money balances will induce people to purchase more goods and services as the price level declines. In addition, a lower price level may also reduce the amount of money households and businesses want to hold in order to make purchases and conduct their affairs. The decline in the demand for money relative to the fixed supply of money will place downward pressure of interest rates. This, too, will encourage people to purchase more goods and services. Therefore, even though the explanation differs, the aggregate demand curve, like the demand curve for a specific product, slopes downward to the right.

**aggregate supply curve**
A curve indicating the relationship between the nation's price level and the quantity of goods supplied by its producers. In the short run, it is probably an upward-sloping curve, but in the long run most economists believe the aggregate supply curve is vertical (or nearly so).

## Aggregate Supply

In view of the preceding discussion, it should come as no great surprise to the reader that the explanation for the general shape of the **aggregate supply**

**curve** also differs from that for the supply curve of a specific good. When considering aggregate supply, it is particularly important to distinguish between the short run and the long run. In this context, the short run is the time period during which some prices, particularly those in labor markets, are set by prior contracts and agreements. Therefore, in the short run, households and businesses are unable to adjust these prices in light of *unexpected* recent changes, including unexpected changes in the price level. In contrast, the long run is a time period of sufficient duration that people have the opportunity to learn more fully about recent price changes and to modify their prior choices in response to them. We now consider both the short-run and long-run aggregate supply curves (Exhibit 13.3).

**SHORT-RUN AGGREGATE SUPPLY** The *short-run aggregate supply (SRAS)* curve indicates the various quantities of goods and services that firms will supply at different price levels during the period immediately following a

**EXHIBIT 13.3** **Aggregate Supply Curve in Short Run and Long Run**

The aggregate supply curve shows the relationship between the price level and the domestic output of goods and services. In the short run, firms will generally expand output as the price level increases. This is because the higher prices for goods and services will temporarily improve profit margins, since many components of costs are "fixed" in the short term (frame a). In the long run, however, long-term commitments will be revised, and higher resource prices will eliminate the short-term profits. An economy's sustainable potential output rate is determined by the supply of resources, level of technology, and the structure of institutions. A higher price level will not loosen these constraints. Therefore, in the long run, the aggregate supply curve is vertical (frame b).

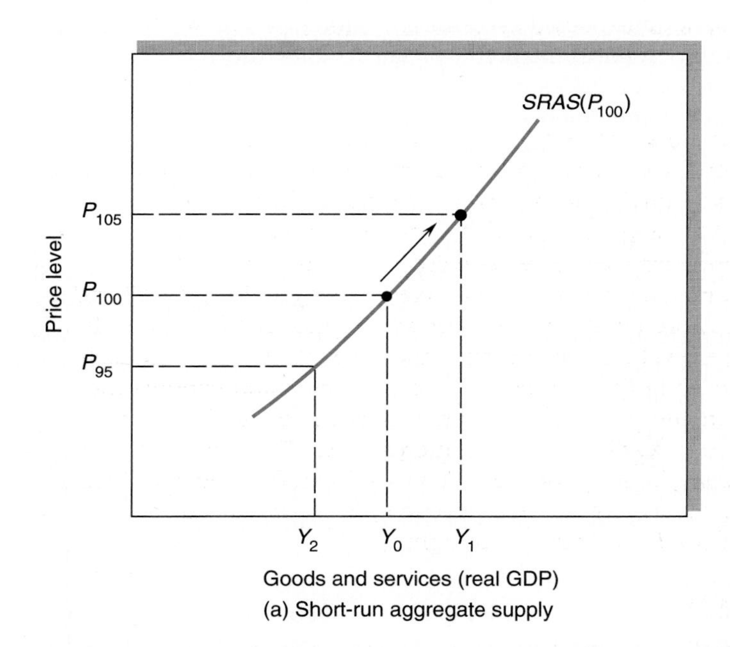

(a) Short-run aggregate supply

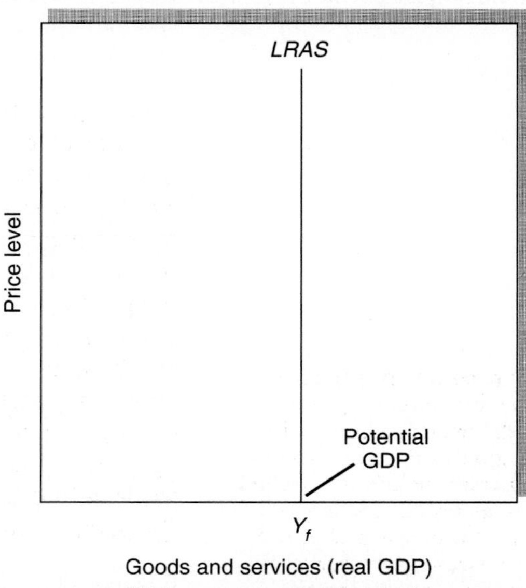

(b) Long-run aggregate supply

change in the price level. As Exhibit 13.3a illustrates, the *SRAS* curve slopes upward to the right, reflecting the fact that in the short run an unexpected increase in the price level will improve the profitability of firms, and they will respond with an expansion in output.

The *SRAS* curve is based on a specific expected price level, $P_{100}$ in the case of Exhibit 13.3. When that price level is achieved, firms will earn normal profits and supply output $Y_0$. Why will an increase in the price level (to $P_{105}$, for example) enhance profitability, at least in the short run? Profit per unit equals price minus the producer's per unit costs. Important components of producers' costs will be determined by long-term contracts. Interest rates on loans, collective bargaining agreements with employees, lease agreements on buildings and machines, and other contracts with resource suppliers will influence production costs during the current period. The prices incorporated into these long-term contracts at the time of the agreement are based on the expectation of price level ($P_{100}$) for the current period. These resource costs tend to be temporarily fixed. If an increase in demand causes the price level to rise unexpectedly during the current period, prices of goods and services will increase relative to the temporarily fixed components of costs. Profit margins will improve, and business firms will happily respond with an expansion in output (to $Y_1$).

An unexpected reduction in the price level to $P_{95}$ would exert just the opposite effects. It would decrease product prices *relative to costs* and thereby reduce profitability. In response, firms would reduce output to $Y_2$. Therefore, *in the short run,* there will be a direct relationship between amount supplied and the price level in the goods and services market.

**LONG-RUN AGGREGATE SUPPLY** The *long-run aggregate supply* (*LRAS*) curve indicates the relationship between the price level and quantity of output after decision-makers have had sufficient time to adjust their prior commitments in light of any previously unexpected changes in market prices. A higher price level in the goods and services market will fail to alter the relationship between product and resource prices in the long run. Once people have time to adjust fully their prior commitments, competitive forces will restore the usual relationship between product prices and costs. *Profit rates will return to normal,* removing the incentive of firms to supply a larger rate of output. Therefore, as Exhibit 13.3b illustrates, the *LRAS* curve is vertical.

The forces that provided for an upward-sloping *SRAS* curve are absent in the long run. Costs that are temporarily fixed due to long-term contracts will eventually rise. With time, the long-term contracts will expire and be renegotiated. Once the contracts are renegotiated, resource prices will increase in the same proportion as product prices. A proportional increase in costs and product prices will leave the incentive to produce unchanged. Consider how a firm with a selling price of $20 and per unit costs of $20 will be affected by the doubling of both product and resource prices. After the price increase, the firm's sales price will be $40, but so, too, will its per unit costs. Thus, neither the firm's profit rate nor the incentive to produce is changed. Therefore, in the long run an increase in the nominal value of the price level will fail to exert a lasting impact on aggregate output.

Reflecting on the production possibilities of an economy also sheds light on why the long-run aggregate supply curve is vertical. As we discussed in Chapter 1, at a point in time, our production possibilities are constrained by

## THUMBNAIL SKETCH

**General Characteristics of Aggregate Demand and Aggregate Supply**

1. Why is the aggregate quantity demanded inversely related to the price level?

   *When the supply of money is constant, a lower price level will increase the wealth of people and tend to lower interest rates, both of which will increase the amount of goods and services purchased.*
2. Why is the short-run aggregate quantity supplied directly related to the price level?

   *As the price level increases, profit margins of firms increase, because initially product prices increase relative to costs (important components of which are fixed by long-term contracts).*
3. Why is the long-run aggregate supply curve vertical?
   - *a. Once people have the time to adjust fully to a new price level, the normal relationship between product prices and resource costs is restored.*
   - *b. The sustainable potential output of a national economy is determined by its quantity of resources, technology, and the efficiency of its institutional structures rather than by the price level.*

the supply of resources, level of technology, and institutional arrangements that influence the efficiency of resource use. A higher price level does not loosen these constraints. For example, a doubling of prices will not improve technology. Neither will it expand the availability of productive resources (once expectations have adjusted to the change) nor improve the efficiency of our economic institutions. Thus, there is no reason for a higher price level to increase our ability to produce goods and services. This is precisely what the vertical *LRAS* curve implies. The accompanying "Thumbnail Sketch" summarizes the factors that explain the general characteristics of aggregate demand, short-run aggregate supply, and long-run aggregate supply.

# EQUILIBRIUM IN GOODS AND SERVICES MARKET

**equilibrium** A balance of forces permitting the simultaneous fulfillment of plans by buyers and sellers.

We are now ready to combine our analyses of aggregate demand and aggregate supply and consider how the two forces act to determine the price level and rate of output. When a market is in **equilibrium,** there is a balance of forces such that the actions of buyers and sellers are consistent with one another.

## Short-Run Equilibrium

As Exhibit 13.4 illustrates, short-run equilibrium is present in the goods and services market at the price level ($P$) where the aggregate quantity demanded is equal to the aggregate quantity supplied. This occurs at the output rate ($Y$) where the *AD* and *SRAS* curves intersect.

**EXHIBIT 13.4**

**Short-Run Equilibrium in Goods and Services Market**

Short-run equilibrium in the goods and services market occurs at the price level (*P*) where *AD* and *SRAS* intersect. If the price level were lower than *P*, general excess demand in goods and services markets would push prices upward. Conversely, if the price level were higher than *P*, excess supply would result in falling prices.

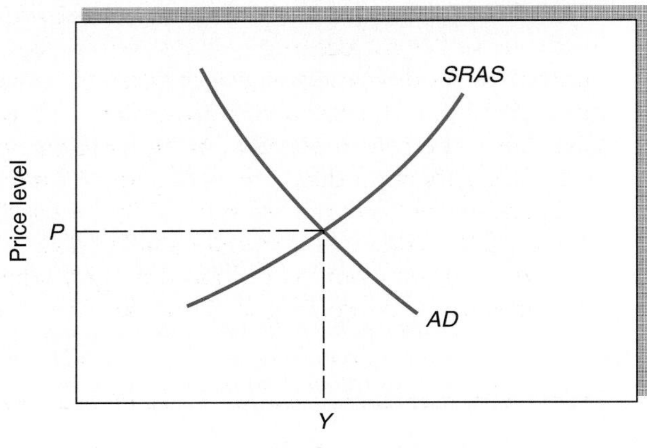


If a price level of less than *P* were present, the aggregate quantity demanded would exceed the aggregate quantity supplied. Purchasers would be seeking to buy more goods and services than producers were willing to produce. This excess demand would place upward pressure on prices, causing the price level to rise toward *P*. On the other hand, at a price level greater than *P*, the aggregate quantity supplied would exceed the aggregate quantity demanded. Producers would be unable to sell all the goods produced. This would result in downward pressure (toward *P*) on prices. Only at the price level *P* would there be a balance of forces between the amount of goods demanded by consumers, investors, governments, and foreigners, and the amount supplied by domestic firms.

## Long-Run Equilibrium

The price level in the economy-wide goods and services market will tend to bring quantity demanded and quantity supplied into balance. However, a second condition is required for long-run equilibrium: the buyers and sellers must be happy with their prior choices. If they are not satisfied, they will want to change their actions in the future. Thus, long-run equilibrium requires that decision-makers who agreed to long-term contracts influencing current prices and costs must have *correctly anticipated the current price level at the time they arrived at the agreements*. If this was not the case, they will modify those agreements when the long-term contracts expire. In turn, their modifications will affect costs, profit margins, and output.

Exhibit 13.5 illustrates a long-run equilibrium in the goods and services market. As in Exhibit 13.3a, the subscripts attached to the *SRAS* and *AD* curves indicate the price level (an index of prices) that was anticipated by decision-makers at the time they made decisions affecting the schedules. In this case, when buyers and sellers made their purchasing and production choices, they anticipated that the price level during the current period would be $P_{100}$, where the 100 refers to an index of prices during an earlier base year. As the intersection of the *AD* and *SRAS* curves reveals, the $P_{100}$ was actually attained.

When the price-level expectations imbedded in the long-term contracts turn out to be correct, there is no reason for buyers and sellers in resource markets to modify resource prices when their contracts come up for renegotiation. Therefore, the resource prices, costs, and profits will continue into the future. Since the price/cost relationship is unchanged, firms have no incentive to alter either their product prices or rate of output. Thus, the equilibrium price level and output will persist into the future (until changes in other factors alter *AD* or *SRAS*). *A long-run equilibrium is present.*

When an economy is in long-run equilibrium, the interrelationship among the three basic markets—goods and services, resources, and loanable funds—

**EXHIBIT 13.5**

**Long-Run Equilibrium in Goods and Services Market**

When the goods and services market is in long-run equilibrium, two conditions must be present. First, the quantity demanded must equal the quantity supplied at the current price level. Second, the price level anticipated by decision-makers must equal the actual price level. The subscripts on the *SRAS* and *AD* curves indicate that buyers and sellers alike anticipated the price level $P_{100}$, where the 100 represents an index of prices during an earlier base year. When the anticipated price level is actually attained, current output ($Y_f$) will equal the economy's potential GDP when full employment is present.

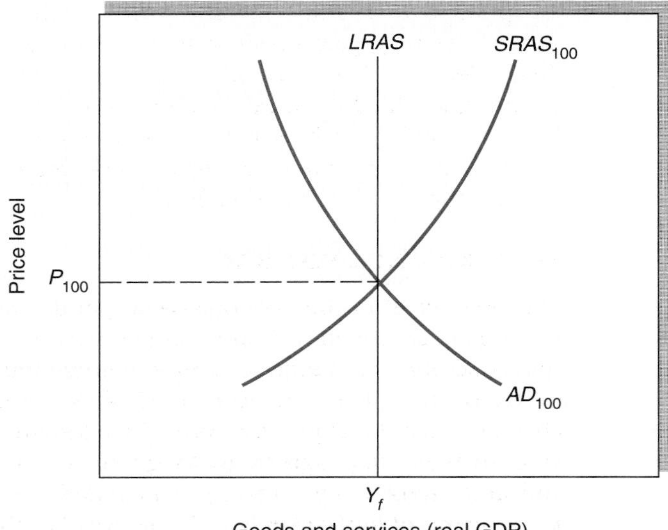

will be in harmony. The price of resources *relative* to the price of goods and services will be such that the business firms, on average, will be just able to cover their cost of production, including a competitive return on their investment. If this were not the case, producers would seek to either contract or expand output. For example, if the prices of resources were so high (relative to producers' prices) that firms were unable to cover their costs, many producers would cut back output or perhaps even discontinue production. Aggregate output would thereby be altered. Conversely, if resource prices were so low that firms were able to earn an above-market return, profit-seeking firms would expand output. New firms would begin production. Again, these forces would alter conditions in the goods and services market.

Similarly, the relationship between interest rates in the loanable funds market and product prices must be such that the typical firm is just able to earn normal returns on their investments. In other words, the typical producer's return to capital must equal the interest rate—that is, the opportunity cost of capital. Higher returns would induce producers to expand output, while lower returns would cause them to cut back on production. Therefore, when macroeconomic equilibrium is present, prices in these three markets will be such that buyers and sellers in each of the markets are willing to continue with the current arrangements.

## Long-Run Equilibrium and Full Employment

When long-run equilibrium is present, the output rate of the economy will be at its maximum *sustainable* rate given the availability of resources, level of technology, and institutional structure. The long-run equilibrium output rate is neither a temporary high nor an abnormal low. Rather, it reflects the normal operation of markets when decision-makers (including those involved in long-term agreements) neither systematically underestimate nor overestimate the current price level.

The long-run equilibrium output rate ($Y_f$ of Exhibit 13.5) also corresponds with the full employment of resources. When full-employment output is present, the job search time of unemployed workers will be normal, given the characteristics of the labor force and the institutional structure of the economy. Cyclical unemployment will be absent. When an economy is at full employment, the unemployment rate that exists is equivalent to the *natural* rate of unemployment. Thus, when an economy is in long-run equilibrium, the actual rate of unemployment will be equal to the natural rate of unemployment.

What happens, however, when changes in the price level catch buyers and sellers by surprise? When the actual price level differs from the level forecast by buyers and sellers, some decision-makers will enter into agreements that they will later regret. Consider a case in which the price level increases more than was anticipated. Failing to foresee the price increase, lenders in the loanable funds market agreed to interest rates that are lower than they are willing to accept once the general increase in prices (inflation) is taken into account. Similarly, anticipating a lower current price level, union officials accept money-wage increases that end up reducing real wages during the period. In the short run, the atypically low interest rates and real wages reduce costs relative to product prices. Profit margins will be abnormally high, and firms will respond with a larger output. Employment will expand. Unemployment will fall below its natural rate. But this abnormally large output and high level of employment is not sustainable. The "mistakes" based on a prior failure to estimate fully the

## HOW LARGE IS THE NATURAL RATE OF UNEMPLOYMENT

When an economy is in long-run equilibrium, unemployment will be at the natural rate. However, since the natural rate of unemployment is a theoretical concept, it cannot be directly observed. It must be estimated.

Economists use two different methods to estimate the natural rate of unemployment. First, they estimate a statistical equation relating aggregate unemployment to changes in the rate of inflation. Conceptually, the natural rate of unemployment is present when the inflation rate is neither rising nor falling. Therefore, when the inflation rate is constant, the equation linking unemployment to the change in the inflation rate provides an estimate for the natural rate of unemployment.

The second method of estimating the natural rate of unemployment uses historical data to estimate the natural rate for several different demographic groups. These estimates are then used to estimate the aggregate natural rate, based on the size of the various demographic groups at different times.

Several researchers have used one or both of these techniques to estimate the natural rate at various times. Perhaps the most widely cited estimates are those by Robert Gordon of Northwestern University, presented in the accompanying chart along with the low and high estimates of other researchers for 1955, 1970, 1980, and 1990.

In the mid-1950s, the natural rate of unemployment was estimated at between 4 percent and 5.5 percent. Gordon's estimate for the natural rate in 1955 was 5.1 percent. Researchers agree that the natural rate increased during the 1960s and 1970s, primarily as the result of a large influx of youthful workers into the labor force. Since younger workers are more likely than their older counterparts both to switch jobs and enter (and reenter) the labor force, the natural unemployment rate increases when youthful workers increase as a proportion of the labor force. By 1980, the estimated natural rate had risen to between 5 percent and 7 percent. As the baby-boom generation matured and the growth of the labor force slowed during the 1980s, the natural rate declined. In the early 1990s, researchers placed the natural rate of unemployment between 4.5 percent and 6.5 percent.

**Estimated Natural Rate of Unemployment**

| Year | Low Estimate | Robert Gordon | High Estimate |
|---|---|---|---|
| 1955 | 4.0 | 5.1 | 5.5 |
| 1970 | 4.5 | 5.6 | 6.0 |
| 1980 | 5.0 | 5.9 | 7.0 |
| 1990 | 4.5 | 6.0 | 6.5 |

**Sources:** Robert Gordon, *Macroeconomics,* 5th ed. (Glenview, IL: Scott Foresman Company, 1990); Stuart E. Weiner, "The Natural Rate of Unemployment: Concepts and Issues," *Economic Review—Federal Reserve Bank of Kansas City,* January 1986, pp. 11–24; Keith M. Carlson, "How Much Lower Can the Unemployment Rate Go?" *Review—Federal Reserve Bank of St. Louis,* July–August 1988, pp. 44–57; and Lowell E. Gallaway and Richard K. Vedder, *The Natural Rate of Unemployment,* Joint Economic Committee, Congress of the United States (Washington: Government Printing Office, 1982).

strength of current demand will be recognized and corrected when contracts expire. Real wages and interest rates will increase and eventually reflect the higher price level and rate of inflation. Profit margins will return to normal. When these adjustments are completed, the temporarily large output rate and high employment level will decline and return to normal.

What would happen if product prices increased less rapidly than decision-makers anticipated? Anticipating larger price increases (a higher inflation rate than actually occurs), borrowers agree to interest rates that later prove to be unacceptably high in terms of the current price level. Similarly, employers agree to wage increases that result in higher real wages than expected, since the price level rises more slowly than was anticipated. The abnormally high interest and wage rates increase costs relative to product prices. As profit margins are squeezed, producers reduce costs by reducing output and by laying off employees. Unemployment rises above the natural rate of unemployment. Current output falls short of the economy's potential GDP.

Many economists think this is precisely what happened during 1982. After inflation rates of 13 percent in 1979 and 12 percent in 1980, price increases plummeted to 4 percent in 1982. This sharp reduction in the inflation rate caught many decision-makers by surprise. Unable to pass along to consumers the large increases in money wages agreed to in 1980 and 1981, employers cut back production and laid off workers. The unemployment rate soared to 10.8 percent in late 1982, up from 7.6 percent in 1981. Eventually, new agreements provided for smaller money wage increases or even wage reductions in 1983 and 1984. Unemployment fell. Nevertheless, in 1982, unemployment was well above its natural rate. The necessary adjustments could not be made instantaneously.

## ANTICIPATED AND UNANTICIPATED CHANGES

**anticipated change** A change that is foreseen by decision-makers in time for them to adjust.

**unanticipated change** A change that decision-makers could not reasonably foresee. Thus, choices made prior to the event did not take the event into account.

It is important to distinguish between anticipated and unanticipated changes in markets. **Anticipated changes** are foreseen by economic participants. Decision-makers have time to adjust to anticipated changes before they occur. For example, suppose that under normal weather conditions, a drought-resistant hybrid seed can be expected to expand the production of feed grain in the Midwest by 10 percent next year. As a result, buyers and sellers will plan for a larger supply and probable lower prices in the future. They will adjust their decision-making and behavior accordingly.

In contrast, **unanticipated changes** catch people by surprise. Our world is characterized by dynamic change. Stock prices rise, incomes change abroad, new products are introduced, demand expands for some goods and contracts for others, technology changes—markets are constantly changing in light of unexpected events. Markets do not adjust instantaneously to unanticipated changes in market conditions. For a time, it may be unclear whether a change in sales, for example, reflects a random occurrence or a lasting change. It takes time to differentiate between temporary and permanent changes. Even after decision-makers are convinced that market conditions have changed, it will take time to carry out new decisions. In some cases, complete adjustment will also be delayed by the presence of long-term contracts.

Since it takes time for markets to adjust, unanticipated changes in aggregate demand and supply will not immediately lead to a new long-run equilibrium. Nonetheless, unpredictable events occur. We now turn to an analysis of factors that alter aggregate demand and aggregate supply and an examination of how macroeconomic markets adjust to various changes.

### Unanticipated Changes in Aggregate Demand

The aggregate demand curve isolates the impact of the price level on the quantity demanded of goods and services. The price level, however, is not the only factor that will influence the choices of buyers in the goods and services market. Changes in various other factors influence the purchasing decisions of consumers, investors, governments, and foreigners, causing the entire aggregate demand schedule to shift, altering the amount purchased at each price. For example, if the wealth of households increases—perhaps as the result of higher stock market prices or a housing boom—people will demand more goods and services. Thus, an increase in wealth will shift the entire demand schedule to the right. More goods and services will be purchased at each price level. Conversely, a reduction in wealth will reduce the demand for goods and services, shifting the demand schedule to the left.

Also, changes in the real interest rate in the loanable funds markets will influence the choices of consumers and investors in the goods and services market. A lower real interest rate makes it cheaper for consumers to buy major appliances, automobiles, and houses now rather than in the future. Simultaneously, a lower rate will also stimulate business spending on capital goods (investment). Thus, both households and business will increase their current expenditures on goods and services in response to a reduction in the real interest rate. As a result, lower real interest rates will stimulate aggregate demand, shifting the entire schedule to the right. Conversely, higher real interest rates will tend to reduce aggregate demand, shifting the schedule to the left.

Expectations about the future direction of the economy will influence current purchasing decisions as well. Consumers are more likely to buy big-ticket items such as automobiles and houses when they expect an expanding economy to provide them with both job security and rising income in the future. Similarly, optimism concerning the future direction of the economy will stimulate current investment. Business decision-makers know that an expanding economy will mean strong sales and improved profit margins. Investment today may be necessary if business firms are going to benefit fully from these opportunities. So increased optimism encourages additional expenditures by both consumers and investors, increasing aggregate demand. And pessimism about the future state of the economy exerts just the opposite impact. Business pessimism leads to a decline in aggregate demand, shifting the demand schedule to the left.

Still another influence is the expected rate of inflation. When consumers and investors believe that the inflation rate is going to accelerate in the future, they have an incentive to spend more during the current period. "Buy now before prices go higher" becomes the order of the day. Thus, the expectation of an acceleration in the inflation rate will stimulate current aggregate demand, shifting the demand schedule to the right. In contrast, the expectation of a deceleration in the inflation rate will tend to discourage current spending. When prices are expected to stabilize (or at least increase less rapidly), the gain obtained by moving expenditures forward in time is reduced. The expectation of a deceleration in the inflation rate will thus reduce current aggregate demand, shifting the curve to the left.

Finally, changes in income abroad and the value of a nation's currency in the exchange rate market can influence net exports. Rapid growth of income in Europe and Japan increases the demand of European and Japanese consumers for U.S.–produced goods. As U.S. exports expand, aggregate demand increases (the demand schedule shifts to the right). Similarly, a depreciation in the exchange rate value of the dollar (this implies an appreciation of the value of foreign currencies) will make U.S. exports cheaper for foreigners and

## THUMBNAIL SKETCH

### Factors Influencing Aggregate Demand

These factors will increase (decrease) aggregate demand:[a]

1. An increase (decrease) in real wealth.
2. A decrease (increase) in the real rate of interest.
3. An increase in the optimism (pessimism) of businesses and consumers about future economic conditions.
4. An increase (decrease) in the expected rate of inflation.
5. Higher (lower) real incomes abroad.
6. A reduction (increase) in the exchange rate value of the nation's currency.

[a]The important factors of macroeconomic policy will be considered later.

foreign goods more expensive to U.S. consumers.[2] Net exports will tend to increase, stimulating aggregate demand. Conversely, declining incomes abroad and appreciation in the dollar will retard net exports, causing a decline in aggregate demand. The accompanying "Thumbnail Sketch" summarizes the major factors causing shifts in aggregate demand.

**UNANTICIPATED INCREASES IN AGGREGATE DEMAND** How will changes in aggregate demand influence price and output in the goods and services market? Exhibit 13.6 will help us answer this question. Here we consider an economy that is initially in long-run equilibrium at output $Y_f$ and price level $P_{100}$ (point $E_1$ of Exhibit 13.6a). Suppose that this equilibrium were disrupted by a stock market boom or burst of business optimism that caused an unanticipated increase in aggregate demand (shift from $AD_1$ to $AD_2$)

At the initial price level, ($P_{100}$), excess demand would be present. Given the excess demand, businesses will increase their prices, improve their profit margins (since product prices increase relative to the cost of resources), and expand their output along SRAS. The economy will move to a short-run equilibrium ($e_2$), at a larger output ($Y_2$) and higher price level ($P_{105}$). (Note: a short-run equilibrium is indicated with a small *e*, while a capital *E* is used to designate a long-run equilibrium.) For a time, many wage rates, interest payments, rents, and other resource prices will still reflect the initial price level ($P_{100}$) and the previously weaker demand. Since markets do not adjust instantaneously, these resource prices and therefore costs, will lag behind prices in the goods and services market. Thus, the higher price level temporarily improves profit margins, which, in turn, provides the incentive for business firms to expand both output and employment in the short run. As a result, the unemployment rate will drop below its natural rate, and output will temporarily exceed the economy's long-run potential output level.

[2]Later, when we consider the topic of international finance, we will analyze in more detail the determinants of the exchange rate and consider more fully the impact of changes in the exchange rate value of a nation's currency.

**EXHIBIT 13.6**

**Unanticipated Increase in Aggregate Demand**

In response to an unanticipated increase in aggregate demand for goods and services (shift from $AD_1$ to $AD_2$), prices will rise (to $P_{105}$) and output will temporarily exceed full-employment capacity in the short run (frame a). However, with the passage of time, prices in resource markets, including the labor market, will rise as the result of the strong demand. As frame b illustrates, the higher resource prices will mean higher costs, which will reduce aggregate supply (to $SRAS_2$, frame b). In the long run, a new equilibrium at a higher price level ($P_{110}$) and an output consistent with the economy's sustainable potential will result. Thus, the increase in demand will expand output only temporarily.

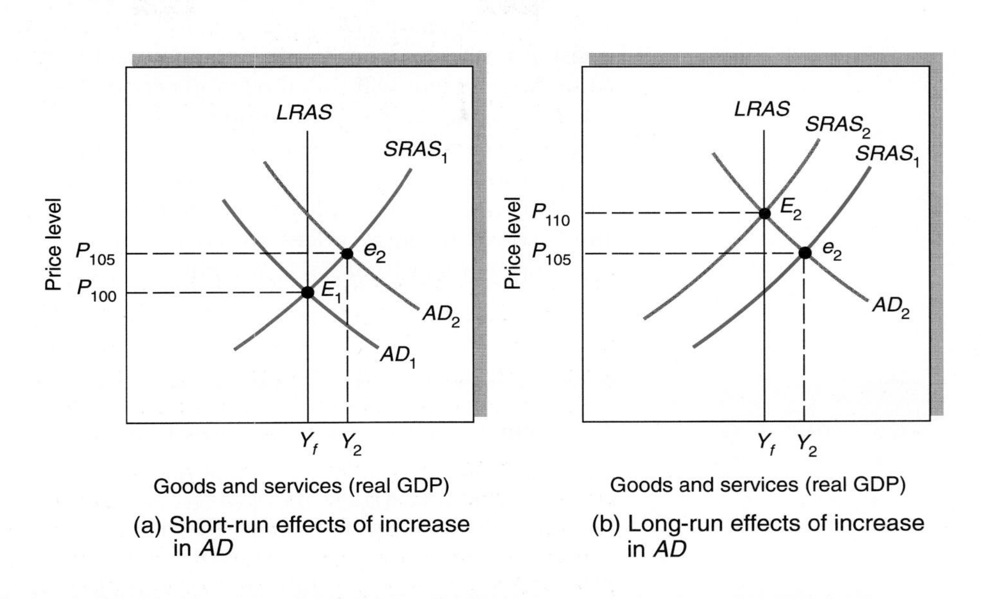


(a) Short-run effects of increase in *AD*

(b) Long-run effects of increase in *AD*

This is not the end of the story, however. The strong demand accompanying this high level of output will place upward pressure on prices in resource and loanable funds markets. With time, the strong demand conditions will push wages, other resource prices, and real interest rates upward. As Exhibit 13.6b illustrates, the rising resource prices and costs will shift the short-run aggregate supply to the left (to $SRAS_2$). Eventually, a new *long-run* equilibrium ($E_2$) will be established at a higher price level ($P_{110}$) that is correctly anticipated by decision-makers.

Thus, the increase in real GDP above the economy's long-run potential is only temporary. It will last only until there is an opportunity to alter the temporarily fixed resource prices (and interest rates) upward in light of the new stronger demand conditions. As this happens, profit margins return to their normal level, output recedes to the economy's long-run potential, and unemployment returns to its natural rate.

Since an increase in aggregate demand does not alter the economy's productive capacity, it cannot permanently expand output (beyond $Y_f$). The expansion in demand temporarily expands output, but over the long term, its major effect will be higher prices (inflation).

**UNANTICIPATED REDUCTIONS IN AGGREGATE DEMAND** How would the goods and services market adjust to an unanticipated reduction in aggregate demand? For example, suppose decision-makers become more pessimistic about the future or that an unexpected decline in income abroad reduces the demand for exports. Exhibit 13.7 will help us analyze this issue. Once again, we consider an economy that is in long-run equilibrium ($E_1$) at output $Y_1$ and price level $P_{100}$ (Exhibit 13.7a). Long-run equilibrium is disturbed by the reduction in aggregate demand: the shift from $AD_1$ to $AD_2$. As the result of the decline in demand, businesses will be unable to sell $Y_f$ units of output at the initial price level ($P_{100}$). In the short run, business firms will both reduce output (to $Y_2$) and cut prices (to $P_{95}$) in response to the weak demand conditions. Since many costs of business firms are temporarily fixed, profit margins will decline. Workers will be laid off, causing unemployment to increase to an abnormally high rate. The actual rate of unemployment will rise above the economy's natural rate of unemployment. Weak demand and excess supply will be widespread in resource markets. These forces will place downward pressure on resource prices.

If resource prices quickly adjusted downward in response to the weak demand and rising unemployment, then the decline in output to $Y_2$ would be brief. Lower resource prices would reduce costs and thereby increase aggregate supply (shift to $SRAS_2$). As Exhibit 13.7b illustrates, the result would be a

**EXHIBIT 13.7**

**Unanticipated Reduction in Aggregate Demand**

As frame a illustrates, the short-run impact of an unanticipated reduction in aggregate demand (shift from $AD_1$ to $AD_2$) will be a decline in output (to $Y_2$) and a lower price level ($P_{95}$). Temporarily, unemployment will rise above its natural rate. In the long run, weak demand and excess supply in the resource market will lead to lower wage rates and resource prices. This will reduce costs, leading to an expansion in short-run aggregate supply (shift to $SRAS_2$, frame b). However, this method of restoring equilibrium ($E_2$) may be both highly painful and quite lengthy.

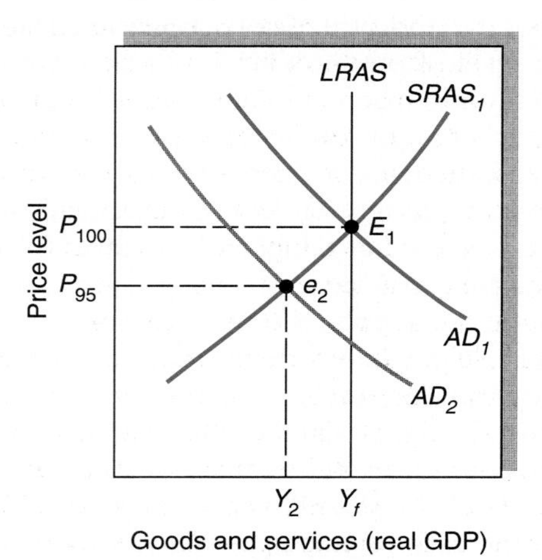


(a) Short-run effects of decline in *AD*

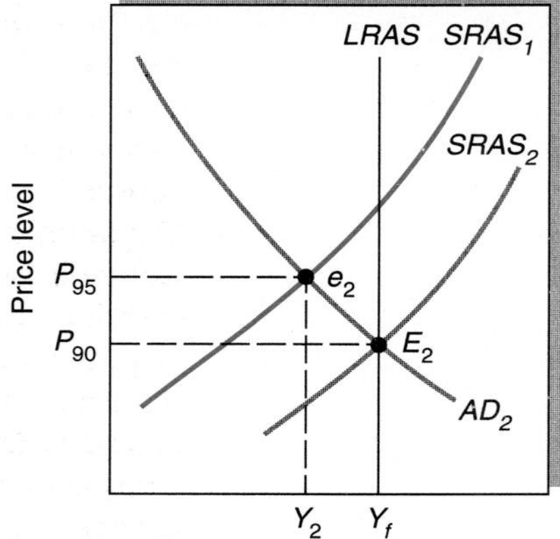


(b) Long-run effects of decline in *AD*

new equilibrium ($E_2$) at the economy's full employment output rate ($Y_f$) and a lower price level ($P_{90}$).

Resource prices, though, may not adjust quickly. Long-term contracts and uncertainty as to whether the weak demand conditions are merely temporary will slow the adjustment process. In addition, individual workers and union officials may be highly reluctant to be the first to accept lower nominal wages.

If resource prices are inflexible in a downward direction, as many economists believe, the adjustment to a reduction in aggregate demand will be both lengthy and painful. Prolonged periods of economic recession—below capacity output rates and abnormally high unemployment—may occur before long-run equilibrium is restored.

## Unanticipated Changes in Aggregate Supply

What happens if aggregate demand stays the same but aggregate supply changes? The answer to this question depends on whether the aggregate supply change is long-run or short-run. By a long-run change in aggregate supply, we mean a change in the economy's long-run production possibilities (sustainable potential output). For example, the invention of a more efficient source of energy would cause a long-run change in aggregate supply. In such a situation, both long-run (*LRAS*) and short-run (*SRAS*) aggregate supply would change.

In contrast, changes that *temporarily* alter the productive capability of an economy will shift the short-run aggregate supply curve, but not long-run aggregate supply. A drought in California would be an example of such a short-run change. The drought will hurt in the short run, but it will eventually end, and output will return to the long-run normal rate. Changes that are temporary in nature will shift only the *SRAS* curve. Let us now consider the major factors capable of shifting the long-run and short-run aggregate supply schedules.

## Changes in Long-Run Aggregate Supply

When constructing the long-run aggregate supply curve, the quantity of resources, level of technology, and institutional arrangements that influence the productivity and efficiency of resource use are held constant. Changes in any of these three determinants of output would cause the *LRAS* curve to shift.

With the passage of time, net investment can expand the supply of physical capital, natural resources, and labor (human resources). Investment in physical capital can expand the supply of buildings, machines, and other physical assets. Search and discovery can increase the supply of natural resources. With the passage of time, changes in population and labor force participation may affect the supply of labor. Similarly, education, training, and skill-enhancing experience can improve the quality of the labor force, and thereby expand the supply of human resources.

Such increases in the economy's resource base will make it possible to produce and sustain a larger rate of output. Both the *LRAS* and *SRAS* curves will increase (shift to the right). On the other hand, a lasting reduction in the quantity (or quality) of resources will reduce both the current and long-term production capacity of the economy, shifting both *LRAS* and *SRAS* curves to the left.

Improvements in technology—the discovery of economical new products or less costly ways of producing goods and services—also permit us to squeeze a larger output from a specific resource supply. For example, the development of the microchip vastly expanded our productive capacity in the 1970s and 1980s. The *LRAS* curve shifted to the right as a result.

Finally, institutional changes may also influence the efficiency of resource use and thereby alter the *LRAS* schedule. Changes in public policy that improve the efficiency of resource use—for example low-cost provision of public goods—will increase long-run aggregate supply. In contrast, institutional changes that reduce the efficiency of resource use will reduce it.

## Changes in Short-Run Aggregate Supply

Changes can sometimes influence current output without altering the economy's long-run capacity. When this is the case, the *SRAS* curve will shift, even though *LRAS* is unchanged.

When we derived the *SRAS* schedule, resource prices were held constant. Changes in resources prices will shift the *SRAS* curve. A reduction in resource prices will lower costs and therefore shift the curve to the right. However, unless the lower prices of resources reflect a *long-term* increase in the supply of resources, they will not alter the *LRAS* schedule. Conversely, an increase in the price of resources will increase costs, shifting the *SRAS* curve to the left. But unless the higher prices are the result of a long-term reduction in the size of the economy's resource base, they will not alter the *LRAS* schedule.

**supply shock** An unexpected event that temporarily either increases or decreases aggregate supply.

In addition, various **supply shocks,** surprise occurrences that temporarily increase or decrease current output, may also alter current output without directly affecting the productive capacity of the economy. For example, adverse weather conditions, a natural disaster, or a temporary increase in the price of imported resources (perhaps oil in the case of the United States) will reduce current supply, even though they do not alter the economy's long-term production capacity. They will thus decrease short-run aggregate supply (shift *SRAS* to the left) without directly affecting *LRAS*. On the other hand, favorable weather conditions or temporary reductions in the world price of imported resources will increase current output, even though the economy's long-run capacity remains unchanged.

The accompanying "Thumbnail Sketch" summarizes the major factors influencing both long-run and short-run aggregate supply. Of course, macroeconomic policy may also influence aggregate supply. As in the case of aggregate

### THUMBNAIL SKETCH

**Factors Influencing Short-Run and Long-Run Aggregate Supply**

These factors will increase (decrease) long-run aggregate supply (*LRAS*):[a]

1. An increase (decrease) in the supply of resources.
2. An improvement (deterioration) in technology and productivity.
3. Institutional changes that increase (reduce) the efficiency of resource use.

These factors will increase (decrease) short-run aggregate supply (*SRAS*):[a]

1. A decrease (increase) in resource prices, that is, production costs.
2. Favorable (unfavorable) supply shocks such as good (bad) weather.
3. A decrease (increase) in the world price of imported resources.

[a]The important factors of macroeconomic policy will be considered later.

demand, we will consider the impact of macroeconomic policy on supply in subsequent chapters.

## Adjusting to Changes in Aggregate Supply

Steady increases in the productive capacity of an economy resulting from such things as net investment, technological advancement, and improvement in the size and quality of the labor force will increase long-run aggregate supply. Since changes of this type take place quite gradually, they need not disrupt the economy's macro equilibrium. Changes in factors that influence the short-run aggregate supply curve, however, are likely to be unanticipated. By their very nature, supply shocks are unpredictable.

What would happen if highly favorable weather conditions or a temporary decline in the world market price of a critical imported resource increased the current output and income of a nation? Since the temporarily favorable supply conditions cannot be counted on in the future, they will not directly alter the economy's *long-term* production capacity. Given that the favorable supply conditions are temporary, *SRAS* will increase (shift to the right), while *LRAS* will remain constant. Output (and income) will temporarily expand beyond the economy's full employment constraints. The increase in current supply will place downward pressure on the price level. However, once the temporary favorable supply shock reverses itself, the rate of output will return to the economy's long-run sustainable level.

In recent decades, the U.S. economy has been jolted by several unfavorable supply-side factors. In 1973, and again in 1979, the United States and other oil-importing countries were hit with sharply higher oil prices as the result of unstable conditions in the Middle East. During the summer of 1988, the most severe drought conditions in 50 years resulted in an extremely poor harvest in the U.S. agricultural belt. In August of 1990, Iraq suddenly invaded Kuwait and threatened the oil fields of Saudi Arabia. Once again the world price of oil shot up, sharply increasing the cost of energy in the United States and other oil-importing countries.

How do such adverse supply shocks influence macroeconomic markets? Exhibit 13.8 illustrates the answer. Both an unfavorable harvest due to adverse weather conditions and a higher world price of oil will reduce the supply of resources (from $S_1$ to $S_2$ in Exhibit 13.8a) in the domestic market. Resource prices will rise (to $P'_r$). In turn, the higher resource prices will reduce short-run aggregate supply (the shift from $SRAS_1$ to $SRAS_2$ in Exhibit 13.8b) in the goods and services market. Since supply shocks of this type are generally unanticipated, initially they will reduce output and place upward pressure on prices (the rate of inflation) in the goods and services market.

If an unfavorable supply shock is expected to be temporary, as will generally be the case for a bad harvest, long-run aggregate supply will be unaffected. After all, unfavorable growing conditions for a year or two do not represent a permanent change in climate. Therefore, as normal weather patterns return with the passage of time, both supply and price conditions in the resource market will return to normal, permitting the economy to return to long-run equilibrium at output $Y_f$.

When an adverse supply-side factor is more permanent, as in the case of a long-term increase in the price of oil imports, the long-run supply curve would also shift to the left. Under these circumstances, the economy would have to adjust to a lower level of real output.

**EXHIBIT 13.8**

**Effects of Adverse Supply Shock**

Suppose there is an unanticipated reduction in the supply of resources, perhaps as the result of a crop failure or sharp increase in the world price of a major imported resource such as oil. Resource prices would rise (from $P_r$ to $P'_r$, frame a). The higher resource prices would shift the *SRAS* curve to the left. In the short run, the price level would rise (to $P_{110}$, frame b) and output would decline (to $Y_2$). What happens in the long run depends on whether the reduction in the supply of resources is temporary or permanent. If it is temporary, resource prices will fall in the future, permitting the economy to return to its initial equilibrium ($E_1$). Conversely, if the reduced supply of resources is permanent, the productive potential of the economy will shrink (*LRAS* will shift to the left) and $e_2$ will become a long-run equilibrium.

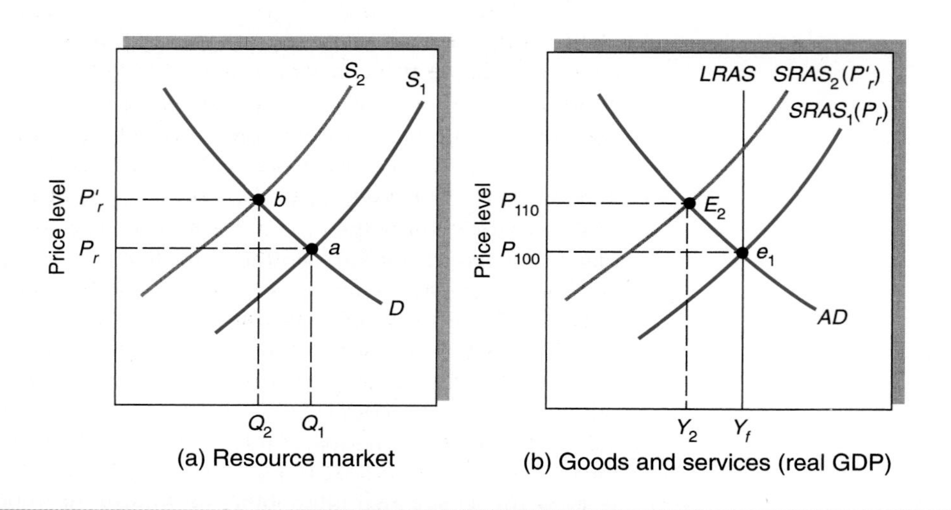

(a) Resource market

(b) Goods and services (real GDP)

Regardless of whether the decline in aggregate supply is temporary or permanent, other things constant, the price level will rise. Similarly, output will decline, at least temporarily. Theory thus indicates that the adverse supply shocks of recent years contributed to the sluggish growth and inflation of the era.

## SELF-CORRECTING MECHANISM

In a dynamic world of changing demand conditions and supply shocks, economic ups and downs are inevitable. Sometimes (during periods of economic boom) output will exceed the economy's long-run capacity, while at other times (during periods of recession) output will fall short of its potential. Are there market forces that will help stabilize an economy and cushion the effects of economic shocks? Does a market economy have a built-in mechanism that will prevent an economic downturn from plunging into a depression? There are three reasons to believe that the answer to both of these questions is yes.

1. *Consumption, the largest component of aggregate demand, is relatively stable over the business cycle.* When income declines during a recession,

people generally dip into their savings or borrow in order to maintain a high level of current consumption. Thus, consumer demand will decline by less than income during a recession. This relative stability of consumer demand will help stabilize aggregate demand and reverse an economic downturn.

Similarly, during an economic expansion, a substantial amount of the above-normal gains in income enjoyed by most households will be allocated to saving. So, consumption demand will increase less rapidly than income during a business expansion. Thus, during an economic boom, the stability of consumption will dampen the growth of aggregate demand and the accompanying inflationary forces. In this manner, the stability of consumption will help keep a market economy on track.

2. *Changes in real interest rates will help to stabilize aggregate demand and redirect economic fluctuations.* During an economic downturn, business demand for new investment projects and therefore loanable funds is generally quite weak. The weak demand, however, leads to a lower real interest rate. In turn, the lower interest rate both encourages current consumption and reduces the opportunity cost of investment projects, dampening the decline in aggregate demand. On the other hand, the real interest rate increases as many businesses borrow in order to undertake investment projects during an economic expansion. The higher real interest rate discourages both consumption and investment and thereby minimizes the increase in aggregate demand during a business expansion. Thus, the interest rate acts as a shock absorber, helping both to stabilize aggregate demand and redirect economic fluctuations.

3. *Changes in real resource prices will redirect economic fluctuations.* Price adjustments in the resource market will also help to keep the economy on an even keel. When the current output of an economy is less than its full employment potential ($Y_f$), weak demand and slack employment in resource markets will place downward pressure on *real* resource prices. Under these conditions, real wages and other resource prices will decline (or increase at a very slow rate). In contrast, when an economy is operating beyond its full employment capacity ($Y_f$)—when unemployment is less than the natural unemployment rate—strong demand will push the real price of resources up rapidly.

Exhibit 13.9 indicates the significance of this pattern of dynamic change in resource prices in response to business conditions. Exhibit 13.9a illustrates the supply and demand conditions in the goods and services market such as might result from an unanticipated increase in aggregate demand. Current output exceeds the economy's full-employment capacity. Given the strong demand, the actual rate of unemployment will be less than the natural rate in the labor market. This high rate of output, however, will not be sustainable. As the result of the strong demand, resource prices will rise with the passage of time. The higher resource prices will push costs upward, and thereby reduce short-run aggregate supply (shift the curve to $SRAS_2$ in Exhibit 13.9a). As costs increase, profit margins will decline to normal competitive rates, and output will recede to its long-run potential. Thus, market forces will help direct the overemployment economy back to long-run equilibrium.

Exhibit 13.9b illustrates an economy initially operating at less than full-employment capacity. When current output is less than an economy's long-run potential, resource prices will decline *relative to product prices*. An abnormally high unemployment rate (in excess of the natural rate) in resource markets will eventually induce suppliers to accept lower wage rates and

**EXHIBIT 13.9**

**Resource Prices and Long-Run Equilibrium**

In the short run, output may either exceed or fall short of the economy's full-employment capacity ($Y_f$). If output is temporarily greater than the economy's potential (frame a), resource prices and production costs will rise. The higher production costs will decrease aggregate supply (to $SRAS_2$, frame a), restoring equilibrium at full-employment capacity and a higher price level ($P_{105}$).

When an economy is temporarily operating at less than capacity (frame b), abnormally high unemployment and an excess supply in the resource market may lead to lower resource prices and production costs. The lower cost would increase aggregate supply (to $SRAS_2$, frame b). Thus, the output of a market economy would tend to move toward full-employment capacity. However, this self-correction process may require considerable time. As we proceed, we will consider alternative methods of attaining full-employment equilibrium more rapidly.

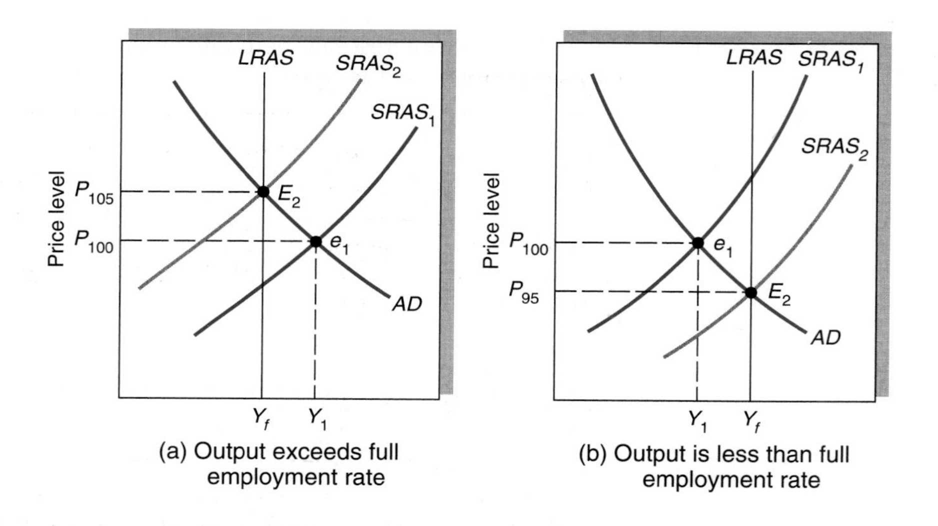


(a) Output exceeds full employment rate

(b) Output is less than full employment rate

prices for other resources. The declining real cost of labor and other resources will shift *SRAS* to the right. With time, the lower resource prices will restore long-run equilibrium ($E_2$) at the full-employment rate of output.

## Speed of Self-Correction

Following the Great Depression, many economists thought that market economies were inherently unstable. They argued that unless monetary and fiscal policy were used to stimulate and guide the macroeconomy, prolonged recessions would result. Influenced by both a reevaluation of the 1930s and the experience of the last 50 years, most modern economists reject this stagnation view of market economies.[3] Today, there is a widespread consensus that market economies possess stabilizing forces.

What divides economists is disagreement about how rapidly the self-corrective forces work. This is a key issue. If the self-corrective process

[3]A detailed analysis of the forces causing and prolonging the Great Depression is presented in Chapter 16.

works quite slowly, then market economies will still experience prolonged periods of abnormally high unemployment and below-capacity output. Many economists believe this is the case. Accordingly, they recommend active use of fiscal and monetary policy by the government to keep the market economy from swinging back and forth between inflationary economic booms and severe business recessions.

Conversely, other economists believe that the self-corrective mechanism of a market economy works reasonably well *when monetary and fiscal policy follow a stable course*. This latter group argues that macroeconomic policy mistakes are the major source of economic instability. Because of this, they call for the use of policy rules, such as a constant growth rate in the supply of money and balanced budgets, rather than discretionary use of macroeconomic policy. As we proceed with our analysis, we will consider this debate in more detail.

## LOOKING AHEAD

In this chapter, we assumed that fiscal policy (government expenditures and taxes) and monetary policy (the supply of money) were unchanged. With regard to fiscal policy, we are now prepared to relax this assumption. In the next chapter, we will use the macroeconomic model of this chapter to analyze the impact of fiscal policy. Later, the model will be utilized to analyze the effects of monetary policy.

## CHAPTER SUMMARY

1. The circular flow of income illustrates the significance of three highly aggregated markets: (a) goods and services, (b) resources, and (c) loanable funds. The resource market coordinates the exchange of labor and other inputs between the household and business sectors. The goods and services market coordinates the demand of households, business investors, governments, and foreigners with the supply of commodities produced. The loanable funds market coordinates the actions of borrowers and lenders, and thereby channels the *net* saving of households back into the flow of income as investment or government expenditures.
2. The aggregate demand curve indicates the quantity of output that consumers, investors, governments, and foreigners will want to buy at different price levels. Assuming the money supply is constant, a reduction in the price level will increase the wealth of people holding the "fixed" quantity of money and place downward pressure on the interest rate. Both of these factors will increase the quantity of goods and services demanded. Therefore, the aggregate demand curve will slope downward to the right.
3. The aggregate supply curve indicates the various quantities of goods and services suppliers will offer to sell at different price levels. In the short run, the aggregate supply curve will generally slope upward to the right. This is because a higher price level temporarily improves profit margins, since important cost components are fixed in the short run.

4. Once decision-makers adjust fully to a higher price level, the factors that justified the upward-sloping short-run aggregate supply curve are no longer present. Output is constrained by factors such as technology and resource supply. A higher price level does not loosen these constraints. Thus, the long-run aggregate supply curve is vertical.
5. Two conditions are necessary for long-run equilibrium in the goods and services market: (a) quantity demanded must equal quantity supplied and (b) the actual price level must equal the price level decision-makers anticipated when they made buying and selling decisions for the current period. When an economy is in long-run equilibrium, output will be at its maximum *sustainable* level. Similarly, the actual rate of unemployment will equal the natural rate (the lowest rate of unemployment that can be sustained over a long period of time). Economists would say that the economy is operating at full employment in this case.
6. When dynamic changes result in a price level that differs from that anticipated, output will differ from the economy's long-run capacity. When the current price level is higher than was anticipated, real wages and interest rates will be abnormally low (relative to the prices of goods and services). Unemployment will temporarily fall below its natural rate. Current output will temporarily exceed the economy's long-run capacity. In contrast, when the current price level is lower than was anticipated, real wages and interest rates will be abnormally high. Unemployment will exceed its natural rate. Under such circumstances, current output will be lower than the economy's long-run capacity.
7. An increase in aggregate demand involves a shift of the entire aggregate demand schedule to the right. Other than policy, major factors causing an increase in aggregate demand are (a) an increase in real wealth, (b) a lower real interest rate, (c) increased optimism on the part of businesses and consumers, (d) an increase in the expected rate of inflation, (e) higher real income abroad, and (f) a reduction in a nation's exchange rate. Conversely, if these factors change in the opposite direction, a decrease in aggregate demand will result.
8. When the long-run equilibrium of an economy is disrupted by an unanticipated increase in aggregate demand, output will temporarily increase beyond the economy's long-run capacity, and unemployment will fall below its natural rate. However, as decision-makers adjust to the increase in demand, resource prices will rise, and output will recede to long-run capacity. In the long run, the major impact of the increase in aggregate demand will be a higher price level (inflation).
9. An unanticipated reduction in aggregate demand will temporarily reduce output below capacity and push unemployment above its natural rate. Eventually, unemployment and excess supply in resource markets will reduce wage rates and resource prices. Costs will decline, and output will return to its long-run potential. However, if wages and prices are inflexible downward, less-than-capacity output and abnormally high unemployment may persist for a substantial period of time.
10. Changes that alter the economy's maximum sustainable output will shift the *LRAS* curve. The following factors will increase *LRAS:* (a) increases in the supply of labor and capital resources, (b) improvements in technology

and productivity, and (c) institutional changes improving the efficiency of resource use.

11. In the short run, output may change as the result of temporary factors that do not directly alter the economy's long-run capacity. The major factors leading to an increase in *SRAS* (a shift of the schedule to the right) are (a) a reduction in resource prices, (b) favorable weather conditions, and (c) a decline in the world price of imported resources. Conversely, if these factors changed in the opposite direction, *SRAS* would decline (shift to the left).
12. An adverse supply shock (decrease in *SRAS*) will reduce output and increase the price level. Many economists think adverse supply shocks, particularly the sharp increase in the price of imported oil, contributed to the slow rate of growth and rapid increase in the price level during the 1970s.
13. When output and employment exceed the rates associated with an economy's long-run equilibrium, real interest rates and resource prices (including real wages) will rise, increasing costs and thereby shifting the *SRAS* to the left until long-run equilibrium is restored at full-employment output and a higher price level. Similarly, when current output is less than the economy's potential GDP, lower real interest rates and falling real resource prices (and wages) will reduce costs and thereby shift *SRAS* to the right until long-run equilibrium is restored. These forces provide the economy with a self-corrective mechanism, directing it toward the full-employment rate of output.
14. Many economists believe the economy's self-corrective mechanism works quite slowly and that discretionary monetary and fiscal policy changes are therefore necessary to minimize economic instability. Others believe that the self-corrective mechanism works reasonably well and that discretionary policy is likely to do more harm than good.

# *Study Guide*

## CHAPTER 13

## Developing the Economic Way of Thinking

## CRITICAL-ANALYSIS QUESTIONS

1. In your own words, explain why aggregate demand is inversely related to the price level. Why isn't the aggregate demand curve simply a reflection of the downward-sloping demand curve for an individual good?
2. What are the major factors influencing aggregate supply in the long run? Why doesn't the long-run aggregate supply curve slope upward to the right like *SRAS?*

*3. In Chapters 3 and 4, we indicated the other things that are held constant when the supply and demand schedules *for a specific good* are constructed. What were they? What are the key "other things" held constant when the aggregate supply, *LRAS,* and *SRAS* schedules are constructed?

*4. Suppose prices had been rising at a 3 percent annual rate in recent years. A major union signs a three-year contract calling for increases in money wage rates of 6 percent annually. What will happen to the real wages of the union members if the price level is constant (unchanged) during the next three years? If other unions signed similar contracts, what will probably happen to the unemployment rate? Why? Answer the same questions under conditions in which the price level increases at an annual rate of 8 percent during the next three years.

5. Under what conditions would the actual unemployment rate be less than the natural rate? Can this condition be sustained in the future? Why or why not?
6. What conditions are present when an economy is in long-run equilibrium? When an economy is in long-run equilibrium, how are the following related to each other?
   a. The actual price level and the price level that was expected for the current period.
   b. Actual GDP and the "full employment" rate of output.
   c. The actual rate of unemployment and the natural rate of unemployment.

*7. Explain how and why each of the following factors would influence current aggregate demand in the United States:
   a. An increase in recession fears.
   b. Increased fear of inflation.
   c. Rapid growth in real income in Japan and Western Europe.
   d. A reduction in the real interest rate.
   e. A higher price level (be careful).

*8. Indicate how each of the following would influence U.S. aggregate supply in the short run:
   a. An increase in real wage rates.
   b. A severe freeze that destroys half of the orange trees in Florida.
   c. A drought in the midwestern agricultural states.
   d. An increase in the world price of oil, a major import.
   e. Abundant rainfall during the growing season of agricultural states.

*Asterisk denotes critical-analysis questions for which answers are given in Appendix A.

9. What is the difference between an anticipated and an unanticipated increase in aggregate demand? Provide an example of each. Which is most likely to result in a temporary spurt in the growth of real output?
10. Suppose that the key macroeconomic markets are initially in long-run equilibrium. How will an unanticipated reduction in aggregate demand affect real output, employment, and the price level in the short run? In the long run?
11. When the actual output exceeds the long-run capacity of the economy, how will the self-correcting mechanism direct the economy to long-run equilibrium? Why can't the above-normal output be maintained?
*12. An unexpectedly rapid growth in real income abroad leads to a sharp increase in demand for U.S. exports. What impact will this change have on the price level, output, and employment in the short run? What is the likely impact in the long run?
13. If the money interest rate is 10 percent and the inflation rate in recent years has been steady at 7 percent, what is the estimated real interest rate?
*14. Suppose consumers and investors suddenly become more pessimistic about the future and therefore decide to reduce their consumption and investment spending. How will a market economy adjust to this increase in pessimism?

## MULTIPLE-CHOICE SELF-TEST

1. The portion of disposable income a consumer does not spend on current consumption is called
   a. Investment.
   b. Saving.
   c. Supply.
   d. Temporary income.
2. Which one of the following factors helps explain why the aggregate quantity demanded of goods and services is inversely related to the price level?
   a. As the price level falls, domestic consumers will purchase more imported goods and fewer domestically produced goods.
   b. As the price level falls, the monetary authorities will have to increase the supply of money, which will lead to an increase in amount purchased.
   c. As the price level falls, the government will have to reduce taxes, which will lead to an increase in amount purchased.
   d. As the price level falls, the wealth of people holding the fixed quantity of money increases, inducing them to expand their purchases.
3. In the short run, an increase in the price level in the goods and services market will
   a. Increase the purchasing power of money.
   b. Improve profit margins and thereby induce suppliers to expand output.
   c. Increase resource prices, squeeze profit margins, and lead to a decline in output.
   d. Reduce the natural rate of unemployment.

4. A vertical long-run aggregate supply curve indicates that
   a. An increase in the price level will not expand an economy's output capacity in the long run.
   b. Output rates greater than the long-run supply constraint cannot be achieved.
   c. An increase in the price level will permit the economy to achieve a higher level of output.
   d. An increase in the price level will promote technological change and more rapid economic growth.
5. Long-run equilibrium in the goods and services market requires that decision-makers who agreed to long-term contracts that influence current prices and costs must have
   a. Incorrectly anticipated the current price level when they made the agreements.
   b. Correctly anticipated the current price level when they made the agreements.
   c. Correctly anticipated the natural rate of unemployment when they made the agreements.
   d. Correctly anticipated the actual rate of unemployment when they made the agreements.
6. Which of the following will lead to an increase in current aggregate demand in the United States?
   a. A higher price level.
   b. An increase in the real interest rate.
   c. An increase in wealth resulting from a rally in the stock market.
   d. A decline in real income in Japan and Western Europe.
7. Starting with initial long-run equilibrium in the goods and services market (the aggregate demand/aggregate supply model), a sudden decrease in optimism about future business conditions will temporarily cause
   a. An increase in output and a reduction in the price level (or inflation rate).
   b. An increase in both output and the price level (or inflation rate).
   c. A reduction in both output and the price level (or inflation rate).
   d. A reduction in output and an increase in the price level (or inflation rate).
8. In the aggregate demand/aggregate supply model, when the current output of an economy is less than its long-run potential capacity, the economy will experience
   a. Falling real wages and resource prices that will stimulate employment and real output.
   b. Rising interest rates that will stimulate aggregate demand and restore full employment.
   c. A budget surplus that will stimulate demand and thereby help restore full employment.
   d. Rising resource prices that will restore equilibrium at a higher price level.
9. For an oil-importing country such as the United States, the immediate effect of a supply shock caused by an increase in the price of imported oil would tend to be

a. An increase in real output and a decrease in the price level.
b. A decrease in real output and employment, and an increase in the price level.
c. A decrease in the price level, real output, and employment.
d. An increase in the price level, real output, and unemployment.

10. If the actual rate of unemployment exceeds the natural rate of unemployment, the aggregate demand/aggregate supply model indicates that full employment
a. Cannot be restored without an increase in aggregate demand.
b. Cannot be restored without a permanent reduction in the rate of output.
c. Will be restored quickly.
d. Will be restored, but the model does not indicate how rapidly it will occur.

## PROBLEMS

1. Construct the *AD, SRAS,* and *LRAS* curves for an economy experiencing a recession. Do the same for economies experiencing (a) full employment (long-run equilibrium) and (b) an economic boom.

2. The accompanying table contains hypothetical information about real GDP (in billions of dollars) and the price level index *(P)*:

| *AD* | *P* | *SRAS* |
|---|---|---|
| $270 | 160 | $330 |
| 290 | 140 | 310 |
| 310 | 120 | 290 |
| 330 | 100 | 270 |
| 350 | 80 | 250 |

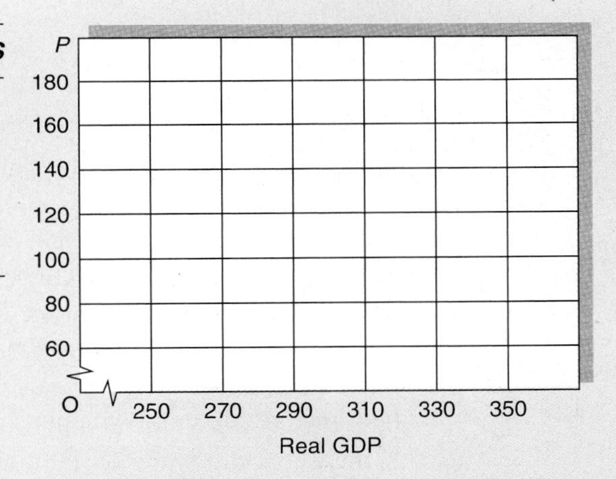


a. Plot the above data in an aggregate demand/aggregate supply model. What is the current equilibrium level of real GDP? What is the price level?
b. What is the current value of nominal GDP?
c. Suppose the level of full-employment real GDP is $320 billion. Add a *LRAS* curve to your diagram.
d. Is this economy currently experiencing full employment, a recession, or a boom? Explain briefly.
e. What was the expected price level for the current period? Did producers and workers overestimate, underestimate, or correctly predict the current price level?

f. Based on your answer to part e, why is the economy producing at its current level relative to full employment?

3. Use the accompanying diagrams to help you label each of the statements below as true or false:

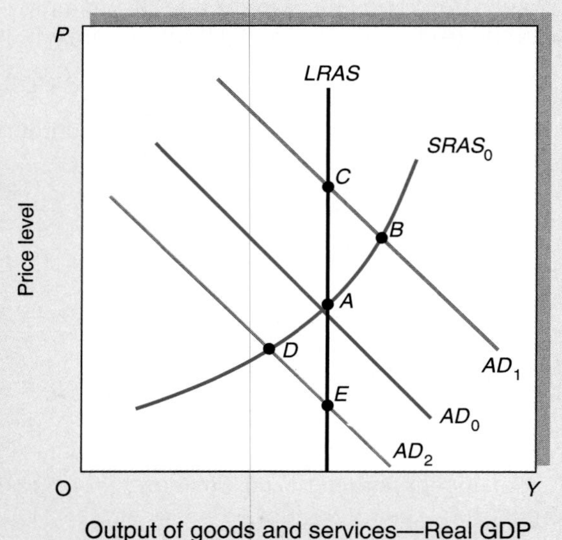


_____ a. Profits are higher at point *B* than at *D*.

_____ b. Profits are higher at point *G* than at *I*.

_____ c. Inflationary expectations are higher at point *B* than at *D*.

_____ d. Over time, if the economy were at point *B*, inflationary expectations would tend to fall, while if the economy were at point *D*, inflationary expectations would tend to rise.

_____ e. If the economy were at point *G*, the real price of resources would tend to decline in the future.

_____ f. If the economy were at point *D*, a fall in interest rates would help restore full employment.

_____ g. If the economy were at point *B*, an increase in U.S. net exports would help restore full employment.

_____ h. If the economy were at point *G*, the actual rate of unemployment would exceed the natural rate.

4. Illustrate the changes in aggregate demand (*AD*), short-run aggregate supply (*SRAS*), long-run aggregate supply (*LRAS*), the price level (*P*), and real gross domestic product (*RGDP*) in the short run as the result of the events described to the left of the diagrams. First draw new curves in the AD/AS diagram to show how *AD*, *SRAS* and/or *LRAS* shift as the result of the event0, and then fill in the table to the right of the diagrams using + to indicate increase, – to indicate decrease, 0 to indicate no change, and ? to indicate that either a decrease or an increase is possible.

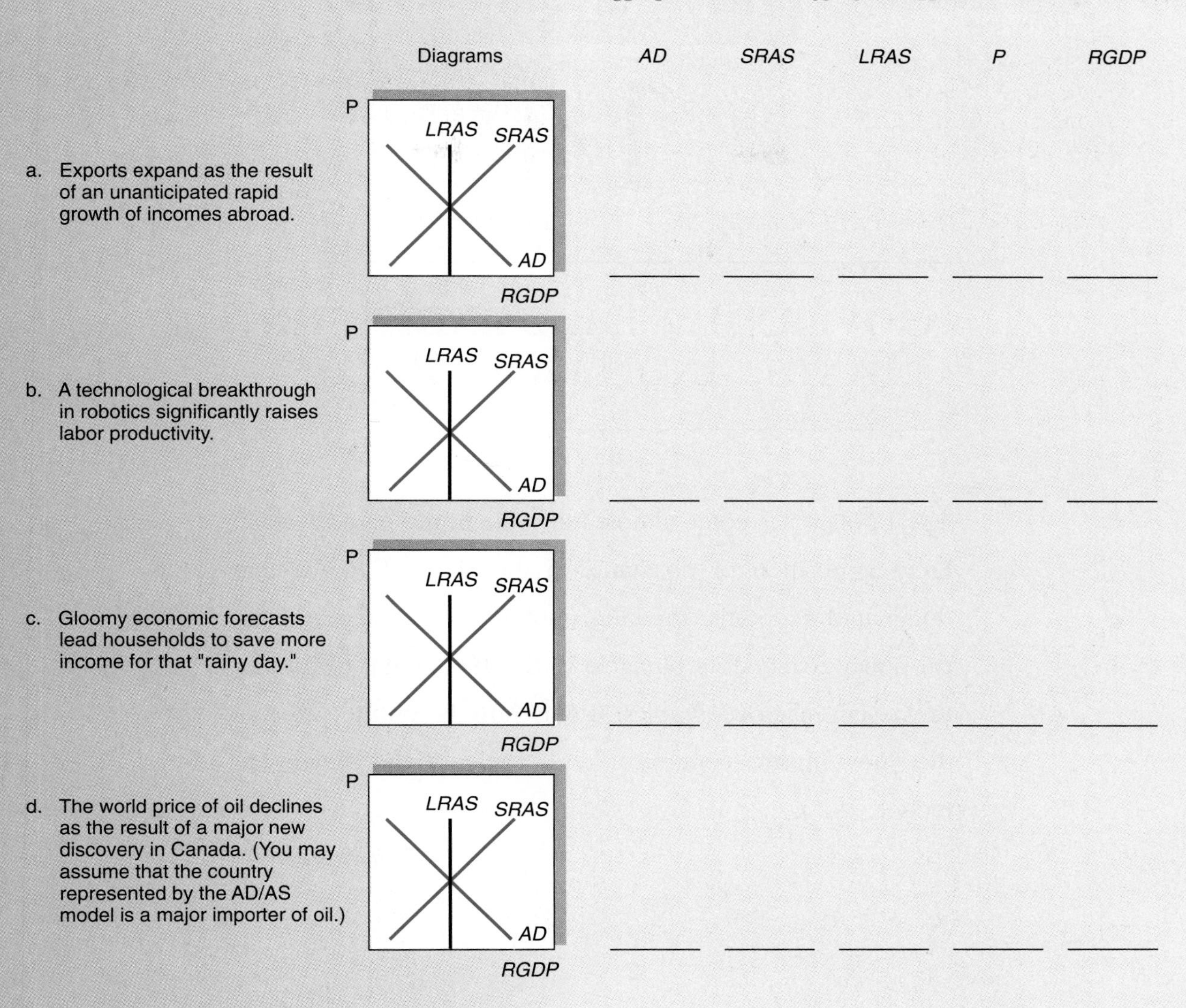
Diagrams
AD
SRAS
LRAS
P
RGDP
a. Exports expand as the result of an unanticipated rapid growth of incomes abroad.
P
LRAS
SRAS
AD
RGDP
b. A technological breakthrough in robotics significantly raises labor productivity.
P
LRAS
SRAS
AD
RGDP
c. Gloomy economic forecasts lead households to save more income for that "rainy day."
P
LRAS
SRAS
AD
RGDP
d. The world price of oil declines as the result of a major new discovery in Canada. (You may assume that the country represented by the AD/AS model is a major importer of oil.)
P
LRAS
SRAS
AD
RGDP

CHAPTER

# 14

# GOVERNMENT EXPENDITURES, TAXES, AND FISCAL POLICY

Fiscal policy has come almost full cycle in the past 50 years. From a position of no status in the classical model that dominated economic thinking until 1935, contracyclical fiscal policy reached its pinnacle in the 1960s—the heyday of Keynesian macroeconomics. It may now be on the wane as the "new macroeconomics" . . . replaces the Keynesian model.

*J. Ernest Tanner*[1]

## CHAPTER FOCUS

- How big is government? How does the size of government vary among countries?
- Why have the government expenditures of the United States grown substantially in recent decades?
- What are the objectives of fiscal policy? How does fiscal policy affect aggregate demand?
- Why do economists now believe that fiscal policy is less potent than they previously thought?
- Can fiscal policy help smooth the business cycle?
- Are there supply-side effects of fiscal policy?
- How do taxes influence the behavior of people? If a tax rate is increased by 10 percent, will revenue from the tax increase by 10 percent?

We are now ready to integrate government spending and taxation into our analysis. After considering the size of government expenditures in several countries and the growth of the public sector in the United States, we will analyze how fiscal policy influences the level of aggregate economic activity.

As we developed the aggregate demand/aggregate supply model in the previous chapter, we assumed the government's taxing and spending policies—that is, its fiscal policies—remained unchanged. We will now relax that assumption. However, we want to isolate the impact of changes in fiscal policy from changes in monetary policy. Because of this, we will continue to assume that the monetary authorities maintain a constant supply of money. The impact of monetary policy will be considered in Chapters 15 and 16.

## SIZE OF GOVERNMENT

The activities of governments have an enormous impact on our lives. Governments define property rights, enforce contracts, establish a legal framework, punish criminals, and administer justice through a system of courts. These activities are often referred to as the "protective function" of government, since they involve the protection of people's lives and property from abuse by others. In most countries, governments also provide goods and services such as national defense, fire protection, highways, education, parks, and electricity. Sometimes users are charged for services, but often they are paid for by taxes. Many governments also tax funds from some people in order to provide income transfers to others.

[1] J. Ernest Tanner, "Fiscal Policy: An Ineffective Stabilizer?" *Economic Review: Federal Reserve Bank of Atlanta,* August 1982.

The range of government activities varies substantially among countries. In a few countries, government does little more than provide a legal structure and a few goods like roads and national defense that are difficult to provide through the private sector. In other countries, government is involved in all sorts of activities, including the operation of businesses like hotels, theaters, mining, airlines, radio and television broadcasting, and steel manufacturing. As Exhibit 14.1 illustrates, there is substantial variation in government expenditures as a share of GDP among countries.

Government spending sums to nearly three-fifths of the total output in Denmark, Sweden, and the Netherlands. Approximately one-half of the total income of Italy, Austria, Greece, France, Belgium, and Germany is channelled through the public sector. The high level of government spending in these countries primarily reflects greater public-sector involvement in the provision of housing, health care, retirement benefits, and aid to the poor and unemployed. In Canada, public-sector spending summed to almost 45 percent of total output in 1989. The size of the public sectors in Australia, Japan, and Switzerland are approximately the same as in the United States. Interestingly, the size of government in South Korea, Singapore, Thailand, and Hong Kong, four Asian nations where income has grown very rapidly in recent decades, is substantially smaller than for the United States.

In recent decades, the size of government has grown in the United States, Canada, Australia, Japan and the industrial countries of Europe. Exhibit 14.2 illustrates the growth of government expenditures as a share of GDP for the United States. In 1950 the total expenditures of the federal, state, and local governments summed to 22 percent of the economy. Through the years, this ratio has grown. By 1992 government expenditures had risen to 34.7 percent of GDP.

## Government Purchases and Transfer Payments

**government purchases**
Current expenditures on goods and services provided by federal, state, and local governments; they exclude transfer payments.

It is important to distinguish between (1) government purchases of goods and services and (2) transfer payments. **Government purchases** are expenditures incurred when goods and services are supplied through the public sector. They include items such as jet planes, missiles, highway construction and maintenance, police and fire protection, and computer equipment. Governments also purchase the labor services of teachers, clerks, lawyers, accountants, and public relation experts to produce goods ranging from public education to administrative services. Government purchases both contribute to the aggregate demand for goods and services and reduce the supply of resources available to produce private consumption and investment goods.

**transfer payments**
Payments to individuals or institutions that are not linked to the current supply of a good or service by the recipient.

**Transfer payments** are transfers of income from taxpayers to recipients who do not provide current goods and services in exchange for these payments. Simply put, transfer payments take income from some to provide additional income to others. Social Security benefits, pensions of retired government employees, and Aid to Families with Dependent Children (AFDC) are examples of transfer payments. Even though transfer payments do not directly reduce the resources available to the private sector, they may reduce the incentive of people to work and save, and thereby indirectly alter the size of the economic pie.

**EXHIBIT 14.1**

**Size of Government—An International Comparison, 1989**

The size of government varies substantially across countries. Government expenditures comprise nearly 60 percent of GDP in Denmark, Sweden, and the Netherlands. In contrast, government spending amounts to only about one-third of GDP in the United States, Australia, Japan, and Switzerland. In South Korea and Hong Kong, two rapidly growing Asian countries, the size of government is still smaller.

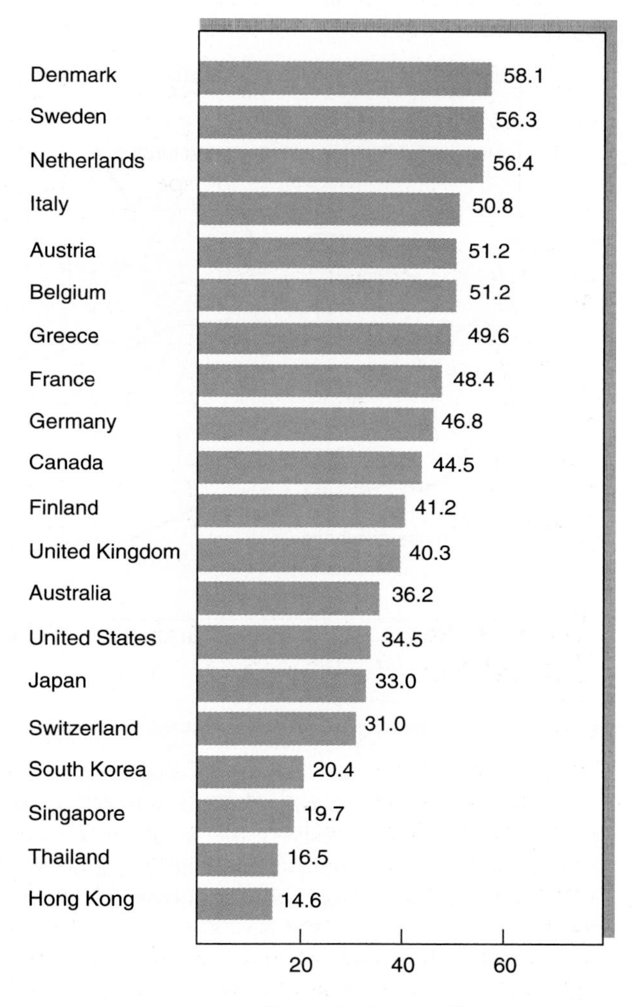


**Source:** *OECD Economic Outlook*, June 1990; Government Information Services: Hong Kong, *Hong Kong 1990*; and International Monetary Fund, *Government Finance Statistics Yearbook*, 1992.

**EXHIBIT 14.2**

**Government Expenditures and Income Transfers as Share of GDP, 1950–1992**

As a percent of GDP, total government expenditures have grown from approximately 25 percent in the mid-1950s to 34.7 percent in 1992. As shown here, growth of income transfers has been the primary source of the increasing size of government. During the last four decades, government purchases of goods and services have been approximately constant at about 20 percent of GDP, while defense expenditures have actually declined relative to the size of the economy.

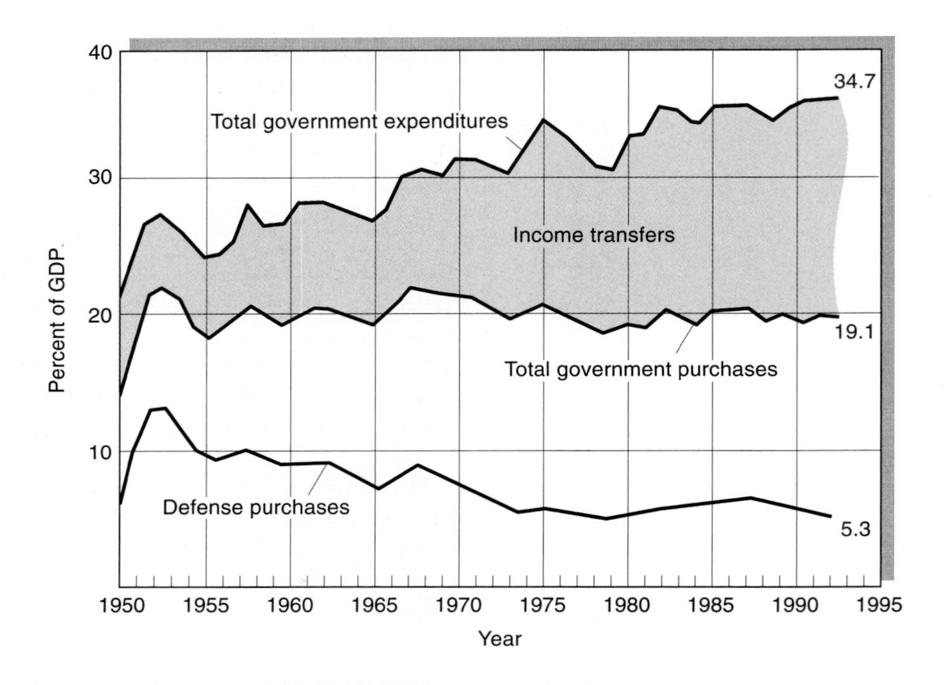


As Exhibit 14.2 shows, the growth of government during the last four decades is almost exclusively the result of increased government involvement in income transfer activities. Interestingly, government purchases of goods and services have fluctuated within a narrow band, around 20 percent of GDP, for the last four decades. Defense expenditures have declined from more than 10 percent of GDP to approximately 5 percent in the early 1990s. In contrast, income transfers have increased substantially. In 1950 transfers comprised less than 5 percent of GDP, and more than half of this total was for veteran pensions. Since the mid-1970s, though, the government has generally taxed approximately 15 percent of total output away from producers and channelled it to the elderly, the unemployed, farmers, children in single-parent families, persons with disabilities, and other transfer recipients.

## GOVERNMENT BUDGET AND FISCAL POLICY

The government budget provides information on government expenditures and revenues. When government revenues from all sources are equal to

**balanced budget** A situation in which current government revenue from taxes, fees, and other sources is just equal to current expenditures.

**budget deficit** A situation in which total government spending exceeds total government revenue during a specific time period, usually one year.

**budget surplus** A situation in which total government spending is less than total government revenue during a time period, usually a year.

government expenditures (including both purchases of goods and services and transfer payments), the government has a **balanced budget**. The budget need not be in balance, however. A **budget deficit** is present when total government spending exceeds total revenue from taxes and user charges. When the government runs a budget deficit, where does it get the money to finance the excess of its spending relative to revenue? It borrows by issuing interest-bearing bonds that we refer to as the *national debt*. This borrowing generates additional demand for loanable funds. A **budget surplus** is present when the government's revenues from taxes and user charges exceed the government's spending. A budget surplus reduces the demand for loanable funds.

The federal budget is much more than merely a revenue and expenditure statement of a large organization. Of course, its sheer size means that it exerts a substantial influence on the economy. Its importance, though, emanates from its position as a policy variable. The federal budget is the primary tool of fiscal policy. In contrast with private organizations that are directed by the pursuit of income and profit, the federal government may alter its budget with an eye toward influencing the future direction of the economy.

While the potency of fiscal policy is a point of controversy, most economists believe that fiscal policy does exert some impact on aggregate demand. As we noted in the previous chapter, an unanticipated decline in aggregate demand can cause recession and unemployment. In contrast, an increase in aggregate demand can lead to an inflationary boom. If fiscal policy could help keep aggregate demand at a level consistent with full employment and stable prices, it would reduce economic instability. Thus, fiscal policy is a potential tool for policymakers to use in combating the ups and downs of the business cycle. Fiscal policy can also influence the incentive of people to work, invest, and use resources efficiently. As a result, it may also affect aggregate supply. Thus, if properly conducted, fiscal policy can help a nation achieve two important objectives: (1) greater economic stability and (2) a larger rate of output.

## Keynesian View of Fiscal Policy

The perception of fiscal policy as a policy tool originated with the writings of the eminent English economist, John Maynard Keynes (pronounced "canes"). Prior to the Great Depression and the work of Keynes, almost everybody thought that government should balance its budget—that government expenditures should be equal to government revenues. In the midst of the widespread unemployment and economic decline of the 1930s, Keynes challenged the balanced-budget view. Keynes believed that the economies of Europe and North America were languishing in economic decline because there was too little demand for goods, and he argued that the solution was readily available: government could use fiscal policy to stimulate aggregate demand and direct the economy to full employment. Against the background of the Great Depression, this was a potent message.

How can fiscal policy—the government's spending and taxing—influence aggregate demand? First, government purchases contribute directly to aggregate demand. The demand for goods and services expands as the government spends more on highways, education, national defense, and medical services, for example. Second, changes in tax policy also influence demand. A reduction in personal taxes increases the disposable income of households. As their after-tax income rises, individuals spend more on consumption. Similarly, a reduction in business taxes increases after-tax profitability and thereby encourages business investment spending.

Keynes argued that businesses would produce only the quantity of goods and services that they believed consumers, investors, governments, and foreigners would buy. If current demand was weak, businesses would only produce a small output, less than the economy's full-employment capacity. If, however, demand could be stimulated, business would expand output and employment. Thus, when unemployment is high and factories are operating well below capacity, the appropriate policy response is **expansionary fiscal policy,** an increase in government purchases of goods and services or a reduction in taxes.

**expansionary fiscal policy** An increase in government expenditures and/or a reduction in tax rates such that the expected size of the budget deficit expands.

Exhibit 14.3 uses our aggregate demand/aggregate supply model to illustrate this point. Initially, the economy is experiencing abnormally high unemployment and economic recession. The initial output is $Y_1$ (short-run equilibrium *e*), well below the economy's full-employment capacity, $Y_f$. As we have previously discussed, if there is no change in policy, abnormally high unemployment and excess supply in the resource market would eventually reduce real wages and other resource prices. The accompanying lower costs would increase supply (shift to dotted $SRAS_3$) and guide the economy to a full-

**EXHIBIT 14.3**

**Expansionary Fiscal Policy to Promote Full Employment**

Here we illustrate an economy operating in the short run at $Y_1$, below its potential capacity $Y_f$. There are two routes to a long-run full-employment equilibrium. First, policymakers could wait for lower wages and resource prices to reduce costs, increase supply to $SRAS_3$, and restore equilibrium at $E_3$. Keynesians believe this market-adjustment method will be slow and uncertain. Alternatively, expansionary fiscal policy could stimulate aggregate demand (shift to $AD_2$) and guide the economy to $E_2$.

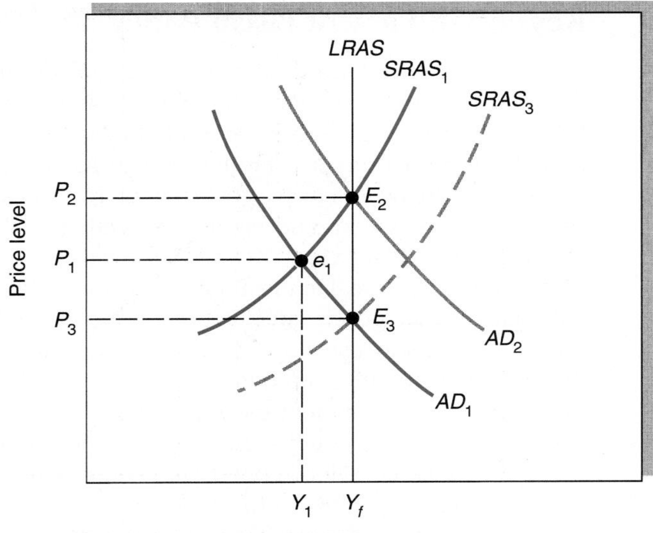

employment equilibrium ($E_3$) at a lower price level ($P_3$). In addition, lower real interest rates resulting from weak business demand for investment funds may help stimulate aggregate demand and restore full employment.

Most Keynesian economists, however, do not believe that this self-corrective mechanism will work very rapidly. Thus, Keynesians argue that policymakers should use a more expansionary policy and thereby speed the recovery process. An increase in government purchases would stimulate aggregate demand directly. Alternatively, taxes could be reduced. A reduction in income taxes would expand the after-tax income of households, stimulating consumption. Similarly, business taxes could be reduced, which would help stimulate private investment. An appropriate dosage of fiscal policy, if timed properly, would stimulate aggregate demand (shift the curve to $AD_2$) and guide the economy to full-employment equilibrium ($E_2$).

**restrictive fiscal policy** A reduction in government expenditures and/or an increase in tax rates such that the expected size of the budget deficit declines (or the budget surplus increases).

The Keynesian view also provides a fiscal policy remedy for inflation. Suppose that an economy is experiencing an inflationary economic boom as the result of excessive aggregate demand. As Exhibit 14.4 illustrates, in the absence of a change in policy, the strong demand ($AD_1$) would push up wages and other resource prices. In time, the higher resource prices would increase costs, reduce aggregate supply (from $SRAS_1$ to $SRAS_3$), and lead to a higher price level ($P_3$). The basic Keynesian model, however, indicates that **restrictive fiscal policy** could be used to reduce aggregate demand (shift to $AD_2$)

**EXHIBIT 14.4**

**Restrictive Fiscal Policy to Combat Inflation**

Strong demand such as $AD_1$ will temporarily lead to an output rate beyond the economy's long-run potential ($Y_f$). If maintained, the high level of demand will lead to long-run equilibrium ($E_3$) at a higher price level. However, restrictive fiscal policy could restrain demand to $AD_2$ (or better still, prevent demand from expanding to $AD_1$ in the first place) and thereby guide the economy to a noninflationary equilibrium ($E_2$).

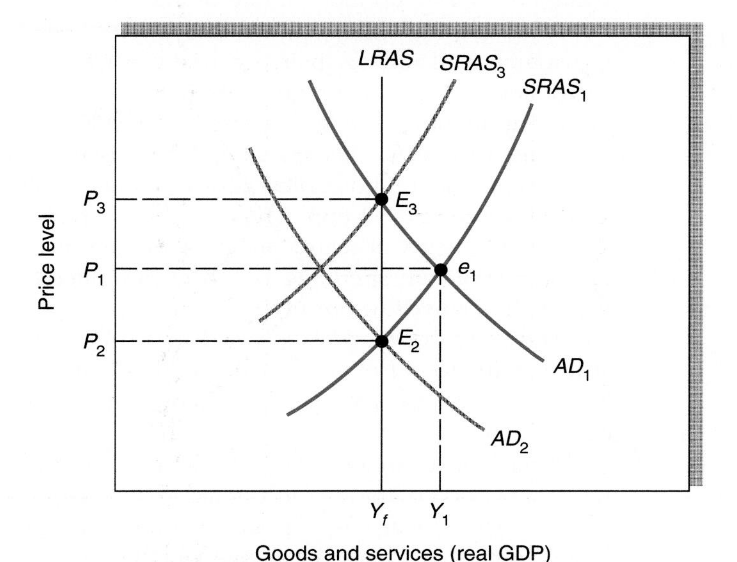

and guide the economy to a noninflationary equilibrium ($E_2$). A reduced level of government purchases would diminish aggregate demand directly. Alternatively, higher taxes on households and businesses could be used to dampen consumption and private investment. The restrictive fiscal policy—a spending reduction and/or increase in taxes—would tend to shift the government budget toward a surplus (or smaller deficit). The Keynesian analysis suggests that this is precisely the proper policy prescription with which to combat inflation generated by excessive aggregate demand.

In the Keynesian view, general economic conditions replace the concept of the annually balanced budget as the proper criterion for evaluating the appropriateness of budget policy. **Countercyclical policy** suggests the government should adopt policies that will shift its budget toward a deficit when the economy is threatened by a recession. In contrast, fiscal policy should shift the budget toward a surplus in response to the threat of inflation. According to the Keynesian view, fluctuations in aggregate demand are the major source of business disturbances, and fiscal policy can help stabilize demand at a level consistent with both full employment and price stability.

**countercyclical policy** A policy that tends to move the economy in an opposite direction from the forces of the business cycle. Such a policy would stimulate demand during the contraction phase of the business cycle and restrain demand during the expansionary phase.

## Interest-Rate Crowding-Out

The early Keynesian view stressed the potency of fiscal policy—how changes in the budget would exert a powerful impact on aggregate demand and output. More recently, however, economists have noted that there are secondary effects that will tend to offset, at least partially, the effects of a fiscal policy change.

Holding the supply of money constant, when the government runs a deficit, it must borrow from private lenders. Typically, the government will finance its deficit by issuing bonds. As the government issues bonds to finance its deficit, it is in effect increasing the demand for loanable funds. The increased government borrowing and expansion in demand for loanable funds will tend to drive up the real rate of interest.

What impact will a higher real interest rate have on private spending? Consumers will reduce their purchases of interest-sensitive goods such as automobiles and consumer durables in response to a higher real interest rate. More importantly, a higher interest rate will increase the opportunity cost of investment projects. Businesses will postpone spending on plant expansions, heavy equipment, and capital improvements. Residential housing construction and sales will also be hurt. Thus, the higher real interest rates emanating from the larger deficit will retard private spending. Economists refer to this squeezing out of private spending by a deficit-induced increase in the real interest rate as the **crowding-out effect.**

**crowding-out effect** A reduction in private spending as a result of higher interest rates generated by budget deficits that are financed by borrowing in the private loanable funds market.

This reduction in private spending as the result of higher interest rates will at least partially offset additional spending emanating from the deficit. Thus, a budget deficit may not exert a very powerful impact on demand, output, and employment.

While most modern economists accept the logic of the crowding-out effect, many would argue that it is unlikely to be very important during a recession. If expansionary fiscal policy is applied when an economy is operating at less than capacity, then the accompanying demand stimulus will lead to an increase in both real output and income. At the higher income level, households will save more, which will permit the government to finance its enlarged deficit without much upward pressure on interest rates. In addition, when applied during a recession, the demand stimulus may improve business profit expectations and thereby stimulate additional private investment. Consequently, an increase in the size of the deficit as the result of more government spending or a tax cut during a recession may not crowd out much private spending.

The implications of the crowding-out analysis are symmetrical. Restrictive fiscal policy will "crowd in" private spending. If the government increases taxes and/or cuts back on expenditures and thereby reduces its demand for loanable funds, the real interest rate will decline. The lower real interest rate will stimulate additional private investment and consumption. So the fiscal policy restraint will be at least partially offset by an expansion in private spending. As the result of this crowding-in, restrictive fiscal policy may not be very effective as a weapon against inflation.

## Debt and Future Taxes—The New Classical View

Some economists stress still another possible secondary effect of budget deficits—the impact of the deficits on saving. Until now, we have implicitly assumed that the current saving decisions of taxpayers are unaffected by the higher future taxes implied by budget deficits. Some economists argue that this is an unrealistic view. During the 1970s, Robert Lucas (University of Chicago), Thomas Sargent (University of Minnesota), and Robert Barro (Harvard University) were leaders among a group of economists who argued that taxpayers would reduce their current consumption and increase saving in anticipation of higher future taxes implied by debt financing. Since this position has its foundation in classical economics, these economists and their followers are referred to as **new classical economists.**

**new classical economists**
Modern economists who believe there are strong forces pushing a market economy toward full employment equilibrium and that macroeconomic policy is an ineffective tool with which to reduce economic instability.

In the basic Keynesian model, a reduction in current taxes financed by borrowing increases the current disposable income of households. Given their additional disposable income, households increase their current consumption. New classical economists argue that this analysis is incorrect because it ignores the higher future taxes implied by the budget deficit and the additional borrowing to finance it. The public will have to pay higher future taxes to finance the interest payments on the additional bonds. Thus, debt financing affects the *timing* of taxes, rather than their magnitude. It merely substitutes higher future taxes for lower current taxes.

Since budget deficits merely affect the timing of the tax liability, new classical economists argue that additional government debt (and the higher taxes that it implies) will reduce the current consumption of households just as surely as an equivalent amount of current taxes. Therefore, according to the new classical view, the current consumption of households will not increase when current taxes are cut and government debt is increased by an equivalent amount. In essence, households will simply save the reduction in their current taxes so they will have the income with which to pay the higher future taxes implied by the additional government debt. Since current consumption declines as the result of the additional debt—just as it would have declined if the equivalent amount of taxes had been levied—new classical economists do not believe that the substitution of debt for taxes will stimulate either private consumption or aggregate demand. According to this view, taxes and debt financing are essentially equivalent.

Exhibit 14.5 illustrates the implications of the new classical view as to the potency of fiscal policy. Suppose the fiscal authorities issue $50 billion of additional debt in order to cut taxes by an equal amount. The government borrowing increases the demand for loanable funds (shift from $D_1$ to $D_2$ in Exhibit 14.5b) by $50 billion. If the taxpayers did not recognize the higher future taxes implied by the debt, they would expand consumption in response to the lower taxes and the increase in disposable income. Under such circumstances, aggregate demand in the goods and services market would expand to $AD_2$. In the new classical model, though, this will not be the case. Recognizing the higher future taxes, taxpayers will cut back their spending and increase their savings by $50 billion—the amount of saving necessary to generate the income required to pay the higher future taxes implied by the additional debt. This additional saving will allow the government to finance its deficit without an increase in the real interest rate. Since debt financing, like tax financing, causes taxpayers to reduce their expenditures, aggregate demand in the goods and services market is unchanged (at $AD_1$). In this polar case, fiscal policy exerts no demand stimulus. Output, employment, and the price level are all unchanged.

**EXHIBIT 14.5**

**New Classical View—Higher Expected Future Taxes Crowd Out Private Spending**

New classical economists emphasize that budget deficits merely substitute future taxes for current taxes. If households did not anticipate the higher future taxes, aggregate demand would increase to $AD_2$ (frame a). However, demand remains unchanged at $AD_1$ when households fully anticipate the future increase in taxes. Simultaneously, the additional saving to meet the higher future taxes will increase the supply of loanable funds to $S_2$ (frame b) and permit the government to borrow the funds to finance its deficit without pushing up the real interest rate. In this model, fiscal policy exerts no effect. The real interest rate, real GDP, and level of employment all remain unchanged.

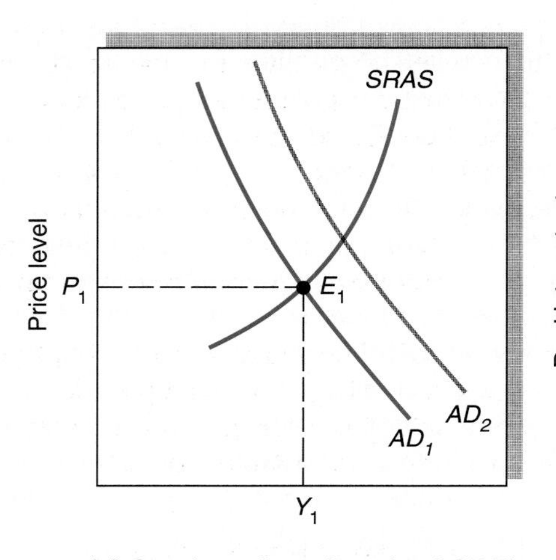


(a) Goods and services (real GDP)

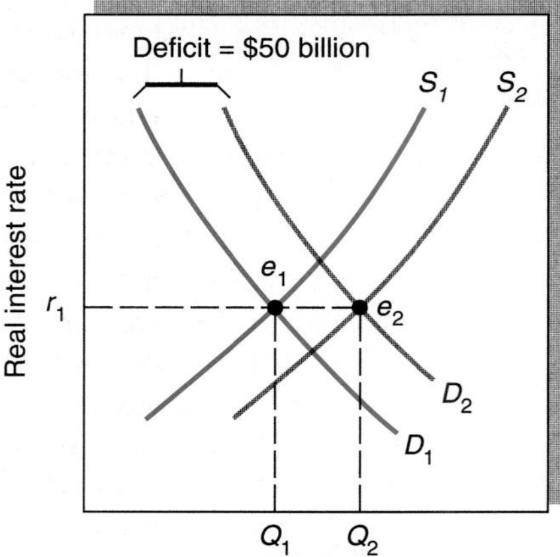


(b) Loanable funds

The new classical theory of fiscal policy is controversial.[2] The critics argue that it is unrealistic to expect that taxpayers will anticipate all or even most of the increase in future taxes implied by additional government debt. In addition, even if people did anticipate the higher future taxes, in our world of limited life spans, many would recognize that they will not be around to pay, at least not in full, the future tax liability implied by debt financing. Thus, many economists reject the new classical view of fiscal policy, at least in its pure form. Nonetheless, the significance of the new classical theory and its implications with regard to fiscal policy continue to provide one of the lively topics of debate in modern macroeconomics.

## TIMING OF FISCAL CHANGES

If fiscal policy is going to reduce economic instability, changes in policy must inject stimulus during a recession and restraint during an inflationary boom. Proper timing of fiscal policy is not an easy task. There are several potential sources of error. To a large extent, macroeconomic policymaking is a little like lobbing a ball at a moving target that sometimes changes directions in an unpredictable manner. Since our ability to forecast a forthcoming recession or boom is a highly imperfect science, policymakers cannot be sure precisely where the economy is headed. Thus, there may be a time lag between when a change in policy is called for and when it is widely recognized by policymakers.

In addition, there is generally a lag between the time when the need for a fiscal policy change is recognized and the time when it is actually instituted. In order to bring about a change in policy, Congress must act. Experts must study the problem. Congressional committees must meet, hear testimony, and draft legislation. And key legislators may choose to delay action if they can use their positions to obtain special favors for their constituencies. A majority of the lawmakers must be convinced that a proposed action is in the interest of the country and that of their own districts and supporters. All of these things take time.

Finally, there is still another factor that adds to the complexity of fiscal policymaking: even after a policy is adopted, it may be 6 to 12 months before its major impact is felt. If government expenditures are going to be increased, time will be required for competitive bids to be submitted and new contracts granted. Contractors may be unable to begin work right away. While a tax reduction will generally exert demand stimulus more quickly, it will take time for these effects to work their way through the economy. Given that we live in a world characterized by dynamic change and unpredictable events, policy errors are inevitable.

Unfortunately, when errors are made, fiscal policy can be a source of instability rather than stability. For example, delays may result in the adoption of a fiscal policy stimulus package as the economy is recovering from a recession. By the time the stimulus begins to exert its primary impact, the

[2]See Robert J. Barro, "Are Government Bonds Net Wealth?" *Journal of Political Economy,* November–December 1974, pp. 1095–1117; James M. Buchanan, "Barro on the Ricardian Equivalence Theorem," *Journal of Political Economy,* April 1976, pp. 337–342; Gerald P. O'Driscoll, Jr., "The Ricardian Nonequivalence Theorem, *Journal of Political Economy,* February 1977, pp. 207–210; and R. G. Holcombe, John D. Jackson, and A. Zardkoohi, "The National Debt Controversy," *Kyklos* 34, 1981, pp. 186–202.

economy's self-corrective mechanism may have already restored full employment. If so, the fiscal stimulus may cause excessive demand and inflation. Alternatively, if a restrictive fiscal policy is adopted as an economy is slipping into a recession, the policy may increase both the depth and length of an economic downturn. In the real world, a fiscal policy change is like a two-edged sword; it can both harm and help. If timed correctly, it will reduce economic instability. If timed incorrectly, however, the fiscal change will increase rather than reduce economic instability.

## Automatic Stabilizers

**automatic stabilizers** Built-in features that tend automatically to promote a budget deficit during a recession and a budget surplus during an inflationary boom, even without a change in policy.

Fortunately, there are a few fiscal programs that tend automatically to apply demand stimulus during a recession and demand restraint during an economic boom. Programs of this type are called **automatic stabilizers.** They are automatic in that, *without any new legislative action,* they tend to increase the budget deficit (or reduce the surplus) during a recession as well as increasing the surplus (or reducing the deficit) during an economic boom.

The major advantage of automatic stabilizers is that they institute countercyclical fiscal policy without the delays that inevitably accompany legislation. Thus, they minimize the problem of proper timing. When unemployment is rising and business conditions are slow, these stabilizers automatically reduce taxes and increase government expenditures, giving the economy a shot in the arm. On the other hand, automatic stabilizers help to apply the brakes to an economic boom, increasing tax revenues and decreasing government spending. Three of these built-in stabilizers deserve specific mention.

1. *Unemployment compensation.* When unemployment is high, the receipts from the unemployment compensation tax will decline because of the reduction in employment. Payments will increase because more laid-off workers are now eligible to receive unemployment compensation benefits. The program will automatically run a deficit during a business slow-down. In contrast, when the unemployment rate is low, tax receipts from the program will increase because more people are now working. The amount paid in benefits will decline because fewer people are unemployed. The program will automatically tend to run a surplus during good times. So, without any change in policy, the program has the desired countercyclical effect on aggregate demand.[3]

2. *Corporate profit tax.* Corporate profits are highly sensitive to cyclical conditions. Under recessionary conditions, they decline sharply, along with corporate tax payments. This sharp decline in tax revenues tends to enlarge the size of the government deficit. Conversely, during an economic expansion, corporate profits typically increase much more rapidly than wages, income, or consumption. This increase in corporate profits results in a rapid increase in the "tax take" from the business sector during an expansion. Thus, corporate tax payments will go up during an expansion and fall rapidly during a contraction without any change in tax policy.

3. *Progressive income tax.* When income grows rapidly, the average personal tax liability of individuals and families increases. With rising incomes,

[3]Although unemployment compensation has the desired countercyclical effects on demand, it also reduces the incentive to accept available employment opportunities. As a result, researchers have found that the existing unemployment compensation system actually increases the long-run normal unemployment rate.

more people will find their income above the "no tax due" cutoff. Others will be pushed into a higher tax bracket. Therefore, during an economic expansion, revenue from the personal income tax increases more rapidly than income. Other things constant, the budget moves toward a surplus (or smaller deficit), even though the economy's tax rate structure is unchanged. On the other hand, when income declines, many individuals will be taxed at a lower rate or not at all. Income tax revenues will fall more rapidly than income, automatically enlarging the size of the budget deficit during a recession.

## FISCAL POLICY: A SUMMARY OF THE MODERN SYNTHESIS

The views of economists concerning the efficacy of fiscal policy as a tool to promote economic stability and growth have changed in recent decades. During the 1960s, the basic Keynesian view was widely accepted. Fiscal policy was thought to be highly potent. Furthermore, it was widely believed that policymakers—no doubt with the assistance of their economic advisors—would adopt fiscal changes in a manner that would help stabilize the economy.

With the passage of time, most macroeconomists have come to accept a more cautious view—a synthesis as follows:

1. *During a depression or severe recession, expansionary fiscal policy can stimulate real output and thereby help to minimize economic instability.* During serious recessions, budget deficits stimulate aggregate demand and therefore output and employment, much as the basic Keynesian model implies. Fiscal policy can help prevent a recurrence of anything like the experiences of the 1930s. This is a major accomplishment that those who grew up during the *relatively* stable post–Second World War era often fail to appreciate.

2. *During more normal times, the ability of fiscal policy to influence real output is far more limited than the Keynesian view implies.* The major debate among macroeconomists now about the impact of fiscal policy during normal times is not whether crowding out takes place, but rather, how it takes place. The interest-rate crowding-out and new classical models highlight this point. Both models indicate that there are side effects of the deficits that substantially, if not entirely, offset increases in aggregate demand emanating from the deficits. In the one, higher real interest rates crowd out private demand, while higher anticipated future taxes accomplish the task in the other. In both cases, however, business and household decision-makers adjust in a manner that largely offsets the potency of fiscal policy—particularly its ability to promote more rapid growth of real output.

3. *Proper timing of discretionary fiscal policy is both highly difficult to achieve and of crucial importance.* Given the potential of ill-timed policy changes to add to economic instability, active discretionary fiscal policy should respond only to major economic disturbances. During the 1950s and 1960s, many macroeconomists thought that fiscal policy changes could smooth even minor economic fluctuations. Few now adhere to that position. It is widely recognized now that in a world of dynamic change and imperfect information concerning the future, active changes in fiscal policy in response to minor economic ups and downs can themselves become a source of economic instability.

## Supply-Side Effects of Fiscal Policy

**tax rate** The per unit or percentage rate at which an economic activity is taxed.

**supply-side economists** Modern economists who believe that changes in marginal tax rates exert important effects on aggregate supply.

**marginal tax rate** Additional tax liability divided by additional income. Thus, if $100 of additional earnings increases one's tax liability by $30, the marginal tax rate is 30 percent.

Thus far, we have focused on the potential demand-side effects of fiscal policy. However, when fiscal changes alter **tax rates,** they influence the incentive of people to work, invest, and use resources efficiently. Thus, tax changes may also influence aggregate supply. Prior to 1980 most economists ignored the impact of changes in tax rates, thinking they were of little importance. This view has been seriously challenged by **supply-side economists** in recent years.

From a supply-side view, the marginal tax rate is of crucial importance. The **marginal tax rate** (MTR) can be expressed as follows:

$$\text{MTR} = \frac{\text{change in tax liability}}{\text{change in income}}$$

The marginal tax rate reveals both how much of one's additional income can be retained and how much must be turned over to the tax collector. For example, when the marginal tax rate is 25 percent, $25 of every $100 of additional earnings must be paid to the taxing authority. The individual is permitted to keep $75 of his or her additional income. As marginal tax rates increase, the share of additional earnings that individuals are permitted to keep declines. Lower tax rates, on the other hand, increase the payoff, or reward, from earning activities.

### Why Marginal Taxes Retard Output

Supply-side economists believe that high marginal tax rates will retard output because they (1) discourage work effort and thus reduce the productive efficiency of labor, (2) reduce both the level and efficiency of capital formation, and (3) encourage the substitution of tax-deductible goods for nondeductible ones. Let's look at the reasoning behind each of these three points.

First, when marginal tax rates soar to 55 percent or 60 percent, individuals get to keep less than half of what they earn—and when the payoff from working declines, people tend to work less. Some (for example, someone with a working spouse) will drop out of the labor force. Others will simply work fewer hours. Still others will decide to take more lengthy vacations, forgo overtime opportunities, retire earlier, be more particular about accepting jobs when unemployed, or forget about pursuing that promising but risky business venture. In some cases, high tax rates will even drive highly productive citizens to other countries where taxes are lower. High tax rates will also result in inefficient utilization of labor. Some individuals will substitute less-productive activities that are not taxed (for example, do-it-yourself projects) for work opportunities yielding taxable income.

Second, high tax rates affect capital formation in that they repel foreign investment and cause domestic investors to search for investment projects abroad where taxes are lower. Domestic investors will also turn to projects that shelter current income from taxation and away from projects with a higher rate of return but fewer tax-avoidance benefits. Business ventures that are designed to show an accounting loss in order to shelter income from the tax collector will become more widespread. As the result of the tax-shelter benefits, people are often able to gain from projects that reduce the value of resources. Scarce capital is wasted and resources are channeled away from their most productive uses.

Third, high marginal tax rates encourage individuals to substitute less desired tax-deductible goods for more desired, nondeductible goods. Here the inefficiency stems from the fact that individuals do not bear the full cost of tax-deductible purchases. High marginal tax rates make tax-deductible expenditures cheap for persons in high tax brackets. Since the personal cost, *but not the cost to society,* is cheap, taxpayers confronting high marginal tax rates will spend more money on pleasurable, tax-deductible items, such as plush offices, Hawaiian business conferences, and various fringe benefits (for example, a company luxury automobile, business entertainment, and a company retirement plan). Since such tax-deductible purchases reduce their taxes, people will often buy such goods even though they do not value them as much as the cost of producing them.

Supply-side economists believe that these factors are powerful enough to reduce both the size of the available resource base and the efficiency of its use significantly—causing a decline in aggregate supply. On the other hand, a reduction in marginal tax rates—particularly in exceedingly high rates—will, they believe, increase aggregate supply.

## Taxes and Shifts in Aggregate Supply

The source of the supply-side effects accompanying a change in tax rates is fundamentally different than the source of the demand-side effects. A change in tax rates affects aggregate demand through its impact on disposable income and the flow of expenditures. In contrast, it affects aggregate supply through changes in marginal tax rates, which influence the relative attractiveness of productive activity in comparison to leisure and tax avoidance.

Exhibit 14.6 graphically depicts the impact of a supply-side tax cut, one that reduces marginal tax rates. The lower marginal tax rates increase aggregate supply as the new incentive structure encourages taxpayers to earn additional income and use resources more efficiently. If the tax change is perceived as long-term, both *LRAS* and *SRAS* will increase. Real output and income expand. Of course, the increase in real income will also increase demand (shift to $AD_2$). If the lower marginal rates are financed by a budget deficit, depending on the strength of the crowding-out effect and the anticipation of higher future taxes (new classical theory), aggregate demand may increase by more than aggregate supply. If this is the case, the price level will rise.

Supply-side economics should not be viewed as a short-run countercyclical tool. It will take time for changing market incentives to move resources out of tax-motivated investments and into higher-yield activities. The full positive effects of lower marginal tax rates will not be observed until labor and capital markets have time to adjust fully to the new incentive structure. Clearly, supply-side economics is a long-run growth-oriented strategy.

**tax base** The level of the activity that is taxed. For example, if an excise tax is levied on each gallon of gasoline, the tax base is the number of gallons of gasoline sold. Since higher tax rates generally make the taxed activity more expensive, the size of the tax base is inversely related to the rate at which the activity is taxed.

## Tax Rates, Tax Revenues, and Laffer Curve

Governments generally levy taxes in order to raise revenues. The supply-side view indicates that it is important to distinguish between a change in *tax rates* and a change in *tax revenues.* When a tax is levied on an activity, people will choose less of it. They will shift to substitutes. Therefore, as the tax rate increases, the quantity or level of the activity that is taxed—the **tax base**—will

**EXHIBIT 14.6**

**Tax Rate Effects and Supply-Side Economics**

Here we illustrate the supply-side effects of a reduction in marginal tax rates. The lower marginal tax rates increase the incentive to earn and to use resources efficiently. Since these effects are long-run as well as short-run, both *LRAS* and *SRAS* increase (shift to the right). Real output expands. If the lower tax rates are financed by a budget deficit, aggregate demand may expand by a larger amount than aggregate supply, leading to an increase in the price level.

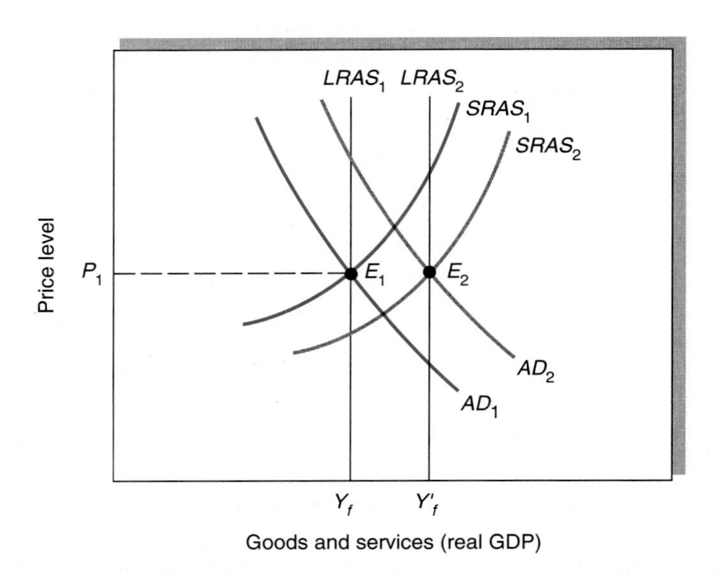


decline. If there are attractive substitutes, the decline in the activity due to the higher tax may be substantial.

Perhaps a real-world example will help clarify this point. In 1981 the District of Columbia increased the tax rate on gasoline from 10 cents to 13 cents per gallon, a 30 percent increase. Tax revenues, however, did not increase by 30 percent—they expanded by only 12 percent. Why? The higher tax rate discouraged motorists from purchasing gasoline in the District of Columbia. There was a pretty good alternative to the purchase of the more highly taxed (and therefore higher-priced) gasoline—the purchase of gasoline in Virginia and Maryland, where the tax rates (and therefore prices) were slightly lower. The revenue gains associated with the higher tax rates were partially eroded by a decline in the tax base. When taxpayers can easily shift to substitutes or escape the tax by altering their behavior, an increase in tax rates will lead to a less-than-proportional increase in tax revenues.

**Laffer curve** A curve illustrating the relationship between tax rates and tax revenues. It reflects the fact that tax revenues are low for both very high and very low tax rates.

Economist Arthur Laffer has popularized the idea that higher tax rates can sometimes shrink the tax base so much that tax revenues will decline despite the higher tax rates. The curve illustrating the relationship between tax rates and tax revenues, called the **Laffer curve,** is shown in Exhibit 14.7. Obviously, tax revenues would be zero if the tax rate were zero. What is not so obvious is that tax revenues would also be zero (or at least very close to zero) if

**EXHIBIT 14.7**

**Laffer Curve**

Since taxation affects the amount of the activity being taxed, a change in tax rates will not lead to a proportional change in tax revenues. As the Laffer curve indicates, beyond some point *(B)*, an increase in tax rates may actually cause tax revenues to fall. Since large tax rate increases will lead to only a small expansion in tax revenue as *B* is approached, there is no presumption that point *B* is an ideal rate of taxation.

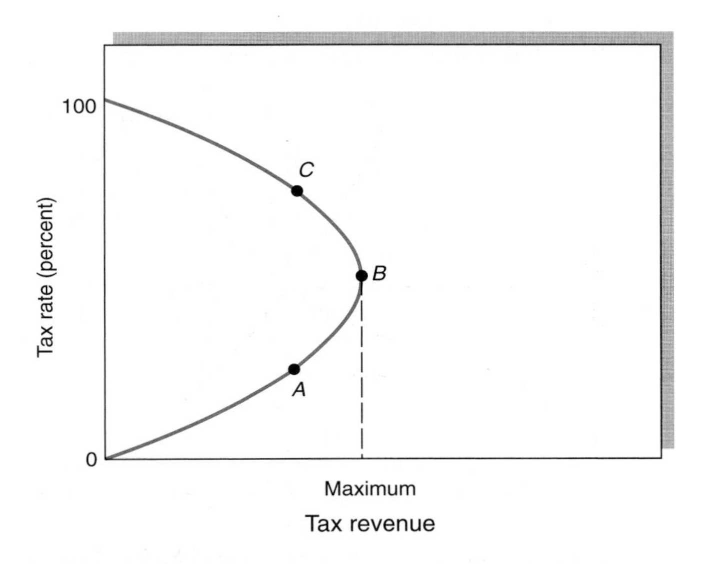


the tax rate were 100 percent. Confronting a 100 percent tax rate, most individuals would go fishing—or find something else to do rather than engage in taxable productive activity, since the 100 percent tax rate would completely remove the material reward derived from earning taxable income.

As tax rates are reduced from 100 percent, the incentive to work and earn taxable income increases, income expands, and tax revenues rise. Similarly, as tax rates increase from zero, tax revenues expand. Clearly, at some rate greater than zero but less than 100 percent, tax revenues will be maximized (point *B* of Exhibit 14.7). This is not to imply that the tax rate that maximizes revenue is ideal. In fact, as the maximum revenue point *(B)* is approached, relatively large tax rate increases will be necessary to expand tax revenues. In this range, the excess burden of taxation in the form of reductions in gains from trade will be substantial.

**progressive income tax**
A tax that requires those with higher taxable incomes to pay a larger percentage of their incomes to the government than those with lower taxable incomes. Under this type of system the marginal tax rate of taxpayers will increase as their income rises.

The Laffer curve analysis indicates that under a **progressive income tax** system, the impact of a change in tax rates on tax revenues will vary across tax brackets (and income groupings). When people confront a low tax rate (for example, the 25 percent rate associated with point *A* in Exhibit 14.7), a rate reduction will reduce revenues. Similarly, a rate increase from, say, 25 percent to 30 percent, will increase tax revenues. On the other hand, for high-income taxpayers confronting extremely high rates (for example, the 75 percent rate associated with point *C* in Exhibit 14.7), a rate reduction would actually increase the revenues collected from this group. Similarly, an increase in the high tax rate would reduce the revenues the government would collect from high-income groups.[4]

When the rates of some taxpayers are above and others are below the revenue maximum point (*B* in Exhibit 14.7), the implications of the Laffer curve are significant. Under these circumstances, a general reduction in tax rates would reduce the revenues collected from low-income taxpayers, while increasing the revenues deriving from high-income taxpayers. A general tax increase would have just the opposite effect—more revenue would be collected from those in lower income brackets while less would be collected from the rich.

## The Laffer Curve and Tax Changes in the 1980s

It is interesting to view the tax changes instituted in the United States during the 1980s within the framework of the Laffer curve. During the 1980s the top marginal tax rates—the rates confronted by high-income taxpayers—were reduced sharply by major legislation passed in 1981 and 1986. At the beginning of the decade, the United States had fourteen different marginal tax brackets ranging from a beginning rate of 14 percent to a top rate of 70 percent. By 1988 the number of brackets had been reduced to only three, with marginal rates of 15, 28, and 33 percent. The personal exemption allowance for each taxpayer, spouse, and dependent and the standard deduction (the amount of tax-free income granted each taxpayer) were also increased. In effect, these latter changes reduced the tax rates of low-income taxpayers. In many cases, the tax liabilities of low-income recipients were completely eliminated.

Focusing on the sharp reduction in the top rates (from 70 percent to 33 percent during the decade), critics charged that the 1980s' tax policies were a bonanza for the rich. In analyzing the position of the critics, once again it is important to distinguish between changes in *tax rates* and changes in *tax revenues.* As the Laffer curve analysis indicates, reduction in high marginal tax rates can sometimes increase the tax revenue collected from high-income taxpayers. When high marginal rates—for example, tax rates of 45 percent or more—are reduced, high-income taxpayers are encouraged to work more hours and make fewer tax-shelter investments. As this happens, their taxable income will grow rapidly. This increase in the tax base as high tax rates are reduced will, at least partially, replace revenues lost as a result of the rate cuts.

Exhibit 14.8 presents data on the real tax revenue collected from various income categories for 1980, 1985, and 1990. Measured in 1982–1984 dollars, the income tax revenue collected from high-income taxpayers rose throughout the decade. Even though their marginal rates were cut sharply, the *real* tax revenue collected from the top 1 percent of earners rose a whopping 51.4 percent between 1980 and 1990. Per tax return, the real taxes paid by this top

[4]Similar rate reductions generally increase the after-tax earnings, and therefore the incentive to earn, more in the upper tax brackets than the lower brackets. Consider how a reduction in a marginal tax rate from 70 percent to 50 percent will influence the incentive of a high-income professional or business executive to earn taxable income. When confronting a 70 percent marginal tax rate, the taxpayer gets to keep only 30 cents of each additional dollar earned by cutting costs, producing more, or investing more wisely. However, after the tax cut, take-home pay from each dollar of taxable income jumps to 50 cents—a whopping 67 percent increase in the incentive to earn. In contrast, consider the incentive effects of an identical percentage rate reduction in lower tax brackets. Suppose the 14 percent marginal rate were cut to 10 percent. Take-home pay, per dollar of additional earnings, would expand from 86 cents to 90 cents, only a 5 percent increase. Since the incentive effects are greater in the upper brackets, changes in the tax base (taxable income) will tend to, at least partially if not entirely, offset changes in revenues resulting from increases (and decreases) in high marginal tax rates.

**EXHIBIT 14.8**

**The Change in Federal Income Tax Revenue Derived from Various Income Groups, 1980–1990**

| | Tax Revenue Collected from Group (in billions of 1982–1984 dollars) | | | | |
|---|---|---|---|---|---|
| **Income Group** | **1980** | **1985** | **1990** | **Percent Change 1980–1990** | |
| | | | | Group | Per Return[a] |
| Top 10 percent of Earners | 149.0 | 154.0 | 191.9 | +28.8 | +5.6 |
| Top 1 percent | 57.6 | 65.3 | 87.2 | +51.4 | +24.1 |
| Top 5 percent | 111.4 | 116.0 | 151.4 | +35.9 | +11.4 |
| Next 40 percent | 132.0 | 123.8 | 133.5 | +1.1 | −17.1 |
| Bottom 50 percent | 21.3 | 21.4 | 19.5 | −8.5 | −25.0 |
| Total | 302.3 | 299.2 | 344.9 | +14.1 | −6.5 |

[a]The number of returns in each category increased by 22 percent between 1980 and 1990.

**Source:** U.S. Department of Treasury, Internal Revenue Service.

group increased 24.1 percent. During the decade, the real revenues collected from the top 5 percent and top 10 percent of returns rose by 35.9 percent and 28.8 percent, respectively. The real revenues per return in these categories also increased. The picture was quite different for other taxpayers. While the real revenues for those between the 50th and 90th percentile changed little, the bottom 50 percent of taxpayers paid less in 1990 than 1980. Per return, the average real tax liability of the bottom 90 percent of taxpayers declined between 1980 and 1990. Perhaps surprising to some, the rich paid more while others paid less as the result of the 1980s tax changes.

Overall, the real revenue on the average return declined by 6.5 percent during the 1980s. Failing to understand the implications of the Laffer curve, some suggested that across-the-board lower rates would increase tax revenues. Clearly, this is not the case. The Laffer curve suggests rather that a reduction in low marginal rates—say, rates of 30 percent or less—will reduce revenues. The decline in revenues per return for the bottom 90 percent of taxpayers indicates that most taxpayers fall into this category. However, when marginal rates are high—say, 45 percent or more—lower rates may indeed lead to an increase in revenues.[5] The increase in revenues collected from a small group of high-income taxpayers indicates that these taxpayers may well have been on the backward-bending portion of the Laffer curve in 1980.

[5]Harvard economists Lawrence Lindsey, now a governor of the Federal Reserve System, estimates that, in the United States, marginal personal income rates above 43 percent reduce tax revenues. See Lawrence Lindsey, *Estimating the Revenue Maximizing Top Personal Tax Rate* (New York: National Bureau of Economic Research—Working Paper 1761, 1985) and *The Growth Experiment: How the New Tax Policy Is Transforming the U.S. Economy* (New York: Basic Books, 1989). Also see James E. Long and James D. Gwartney, "Income Tax Avoidance: Evidence from Individual Tax Returns," *National Tax Journal,* December 1987, for additional evidence on this topic.

## Taxes around the World

High-income industrial countries rely extensively on income and employment taxes for their revenues. When both income and employment taxes are considered, top marginal tax rates in the industrial countries generally exceed 50 percent. However, there is substantial variation among these countries in the tax treatment of savings, investment, income from capital gains, and deductibility of various expenditures. Thus, it is difficult to compare the impact of taxes among these countries.

Among the developing countries of Asia, Africa, and Latin America, there is more variation in marginal tax rates. The most detailed study of the impact of high marginal tax rates on the economic growth of such countries has been conducted by Alvin Rabushka of Stanford University.[6] Rabushka undertook the tedious task of reconstructing the 1960–1982 tax structure for 54 less developed countries for which data could be obtained. He found that some countries levied very high marginal tax rates, which took effect only at very high income thresholds. Others levied high marginal rates on even modest levels of income. A few countries imposed only low or medium tax rates.

Rabushka found that countries which kept marginal tax rates low generally experienced more rapid economic growth. He summarized the findings of his study thus:

> Good economic policy, including tax policy, fosters economic growth and rising prosperity. In particular, low marginal income tax rates, or high thresholds for medium- and high-rate tax schedules, appear consistent with higher growth rates. The key in any system of direct taxation is to maintain low tax rates or high (income) thresholds.[7]

Exhibit 14.9 presents data similar to that used by Rabushka in his study. The ten developing countries with the lowest top marginal rates during the 1980s and the ten with the highest marginal rates are included in the table. Several developing countries imposed exceedingly high marginal tax rates and applied them at a very low income level. For example, Zambia, Tanzania, Zaire, Ghana, and Uganda levied marginal tax rates of 50 percent or more beginning at an equivalent income level of less than $10,000 (1982–1984 dollars). Among the ten high-tax countries, only two (Morocco and Uganda) were able to achieve a positive growth rate of per capita GDP during the 1980–1990 period. None of the high-tax countries were able to do better than an annual growth rate of 1.4 percent during the 1980s. The average annual change in GDP of the high-tax countries was minus 0.6 percent.

Among the low-tax countries, the average growth of per capita GDP was 2.0 percent. Seven of the ten low-tax countries experienced a growth rate of 1.7 percent or more, while three of the ten (Uruguay, Paraguay, and Guatemala) experienced declines in per capita GDP. Clearly, low taxes alone are not sufficient to guarantee economic growth. Other factors such as monetary stability, low trade barriers, an efficient capital market, and political stability are necessary. However, the record of the high-tax countries does suggest

[6]See Alvin Rabushka, "Taxation, Economic Growth, and Liberty," *Cato Journal,* Spring–Summer 1987, pp. 121–148.

[7]Alvin Rabushka, "Taxation and Liberty in the Third World," paper presented to a conference on Taxation and Liberty held in Santa Fe, New Mexico, September 26–27, 1985.

**EXHIBIT 14.9**

**Growth Rate of Developing Countries with Highest and Lowest Marginal Tax Rates**

| | Top Marginal Rate | | Annual Growth Rate of per Capita GDP, 1980–1990 |
|---|---|---|---|
| | 1984 | 1989 | |
| **High Tax Countries** | | | |
| Iran | 90 | 75 | −1.2 |
| Morocco | 87 | 87 | 1.4 |
| Zambia | 80 | 75[a] | −2.9 |
| Dominican Republic | 73 | 73 | −0.1 |
| Tanzania | 95 | 50[a] | −0.3 |
| Zimbabwe | 63 | 60 | −0.5 |
| Zaire | 60[a] | 60[a] | −1.4 |
| Cameroon | 60 | 60 | −0.7 |
| Ghana | 60[a] | 55[a] | −0.4 |
| Uganda | 70[a] | 50[a] | 0.3 |
| **Average Growth Rate** | | | **−0.6** |
| **Low Tax Countries** | | | |
| Uruguay | 0 | 0 | −0.3 |
| Hong Kong | 25 | 25 | 5.7 |
| Paraguay | 30 | 30 | −0.7 |
| Mauritius | 30 | 35 | 5.0 |
| Indonesia | 35 | 35 | 3.7 |
| Singapore | 40 | 33 | 4.2 |
| Colombia | 49 | 30 | 1.7 |
| Guatemala | 48 | 34 | −2.1 |
| Malaysia | 45 | 45 | 2.6 |
| **Average Growth Rate** | | | **2.0** |

[a]Indicates that the top rate applied at an equivalent income level of less than $10,000.

**Source:** The marginal tax rate data are from Price Waterhouse, *Individual Tax Rates, 1984 and 1989* (New York: Price Waterhouse, 1991). The growth rate data are from the World Bank, *World Development Report,* (Oxford: Oxford University Press, 1992).

that high marginal tax rates will deter economic growth. Government officials wanting to promote prosperity would do well to keep this evidence in mind.

## LOOKING AHEAD

In this chapter we focused on how fiscal policy—government expenditures and taxes—can influence economic activity. We are now ready to integrate the monetary system into our analysis. Once we understand how both fiscal and monetary policy work, we will be better able to comprehend the potential of macroeconomic policy overall as a tool for promoting high employment, stable prices, and the growth of income.

## CHAPTER SUMMARY

1. There is substantial variation among countries in the size of government expenditures as a share of the economy. In the United States, total government expenditures account for a little more than one-third of GDP. The size of government expenditures in Japan and Switzerland is similar to that of the United States. In Canada and most Western European countries, it is larger.
2. As a share of GDP, government expenditures in the United States have grown from approximately 25 percent in the early 1950s to approximately 35 percent in the early 1990s. The growth of transfer payments accounts for most of this increase.
3. The primary fiscal policy weapon is the government's budget. Fiscal policy involves changes in spending and/or taxes that influence the size of the government's budget deficit or surplus.
4. Fluctuations in aggregate demand are a potential source of economic instability. Fiscal policies that help maintain aggregate demand at a level consistent with full-employment output and stable prices will reduce economic instability.
5. When an economy's resources are underutilized, the Keynesian view stresses that expansionary fiscal policy—that is, an increase in government spending and/or reduction in taxes—will stimulate aggregate demand and help direct the economy toward its full-employment capacity. Conversely, restrictive fiscal policy—higher taxes and/or a reduction in government expenditures—can be used to combat inflationary pressures resulting from excess aggregate demand. The Keynesian view stresses that the government's budget should be shifted toward a larger deficit during a recession and toward a budget surplus (or smaller deficit) during an inflationary boom.
6. Modern macroeconomic analysis also stresses the importance of potential secondary effects associated with fiscal policy changes. The crowding-out model stresses one of these effects—that budget deficits increase the demand for loanable funds and thereby increase the real interest rate. In turn, the higher real interest rate will crowd out private spending, particularly investment, and thereby dampen the stimulus effects of expansionary fiscal policy. Similarly, restrictive fiscal policy will reduce the demand for loanable funds and lower the real interest rate. The decline in the interest rate will stimulate private spending and thereby retard the effectiveness of restrictive policy as an anti-inflation weapon.
7. The new classical model introduces another secondary effect—the impact of debt on future taxes. New classical economists argue that substitution of debt for tax financing merely changes the timing, not the level, of taxes. According to this view, taxpayers will anticipate the higher future taxes implied by additional government debt, save more to pay the high future taxes, and as a result, reduce their current consumption just as if the

equivalent taxes had been levied during the current period. The expansion in saving will permit the government to finance its deficit without an increase in the real interest rate. According to the new classical view, substitution of debt for tax financing will leave real interest rates, aggregate demand, output, and employment unchanged.

8. Fiscal policy changes must be properly timed if they are going to exert a stabilizing effect on the economy. Dynamic change and limited ability to forecast the future level of economic activity reduce the effectiveness of fiscal policy as a stabilization tool. The problem of proper timing is reduced in the case of automatic stabilizers, programs that apply stimulus during a recession and restraint during a boom, even though no legislative action has been taken. Unemployment compensation, corporate profit taxes, and the progressive income tax are examples of automatic stabilizers.
9. The modern synthesis of fiscal policy emphasizes three major points: (a) during a depression or severe recession, expansionary fiscal policy can stimulate real output as the Keynesian analysis implies; (b) during normal times, higher real interest rates and/or higher expected future taxes substantially dampen the stimulative effects of expansionary fiscal policy; and (c) since discretionary changes in fiscal policy are difficult to time properly, fiscal policy should be altered only in response to major disturbances.
10. Changes in marginal tax rates alter the share of additional earnings that taxpayers are permitted to keep, and thus their incentive to earn and engage in tax-avoidance activities. When fiscal policy changes marginal tax rates, it influences aggregate supply by altering the relative attractiveness of productive activity compared to leisure and tax avoidance. Other things constant, lower marginal tax rates will increase aggregate supply. Most economists believe that the demand-side effects of changes in taxes will dominate the supply-side effects in the short run. Supply-side economics should be viewed as a long-run strategy, not a countercyclical tool.
11. It is important to distinguish between a change in tax rates and a change in tax revenues. The size of the tax base will generally be inversely related to the rate of taxation. Therefore, an increase in tax rates will lead to a less-than-proportional increase in tax revenues, as individuals turn to substitutes for those things that are taxed.
12. When tax rates on income are relatively low, say, 30 percent or less, tax rates and tax revenues will change in the same direction. As the Laffer curve illustrates, however, when the marginal tax rates imposed on a group are exceedingly high, a change in tax rates may cause the revenues derived from the group to change in the opposite direction.

# Study Guide

## CHAPTER 14

## DEVELOPING THE ECONOMIC WAY OF THINKING

## CRITICAL-ANALYSIS QUESTIONS

1. Given the current rates of unemployment, inflation, and growth of real income, what changes in fiscal policy, if any, would you recommend? Justify your answer.
2. "The change in the size of a budget deficit or surplus is a better measure of fiscal policy than the mere size of the deficit or surplus." Do you agree with this statement? Explain.
3. Suppose that the government increases its spending on highways in order to increase aggregate demand during a recession. Should taxes be increased in order to finance the additional expenditures? Why or why not?

*4. What are automatic stabilizers? Explain their major advantage.

*5. What is the crowding-out effect? How does the crowding-out effect modify the implications of the basic Keynesian analysis with regard to fiscal policy? How does the new classical theory of fiscal policy differ from the crowding-out model?

*6. Some people argue that the growth of output and employment in the 1980s was the result of the large budget deficits. As one politician put it, "Anyone could create prosperity, if they wrote $200 billion of hot checks every year." Evaluate this view.

7. Suppose the federal government decided to systematically reduce the budget deficit by $25 billion each year and eventually run a budget surplus which would be used to reduce its outstanding debt. What would be the consequences of this policy?

*8. "If we set aside our reluctance to use fiscal policy as a stabilization force, it is quite easy to achieve full employment and price stability. When output is at less than full employment, we run a budget deficit. If inflation is a problem, we run a budget surplus. Quick implementation of proper fiscal policy will stabilize the economy." Evaluate this view.

*9. How would a reduction in marginal tax rates influence the incentive of a taxpayer to incur a tax-deductible expenditure?

10. As of 1990, capital gains (income from assets sold for more than the purchase price paid during an earlier time period) were taxed at the same rate as other income. Explain why during a period of inflation, taxing people on the nominal difference between the sale and purchase price of an asset may result in very high marginal tax rates on the real value of capital gains. Use hypothetical numbers if they will help you explain your answer.
11. Are government liabilities such as bonds the same thing as future taxes? Which would you prefer: (a) $100 in additional taxes this year or (b) $15 in additional taxes for each of the next ten years? Why?
12. "Budget deficits absorb private saving and divert it from investment. Therefore, the deficits retard economic growth." Indicate why you either agree or disagree with this statement.

*Asterisk denotes critical-analysis questions for which the answers are given in Appendix A.

# MULTIPLE-CHOICE SELF-TEST

1. Which of the following statements is true with regard to the pattern of total government spending in the United States *during the last four decades?*
   a. Government expenditures have declined as a percent of GDP, while government purchases of goods and services have increased as a percent of GDP.
   b. Both government expenditures and government purchases of goods and services have increased as a percent of GDP.
   c. Both government expenditures and government purchases of goods and services have declined as a percent of GDP.
   d. Government expenditures have increased as a percent of GDP, while government purchases of goods and services have fluctuated in a narrow band around 20 percent of GDP.
2. According to the Keynesian view, if policymakers thought the economy was about to fall into a recession, which of the following would be most appropriate?
   a. An increase in taxes.
   b. A planned increase in the budget deficit.
   c. A reduction in government expenditures.
   d. A balanced budget.
3. The prevailing budget philosophy prior to Keynes called for a balanced budget. Keynes argued that the government's tax and spending policies should be determined by the
   a. Supply-side impact of marginal tax rates.
   b. Current output of the economy relative to its potential.
   c. Size and quality of the labor force.
   d. Public's willingness to accept or reject tax changes.
4. Which of the following statements best expresses the central idea of countercyclical fiscal policy?
   a. Planned budget deficits are experienced during economic booms, and planned surpluses during economic recessions.
   b. The balanced-budget approach is the proper criterion for determining annual budget policy.
   c. Budget deficits during periods of inflation should equal budget surpluses during periods of deflation (declines in the price level).
   d. Deficits are planned during economic recessions, and surpluses are utilized to restrain inflationary booms.
5. "The large budget deficits of the 1980s were associated with historically high real interest rates." This finding is most clearly supportive of which of the following views?
   a. Keynesian theory of fiscal policy.
   b. Crowding-out theory of fiscal policy.
   c. New classical theory of fiscal policy.
   d. Supply-side view of fiscal policy.
6. According to the new classical theory, a $50 billion increase in government expenditures financed by a $50 billion increase in the budget deficit will

a. Cause both aggregate demand and real output to expand by at least $50 billion.
b. Exert little impact on real output, because higher real interest rates will crowd out private spending.
c. Stimulate aggregate demand, causing the price level to rise (inflation).
d. Be largely offset by a reduction in private spending, because individuals will anticipate higher future taxes.

7. Automatic stabilizers are government programs that tend to
   a. Reduce the ups and downs in aggregate demand without legislative action.
   b. Bring expenditures and revenues automatically into balance without legislative action.
   c. Signal Congress that legislative changes are needed.
   d. Increase tax collections automatically during a recession.
8. The modern synthesis view of fiscal policy stresses
   a. Our capability of timing fiscal policy changes in a manner that would eliminate the business cycle.
   b. The impotency of fiscal policy, even during periods of widespread unemployment.
   c. The difficulties involved in timing fiscal policy changes so they will exert a stabilizing influence on the economy.
   d. The use of expansionary fiscal policy as a tool to reduce the natural rate of unemployment.
9. Susan Harper's annual income increased from $20,000 to $25,000. If these income figures place Susan in the 60 percent marginal tax bracket, the $5,000 increase in income will increase Susan's after-tax income by
   a. $2,000.
   b. $3,000.
   c. $3,600.
   d. $5,000.
10. The Laffer curve illustrates the concept that
    a. An increase in tax rates will always cause tax revenues to increase.
    b. An increase in tax rates will always cause tax revenues to decline.
    c. When marginal tax rates are quite high, a reduction in the high rates may increase tax revenues.
    d. When marginal taxes are quite low, an increase in the rates will usually cause tax revenues to decline.

## PROBLEMS

1. Label each of the following statements as most likely to be made by a Keynesian (K), a Keynesian critic concerned about crowding out (C), a new classical economist (NC), or a supply-sider (SS):

   _____ a. "The output lost due to resources left idle during a recession can never be recovered."

   _____ b. "The large budget deficits of the 1980s have been accompanied by historically high real interest rates."

_____ c. "Most research indicates that there is no link between budget deficits and interest rates; higher deficits may simply be matched by higher savings."

_____ d. "A budget deficit during a recession can actually promote crowding in of investment by making investors feel more optimistic."

_____ e. "A budget surplus is not likely to be a very effective weapon against inflation. The surplus will lower interest rates, which will offset the restrictive effects of the surplus."

_____ f. "Lower marginal tax rates stimulate people to work, save, and invest, resulting in more output and a larger tax base."

_____ g. "Since taxpayers are concerned about the welfare of succeeding generations, they consider debt financing of government spending to be equivalent to tax financing."

2. Both the initial tax structure and the tax structure after a 20 percent rate reduction are indicated in the accompanying table.
   a. Fill in the missing blanks.
   b. By what percent did the tax cut increase the amount of additional earnings that people making less than $10,000 were allowed to keep?
   c. By what percent did the tax cut increase the amount of additional earnings that people making more than $70,000 were allowed to keep?
   d. How will the tax cut affect the revenues derived from people making less than 10,000 per year? Be specific. How will the rate cut affect the revenues derived from those making more than $70,000 per year? Explain.

| | Initial Tax Structure | | Tax Structure after a 20% Rate Cut | |
|---|---|---|---|---|
| **Annual Taxable Income (in dollars)** | **Marginal Tax Rate** | **Percent of Additional Earnings Taxpayers Get to Keep** | **Marginal Tax Rate** | **Percent of Additional Earnings Taxpayers Get to Keep** |
| Less than 10,000 | 10 | ____ | 8 | ____ |
| 10,000 to 20,000 | 20 | ____ | 16 | ____ |
| 20,000 to 30,000 | 30 | ____ | ____ | ____ |
| 30,000 to 50,000 | 50 | ____ | ____ | ____ |
| 50,000 to 70,000 | 70 | ____ | ____ | ____ |
| More than 70,000 | 90 | ____ | ____ | ____ |

3. Smith purchased 500 shares of stock in 1980 and sold them in 1992. The nominal purchase and sales prices are indicated in the table on page 372.
   a. If Smith is liable for a 28 percent tax on the nominal capital gain derived from the stock, calculate her capital gain tax liability as the result of the stock sale.
   b. Fill in the blanks in the last column of the table. What was Smith's real capital gain measured in 1992 dollars?
   c. What was Smith's marginal tax rate on the real capital gain?
   d. If the inflation rate and the increase in the nominal price of the stock

have both been 20 percent greater during the 1980–1992 period, what would have happened to Smith's marginal tax rate on her real capital gain?

| | Price of 500 Shares of Stock | Price Index (1980 = 100) | Real Price of Stock (1992 dollars) |
|---|---|---|---|
| Bought in 1980 | $2,500 | 100 | ______ |
| Sold in 1992 | $4,950 | 180 | ______ |

CHAPTER

# 15

# BANKING AND THE CONTROL OF THE MONEY SUPPLY

Money is whatever is generally accepted in exchange for goods and services—accepted not as an object to be consumed but as an object that represents a temporary abode of purchasing power to be used for buying still other goods and services.

*Milton Friedman*[1]

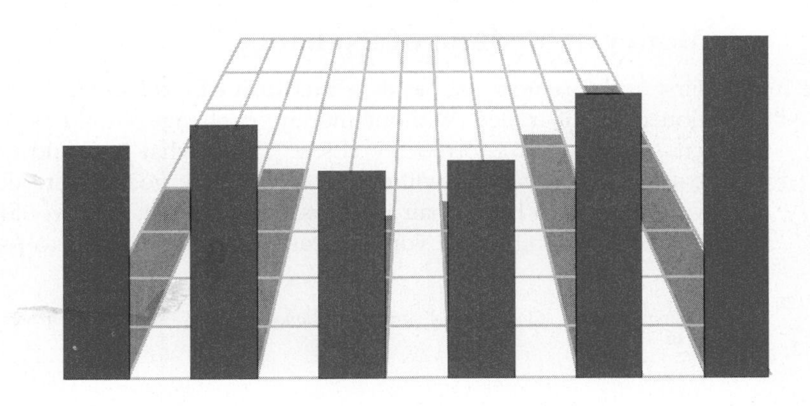

### CHAPTER FOCUS

- What is money? Why is it important?
- How is the money supply defined?
- What is a fractional reserve banking system? How does it influence the ability of banks to create money?
- What are the major tools with which the Federal Reserve controls the supply of money? How do changes in Fed policy influence the supply of money?
- How does the Fed differ from the U.S. Treasury? What are the functions of each?

This chapter focuses on money—why it is important, and how the policies of central banks influence its supply. Economists are interested in how monetary policies influence the way the economy works. In the next chapter, we will analyze how monetary policy affects the level of prices, output, employment, and other important economic variables. But before we are able to deal with that topic, we need to know something about the nature of money, how it is measured, and the factors that influence its availability.

## WHAT IS MONEY AND WHY IS IT IMPORTANT?

The simple model we have developed thus far in this text has three major markets: (1) goods and services, (2) resources, and (3) loanable funds. However, when people make exchanges in any of these markets, they generally use money. They trade money for resource services—labor, for example—and for all types of goods and services, as well as bonds. Money is an asset that not only serves as a medium of exchange, but also as an accounting unit and a store of value.

### Money as Medium of Exchange

**medium of exchange** An asset used to buy and sell goods and services.

First and foremost, money is a **medium of exchange.** It reduces the transaction costs of trades. Without money, exchange would be complicated, time-consuming, and enormously costly. Think what it would be like to live in a barter economy—one without money, where goods were traded for goods. If you wanted to buy a pair of jeans, for example, you would have to first find someone willing to sell you the jeans who also wanted to purchase something

[1]Milton Friedman, *Money Mischief: Episodes in Monetary History* (New York: Harcourt Brace Jovanovich, 1992), p. 16.

you were willing to supply. Such an economy would be highly inefficient. Money oils the wheels of trade and makes it possible for each of us to specialize in the supply of those things that we do best and to purchase (and consume) a broad cross-section of goods and services consistent with our individual preferences. People simply sell their productive services or assets for money and, in turn, use the money to buy precisely the goods and services they want. For example, if a farmer wants to exchange a cow for electricity and medical services, the cow is sold for money, which is then used to buy the electricity and the medical services. Money permits a society to escape the cumbersome procedures of a barter economy.

### Money as Accounting Unit

Since money is widely used in exchange, it also serves as a yardstick with which the value (and costs) of goods and services can be compared. If consumers are going to spend their income wisely, they must be able to compare the value of a vast array of goods and services. Similarly, sound business decision-making will require comparisons among vastly different productive services. Money serves as a unit of account, a common denominator in which the current value of all goods and services can be expressed.

### Money as Store of Value

Money is a financial asset; it allows us to move purchasing power from one time period to another. There are some disadvantages to using money as a vehicle for storing value (wealth), though. Many methods of holding money do not yield an interest return. During a time of inflation, the purchasing power of money will decline, imposing a cost on those who are holding wealth in the form of money. There is, however, one big advantage to using money as a store of value; it can be easily and quickly transformed into other goods at a low transaction cost and without an appreciable loss in its nominal value. Because of this, most people hold some of their wealth in the form of money. It provides readily available purchasing power for dealing with an uncertain future.

## MEASUREMENT OF THE MONEY SUPPLY

**demand deposits** Non-interest-earning deposits that either can be withdrawn from a bank or made payable on demand to a third party via check. In essence, they are "checkbook money" because they permit transactions to be paid for by check rather than by currency.

**interest-earning checkable deposits** Deposits that earn interest and are also available for checking.

Measuring the supply of money in an economy involves more than a count of currency and coins. Since money is defined primarily as a means of exchange, and since most business in the United States—more than 75 percent of the total—is conducted by check, checkable deposits are also included in the supply of money. There are two general categories of checking deposits. First, there are **demand deposits,** non-interest-earning deposits with banking institutions that are available for withdrawal "on demand," at any time without restrictions. These are usually withdrawn by writing a check. Second, there are **interest-earning checkable deposits** that carry some restrictions on their transferability. Interest-earning checkable deposits generally either limit the number of checks written each month or require the depositor to maintain a substantial minimum balance ($1,000, for example). Like currency and demand deposits, interest-earning checkable deposits are available for use as a medium of exchange. Traveler's checks are also a means of exchange and thus included in the economists' definition of money.

**money supply** Defined two ways: *M1* is the sum of (1) currency in circulation (including coins), (2) demand deposits, (3) other (interest-earning) checkable deposits of depository institutions, and (4) traveler's checks. *M2* is the combined amount of M1 plus (1) savings and time deposits (accounts of less than $100,000) of all depository institutions, (2) money market mutual fund shares, (3) money market deposit accounts, (4) overnight loans from customers to commercial banks, and (5) overnight Eurodollar deposits held by U.S. residents.

**Eurodollar deposits** Deposits denominated in U.S. dollars at banks and other financial institutions outside the United States. Although this name originated because of the large amounts of such deposits held at banks in Western Europe, similar deposits in other parts of the world are also called Eurodollars.

The narrowest definition of the **money supply**—economists call it *M1*—includes only assets that are directly used as a medium of exchange: (1) currency (and coins) in circulation, (2) demand deposits, (3) other (interest-earning) checkable deposits, and (4) traveler's checks. A broader concept, called *M2,* includes savings that can easily be converted to checking deposits or currency. Since in modern economies, financial assets are used both for the conduct of transactions and for saving, the line between money and "near monies" is a fine one. This is why some economists—particularly those who stress the store-of-value function of money—prefer the M2 definition, which includes M1 plus (1) savings and small-denomination time deposits at all depository institutions, (2) money market mutual fund shares, (3) money market deposit accounts, (4) overnight loans of customers to commercial banks (called repurchase agreements) and (5) overnight **Eurodollar deposits** of U.S. residents—deposits denominated in U.S. dollars at banks and other financial institutions outside the United States. The owners of these financial assets may perceive of them as funds available for use as payment. In some cases, the assets may even be directly used as a means of exchange. So, regardless of whether they are counted as part of the money supply, the additional assets incorporated into M2 are close substitutes for money.

Recent developments in financial markets have, to some extent, changed the nature of the M1 money supply. During the 1970s M1 was almost entirely composed of currency and demand deposits, neither of which earned interest. The situation changed substantially during the 1980s. Responding to the availability of interest-earning checking accounts, many depositors held some of their savings in these accounts. By 1990 these interest-earning checking accounts exceeded demand deposits, and they comprised more than one-third of the M1 money supply.

Since they earn interest, interest-earning checking accounts are less costly to hold than currency and demand deposits. In essence, interest-earning checking accounts are partly medium-of-exchange money and partly savings. The rapid growth of interest-earning checking accounts during the mid-1980s accelerated the growth rate of the M1 money supply. But they also reduced its comparability with earlier data. Today the M1 money supply has a larger savings component and a smaller medium-of-exchange component than was true during the 1970s.

The changes in the nature of M1 during the 1980s caused economists and monetary planners to pay more attention to M2. Since both savings and interest-earning checking accounts are components of M2, the financial innovations of the 1980s exerted less impact on M2 than on M1. Most analysts now rely more extensively on M2 (rather than M1) when making comparisons of the money supply (and its growth rate) across time periods that include the 1980s. Reflecting these views, when we use money supply data over the last several decades to assess the impact of monetary policy, we will generally use the M2 definition of money.

As Exhibit 15.1 shows, the total M1 money supply in the United States was $1,024 billion in December 1992. Demand and other checkable deposits accounted for 70 percent of this amount. The M2 money supply added another $2,480 billion to M1, bringing the total to $3,504 billion.

**EXHIBIT 15.1**

**Composition of Money Supply in United States**

The size (as of December 1992) of two alternative measures of the money supply are shown. M1 is the narrowest and most commonly used definition of the money supply. M2, which contains M1 plus the various savings components indicated, is approximately four times the size of M1.

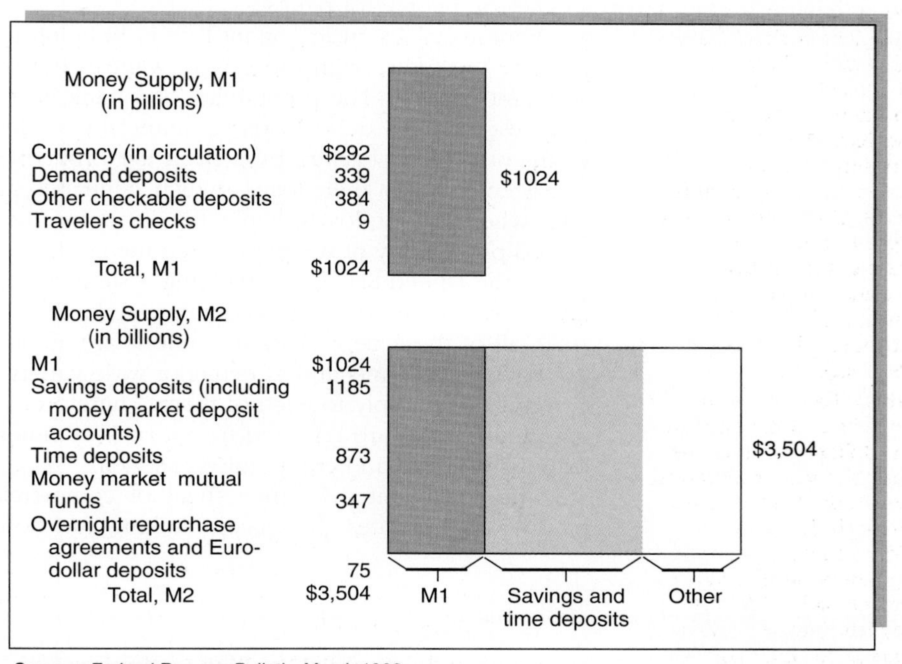

Money Supply, M1
(in billions)
Currency (in circulation) $292
Demand deposits 339
Other checkable deposits 384
Traveler's checks 9
Total, M1 $1024
$1024
Money Supply, M2
(in billions)
M1 $1024
Savings deposits (including money market deposit accounts) 1185
Time deposits 873
Money market mutual funds 347
Overnight repurchase agreements and Euro-dollar deposits 75
Total, M2 $3,504
$3,504
M1
Savings and time deposits
Other


**Source:** *Federal Reserve Bulletin,* March 1993.

## Why Credit Cards Are Not Money

**credit** Funds acquired by borrowing.

It is important to distinguish between money and credit. Money is a financial *asset* that provides the holder with future purchasing power. **Credit** is *liability* acquired when one borrows funds. This distinction sheds light on a question students frequently ask, "Since credit cards are often used to make purchases, why aren't credit card expenditures part of the money supply?" In contrast with money, credit cards are not purchasing power. They are merely a convenient means of arranging a loan. When you use your Visa or MasterCard to buy a disc player, for example, you are not using money to pay for the player. Instead, you are merely taking out a loan from the institution issuing your card. Payment is not made until later when you write a check to settle your credit card bill and thereby reduce your money balances. Thus, credit card purchases differ from money in that they are a *liability* in the form of an easy and convenient personal loan rather than an *asset* representing future purchasing power.

## FRACTIONAL RESERVE BANKING SYSTEM

The banking system is an important component of the capital market. Like other private businesses, banks are profit-seeking operations. Banks provide services (for example, safekeeping of funds and checking-account services) and pay interest in order to attract deposits. Most of these deposits are then used to extend loans and undertake investments, which are the primary sources of income for banks.

Banking plays an important role in bringing together people who want to save for the future with those who want to borrow in order to undertake investment projects. The profitability of a bank is very much linked to its ability to invest in and extend loans to financially successful projects. When the investment projects backed by a bank are profitable, borrowers will be able to consistently repay their loans, which generates income for the bank. Therefore, when making loans, banks have a strong incentive to judge both the expected profitability of the project and the creditworthiness of the borrower.

In the United States, the banking system consists of savings and loan institutions, credit unions, and commercial banks. Under legislation passed in 1980, all of these depository institutions are authorized to offer both checking and savings accounts and to extend a wide variety of loans to customers. Similar regulations apply to each of them. Therefore, when we speak of the banking industry, we are referring to not only commercial banks, but savings and loan associations and credit unions as well.

The consolidated balance sheet of commercial banking institutions (Exhibit 15.2) illustrates the major banking functions. It shows that the major

**EXHIBIT 15.2**

**Functions of Commercial Banking Institutions**

Banks provide services and pay interest to attract checking, savings, and time deposits (liabilities). A portion of their assets is held as reserves (either vault cash or deposits with the Fed) to meet their daily obligations toward their depositors. Most of the rest is invested and loaned out, providing interest income for the bank.

**Consolidated Balance Sheet of Commercial Banking Institutions, December 30, 1992 (billions of dollars)**

| Assets | | Liabilities | |
|---|---|---|---|
| Vault cash | $ 36 | Checking deposits | $ 799 |
| Deposits with the Fed | 29 | Savings and time deposits | 1,742 |
| Loans outstanding | 2,285 | Borrowings | 499 |
| U.S. government securities | 635 | Other liabilities | 343 |
| Other securities | 163 | Net worth | 268 |
| Other assets | 503 | | |
| Total | $3,651 | Total | $3,651 |

**Source:** *Federal Reserve Bulletin*, March 1993.

liabilities of banks are transactions, savings, and time deposits. From the viewpoint of a bank, these are liabilities because they represent an obligation of the bank to its depositors. Outstanding interest-earning loans comprise the major class of banking assets. In addition, most banks own sizable amounts of interest-earning securities, both government and private.

Banking differs from most businesses in that a large portion of its liabilities are payable on demand. However, even though it would be possible for all depositors to demand the money in their checking accounts on the same day, the probability of this occurring is quite remote. Typically, while some individuals are making withdrawals, others are making deposits. These transactions tend to balance out, eliminating sudden changes in the total amount of demand deposits.

**Federal Reserve System** The central bank of the United States; it carries out banking regulatory policies and is responsible for the conduct of monetary policy.

**bank reserves** Vault cash plus deposits of the bank with Federal Reserve Banks.

Thus, banks maintain only a fraction of their assets in reserves to meet the requirements of depositors. Some of these reserves are held in the form of deposits of the private banks with the **Federal Reserve System,** the central bank of the United States. We will discuss the Federal Reserve in detail later in this chapter. For now, though, we will simply note its role in the maintenance of **bank reserves,** which consist of vault cash plus deposits at a Federal Reserve Bank. As Exhibit 15.2 illustrates, bank reserves were only $55 billion ($36 billion vault cash plus $29 billion in deposits with the Fed) at year-end 1992, compared to checking deposits of $799 billion. Thus, on average, banks were maintaining less than 10 percent of their assets in reserve against the checking deposits of their customers.

## Fractional Reserve Goldsmithing

Economists often like to draw an analogy between the goldsmith of the past and our current banking system. When gold was used as the means of making payments, people would store it with a goldsmith for safekeeping, just as many of us open a checking account for safety reasons. Gold owners received a certificate granting them the right to withdraw their gold (their "money") any time they wished. If they wanted to buy something, they would go to the goldsmith, withdraw gold, and use it as a means of making a payment. Thus, the money supply was equal to the amount of gold in circulation plus the gold deposited with goldsmiths.

The day-to-day deposits of and requests for gold were always only a fraction of the total amount of gold deposited. A major portion of the gold simply lay idle in the goldsmiths' vaults. Taking notice of this fact, goldsmiths soon began loaning gold to local merchants. After a time, the merchants would pay back the gold, plus pay interest for its use. What happened to the money supply when a goldsmith extended loans to local merchants? The deposits of persons who initially brought their gold to the goldsmith were not reduced. Depositors could still withdraw their gold anytime they wished (as long as they did not all try to do so at once). The merchants were now able to use the gold they borrowed from the goldsmith as a means of payment. As goldsmiths lent gold, they increased the amount of gold in circulation, thereby increasing the money supply.

It was inconvenient to make a trip to the goldsmith every time one wanted to buy something. Since people knew that the certificates were redeemable in gold, certificates began circulating as a means of payment. The depositors were pleased with this arrangement because it eliminated the need for a trip to the goldsmith every time something was exchanged for gold. As long as they had confidence in the goldsmith, sellers were glad to accept the certificates as payment.

Since depositors were now able to use the gold certificates as money, the daily withdrawals and deposits with goldsmiths declined even more. Local goldsmiths would keep about 20 percent of the total gold deposited with them so they could meet the current requests to redeem gold certificates in circulation. The remaining 80 percent of their gold deposits would be loaned out to business merchants, traders, and other citizens. Therefore, 100 percent of the gold certificates was circulating as money; and that portion of gold that had been loaned out, 80 percent of the total deposits, was also circulating as money. The total money supply, gold certificates plus gold, was now 1.8 times the amount of gold that had been originally deposited with the goldsmith. Since the goldsmiths issued loans and kept only a fraction of the total gold deposited with them, they were able to increase the money supply.

As long as the goldsmiths held enough reserves to meet the current requests of the depositors, everything went along smoothly. Most gold depositors probably did not even realize that their gold was not in actual fact sitting in the goldsmiths' vaults.

Goldsmiths derived income from loaning gold. The more gold they loaned, the greater their total income. Some goldsmiths, trying to increase their income by extending more and more interest-earning loans, depleted the gold in their vaults to imprudently low levels. If an unexpectedly large number of depositors had wanted their gold, these greedy goldsmiths would have been unable to meet their requests. They would have lost the confidence of their depositors, and the system of fractional reserve goldsmithing would tend to break down.

## How Banks Create Money by Extending Loans

**fractional reserve banking** A system that enables banks to keep less than 100 percent reserves against their deposits. Required reserves are a fraction of deposits.

**required reserves** The minimum amount of reserves that a bank is required by law to keep on hand to back up its deposits. Thus, if reserve requirements were 15 percent, banks would be required to keep $150,000 in reserves against each $1 million of deposits.

In principle, our modern **fractional reserve banking system** is very similar to goldsmithing. Banks are required to maintain only a fraction of their deposits in the form of cash and other reserves. Just as the early goldsmiths did not have enough gold to pay all their depositors simultaneously, neither do our banks have enough reserves (vault cash and deposits with Federal Reserve banks) to pay all their depositors simultaneously (see Exhibit 15.2). The early goldsmiths expanded the money supply by issuing loans. So do present-day bankers. The amount of gold held in reserve to meet the requirements of depositors limited the ability of the goldsmiths to expand the money supply. The amount of cash and other **required reserves** limits the ability of present-day banks to expand the money supply.

However, there are also important differences between modern banking and early goldsmithing. Today the actions of individual banks are regulated by a central bank (the Federal Reserve System, in the case of the United States). The central bank is supposed to follow policies designed to promote a healthy economy. It also acts as a lender of last resort. If all depositors in a specific bank suddenly attempted to withdraw their funds simultaneously, the central bank would intervene and supply the bank with enough funds to meet the demand.

Under a fractional reserve system, an increase in reserves will permit banks to extend additional loans and thereby create additional checking deposits. Since checking deposits are money, the extension of the additional loans expands the supply of money.

To enhance our understanding of this process, let us consider a banking system without a central bank, one in which only currency acts as a reserve against deposits. Initially, we will assume that all banks are required by law to maintain vault currency equal to at least 20 percent of the checking accounts of their depositors. Suppose you found $1,000 that your long-deceased uncle had apparently hidden in the basement of his house. How much would this newly found $1,000 of currency expand the money supply? You take the bills to the First National Bank, open a checking account of $1,000, and deposit the cash with the banker. First National is now required to keep an additional $200 in vault cash, 20 percent of your deposit. However, it received $1,000 in additional cash, so after placing $200 in the bank vault, First National has $800 of **excess reserves,** reserves over and above the amount it is required by law to maintain. Given its current excess reserves, First National can now extend an $800 loan. Suppose it loans $800 to a local citizen to buy a car. At the time the loan is extended, the money supply will increase by $800 as the bank adds the funds to the checking account of the borrower. No one else has less money. You still have your $1,000 checking account and the borrower has $800 for a new car.

**excess reserves** Actual reserves that exceed the legal requirement.

When the borrower buys a new car, the seller accepts a check and deposits the $800 in a bank, Citizen's State Bank. What happens when the check clears? The temporary excess reserves of the First National Bank will be eliminated when it pays $800 to the Citizen's State Bank. But when Citizen's State Bank receives $800 in currency (or as a deposit in its account with a Federal Reserve bank), it will now have excess reserves. It must keep 20 percent, an additional $160, in the reserve against the $800 checking account deposit of the automobile seller. The remaining $640 could be loaned out. Since Citizen's State, like other banks, is in business to make money, it will be quite happy to "extend a helping hand" to a borrower. When the second bank loans out its excess reserves, the deposits of the persons borrowing the money will increase by $640. Another $640 has now been added to the money supply. You still have your $1,000, the automobile seller has an additional $800, and the new borrower has just received an additional $640. Because you found the $1,000 that had been stashed away by your uncle, the money supply has increased by $2,440.

Of course, the process can continue. Exhibit 15.3 follows the potential creation of money resulting from the initial $1,000 through several additional stages. In total, the money supply can increase by a maximum of $5,000, the $1,000 initial deposit plus an additional $4,000 in demand deposits that can be created by extending new loans.

The amount by which additional reserves can increase the supply of money is inversely related to the ratio of required reserves to checkable deposits. The lower the percentage of the reserve requirement, the greater the potential expansion in the money supply resulting from the creation of new reserves. The fractional reserve requirement places a ceiling on potential money creation from new reserves.

When new reserves are injected into the banking system, the money supply will expand by less than our simple analysis indicates. There are two reasons why. First, the public will generally hold some of the additional reserves in the form of currency rather than checking deposits. This will reduce the

**EXHIBIT 15.3**

**Creating Money from New Reserves**

When banks are required to maintain 20 percent reserves against demand deposits, the creation of $1,000 of new reserves will potentially increase the supply of money by $5,000.

| Bank | New Cash Deposits (Actual Reserves) | New Required Reserves | Potential Demand Deposits Created by Extending New Loans |
|---|---|---|---|
| Initial deposit (Bank A) | $1,000.00 | $ 200.00 | $ 800.00 |
| Second stage (Bank B) | 800.00 | 160.00 | 640.00 |
| Third stage (Bank C) | 640.00 | 128.00 | 512.00 |
| Fourth stage (Bank D) | 512.00 | 102.40 | 409.60 |
| Fifth stage (Bank E) | 409.60 | 81.92 | 327.68 |
| Sixth stage (Bank F) | 327.68 | 65.54 | 262.14 |
| Seventh stage (Bank G) | 262.14 | 52.43 | 209.71 |
| All others (other banks) | 1,048.58 | 209.71 | 838.87 |
| Total | $5,000.00 | $1,000.00 | $4,000.00 |

reserves available to banks, and thereby retard their ability to expand the money supply through the extension of additional loans. Second, banks may not loan out all of the additional reserves that they acquire. To the extent that banks fail to use their additional reserve to extend more loans, the expansion in the money supply will fall below its potential. Thus, both currency leakages and idle bank reserves will result in an actual expansion in the money supply that is less than its potential. These factors, however, do not negate the major point: Injection of new reserves into the banking system will result in an expansion in the money supply that is substantially greater than the increase in the additional reserves.

## CONTROLLING THE MONEY SUPPLY

Most countries have a central banking authority that controls the money supply and conducts monetary policy. In the United States, the central bank is the Federal Reserve System, often referred to as "the Fed." In the United Kingdom, the central bank is the Bank of England; in Germany, it is the Bundesbank.

The central bank of a nation conducts the country's monetary policy. In some cases, this central bank is largely independent of the political authorities. The Bundesbank provides an example. In other instances, central banks are directly beholden to political officials. The central banks of most Latin American countries fit into this category.

### Structure and Function of the Fed

In the United States, the Federal Reserve System, or the Fed, operates with considerable independence of both Congress and the executive branch of government. The Board of Governors is the decision-making center of the Fed. This powerful board consists of seven members, each appointed to a staggered 14-year term by the president with the advice and consent of the Senate. The president designates one of the seven members as chair for a four-year term. However, since a new member of the governing board is appointed only every other year, each president has only limited power over the Fed. This enhances the independence of the Fed and makes monetary policy less subject to political manipulation.

Unlike commercial banks, the Federal Reserve is not a profit-seeking institution. Rather it is an institution set up to establish "a stable monetary climate for the economy of the United States." The Board of Governors establishes rules and regulations applicable to all depository institutions. It sets the reserve requirements and regulates the composition of the asset holdings of depository institutions. The board is the rule-maker, and often the umpire, of the banking industry.

In addition to the Board of Governors, the Federal Open Market Committee (FOMC) exerts an important influence on monetary policy. This powerful policymaking arm of the Fed is made up of (1) the seven members of the Board of Governors, (2) the president of the New York District Bank, and (3) four (of the remaining eleven) additional presidents of the Fed's district banks, who rotate on the committee. While they do not always have a vote, all 12 presidents of the Federal Reserve regional banks attend the FOMC meetings, held every five to eight weeks. The FOMC determines the Fed's policy with respect to the purchase and sale of government bonds. As we shall soon see, this is the Fed's most frequently used method of controlling the money supply in the United States.

The Federal Reserve is a bankers' bank; its customers are commercial banks and depository institutions, not private citizens and corporations. Banks, including savings and loan institutions and credit unions, maintain balances with the Fed, which, like vault cash, count as reserves for the bank. The Fed audits the books of depository institutions regularly to assure regulatory compliance and the protection of depositors against fraud. The Fed also plays an important role in the clearing of checks through the banking system. Since most banks maintain deposits with the Fed, the clearing of checks becomes merely an accounting transaction.

## How the Fed Controls the Money Supply

The Fed has three major means of controlling the money stock: (1) establishing reserve requirements for depository institutions, (2) buying and selling U.S. government securities in the open market, and (3) setting the interest rate at which it will loan funds to commercial banks and other depository institutions. We will analyze in detail how each of these tools can be used to regulate the amount of money in circulation.

**RESERVE REQUIREMENTS** The Federal Reserve System requires banking institutions (including credit unions and savings and loan associations) to maintain reserves against the demand deposits of its customers. The reserves of banking institutions are composed of (1) currency held by the bank (vault cash) and (2) deposits of the bank with the Federal Reserve System. A bank can always obtain additional currency by drawing on its deposits with the Federal Reserve. So both cash-on-hand and the bank's deposits with the Fed can be used to meet the demands of depositors. Both therefore count as reserves.

**required reserve ratio** A percentage of a specified liability category (for example, checking accounts) that banking institutions are required to hold as reserves against this type of liability.

Larger banks are required to maintain a higher ratio of their assets as reserves against their checking deposits. On average, the **required reserve ratio** for banks was approximately 10 percent of checking deposits at year-end 1992. Why are commercial banks required to maintain assets in the form of reserves? One reason is to prevent imprudent bankers from overextending loans and thereby placing themselves in a poor position to deal with any sudden increase in withdrawals by depositors. The quantity of reserves needed to meet such emergencies is not left totally to the judgment of individual bankers. The Fed sets the rules.

The Fed's control over reserve requirements, however, is important for another reason. By altering reserve requirements, the Fed can alter the money supply. Commercial banks are free to maintain reserves over and above those required by the Fed. However, since banks are profit-seeking institutions, they prefer to hold interest-bearing assets such as loans rather than large amounts of non-interest-earning reserves. Clearly, profit-seeking banks will want to minimize their excess reserves, those over and above what the Fed requires that they maintain.

If the Fed reduced the required reserve ratio, it would free additional reserves that banks could loan out. Profit-seeking banks would not allow these excess reserves to lie idle—they would extend additional loans. The extension of new loans would then expand the money supply.

What would happen if the Fed increased the reserve requirements? Since banks typically have very small excess reserves, they would have to extend fewer loans in the future. This reduction in loans outstanding would then cause a decline in the money supply.

Reserve requirements are an important determinant of the money supply because they increase the ability of commercial banks to extend loans and thereby alter the money supply. When the Fed increases reserve requirements, banks will tend to extend fewer loans and, as a result, the money supply will decline. On the other hand, a decline in the required reserve ratio will encourage banks to extend more loans, which will expand the money supply.

**OPEN MARKET OPERATIONS** Unlike individuals, businesses, and even other government agencies, the Fed can write a check without having funds in its account. When the Fed buys things, it creates money. The primary thing that the Fed buys is the national debt, bonds that were originally issued by the U.S. Treasury and sold to private parties in order to finance budget deficits. The Fed's purchase and sale of these U.S. securities influences the amount of reserve available to the banking system.

**open market operations** The buying and selling of U.S. government securities (national debt) by the Federal Reserve.

Since the Fed's buying and selling of U.S. securities takes place in the open market, such activity is often referred to as **open market operations.** By far, open market operations are the most important tool that the Fed uses to control the money supply. When the Fed purchases U.S. securities, it injects "new money"—additional potential reserves—into the economy. This new money shows up as an increase in either bank reserves or currency in circulation. The sellers of the securities receive checks drawn on a Federal Reserve Bank. If a seller cashes the check, the amount of currency in circulation expands. If, as is more likely to be the case, the seller deposits the check with a commercial bank, the supply of checking-account money increases directly and new bank reserves are created. When the check is deposited in a bank, the receiving bank acquires a deposit or credit with the Federal Reserve as the check clears. This increases the reserves of the bank, placing it in a position to extend additional loans. As the new loans are extended, the money supply expands by a still larger amount. Eventually, the money supply will increase by two or three times the amount of the securities purchased by the Fed.

Let us consider a hypothetical case. Suppose the Fed purchases $10,000 of U.S. securities from Mary Jones. The Fed receives the securities, and Jones receives a check for $10,000, which she deposits in her checking account at City Bank. Her deposit increases the money supply by $10,000, only a fraction of which must be held as required reserves against the new deposits of Jones. Assuming a 10 percent required reserve ratio, City Bank can now extend new loans of up to $9,000 while maintaining its initial reserve position. As we explained when discussing Exhibit 15.3, extension of these loans will contribute to a further expansion in the money supply. Part of the new loans will eventually be deposited in other banks, and they also will be able to extend additional loans. As the process continues, the money supply expands by a multiple of the securities purchased by the Fed.

Open market operations can also be used to reduce the money stock, or reduce its rate of increase. If the Fed wants to reduce the money stock, it sells some of its current holdings of government securities. When the Fed sells securities, the buyer pays for them with a check drawn on a commercial bank. As the check clears, the reserves of that bank with the Fed will decline. The reserves available to commercial banks are reduced, and the money stock falls.

Every dollar of securities that the Fed buys increases the money supply by several dollars. Conversely, every dollar of securities that the Fed sells reduces the money supply by several dollars. This happens because open market operations affect not only the money supply directly, but they also affect the potential reserves available to the banking system.

**THE DISCOUNT RATE—THE COST OF BORROWING FROM THE FED** When banking institutions borrow from the Federal Reserve, they must pay interest on the loan. This interest rate is called the **discount rate.** Borrowing from the Fed is a privilege, not a right. The Fed does not have to loan funds to banking institutions. Banks borrow from the Fed primarily to meet temporary shortages of reserves. They are most likely to borrow for a brief period of time while they are making other adjustments in their loan and investment portfolios that will permit them to meet their reserve requirement.

**discount rate** The interest rate the Federal Reserve charges banking institutions for borrowing funds.

An increase in the discount rate makes it more expensive for banking institutions to borrow from the Fed. Borrowing is thus discouraged, and banks are more likely to build up their reserves to ensure that they will not have to borrow from the Fed. An increase in the discount rate is therefore restrictive. It tends to discourage banks from shaving their excess reserves to a low level.

In contrast, a reduction in the discount rate is expansionary. At the lower interest rate, it costs banks less if they have to turn to the Fed to meet a temporary emergency. Therefore, as the cost of borrowing from the Fed declines, banks are more likely to reduce their excess reserves to a minimum, extending more loans and increasing the money supply.

## Controlling the Money Supply—A Summary

The accompanying "Thumbnail Sketch" summarizes the effects of the tools used by the Fed to control the supply of money. The Fed can determine the amount of reserves available to the economy through its buying and selling of securities and its discount rate policy. It can also use adjustments in the reserve

## THUMBNAIL SKETCH

**Monetary Tools of the Fed for Expanding or Restricting Money Supply**

| Federal Reserve Policy | Expansionary Monetary Policy | Restrictive Monetary Policy |
|---|---|---|
| 1. Reserve requirements | *Reduce reserve requirements,* because this will free additional excess reserves and induce banks to extend additional loans, which will expand the money supply | *Raise reserve requirements,* because this will reduce the excess reserves of banks, causing them to make fewer loans; as the outstanding loans of banks decline, the money stock will be reduced |
| 2. Open market operations | *Purchase additional U.S. securities,* which will expand the money stock directly, and increase the reserves of banks, inducing bankers in turn to extend more loans; this will expand the money stock indirectly | *Sell previously purchased U.S. securities,* which will reduce both the money stock and excess reserves; the decline in excess reserves will indirectly lead to an additional reduction in the money supply |
| 3. Discount rate | *Lower the discount rate,* which will encourage more borrowing from the Fed; banks will tend to reduce their reserves and extend more loans because of the lower cost of borrowing from the Fed if they temporarily run short on reserves | *Raise the discount rate,* thereby discouraging borrowing from the Fed; banks will tend to extend fewer loans and build up their reserves so they will not have to borrow from the Fed |

requirements to influence the size of checking deposits relative to bank reserves. If the Fed wants to follow an expansionary policy, it can decrease reserve requirements, purchase additional U.S. securities, and/or lower the discount rate. If it wants to reduce the money stock, it can increase the reserve requirements, sell U.S. securities, and/or raise the discount rate. Since the Fed typically seeks only small changes in the money supply (or its rate of increase), it typically uses only one or two of these tools at a time to accomplish a desired objective.

As the economy grows, the money supply is generally expanded also. In a dynamic setting, therefore, the direction of monetary policy is best gauged by the *rate of change* in the money supply. When economists say that monetary policy is expansionary, they mean that the rate of growth of the money stock is rapid. Similarly, restrictive monetary policy implies a slow rate of growth or a decline in the money stock.

### The Fed and the Treasury

Many students have a tendency to confuse the Federal Reserve and the U.S. Treasury, probably because both sound like monetary agencies. The two, however, are independent of each other and each has a different function. The Treasury is a budgetary agency. If there is a budget deficit, the Treasury will issue U.S. securities as a method of financing the deficit. Newly issued U.S. securities are almost always sold to private investors (or invested in government trust funds). Bonds issued by the Treasury to finance a budget deficit are seldom purchased directly by the Fed. In any case, the Treasury is primarily interested in obtaining funds so it can pay Uncle Sam's bills.

In contrast, the Fed is concerned primarily with the availability of money and credit for the entire economy. The Fed does not issue U.S. securities. It merely purchases and sells government securities issued by the Treasury as a means of controlling the economy's money supply. Unlike the Treasury, the Fed can purchase government bonds by writing a check on itself without having deposits, gold, or anything else to back it up. In doing so, the Fed creates money out of thin air. The Treasury does not have this power. The Fed does not have an obligation to meet the financial responsibilities of the U.S. government. That is the domain of the Treasury. The Fed's responsibility is to provide a stable monetary framework for the entire economy.

## LOOKING AHEAD

We are now ready to introduce money into our aggregate demand/aggregate supply model. The following chapter analyzes how monetary policy influences prices, output, and employment.

## CHAPTER SUMMARY

1. Money is a financial asset that is widely accepted as a medium of exchange. It also provides a means of storing current purchasing power for the future and acts as a unit of account. Without money, exchange would be both costly and tedious.
2. There is some debate among economists as to precisely how the money supply should be defined. The narrowest definition of the money supply (M1) includes only (a) currency in the hands of the public, (b) demand deposits, (c) other (interest-earning) checkable deposits in depository institutions, and (d) traveler's checks.
3. The broader definition of money supply (M2) includes M1 plus (a) savings and small-denomination time deposits, (b) money market mutual fund shares, (c) money market deposit accounts, (d) overnight loans of customers to commercial banks, and (e) Eurodollar deposits. The introduction of interest-earning checkable deposits has changed the nature of M1 and reduced the comparability of M1 data over time. As a result, most analysts now rely more extensively on M2 data when making comparisons of money supply growth rates across time periods that include the 1980s.
4. Banking is a business. Banks provide their depositors with safekeeping of money, check-clearing services on checkable deposits, and interest

payments on time deposits and certain checking deposits. Banks derive most of their income from the extension of loans and investments in interest-earning securities.

5. Under legislation adopted in 1980, savings and loan associations and credit unions are permitted to provided essentially the same services as commercial banks. All of these depository institutions are regulated by the Federal Reserve. In essence, they are all part of an integrated banking system.
6. Under a fractional reserve banking system, banks are required to maintain only a fraction of their deposits in the form of reserves (vault cash or deposits with the Fed). Excess reserves may be invested or loaned to customers. When banks extend additional loans, they create additional deposits and thereby expand the money supply.
7. The Federal Reserve System is a central banking authority designed to provide a stable monetary framework for the entire economy. It has three major tools with which to control the money supply.
   a. *Establishment of the required reserve ratio.* Under a fractional reserve banking system, reserve requirements limit the ability of banking institutions to expand the money supply by extending more loans. When the Fed lowers the required reserve ratio, it creates excess reserves and allows banks to extend new loans, expanding the money supply. Raising the reserve requirements has the opposite effect.
   b. *Open market operations.* The open market operations of the Fed can directly influence both the money supply and available reserves. When the Fed buys U.S. securities, the money supply will expand because bond buyers will acquire money and the reserves of banks will increase as checks drawn on Federal Reserve Banks are cleared. When the Fed sells securities, the money supply will contract because bond buyers are giving up money in exchange for securities. The reserves available to banks will decline, causing banks to issue fewer loans and thereby reduce the money supply.
   c. *Discount rate.* An increase in the discount rate is restrictive because it discourages banks from borrowing from the Fed to extend new loans. A reduction in the discount rate is expansionary because it makes borrowing from the Fed less costly.
8. For a dynamic, growing economy, monetary policy can best be judged by the *rate of change* in the money supply. Rapid growth of the money supply is indicative of expansionary monetary policy. Conversely, slow growth (or a decline) in the money supply is indicative of restrictive money policy.
9. The Federal Reserve and the U.S. Treasury are distinct agencies. The Fed is concerned primarily with the money supply and the establishment of a stable monetary climate. The Treasury focuses on budgetary matters—tax revenues, government expenditures, and the financing of government debt.

# *Study Guide*

## CHAPTER 15

## DEVELOPING THE ECONOMIC WAY OF THINKING

## CRITICAL-ANALYSIS QUESTIONS

*1. What makes money valuable? Does money perform an economic service? Explain. Could money perform its function better if there were twice as much of it? Why or why not?

2. How has the nature of the M1 money supply changed in recent years? How have these changes influenced the usefulness of M1 as an indicator of monetary policy? Why do many analysts prefer to use M2 rather than M1 when comparing the monetary policy of the 1980s with earlier periods?

*3. Are the following statements true or false?
   a. "You can never have too much money."
   b. "When you deposit currency in a commercial bank, cash goes out of circulation and the money supply declines."
   c. "If the Fed would create more money, Americans would achieve a higher standard of living."

4. If the Federal Reserve does not take any offsetting action, what would happen to the supply of money if the general public decided to increase its holdings of currency and decrease its checking deposits by an equal amount?

5. Why can banks continue to hold reserves that are only a fraction of the demand deposits of their customers? Is your money safe in a bank? Why or why not?

*6. Suppose you withdraw $100 from your checking account. How does this transaction affect (a) the supply of money, (b) the reserves of your bank, and (c) the excess reserves of your bank?

7. Explain how the creation of new reserves would cause the money supply to increase by some multiple of the newly created reserves.

*8. How will the following actions affect the money supply?
   a. A reduction in the discount rate.
   b. An increase in the reserve requirements.
   c. Purchase by the Fed of $10 million of U.S. securities from a commercial bank.
   d. Sale by the U.S. Treasury of $10 million of newly issued bonds to a commercial bank.
   e. An increase in the discount rate.
   f. Sale by the Fed of $20 million of U.S. securities to a private investor.

## MULTIPLE-CHOICE SELF-TEST

1. Without money to serve as a medium of exchange,
   a. The gains from trade would be severely limited.
   b. Our standard of living would probably be increased.
   c. Barter exchange methods would still permit us to enjoy our current level of economic activity.

*Asterisk denotes critical-analysis questions for which the answers are given in Appendix A.

d. Self-sufficiency in production would still permit us to enjoy our current level of economic activity.

2. In the United States, the M1 money supply consists of
   a. Paper currency and coins.
   b. Coins, paper currency, demand deposits, other checkable deposits, and traveler's checks.
   c. Paper currency, coins, demand deposits, and savings deposits.
   d. Government bonds, currency, demand deposits, other (interest-earning) checkable deposits, and traveler's checks.
3. The legal requirement that commercial banks hold reserves equal to some fraction of their deposits
   a. Limits the ability of banks to expand the money supply by extending additional loans.
   b. Prevents the Fed from controlling the supply of money since commercial banks can always offset the actions of the Fed.
   c. Prevents runs on banks by depositors who fear that banks have insufficient assets to meet the claims of their depositors.
   d. Limits the ability of the Treasury to expand the national debt.
4. If Federal Reserve policy increases the excess reserves of banks, why will banks want to expand their loans and investments?
   a. Banks are legally required to expand loans and investments when the Fed expands reserves.
   b. Since excess reserves are a non-interest-earning asset for banks, they will want to extend loans and make investments rather than hold assets that do not earn interest.
   c. If they did not extend additional loans and make additional investments, the interest rate would fall and reduce the banks' profitability.
   d. The banks would interpret the Fed's action as reducing uncertainty for businesses, and thus it would increase the demand for loans and improve investment opportunities.
5. Suppose you withdraw $200 from your checking account. How does this transaction affect the money supply and the resources of your bank?
   a. The money supply increases, and the reserves of your bank decline.
   b. Both money supply and the reserves of your bank increase.
   c. There is no change in the money supply, and the reserves of your bank decline.
   d. The money supply decreases, and the reserves of your bank increase.
6. Suppose the general public decides to increase its holdings of currency and reduce its holdings of checking account funds by an equal amount. If the Fed does not take any offsetting actions, how will the money supply be affected?
   a. The money supply will increase.
   b. The money supply will decrease, since checking deposits are part of the money supply but currency is not.
   c. While the action does not directly affect the money supply, it will reduce the excess reserves of banks and tend to indirectly reduce the money supply.
   d. While the action does not directly affect the money supply, it will increase the excess reserves of banks and tend to indirectly increase the money supply.

7. The discount rate is the interest rate that
   a. Commercial banks charge their low-risk customers for a loan.
   b. Savings and loan associations pay for the use of savings deposit funds.
   c. The U.S. Treasury pays individuals who purchase Treasury bonds in denominations of $10,000 or more.
   d. The Federal Reserve charges banking institutions that borrow funds from the Fed.
8. If the required reserve ratio were increased, then
   a. The outstanding loans of banks would tend to decrease, but the money supply would tend to increase.
   b. Both the outstanding loans of banks and the money supply would tend to decrease.
   c. The outstanding loans of banks would tend to increase, but the money supply would tend to decrease.
   d. Both the outstanding loans of banks and the money supply would tend to increase.
9. When the Federal Reserve purchases government bonds from the public, it
   a. Directly increases the stock of money and increases the reserves of the commercial banking system.
   b. Directly increases the stock of money, while reducing the reserves of the commercial banking system.
   c. Directly reduces the stock of money, while increasing the reserves of the commercial banking system.
   d. Directly reduces the stock of money and decreases the reserves of the commercial banking system.
10. "The Fed could increase the money supply if it issued more government securities." This statement is
    a. True.
    b. False, because this action would decrease the money supply.
    c. False, because the Council of Economic Advisors, not the Fed, issues government securities.
    d. False, because the Treasury, not the Fed, issues government securities.

# PROBLEMS

1. For each of the following, indicate whether the result will create an increase (+), decrease (–), or no change (0) in the money supply and the national debt.

| | Money Supply | National Debt |
|---|---|---|
| a. The Fed purchases $100 million of government securities from the public. | ______ | ______ |
| b. Government purchases exceed tax receipts, and the Treasury responds by selling $10 billion of T-bills to the public. | ______ | ______ |
| c. The Treasury sells $5 billion of T-bills to the Fed and uses the proceeds to cover $5 billion of deficit spending. | ______ | ______ |

| | Money Supply | National Debt |
|---|---|---|
| d. The general public decides to hold more money in the form of currency rather than checking deposits. | ______ | ______ |

2. Assume that the required reserve ratio for the U.S. banking system is 10 percent, that banks loan out any excess reserves, and that the public maintains 10 percent of its money balances in the form of currency (and the other 90 percent as checking deposits).
   a. If the Fed buys $100,000 of U.S. securities from Mr. Midas, how will this transaction affect the money supply?
   b. Midas maintains $10,000 in currency and deposits $90,000 in his checking account at the First Union Bank. Complete the following table, indicating the changes in the money supply resulting from the Fed's action:

| | Change in Checking Deposits | Required Reserves | Additional Loans | Amount of Loans Held as Currency Outside Banks |
|---|---|---|---|---|
| Round 1 | $90,000 | | | |
| Round 2 | | | | |
| Round 3 | | | | |
| Round 4 | | | | |
| Round 5 | | | | |
| Total (5 rounds) | | | | |

   c. By approximately how much did the Fed's purchase of the $100,000 of securities increase the money supply (through five rounds)?

CHAPTER

16

# MONETARY POLICY

In the early editions of the book, fiscal policy was top banana. In later editions that emphasis changed to equality. In this edition we've taken a stand that monetary policy is most important.

*Paul Samuelson*

(*1985 comment on the 12th edition of his classic text* Economics)[1]

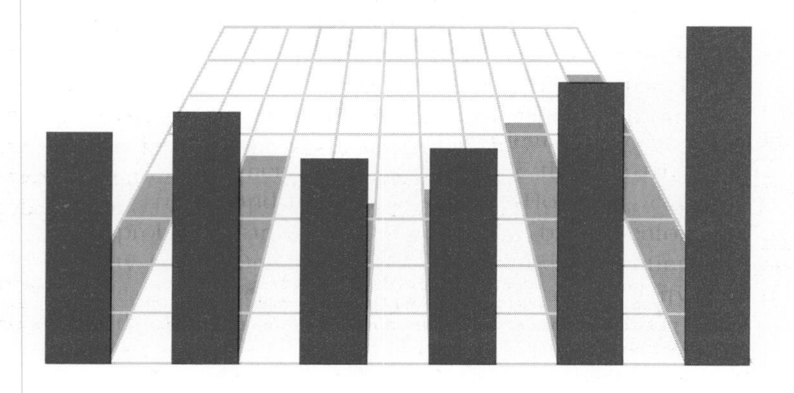

## CHAPTER FOCUS

- What determines the amount of money that people will want to hold?
- How does an increase in the supply of money influence output and prices in the short run? In the long run?
- How does a shift to a more restrictive monetary policy influence the economy?
- Can monetary policy help promote stable growth?
- What impact does monetary instability have on the economic health of a country?
- Did macroeconomic policy cause the Great Depression?

Money plays a central role in an exchange economy. Most countries have a national currency and a central bank that conducts monetary policy. This chapter focuses on monetary policies—how the policies of the central monetary authorities influence the output, price level, and interest rates of a country.

## DEMAND AND SUPPLY OF MONEY

How do people decide how much of their wealth to hold in the form of stocks, automobiles, consumer durables, and other assets and how much to hold in the form of money—cash and checking deposits? Two major forces determine the size of the money balances that people will hold: (1) the usefulness of money and (2) the cost of holding money balances.

Money is useful because it makes transactions easier to conduct and provides a means of storing purchasing power for future use. With money, the exchange process is greatly simplified, since the generalized purchasing power of money can be used to buy a multitude of goods and services. Money is also useful as a means of storing purchasing power for the future, when, for example, one might encounter an emergency medical expense or an unexpected opportunity to purchase a commodity or asset at a bargain price. Of course, other assets such as stocks and bonds can also be used to store purchasing power for the future. Usually, however, it is more convenient to use money for this purpose, provided the stability of its purchasing power is assured.

**demand for money** At any given interest rate, the amount of wealth that people desire to hold in the form of money balances; that is, cash and checking account deposits. The quantity demanded is inversely related to the interest rate.

The **demand for money**—the amount of money balances that people will want to hold—is inversely related to the nominal interest rate. Rather than maintaining $1,000 in cash or in a checking account that does not pay interest,

[1]Prior to the 1970s, most economists thought that fiscal policy was far more important than monetary policy. As the statement of Nobel laureate Paul Samuelson implies, this is no longer true. Since Professor Samuelson is a long-time Keynesian economist, the change in his views concerning the importance of monetary policy is particularly revealing.

**EXHIBIT 16.1** **Demand and Supply of Money Balances**

The demand for money indicates the amount of money balances that households and businesses will want to hold at different interest rates. Since an increase in the money interest rate makes it more costly to hold money balances, the demand for money is inversely related to the money rate of interest. Since the quantity of money is determined by the central monetary authorities (the Fed) through their open market operations, discount rate policy, and reserve requirements, the supply curve is vertical.

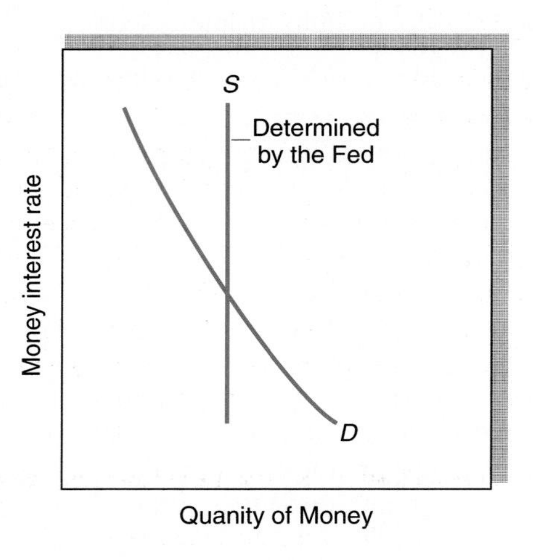


you could earn interest by purchasing a $1,000 bond. Even if you are maintaining money balances in an interest-earning checking account, you could earn a higher rate of interest if you are willing to tie up the funds in a bond or some other less liquid form of savings. As Exhibit 16.1 illustrates, the higher the nominal interest rate, the more costly it is to continue holding money balances. At the higher interest rate, individuals and businesses will try to manage their affairs with smaller money balances—hence, the inverse relationship between the quantity of money demanded and the interest rate.

**supply of money** The amount of cash and checking account deposits present. It is determined by the policies of the central monetary authority, the Fed in the case of the United States. For some purposes, the quantity of various savings accounts that can easily be converted to cash or checking deposits may also be included in the supply of money.

Since the **supply of money** is determined by the monetary authorities (the Fed in the United States), the supply curve of Exhibit 16.1 is vertical. This implies that the supply of money is insensitive to the interest rate. It is whatever the Fed decides it should be, largely independent of the interest rate. In equilibrium, the quantity of money demanded must equal the quantity supplied at the economy's money interest rate.

## MONETARY POLICY

When analyzing conditions in the goods and services, resources, and loanable funds markets, we previously assumed that the supply of money was constant. We are now ready to relax this assumption and consider how conditions in the market for money balances influence output, employment, and the price level in our increasingly complex aggregate demand/aggregate supply model.

## Expansionary Monetary Policy

**expansionary monetary policy** An acceleration in the growth rate of the money supply.

**excess supply of money** Situation in which the actual money balances of individuals and business firms are in excess of their desired level. Thus, decision-makers will increase their spending on other assets and goods until they reduce their actual balances to the desired level.

Suppose that the Fed shifts to a more **expansionary monetary policy**—that is, it unexpectedly begins to increase the money supply more rapidly. How would this increase in the supply of money influence the economy? As Exhibit 16.2 illustrates, if the market for money balances was initially in equilibrium, an increase in the supply of money from $S_1$ to $S_2$ will leave households and businesses with larger money balances than they desire to hold. The public will take steps to reduce its **excess supply of money.** There are two general ways to do this. First, people can transfer funds from their checking accounts into savings accounts, bonds, stocks, and other financial assets. To the extent that they reduce their money balances by this route, the supply of loanable funds will increase, placing downward pressure on the real rate of interest. In turn, a lower real interest rate will make potential investment projects more profitable and current consumption goods cheaper. At the lower real interest rate, entrepreneurs will undertake some investment projects they otherwise would have forgone. Spending by firms on plant and equipment will increase. Similarly, consumers will decide to expand their purchases of automobiles and consumer durables, which can now be enjoyed with smaller monthly payments. This increase in spending by both investors and consumers will increase aggregate demand.

**EXHIBIT 16.2**

**Impact of Monetary Policy on Aggregate Demand**

An unanticipated increase in the money supply (shift to $S_2$ in frame a) will create an excess supply of money balances. People will respond by either shifting some of their money into savings (increasing the supply of loanable funds) or spending more on goods and services. The latter will directly stimulate aggregate demand, while the former will place downward pressure on the real interest rate, which will encourage both investment and current consumption, and thereby stimulate aggregate demand. Therefore, a shift to a more expansionary monetary policy will increase demand (shift from $AD_1$ to $AD_2$) in the goods and services market.

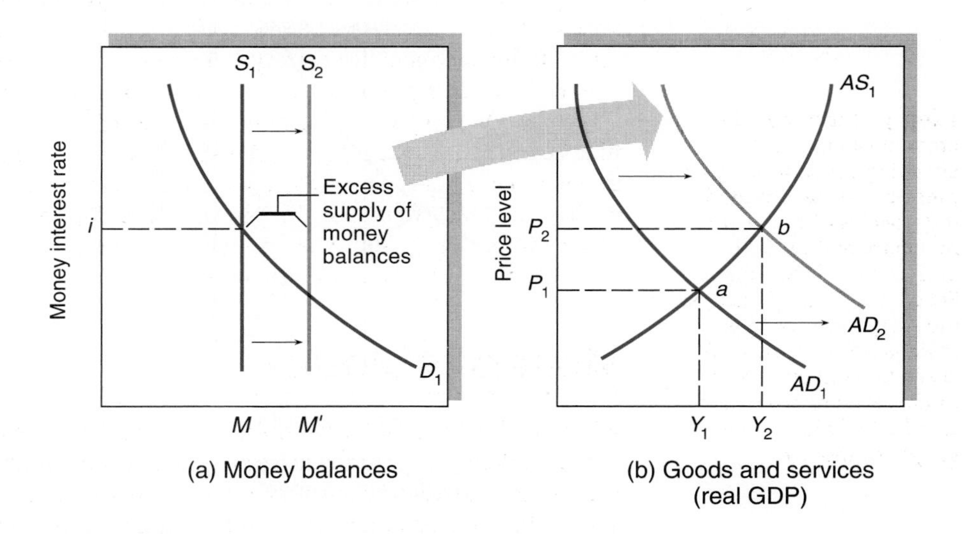

Second, people can reduce their money balances by spending more on goods and services—clothes, television sets, cameras, recreational activities, and so on. This action, of course, will directly increase demand for goods and services.

As Exhibit 16.2 illustrates, an unexpected increase in the supply of money will increase the demand for goods and services, either indirectly via a reduction in the real rate of interest or directly as people spend more in order to reduce their money balances. In turn, the increase in aggregate demand will expand real output and employment in the short run.

Exhibit 16.3a illustrates the potential of expansionary monetary policy to direct a recessionary economy to full-employment capacity. Consider an economy initially at output $Y_1$, less than the full-employment income level ($Y_f$). Expansionary monetary policy will increase aggregate demand (to $AD_2$). Real output will expand (to $Y_f$). In essence, the expansionary monetary policy provides an alternative to the economy's self-corrective mechanism. In the absence of demand stimulus, declining resource prices and real interest rates would eventually restore full employment. But many economists believe that

**EXHIBIT 16.3**

**Initial Economic Conditions and the Effects of Expansionary Monetary Policy**

If the impact of an increase in aggregate demand accompanying expansionary monetary policy is felt when the economy is operating below capacity, the policy will help direct the economy to a long-run full-employment equilibrium (frame a). In this case, the increase in output from $Y_1$ to $Y_f$ will be long term. In contrast, if the demand stimulus effects are imposed on an economy already at full employment (frame b), they will lead to inflation. Output will temporarily increase (to $Y_2$, frame b). However, in the long run, the strong demand will push up resource prices, shifting short-run aggregate supply to $SRAS_2$. The price level will rise to $P_3$, and output will recede (to $Y_f$) from its temporary high.

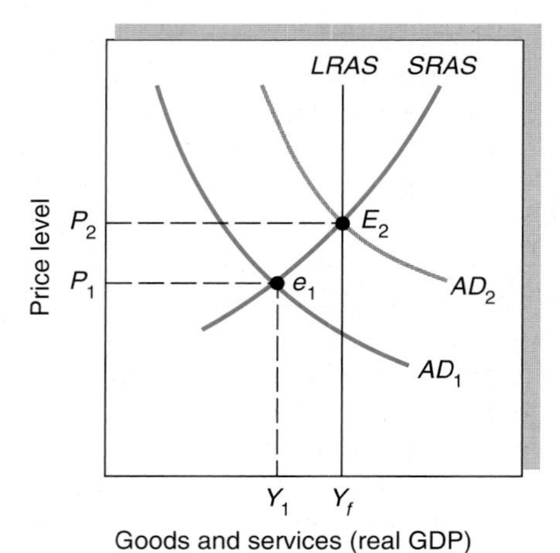


(a) Output is initially at less than full employment

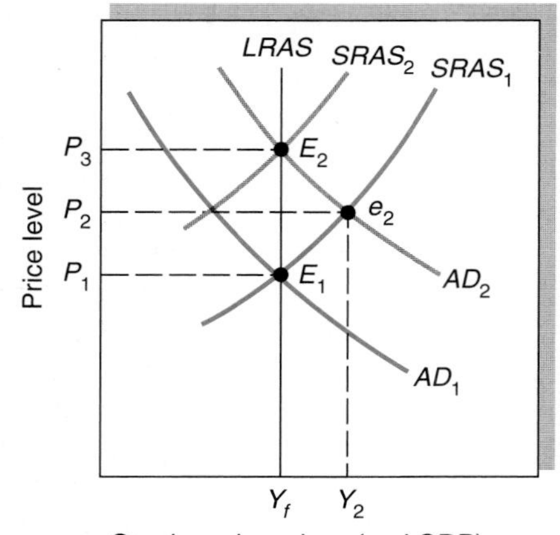


(b) Output is initially at full employment

this mechanism works too slowly. If this is the case, expansionary monetary policy will restore long-run, full-employment equilibrium more rapidly.

How would a shift to expansionary monetary policy influence output and the price level if the economy were already at full employment? While this is generally not a desirable strategy, nonetheless, it is instructive to analyze the outcome. As Exhibit 16.3b illustrates, in the short run, an unanticipated increase in aggregate demand resulting from a shift to a more expansionary monetary policy will temporarily push real output (to $Y_2$) beyond the economy's long-run capacity ($Y_f$). Since important components of costs (for example, union wage contracts, fixed-interest loans, and lease agreements) are fixed in the short run, the strong demand for goods and services will temporarily increase product prices relative to costs. Profit margins will improve, providing the incentive for business firms to produce the larger output. Unemployment will fall below the natural rate of unemployment.

However, the high rate of output ($Y_2$, Exhibit 16.3b) and employment will not be sustainable. Eventually, long-term contracts based on the previously weaker demand ($AD_1$) will expire. New agreements will reflect the stronger demand. Resource prices will rise, shifting *SRAS* upward to the left. Eventually, long-run equilibrium ($E_2$, Exhibit 16.3b) will result at a higher price level ($P_3$). Output will recede to $Y_f$. Therefore, when an economy is already at full employment, an unexpected increase in the money supply will temporarily increase output, but in the long run it merely leads to higher prices. Hence, the wisdom of a shift to a more expansionary monetary policy is highly questionable when an economy is already operating at (or beyond) its full-employment capacity.

## Restrictive Monetary Policy

**restrictive monetary policy** A deceleration in the growth rate of the money supply.

Suppose the Fed moves toward a more **restrictive monetary policy** and reduces the money supply (or in dynamic terms, reduces its rate of growth). How would a reduction in the money supply influence the economy? To stimulate your thoughts on this topic, consider what would happen if someone, perhaps a foreign agent, destroyed half of the U.S. money stock. We simply awake one morning and find that half of the cash in our billfolds and half of the checkable deposits in our banks are gone. Ignore, for the sake of analysis, the liability of bankers and the fact that the federal government would take corrective action. Just ask yourself, "What has changed because of the drastic reduction in the money supply?" The work force is the same. Our buildings, machines, land, and other productive resources are untouched. There are no consumer durables missing. Only the money, half of yesterday's money supply, is gone.

Exhibit 16.4 sheds some light on the situation. To make things simple, let us assume that before the calamity, the money balances of individuals and businesses were at the desired level, given current incomes and interest rates. Hence, the reduction in the supply of money (shift from $S_1$ to $S_2$) leaves people with less than the desired amount of money. People want to hold larger money balances, but the reduction in the money stock prevents them from doing so. Attempting to remedy the situation, people will try to restore at least part of their shrunken money balances.

How do people increase their money balances? Answer: they draw on their past savings, sell bonds and other assets, and cut back on their current spending. As people reduce their savings and purchase fewer bonds, the

**EXHIBIT 16.4**

**Short-Run Effects of a Reduction in Money Supply**

A reduction in the money supply creates an excess demand for money balances. Economic agents will seek to restore their money balances by drawing on their savings, purchasing fewer bonds, and/or spending less on goods and services. As a result, aggregate demand will decline (shift to $AD_2$). If the demand restraint comes during a period of strong demand and an overheated economy, then it will limit or even prevent the occurrence of an inflationary boom. In contrast, if the reduction in aggregate demand takes place when the economy is at or below full employment, the restrictive policy will contribute to a recession and limit the ability of the economy's self-corrective mechanism to restore full employment.

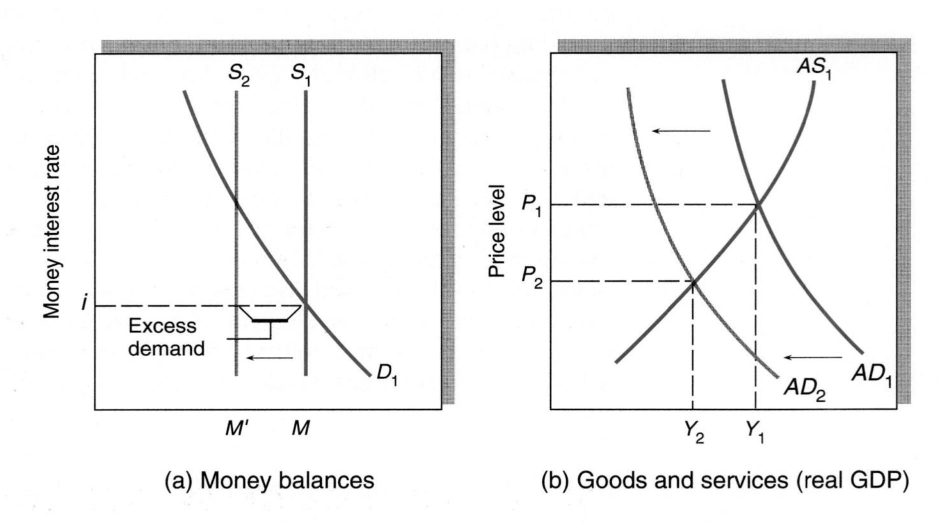


(a) Money balances

(b) Goods and services (real GDP)

supply of loanable funds will fall (relative to demand), causing the real rate of interest to increase. In turn, the higher real interest rate will induce both investors and consumers to cut back on their purchases of current goods and services. Simultaneously, others will seek to rebuild their money balances directly by spending less during the current period. Both the higher real interest rate and the direct reduction in current purchases will reduce aggregate demand (shift from $AD_1$ to $AD_2$, Exhibit 16.4b).

In turn, the unexpected decline in the demand for goods and services will place downward pressure on prices, squeeze profit margins, and reduce output. As Exhibit 16.4b illustrates, the price level tends to move toward $P_2$ and output tends to move toward $Y_2$ as the result of the restrictive monetary policy.

## Proper Timing

As with fiscal policy, monetary policy must be properly timed if it is to help stabilize an economy. When an economy is operating below its long-run capacity, expansionary monetary policy can stimulate demand and push the output of the economy to its sustainable potential (Exhibit 16.3a). Similarly, if the effects of a shift to a more restrictive policy come at a time when excessive aggregate demand is placing upward pressure on prices, the policy will help control (or prevent) inflation. On the other hand, if improperly timed, monetary policy can be destabilizing. Expansionary monetary policy is a source of inflation if the effects of the policy are felt when the economy is already at or beyond its capacity (Exhibit 16.3b). Similarly, if the effects of a restrictive policy come when an economy is operating at its potential GDP, recession is the likely outcome. Worse still, the impact of restrictive policy may be disastrous if imposed on an economy already in the midst of a recession (see the boxed feature, "What Caused the Great Depression?").

Proper timing of monetary policy is not an easy task. In contrast with fiscal policy changes requiring time-consuming congressional action, the Federal Reserve can institute a change in monetary policy quite rapidly. However, as an economy drifts toward a recession or an inflationary boom, policymakers may not immediately recognize the need for a change. Thus, there may be a time lag of several months between the time that a change becomes warranted and the time that policymakers at the Fed realize it is warranted. More importantly, there will be an additional time lag between the institution of a policy and when it exerts an impact on aggregate demand. Economists who have studied this issue estimate that this *effectiveness lag* will be 5 or 6 months at a minimum. Some economists believe that the primary impact of a change in monetary policy *on the price level* is sometimes as much as 18 to 36 months after the change is instituted. Given our limited ability to forecast the future, such time lags make it extremely difficult to institute changes in monetary policy in a countercyclical manner. Therefore, most economists now believe that monetary policymakers should respond only to major economic disturbances, rather than attempting to smooth out every turn in the economic road.

## MONETARY POLICY IN THE LONG RUN

Thus far, we have focused on the impact of monetary policy in a static framework. Of course, in a static framework, an increase in the price level implies inflation. However, inflation is a dynamic concept—a *rate of increase* in prices, not a once-and-for-all movement to a higher price level. It is also important to distinguish between the static and dynamic with regard to the money supply. Static analysis focuses on the change in the supply of money. In a dynamic setting, though, a change in the *growth rate* of the money supply is more indicative of the direction of monetary policy.

In this section, we want to recast our analysis slightly so we can better illustrate both dynamic factors and the long-run adjustment process. We will begin with a simple dynamic case. Suppose that the output of an economy is growing at a 3 percent annual rate and that the monetary authorities are expanding the money supply by 3 percent each year. In addition, let's assume that the **velocity of money**—the average number of times a unit of money is used to purchase goods and services during a time period—is constant. This would imply that, since output is growing at 3 percent each year, people will want to increase their money balances by 3 percent each year. Under these circumstances, the 3 percent monetary growth would be consistent with stable prices (zero inflation). Initially, we will assume that the economy's real interest rate is 4 percent. Since the inflation rate is zero, the nominal rate of interest is also equal to 4 percent. Exhibits 16.5 and 16.6 illustrate an economy initially (Period 1) characterized by these conditions.

**velocity of money** The average number of times a unit of money (e.g., a dollar) is used to purchase final goods and services during a year. It is equal to GDP divided by the stock of money.

**EXHIBIT 16.5**

**Long-Run Effects of More Rapid Expansion in the Money Supply—The Goods and Services Market**

Here we illustrate the long-term impact of an increase in the annual growth rate of the money supply from 3 to 8 percent. Initially, prices are stable ($P_{100}$) when the money supply is expanding 3 percent annually. The acceleration in the growth rate of the money supply increases aggregate demand (shift to $AD_2$). At first, real output may expand beyond the economy's potential ($Y_f$). However, abnormally low unemployment and strong demand conditions will create upward pressure on wages and other resource prices, shifting aggregate supply to $AS_2$. Output will return to its long-run potential and the price level will increase to $P_{105}$($e_2$). If the more rapid monetary growth continues in subsequent periods, *AD* and *AS* will continue to shift upward, leading to still higher prices ($e_3$ and points beyond). The net result of this process is sustained inflation.

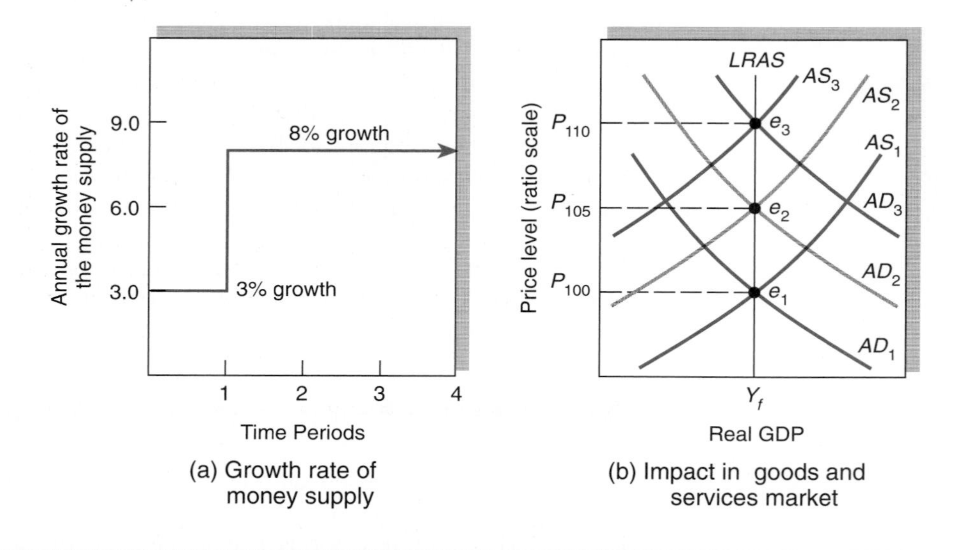


(a) Growth rate of money supply

(b) Impact in goods and services market

What will happen if the monetary authorities permanently increase the growth rate of the money supply from 3 percent to 8 percent annually (Exhibit 16.5a, beginning in Period 2)? In the short run, the expansionary monetary policy will reduce the real interest rate and stimulate aggregate demand (shift to $AD_2$), just as we previously explained (Exhibit 16.2). For a time, real output may exceed the economy's potential. However, as they confront strong demand conditions, many resource suppliers (who previously committed to long-term agreements) will wish they had anticipated the strength of demand and driven harder bargains. With the passage of time, more and more resource suppliers (including labor represented by union officials) will have the opportunity to raise prices and wages in order to rectify past mistakes. As they do so, costs will rise and profit margins will be squeezed. The higher costs will reduce aggregate supply (shift to $AS_2$). As the rapid monetary growth continues in subsequent periods (3, 4, 5, and so on), both *AD* and *AS* will shift upward. The price level will rise to $P_{105}$, $P_{110}$, and on to still higher levels as the money supply continues to grow more rapidly than the monetary growth rate

**EXHIBIT 16.6**

**Long-Run Effects of More Rapid Expansion in the Money Supply—The Loanable Funds Market**

When prices are stable, supply and demand in the loanable funds market are in balance at a real and nominal interest rate of 4 percent. If more rapid monetary expansion leads to a long-term 5 percent inflation rate (see Exhibit 16.5), borrowers and lenders will build the higher inflation rate into their decision-making. As a result, the nominal interest rate (*i*) will rise to 9 percent—the 4 percent real rate plus a 5 percent inflationary premium.

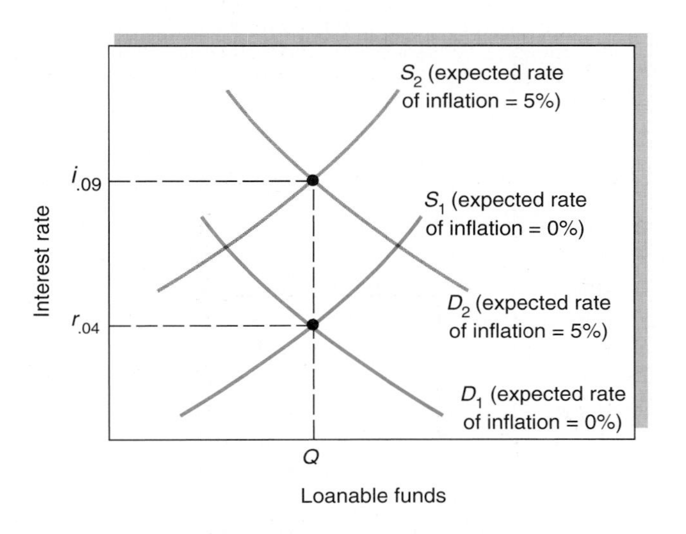


consistent with stable prices. The rapid monetary growth leads to a continual rise in the price level—that is, a sustained inflation.

Suppose an inflation rate of 5 percent eventually emerges from the more rapid growth rate (8 percent rather than 3 percent) of the money supply. With the passage of time, more and more people will adjust their decision-making in light of the persistent 5 percent inflation. In the resource market, both buyers and sellers will eventually incorporate the expectation of the 5 percent inflation rate into long-term contracts such as collective bargaining agreements. Once that happens, resource prices and costs will rise as rapidly as prices in the goods and services market. *When the inflation rate is anticipated fully, it will fail to either reduce real wages or improve profit margins.* Unemployment will return to its natural rate.

Exhibit 16.6 illustrates the adjustments in the loanable funds market once borrowers and lenders expect the 5 percent inflation rate. When lenders anticipate a 5 percent annual increase in the price level, a 9 percent interest rate will be necessary to provide them with as much incentive to supply loanable funds as 4 percent interest provided when stable prices were expected. Thus, the supply of loanable funds will shift vertically by the 5 percent expected rate of inflation. Simultaneously, borrowers who were willing to pay 4 percent interest on loans when they expected stable prices will be willing to pay 9 percent when they expect prices to increase 5 percent annually. The demand for

## The Quantity Theory of Money

For centuries, both laypersons and economists recognized that increases in the money supply were a major determinant of changes in price level. Even prior to Adam Smith, early social philosophers such as David Hume argued that rapid growth in the supply of money caused inflation. Nearly a hundred years ago, the great classical economists, Englishman Alfred Marshall and American Irving Fisher, formalized a theory in support of this view. Economists refer to the theory as the *quantity theory of money*. The theory implies that an increase in the supply of money will lead to a proportional increase in the price level.

The quantity theory of money can be easily understood once we recognize that there are two ways of viewing GDP. As we previously discussed, nominal GDP is the sum of the price, $P$, times the output, $Y$, of each "final-user" good purchased during the period. In aggregate, $P$ represents the economy's price level, while $Y$ indicates real income or real GDP. There is also a second way of visualizing GDP. When the existing money stock, $M$, is multiplied by the number of times, $V$, that money is used to buy final products, this, too, yields the economy's nominal GDP. Therefore,

$$PY = GDP = MV$$

The *velocity of money (V)* is simply the average number of times a dollar is used to purchase a final product or service during a year. Velocity is equal to nominal GDP divided by the size of the money stock. For example, in 1992 GDP was equal to $5,951 billion while the M1 money supply was $1,027 billion. On average, each dollar in the M1 money supply was used 5.8 times to purchase final-user goods and services included in GDP. The velocity of the M1 money stock therefore was 5.8. The velocity of the M2 money stock can be derived in a similar manner. In 1992, the M2 money stock was $3,497 billion. Thus, the velocity of M2 was 1.70 ($5,951 billion ÷ $3,497 billion).

When considering the behavior of prices, output, money, and velocity over time, we can write the quantity theory equation in terms of growth rates:

Rate of inflation + growth of real output = growth rate of the money supply + growth rate of velocity

The $MV = PY$ relationship is simply an identity, or a tautology. The quantity theory of money, however, postulates that $Y$ and $V$ are determined by factors other than the amount of money in circulation. Classical economists believed the real output $Y$ was determined by such factors as technology, the size of the economy's resource base, and the skill of the labor force. These factors were thought to be insensitive to changes in the money supply.

Similarly, classical economists thought the velocity of money was determined primarily by institutional factors such as the organization of banking and credit, the frequency of income payments, the rapidity of transportation, and the communication system. These factors would change quite slowly. Thus, classical economists thought that for all practical purposes, the velocity or "turnover" rate of money in the short run was constant.

If both $Y$ and $V$ are constant, the $MV = PY$ relationship indicates that an increase in the money supply will lead to a proportional increase in the price level. For classical economists, the link between the money supply and the price level was quite mechanical: an increase in the quantity of money would cause a proportional increase in the price level. Of course, they recognized that the link might not always be exact. For the purposes of theory, though, it was a reasonably close approximation to reality according to the classical theory.

Modern analysis indicates that the quantity theory of money is an oversimplification—in the short run it is unlikely to hold. However, *in the long run* the insights of the quantity theory of money are basically correct—growth of the money supply will primarily affect the price level, and the more rapidly the increase in the money supply, the higher the rate of inflation.

loanable funds will therefore also increase (shift vertically) by the expected rate of inflation. Once borrowers and lenders anticipate the higher (5 percent) inflation rate, the equilibrium money interest rate will rise to 9 percent. Of course, the real interest rate is equal to the money interest rate (9 percent) minus the expected rate of inflation (5 percent). In the long run, a 4 percent real interest rate will emerge with inflation, just as it did with stable prices.[2] Inflation will fail to reduce the real interest rate in the long run.

Modern analysis indicates that the long-run effects of rapid monetary growth differ from the short-run effects of an *un*anticipated move to expansionary monetary policy. In the long run, the major consequences of rapid monetary growth are inflation and higher nominal interest rates. Rapid monetary growth will neither reduce unemployment nor stimulate real output in the long run.

## IMPORTANT SOURCE OF PROSPERITY: STABLE MONEY AND PRICES

As we previously discussed, money is useful because it reduces transaction costs and provides a convenient method of storing purchasing power for the future. Its ability to perform these functions, however, is reduced when the purchasing power of the monetary unit changes rapidly and unpredictably. The productive contribution of money is directly related to the stability of its value. In this regard, money is to an economy what language is to communication. Without words that have clearly defined meanings to both the speaker and listener, communication is limited. So it is with money. If money does not have a stable and predictable value, it will be more costly for borrowers and lenders to conduct exchanges; saving and investing will involve additional risks; and time-dimension transactions (for example, the payment of the purchase price for a house or automobile over a time period) will be fraught with additional danger.

There are three major reasons why inflation and monetary instability tends to retard economic progress.

1. *Inflation distorts the information delivered by prices and changes the intent of long-term contracts in unpredictable ways.* Some prices will respond quickly to inflationary policies, while other prices such as rental lease agreements, utility rates, and mortgage interest rates will change more slowly, since they generally reflect long-term contracts or regulatory policies. Thus, an unanticipated inflation will change relative prices, as well as the general price level. Producers and resource suppliers will often be led astray by the unreliable price signals stemming from the inflation. This will be particularly true in the case of capital investment decisions. Unexpected changes in the inflation

[2]Higher rates of inflation are generally associated with an increase in the *variability* of the inflation rate. Thus, greater risk (the possibility of either a substantial gain or loss associated with a sharp change in the inflation rate) accompanies exchange in the loanable funds market when inflation rates are high. This additional risk may result in *higher* real interest rates than would prevail at lower rates of inflation. The text discussion does not introduce this consideration.

rate can quickly turn an otherwise profitable project into a personal economic disaster. Planning and undertaking capital investment is extremely hazardous in an inflationary environment. Given the additional uncertainty associated with the inflation, many decision-makers will simply forgo capital investments and other transactions involving long-term commitments. Because of this, mutually advantageous trades will be curtailed and the potential gains from these exchanges lost.

As we have stressed throughout this text, our modern living standards are linked to the realization of gains from specialization, capital formation, and economies accompanying the adoption of mass-production methods. The realization of these gains is directly related to our ability to cooperate with each other through voluntary exchange. High, variable rates of inflation make exchange more hazardous. As a result, people will engage in fewer productive activities and the level of social cooperation will decline!

2. *People will respond to the inflation and monetary instability by spending less time producing and more time trying to protect their wealth.* Since failure to anticipate accurately the rate of inflation can have a substantial effect on one's wealth, individuals will divert scarce resources away from the production of goods and services and into the acquisition of information on the future rate of inflation. Under these circumstances, the ability of business decision-makers to forecast changes in prices becomes more valuable than their ability to manage and organize production. Speculative practices are encouraged as people try to outwit each other with regard to the future direction of prices. Funds flow into speculative investments like gold, silver, and art objects rather than into productive investments like buildings, machines, and technological research. And as resources move from productive to unproductive activities, the production possibilities of the country decline.

3. *Inflation and monetary instability undermine the credibility of government.* At the most basic level, people expect government to protect their person and property from intruders who would take what does not belong to them. When government become an intruder—when it cheats citizens by "watering down" the value of their currency—how can people have any confidence that the government will protect their property against other intrusions, enforce contracts, or punish unethical and criminal behavior? When the government "waters down" its currency, it is in a weak position to punish, for example, an orange juice producer that defrauds consumers by diluting juice sold to customers or a business that waters down its stock (issues additional stock without permission of current stockholders).

## EFFECTS OF MONETARY POLICY—A SUMMARY

Our analysis indicates that the impact of monetary policy in the short run will differ substantially from its impact in the long run. The accompanying "Thumbnail Sketch" summarizes the major implications for both the short run and the long run. Five predictions flow from our analysis of monetary policy.

1. *An unanticipated shift to a more expansionary (restrictive) monetary policy will temporarily stimulate (retard) output and employment.* As Exhibit

## THUMBNAIL SKETCH

**Impact of Monetary Policy—A Summary**

| | The Short-Run Effects When the Policy Is Unanticipated (1) | The Long-Run Effects (2) |
|---|---|---|
| **Impact of expansionary monetary policy on:** | | |
| Inflation rate | Only a small increase, particularly if excess capacity is present | Increases |
| Real output and employment | Long-term increase if excess capacity is present; otherwise they increase temporarily | No change |
| Real interest rate | Decreases | No change |
| **Impact of restrictive monetary policy on:** | | |
| Inflation rate | Only a small decrease | Decreases |
| Real output and employment | Decrease, particularly if economy is at less than capacity | No change |
| Real interest rate | Increases | No change |

16.2 illustrates, an increase in aggregate demand emanating from an unanticipated increase in the money supply will lead to a short-run expansion in real output and employment. Conversely, as Exhibit 16.4 shows, an unanticipated move toward more restrictive monetary policy reduces aggregate demand and retards real output.

2. *The stabilizing effects of a change in monetary policy are dependent upon the state of the economy when the effects of the policy change are observed.* If the effects of an expansionary policy come when the economy is operating at less than capacity, then the demand stimulus will push the economy toward full employment. However, if the demand stimulus comes when the economy is operating at or beyond capacity, it will contribute to an acceleration in the inflation rate. Correspondingly, restrictive policy will help to control inflation if the demand-restraining effects are felt when output is beyond the economy's long-run capacity. On the other hand, restrictive policy will result in recession if the reduction in demand comes when the economy is at or below long-run capacity.

3. *Persistent growth of the money supply at a rapid rate will cause inflation.* While the short-run effects of expansionary monetary policy may be primarily on output, particularly if excess capacity is present, a persistent expansion in the money supply at a rate greater than the growth of real output will cause inflation. The more rapid the sustained growth rate of the money supply (relative to real output), the higher the accompanying rate of inflation will be.

4. *Money interest rates and the inflation rate will be directly related.* As the inflation rate rises, money interest rates will increase because both borrowers and lenders will begin to expect the higher rate of inflation and build it

into their decision-making. Conversely, as the inflation rate declines, a reduction in the expected rate of inflation will lead to lower money interest rates. Therefore, when monetary expansion leads to an acceleration in the inflation rate, it will also result in an increase in nominal interest rates.

5. *Monetary policies that lead to high and variable rates of inflation will undermine economic progress.* Monetary and price instability reduces the ability of people to plan for the future; it diverts resources away from production and toward speculation; and it undermines the credibility of government.

## TESTING THE MAJOR IMPLICATIONS OF MONETARY THEORY

Is the real world consistent with our analysis? The next four exhibits provide evidence on this topic.

Our analysis indicates that a shift to more expansionary monetary policy will initially stimulate output, while a shift to monetary restriction will retard it. Exhibit 16.7 shows the relationship between changes in the growth rate of the

**EXHIBIT 16.7**

**Monetary Policy and Real Output**

Periods of sharp acceleration in the growth rate of the money supply, such as 1961–1964, 1971–1972, and 1976 have generally been followed by a rapid growth of GDP. In contrast, sharp declines in the growth rate of the money supply such as those experienced in 1968–1969, 1973–1974, 1977–1979, and 1989–1991 have often been associated with (or closely followed by) reductions in real GDP and economic recession. The shaded years represent periods of recession.

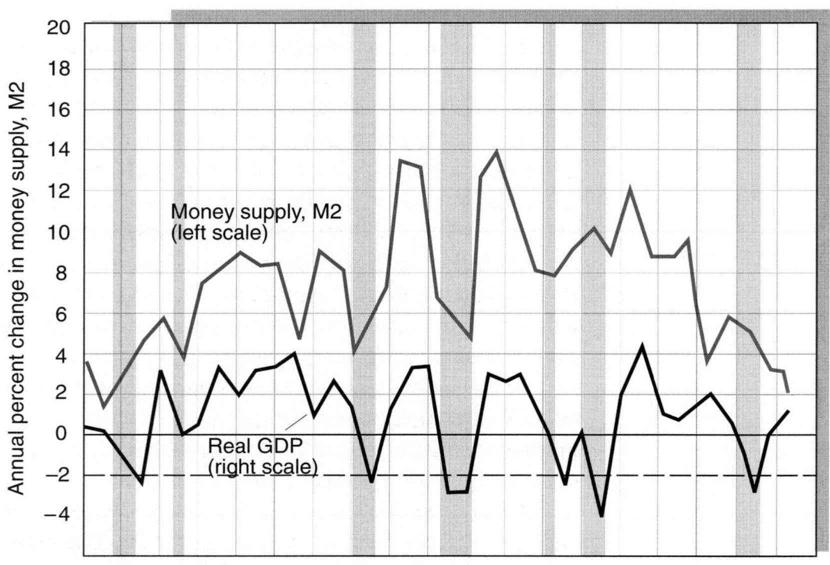

money supply and real output since the mid-1950s for the United States. Since the introduction of interest-earning checking accounts changed the nature of M1 (and affected its growth rate) during the 1980s, the M2 money supply measure is used here. Of course, factors other than monetary policy (for example, supply shocks, fiscal policy, or changes in incomes abroad) will influence the growth of output. Thus, the relationship between changes in the money supply and the growth of real GDP will be far from perfect. However, close inspection of the data reveals that periods of sharp acceleration in the growth rate of the money supply were often associated with an acceleration in the growth rate of real GDP. For example, an acceleration in the growth rate of the money supply during 1961–1964, 1971–1972, 1976, and 1983 was associated with an increase in the growth rate of real GDP during each of the periods. The converse was also true: periods of sharp deceleration in the growth rate of the money supply were generally associated with (or followed by) economic recession. A decline in the growth rate of the money supply preceded the recessions of 1958, 1960, 1970, and 1974–1975. Similarly, a sharp decline in the growth rate of the money stock from 13.7 percent in 1976 to 8 percent in 1978–1979 preceded the recession and sluggish growth of 1979–1982. Most recently, the recession and sluggish growth of 1989–1991 was preceded by a substantial deceleration in the growth rate of the money supply. Hence, just as our theory predicts, there does appear to be a relationship between shifts in monetary policy and changes in real GDP. (See the boxed feature, "What Caused the Great Depression" for further evidence on the impact of a decline in the money supply on real output and employment.)

Exhibit 16.8 presents a graphic picture of the relationship between monetary policy and the inflation rate for the United States. While our theory indicates that persistent, long-term growth of the money supply will be closely associated with inflation, it also indicates that it will take time for a monetary expansion (or contraction) to alter demand relationships and influence prices. Most economists believe that the time lag between shifts in monetary policy and observable changes in the level of prices is often two or three years. Reflecting these views, Exhibit 16.8 compares the current money supply (M2) data with the inflation rate three years in the future. Once again, while the linkage is far from perfect, a definite positive relationship is observable. Most noticeably, the rapid monetary acceleration during 1971–1973 was followed by a similar acceleration in the inflation rate during 1973–1975. Similarly, the sharp monetary contraction of 1974–1975 was accompanied by not only the recession of 1974–1975, but also a sharp deceleration in the inflation rate during 1976–1977. However, as monetary policy again shifted toward expansion in 1976–1977, the double-digit inflation rates of 1979–1980 were soon to follow. During the 1980s, the linkage between monetary growth and the inflation rate a few years later appeared to weaken. To some degree this may reflect the financial innovations and changing nature of money during the 1980s. A closer relationship, however, appears to be reemerging. The money supply growth declined to its lowest level in 30 years during the 1988–1992 period; so, too, did the inflation rate.

A major implication of our analysis is that rapid growth rates in the money supply over long periods of time will be associated with high rates of inflation. Exhibit 16.9 presents data on the annual growth rate of the money supply and the rate of inflation for 54 countries during the 1980–1990 period. The results clearly illustrate the linkage between monetary policy and the inflation rate. The annual growth rate of the money supply was less than 6 percent for 11 of

**EXHIBIT 16.8**

**Effect of Changes in Money Supply on Inflation**

Here we illustrate the relationship between the rate of growth in the money supply (M2) and the annual inflation rate *three years later.* While the two are not perfectly correlated, the data do indicate that periods of monetary acceleration (for example: 1971–1972 and 1975–1976) tend to be associated with an increase in the inflation rate about three years later.

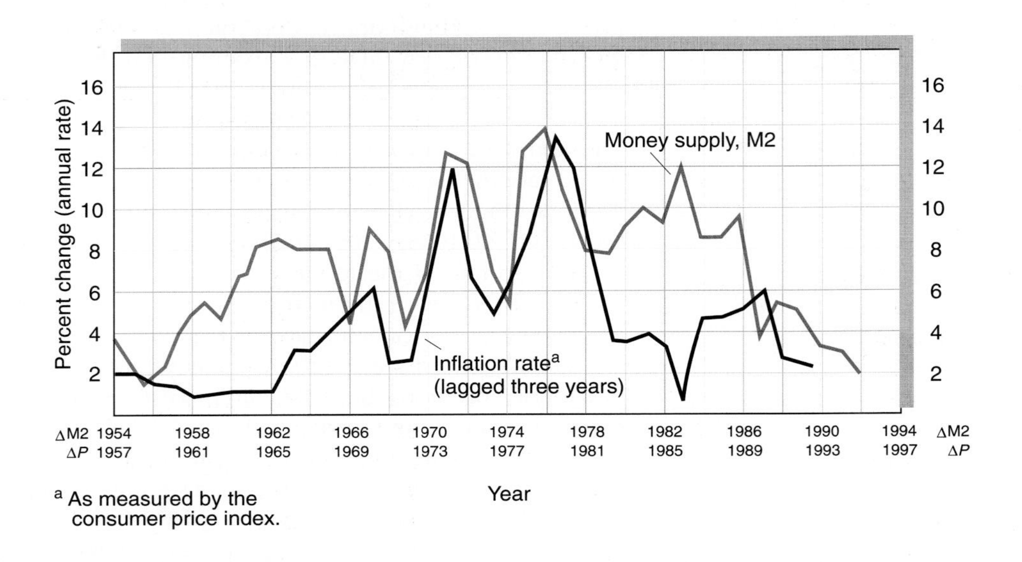


[a] As measured by the consumer price index.

the countries; the accompanying inflation rate of these countries was also less than 6 percent. All 20 countries that expanded the supply of money at a single-digit annual rate during the 1980–1990 period also experienced a single-digit average rate of inflation. In contrast, of the 30 countries that expanded the money supply at an annual rate in excess of 12 percent, all but two (Bangladesh and Indonesia) experienced a double-digit average inflation rate during 1980–1990. Seven countries (Ecuador, Zambia, Ghana, Turkey, Poland, Mexico, and Zaire) expanded the supply of money at annual rates between 30 percent and 70 percent. These seven countries experienced average inflation rates within the same range. Four countries (Brazil, Peru, Argentina, and Bolivia) had triple-digit rates of monetary growth; these four countries also experienced triple-digit annual rates of inflation.

Clearly, the data of Exhibit 16.9 provide strong evidence that in the long run there is a close relationship between monetary expansion and the rate of inflation. Countries that expand the money supply at a slow rate tend to experience low rates of inflation. Conversely, countries that expand their money supply rapidly experience high rates of inflation. This link between rapid monetary growth and inflation is one of the most consistent relationships in all of economics.

Finally, our analysis indicates that monetary stability will help promote economic growth. Exhibit 16.10 presents data on this topic. The countries are rated on the basis of the *stability* of both monetary growth and the price level.

**EXHIBIT 16.9** **Money and Inflation—An International Comparison**

| Country (ranked according to low rate of money growth) | Average Annual Growth Rate of Money Supply 1980–1990[a] | Average Annual Inflation Rate 1980–1990 | Country (ranked according to low rate of money growth) | Average Annual Growth Rate of Money Supply 1980–1990[a] | Average Annual Inflation Rate 1980–1990 |
|---|---|---|---|---|---|
| Germany | 4.0 | 2.7 | Guatemala | 14.9 | 14.6 |
| Cote d'Ivoire | 4.1 | 2.7 | Philippines | 15.2 | 14.9 |
| Netherlands | 4.4 | 1.9 | South Africa | 15.3 | 14.4 |
| United Kingdom | 4.8 | 5.8 | Madagascar | 16.4 | 17.1 |
| Japan | 4.9 | 1.5 | Venezuela | 16.8 | 19.3 |
| United States | 5.0 | 3.7 | Egypt | 16.9 | 11.9 |
| Switzerland | 5.1 | 3.7 | Syria | 17.3 | 14.7 |
| Belgium | 5.1 | 4.4 | Bangladesh | 17.3 | 9.6 |
| Austria | 5.2 | 3.6 | Tanzania | 18.7 | 25.7 |
| Canada | 5.2 | 4.4 | Indonesia | 20.3 | 8.4 |
| Cameroon | 5.6 | 5.6 | New Zealand | 22.1 | 10.5 |
| Pakistan | 7.0 | 6.7 | Dominican Republic | 24.8 | 21.8 |
| Spain | 7.3 | 9.2 | Greece | 25.7 | 18.0 |
| Malaysia | 7.4 | 1.6 | Chile | 27.1 | 20.5 |
| Sweden | 7.6 | 7.4 | Ecuador | 33.5 | 36.7 |
| France | 7.7 | 6.1 | Zambia | 39.4 | 42.3 |
| Hungary | 9.1 | 9.0 | Ghana | 41.8 | 42.7 |
| Australia | 9.4 | 7.4 | Turkey | 46.8 | 43.2 |
| Thailand[b] | 9.5 | 4.2 | Poland | 49.7 | 54.3 |
| Italy | 9.6 | 9.9 | Mexico | 61.4 | 70.4 |
| Kenya | 10.7 | 9.2 | Zaire | 67.3 | 60.9 |
| Korea | 11.3 | 5.1 | Uganda | 84.5 | 107.0 |
| India | 11.4 | 7.9 | Israel | 98.6 | 101.4 |
| Zimbabwe | 12.0 | 10.8 | Brazil[c] | 119.6 | 151.8 |
| Nigeria | 12.7 | 18.2 | Peru | 157.3 | 233.7 |
| Portugal | 13.2 | 18.2 | Argentina | 368.9 | 395.1 |
| Iran | 14.2 | 13.2 | Bolivia | 444.3 | 318.4 |

[a]The money supply data are for the actual growth rate of the money supply minus the growth rate of real GDP. Thus, it is the actual supply of money adjusted to reflect the country's growth rate of real output.

[b]Data are for 1981–1990.

[c]Data are for 1980–1985.

**Source:** World Bank, *World Development Report: 1992* (Washington, DC: World Bank, 1992); and International Monetary Fund, *Monthly International Financial Statistics* (Washington, DC: IMF, 1992). Only countries with a population of more than 6 million in 1992 were included.

**EXHIBIT 16.10**

**The per Capita Growth of GDP for the Ten Countries with the Most Stable and Least Stable Money and Prices During the 1980–1990 Period**

| Countries | Average Annual Growth Rate of Money Supply | Average Annual Inflation Rate | Growth of GDP per Capita 1980–1990 |
|---|---|---|---|
| **Ten Most Stable**[a] | | | |
| Netherlands | 4.4 | 1.9 | 1.4 |
| Japan | 4.9 | 1.5 | 3.5 |
| Germany | 4.0 | 2.7 | 2.0 |
| Malaysia | 7.4 | 1.6 | 2.6 |
| Singapore | 6.9 | 1.7 | 4.2 |
| United States | 5.0 | 3.7 | 2.5 |
| Switzerland | 5.1 | 3.7 | 1.6 |
| Austria | 5.2 | 3.6 | 1.9 |
| Belgium | 5.1 | 4.4 | 1.9 |
| Canada | 5.2 | 4.4 | 2.4 |
| **Average Growth Rate** | | | **2.4** |
| **Ten Least Stable**[a] | | | |
| Nicaragua | 165.0[b] | 432.0 | –5.6 |
| Argentina | 368.9 | 395.1 | –1.7 |
| Bolivia | 444.3 | 318.4 | –2.6 |
| Brazil | 119.6 | 284.4 | 0.5 |
| Peru | 157.3 | 233.7 | –2.6 |
| Uganda | 84.5 | 107.0 | 0.3 |
| Israel | 98.6 | 101.4 | 1.4 |
| Mexico | 61.4 | 70.4 | –1.0 |
| Uruguay | 65.6 | 61.4 | –0.3 |
| Zaire | 67.3 | 60.9 | –1.4 |
| **Average Growth Rate** | | | **–1.3** |

[a]The countries are rated on the basis of the *stability* of money and prices. However, countries with lower growth rates of the money supply and the price level also tend to have less variability in these variables.

**Source:** Derived from International Monetary Fund, *International Financial Statistics Yearbook, 1992.*

[b]Data are for 1980–1987.

The ten countries that followed the most stable monetary policies all experienced a positive growth rate in per capita GDP during 1980–1990. On average, the output per person of these countries expanded at an annual rate of 2.4 percent. Data are also presented for the ten countries that followed the most unstable monetary policies during 1980–1990. Annual rates of inflation in these countries ranged from 60.9 percent in Zaire to 432 percent in Nicaragua. The

APPLICATIONS IN ECONOMICS

## What Caused the Great Depression?

As we previously discussed, the Great Depression exerted an enormous impact both on economic thought and on economic institutions. Prior to and since the Great Depression, business recessions in the United States, as well as in other countries, have reversed themselves after a year or two. The Great Depression, though, was different. Exhibit 16.11 presents the economic record during the period. For four successive years (1930–1933), real output fell. Unemployment soared to nearly one-quarter of the work force in 1932 and 1933. Although recovery did take place during 1934–1937, the economy again fell into the depth of depression in 1938. Ten years after the catastrophe began, real GDP was virtually the same as it had been in 1929.

Why did the economic system break down? Armed with knowledge of how monetary and fiscal policy work, we are now in a position to answer this question. Let us consider four important factors that contributed to the economic collapse of the 1930s.

1. *A sharp reduction in the supply of money during 1930–1933 reduced aggregate demand and real output.* The supply of money expanded slowly but steadily throughout the 1920s.[1] As Exhibit 16.11 shows, monetary policy suddenly shifted in 1930. The supply of money *declined* by 6.9 percent during 1930, by 10.9 percent in 1931, and by 4.7 percent in 1932. Banks failed, and the Fed also failed to act as a lender of last resort to head off the huge decline in the supply of money. From 1929 to 1933, the quantity of money in circulation declined by 27 percent!

What is the predicted impact of a sharp unexpected reduction in the money supply? Our analysis indicates it will lead to reductions both in prices and in real output (see Exhibit 16.4). This is precisely what happened. By 1933 prices were 24 percent below the level of 1929. Real output also plunged. By 1933, real GDP was 29 percent lower than the 1929 level. Changes in the purchasing power of money altered the terms of long-term contracts. During the 1930s, farmers, business people, and others who had signed long-term contracts (for example, mortgages) in the 1920s were unable to meet their fixed money commitments in an economy dominated by falling prices and wages. Bankruptcies resulted. Those trends bred fear and uncertainty, causing still more people to avoid investments involving long-term money commitments. Production and exchange dropped substantially. Gains previously derived from comparative advantage, specialization, and exchange were lost.[2]

2. *A large tax increase in the midst of a severe recession made a bad situation worse.* Prior to the Keynesian revolution, the dominant view was that the federal budget should be balanced. Reflecting the ongoing economic downturn, the federal budget ran a deficit in 1931, and an even larger deficit was shaping up for 1932. Assisted by the newly elected Democratic majority in the House of Representatives, the Republican Hoover administration passed the largest peacetime tax-rate increase in the history of the United States. At the bottom of the income scale, marginal tax rates were raised from 1.5 percent to 4 percent in 1932. At the top of the scale, tax rates were raised from 25 percent to 63 percent.

Our prior analysis of fiscal policy indicates the counterproductiveness of higher tax rates during a

[1] From 1921 through 1929, the money stock expanded at an annual rate of 2.7 percent, slightly less rapidly than the growth in the output of goods and services. Thus, the 1920s were a decade of price stability, even of slight deflation.

[2] For a detailed analysis of the role of monetary policy during the 1930s, see Milton Friedman and Anna J. Schwartz, *A Monetary History of the United States, 1867–1960* (Princeton: Princeton University Press, 1963), particularly the chapter, "The Great Contraction."

*Continued on next page*

(Continued from previous page)

**EXHIBIT 16.11** **The Economic Record of the Great Depression**

| Year | Real GDP in 1989 Dollars (billions) | Implicit GDP Deflator (1929 = 100) | Unemployment Rate | Changes in the Money Supply (M1) |
|---|---|---|---|---|
| 1929 | 821.8 | 100.0 | 3.2 | + 1.0 |
| 1930 | 748.9 | 96.8 | 8.7 | − 6.9 |
| 1931 | 691.3 | 88.0 | 15.9 | −10.9 |
| 1932 | 599.7 | 77.6 | 23.6 | − 4.7 |
| 1933 | 587.1 | 76.0 | 24.9 | − 2.9 |
| 1934 | 632.6 | 82.4 | 21.7 | +10.0 |
| 1935 | 681.3 | 84.8 | 20.1 | +18.2 |
| 1936 | 777.9 | 84.8 | 16.9 | +13.9 |
| 1937 | 811.4 | 89.6 | 14.3 | + 4.7 |
| 1938 | 778.9 | 87.2 | 19.0 | − 1.3 |
| 1939 | 840.7 | 86.4 | 17.2 | +12.1 |

**Source:** Economic Report of the President: 1993, Washington, D.C.: U.S. Government Printing Office, 1993; and Bureau of the Census, *The Statistical History of the United States from Colonial Times to Present* (New York: Basic Books, 1976).

recession. Predictably, the tax increase reduced disposable income and placed still more downward pressure on aggregate demand, which had already fallen sharply in response to the monetary contraction. Simultaneously, the higher marginal tax rates reduced the incentive to earn taxable income. The restrictive fiscal policy further added to the severity of the economic decline. Exhibit 16.11 shows the degree to which this happened. As tax rates were increased in 1932, real GDP fell by 13.3 percent. Unemployment rose from 15.9 percent in 1931 to 23.6 percent in 1932.

3. *Tariff increases retarded international exchange.* Concern about low agricultural prices, an influx of imports, rising unemployment, and declining tax revenues generated public sentiment for trade restraints. Responding to this pressure, the Hoover administration pushed for a substantial increase in tariffs on a wide range of products in early 1930. The tariff legislation took effect in June of 1930. Other countries promptly responded by increasing their tariffs, further slowing the flow of goods between nations. A tariff is, of course, nothing more than a tax on exchanges between parties residing in different countries. Since the increase in tariff rates made such

transactions more costly and reduced their volume, additional gains from specialization and exchange were lost.

The high-tariff policy of the Hoover administration not only retarded the ability of the United States to generate output, it was also ineffective as a revenue measure. The tariff legislation increased the duty (tax) rate on imports into the United States by approximately 50 percent. However, the value of the goods and services imported declined even more sharply. Thus, tariff revenues fell from $602 million in 1929 to $328 million in 1932. Like the monetary and fiscal policies of the era, tariff policy retarded exchange and contributed to the uncertainty of the period.

4. *The stock market crash and the business pessimism that followed reduced both consumption and investment demand.* Economists generally think of the stock market as an economic thermometer. Although it may register the temperature, it is not the major cause of the fever. While historians may exaggerate the importance of the stock market crash of 1929, there is reason to believe that it was of significance. As the stock market rose substantially during the 1920s, business optimism soared. In contrast, as stock prices plummeted, beginning in October of 1929, aggregate demand fell. The falling stock prices reduced the wealth in the hands of consumers. This decline in wealth contributed to the sharp reduction in consumption expenditures in the early 1930s. In addition, the stock market crash changed the expectations of consumers and investors. Both reduced their expenditures as they became more pessimistic about the future. As spending continued to decline, unemployment rose and the situation worsened. Given the impact of both the business pessimism and the perverse policies previously discussed, a minor recession was turned into an economic debacle.

**Could It Happen Again?**

This question was on the minds of many people following the stock market crash of October 1987. Numerous parallels were drawn between the crash of 1929 and the crash of 1987. In both cases, the stock market lost a third of its value in just a few days. But that is where the parallel ends. The Great Depression was the result of disastrous macroeconomic policy, not an inevitable consequence of a stock market crash. The experience following the October 1987 crash illustrates this point. In contrast with the crash of 1929, in 1987 the Fed moved quickly to supply reserves to the banking system. The money supply did not fall. Tax rates were not increased. And even though there was a lot of political rhetoric about "the need to protect American businesses," trade barriers were not raised. In short, sensible policies were followed subsequent to the crash of 1987. Continued growth and stability were the result. Inadvertently, perverse macroeconomic policies were followed subsequent to the crash of 1929. Economic disaster was the result.

There is no law able to guarantee that we will not pursue perverse policies again. However, given our current knowledge of macroeconomics, most economists believe that the likelihood of another Great Depression is remote.

average growth of per capita GDP of these ten countries was *minus* 1.3 percent. Seven of the ten countries experienced declines in per capita GDP. None of the ten was able to achieve even the average growth rate of the countries following stable monetary polices. Just as the theory implies, these data indicate that monetary stability is an important source of economic prosperity.

## LOOKING AHEAD

We are now in a position to begin pulling together our analysis of macroeconomics and consider both the achievable objectives and limitations of macroeconomic policy. Can monetary and fiscal policy accelerate the growth rate of an economy? Can macroeconomic policy smooth the business cycle? And what about the budget deficit and the national debt—how do they influence our future economic health? The next chapter will focus on these issues and related topics.

## CHAPTER SUMMARY

1. Households and businesses demand (hold) money balances because they make it easier to conduct transactions and provide a means of storing purchasing power for the future. The quantity of money demanded is inversely related to the nominal interest rate. The quantity of money supplied is determined by the central monetary authority (the Fed in the United States).
2. A shift to a more expansionary monetary policy will create an excess supply of money. To the extent people respond to their excess money balances by buying more bonds (and other financial assets), real interest rates will decline, which will increase aggregate demand. To the extent people reduce their money balances by spending more on goods and services, aggregate demand will increase directly. Initially, the monetary expansion and increase in aggregate demand will tend to increase output.
3. A shift to a more restrictive monetary policy will create an excess demand for money balances, place upward pressure on the real rate of interest, and reduce aggregate demand. In the short run, the primary effect of a shift to a more restrictive monetary policy is likely to be declining output.
4. Monetary policy is a potential tool of economic stabilization. If the effects of expansionary monetary policy are felt when aggregate output is at less than capacity, then the policy will stimulate demand, and push the economy toward full employment. Correspondingly, if restrictive monetary policy is properly timed, then it can help to control inflation.
5. In the long run, the primary impact of monetary policy will be on prices rather than on real output. Rapid growth in the supply of money is the basic cause of persistent inflation.
6. When expansionary monetary policy leads to rising prices, decision-makers eventually anticipate the higher inflation rate and build it into their choices. As this happens, money interest rates will reflect the expectation of inflation. Thus, money interest rates and the rate of inflation are directly related.

7. Monetary instability and inflation create uncertainty, which makes exchange, capital investments, and long-term contracts more hazardous. Monetary instability also tends to encourage speculation rather than production, and it tends to undermine the credibility of government. Thus, monetary instability tends to deter economic progress and the growth of income. In contrast, monetary stability reduces uncertainty and helps provide an environment conducive to economic growth.
8. Both international comparisons and the U.S. experience strongly indicate that prolonged, rapid growth in the money supply is closely linked with inflation. The international data show that countries with low (high) rates of growth in the money supply tend to experience low (high) rates of inflation. Similarly, the U.S. data illustrate that shifts to rapid monetary growth for an extended period of time are generally followed by an acceleration in the inflation rate.
9. The empirical evidence also indicates that changes in monetary policy influence real GDP in the short run. *Shifts* toward monetary acceleration tend to be associated with a temporary increase in the growth rate of real GDP. Conversely, *shifts* toward monetary contraction have generally been associated with a slowdown in real output.
10. Analysis of the Great Depression suggests that the depth of the economic plunge, if not its onset, was the result of perverse monetary and fiscal policies. The 27 percent reduction in the money supply between 1929 and 1933 is without parallel in United States history. It reduced aggregate demand, changed the intended real terms of time-dimension exchanges, and created enormous uncertainty. The substantial increase in tariffs (taxes on imports) in 1930 and the huge increases in tax rates in 1932 further reduced aggregate demand and the incentive to earn taxable income. Lacking understanding of monetary and fiscal tools, policymakers followed precisely the wrong course during this period.

# *Study Guide*

**CHAPTER**

**16**

# DEVELOPING THE ECONOMIC WAY OF THINKING

## CRITICAL-ANALYSIS QUESTIONS

1. Why do people hold money? How will an increase in the interest rate influence the amount of money that people will want to hold? Are money balances a component of income? Are they a component of wealth?

*2. What is the opportunity cost of (a) obtaining a $100,000 house? (b) holding the house during the next year? (c) obtaining a dollar? and (d) holding the dollar during the next year?

3. Political officials often call on the monetary authorities to expand the money supply more rapidly so that interest rates can be reduced. Nonetheless, the highest interest rates in the world are found in countries that expand the supply of money rapidly. Can you explain these seemingly contradictory facts?

*4. If the supply of money is constant, how will an increase in the demand for money influence aggregate demand?

5. Historically, shifts toward a more expansionary monetary policy have often been associated with increases in real output. Why? Would a more expansionary policy increase the long-term growth rate of real GDP? Why or why not?

6. "Inappropriate monetary and fiscal policy was the major cause of economic instability during the 1930s, and it was the major cause of inflation in the 1970s." Evaluate this view, presenting empirical evidence to defend your position.

7. It is commonly held that the stock market crash caused the Great Depression. Do you think it did? Why or why not? If not, why has the belief that it did been so widely accepted?

*8. "Historically, when interest rates are high, the inflation rate is high. High interest rates are a major cause of inflation." Evaluate this statement.

9. Do you think the monetary authorities should increase or decrease the growth rate of the money supply during the next 12 months? Why or why not?

10. Suppose that the legislators of a country are trying to decide whether a government-provided health care program will be financed with tax revenues or borrowing from the country's central bank. Which of these two options do you think would be best? Why? Why do governments often use "printing press" money rather than taxes to finance government programs?

11. Politicians often blame inflation on greedy businesses, powerful labor unions, or foreigners that raise the prices of the goods or services they supply. Do you think that businesses, labor unions, or foreigners can cause inflation? Why or why not?

*12. "During the last decade, wages and salaries have increased 50 percent. Prices, however, have increased almost as rapidly. In essence, inflation has robbed workers of the pay increases that they earned." Evaluate this statement.

*Asterisk denotes critical-analysis questions for which the answers are given in Appendix A.

## MULTIPLE-CHOICE SELF-TEST

1. The demand curve for money
   a. Shows the amount of money balances that individuals and businesses wish to hold at various interest rates.
   b. Reflects the open market operations policy of the Federal Reserve.
   c. Shows the amount of money that individuals and businesses wish to hold at various price levels.
   d. Reflects the discount rate policy of the Federal Reserve.
2. Starting from an initial long-run equilibrium, an unanticipated shift to more expansionary monetary policy would tend to result in an
   a. Increase in unemployment in the short run, but not in the long run.
   b. Increase in real output in the short run, but not in the long run.
   c. Increase in nominal GDP in the long run, but not in the short run.
   d. Increase in real output in both the long run and the short run.
3. If the Fed *unexpectedly* shifts to a more restrictive monetary policy, which of the following is most likely to occur in the short run?
   a. A decrease in the real interest rate.
   b. A decrease in employment.
   c. An increase in real GDP.
   d. An increase in the inflation rate.
4. "The more money there is in the economy, the more people spend. The more people spend, the higher national income is. Therefore, rapid growth in the supply of money stimulates output and promotes prosperity." This view is
   a. Essentially correct.
   b. Incorrect, because an increase in the supply of money usually does not lead to an increase in spending.
   c. Incorrect, because an increase in spending will usually cause national income to decline rather than rise.
   d. Incorrect, because the real income (and output) of the economy is limited by the economy's productive capacity.
5. A shift to a more restrictive macroeconomic policy in order to halt inflation is likely to cause
   a. An increase in the unemployment rate in the short run.
   b. A reduction in the unemployment rate in the short run.
   c. A reduction in the natural rate of unemployment.
   d. An increase in the natural rate of unemployment.
6. If restrictive macroeconomic policy is going to reduce inflation emanating from excess aggregate demand, *ideally* the policy should be undertaken
   a. When the inflation rate is at its highest level.
   b. When the inflation rate begins to increase.
   c. Before the inflation rate begins to increase.
   d. About 6 months after the inflation rate reaches its peak.
7. Which of the following is the most likely impact of a rapid growth rate of the money supply over a long period of time?
   a. Inflation and rapid growth of real GDP.
   b. Inflation and slow growth, or even a decline, in real GDP.
   c. Declining prices and rapid growth of real GDP.
   d. Declining prices and slow growth, or even a decline, in real GDP.

8. Which of the following is most likely to result from a shift to a more expansionary monetary policy?
   a. A short-run decrease in output and a long-run increase in the inflation rate.
   b. A short-run increase in output and a long-run increase in the inflation rate.
   c. A short-run increase in the inflation rate, but the primary effect will be a larger output rate in the long run.
   d. A short-run decrease in the inflation rate, but the primary effect will be a smaller output rate in the long run.
9. An analysis of countries experiencing rapid rates of inflation indicates that inflation is generally
   a. Caused by strong labor unions.
   b. The result of restrictive macropolicy, which pushes up interest rates.
   c. Caused by the impulse buying of consumers, who continue to purchase the same goods even when prices go up.
   d. The result of the failure of monetary planners to restrict the rate of growth of the money supply to approximately the growth rate of real output.
10. Analysis of the Great Depression indicates that
   a. Even though monetary and fiscal policies were highly expansionary, they were unable to offset the economic plunge.
   b. Even though monetary policy was expansionary, restrictive fiscal policy dominated during the 1930s.
   c. A reduction in tax rates was unable to prevent the economic downturn from spiraling into a depression.
   d. The depth of the economic plunge, if not its onset, was the result of a highly restrictive monetary policy and a major tax increase.

# PROBLEMS

1. The accompanying graphic illustrates a macroeconomy in equilibrium initially at real GDP level $Y_f$ (the full-employment level) and price level $P_1$.

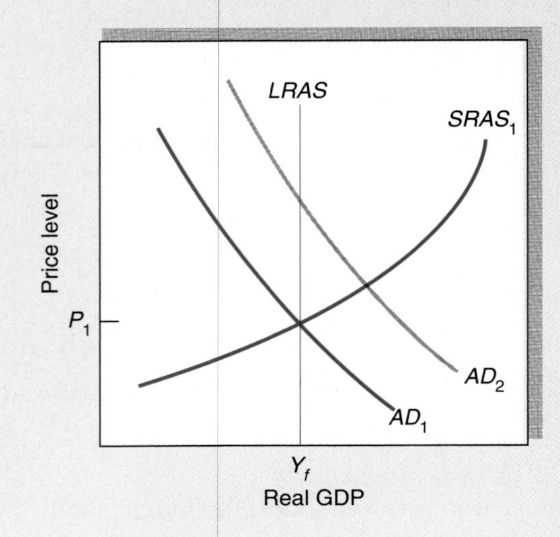

There is no long-run growth of real GDP, and initially the money supply is constant. Therefore, prices are stable at $P_1$. Suppose now that, all else being equal, the Fed increases the money supply at a 5 percent constant rate per period.

a. If the increase in the money supply raises aggregate demand in the second period to $AD_2$, what will be the short-run impact on real GDP and the price level? Explain briefly.
b. Will the change in real GDP you described in part "a" be sustainable in the long run? Explain, modifying the diagram as necessary.
c. What will happen in the long run if there is no growth in real GDP and the Fed continues to increase the money supply so that aggregate demand continues to increase? Explain briefly the process.

2. The accompanying chart presents data on the money supply, price level, and real GDP for three countries during the 1986–1990 period.

| | Money Supply (in billions of local currency) | GDP Deflator (1987=100) | Nominal GDP (in billions of local currency) | Real GDP (1987 currency units) | Rate of Change | |
|---|---|---|---|---|---|---|
| | | | | | Money supply | Price Level |
| **United States** | | | | | | |
| 1986 | 2811.1 | 96.9 | 4268.6 | ____ | X | X |
| 1987 | 2910.8 | 100.0 | 4539.9 | ____ | ____ | ____ |
| 1988 | 3071.1 | 103.9 | 4900.4 | ____ | ____ | ____ |
| 1989 | 3227.3 | 108.5 | 5250.8 | ____ | ____ | ____ |
| **Turkey** | | | | | | |
| 1986 | 12357 | 72.4 | 38172 | ____ | X | X |
| 1987 | 17992 | 100.0 | 56763 | ____ | ____ | ____ |
| 1988 | 27881 | 166.7 | 97929 | ____ | ____ | ____ |
| 1989 | 47958 | 274.0 | 163969 | ____ | ____ | ____ |
| **Argentina** | | | | | | |
| 1986 | 17.8 | 43.9 | 70.1 | ____ | X | X |
| 1987 | 48.4 | 100.0 | 163.5 | ____ | ____ | ____ |
| 1988 | 259.9 | 487.9 | 776.6 | ____ | ____ | ____ |
| 1989 | 5958.4 | 15483.0 | 22892.6 | ____ | ____ | ____ |

**Source:** World Bank: *World Tables, 1992.*

a. Fill in the missing data.
b. Which country followed the most expansionary monetary policy?
c. Which country experienced the highest annual rate of inflation for the years 1987, 1988, and 1989?
d. Which country experienced the most rapid increase in real output during the 1986–1989 period?

CHAPTER

# 17

# THREE KEY MACROECONOMIC POLICY ISSUES: UNEMPLOYMENT, ECONOMIC STABILITY, AND GOVERNMENT DEBT

Inflation does give a stimulus . . . when it starts from a condition that is noninflationary. If the inflation continues, people get adjusted to it. But when people get adjusted to it, when they expect rising prices, the mere occurrence of what has been expected is no longer stimulating.

*Sir John R. Hicks*[1]

## CHAPTER FOCUS

- Can expansionary macroeconomic policy reduce the rate of unemployment?
- Can macroeconomic policy moderate the business cycle? Would the economy be more stable if policymakers merely followed stable policies rather than responding to economic conditions?
- Are budget deficits harmful to the economy? Do they mortgage the future of our children and grandchildren? Why have budget deficits been so large in recent years?

Now that we have analyzed how fiscal and monetary policy work, we are in a position to consider both the potential and limitations of macropolicy. In recent decades, three key issues keep coming up in macroeconomic policy debates. First, there is the issue of employment—can macroeconomic policy stimulate output and employment and thereby reduce the rate of unemployment? Second, there is the issue of stability—what can macroeconomic policy do to reduce the economic ups and downs of the business cycle? Finally, there are concerns about budget deficits and government debt—what impact will growing government debt have on the future economic health of a nation? This chapter will focus on these important issues.

# CAN MACROECONOMIC POLICY PROMOTE GROWTH AND REDUCE UNEMPLOYMENT?

In an influential article published in 1958, the British economist A.W. Phillips noted that there had been an inverse relationship between the rate of change in wages and the unemployment rate for nearly a century in the United Kingdom. When wages were rising rapidly, unemployment was low. Correspondingly, wage rates rose more slowly when the unemployment rate was high.[2] Others noted that a similar inverse relationship was present between inflation and unemployment during the post–Second World War period in the United States. Since it is based on Phillips's earlier work, a curve indicating the relationship between the rate of inflation and the rate of unemployment is known as the **Phillips curve.**

**Phillips curve** A curve that illustrates the relationship between the rate of change in prices (or money wages) and the rate of unemployment.

## Early Views about the Phillips Curve

Phillips did not draw any policy implications from his analysis, but others did. As early as 1959, Paul Samuelson and Robert Solow (each of whom would

[1]J. R. Hicks, "Monetary Theory and Keynesian Economics," in R. W. Clower (ed.), *Monetary Theory* (Harmondsworth: Penguin, 1969), p. 260.

[2]A. W. Phillips, "The Relationship between Unemployment and the Rate of Change of Money Wages in the United Kingdom, 1861–1957," *Economica* 25 (1958), pp. 238–299.

later win a Nobel Prize in economics) argued that we could trade a little more inflation for less unemployment. Samuelson and Solow told the American Economic Association,

> In order to achieve the nonperfectionist's goal of high enough output to give us no more than 3 percent unemployment, the price index might have to rise by as much as 4 to 5 percent per year. That much price rise [inflation] would seem to be the necessary cost of high employment and production in the years immediately ahead.[3]

During the 1960s many leading economists thought that expansionary macroeconomic policy—that is, budget deficits and rapid growth in the money supply—would stimulate output and reduce the rate of unemployment if we were willing to tolerate a little higher rate of inflation. As Exhibit 17.1 indicates, even the prestigious annual *Economic Report of the President* argued that moderate inflation would reduce the unemployment rate.

Beginning in the mid-1960s, both fiscal and monetary policy were more expansionary. Budget deficits were larger and the money supply grew more rapidly. In the latter half of the 1960s, the inflation rate began to creep upward from less than 2 percent in the early 1960s to 3.5 percent in 1966 and 5 percent in 1969. During the 1970s, the inflation rate accelerated to still higher levels.

For a while, it appeared that the more expansionary macroeconomic policies were working as advertised. In the late 1960s the unemployment rate fell to less than 4 percent as the inflation rate increased. Things began to change, however, in the early 1970s. In 1971 the unemployment rate rose to 5.8 percent, while the price level continued to rise at an annual rate of more than 5 percent. By 1975 the unemployment rate had soared to 8.3 percent, even though the inflation rate had accelerated to almost 10 percent. Contrary to expectations, as the inflation rate climbed during the 1970s, the rate of unemployment rose rather than fell.

## How Expectations Are Formed

Why did the early optimistic view concerning the Phillips curve prove to be incorrect? The answer lies in the idea of people's *expectations.* What people think is going to happen in the future is important because it affects the choices that they make in the present. There are two views concerning how people form expectations about the future. The simplest theory of expectations is that people expect the future to be pretty much like the recent past. According to this theory, which economists call the **adaptive expectations hypothesis,** decision-makers believe that the best indicator of the future is what has happened in the recent past. For example, under adaptive expectations, people would expect the price level to be stable next year if stable prices had been present during the last two or three years. Similarly, if prices had risen at an annual rate of 4 or 5 percent during the last several years, adaptive expectations implies that similar increases will be expected next year.

**adaptive expectations hypothesis** The hypothesis that economic decision-makers base their expectations of the future on actual outcomes observed during recent periods. For example, according to this view, the rate of inflation actually experienced during the last two or three years would be the major determinant of the rate of inflation expected for next year.

With adaptive expectations, therefore, past experience determines the future expectations of decision-makers. If the inflation rate has been low (high) in the recent past, individuals will anticipate a continuation of the low (high) rate in the future.

[3]Paul A. Samuelson and Robert Solow, "Our Menu of Policy Changes," *American Economic Review,* May 1960.

**EXHIBIT 17.1**

**The Phillips Curve—Before Inflation of 1970s**

This exhibit is from the 1969 *Economic Report of the President,* prepared by the President's Council of Economic Advisers. Each dot on the diagram indicates, as a coordinate point on the graph, the inflation rate and unemployment rate for the year. The report stated that the chart "reveals a fairly close association of more rapid price increases with lower rates of unemployment." Economists refer to this link as the Phillips curve. In the 1960s, it was widely believed that policymakers could pursue expansionary macroeconomic policies and thereby permanently reduce the unemployment rate. More recent experience has caused most economists to reject this view.

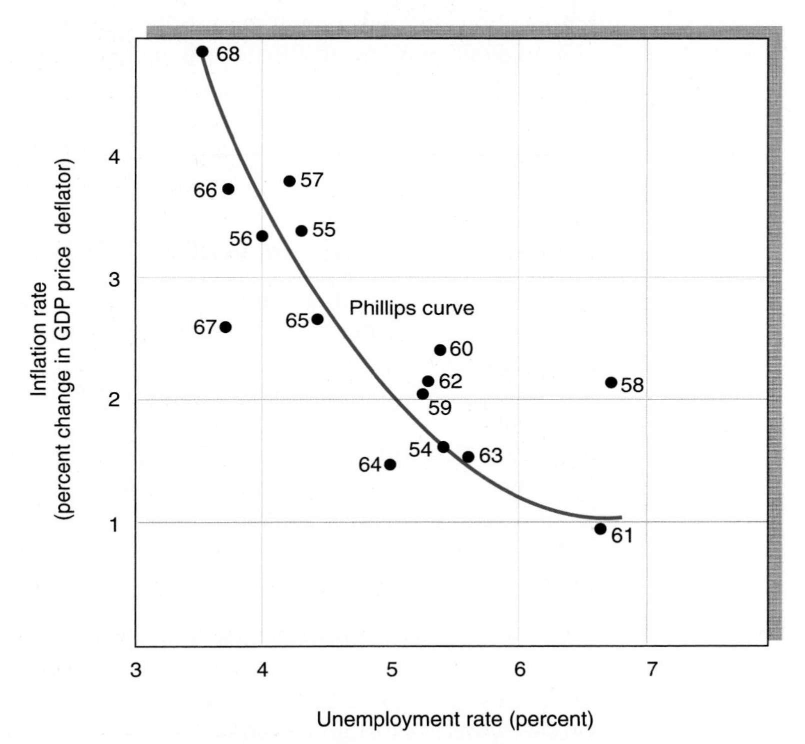


**Source:** *Economic Report of the President, 1969* (Washington, D.C.: U.S. Government Printing Office, 1969), p. 95. The Phillips curve is fitted to the points to illustrate the relationship.

**rational expectations hypothesis** The hypothesis that economic decision-makers base their expectations of the future on all available evidence, including information concerning the probable effects of current and future economic policy, not just on observed actual outcomes in recent periods.

An alternative theory, which economists refer to as the **rational expectations hypothesis,** is based on the idea that all available information, including information about how policy changes affect the economy, will influence the expectations of people. According to this view, rather than merely assuming the future will be pretty much like the immediate past, people also consider the expected effects of changes in policy. Based on their understanding of economic policy, people alter their expectations with regard to the future when the government, for example, runs a larger deficit, expands the supply of money more rapidly, or cuts the size of its expenditures.

Perhaps an example will help clarify the rational expectations hypothesis. Suppose prices had increased at an annual rate of 6 percent during each of the last three years. In addition, let us assume that decision-makers believe there is a relationship between the growth rate of the money supply and rising prices. Individuals note that the money stock has expanded at a 12 percent annual rate during the last nine months, up from the 7 percent rate of the past several years. According to the rational expectations hypothesis, decision-makers will integrate the recent monetary acceleration into their forecast of the future inflation rate. With rational expectations, decision-makers will project an acceleration in the inflation rate, perhaps to the 10 to 12 percent range, since they believe the future inflation rate will respond to the more rapid growth of the money supply.

Contrary to the views of some, the rational expectations hypothesis does not assume that people do not make forecasting errors. Under rational expectations, however, errors will tend to be random. For example, sometimes decision-makers may overestimate the increase in the inflation rate caused by monetary expansion, and at other times they may underestimate it. But, since they learn from prior experience, people will not continue to make *systematic* errors year after year. Consequently, underestimation errors are as likely as overestimation errors.

## Adaptive Expectations and the Phillips Curve

Integration of expectations into the analysis of the Phillips curve helps explain why expansionary macroeconomic policy reduced the unemployment rate during the late 1960s, but failed to do so during the 1970s. As we have previously discussed, a shift to a more expansionary macroeconomic policy—for example, a tax cut or acceleration in the growth rate of the money supply—will increase aggregate demand. As Exhibit 17.2 illustrates, product prices will rise. Since many resource prices are "fixed" in the short run, however, the increase in product prices will initially improve profit margins, providing firms with the incentive to expand output (to $Y_2$) and employment. The unemployment rate will recede below the economy's natural rate. For a time, therefore, the economy will experience both rising prices and an output beyond its full-employment potential (point *B*). Under adaptive expectations, however, this high level of output will not be long-lasting. After a period of time, people will begin to anticipate the rising prices. When this happens, resource prices (and costs) will rise *relative to product prices,* causing the *SRAS* curve to shift to the left. As the previous relationship between resource prices and product prices is restored, output will recede to the economy's full-employment equilibrium level (point *C*).

Exhibit 17.2b illustrates the same case within the Phillips curve framework. Since initially stable prices are present and the economy is in long-run equilibrium, unemployment is equal to the natural rate of unemployment (point *A*). We assume that the economy's natural rate of unemployment is 5 percent. The condition of long-run equilibrium implies that the stable prices are both anticipated and observed. Under adaptive expectations, an unanticipated shift to a more expansionary policy will temporarily increase output and reduce unemployment. It will also place upward pressure on prices. Suppose that demand stimulus policies lead to 4 percent inflation and a reduction in the unemployment rate from 5 percent to 3 percent (move from *A* to *B* along the short-run Phillips Curve $PC_1$). While point *B* is *attainable,* it will not be *sustainable.* After an extended period of 4 percent inflation, decision-makers will begin to anticipate the higher rate of inflation. Workers and their union representatives will take the higher expected rate of inflation into account in their job search

**EXHIBIT 17.2**

**Adaptive Expectations and Phillips Curve**

When stable prices are observed *and* anticipated, both full-employment output and the natural rate of unemployment will be present (*A* in both panels). With adaptive expectations, a shift to a more expansionary policy will increase prices, expand output beyond its full-employment potential, and reduce the unemployment rate below its natural level (move from *A* to *B* in both panels). Decision-makers, though, will eventually anticipate the rising prices and incorporate them into their decision-making. When this happens, the *SRAS* curve shifts to the left, output recedes to the economy's full-employment potential, and unemployment returns to the natural rate (move from *B* to *C* in both panels). Inflation fails to reduce the unemployment rate when it is anticipated by decision-makers. Thus, the *long-run* Phillips curve is vertical at the natural rate of unemployment.

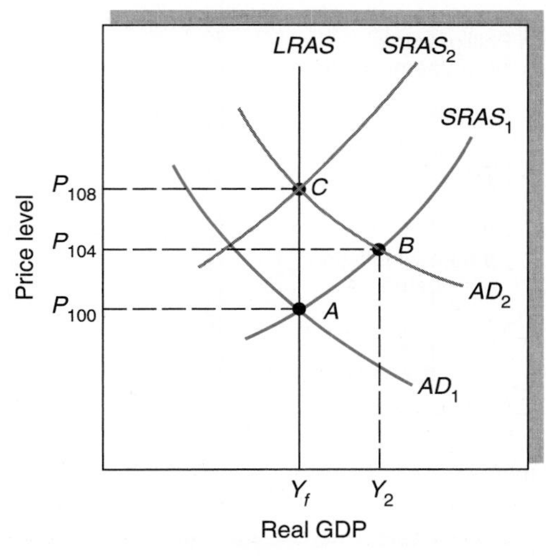

(a) Goods and services market

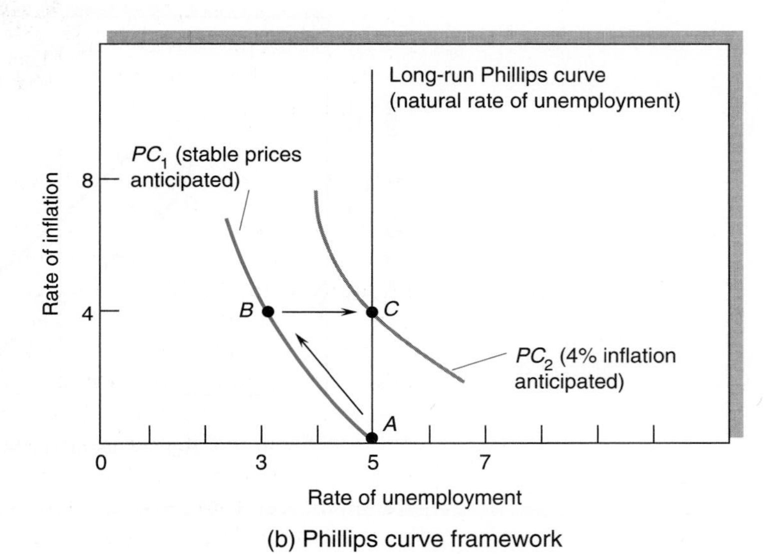

(b) Phillips curve framework

and collective-bargaining decision-making. Once the 4 percent rate of inflation is fully anticipated, the economy will confront a new, higher short-run Phillips curve ($PC_2$). The rate of unemployment will return to the long-run natural rate of 5 percent, even though prices will continue to rise at an annual rate of 4 percent (point *C*).

The moves from *A* to *B* in Exhibits 17.2a and 17.2b are simply alternative ways of representing the same phenomenon—a temporary increase in output and reduction in unemployment as the result of an unanticipated increase in aggregate demand. Similarly, the moves from *B* to *C* in the two panels also represent the same thing: the return of output to its long-run potential and unemployment to its natural rate, once decision-makers fully anticipate the observed rate of inflation.

What would happen if the macroplanners attempted to keep the unemployment rate low (below its natural rate) by shifting to a still more expansionary policy? As Exhibit 17.3 illustrates, this course of action will accelerate the

**EXHIBIT 17.3**

**Adaptive Expectations and Shifts in the Short-Run Phillips Curve**

Continuing with the example of Exhibit 17.2b, point *C* illustrates an economy experiencing 4 percent inflation that was anticipated by decision-makers. Since the inflation was anticipated, the natural rate of unemployment is present. With adaptive expectations, demand stimulus policies that result in a still higher rate of inflation (8 percent, for example) would once again temporarily reduce the unemployment rate below its long-run, normal level (move from *C* to *D* along $PC_2$). After a time, however, decision-makers would come to anticipate the higher inflation rate, and the short-run Phillips curve would shift still further to the right to $PC_3$ (move from *D* to *E*). Once the higher rate is anticipated, if macroplanners try to decelerate the rate of inflation, unemployment will temporarily rise above its long-run natural rate (for example, move from *E* to *F*).

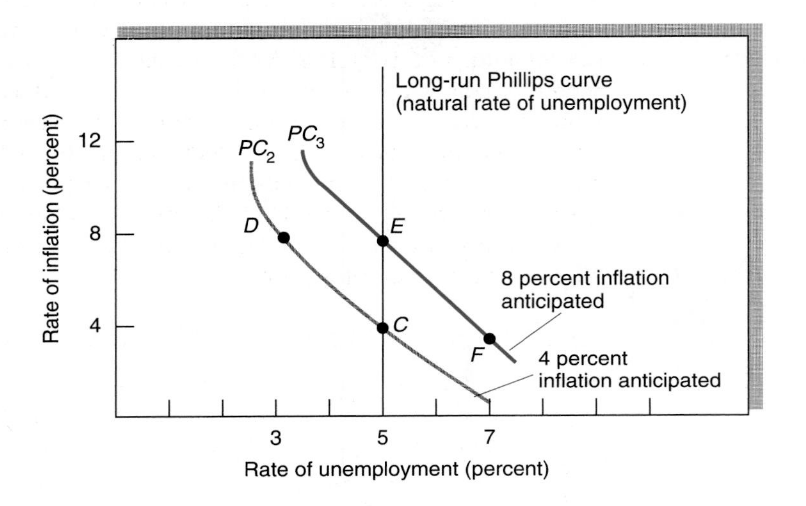


inflation rate to still higher levels. Under adaptive expectations, once the 4 percent inflation rate is anticipated, the rate of unemployment can, for a time, be reduced to 3 percent only if the macroplanners are willing to tolerate 8 percent inflation (movement from *C* to *D*). Of course, once the 8 percent rate has persisted for a while, it, too, will be fully anticipated. The short-run Phillips curve will again shift to the right (to $PC_3$), unemployment will return to its long-run natural rate, and inflation will continue at a rate of 8 percent (point *E*).

Once decision-makers anticipate a higher rate of inflation (for example, the 8 percent rate), what will happen if macroplanners shift to a more restrictive policy designed to reduce the rate of inflation? When the inflation rate is declining, decision-makers will systematically *over*estimate the future inflation rate under the adaptive expectations hypothesis. Suppose that wage rates are based on agreements that anticipated a continuation of the 8 percent inflation rate (point *E* of Exhibit 17.3). If the actual inflation rate falls to 4 percent when 8 percent inflation was expected, the real wages of workers will exceed the real wage present when the actual and expected rates of inflation were equal at 8 percent. The more the actual inflation rate falls short of the expected rate, the higher the real wages of workers. Similarly, the search time of job seekers will be longer when they overestimate the impact of inflation on money wage rates. Unaware that the attractive money wage offers they seek are unavailable, job hunters will lengthen their job search. In the short run, rising unemployment will be a side effect of the higher real wages and more lengthy job searches.

As Exhibit 17.3 illustrates, with adaptive expectations, once a high (8 percent) inflation rate is anticipated by decision-makers, a shift to a more restrictive policy designed to decelerate the inflation rate will cause abnormally high unemployment (the move from *E* to *F* along $PC_3$) and economic recession. The abnormally high unemployment rate will continue until a lower rate of inflation convinces decision-makers to alter their inflationary expectations downward and revise long-term contracts accordingly.

We can now summarize the implications of adaptive expectations for the Phillips curve. Under adaptive expectations, decision-makers will underestimate the future inflation rate when the rate is rising and overestimate it when the inflation rate is falling. As the result of this systematic pattern, a shift to a more expansionary policy will temporarily reduce the unemployment rate, while a move to a more restrictive policy will temporarily increase it. As an inflation rate persists over time, decision-makers will eventually anticipate the rate, and unemployment will return to its natural rate. There is no long-run (permanent) trade-off between inflation and unemployment under adaptive expectations. Like the *LRAS* curve, the long-run Phillips curve is vertical at the natural rate of unemployment.

## Rational Expectations and the Phillips Curve

How would the Phillips curve analysis be altered if the rational expectations hypothesis was correct? In a world of rational expectations, people quickly anticipate the effects of policy changes and adjust their actions accordingly. For example, if people see a surge in the money supply or a tax cut coming, they will adjust their expectations in light of the shift toward expansionary policy. Anticipating the strong future demand, workers and union representatives will immediately press for higher wages and/or inclusion of cost-of-living provisions to prevent the erosion of their real wages by inflation. Business firms, also anticipating the increase in demand, will consent to the demands of labor, but they will also raise prices. By the time the demand stimulus arrives, it will have *already been counteracted* by higher money wages, costs, and product prices.[4] If decision-makers accurately anticipate the inflationary effects of a more expansionary macroeconomic policy, the demand stimulus will merely increase the price level (inflation rate) without altering output or employment.

Of course, rational expectations does not imply that decision-makers are always right. People may either underestimate or overestimate the inflationary effects of the demand stimulus. When they *under*estimate the inflationary effects, the increase in resource prices will lag behind the increase of product prices. As was true under adaptive expectations, output and employment will expand temporarily when people underestimate the inflationary effects of a more expansionary macroeconomic policy.

In contrast, when individuals *over*estimate the increase in inflation, the current unemployment rate will temporarily increase. For example, if

[4]As we discussed in the last chapter, expansionary monetary policy will also increase the expected rate of inflation and lead to a higher money interest rate in the loanable funds markets. The rational expectations hypothesis also implies that money interest rates will rise quickly in response to expansionary monetary policy.

decision-makers expect the inflation rate to rise to 10 percent while the expansionary policies generate an increase to only 8 percent, resource prices will increase even more rapidly than product prices. As a result, profit margins will be squeezed and firms will reduce both output and employment. In the short run, unemployment will rise above its long-run natural rate. Under these circumstances, the effects of the expansionary policy are opposite of what was intended.

How can policymakers know whether rational decision-makers will over- or underestimate the effects of a policy change? According to the proponents of rational expectations, they cannot. If the errors of decision-makers are random, as the rational expectations theory assumes, people will be as likely to overestimate as underestimate the inflationary impact of demand stimulus policies. Under rational expectations, then, the impact of expansionary policy on real output and employment is *unpredictable,* even in the short run. If decision-makers accurately anticipate the inflationary impact of expansionary policy, the unemployment rate will remain unchanged even though the inflation rate accelerates. However, if they underestimate the future inflation impact, the unemployment rate will temporarily decline. Conversely, the unemployment rate will temporarily rise if they overestimate the inflationary impact of the policy.

## Expectations and the Modern View of the Phillips Curve

Expectations substantially alter the 1960s view of the Phillips curve. Demand stimulus policies will reduce the rate of unemployment only when they catch people by surprise. Once people fully anticipate the inflationary side effects of expansionary policies, resource prices will rise, profit margins will return to normal levels, and unemployment will return to its natural rate. Under adaptive expectations, this will happen only after the higher inflation rates have been observed for a period of time, say, a year or so. Under rational expectations, the adjustment process will occur more rapidly. If people accurately anticipate the inflationary effects, the demand stimulus policies may fail to reduce, even temporarily, the unemployment rate when expectations are rational. Perhaps more importantly, in the long run the implications of adaptive and rational expectations are identical—persistent expansionary policy will lead to inflation without permanently reducing the unemployment rate. Neither the adaptive nor the rational expectations hypothesis indicates that expansionary policies can sustain unemployment below its natural rate.

When the inflation rate is steady—when it is neither rising nor falling—the actual rate of unemployment will equal the economy's natural rate of unemployment. If the inflation rate of an economy is constant (or approximately so), decision-makers will come to anticipate the rate. This rate will be reflected in both long-term contracts and the job search of workers. Once this happens, unemployment will return to its natural rate. In fact, the natural rate of unemployment is sometimes defined as the unemployment rate present when the inflation rate is neither rising nor falling (see boxed feature, "The Natural Rate of Unemployment in Europe, Canada, Japan, and the United States").

## The Phillips Curve in the United States, 1961–1992

Once we understand the importance of expectations, the U.S. data on inflation and unemployment in recent decades are understandable. After nearly 20 years of low inflation (and moderate monetary and fiscal policy) following the

Second World War, decision-makers were accustomed to relative price stability. Against this background, the *expected* rate of inflation was low. As a result, the shift toward expansionary policies in the mid-1960s caught people by surprise. Therefore, as Exhibit 17.1 shows, these policies initially reduced the unemployment rate.

Contrary to the popular view of the 1960s, though, the abnormally low unemployment did not last. Exhibit 17.4, which is an updated version of Exhibit 17.1, makes this point clear. Just as our theory predicts, the inflation-unemployment conditions worsened substantially as the expansionary policy persisted. The Phillips curve consistent with the 1970–1973 data ($PC_2$) was well to the right of $PC_1$. During the 1974–1983 period, still higher rates of inflation were observed. As inflation rates in the 6 to 10 percent range became commonplace in the latter half of the 1970s, the Phillips curve once again shifted upward to $PC_3$. As monetary policy tightened in 1981–1983 and the Reagan administration promised to bring inflation under control, the inflation rate

**EXHIBIT 17.4**

**Inflation and Real-World Shifts in the Phillips Curve**

The 1982 *Report of the Council of Economic Advisers* (CEA) contained this unemployment-inflation rate chart. While the 1961–1969 data mapped Phillips curve $PC_1$, as demand stimulus policies led to higher inflation rates, the Phillips curve shifted out to $PC_2$ (for the 1970–1973 period) and $PC_3$ (for the 1974–1982 period). In contrast with the 1969 CEA report (see Exhibit 17.1), the 1982 report stated:

> Nothing in Phillips' works or in subsequent studies showed that higher inflation was associated with sustainable lower unemployment, and nothing in economic theory gave reason to believe that the relationship uncovered by Phillips was a dependable basis for policies designed to accept more inflation or less unemployment.

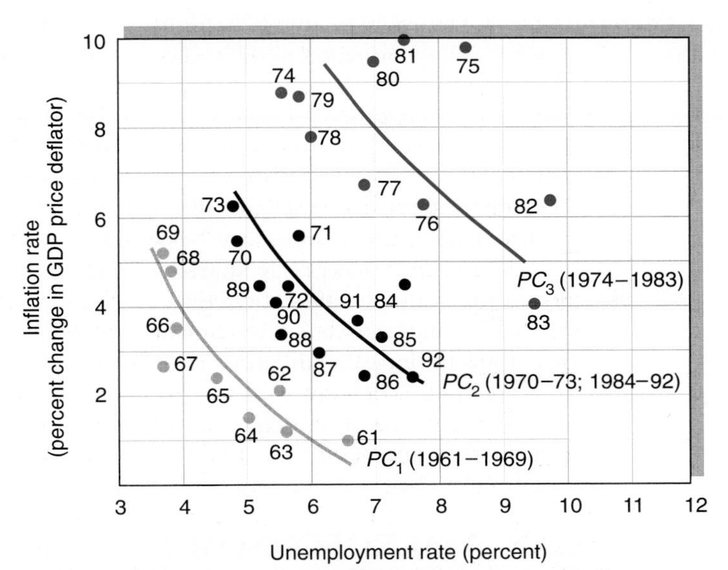


**Source:** *Economic Report of the President, 1982* (Washington, D.C.: U.S. Government Printing Office, 1982), p. 51. The Phillips curves have been fitted and the 1982–1990 data added to the chart.

## THE NATURAL RATE OF UNEMPLOYMENT IN EUROPE, CANADA, JAPAN, AND THE UNITED STATES

Our analysis indicates that when the inflation rate of a country is steady (when it is neither rising nor falling) for an extended period of time, people will anticipate the rate, and unemployment will move to the economy's natural rate of unemployment. Interestingly, the inflation rates in the United States, Canada, Europe, and Japan were quite steady during 1986–1990. The inflation rate averaged approximately 4 percent during 1986–1990 in the United States, Europe, and Canada. More importantly, in each of these areas the inflation rate fluctuated within a narrow band (between 3 percent and 5 percent) during the five-year period. In Japan, the inflation rate was lower, and it was virtually constant at approximately 1.5 percent during 1986–1990.

Given these steady rates of inflation, the actual unemployment rates during the latter part of the period should approximate the natural rate of unemployment for each of these economies. The unemployment rates in 1989 and 1990 were:

| | 1989 | 1990 |
|---|---|---|
| United States | 5.3 | 5.5 |
| Europe (11 EEC Countries) | 7.3 | 7.0 |
| Canada | 7.5 | 8.1 |
| Japan | 2.3 | 2.1 |

Thus, after an extended period of inflation at a steady rate, the unemployment rate during 1989–1990 was approximately 5.5 percent in the United States, approximately 7 percent in Europe, 8 percent in Canada, and 2 percent in Japan. These numbers imply that, compared to the United States, the natural rate of unemployment in the late 1980s was higher in Europe and Canada, but lower in Japan.

Why might the natural rate of unemployment be high in Europe and Canada but low in Japan? There are two major reasons. First, wages tend to be more flexible in Japan, but less flexible in Europe and Canada, than in the United States. Unions in Japan are almost exclusively of the "company union" variety. They seldom set wages for an entire industry, and they are much more likely than their U.S. counterparts to accept wage cuts during a period of declining demand for the products that they produce. Compared to the United States, a decline in demand in an industry in Japan is more likely to result in wage reductions

decelerated sharply in the mid-1980s. Just as our theory predicts, initially the unemployment rate soared, to 9.7 percent in 1982 and 9.6 percent in 1983 (see Exhibit 17.4) as macropolicy shifted toward restraint. However, as the restraint continued, people scaled their expectations for the inflation rate downward, and the Phillips curve shifted inward. As Exhibit 17.4 indicates, during the 1984–1992 period, the inflation rate declined from the high rates of the late 1970s to the 2.5 percent to 4.5 percent range. Soon after the decline in inflation, people began to anticipate the lower rates, and the Phillips curve shifted inward (from $PC_3$ to $PC_2$).

## CAN MACROECONOMIC POLICY REDUCE ECONOMIC INSTABILITY?

There is widespread agreement concerning the goals of macroeconomic policy. Economists of all persuasions believe that the performance of a market economy would be improved if economic fluctuations were minimal, prices and less likely to result in termination and worker layoffs. In contrast, wages tend to be less flexible in Europe and Canada than in the United States. Unionism is more prevalent in Europe and Canada than in the United States. For example, between 40 percent and 50 percent of the nonagricultural labor force is unionized in the United Kingdom, Italy, and Germany.[1] In Canada, 37 percent of the nonfarm workers belong to a union. By way of comparison, only 16 percent of the U.S. nonagricultural labor force is unionized. To the extent that strong unions in Europe and Canada push wages above the market level and reduce wage flexibility, they tend to increase the natural rate of unemployment. In addition, many of the governments in Europe set wages—often at or above equilibrium rates—in various occupations and industries. This, too, contributes to wage rigidity and tends to push the natural rate of unemployment up.

Second, the unemployment compensation system is generally more lucrative (and less restrictive with regard to eligibility) in Europe and Canada than in the United States.[2] This encourages more lengthy periods of job search and thereby pushes up the natural rate of unemployment in Europe and Canada. In contrast, unemployment compensation and other income transfer programs are less lucrative in Japan than in the United States. This, too, contributes to the low natural rate of unemployment in Japan.

Restrictions limiting the mobility of workers and businesses across national boundaries may also contribute to the high unemployment rate in Europe. Many of these barriers are declining with European unification. Thus, it will be interesting to follow the natural rate of unemployment in Europe during the 1990s as the unification process continues.

[1]Richard B. Freeman, "Contraction and Expansion: The Divergence of Private and Public Sector Unionism in the United States," *Journal of Economic Perspectives*, Spring 1988, pp. 63–88.

[2]See Vivek Moorthy, "Unemployment in Canada and the United States: The Role of Unemployment Insurance Benefits," *Federal Reserve Bank of New York: Quarterly Review*, Winter 1990, pp. 48–61.

were stable, and employment were at a high level (keeping unemployment at the natural rate). How to achieve these goals is, however, a hot topic of debate among macroeconomists.

## Activist View

**activist strategy** The view that deliberate changes in monetary and fiscal policy can be used to inject demand stimulus during a recession and apply restraint during an inflationary boom, thereby minimizing economic instability.

Most macroeconomists are proponents of an **activist strategy** in which political officials and other policymakers monitor important economic indicators and modify fiscal and monetary policy accordingly. Activists generally do not believe that a market economy's self-corrective mechanism works very well. Some even charge that market economies are inherently unstable—that both economic expansions and contractions tend to feed on themselves. Other activists—probably the majority—argue that the self-corrective mechanism of a market economy works too slowly. They emphasize that restoration of full employment via lower real wage rates and interest rates is likely to be an unacceptably lengthy process without the prudent use of monetary and fiscal policy to speed it along.

Exhibit 17.5 illustrates the basic idea of the activists' strategy. Ideally, macroeconomic policy would apply demand restraint during an economic

**EXHIBIT 17.5**

**Activists' Countercyclical Policy—Hypothetical Ideal**

Activists believe that macropolicy based on economic conditions can help stabilize the economy. Here we illustrate the hypothetical ideal in which both monetary and fiscal policy restrain demand during an inflationary boom and add stimulus during a recession.

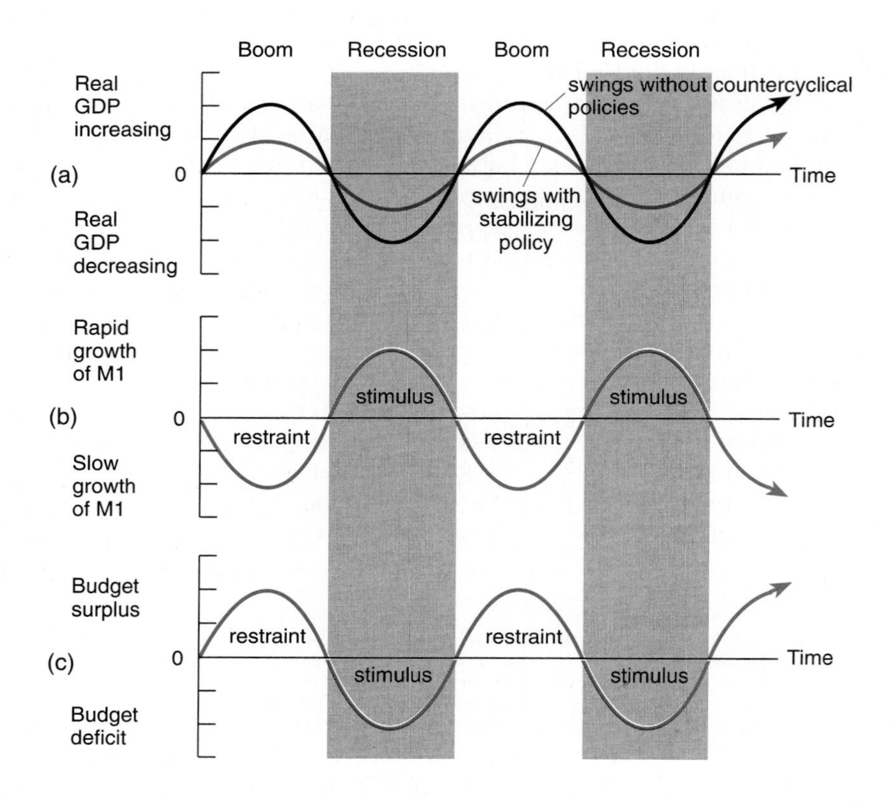


boom and apply demand stimulus during a recession. During an economic boom, then, proper macroeconomic policy would couple a deceleration in the growth rate of the money supply with movement toward a budget surplus (or smaller deficit). This would help restrain aggregate demand and thereby minimize the potential inflationary side effects of the boom. In contrast, when the economy dips into a recession, activist stabilization policy would shift toward stimulus. The money supply would be expanded more rapidly than normal, while budgetary policy would plan a budget deficit. When macroeconomic policy is applied in this manner, it will reduce the swings in real GDP (as illustrated in Exhibit 17.5a) and employment.

If it is going to reduce instability, however, macroeconomic policy must inject stimulus and apply restraint at the proper phase of the business cycle. Proper timing is the key to an effective stabilization policy. Since it takes time for a policy change to work, policymakers need to allow for that lag.

How can policymakers know whether they should be stimulating aggregate demand (in order to combat a recession six or eight months from now) or apply the economic brakes (in order to retard future inflation)? Economic variables such as growth of real GDP, the rate of unemployment, and the consumer price index will provide information on current conditions, but for future conditions a forecasting device is needed. The most widely used such device is the **index of leading indicators,** a composite statistic based on eleven key variables that generally turn down prior to a recession and turn up before the beginning of a business expansion. This index has forecast each of the eight recessions since 1950. Generally, the turndown occurs eight to eleven months prior to a recession, providing policymakers with sufficient lead time to modify policy, particularly monetary policy. Sometimes, though, the lead time is exceedingly short—it was only three months prior to the 1982 recession and only four months prior to the recession of 1954.

**index of leading indicators** An index of economic variables that historically has tended to turn down prior to the beginning of a recession and turn up prior to the beginning of a business expansion.

Worse still, the index is sometimes completely inaccurate as a forecaster. On three occasions (1950–1951, 1962, and 1966) a downturn forecast a recession that never materialized. This has given rise to the quip that the index has accurately forecast eleven of the last eight recessions.

Many activists also believe that auction markets—such as markets for commodities—provide important information about the future direction of inflation. Elaborate computer forecasting models are another source of information, although the record of these models is mixed.

The activists' view holds that the index of leading indicators and other forecasting tools will provide an early warning of impending turns in the economic road, and that, armed with this information, policymakers can modify monetary and fiscal policy in a manner that will reduce the ups and downs of the business cycle.

## Nonactivist View

In contrast to the activist strategy, the **nonactivist strategy** is based on the view that the economy would be more stable if policymakers simply followed stable policies rather than modifying them in response to changing business cycle conditions. Nonactivists argue that the self-corrective mechanism of a market economy works quite well. If it is not stifled by perverse macroeconomic policy, they believe, the self-corrective mechanism will prevent prolonged periods of economic decline and high unemployment. Furthermore, nonactivists charge that the *discretionary* use of monetary and fiscal policy in response to changing economic conditions is likely to do more damage than good. They note that the really serious cases of economic instability, such as the Great Depression and the inflation of the 1970s, were primarily the result of policy errors, not inherent instability of markets. Thus, nonactivists believe that we can best moderate the business cycle by adopting rules and guidelines (for example, a constant growth rate in the money supply and a balanced budget over the business cycle) that provide for stable monetary and fiscal policy, *independent of current economic conditions.*

**nonactivist strategy** The view that the economy would be more stable if macroeconomic policymakers followed stable monetary and fiscal policies rather than modifying these policies in response to changing economic indicators.

Exhibit 17.6 illustrates the difference between the views of the activists and nonactivists. When the economy begins to dip into a recession, activists argue that policymakers can reasonably be expected to recognize the danger and shift to a more expansionary policy at *B*. If the demand stimulus effects are felt quickly (before the economy gets to *C*), the shift to the

**EXHIBIT 17.6** **Time Lags and Effects of Discretionary Policy**

Beginning with *A,* we illustrate the path of a hypothetical business cycle. If a forthcoming recession can be recognized quickly and a more expansionary policy instituted at point *B,* the policy may add stimulus at point *C* and help to minimize the magnitude of the downturn. Activists believe that discretionary policy is likely to achieve this outcome.

However, if delays result in the adoption of the expansionary policy at *C,* and if it does not exert its major impact until *D,* the demand stimulus will exacerbate the inflationary boom. In turn, an anti-inflationary strategy instituted at *E* may exert its primary effects at *F,* just in time to increase the severity of a recession beyond *F.* Nonactivists fear that improper timing of discretionary macropolicy will exert such destabilizing effects.

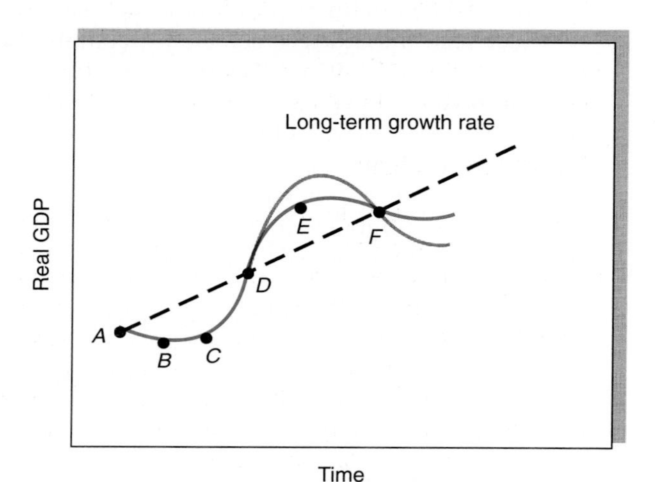


more expansionary macropolicy will help to minimize the decline in output accompanying the business downturn. In contrast, nonactivists believe that policymakers are unlikely to act so quickly, and even if they did, the time lags accompanying changes in monetary and fiscal policies are likely to be both lengthy and unpredictable. Thus, the nonactivists fear that the shift to the more expansionary policy will not come until *C,* and that its *effects* will not be significant until *D.* If this is the case, the expansionary policy will contribute to the severity of the inflationary boom (gray line beyond *D*). Similarly, a subsequent shift to an anti-inflationary policy may begin to exert its major impact at *F,* just in time to make an oncoming recession worse (gray line beyond *F*). Therefore, nonactivists believe that discretionary policy shifts are likely to be destabilizing rather than stabilizing.

Nonactivists point out that monetary instability, in particular, has been a major source of economic instability. Monetary planners have often expanded the money supply more rapidly than the economy's long-term growth rate, and thereby caused inflation. Then, responding to an acceleration in the inflation rate, the monetary authorities have often stepped on the monetary brakes and thrown the economy into a recession. As Milton Friedman stated in an address to the American Economic Association, "Every major contraction in this country has been either produced by monetary disorder or greatly exacerbated by monetary disorder. Every major inflation has been produced by monetary expansion."[5]

Rather than respond to forecasts and current economic indicators, nonactivists recommend that policymakers choose a long-run policy path and pursue it regardless of cyclical ups and downs. With regard to monetary policy, most nonactivists would favor slow, steady growth in the supply of money at an annual rate equal to the economy's long-term growth of real output (approximately 3 percent in the United States). In the areas of fiscal policy they would oppose changes in tax rates or increases in government spending in response to cyclical conditions. The nonactivists theorize that as policymakers stay on a steady course, they will gain credibility. The public will develop confidence in the future stability of the policy. Uncertainty will be reduced, thereby increasing the efficiency of private decision-making. Nonactivists are confident this strategy would result both in less instability and in more rapid growth than Western economies have experienced under more activist policies.

### Consensus View

While it is important to understand the fundamental differences between the activists' and nonactivists' viewpoints, we must not forget that most economists are hybrids, influenced by the analysis of alternative schools of thought. Also, activists and nonactivists actually share a great deal of common ground. Both recognize that the wrong use of policy is a potential source of economic instability. Both are sensitive to the potential destructiveness of policy swings like those that were followed during the 1930s. Similarly, both recognize the uncertainty and inflationary effects of rapid monetary growth.

Compared to their counterparts of the 1960s, economists in the 1990s are more aware of both the limitations and dangers of macroeconomic policy. Macroeconomic policy is a two-edged sword. If properly timed, it can help smooth business ups and downs, but proper timing is not easily achieved, and if the effects of a policy shift are improperly timed, they will be destabilizing. Consequently, fine-tuning, the idea that policymakers can successfully promote stability by responding to each short-term bump in the economic road, has lost most of its luster. Today, most economists favor a policy response only in the case of major cyclical disturbances. Economists of all persuasions are more cautious than they were a couple of decades ago. More stable policies are likely to flow from this caution.

## BUDGET DEFICITS AND NATIONAL DEBT

When the spending of a government exceeds its revenues, a *budget deficit* results. Deficit spending has become a way of life for modern governments. During the 1970s and 1980s, the governments of every major industrial country consistently ran budget deficits. They financed a portion of their expenditures by borrowing rather than taxing. When governments borrow funds, they

[5]Milton Friedman, "The Role of Monetary Policy," *American Economic Review* (March 1968), p. 12.

**national debt** The sum of the indebtedness of the federal government in the form of outstanding interest-earning bonds. It reflects the cumulative impact of budget deficits and surpluses.

generally issue interest-bearing bonds, such as a savings bond, which are sold to private investors. These interest-bearing bonds comprise the **national debt.**

The budget deficit and the national debt are directly related. The deficit is a "flow" concept (like water running into a bathtub), while the national debt is a "stock" figure (like the amount of water in the tub at a point in time). In essence, the national debt represents the cumulative effect of all the prior budget deficits and surpluses. A budget deficit increases the size of the national debt by the amount of the deficit. Conversely, a budget surplus allows the government to pay off bondholders and thereby reduce the size of the national debt.

When analyzing the significance of budget deficits and the national debt, it is important to consider their size relative to the entire economy. Exhibit 17.7 presents data for the United States during the last four decades for both the federal budget deficit and the national debt *as a percent of GDP.* Since the defense effort during the Second World War was financed substantially with debt rather than with taxes, the national debt was quite large at the end of the war. Following the war, the combination of economic growth and small budget deficits reduced the size of the national debt as a percent of GDP. During the 1950–1974 period, budget deficits averaged less than 1 percent of GDP. Historically, real output in the United States has grown at an annual rate of approximately 3 percent. As long as the budget deficit *as a percent of GDP* is less than the growth of real output, the federal debt will get smaller relative to the size of the economy. This is precisely what happened during the 1950–1974 period. By 1974 the national debt had fallen to 34 percent of GDP, down from 89 percent in 1950 (and 127 percent in 1946).

This situation reversed in the mid-1970s. Since 1974, federal budget deficits have been much larger, averaging nearly 4 percent of GDP (Exhibit 17.7a). When the budget deficit as a percent of GDP exceeds the growth of real GDP, the national debt will increase relative to the size of the economy. As Exhibit 17.7 illustrates, this was the case during the 1975–1992 period. Pushed along by the large budget deficits of the 1980s, the national debt expanded to 68 percent of GDP in 1992, up from 34 percent in 1974.

## Who Owns the National Debt?

As Exhibit 17.8 illustrates, the biggest share of the national debt (55.4 percent) is held internally by U.S. citizens and private institutions, such as insurance companies and commercial banks. Foreigners hold approximately one-eighth of the total.

**external debt** The portion of the national debt owed to foreign investors.

The portion owned by foreigners is sometimes referred to as **external debt.** Currently, 25 percent of the debt is held by agencies of the federal government. For example, social security trust funds are often used to purchase U.S. bonds. When the debt is owned by a government agency, it is little more than an accounting transaction indicating that one government agency (for example, the Social Security Administration) is making a loan to another (the U.S. Treasury). Even the interest payments, in this case, represent little more than an internal government transfer.

Approximately 7 percent of the public debt is held by the Federal Reserve System. As we have previously discussed, when the Fed purchases U.S. securities, it creates money. The bonds held by the Fed, therefore, are indicative of prior government expenditures that have been paid for with "printing press" money—money created by the central bank. As in the case of the securities

**EXHIBIT 17.7**

**Budget Deficits and the National Debt as a Percent of GDP**

Throughout most of the 1950s and 1960s, federal budget deficits were small as a percent of GDP, and occasionally the government ran a budget surplus (frame a). During this period, the national debt declined as a proportion of GDP (frame b). Since 1974, however, the budget deficits have been quite large, larger (as a percent of GDP) than the growth of real GDP. As a result, the national debt has increased as a percent of GDP in recent years.

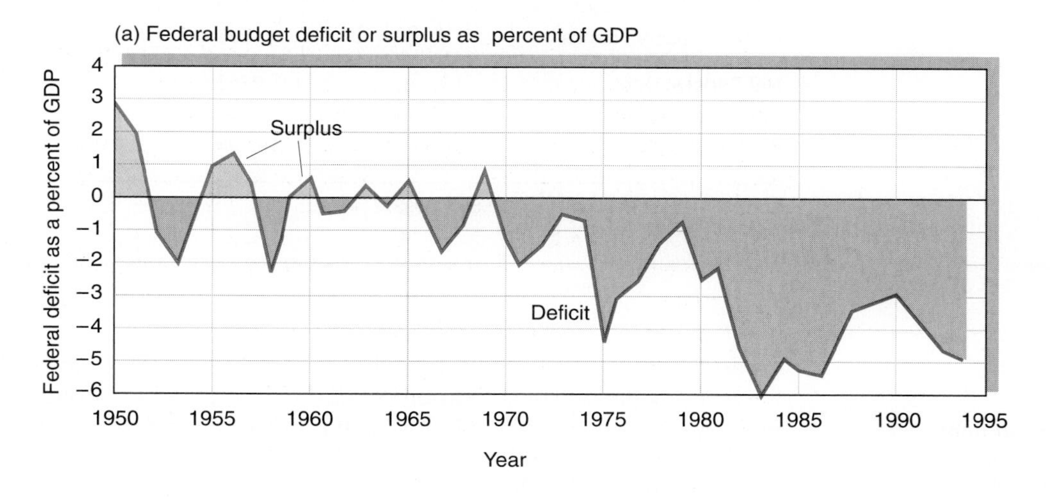


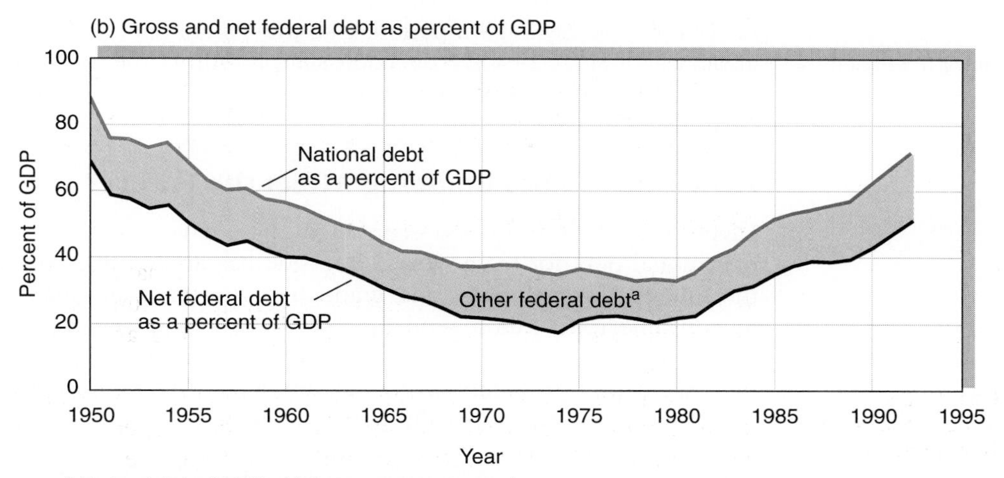


[a] Federal debt held by U.S. government agencies and Federal Reserve banks.

held by government agencies, the interest on the bonds held by the Fed is returned to the Treasury after the Fed has covered its costs of operation.

Since the government both pays and receives the interest on the bonds held by government agencies and the Federal Reserve (minus Fed expenses), these bonds do not represent a net interest obligation. Only the bonds held by

**EXHIBIT 17.8** **Ownership of the National Debt (September 30, 1992)**

| Ownership of U.S. Securities | Dollar Value (in billions) | Percent of National Debt |
|---|---|---|
| **Total National Debt** | $4065 | 100.0 |
| U.S. government agencies | 1016 | 25.0 |
| Federal Reserve banks | 296 | 7.3 |
| **Net Federal Debt** | 2753 | 67.7 |
| Domestic investors | 2254 | 55.4 |
| Foreign investors | 499 | 12.3 |

**Source:** *Federal Reserve Bulletin,* March 1993.

**net federal debt** The portion of the national debt owed to domestic and foreign investors. It does *not* include bonds held by agencies of the federal government or the Federal Reserve.

domestic and foreign investors will require additional taxes to meet future net interest payments. Thus, the portion of the debt owed to domestic and foreign investors is sometimes referred to as the **net federal debt** (or *net public debt*). As Exhibit 17.8 illustrates, the net federal debt accounted for 67.7 percent of the national debt in 1992.

Exhibit 17.7b presents data on the size of the net federal debt as a percent of GDP for the 1950–1992 period. Like the overall national debt, the net federal debt as a share of GDP declined sharply during the 1950s and moderately during the 1960–1974 period. However, since 1974, it too, has been rising as a percent of GDP.

## How Does Debt-Financing Affect the Future?

Laypersons, politicians, and economists alike have debated about the burden of national debt for many years. One side has argued that we are mortgaging the future of our children and grandchildren—that debt-financing permits us to consume today, then send the bill to future generations. The other side, noting that most of the national debt is held by domestic citizens and government agencies (see Exhibit 17.8), has retorted, "we owe it to ourselves."

Does debt-financing really permit us to have a party today and send the bill to our grandchildren? Clearly, this view overstates the case. The ability of debt to shift the cost of government into the future is limited. In the United States, most of the government debt is owed to Americans. Future generations of Americans will have to pay higher taxes in order to meet the interest payments on the national debt. At the same time, however, most of the interest income will also be received by future generations of Americans. Thus, in the case of domestically held debt, our children and grandchildren will both pay the taxes to service the debt and receive the interest payments.

When current resources are used to produce government services, these resources are not available to produce other things. This will be true regardless of whether the government finances these services with debt or taxes. For example, when the government builds a highway, it draws resources with alternative uses away from the private sector. *Current* output of goods for private consumption and investment will decline as a result of the government's use of resources. This cost is incurred in the present; debt-financing cannot push it into the future.

If the opportunity cost of resources occurs during the current period, does this mean that there is little reason to be concerned about an adverse impact of deficits on future generations? Not necessarily. Debt-financing influences future generations primarily through its potential impact on saving and capital formation. If the current generation bequeaths lots of factories, machines, houses, knowledge, and other productive assets to its children, then the productive potential of the next generation will be high. Alternatively, if fewer productive assets are passed along to the next generation, then its productive capability will decline accordingly. Thus, the true measure of how government debt influences future generations involves knowledge of its impact on capital formation.

The impact of budget deficits on capital formation and the welfare of future generations is a complex issue. There are two broad alternative theories. Most embrace the traditional one, that deficits push interest rates upward, crowd out private investment, and thereby reduce the stock of capital assets that will be available to Americans in the future. According to this view, people will tend to treat their additional holdings of government bonds (used to finance the debt) as wealth. After all, the bonds represent future income to their holders. On the other hand, proponents of the traditional view argue that it is absurd to believe that taxpayers think through the implications of the budget deficit for their future taxes. If bondholders recognize the asset value of the government bonds while taxpayers fail to recognize fully the accompanying tax liability, then the general populace will have an exaggerated view of its true wealth position. Wealth is an important determinant of consumption. With an exaggerated view of their wealth, people will consume more and save less than they would otherwise. Given the high consumption and low saving rates, the strong government demand for loanable funds to finance its deficit will push real interest rates upward. In turn, the higher interest rates will crowd-out private investment and reduce the growth rate of the capital stock. Since future generations will inherit less capital (fewer productivity-enhancing tools and machines), their productivity and wages will be lower than would have been the case had the budget deficits not crowded out private investment. Thus, according to the traditional view, budget deficits will retard the growth rate of income and thereby reduce the living standard of future generations of Americans.

An alternative view of debt-financing, most closely associated with Robert Barro of Harvard University, stresses that additional debt implies an equivalent amount of future taxes. If, as the new classical model of fiscal policy assumes, individuals fully anticipate the added future tax liability accompanying the debt, current consumption will be unaffected when the taxes are levied. According to this view, if future taxes (debt) are substituted for current taxes, then people will save the reduction in current taxes so that they will have the required income to pay the higher future taxes implied by the additional debt. As a result, the increase in the demand for loanable funds emanating from the budget deficit is offset by an equivalent increase in private saving. Therefore, neither real interest rates nor private investment is altered. Since capital formation is unaffected, the substitution of debt for taxes does not affect the welfare of future generations in the new classical model. To date, most economists believe that the empirical evidence is more consistent with the traditional view. The issue, however, is by no means resolved, and empirical work continues in this area.

## Could Budget Deficits Cause Economic Collapse?

Some people fear that economic collapse is imminent if the size of the budget deficit is not reduced. When considering this issue, it is important to recognize that borrowing is a standard method of doing business. Many large and profitable corporations continually have debt outstanding. As long as the net income of a business firm is large relative to its interest liability, the outstanding debt poses little problem. So it is with the federal government. As long as people have confidence that it can raise the tax revenue necessary to meet its debt obligations, the federal government will have no trouble financing and refinancing its outstanding debt.

Thus, the key to creditworthiness is expected future income relative to interest liability. This is true for individuals, private businesses, and governments. What is happening to the creditworthiness of the U.S. federal government? In the late 1940s, approximately 10 percent of U.S. federal revenues went to pay the interest on the national debt. As Exhibit 17.9 illustrates, net

**EXHIBIT 17.9**

**Net Interest Cost as Percent of Government Revenues, 1950–1992**

During the period from 1950 to 1975, the net interest cost of the federal government consumed approximately 7 percent of federal revenues. By 1980 the ratio had jumped to 10 percent, and by 1992 it had risen to 18.5 percent. Obviously, interest costs cannot continue to increase as a share of federal revenue.

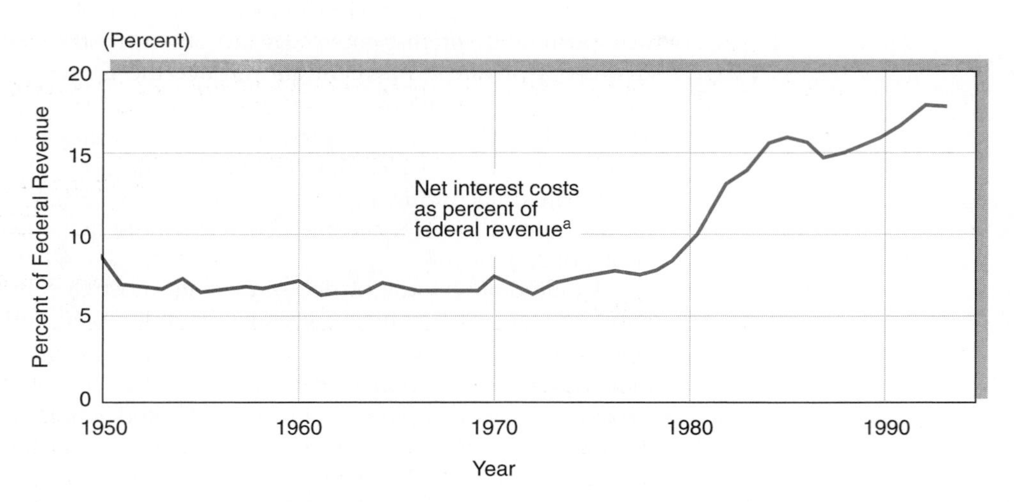


[a] The net interest costs include only the interest paid to private investors. The interest on debt held by federal government agencies and Federal Reserve banks is omitted.

**Source:** *Economic Report of the President* (various issues).

interest costs were approximately 7 percent of federal revenues throughout the 1951–1974 period. Since that time, interest costs as a share of federal revenues have risen, soaring to 10 percent in 1980, 14 percent in 1983, and 18.5 percent in 1992.

This is a trend that cannot continue, at least not without serious consequences. If the interest costs continue to rise relative to federal revenues, people will become increasingly fearful that the government might resort to "printing press" money in an effort to escape its loan obligations. If this should happen, the fear of rapid money growth and inflation would push interest rates up and make it even more difficult for the government to meet its debt obligations. If sufficiently intense, the fear of inflation alone could seriously disrupt the long-term capital market, not only for the federal government, but for other borrowers as well. And if the government did resort to "printing press" money in order to pay off its debt, hyperinflation and a breakdown in the exchange system would result. The economy would be severely crippled.

Excessive debt has led to financial crises elsewhere. The economies of several countries, including Bolivia, Argentina, Chile, Brazil, and Israel have been ravaged in recent years by excessive debt, money creation, and runaway inflation. If the interest liability of the federal government continued to grow more rapidly than revenues, clearly the United States would not be immune to such an occurrence.

## Budget Deficits in Other Countries

The United States has not been alone in its reliance on deficit financing. As Exhibit 17.10 shows, other industrial countries have also run substantial deficits in recent years. When all levels of government are considered, only Japan and the United Kingdom ran surpluses during the 1988–1992 period. As a share of the economy, except for Italy, the central governments of the seven industrial

**EXHIBIT 17.10** **Budget Deficits of Seven Industrial Countries, 1988–1992**

| | Average Budget Deficit as a Percent of Economy 1988–1992 | |
|---|---|---|
| **Country** | **All Government Units** | **Central Government Only** |
| Canada | –3.7 | –3.4 |
| United States | –2.4 | –3.1 |
| Japan | +2.7 | –1.0 |
| France | –1.4 | –1.5 |
| Germany | –2.4 | –1.7 |
| Italy | –10.1 | –10.6 |
| United Kingdom | +0.3 | –1.5 |

**Source:** International Monetary Fund, *World Economic Outlook,* October 1992, tables A16, A17.

nations ran deficits of similar size as a share of their economies. Compared to other industrial countries, Italy has consistently run large budget deficits. In recent years, the expenditures of the Italian government have exceeded revenues by 20 to 30 percent. During the 1988–1992 period, the budget deficits of the Italian government summed to more than 10 percent of GDP.

## The Politics of Budget Deficits

Why do governments around the world use debt to finance expenditures? Many *public choice economists,* including the 1986 Nobel laureate James Buchanan, believe that their analysis provides the answer. Buchanan and others charge that politicians like to spend money in order to buy the favor of various interest groups and voting blocs, but they dislike taxes that impose visible costs on voting constituents. However, government expenditures must be financed in some manner. Borrowing provides an alternative to current taxation. Since they push the taxes into the future, deficits are less visible to people than current taxation. In essence, the substitution of debt for taxes permits politicians to conceal the full cost of government from voters. People imagine that government services cost less than is really the case. Thus, borrowing allows politicians to supply voters with *immediate* benefits without having to impose a parallel visible cost in the form of higher taxes or user charges.

Prior to the Keynesian analysis of the Great Depression, almost everyone thought that the government should balance its budget. The Keynesian revolution changed opinions, first among economists and later among non-economists. In essence, the Keynesian view eroded the discipline that emanated from the implicit balanced-budget concept. Released from the balanced-budget constraint, politicians consistently spend more than they are willing to tax.

Public choice analysis explains why each representative has a strong incentive to fight hard for expenditures beneficial to his or her constituents and little incentive to oppose spending by others. A legislator who is a spending "watchdog" will incur the wrath of colleagues favoring special programs for their districts. More importantly, the benefits (for example, tax reductions and lower interest rates) of spending cuts and deficit reductions will be spread thinly among the voters in all districts. Thus, the legislator's constituents will reap only a small part of these benefits.

It is as if 535 families go out to dinner knowing that after the meal each will receive a bill for 1/535th of the cost. No family feels compelled to order less, because their restraint will exert little impact on the total bill. Why not order shrimp for an appetizer, entrees of steak and lobster, and a large piece of cheesecake for dessert? After all, the extra spending will add only a few pennies to each family's share of the total bill. However, when everybody follows this course of action, many items are purchased that are valued less than their cost.[6]

Budget deficits are a natural outgrowth of the current political structure. Reducing the deficit will probably require some structural modifications that

[6]As E. C. Pasour, Jr., of North Carolina State University, has pointed out to the authors, the federal "dinner check" analogy can be carried one step further. Suppose the check is to be divided evenly among the large group, but the ordering will be done by committee so there will be separate committees for drinks, appetizers, entrees, salads, and desserts. Since each person can serve on the committees of his (or her) choice, lushes end up on the drinks committee, vegetarians on the salad committee, sweet-tooths on the dessert committee, and so on. This arrangement further exacerbates the tendency toward over-ordering and over-spending. The arrangement just described closely resembles the committee structure of the U.S. Congress.

will make it more difficult for politicians to spend more than they are willing to tax. There are several ways this might be done. The Constitution might be amended to require the federal government to balance its budget, even as most state governments are required to balance their budgets. A constitutional amendment requiring two-thirds or three-fourths approval of both houses for spending proposals and increases in the federal government's borrowing power might be sought. This year's spending might be limited to last year's level of revenues. Proposed rule changes of this type would make it more difficult for legislators to spend, unless they were willing to tax or charge for the government services. Such rule changes would stiffen the government's budget constraint, discourage "pork barrel" spending, and force both legislators and voters to consider more carefully the cost of government programs.

## LOOKING AHEAD

In our modern world, trade is often between people who live in different countries. The next two chapters will focus on international trade and accompanying issues that arise from it.

## CHAPTER SUMMARY

1. The Phillips curve indicates the relationship between the unemployment rate and the inflation rate. Prior to the 1970s, there was a widespread belief that higher inflation would lower the rate of unemployment. This was not the case during the 1970s. As the inflation rate rose during the 1970s, so, too, did the rate of unemployment.
2. There are two major theories as to how expectations are formed: (a) the adaptive expectations hypothesis and (b) the rational expectations hypothesis. According to the adaptive expectations hypothesis, individuals base their expectations for the future on observations of the recent past. Expectations for the future will lag behind observed changes. The rational expectations hypothesis assumes that people use all pertinent information, including data on the conduct of current policy, when formulating their expectations about the future. While decision-makers make forecasting errors under rational expectations, the errors are not systematic. That is, they are equally likely to either overestimate or underestimate the future change in an economic variable.
3. Integration of expectations into macroeconomics makes it clear why inflation will not reduce the unemployment rate, at least not for very long. With adaptive expectations, expansionary macroeconomic policies will temporarily reduce the unemployment rate, but eventually people will come to expect the higher rate of inflation and alter their decisions accordingly. Once people expect a given inflation rate, it will fail to reduce the rate of unemployment.
4. With rational expectations, there is no consistent unemployment-inflation trade-off, even in the short run. The impact of expansionary macropolicy is unpredictable. If decision-makers accurately forecast the inflationary effects, expansionary policies will cause inflation while leaving the

unemployment rate unchanged. However, if expansionary policy leads to an increase in inflation that exceeds (is less than) the expected increase, unemployment will temporarily fall below (rise above) its long-run normal level.

5. There is no evidence that in the long run inflationary policies can reduce the unemployment rate—that inflation can be "traded off" for unemployment. Neither the adaptive nor the rational expectations hypothesis indicates that expansionary policy can sustain unemployment below its natural rate.
6. Proponents of an activist macroeconomic strategy argue that the self-corrective mechanism of a market economy is unreliable and works slowly. Thus, discretionary policy modifications can help stabilize aggregate demand, stimulating the economy when it is threatened by recession and restraining it during an inflationary boom.
7. Nonactivists stress that inability to accurately forecast the future and quickly modify macroeconomic policy, along with uncertainty as to when a policy change will exert its primary impact, substantially reduce the effectiveness of discretionary policy as a stabilization tool. Nonactivists argue that policy shifts in response to business cycle conditions are likely to do more harm than good. Nonactivists believe that stability would be enhanced if policymakers simply pursued stable, predictable policies.
8. Despite their differences, activists and nonactivists agree on several important points. Both agree that (a) it is more difficult to properly time stabilization policy than was generally perceived during the 1960s, (b) past errors have contributed to economic instability, and (c) it is a mistake for policymakers to respond to minor changes in economic indicators.
9. The national debt is the sum of the outstanding bonds of the government. Budget deficits increase the national debt. In fact, the national debt reflects the cumulative effect of all prior budget deficits and surpluses.
10. Approximately one-third of the national debt is owned by U.S. government agencies and Federal Reserve banks. For this portion of the debt, the government both pays and receives (except for the expenses of the Fed) the interest. Therefore, only the net federal debt—the portion of the national debt owned by domestic and foreign investors—generates a net interest liability for the government. Most of the net federal debt is owed to domestic investors.
11. Budget deficits affect future generations through their impact on capital formation. When an economy is operating below capacity, a budget deficit may stimulate output and expand the stock of future capital assets available to future generations.
12. According to the traditional view, the substitution of debt-financing for taxes during normal times will indirectly alter the composition of private spending toward consumption and away from investment. Since households are unlikely to recognize fully the future taxes implied by the government's outstanding bonds, they will tend to view the securities as wealth, and therefore have an exaggerated view of their true wealth position. As a result, they will consume more and invest less than if government were fully financed by current taxation. The reduction in investment

will reduce the amount of physical capital inherited by future generations, and thereby adversely affect their standard of living.

13. In contrast with the traditional view, the new classical theory argues that households will anticipate fully the added future tax liability implied by debt-financing and increase their savings in order to meet the higher future taxes. This increase in saving offsets the increase in demand for loanable funds emanating from the debt. In the new classical model, the substitution of debt for taxes leaves interest rates, consumption, and investment unaffected.
14. Many public choice economists believe that the current budget process is structurally unsound. They argue that it encourages debt-financing and fails to confront Congress with a firm budget constraint. These economists believe that structural changes are necessary to deal with the "budget problem."

*Study Guide*

CHAPTER

# 17

## DEVELOPING THE ECONOMIC WAY OF THINKING

## CRITICAL-ANALYSIS QUESTIONS

*1. Prior to the mid-1970s, many economists thought a higher rate of inflation would reduce the rate of unemployment. Why? How does the modern view of the Phillips curve differ from the earlier view?

2. After a period of persistent inflation, such as was experienced in the United States during the 1974–1981 period, most economists believe that a shift to restrictive monetary policy to reduce the inflation rate will cause a recession. Why? How could the monetary authorities minimize the danger of a severe, lengthy recession?

3. State in your own words the adaptive expectations hypothesis. Explain why adaptive expectations imply that macroacceleration will only temporarily reduce the rate of unemployment.

*4. How would you expect the actual unemployment rate to compare with the natural unemployment rate in the following cases?
   a. Prices are stable and have been stable for the last four years.
   b. The current inflation rate is 3 percent, and this rate was widely anticipated more than a year ago.
   c. Expansionary policies lead to an unexpected increase in the inflation rate from 3 percent to 7 percent.
   d. There is an unexpected reduction in the inflation rate from 7 percent to 2 percent.

*5. Why do most nonactivists favor a monetary rule such as expansion of the money supply at a constant annual rate? What are some of the potential problems with a monetary rule? Do you think a monetary rule could be devised that would reduce economic instability? Why or why not?

6. "The Great Depression indicates that the self-correcting mechanism of a market economy is weak and unreliable." Evaluate.

7. Evaluate the effectiveness of monetary and fiscal policy during the last three years. Has it helped to promote stable prices, rapid growth, and high employment? Do you think policymakers have made mistakes during this period? If so, indicate why.

8. Compare the views of activists and nonactivists with regard to the following points: (a) the self-stabilizing characteristics of a market economy; (b) the ability of policymakers to forecast the future; (c) the validity of the rational expectations hypothesis; and (d) the use of rules versus discretion in the institution of monetary and fiscal policy.

*9. Does the national debt have to be paid off at some time in the future? What will happen if it is not?

10. "The national debt is a mortgage against the future of our children and grandchildren. We are forcing them to pay for our current consumption of goods and services." Evaluate.

*11. If citizen-taxpayers fail to anticipate the future tax liability accompanying debt-financing, what does this imply about their perception of the cost of government? How do you think this affects the political popularity of debt-financing relative to taxes?

*Asterisk denotes critical-analysis questions for which the answers are given in Appendix A.

*12. Even if it were unable or unwilling to raise taxes in order to meet the interest payments on outstanding debt, the federal government would be unlikely to default on its outstanding bonds. Why? What would happen in the event of such a crisis?

13. Are the large deficits of the federal government a threat to our economy? Why or why not? Would our economy be healthier if taxes were raised sufficiently to generate a substantial budget surplus? Why or why not?

## MULTIPLE-CHOICE SELF-TEST

1. If a shift to a more expansionary monetary policy leads to an unanticipated acceleration in the inflation rate, then
   a. The actual rate of unemployment will decline in the short run.
   b. The natural rate of unemployment will decline.
   c. The real interest rate will rise in the short run.
   d. The nominal interest rate will fall in the long run.
2. The Phillips curve depicts the relationship between
   a. The rate of change in the money supply and the rate of change in unemployment.
   b. Wage rates and aggregate demand.
   c. The equilibrium level of income and the employment rate.
   d. The rate of inflation and the rate of unemployment.
3. The view that the current expectations of decision-makers about the future are based on the actual outcomes observed during the recent past is called the
   a. Rational expectations hypothesis.
   b. Adaptive expectations hypothesis.
   c. Permanent income theory.
   d. Phillips curve theory.
4. In terms of the Phillips curve, the experience of the 1970s indicates that macropolicy
   a. Can permanently reduce the rate of unemployment, if we are willing to tolerate a higher rate of inflation.
   b. Can reduce the unemployment rate in the long run, if we are willing to tolerate a higher rate of inflation.
   c. May be able to reduce the unemployment rate, but cannot retard the rate of inflation.
   d. May be able to reduce the unemployment rate in the short run, but there is little evidence that expansionary policies can reduce the rate of unemployment permanently.
5. Which of the following is the major area of disagreement between activists and nonactivists?
   a. Activists believe that discretionary macroeconomic policy can be applied in a manner that will lead to greater economic stability than would result from inflexible rules. Nonactivists disagree.
   b. Activists believe that monetary policy is more potent than fiscal policy. Nonactivists disagree.
   c. Activists believe that changes in monetary and fiscal policy exert their effects instantaneously. Nonactivists think they work only with a substantial lag.

d. Activists think that macroeconomic policy is sometimes motivated by the pursuit of political gain. Nonactivists disagree.

6. If the index of leading indicators and other forecasting devices suggested that the economy was sliding into a recession, activists' macroeconomic policy would call for
   a. A shift to a more restrictive monetary and fiscal policy.
   b. An increase in the growth rate of the money supply and a shift toward a larger budget deficit (or smaller surplus).
   c. An increase in the growth rate of the money supply and a tax increase in order to balance the budget should the recession materialize.
   d. A continuation of the current policies already in place.

7. Which one of the following is the most serious obstacle limiting the effectiveness of monetary and fiscal policy as stabilization tools?
   a. Our data on the current state of the economy is inadequate.
   b. Our ability to forecast accurately future changes in the state of the economy is limited.
   c. Our ability to tell whether a change in monetary and fiscal policy will stimulate or restrain aggregate demand is inadequate.
   d. Our ability to institute a monetary policy change without simultaneously triggering an offsetting fiscal policy change is inadequate.

8. Which of the following is true?
   a. An increase in the national debt indicates that the federal government is expanding the supply of money in order to finance its expenditures.
   b. The national debt represents the cumulative effect of all prior budget deficits and surpluses.
   c. A budget deficit reduces the size of the national debt by the amount of the deficit.
   d. Since 1974 the national debt has grown at a slower rate than the GDP.

9. Which of the following is a valid concern about the national debt for a country whose debt is held entirely by its citizens?
   a. The welfare of future generations will be directly related to the per capita size of the national debt that they inherit.
   b. Growth of the national debt will eventually lead to the bankruptcy of the government.
   c. When the debt comes due, future generations may be unable to pay it off.
   d. If increases in the national debt reduce investment, future generations may have lower incomes, because they will inherit a smaller stock of capital.

10. Public choice theory indicates that budget deficits
    a. Are a surprising occurrence, since each legislator has a strong incentive to favor high taxes rather than additional borrowing.
    b. Are a natural outgrowth of the ordinary political process, since borrowing allows politicians to supply voters with immediate benefits without having to impose an equal, visible cost on the voter-taxpayer.
    c. Reduce the opportunity cost of government and thereby enhance the welfare of future generations.
    d. Stimulate both real output and employment, and thereby promote economic growth.

## PROBLEMS

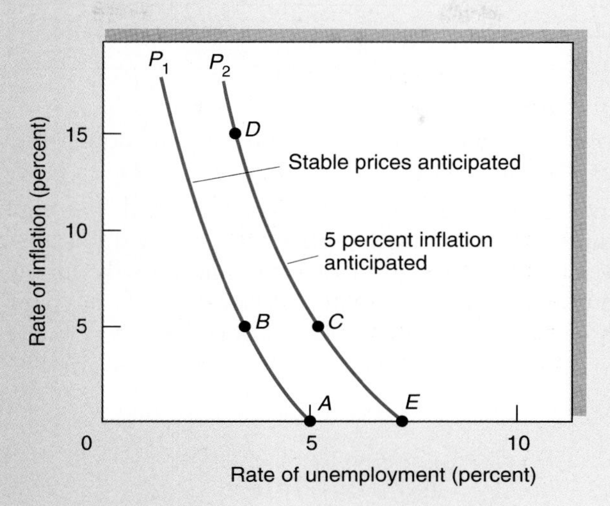


1. a. Assume the economy was initially at point *A* on the Phillips curve $P_1$ of the accompanying diagram. The unemployment rate was 5 percent, and decision-makers expected stable future prices. Suppose that political entrepreneurs, perhaps trying to stimulate the economy before the next election, followed an expansionary macropolicy. What would happen to the rates of unemployment and inflation in the short run? In the long run? Explain.

   b. Suppose the economy were at point *C* on the Phillips curve $P_2$. How could the short-run rate of unemployment be reduced to less than 5 percent? What would happen to prices? Could the lower rate of unemployment be maintained?

   c. If the economy were at point *C*, what would happen if the macropolicymakers pursued a course that would return the economy to price stability? Would this course be attractive to political entrepreneurs? Explain.

   d. In what ways are your answers affected by the manner in which expectations are developed?

2. Consider the following hypothetical information (figures are in billions of dollars):

| | |
|---|---|
| Budget receipts in 1993: | 1,150 |
| Budget expenditures in 1993: | 1,300 |
| Annual growth rate of GDP: | 6 percent |

   a. Complete the following table (some information has already been provided):

| | Budget Deficit | National Debt | GDP | Budget Deficit as Share of GDP | National Debt as Share of GDP |
|---|---|---|---|---|---|
| 1992 | $145 | $4,200 | $6,000 | ______ | ______ |
| 1993 | ______ | ______ | ______ | ______ | ______ |

b. Why did the national debt fall as a share of GDP even though the budget deficit rose?

3. The Chair of the Council of Economic Advisers has requested that you write a short paper indicating how economic policy can be used to stabilize the economy and achieve a high level of economic growth during the next five years. Be sure to make specific proposals. Indicate why your recommendations will work. You may submit your paper to your instructor.

# PART IV

## INTERNATIONAL ECONOMICS

CHAPTER

# 18

## GAINS FROM TRADE AND THE GLOBAL ECONOMY

Free trade consists simply in letting people buy and sell as they want to buy and sell. . . . Protective tariffs [trade restrictions] are as much applications of force as are blockading squadrons, and their objective is the same—to prevent trade. The difference between the two is that blockading squadrons are a means whereby nations seek to prevent their enemies from trading; protective tariffs are a means whereby nations attempt to prevent their own people from trading.

*Henry George (1886)*[1]

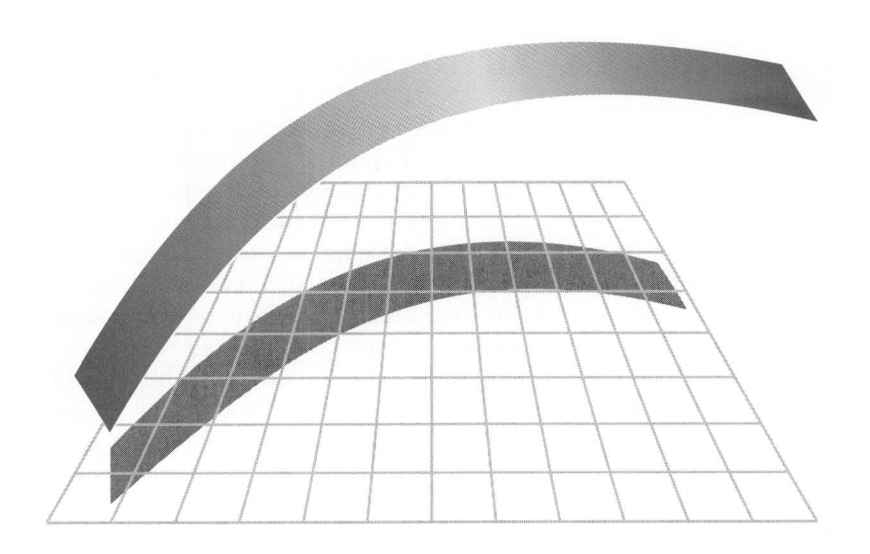

CHAPTER FOCUS

- How does the size of the international trade sector vary across countries?
- How does international trade affect the economic prosperity of nations?
- What impact do trade restrictions have on an economy? Do trade restrictions create jobs?
- Will free trade with low-wage countries cause wage rates in high-wage countries to decline?
- Why do nations adopt trade restrictions?
- How does the economic record of countries that impose trade restrictions compare with that of countries following free-trade policies?

We live in a shrinking world. Wheat raised on the flatlands of western Kansas may be processed into bread in a Russian bakery. The breakfast of many Americans might include bananas from Honduras, coffee from Brazil, or hot chocolate made from Nigerian cocoa beans. The volume of international trade, enhanced by improved transportation and communications, has grown rapidly in recent years. Approximately 21 percent of the world's total output is now sold in a country other than that in which it was produced—double the figure of three decades ago.

Perhaps surprising to some, most international trade is not between the governments of the nations involved. Instead, international buying and selling of goods and services take place between individuals (or business firms) that happen to be located in different countries. International trade, like other voluntary exchange, results because both the buyer and the seller gain from it. If both parties did not expect to gain, there would be no trade.

## SIZE OF TRADE SECTOR

The size of the trade sector varies substantially among nations. Some of the difference is due to size of country. For industries in which economies of scale are important, the domestic market of a sparsely populated country may not be large enough to support cost-efficient firms. Therefore, in small countries firms in such industries will tend to export a larger share of their output and consumers will be more likely to purchase goods produced abroad. As a result, the size of the trade sector *as a share of the economy* tends to be inversely related to the population of the country.

Exhibit 18.1 illustrates the variation in the size of the trade sector (as measured by exports) as a share of total output for countries of similar size.

[1]Henry George, *Protection or Free Trade* (1886; reprinted edition, New York: Robert Schalkenbach Foundation, 1980), p. 47.

**EXHIBIT 18.1**

**Size of Trade Sector of Selected Countries**

| | Exports as Percent of Total Output | |
|---|---|---|
| | 1965 | 1990 |
| *Large Countries*[a] | | |
| Indonesia | 5% | 26% |
| Japan | 11 | 11 |
| United States | 5 | 10 |
| Brazil | 8 | 7 |
| India | 4 | 8 |
| *Mid-size*[b] | | |
| Thailand | 16 | 38 |
| Germany | 18 | 32 |
| South Korea | 9 | 32 |
| United Kingdom | 19 | 25 |
| France | 13 | 23 |
| Italy | 15 | 21 |
| Egypt | 18 | 20 |
| Turkey | 6 | 19 |
| Iran | 20 | 15 |
| *Small Countries*[c] | | |
| Singapore | 123 | 190 |
| Hong Kong | 71 | 137 |
| Belgium | 43 | 74 |
| Norway | 41 | 44 |
| Switzerland | 29 | 37 |
| Costa Rica | 23 | 34 |
| Israel | 19 | 32 |
| Sweden | 22 | 30 |
| Bolivia | 21 | 21 |
| Guatemala | 17 | 21 |
| Haiti | 13 | 12 |

[a]Population more than 120 million.
[b]Population between 40 and 65 million.
[c]Population less than 10 million.
**Source:** World Bank, *World Development Report,* 1992 (Table 9).

Among the countries with a large population, the trade sector is largest in Indonesia and smallest in Brazil and India. The United States and Japan are between these two extremes. For the mid-size countries of Exhibit 18.1, the size of the trade sectors of Thailand, Germany, and South Korea are larger than those of Iran, Turkey, Egypt, Italy, France, and the United Kingdom.

As a share of domestic output, Singapore and Hong Kong have the largest international trade sectors in the world. Both of these countries import large quantities of raw materials and unfurnished goods and manufacture them into products that are often exported abroad. Therefore, the gross exports of these two vibrant trade centers actually exceed their gross domestic product. In contrast, the exports of Haiti, Guatemala, and Bolivia are quite small, given the size of these countries.

The data of Exhibit 18.1 illustrate the growth of trade in recent decades. Note that in almost every case, exports comprised a larger share of the aggregate economy in 1990 than in 1965.

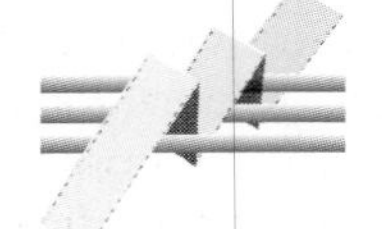

## IMPORTANT SOURCE OF PROSPERITY: INTERNATIONAL TRADE

> *If a foreign country can supply us with a commodity cheaper than we ourselves can make it, [we had] better buy it of them with some part of our own industry, employed in a way in which we have some advantage.*
>
> Adam Smith[2]

As we discussed in Chapter 2, the law of comparative advantage explains why a group of individuals, regions, or nations can gain from specialization and exchange. Trading partners are better off if each specializes in the production of goods for which it is a low opportunity-cost producer and trades for those goods for which it is a high opportunity-cost producer. Specialization in the area of one's **comparative advantage** minimizes the cost of production and leads to maximum joint output.

**comparative advantage** The ability to produce a good at a lower opportunity cost than others can produce it. Relative costs determine comparative advantage. A nation will have a comparative advantage in the production of a good when its production costs for the good are low relative to its production costs for other goods.

International trade leads to mutual gain because it allows each country to specialize more fully in the production of those things that it does best. Labor force skills and resource endowments differ substantially across countries. These differences influence costs. Therefore, a good that is quite costly to produce in one country may be economically produced in another country. For example, the warm, moist climate of Brazil and Colombia enhance the economical production of coffee. Countries like Saudi Arabia and Venezuela with rich oil fields can produce petroleum cheaply. Countries with an abundance of fertile land, like Canada and Australia, are able to produce products like wheat, feed grains, and beef at a low cost. In contrast, land is scarce in Japan, a nation with a highly skilled labor force. The Japanese therefore specialize in manufacturing, using their comparative advantage to produce cameras, automobiles, and electronic products for export. With international trade, each country can gain by specializing in the production of goods that it can produce economically and use the proceeds to import goods that would be expensive to produce domestically.

While the potential gains from trade are relatively too easy to see when each trading partner is quite good at producing a product, it is important to recognize that mutual gain is still possible even when it looks like one country is a lower-cost producer of almost all goods. Since failure to comprehend the principle of mutual gains from trade is often a source of "fuzzy thinking," we will take the time to illustrate the principle in detail.

In order to keep things simple, we will consider a case involving only two countries, the United States and Japan, and two products, food and clothing.

[2]Adam Smith, *An Inquiry into the Nature and Causes of the Wealth of Nations* (1776; Cannan's ed., Chicago: University of Chicago Press, 1976), pp. 478–479.

Furthermore, we will assume that labor is the only resource used to produce these products. In addition, since we want to illustrate that gains from trade are nearly always possible, we are going to assume that the Japanese workers are more efficient than Americans in the production of both commodities. Exhibit 18.2 illustrates this situation. Perhaps due to their prior experience or higher skill level, Japanese workers can produce three units of food per day, compared with only two units per day for U.S. workers. Similarly, Japanese workers are able to produce nine units of clothing per day, compared to one unit of clothing per day for U.S. workers.

The question is, can two countries gain from trade if one of them can produce both goods with fewer resources? Perhaps surprising to some, the answer is yes. As long as *relative* production costs of the two goods differ between Japan and the United States, gains from trade will be possible. Consider what would happen if the United States shifted three workers from the clothing industry to the food industry. This reallocation of labor would allow the United States to expand its food output by six units (two units per worker), while clothing output would decline by three units (one unit per worker). Suppose Japan reallocates labor in the opposite direction. When Japan moves one worker from the food industry to the clothing industry, Japanese clothing production expands by nine units while food output declines by three units. Look how this reallocation of labor *within* the two countries affects output. As the exhibit illustrates, the joint output of the two countries has increased by three units of food and six units of clothing.

The source of this increase in output is straightforward: aggregate output is expanded when each country uses more of its resources to produce those goods that it can produce at a *relatively* low cost. Our old friend, the opportunity-cost concept, reveals the low-cost producer of each good. If Japanese

**EXHIBIT 18.2**

**Gains from Specialization and Trade**

Columns 1 and 2 indicate the daily output of either food or clothing of each worker in the United States and Japan. If the United States moves 3 workers from the clothing industry to the food industry, it can produce 6 more units of food and 3 fewer units of clothing. Similarly, if Japan moves 1 worker from food to clothing, clothing output will increase by 9 units while food output will decline by 3 units. With this reallocation of labor, the United States and Japan are able to increase their aggregate output of both food (3 additional units) and clothing (6 additional units).

| | Output per Worker Day | | Potential Change in Output[a] | |
|---|---|---|---|---|
| Country | Food (1) | Clothing (2) | Food (3) | Clothing (4) |
| United States | 2 | 1 | +6 | −3 |
| Japan | 3 | 9 | −3 | +9 |
| Change in Total Output | | | +3 | +6 |

[a] Change in output if the United States shifts three workers from the clothing to the food industry and if Japan shifts one worker from the food to the clothing industry.

workers produce one additional unit of food, they sacrifice the production of three units of clothing. Therefore, in Japan the opportunity cost of one unit of food is three units of clothing. On the other hand, one unit of food in the United States can be produced at an opportunity cost of only one-half unit of clothing. U.S. workers are therefore the low opportunity-cost producers of food, even though they cannot produce as much food per day as the Japanese workers. Simultaneously, Japan is the low opportunity-cost producer of clothing. The opportunity cost of producing a unit of clothing in Japan is only one-third unit of food, compared to two units of food in the United States. The reallocation of labor illustrated in Exhibit 18.2 expanded joint output because it moved resources in both countries toward areas where they had a comparative advantage.

As long as the relative costs of producing the two goods differ in the two countries, gains from specialization and trade will be possible. When this is the case, each country will find it cheaper to trade for goods that can be produced only at a high opportunity cost. For example, both countries can gain if the United States trades food to Japan for clothing at a trading ratio greater than 1 unit food = 1/2 unit clothing (the U.S. opportunity cost of food) but less than 1 unit food = 3 units clothing (the Japanese opportunity cost of food). Any trading ratio between these two extremes will permit the United States to acquire clothing more cheaply than it can be produced within the country and simultaneously permit Japan to acquire food more cheaply than it could be produced within that country.

## How Trade Expands Consumption Possibilities

Since trade permits nations to expand their joint output, it also allows each nation to expand its consumption possibilities. The production possibilities concept can be used to illustrate this point. Suppose that there were 200 million workers in the United States and 50 million in Japan. Given these figures and the productivity of workers indicated in Exhibit 18.2, the production possibilities curves for the two countries are presented in Exhibit 18.3. If the United States used all of its 200 million workers in the food industry, it could produce 400 million units of food per day (2 units per worker) and zero units of clothing. Alternatively, if the United States used all of its workers to produce clothing, daily output would be 200 million units of clothing and no food. Intermediate output combinations along the production possibilities line (*MN*) intersecting these two extreme points also would be achievable. For example, the United States could produce 150 units of clothing and 100 units of food (point $US_1$).

Exhibit 18.3b illustrates the production possibilities of the 50 million Japanese workers. Japan could produce 450 million units of clothing and no food (*R*), 150 million units of food and no clothing (*S*), or various intermediate combinations like 225 million units of clothing and 75 million units of food ($J_1$). The slope of the production possibilities constraint reflects the opportunity cost of food relative to clothing. Since Japan is the high opportunity-cost producer of food, its production possibilities constraint is steeper than the constraint for the United States.

In the absence of trade, the consumption of each country is constrained by the country's production possibilities. Trade, however, expands the consumption possibilities of both. As we previously indicated, both countries can gain from specialization if the United States trades food to Japan at a price greater than 1 unit of food = 1/2 unit of clothing but less than 1 unit of food =

**EXHIBIT 18.3**

**Production Possibilities of United States and Japan before Specialization and Trade**

Here we illustrate the daily production possibilities of a U.S. labor force of 200 million workers and a Japanese labor force of 50 million workers, given the cost of producing food and clothing presented in Exhibit 18.2. In the absence of trade, consumption possibilities will be restricted to points such as $US_1$ in the United States and $J_1$ in Japan along the production possibilities curve of each country.

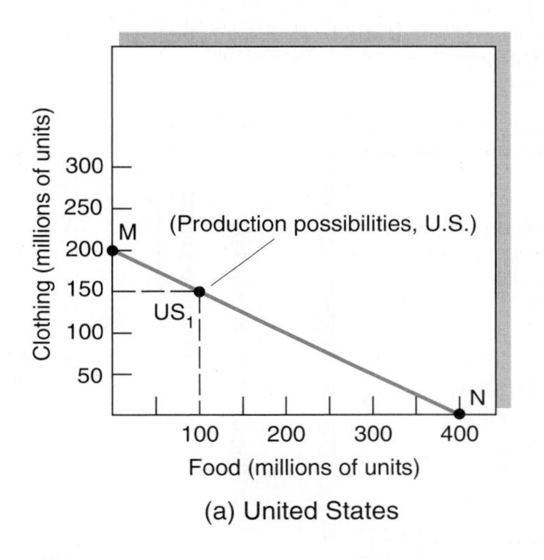

(a) United States

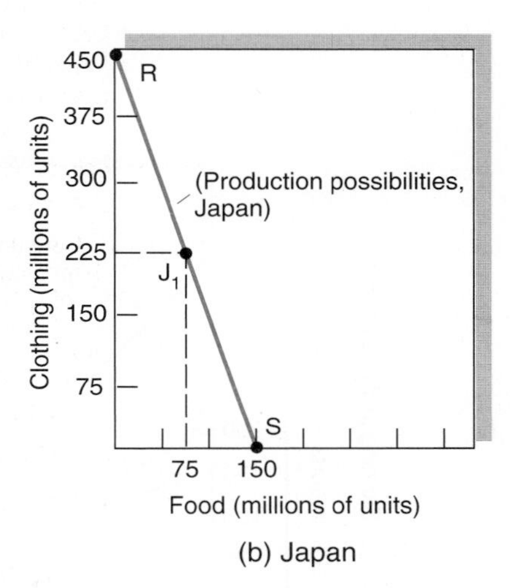

(b) Japan

3 units of clothing. Suppose that they agree on an intermediate price of 1 unit of food = 1 unit of clothing. As Exhibit 18.4a illustrates, when the United States specializes in the production of food (where it has a comparative advantage) and trades food for clothing (at the price ratio where 1 unit of food = 1 unit of clothing), it can consume along the line *ON*. If the United States insisted on self-sufficiency, it would be restricted to consumption possibilities like $US_1$ (100 million units of food and 150 million units of clothing) along its production possibilities constraint of *MN*. With trade, however, the United States can achieve combinations such as $US_2$ (200 million units of food and 200 million units of clothing) along the line *ON*. Trade permits the United States to expand its consumption of both goods.

Simultaneously, Japan is also able to expand its consumption of both goods when it is able to trade clothing for food at the one-to-one price ratio. As Exhibit 18.4b illustrates, Japan can specialize in the production of clothing and consume along the constraint *RT* when it can trade one unit of clothing for one unit of food. Without trade, consumption in Japan would be limited to points like $J_1$ (75 million units of food and 225 million units of clothing) along the line *RS*. With trade, however, it is able to consume combinations like $J_2$ (200 million units of food and 250 million units of clothing) along the constraint *RT*.

Look what happens when Japan specializes in clothing and the United States specializes in food. Japan can produce 450 million units of clothing, export 200 million to the U.S. (for 200 million units of food), and still have 250

**EXHIBIT 18.4**

**Consumption Possibilities with Trade**

With specialization and trade, the consumption possibilities of a country can be expanded. If the United States can trade one unit of clothing for one unit of food, it can specialize in the production of food and consume along the *ON* line (rather than its original production possibilities constraint, *MN*). Similarly, when Japan is able to trade one unit of clothing for one unit of food, it can specialize in the production of clothing and consume any combination along the line *RT*. For example, with specialization and trade, the United States could increase its consumption from $US_1$ to $US_2$, gaining 50 million units of clothing and 100 million units of food. Simultaneously, Japan could increase consumption from $J_1$ to $J_2$, a gain of 125 million units of food and 25 million units of clothing.

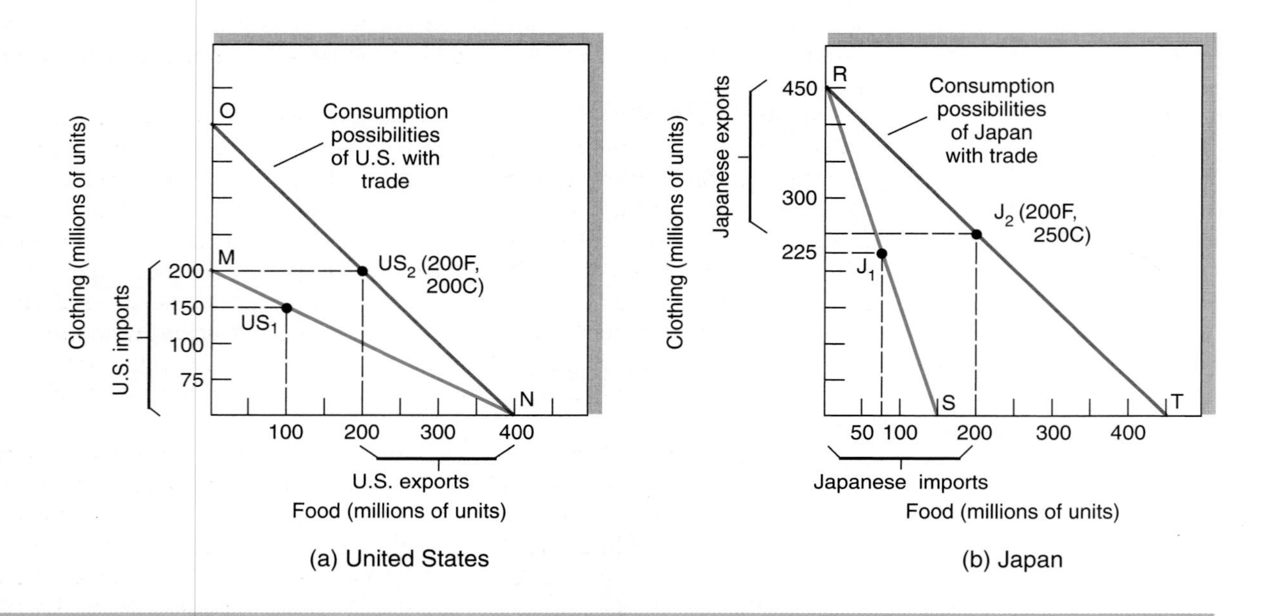


million units of clothing remaining for domestic consumption. Simultaneously, the United States can produce 400 million units of food, export 200 million to Japan (for 200 million units of clothing), and still have 200 million units of food left for domestic consumption. After specialization and trade, the United States is able to consume at the point of $US_2$ and Japan $J_2$, consumption levels that would otherwise be unattainable. Specialization and exchange permits the two countries to expand their joint output, and as a result, *both* countries can increase their consumption of *both* commodities.

The implications of the law of comparative advantage are clear: trade between nations will lead to an expansion in total output and mutual gain for each trading partner when each country specializes in the production of goods it can produce at a relatively low cost and uses the proceeds to buy goods that it could produce only at a high cost. It is comparative advantage that matters. As long as there is some variation in the *relative* opportunity cost of goods across countries, each country will always have a comparative advantage in the production of some goods.

## Additional Considerations on International Trade

In order to keep things simple, we ignored the potential importance of transportation costs, which, of course, reduce the potential gains from trade. Sometimes transportation costs, both real and artificially imposed, even exceed the mutual gain. In this case, exchange does not occur.

While our hypothetical example illustrates the case of complete specialization, a country need not specialize in the production of just a few products in order to realize gains from trade. The example of complete specialization was used for illustrative purposes only.

We also assumed that the cost of producing each good was constant in each country. This is seldom the case. Beyond some level of production, the opportunity cost of producing a good will often increase as a country produces more and more of it. Rising marginal costs as the output of a good expands will limit the degree to which a country will specialize in the production of a good.

Sometimes, however, an expansion in the size of the market will permit firms to realize economies that accompany large-scale production, marketing, and distribution. Under these circumstances, international trade will allow domestic firms to produce larger outputs and achieve lower costs than would be possible if they were unable to sell abroad. This point is particularly important for small countries. For example, textile manufacturers in Hong Kong, Taiwan, and South Korea would have much higher costs if they could not sell abroad. The domestic textile markets of these countries are too small to support large, low-cost firms in this industry. With international trade, however, textile firms in these countries operate at a large scale and compete quite effectively in the world market.

Simultaneously, international trade benefits domestic consumers, particularly those in small countries, because it permits them to purchase from large-scale producers abroad. The aircraft industry provides a vivid illustration of this point. Given the huge designing and engineering costs, the domestic market of most all countries would be substantially less than the quantity required for the efficient production of jet planes. With international trade, however, consumers around the world are able to purchase planes economically from a large-scale producer such as Boeing or McDonnell Douglas.

Finally, international trade promotes competition in domestic markets and allows consumers to purchase a wide diversity of goods at economical prices. Competition from abroad helps keep domestic producers on their toes. Domestic producers that otherwise might have few rivals will have to constantly be seeking ways to improve quality and keep costs low. Simultaneously, the diversity of goods that is available from abroad provides consumers with a broader array of choices than would be available in the absence of international trade.

# EXPORT-IMPORT LINK

Confusion about the merit of international trade often results because people do not consider all the consequences. Why are other nations willing to export their goods to the United States? So they can obtain dollars. Yes, but why do they want dollars? Would foreigners be willing to continue exporting oil, radios, watches, cameras, automobiles, and thousands of other valuable products to Americans in exchange for pieces of paper? If so, Americans could all be semi-retired, spending only an occasional workday at the dollar printing press office! Of course, foreigners are not so naive. They trade goods for dollars so they can use the dollars to import goods and purchase ownership rights to U.S. assets.

Exports, broadly perceived to include goods, services, and assets, provide the buying power that makes it possible for a nation to import. If a nation did not export goods, it would not have the foreign currency that is required for the purchase of imports. Similarly, if a nation did not import goods from foreigners, foreigners would not have the purchasing power to buy that nation's export products. Therefore, if imports decline, so too, will the demand for the nation's exports. Exports and imports are closely linked.

## SUPPLY, DEMAND, AND INTERNATIONAL TRADE

How does international trade affect prices and output levels in domestic markets? Supply and demand analysis will help us answer this question. Given our modern transportation and communication networks, the market for many commodities is worldwide. When a product can be transported long distances at a low cost (relative to its value) the domestic price of the product is in effect determined by the forces of supply and demand in the worldwide market.

Using soybeans as an example, Exhibit 18.5 illustrates the relationship between the domestic and world markets for an internationally traded commodity. Worldwide market conditions determine the price of soybeans. In an open economy, domestic producers are free to sell and domestic consumers are free to buy the product at the world market price ($P_w$). At the world market price, U.S. producers will supply $Q_p$, while U.S. consumers will purchase $Q_c$. Reflecting their comparative advantage, U.S. soybean producers will export $Q_p - Q_c$ units at the world market price.

Let us compare the open-economy outcome with the situation in the absence of trade. If U.S. producers were not allowed to export soybeans, the domestic price would be determined by the domestic supply ($S_d$) and demand ($D_d$) only. A lower "no-trade" price ($P_n$) would emerge. Who are the winners and losers as the result of free trade in soybeans? Clearly, soybean producers gain. Free trade allows domestic producers to sell a larger quantity ($Q_p$ rather than $Q_n$). As a result, the *net* revenues of soybean producers will rise by $P_w bcP_n$. On the other hand, domestic consumers of soybeans will have to pay a higher price under free trade. Consumers will lose both (1) because they have to pay $P_w$ rather than $P_n$ for the $Q_c$ units they purchase, and (2) because they lose the consumer surplus on the $Q_n - Q_c$ units now purchased at the higher price. Thus, free trade imposes a net cost of $P_w acP_n$ on consumers. As can be seen in Exhibit 18.5, however, the gains of producers outweigh the losses to consumers by the triangle *abc*. Free trade leads to a net welfare gain.

When one focuses only on an export product, it appears that free trade benefits producers relative to consumers. This is potentially quite misleading, however, because it ignores the secondary effects. (Remember, failure to

**EXHIBIT 18.5**

**Producer Benefits from Exports**

As frame b shows, the price of soybeans and other internationally traded commodities is determined by the forces of supply and demand in the world market. If U.S. soybean producers were prohibited from selling to foreigners, the domestic price would be $P_n$ (frame a). Free trade permits the U.S. soybean producers to sell $Q_p$ units at the higher world price ($P_w$). The quantity $Q_p - Q_c$ is exported abroad. Compared to the no-trade situation, the producers' gain from the higher price ($P_w bcP_n$) exceeds the cost imposed on domestic consumers ($P_w acP_n$) by the triangle *abc*.

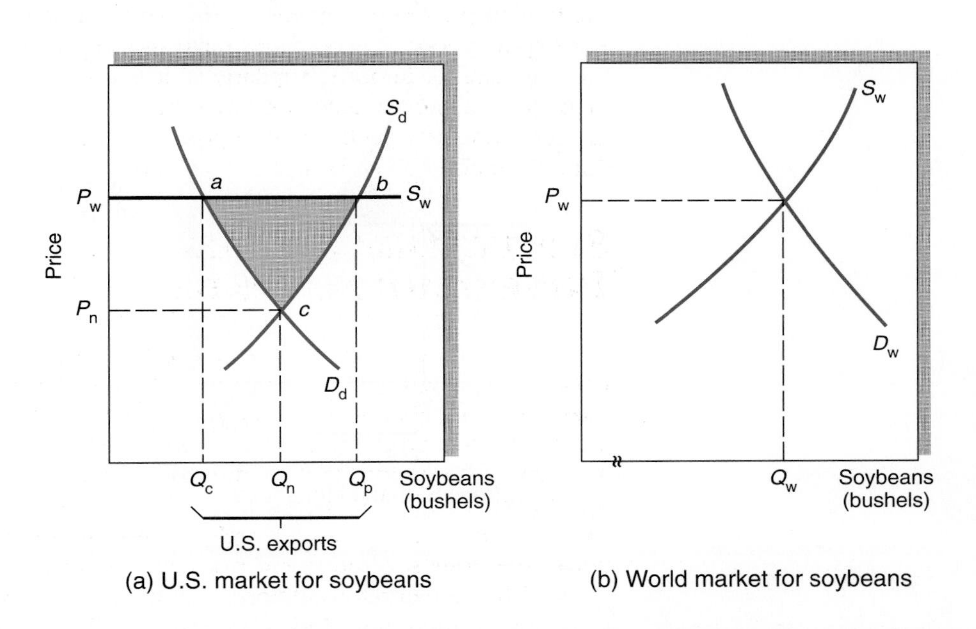


consider the secondary effects is one of the most common sources of error in economics.) How will foreigners generate the dollars they will need to purchase the export products of the United States? If foreigners do not sell goods to us, they will not have the purchasing power necessary to purchase goods from us. U.S. imports—that is, the purchase of goods from low-cost foreign producers—provide foreigners with the dollar purchasing power necessary to buy U.S. exports. In turn, the lower prices in the import-competitive markets will benefit the U.S. consumers who appeared at first glance to be harmed by the higher prices (compared to the no-trade situation) in export markets.

Exhibit 18.6 illustrates the impact of imports, using shoes as an example. In the absence of trade, the price of shoes in the domestic market would be $P_n$, the intersection of the domestic supply and demand curves. However, the world price of shoes is $P_w$. In an open economy, many U.S. consumers would take advantage of the low shoe prices available from foreign producers. At the lower world price, U.S. consumers would purchase $Q_c$ units of shoes, importing $Q_c - Q_p$ from foreign producers.

Compared to the no-trade situation, free trade in shoes results in lower prices and an expansion in domestic consumption. The lower prices lead to a net consumer gain of $P_n abP_w$. Domestic producers lose $P_n acP_w$ in the form of

**EXHIBIT 18.6**

**Consumer Benefits from Imports**

In the absence of trade, the domestic price of shoes would be $P_n$. Since many foreign producers have a comparative advantage in the production of shoes, international trade leads to lower prices. At the world price $P_w$, U.S. consumers will demand $Q_c$ units, of which $Q_c - Q_p$ are imported. Compared to the no-trade situation, consumers gain $P_n abP_w$, while domestic producers lose $P_n acP_w$. A net gain of *abc* results.

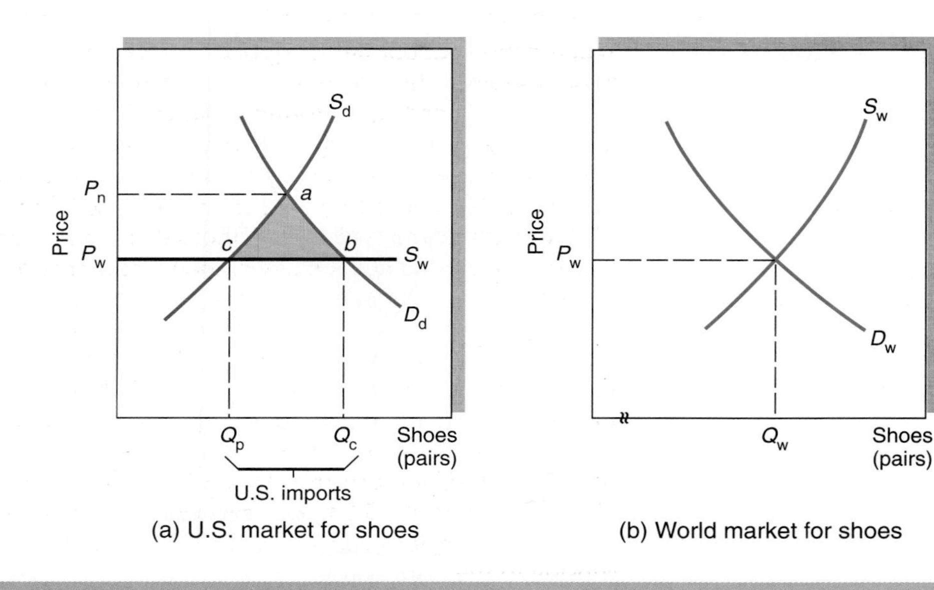


(a) U.S. market for shoes

(b) World market for shoes

lower sales prices and reductions in output. However, the net gain of consumers exceeds the net loss of producers by *abc*.

For an open economy, international competition directs the resources of a nation toward the areas of their comparative advantage. When domestic producers have a comparative advantage in the production of a good, they will be able to compete effectively in the world market and profit from the export of goods to foreigners. In turn, the exports will generate the purchasing power necessary to buy goods that foreigners can supply more economically than can be produced domestically. Relative to the no-trade alternative, international trade and specialization result in lower prices (and higher consumption levels) for imported products and higher prices (and lower consumption levels) for exported products. International markets tend to direct the producers of each nation toward the production of things they do best and away from those things which they do least well. As Exhibit 18.4 illustrated, the result is an expansion in both output and consumption compared to what otherwise could be achieved.

The pattern of U.S. exports and imports is consistent with this view. The United States is a nation with a technically skilled labor force, fertile farmland, and substantial capital formation. Thus, we export computers, aircraft, power generating equipment, scientific instruments, and land-intensive agricultural products—items we are able to produce at a comparatively low cost.

Simultaneously, we import substantial amounts of petroleum, textile (clothing) products, shoes, coffee, and diamonds—goods for which it is costly to produce additional units domestically. Clearly, trade permits us to specialize in those areas in which our comparative advantage is greatest and trade for those products we are least suited to produce.

## IMPACT OF TRADE RESTRICTIONS

When nations adopt tariffs, quotas, exchange rate controls and other types of trade restraints, they increase the transaction costs of exchange. Physical obstacles, like bad roads and stormy weather, that increase transaction costs will retard the gains from trade. So too, will man-made obstacles. Henry George compares trade restrictions to a blockade (see chapter opening quote). Both the blockade imposed by an enemy and a self-imposed blockade in the form of trade restrictions will retard the gains from specialization and trade, and thereby reduce the economic well-being of a nation.

**tariff** A tax levied on goods imported into a country.

A **tariff** is nothing more than a tax imposed on imports but not on the domestic producers of the good. The imposition of a tariff on a good makes it more costly for foreigners to supply the good to consumers in the country imposing the tariff. As the result of the tariff, foreigners will supply less, the domestic market will be less competitive, and consumers will pay higher prices. Consider the impact of a tariff on automobiles. The tariff will reduce the supply of automobiles and thereby push up auto prices in the domestic market. As the result of the higher prices, domestic automobile producers benefit at the expense of domestic automobile consumers. In effect, the tariff provides a subsidy to the domestic automobile producers at the expense of domestic consumers who now face higher prices. Since foreigners will sell less in the domestic market, they will have less purchasing power with which to buy domestic exports. Thus, producers in export industries will experience a decline in the foreign demand for their product. This latter negative effect is often overlooked when considering the impact of tariffs and other trade restraints on output and employment.

**import quota** A specific quantity (or value) of a good permitted to be imported into a country during a given year.

Like tariffs, **import quotas** also restrict the supply of foreign goods, in this case by placing a ceiling on the quantity of various products that can be imported during a given time period (typically a year). Currently, the United States imposes quotas on several products, including brooms, steel, shoes, textile products, sugar, dairy products, and peanuts.

When a quota reduces the supply to the domestic market, the price of the quota-protected good will be higher than otherwise would be the case. Even the foreign suppliers with quota permits will receive the higher price. In many ways, quotas are more harmful than tariffs. With a quota, foreign producers are prohibited from selling additional units regardless of how much lower their costs are relative to domestic producers. In contrast with a tariff, a quota brings in no revenue for the government. While a tariff transfers revenue from U.S. consumers to the Treasury, quotas transfer these revenues to foreign producers. Foreign producers who have permits to market the goods actually benefit from the quotas. Thus, quotas generate two strong interest groups supportive of their continuation. Domestic producers of the "protected" good favor the quotas because the quota permits them to charge domestic consumers a higher price than would otherwise be the case. Similarly, foreign producers with marketing permits are also permitted to sell at the higher price, one that will often be substantially above their production costs. Given the benefits received by both domestic suppliers and some foreign producers, removal of a quota on a good is often even more difficult to achieve than a tariff reduction.

Many countries, particularly less developed countries, fix the exchange rate value of their currency above the market rate. At the official (artificially high) exchange rate, the country's export goods will be extremely expensive to foreigners. As a result, foreigners will purchase goods elsewhere, and the country's exports will be small. In turn, the low level of exports will make it extremely difficult for domestic residents to get their hands on the foreign currency required for the purchase of imports. Such exchange rate controls will both reduce the volume of trade and lead to black-market currency exchanges. A large black-market premium indicates that the country's exchange rate policy is substantially limiting the ability of its citizens to trade with foreigners. The greater the black-market premium, the larger the expected decline in the size of the country's international trade sector as the result of the exchange rate controls.

## FALLACIOUS VIEWS ABOUT TRADE RESTRICTIONS

Fallacious views abound in the area of international trade. Whenever foreign competitors begin to make inroads into markets that have traditionally been supplied by domestic producers, the outcry for "trade restrictions to save jobs" is often heard. In addition, many charge that a high-wage country cannot compete with low-wage countries.

When considering these views, it is important to keep the ultimate source of economic prosperity clearly in mind. Production of things that people value is the source of income and prosperity. Jobs will promote prosperity only if they expand the production of things people want. The people of a nation will prosper in direct proportion to their ability to produce goods and services that people value.

### Import Restrictions and Jobs

Noneconomists often argue that import restrictions will save jobs and promote prosperity. This view is a fallacy that stems from a failure to consider the secondary effects. Tariffs, quotas, exchange rate controls, and other import restrictions may create jobs in industries shielded by the restraints, but they will destroy jobs in other industries. Remember, the sales of foreigners to us (our imports) provides them with the purchasing power required to buy from us (our exports). If foreigners are unable to sell as much to Americans, then they will have fewer of the dollars required to buy from Americans. Therefore, a secondary effect accompanies trade restrictions; the restrictions will indirectly cause a reduction in the foreign demand for goods produced by export industries. Thus, output and employment in export industries will decline, offsetting any jobs saved in protected industries.

In addition, import restrictions push up the price of machine tools, steel, raw materials, delivery trucks, and other resources that are often imported by

American businesses. These high resource prices make it more costly to produce all domestic output. This, too, will reduce exports. Thus, any employment expansion in industries that compete with imports will, to a large degree if not entirely, be offset by a shrinkage of employment in export industries.

In essence, import restraints direct resources away from areas where domestic producers have a comparative advantage and into areas where domestic producers are relatively inefficient. As a result, the value of the goods and services produced by Americans will decline. Correspondingly, the incomes of Americans also will be reduced.

The choice is not whether a product is going to be produced domestically or abroad. The real question is (1) whether the resources of a nation are going to be used to produce things that can be supplied by domestic firms only at a high cost or (2) whether the resources will be used to produce goods that the nation can supply cheaply. With free trade, domestic consumers are permitted to buy whatever they want, wherever they can get the cheapest prices. Similarly, domestic producers are able to sell their products wherever they can get the highest prices. As a result, consumers get more for their money and resource owners produce more value.

Perhaps reflection on the following question will enhance your understanding of this issue. If import restrictions are a good idea, why don't we use them to restrict trade among the 50 states? After all, think of all of the jobs that are lost when, for example, Michigan "imports" oranges from Florida, apples from Washington, wheat from Kansas, and cotton from Georgia. All of these products could be produced in Michigan. However, the residents of Michigan generally find it cheaper to "import" these commodities rather than produce them domestically. Michigan gains by using its resources to produce and "export" automobiles (and other goods it can produce economically) and then using the sales revenue to "import" goods that would be expensive to produce in Michigan.

Most people recognize that free trade among the 50 states is a major source of prosperity for each of the states. Similarly, most recognize that "imports" from other states do not destroy jobs—at least not for long. Instead, the "imports" release workers for employment in "export" industries, where they will be able to produce more value and therefore generate more income. The underlying source of gains from trade among nations is exactly the same as for trade among people in different states. Free trade among the 50 states promotes prosperity; so too, does free trade among nations.

Of course, sudden and complete removal of trade barriers might initially harm producers and workers. It would be costly to effect an immediate transfer of the protected resources to other areas and industries. Gradual removal of such barriers would minimize the cost of relocation and eliminate the shock effect. The government might also cushion the burden by subsidizing the retraining and relocation costs of displaced workers.

## Trade with Low-Wage Countries

Many people in high-wage countries believe that trade restrictions are necessary to protect domestic workers from imported goods produced by cheap labor. This view is false. The exports of low-wage countries provide them with the purchasing power to buy from high-wage countries like the United States. As in other cases, relative prices will determine the direction goods will be traded between high- and low-wage countries. High-wage countries will tend to import things that are relatively cheap abroad and export goods that are relatively cheap at home. Therefore, a high-wage country like the United States will tend to import labor-intensive goods such as wigs, rugs, toys, textiles, and assembled manufactured products. On the other hand, the United States will tend to export goods like computers, aircraft, scientific instruments, and grains, which are produced with high skill labor and fertile farm labor, resources that are relatively abundant in the United States.

When a country can get a good more cheaply from foreigners than it can produce it domestically, it will gain by importing the good and using domestic resources to produce other things. Perhaps an extreme example will illustrate this point. Suppose a foreign producer, perhaps Santa Claus, who pays workers little or nothing, were willing to supply Americans with free winter coats. Would it make sense to enact a tariff barrier to keep out the free coats? Of course not. Resources that were previously used to produce coats could be freed to produce other goods. Output and the availability of goods would expand. It makes no more sense to erect trade barriers to keep out cheap foreign goods than to keep out the free coats of a friendly, foreign Santa Claus.

## WHY NATIONS ADOPT TRADE RESTRICTIONS

*Protectionism is a politician's delight because it delivers visible benefits to the protected parties while imposing the costs as a hidden tax on the public.*

Murry L. Weidenbaum[3]

If trade restrictions promote inefficiency and reduce the potential gains from specialization and trade, why do nations adopt them? Some may want to protect industries for reasons related to national defense. For example, a nation may not want to be dependent on foreign sources of petroleum, ammunition, and weapons in case an international conflict should arise. In addition, less developed countries often find it easier to collect a tariff than an income or sales tax. Therefore, such countries sometimes rely heavily on tariffs as a source of government revenue.

In most situations, however, the presence of trade restrictions reflects the politics of the issue. Politicians have a strong incentive to favor well-organized interest groups at the expense of widely dispersed citizens who are likely to be poorly informed. Trade restrictions are this type of an issue. They tend to benefit producers (and resource suppliers) at the expense of consumers. In general, the former group—investors and workers in a specific industry—are well organized, and "jobs saved" in these industries are often highly visible. Thus, organized interest groups that benefit from trade restrictions frequently provide contributions and other resources to politicians willing to support trade restrictions favorable to their industry. In contrast, consumers, who will pay higher prices for the products of a protected industry, are an unorganized group. Most of them will not associate the higher product prices with the trade restrictions. Similarly, *potential* workers and investors in export industries harmed by the restrictions are often unaware of their impact. Thus, most of the people harmed by trade restrictions are likely to be uninformed and unconcerned about trade policy.

[3]Former chairman of the President's Council of Economic Advisers.

Predictably, well-organized special interests favoring trade restrictions will generally have more political clout that those harmed by the restrictions. As a result, politicians will often be able to gain more votes by supporting trade restrictions that benefit organized interest groups than they could gain from the support of consumers and exporters. In the case of trade restrictions, sound economics often conflicts with a winning political strategy.

## TRADE RESTRICTIONS AND ECONOMIC PERFORMANCE

Our analysis indicates that countries imposing trade barriers will fail to realize their full economic potential. There are various ways—tariffs, quotas, exchange rate controls, and licensing requirements, for example—that countries can restrain international trade. It is not easy to determine the extent to which various countries are restricting trade.

Taxes on international trade are generally lower in high-income industrial countries than the less developed countries of Latin America, Africa, and parts of Asia. Similarly, exchange rate controls are a negligible deterrent to international trade in developed countries, while they are a major factor restricting trade in several less developed countries. Therefore, adjusted for size of country, the size of the trade sector tends to be larger in the high-income industrial countries. This is not surprising, since specialization and international exchange contribute substantially to the prosperity of these countries.

Among less developed countries, there is considerable variation in the height of trade barriers. Some less developed countries impose exceedingly high tariffs. Others impose exchange rate controls. When a country both imposes high tariffs and fixes the value of its currency at unrealistic rates (relative to convertible currencies like the dollar and yen), international trade will be retarded substantially.

Exhibit 18.7 presents data for 10 less developed countries with relatively low trade barriers.[4] Given the size of their population, the trade sectors of these 10 countries are large. Their tariff rates are low, and the exchange rate value of their currencies is pretty much in line with market forces (a low black-market exchange rate premium provides evidence on this point). Data are also provided for 10 countries that impose substantial restrictions on trade. For this latter group, the size of the trade sector is small, tariffs are high, and the black-market exchange rate premium for the conversion of the domestic currency is high. As we previously discussed, a high black-market premium indicates that the country has imposed tight exchange rate controls. Compared to the low-restriction countries, on average, the tax (tariff) rates imposed on international trade were approximately four times higher for the high-restriction countries. Similarly, the black-market exchange rate premium for the domestic currency was much higher in the high-restriction countries.

Look at the growth of per capita GDP during the 1980s for the two groups. Singapore and Hong Kong, two countries that follow free-trade policies—their tariffs are negligible and their currencies are fully convertible—both

[4]The empirical data presented in this section is part of a larger study undertaken by one of the authors. See James Gwartney, Walter Block, and Robert Lawson, "Measuring Economic Freedom," edited by Steven T. Easton and Michael A. Walker, *Rating Global Economic Freedom* (Vancouver, BC: The Fraser Institute, 1992).

**EXHIBIT 18.7** **Economic Growth of Less Developed Countries with Low and High Trade Restrictions**

| | Size of Trade Sector as Percent of GDP, 1989[a] | Average Tax Rate on International Trade | | Black-Market Exchange Rate Premium 1988[b] | Growth of per Capita GDP, 1980–1990 |
|---|---|---|---|---|---|
| | | 1980 | 1989 | | |
| *Low Trade Restrictions*[a] | | | | | |
| Singapore | 184.2 | 0.5 | 0.2 | 0 | 4.2 |
| Hong Kong | 131.5 | 0.0 | 0.0 | 0 | 5.7 |
| Malaysia | 74.7 | 7.7 | 3.2 | 0 | 2.6 |
| Ireland | 74.1 | 3.0 | 2.5 | 2 | 2.9 |
| Taiwan | 45.0 | 3.6 | 2.2 | 1 | 6.5 |
| Portugal | 41.5 | 2.1 | 1.1 | 13 | 2.1 |
| Chile | 39.1 | 2.8 | 3.9 | 29 | 1.5 |
| Thailand | 38.0 | 6.9 | 5.2 | 1 | 5.8 |
| South Korea | 33.1 | 4.1 | 3.0 | 10 | 8.6 |
| Indonesia | 25.6 | 2.9 | 2.2 | 16 | 3.7 |
| **Average** | 68.7 | 3.4 | 2.4 | 7 | **4.4** |
| *High Trade Restrictions*[a] | | | | | |
| Iran | 3.9 | 8.5 | 14.6 | 1030 | –1.2 |
| Brazil | 6.1 | 10.0 | 5.5 | 57 | 0.5 |
| India | 9.5 | 15.5 | 21.6 | 14 | 3.2 |
| Peru | 12.7 | 10.6 | 5.0 | 240 | –2.6 |
| Bangladesh | 13.1 | 13.4 | 12.1 | 318 | 2.0 |
| Rwanda | 13.4 | 13.3 | n.a.[c] | 30 | –2.3 |
| Argentina | 13.8 | 9.5 | 7.0 | 50 | –1.7 |
| Sierra Leone | 17.1 | 13.3 | 11.8 | 1406 | –0.9 |
| Pakistan | 17.4 | 15.3 | 16.1 | 10 | 3.2 |
| Ghana | 21.3 | 17.3 | 11.4 | 36 | –0.4 |
| **Average** | 12.8 | 13.7 | 11.7 | 319 | **0.0** |

[a]The size of the trade sector is equal to one-half of exports plus imports as a percent of GDP. As Exhibit 18.1 shows, the size of the trade sector tends to be inversely related to the population of a country. Given population, the size of the trade sector is generally large in countries with low trade restrictions and small in countries with high trade restrictions.

[b]A sizeable black-market exchange rate premium indicates that the country has imposed exchange rate controls that substantially limit the ability of domestic citizens to convert the national currency to other currencies.

[c]Data not available.

**Source:** Derived from World Bank, *World Tables, 1991* and *World Development Report, 1992;* International Money Fund, *Government Finance Yearbook, 1991;* and International Currency Analysis, *The World Currency Yearbook, 1989–90.*

achieved impressive growth rates during the 1980s. The average annual growth of per capita GDP in the low-restriction countries was 4.4 percent during the 1980s, compared to zero growth in the countries with high trade restrictions. Per capita GDP declined during the 1980s in 6 of the 10 countries that imposed substantial restrictions on international trade. None of the countries with high trade restrictions were able to achieve even the average growth rate of the countries following policies more consistent with free trade. Just as our theory implies, these data indicate that trade barriers are harmful to the economic health of a country.

There is some evidence that several less developed countries are ready to move toward freer trade policies. Among Latin American coutries, Chile reduced its tariffs and began moving toward freer trade policies in the early 1980s. More recently, tariff rates have been cut substantially in Mexico, Argentina, and Bolivia. Exchange rate controls have also been relaxed or eliminated in these and other Latin American countries. Perhaps the stage is now set for many Latin American and other less developed countries to follow the lead of Chile and the trade-oriented countries of Southeast Asia. If so, economic analysis indicates that such a policy shift will contribute to their future prosperity.

## LOOKING AHEAD

There are many similarities between trade within national borders and trade across national boundaries. However, there is also a major difference. In addition to the exchange of goods for money, trade across national borders generally involves the exchange of national currencies. The next chapter deals with the financial arrangements under which international trade is conducted.

## CHAPTER SUMMARY

1. The volume of international trade has grown rapidly in recent decades. In the late 1980s approximately 21 percent of the world's output was sold in a different country than it was produced. The size of the trade sector as a share of the economy varies substantially among countries. It is generally larger in countries with a smaller population.
2. Nations are able to produce a larger joint output when each uses its resources to produce only those goods that it can produce at a relatively low cost. The expansion in output derived from specialization in areas of comparative advantage provides the basis for mutual gains from trade.
3. Comparative advantage is the source of gains from trade. As long as there are differences among countries in the *relative* opportunity cost of producing goods, each country will have a comparative advantage in some areas and therefore each will be able to gain from specialization and trade.
4. International trade expands the size of the potential market. This expansion in the size of the market makes it easier for producers to achieve economies of large-scale operation and for consumers to purchase from larger firms with lower costs and cheaper prices. International trade also promotes competition in domestic markets and increases the diversity of goods available to consumers.
5. Exports and imports are closely linked. The exports of a nation are the primary source of purchasing power used to import goods. When a nation restricts imports, it simultaneously limits the ability of foreigners to acquire the purchasing power necessary to buy the nation's exports.

6. In a market setting, domestic producers will be able to compete effectively in world markets in those areas where they have a comparative advantage. On the other hand, domestic producers will be unable to compete successfully in areas where foreigners have a comparative advantage. International competition tends to direct the resources of each nation into areas where the nation has a comparative advantage.
7. Relative to the no-trade alternative, international exchange and specialization result in lower prices for products that are imported and higher domestic prices for products that are exported. However, the net effect is an expansion in the aggregate output and the consumption possibilities available to a nation.
8. The application of a tariff, quota, or other import restriction to a product reduces the amount of the product that foreigners supply to the domestic market. As a result of diminished supply, consumers face higher prices for the protected product. Essentially, import restrictions are subsidies to producers (and workers) in protected industries at the expense of (a) consumers and (b) producers (and workers) in export industries. Restrictions reduce the ability of domestic producers to specialize in those areas for which their comparative advantage is greatest.
9. In the long run, trade restrictions do not create jobs. Jobs protected by import restrictions are offset by jobs destroyed in export industries. Since this result of restrictions often goes unnoticed, their political popularity is understandable. Nevertheless, trade restrictions are inefficient, since they lead to the loss of potential gains from specialization and exchange.
10. Both high-wage and low-wage countries gain from the opportunity to specialize in the production of goods that they produce at a low opportunity cost. If a low-wage country can supply a good to the United States more cheaply than the United States can produce it, the United States can gain by purchasing the good from the low-wage country and using the scarce resources of the United States to produce other goods for which it has a comparative advantage.
11. Even though trade restrictions promote economic inefficiency, they are often attractive to politicians because they generate visible benefits to special interests—particularly business and labor interests in protected industries—while imposing costs on consumers and taxpayers that are *individually* small and largely invisible.

# *Study Guide*

**CHAPTER**

# 18

# DEVELOPING THE ECONOMIC WAY OF THINKING

## CRITICAL-ANALYSIS QUESTIONS

*1. "Trade restrictions limiting the sale of cheap foreign goods in the United States are necessary to protect the prosperity of Americans." Evaluate this statement made by an American politician.

2. Suppose at the time of the Civil War the United States had been divided into two countries and that through the years no trade existed between the two. How would the standard of living in the "divided" United States have been affected? Explain.

*3. Can both (a) and (b) be true? Explain.
   a. "Tariffs and import quotas promote economic inefficiency and reduce the real income of a nation. Economic analysis suggests that nations can gain by eliminating trade restrictions."
   b. "Economic analysis suggests that there is good reason to expect trade restrictions to exist in the real world."

4. "Tariffs and quotas are necessary to protect the high wages of the American worker." Do you agree or disagree? Why?

5. "The United States is suffering from a huge excess of imports. Cheap foreign products are driving American firms out of business and leaving our economy in shambles." Evaluate this statement from an American politician.

6. Do you think the United States would benefit if all trade barriers with Mexico were eliminated? Would Mexico benefit? Would wages in the United States fall to the level of wages in Mexico? Why or why not?

*7. Tariffs not only reduce the volume of imports, they also reduce the volume of exports. True or false? Explain.

*8. "Getting more Americans to realize that it pays to buy things made in the United States is the heart of the competitiveness issue" (quote from an American business magazine).
   a. Would Americans be better off if more of them paid higher prices in order to "buy American" rather than purchase from foreigners? Would U.S. employment be higher? Explain.
   b. Would Californians be better off if they only bought goods produced in California? Would the employment in California be higher? Explain.

*9. It is often alleged that Japanese producers receive subsidies from their government that permit them to sell their products at a low price in the U.S. market. Do you think we should erect trade barriers to keep out cheap Japanese goods if the source of their low price is governmental subsidies? Why or why not?

10. How do tariffs and quotas differ? Can you think of any reason why foreign producers might prefer that a quota rather than a tariff be imposed on their products? Explain.

## MULTIPLE-CHOICE SELF-TEST

1. Suppose that the United States imposed a tariff on television sets. Which of the following results would be most likely?

*Asterisk denotes critical-analysis questions for which answers are given in Appendix A.

a. The price of televisions to U.S. consumers would increase, and the demand for U.S. export products would rise.
b. The price of televisions to U.S. consumers would fall, and the demand for U.S. export products would fall.
c. The price of televisions to U.S. consumers would increase, and the demand for U.S. export products would fall.
d. The price of televisions to U.S. consumers would fall, and the demand for U.S. export products would rise.

2. As the result of specialization and trade, according to the law of comparative advantage, total output will
   a. Decline, because specialization is costly.
   b. Rise only when there is an accompanying decline in the total output of one's trading partners.
   c. Rise if a nation is a net exporter but will fall if the nation is a net importer of goods and services.
   d. Increase, because resources will be better directed toward their highest-valued use.
3. If the U.S. lumber producers were prohibited from exporting their product abroad, which of the following would be most likely to occur?
   a. The incomes of U.S. lumber producers would rise.
   b. U.S. lumber prices would rise.
   c. U.S. consumers would gain at the expense of foreign producers.
   d. U.S. lumber prices would fall, but U.S. households would have less foreign exchange with which to purchase goods, services, and assets abroad.
4. When both exports and imports are considered, the major advantage of international trade is that it allows us to
   a. Sample foreign products that many of us would otherwise never see.
   b. Consume a larger, more diverse quantity of goods and services at lower prices than would otherwise prevail.
   c. Share our technology and efficiency with less developed countries that would otherwise never have the opportunity to observe modern goods and services.
   d. Maintain jobs for workers who would otherwise have little or nothing to do.
5. The imposition of a restrictive quota on the import of spiked track shoes is likely to
   a. Increase the price of the shoes but decrease the quantity consumed.
   b. Increase both the price of the shoes and the quantity consumed.
   c. Leave the price of the shoes unchanged but decrease the quantity consumed.
   d. Leave the price of the shoes unchanged and also leave the quantity consumed of the shoes unchanged, since domestic producers will expand output in order to make up for a reduction in the supply of the imported shoes.
6. The argument that trade restrictions expand employment in import-competing industries is generally
   a. Correct; but it fails to consider that the restrictions also reduce the efficiency of resource use and retard employment in export industries.
   b. Correct; therefore, it is correct to conclude that the restrictions also expand aggregate employment.

c. Incorrect; trade restrictions generally destroy jobs in import-competing industries.
d. Incorrect; trade restrictions increase the efficiency of resource use, but they do not enlarge employment in import-competing industries.

7. American textile manufacturers and union members have often lobbied successfully for lower quotas that would restrict the quantity of Japanese textile products imported. The major impact of quotas on these Japanese imports is
   a. A permanent reduction in unemployment in the United States.
   b. Lower prices for American consumers and an improvement in the quality of textile products available.
   c. Higher prices for American consumers, a narrower selection of products, and less competition in the U.S. textile industry.
   d. Long-run profits in the U.S. textile industry that are substantially above the market equilibrium level.
8. A reduction in the tariff on imported steel would most likely benefit
   a. Workers in the steel industry.
   b. Domestic consumers of steel.
   c. Domestic producers of steel.
   d. Foreign producers at the expense of domestic consumers.
9. According to the law of comparative advantage, joint output will be greatest when each country
   a. Specializes in the production of those products for which it is the high opportunity-cost producer.
   b. Specializes in the production of those products for which it is the low opportunity-cost producer.
   c. Raises tariff barriers to protect its domestic industries from cheap foreign products.
   d. Lowers tariffs in a manner that will maximize the level of employment in its domestic industries.
10. The political popularity of a tariff on imported goods that compete with products of a well-established domestic industry is
    a. Surprising, since one would expect the political power of consumers to override the interests of even a well-established domestic industry.
    b. Surprising, since one would expect the economic harm resulting from tariffs to be well understood by voters.
    c. Not surprising, since such a tariff would generally benefit an easily recognized interest group at the expense of uninformed, uninterested consumers.
    d. Not surprising, since the tariff enables domestic producers and consumers to gain at the expense of foreigners.

## PROBLEMS

1. Consider the following hypothetical information about the United States and South Korea:

| | Output per Worker per Day | |
|---|---|---|
| | **United States** | **South Korea** |
| Tons of steel | 8 | 4 |
| Bushels of wheat | 80 | 8 |

a. Which country has the comparative advantage in steel production? ________ Wheat production? ________

b. If these countries trade steel and wheat with each other, which country will export steel and import wheat?

c. Suppose that the United States and South Korea agree to a daily trade of 10 tons of Korean steel for 50 bushels of U.S. wheat. One worker in the United States then switches from steel production to wheat production, while four workers in South Korea switch from wheat production to steel production. Complete the following table to show that both countries end up with more steel and more wheat than they had initially:

| **United States** | **Tons of Steel** | **Bushels of Wheat** |
|---|---|---|
| Change in production | −8 | +80 |
| Trade | | |
| Change in consumption | | |

| **South Korea** | **Tons of Steel** | **Bushels of Wheat** |
|---|---|---|
| Change in production | | |
| Trade | | |
| Change in consumption | | |

2. Suppose that the United States can purchase motorcycles from abroad for $3,000 each, and that this price does not vary with the quantity the U.S. purchases. Alternatively, the United States can produce its own motorcycles according to the supply schedule given in the accompanying table, which also shows the United States's demand for motorcycles.

| Price (dollars/unit) | Quantity (thousands/year) | |
|---|---|---|
| | **Supplied** | **Demanded** |
| $4,500 | 1,000 | 700 |
| 4,000 | 900 | 900 |
| 3,500 | 800 | 1,100 |
| 3,000 | 700 | 1,300 |
| 2,500 | 600 | 1,500 |
| 2,000 | 500 | 1,700 |

a. In the absence of international trade, what would be the price of motorcycles in the United States? What quantities would be demanded and supplied?
b. Suppose that motorcycles can be imported into the United States without restriction. What will be their price? What will be the quantities demanded and produced domestically? What will be the quantity of imports? By how much will domestic production decline relative to the no-trade amount?
c. Suppose that workers and management in the domestic motorcycle industry lobby Congress for a tariff on imports on the grounds that they need temporary protection from imports in order to maintain domestic markets while they "retool" to incorporate the latest and most efficient techniques of motorcycle production (a version of the "infant" industry argument). If the government yields to the domestic producers and imposes a tariff on imports of $500 per cycle, what will be the domestic price of motorcycles? By how much will domestic production increase? (This is called the "protective effect" of the tariff.) By how much will U.S. purchases of motorcycles fall? By how much will imports fall?
d. Suppose that instead of the tariff of part c, government imposed a quota limiting imports to 300 motorcycles per year. In this case, what would happen to the price of motorcycles as compared to the unrestricted ("free") trade price? (*Hint:* locate a price at which the domestic quantity supplied plus 300 equals the domestic quantity demanded at that price.) What will be the protective effect (increase in domestic quantity produced) of the quota?
e. Judging from your answers to c and d above, what is the basic difference between a tariff and a quota?

CHAPTER

# 19

# EXCHANGE RATES AND INTERNATIONAL FINANCE

Currencies, like tomatoes and football tickets, have a price at which they are bought and sold. An exchange rate is the price of one currency in terms of another, such as the price of a French franc in U.S. dollars or German marks.

*Gary Smith*[1]

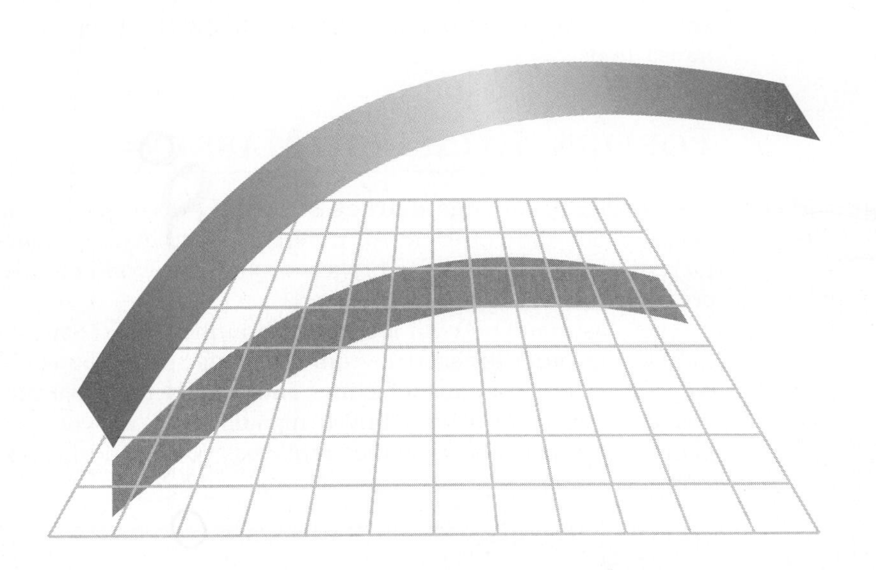

## CHAPTER FOCUS

- What determines the exchange rate value of a currency?
- What are the major factors that would cause the exchange rate value of a currency to change?
- What information is included in the balance-of-payments accounts of a nation? How are these accounts related to the exchange rate market?
- Will the balance-of-payments accounts of a country always be in balance? Will the balance of trade always be in balance?
- Will a healthy economy run a balance-of-trade surplus? Does a balance-of-trade deficit indicate that a nation is in financial trouble?
- What impact do restrictions on the convertibility of a currency have on people in the countries that impose them?

Every nation has a domestic currency that is utilized to buy and sell goods in the domestic market. Germans use marks, the British pounds, the Japanese yens, the Mexicans pesos, and so on. When exchange is between people in different countries, it generally involves the conversion of one currency to another. Farmers in the United States want dollars, not some foreign currency, when they sell their wheat. Therefore, foreign purchasers must exchange their currency for dollars before they buy U.S. wheat. Similarly, French winemakers want to be paid in francs, not dollars. Therefore, U.S. importers must exchange dollars for francs when they purchase French wines (or French exporters must obtain francs before they pay the winemakers).

In this chapter, we analyze how international currencies are linked and how the rates for their exchange are determined. We will also analyze the balance-of-payments accounting that is utilized to keep track of international transactions.

## FOREIGN EXCHANGE MARKET

**foreign exchange market** The market in which the currencies of different countries are bought and sold.

The **foreign exchange market** is a widely dispersed, highly organized market in which the currencies of different countries are bought and sold. Commercial banks and currency brokers around the world are the primary organizers of the market.

Let's assume you own a shoe store in the United States and are preparing to place an order for sandals from a manufacturer. You can purchase the sandals from a domestic manufacturer and pay for them with dollars. Alternately, you can buy them from a British manufacturer, in which case they must be paid for in pounds because the employees of the British manufacturer must be

[1]Gary Smith, *Macroeconomics* (New York: W. H. Freeman and Company, 1985), p. 514.

paid with pounds. If you buy from the British firm, either you will have to change dollars into pounds at a bank and send them to the British producer, or the British manufacturer will have to go to a bank and change your dollar check into pounds. In either case, purchasing the British sandals will involve an exchange of dollars for pounds.

**exchange rate** The domestic price of one unit of foreign currency. For example, if it takes $1.50 to purchase one English pound, the dollar-pound exchange rate is 1.50.

If the British producer sells sandals for 10 pounds per pair, how can you determine whether the price is high or low? To compare the price of the sandals produced by the British firm with the price of domestically produced sandals, you must know the exchange rate between the dollar and the pound. The **exchange rate** is simply the price of one national currency (the pound, for example) in terms of another national currency (such as the U.S. dollar). Exchange rates enable consumers in one country to translate the prices of foreign goods into units of their own currency. For example, if it takes 1.50 dollars to obtain 1 pound, then the British sandals priced at 10 pounds would cost $15.00 (10 times the 1.50 dollar price of the pound).

Suppose the dollar pound exchange rate is $1.50 = 1 pound and you decide to buy 200 pairs of sandals from the British manufacturer at 10 pounds ($15) per pair. You will need 2,000 pounds in order to pay the British manufacturer. If you contact an American bank that handles exchange rate transactions and write the bank a check for $3,000 (the 1.50 exchange rate multiplied by 2,000), it will supply the 2,000 pounds. The bank will typically charge a small fee for handling the transaction.

Where does the American bank get the pounds? The bank obtains the pounds from British importers who want dollars to buy things from Americans. Note that the U.S. demand for foreign currencies (such as the pound) comes from the demand of Americans for things purchased from foreigners. On the other hand, the U.S. supply of foreign exchange comes from the demand of foreigners for things bought from Americans.

Exhibit 19.1 presents data on the exchange rate between the dollar and selected foreign currencies during the 1973-1993 period, as well as an index of the exchange rate value of the dollar against ten major currencies. Under the current flexible system, the exchange rate between currencies changes from day to day and even from hour to hour. Thus, the annual exchange rate data given in Exhibit 19.1 are really averages for each year.

**appreciation** An increase in the value of a domestic currency relative to foreign currencies. An appreciation increases the purchasing power of the domestic currency over foreign goods.

Between 1980 and 1985, the exchange rate value of the dollar appreciated against the major foreign currencies. An **appreciation** in the value of a nation's currency means that fewer units of the currency are now required to purchase one unit of a foreign currency. For example, in 1985 only 34 cents were required to purchase a German mark, down from 55 cents in 1980.[2] As a result of this appreciation in the value of the dollar relative to the mark, German goods became less expensive to Americans. The direction of change in the prices that Germans paid for American goods was just the opposite. An appreciation of the U.S. dollar in terms of the mark is the same thing as a depreciation in the mark relative to the dollar.

**depreciation** A reduction in the value of a domestic currency relative to foreign currencies. A depreciation reduces the purchasing power of the domestic currency over foreign goods.

A **depreciation** makes foreign goods more expensive, since it decreases the number of units of the foreign currency that can be purchased with a unit

[2]Since an appreciation means a *lower* price of foreign currencies, some may think it looks like a depreciation. Just remember that a lower price of the foreign currency means that one's domestic currency will buy more units of the foreign currency and thus more goods and services from foreigners. For example, if the dollar price of the pound falls, this means that a dollar will buy more pounds and thus more goods and services from the British. Therefore, a lower dollar price of the pound means the dollar has appreciated relative to the pound.

EXHIBIT 19.1

**Foreign Exchange Rates, 1973–1993 (U.S. cents per unit of foreign currency)**

| Year | French Franc | German Mark | Japanese Yen | British Pound | Canadian Dollar | Index of Exchange Rate Value of the Dollar (Ten Currencies)[a] |
|---|---|---|---|---|---|---|
| 1973 | 22.5 | 37.8 | 0.369 | 245.10 | 99.9 | 99.1 |
| 1975 | 23.4 | 40.7 | 0.337 | 222.16 | 98.3 | 98.5 |
| 1977 | 20.3 | 43.1 | 0.373 | 174.49 | 94.1 | 103.4 |
| 1979 | 23.5 | 54.6 | 0.458 | 212.24 | 85.3 | 88.1 |
| 1980 | 23.7 | 55.1 | 0.443 | 227.74 | 85.5 | 87.4 |
| 1981 | 18.4 | 44.4 | 0.453 | 202.43 | 83.4 | 103.4 |
| 1982 | 15.2 | 41.2 | 0.402 | 174.80 | 81.0 | 116.6 |
| 1983 | 13.1 | 39.2 | 0.421 | 151.59 | 81.1 | 125.3 |
| 1984 | 11.4 | 35.1 | 0.421 | 133.68 | 77.1 | 138.2 |
| 1985 | 11.1 | 34.0 | 0.419 | 129.74 | 73.2 | 143.0 |
| 1986 | 14.4 | 46.1 | 0.594 | 146.77 | 72.0 | 112.2 |
| 1987 | 16.6 | 55.6 | 0.691 | 163.98 | 75.4 | 96.9 |
| 1988 | 16.8 | 56.9 | 0.780 | 178.13 | 81.3 | 92.7 |
| 1989 | 15.7 | 53.2 | 0.724 | 163.82 | 84.4 | 98.6 |
| 1990 | 18.4 | 61.9 | 0.690 | 178.41 | 85.7 | 89.1 |
| 1991 | 17.7 | 60.2 | 0.743 | 176.74 | 87.3 | 89.3 |
| 1992 | 18.9 | 64.0 | 0.789 | 176.63 | 82.7 | 86.6 |
| 1993 | 17.8 | 61.2 | 0.861 | 149.15 | 80.2 | 90.5 |

[a]March 1973 = 100. In addition to the five currencies listed above, the index includes the Belgian franc, Italian lira, Netherlands guilder, Swedish krona, and Swiss franc.

**Source:** Council of Economic Advisers, *Economic Report of the President* (Washington, D.C.: U.S. Government Printing Office, 1993), and *The Wall Street Journal,* March 22, 1993.

of domestic currency. As Exhibit 19.1 shows, the number of cents required to purchase a French franc, German mark, Japanese yen, or British pound rose substantially between 1985 and 1990. Thus, during this period the dollar depreciated against these currencies, increasing the price of goods purchased by Americans from producers in these countries.

The ten-currency index of the dollar's exchange rate value presented in Exhibit 19.1 provides evidence on what is happening to the dollar's general exchange rate value.[3] An increase in the index implies an appreciation in the dollar, while a decline is indicative of a depreciation in the dollar. During the 1970s, the ten-currency index changed by only small amounts from year to year. However, between 1980 and 1985, the index increased from 87.4 to

[3]In the construction of this index, the exchange rate of each currency relative to the dollar is weighted according to the proportion of U.S. trade with the country. For example, the index weights the dollar–Japanese yen exchange rate more heavily than the dollar–Swiss franc exchange rate because the volume of U.S. trade with Japan exceeds the volume of trade with Switzerland.

143.0, a 60 percent appreciation in the exchange rate value of the dollar during the five-year period. In contrast, the dollar depreciated by a similar amount during the 1986–1990 period.

## Determinants of Exchange Rates

**flexible exchange rates** Exchange rates that are determined by the market forces of supply and demand. They are sometimes called *floating exchange rates.*

The foreign exchange rate market is a highly competitive market characterized by a large number of buyers and sellers. The exchange rate of a currency is a price. Under a system of *floating* or **flexible exchange rates,** the forces of demand and supply will determine the exchange rate value of a currency just as they determine other prices.

The exchange rate system in effect since 1973 might best be described as a managed flexible rate system. The system qualifies as a flexible rate system because all of the major industrial countries allow the exchange rate value of their currencies to float. Several small countries maintain fixed exchange rates against the dollar, the English pound, or some other major currency. Therefore, the exchange rate value of these currencies rises and falls with the major currency to which they are tied. The system is managed because the major industrial nations have from time to time attempted to alter supply and demand in the exchange rate market by buying and selling various currencies. Compared to the size of the exchange rate market, however, these transactions have been relatively small. Thus, the exchange rate value of major currencies like the U.S. dollar, British pound, German mark, Japanese yen, and French franc is determined primarily by market forces.

To simplify our explanation of how the exchange rate market works, let us assume that the United States and Great Britain are the only two countries in the world. When Americans buy and sell with each other, they use dollars. Therefore, American sellers will want to be paid in dollars. Similarly, when the British buy and sell with each other, they use pounds. As a result, British sellers will want to be paid in pounds.

If Americans want to buy from British sellers, they will need to acquire pounds. In our two-country world, the demand for pounds in the exchange rate market originates from the demand of Americans for British goods, services, and assets (either real or financial). For example, when U.S. residents purchase men's suits from a British manufacturer, travel in the United Kingdom, or purchase the stocks, bonds, or physical assets of British business firms, they demand pounds from (and supply dollars to) the foreign exchange rate market to pay for these items.

Similarly, when the British buy from American sellers, they will need to exchange pounds for dollars. The supply of pounds (and demand for dollars) in the exchange rate market comes from the demand of the British for items supplied by Americans. When the British purchase goods, services, or assets from Americans, they supply pounds to (and demand dollars from) the foreign exchange market.

Exhibit 19.2 illustrates the demand and supply curves of Americans for foreign exchange; British pounds in our two-country case. The demand for pounds is downward sloping because a lower dollar price of the pound—this means a dollar will buy more pounds—makes British goods cheaper for American importers. The goods produced by one country are generally good substitutes for the goods of another country. This means that when foreign (British) goods become cheaper, Americans will increase their expenditures on imports

**EXHIBIT 19.2**

**Equilibrium in the Foreign Exchange Market**

The dollar price of the pound is measured on the vertical axis. The horizontal axis indicates the flow of pounds to the foreign exchange market. The equilibrium exchange rate is $1.50 = 1 pound. At the equilibrium price, the quantity demanded of pounds just equals the quantity supplied. A higher price of pounds such as $1.80 = 1 pound would lead to an excess supply of pounds, causing the dollar price of the pound to fall. On the other hand, a lower price, for example $1.20 = 1 pound, would result in an excess demand for pounds, causing the pound to appreciate.

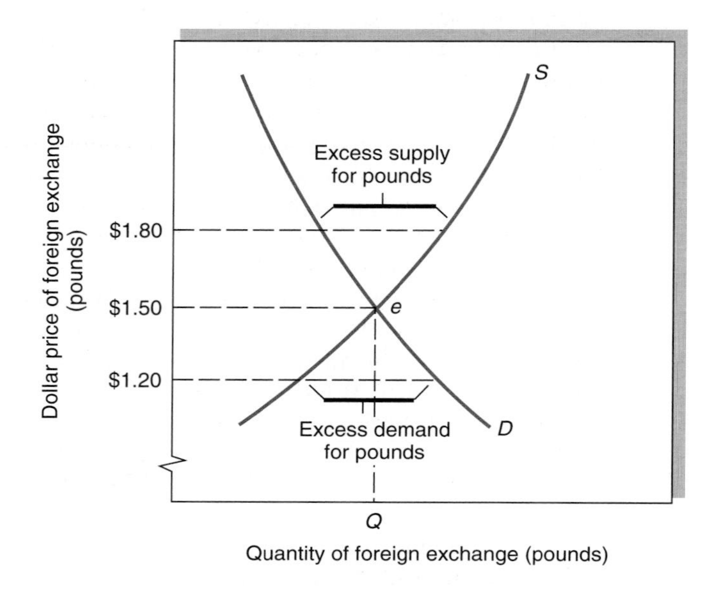


(and therefore the quantity of pounds demanded will increase). Thus, Americans will increase their expenditures on the lower-priced (in dollars) British goods and therefore they will demand more pounds as the pound's dollar price declines.

Similarly, the supply curve for pounds is dependent on the purchases of American goods by the British. An increase in the dollar price of the pound means that a pound will purchase more dollars and more goods priced in terms of dollars. The price (in terms of pounds) of American goods, services, and assets to *British consumers* declines as the dollar price of the pound increases. The British will purchase more from Americans and therefore supply more pounds to the exchange rate market as the dollar price of the pound rises. Because of this, the supply curve for pounds tends to slope upward to the right.

As Exhibit 19.2 shows, equilibrium is present (at $1.50 = 1 pound) when the dollar price of the pound brings the quantity demanded and quantity supplied of pounds into balance. The market-clearing price of $1.50 per pound not only equates demand and supply in the foreign exchange market; it also equates (1) the value of U.S. purchases of items supplied by the British with

(2) the value of items sold by U.S. residents to the British. Demand and supply in the currency market are merely the mirror images of these two factors.

What would happen if the price of the pound were above equilibrium, for example, $1.80 = 1 pound? At the higher dollar price of the pound, British goods would be more expensive for Americans. Americans would cut back on their purchases of English shoes, glassware, textile products, financial assets, and other items supplied by the British. Reflecting this reduction, the quantity of pounds demanded by Americans would decline. Simultaneously, the higher dollar price of the pound would make U.S. exports cheaper for the British. For example, an $18,000 American automobile would cost British consumers 12,000 pounds when one pound trades for $1.50, but it would cost only 10,000 pounds when one pound exchanges for $1.80. If the price of the pound were $1.80, the British would tend to supply more pounds to the exchange rate market to purchase the cheaper American goods. Thus, at the $1.80 = 1 pound price, the quantity of pounds demanded by Americans falls and the quantity supplied by the British increases. As can be seen in Exhibit 19.2, an excess supply of pounds results, causing the dollar price of the pound to decline until equilibrium is restored at the $1.50 = 1 pound price.

At a below-equilibrium price such as $1.20 = 1 pound, an opposite set of forces would be present. The lower dollar price of the pound would make English goods cheaper for Americans and American goods more expensive for the British. The quantity demanded of British goods and pounds by Americans would increase. Simultaneously, the quantity of American goods demanded and pounds supplied by the British would decline. An excess demand for pounds would result at the $1.20 = 1 pound price. The excess demand would tend to cause the dollar price of the pound to rise until equilibrium was restored at $1.50 = 1 pound.

## Changes in Exchange Rates

When exchange rates are free to fluctuate, the market value of a nation's currency will appreciate and depreciate in response to changing market conditions. Any change that alters the quantity of goods, services, or assets bought from foreigners relative to the quantity sold to foreigners will also alter the exchange rate. What types of change will alter the exchange rate value of a currency?

**CHANGES IN INCOME** An increase in domestic income will encourage the nation's residents to spend a portion of their additional income on imports. When the income of a nation grows rapidly, the nation's imports tend to rise rapidly as well. As Exhibit 19.3 illustrates, an increase in imports also increases the demand for foreign exchange, the pound in our two-country case. As the demand for pounds increases, the dollar price of the pound rises (from $1.50 to $1.80). This depreciation of the dollar reduces the incentive of Americans to import British goods and services, while increasing the incentive of the British to purchase U.S. exports. These two forces will restore equilibrium in the foreign exchange market at a new, higher dollar price of the pound.

Just the opposite takes place when the income of a trading partner (Great Britain in our example) increases. Rapid growth of income abroad will lead to an increase in U.S. exports, causing the demand for the dollar to rise. This will result in dollar appreciation—equilibrium at a new, lower dollar price of the pound.

**EXHIBIT 19.3**

**Growth of Income and Growth of Imports**

Other things constant, if incomes grow in the United States, U.S. imports will grow. The increase in the imports will increase the demand for pounds, causing the dollar price of the pound to rise (from $1.50 to $1.80).

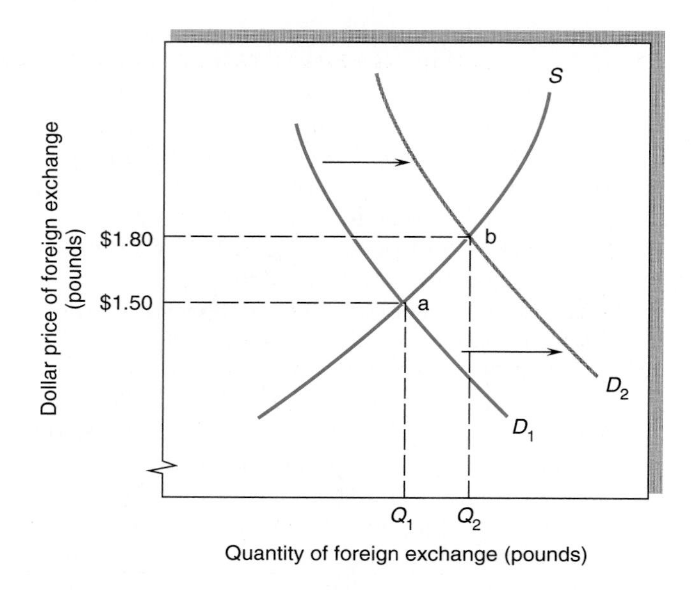


What happens to the exchange rate if income increases in both countries? The key here is to identify the nation that is growing faster. For countries that are similar in size and propensity to import, the country that is growing faster will increase its demand for imports relatively more than will its trading partner, resulting in a decrease in the value of the more rapidly growing nation's currency. Thus, as paradoxical as it may seem, sluggish growth of income relative to one's trading partners tends to cause the slow-growth nation's currency to appreciate, since the nation's imports decline relative to exports.

**DIFFERENCES IN RATES OF INFLATION** Other things constant, domestic inflation will cause a nation's currency to depreciate on the foreign exchange market, whereas deflation will result in appreciation. Suppose prices in the United States rise by 50 percent, while our trading partners are experiencing stable prices. The domestic inflation will cause U.S. consumers to increase their demand for imported goods (and foreign currency). In turn, the inflated domestic prices will cause foreigners to reduce their purchases of U.S. goods, thereby reducing the supply of foreign currency to the exchange market. As Exhibit 19.4 illustrates, the exchange rate will adjust to this set of circumstances. The dollar will depreciate relative to the pound.

Exchange rate adjustments permit nations with even high rates of inflation to engage in trade with countries experiencing relatively stable prices. A depreciation in a nation's currency in the foreign exchange market compensates

**EXHIBIT 19.4**

**Inflation with Flexible Exchange Rates**

If prices were stable in England while the price level increased 50 percent in the United States, the U.S. demand for British products (and pounds) would increase, whereas U.S. exports to Britain would decline, causing the supply of pounds to fall. These forces would cause the dollar to depreciate relative to the pound.

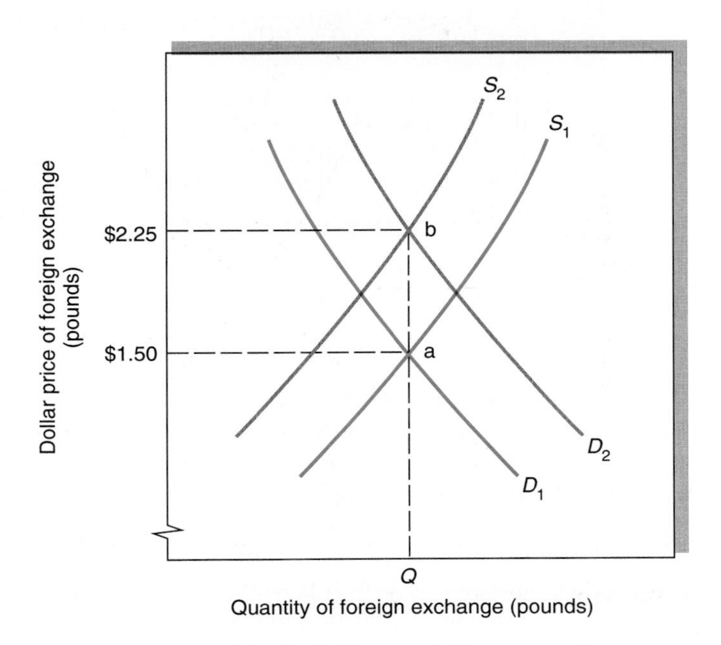


for the nation's inflation rate. For example, if inflation increases the price level in the United States by 50 percent and the value of the dollar in exchange for the pound depreciates 50 percent, then the prices of American goods measured in pounds are unchanged to British consumers. Thus, when the exchange rate value of the dollar changes from \$1.50 = 1 pound to \$2.25 = 1 pound, the depreciation in the dollar restores the original prices of U.S. goods to British consumers even though the price level in the United States has increased by 50 percent.

What if prices in both England and the United States are rising at the same annual rate, say, 10 percent? The prices of imports (and exports) will remain unchanged relative to domestically produced goods. Equal rates of inflation in each of the countries will not cause the value of exports to change relative to imports. Identical rates of inflation will not disturb an equilibrium in the exchange market. Inflation contributes to the depreciation of a nation's currency only when a country's rate of inflation is more rapid than that of its trading partners.

**CHANGES IN INTEREST RATES** Short-term financial investments will be quite sensitive to changes in real interest rates—that is, interest rates adjusted for the expected rate of inflation. International loanable funds will tend to move

THUMBNAIL SKETCH

**Currency Appreciation and Depreciation with Freely Fluctuating Exchange Rates**

These factors will cause a nation's currency to appreciate:

1. A slow rate of growth in income that causes imports to lag behind exports.
2. A rate of inflation that is lower than one's trading partners.
3. Domestic real interest rates that are greater than real interest rates abroad.

These factors will cause a nation's currency to depreciate:

1. A rapid rate of growth in income that stimulates imports relative to exports.
2. A rate of inflation that is higher than one's trading partners.
3. Domestic real interest rates that are lower than real interest rates abroad.

toward areas where the expected real rate of return (after compensation for differences in risk) is highest. If real interest rates increase in the United States relative to Western Europe, borrowers in Britain, France, and Germany will demand dollars (and supply their currencies) in the foreign exchange market in order to purchase the high-yield American assets. The increase in demand for the dollar and supply of European currencies will cause the dollar to appreciate relative to the British pound, French franc, and German mark.

In contrast, when real interest rates in other countries are high relative to the United States, short-term financial investors will move to take advantage of the improved earnings opportunities abroad. As investment funds move from the United States to other countries, there will be an increase in the demand for foreign currencies and an increase in the supply of dollars in the foreign exchange market. A depreciation in the dollar relative to the currencies of countries experiencing the high real interest rates will be the result. The accompanying "Thumbnail Sketch" summarizes the major forces that cause a nation's currency to appreciate or depreciate when exchange rates are determined by market forces.

## BALANCE OF PAYMENTS

**balance of payments** A summary of all economic transactions between a country and all other countries for a specific time period—usually a year. The balance-of-payments account reflects all payments and liabilities to foreigners (debits) and all payments and obligations (credits) received from foreigners.

The **balance of payments** account of a nation summarizes the transactions of the country's citizens, businesses, and governments with foreigners. Basic bookkeeping principles are utilized in balance-of-payments accounting. The entries are closely related to the forces underlying the exchange rate market. Transactions with foreigners that create a demand for the nation's currency (or a supply of foreign currency) in the foreign exchange market are recorded as a credit, or plus item. Exports are an example of a credit item. Similarly, transactions that supply the nation's currency (or create a demand for foreign currency) in the exchange rate market are recorded as debits, or minus items. Imports are an example of a debit item.

The balance-of-payments transactions can be grouped into three basic categories: current account, capital amount, and official reserve account. Let us take a look at each of these.

## Current Account

All payments (and gifts) that are related to the purchase or sale of goods and services and income flows during the designated period are included in the **current account.** In general, there are four major types of current-account transactions: the exchange of merchandise goods, the exchange of services, income from investments, and unilateral transfers.

**current account** The record of all transactions with foreign nations that involve the exchange of merchandise goods and services or unilateral gifts.

**MERCHANDISE TRADE TRANSACTIONS** The export and import of merchandise goods comprise by far the largest portion of a nation's balance-of-payments account. When U.S. producers export their products, foreigners will supply their currency in exchange for dollars in order to pay for the U.S.–produced goods. Since U.S. exports generates a demand for dollars in the foreign exchange market, they are a credit (+) item. In contrast, when Americans import goods, they will supply dollars and demand a foreign currency in the exchange rate market. Thus, imports are a debit (–) item.

As Exhibit 19.5 shows, the United States exported $416 billion of merchandise goods in 1991, compared to imports of $489 billion. The difference between the value of a country's merchandise exports and the value of its

**EXHIBIT 19.5** **U.S. Balance of Payments, 1991**

| | Billions of Dollars | |
|---|---|---|
| | **Amount** | **Deficit (–) or Surplus (+)** |
| **Current Account** | | |
| 1a. U.S. merchandise exports | 416 | |
| 1b. U.S. merchandise imports | –489 | |
| **Balance of merchandise trade** | | –73 |
| 2a. U.S. service exports | 163 | |
| 2b. U.S. service imports | –118 | |
| **Balance on goods and services** | | –28 |
| 3. Net investment income | 16 | |
| 4. Net transfers | 8 | |
| **Balance on current account** | | –4 |
| **Capital Account** | | |
| 5. Capital inflow to U.S. | 48 | |
| 6. Outflow of U.S. capital | –68 | |
| **Balance on capital account** | | –20 |
| **Current and capital account balance** | | –24 |
| **Official reserve account transactions** | | 24 |

**Source:** Survey of Current Business, September 1992.

**balance of merchandise trade** The difference between the value of merchandise exports and the value of merchandise imports for a nation. The balance of trade is only one component of a nation's total balance of payments.

merchandise "imports is known as the **balance of merchandise trade** (or "balance-of-trade"). If the value of a country's merchandise exports falls short of (exceeds) the value of its merchandise imports, it is said to have a balance-of-trade deficit (surplus). In 1991 the United States ran a balance-of-trade deficit of $73 billion.

**SERVICE EXPORTS AND IMPORTS** The export and import of *invisible services,* as they are sometimes called, also exert an important influence on the foreign exchange market. The export of insurance, transportation, and banking services generates a demand for dollars by foreigners just as the export of merchandise does. A French business that is insured with an American company will demand dollars with which to pay its premiums. When foreigners travel in the United States or transport cargo on American ships, they will demand dollars with which to pay for these services. These service exports are thus entered as credits on the current account.

On the other hand, the import of services from foreigners expands the supply of dollars to the foreign exchange market. Therefore, service imports are entered on the balance-of-payments accounts as debit items. Travel abroad by U.S. citizens, the shipment of goods on foreign carriers, and the purchase of other services from foreigners are all debit items, since they supply dollars to the foreign exchange market.

These service transactions are substantial. As Exhibit 19.5 illustrates, in 1991 the U.S. service exports were $163 billion, compared with service imports of $118 billion. Thus, the U.S. ran a $45 billion surplus on its service trade transactions.

**balance on goods and services** The exports of goods (merchandise) and services of a nation minus its imports of goods and services.

When we add the balance of service exports and imports to the balance of merchandise trade we obtain the **balance on goods and services.** In 1991, the United States ran a $28 billion deficit (the sum of the $73 billion trade deficit minus the $45 billion service surplus) in the goods and services account.

**INCOME FROM INVESTMENTS** In the past, Americans have made substantial investments in stocks, bonds, and real assets in other countries. As these investments abroad generate income, dollars will flow from foreigners to Americans. Since the income of Americans from their investments abroad supplies foreign currency (and creates a demand for dollars) in the foreign exchange market, it enters as a credit item on the current account.

Correspondingly, foreigners hold substantial investments in the United States. As these investments earn dividends, interest, and rents, they earn income for foreigners. This income of foreigners leads to an outflow of dollars. As foreigners convert their dollar earnings to their domestic currency, the supply of dollars (and demand for foreign currency) increases on the foreign exchange market. Thus, the income of foreigners from their investments in the United States is a debit item in the balance-of-payments accounts.

In 1991 Americans earned $16 billion more on their investments abroad than foreigners earned on their investments in the United States. Since these items resulted in a net flow of income to the United States, the result is recorded as a credit.

**UNILATERAL TRANSFERS** Monetary gifts to foreigners, such as U.S. aid to a foreign government or private gifts from U.S. residents to their relatives abroad, supply dollars to the exchange market. These gifts are debit items in the balance-of-payments accounts. Monetary gifts to Americans from foreigners are credit items. Gifts in kind are more complex. When products are given to foreigners, goods flow abroad, but there is no offsetting influx of foreign currency—that is, no demand for dollars. Balance-of-payments accountants handle such transactions as though the United States had supplied the dollars with which to purchase the direct grants made to foreigners. So these items are also entered as debits. In 1991 the U.S. government and private U.S. citizens received net transfers of $8 billion from foreigners. This item was entered as a credit in the balance-of-payments accounts.

**balance on current account** The import-export balance of goods and services plus net investment income and net unilateral transfers. If the figure is positive (negative), a current account surplus (deficit) is present.

**BALANCE ON CURRENT ACCOUNT** The difference between (1) the value of a country's current exports and earnings from investments abroad and (2) the value of its current imports and the earnings of foreigners on their domestic assets (plus net unilateral transfers to foreigners) is known as the **balance on current account.** Current-account transactions involve only current exchanges of goods and services and current income flows (and gifts). They do not involve changes in the ownership of either real or financial assets. The current-account balance provides a summary of all current-account transactions. As with the balance of trade, when the value of the current-account debit items (import-type transactions) exceeds the value of the credit items (export-type transactions), we say that the country is running a current-account deficit. Alternatively, if the credit items are greater than the debit items, the country is running a current-account surplus. In 1991 the United States ran a current-account deficit of $4 billion.

## Capital Account

In contrast with current-account transactions, capital-account transactions focus on changes in the ownership of real and financial assets. When foreigners make investments in the United States, for example, by purchasing stocks, bonds, or real assets from Americans, their actions will supply foreign currency and generate a demand for dollars in the foreign exchange market. Thus, these capital-inflow transactions are a credit. On the other hand, capital-outflow transactions are recorded as debits, since U.S. citizens will supply dollars and demand foreign currency when they invest in stocks, bonds, and real assets abroad.

In 1991 foreign investments in the United States (capital inflow) summed to $48 billion while U.S. investments abroad (capital outflow) totaled $68 billion. Since the capital outflow exceeded the inflow, the United States ran a $20 billion capital account deficit in 1991.

**special drawing rights** Supplementary reserves, in the form of accounting entries, established by the International Monetary Fund (also called *paper gold*). Like gold and foreign currency reserves, they can be used to make payments on international accounts.

## Official Reserve Account

Governments maintain official reserve balances in the form of foreign currencies, gold, and **special drawing rights** (SDRs) with the International Monetary Fund (IMF), a type of international central bank. Countries running a deficit on their current-account and capital-account balances can draw on their reserves. Similarly, countries running a surplus can build up their reserves of foreign currencies and reserve balances with the IMF.

Under the current (primarily) flexible rate system, changes in the official reserve account of nations are generally quite small. Changes in the exchange rate are generally relied on to balance the amount of goods, services, and assets purchased from foreigners and the amount sold to foreigners. However, sometimes nations have their central banks buy and sell currencies in an attempt to reduce sharp swings in the exchange rate. During some years, a nation may build up its holdings of foreign currencies, while in other years it may permit them to be drawn out. These official reserve transactions are generally quite modest relative to the total of all international transactions. In 1991 the U.S. official reserve holdings of foreign currencies declined by $24 billion. When a country reduces its official reserve holdings, it supplies foreign currency to the exchange rate market. Therefore, such transactions are a credit item. Similarly, when a country increases its official reserve holdings, the action is a debit, since it increases the demand for foreign currency in the foreign exchange market.

### Balance of Payments Must Balance

The aggregated balance-of-payments accounts must balance according to the following equation:

Current account + capital account + official reserve account = 0

However, the specific components of the accounts need not balance. For example, the debit and credit items of the current account need not be equal. Specific components may run either a surplus or a deficit. Nevertheless, since the balance of payments as a whole must balance, a deficit in one area implies a surplus in another.

In 1991 the United States ran a $4 billion deficit on current-account and a $20 billion deficit on capital-account transactions. This $24 billion combined deficit was exactly offset by a $24 billion surplus on the official reserve–account transactions. Thus, the deficits and surpluses on current-account, capital-account, and official reserve–account transactions summed to zero.

Since countries, to some extent, engage in official reserve transactions, the current system is not a purely flexible rate system. If it were, there would not be any official reserve transactions. Consequently, equilibrium in the exchange rate market would imply that the sum of the credit items in the current and capital accounts was just equal to the sum of the debit items. Therefore, if the current account was running a deficit, the capital account would have to be running a surplus. Similarly, if a nation was running a current-account surplus, it would have to run a capital-account deficit under a purely flexible exchange system.

## TRADE DEFICITS AND SURPLUSES

There is a tendency to think that a balance-of-trade surplus is good and a deficit bad. This is certainly understandable. In other contexts, the implications associated with a surplus are generally preferable to those of a deficit. In the area of trade, however, there are often two ways of viewing transactions.

When the service sector is included, a balance-of-trade deficit means that, in aggregate, the citizens of a nation are buying more goods and services from foreigners than they are receiving from foreigners. A surplus implies that the sales to foreigners (exports) exceed the purchases from foreigners (imports). It is not obvious that a surplus is preferable to a deficit. After all, a nation that is running a deficit is getting more goods and services from others than it is supplying to them. What is so bad about that? Similarly, a trade surplus implies that a nation is producing more goods and services for foreigners to consume than it is receiving from foreigners. Is this something that people will want to continue to do?

A nation's trade deficit or surplus is an aggregation of the voluntary choices of businesses and individuals. In contrast with a budget deficit of an individual, business, or government, there is no legal entity that is responsible for the trade deficit. As Herbert Stein, a former Chairman of the President's Council of Economic Advisers, states:

> The fact is that a certain (unknown) number of Americans bought more abroad than they sold abroad and a certain other (unknown) number of Americans sold more than they bought abroad. The trade deficit is the excess of the net foreign purchases of the first group over the net foreign sales of the second group. The trade deficit does not belong to any individual or institution. It is a pure statistical aggregate, like the number of eggs laid in the U.S. or the number of bald-headed men living here.[4]

Under a flexible exchange rate system, a trade deficit—or more broadly, a current-account deficit—must be financed with a capital-account surplus. A capital-account surplus indicates that foreigners are investing more in the United States than Americans are investing abroad. Is this inflow of real and financial capital bad? The answer to this question depends on why Americans are investing so little abroad and foreigners are investing so much in the United States. If it is because large budget deficits have induced Americans to consume beyond their means, and pushed up interest rates, then there is cause for concern. However, if this is the case, it is important to note that the problem is not the current-account deficit, but rather large budget deficits that are encouraging current consumption and diverting the savings of Americans away from private capital formation. To the extent that Americans save and invest less as the result of budget deficits, the growth of their future income will be slower.

On the other hand, if the capital-account surplus merely reflects that investment opportunities in a country are attractive relative to investment opportunities elsewhere, the inflow of capital reflects positively on the economic health of that country. Under a flexible exchange system, countries with more attractive investment opportunities and a lower saving rate than their trading partners will run current-account deficits. Correspondingly, countries with less attractive investment opportunities and a higher saving rate will run current-account surpluses.

How long can a nation continue to run a current-account deficit? Perhaps surprising to some, the answer is a long time. A current-account deficit is not like business losses or an excess of household spending relative to income—conditions that eventually force decision-makers to alter their ways. The United States ran a current (trade) account deficit almost every year from 1800 to 1875. On the other hand, it consistently ran current-account surpluses from 1946 to 1976. The trade accounts of other countries have followed similar lengthy periods of both deficits and surpluses.

Currently, the United States has a rapidly growing labor force (compared with Europe and Japan), a system of secure property rights, and political

[4]Herbert Stein, "Leave the Trade Deficit Alone," *The Wall Street Journal,* March 11, 1987.

stability. This makes it an attractive country in which to invest. On the other hand, the saving rate of the United States, perhaps as the result of budget deficits, cultural factors, or less favorable tax treatment of saving, is low compared to our major trading partners. A continuation of this combination of factors—attractive investment opportunities and a low saving rate—will result in the long-term inflow of foreign capital and a corresponding current-account deficit.

The forces underpinning the U.S. current-account deficit may change in the near future. The growth rate of the U.S. labor force may slow, reducing the return on investment and the inflow of capital. Or a period of slow growth in the income of Americans may motivate them to save a larger proportion of their income. Correspondingly, as the income of foreigners increases, they may decide to consume more and save less. Perhaps the federal government will reduce the size of its deficit and thereby push U.S. interest rates lower. Changes of this type will close the current-account deficit. But such changes need not take place. And if they do not, the current-account deficit will continue, and there is little reason to believe that it is exerting a harmful impact on the U.S. economy.

## IMPORTANT SOURCE OF PROSPERITY: FREE CONVERTIBILITY OF DOMESTIC CURRENCY

If the people of one country are going to trade with buyers and sellers in other countries, they must be able to convert their domestic currency into foreign currencies. For example, American sellers will not want to be paid in Iranian rials because the Iranian currency cannot be used to buy things in the United States. Neither is it freely convertible to U.S. dollars. Nonconvertibility of one's domestic currency is a major obstacle that will reduce the ability of people to realize gains from trade and specialization in areas where they have a comparative advantage.

Of course, if a country has a flexible exchange rate—if it permits its currency to be freely and legally converted to other currencies in foreign exchange markets, currency convertibility is no problem. Many governments, however, fix the price of their currency and prohibit currency exchanges at other prices. Both a fixed exchange rate and free convertibility of a currency can be maintained *if a country is willing to use its monetary policy to maintain the fixed exchange rate.* Put another way, a country can either (1) follow an independent monetary policy and allow its exchange rate to fluctuate or (2) tie its monetary policy to the maintenance of the fixed exchange rate. It cannot, however, maintain convertibility if it is going to both fix the exchange rate value of its currency and follow an independent monetary policy. It must either give up its monetary independence or allow its exchange rate to fluctuate if its currency is going to be fully convertible with other currencies.

Some countries, particularly small countries, have chosen to forgo monetary independence and tie the exchange rate value of their domestic currency to a widely accepted currency like the U.S. dollar, the German mark, or the French franc. This is not a bad strategy. Worldwide, people already have confidence in currencies like the dollar, mark, and franc. Thus, tying one's currency to those currencies increases its acceptability.

Hong Kong has followed this strategy. It does not have a central bank that conducts monetary policy. Instead it has a currency board that issues Hong Kong dollars in exchange for U.S. dollars at an exchange rate of 7.2 Hong Kong dollars = 1 U.S. dollar. When U.S. dollars are received in exchange for newly issued Hong Kong dollars, the U.S. dollars are invested in U.S. government bonds. Thus, the Hong Kong dollar is fully backed by the U.S. dollar (or U.S. bonds). If prices were to rise in Hong Kong relative to the United States, fewer people would want to use Hong Kong dollars and more would want to use U.S. dollars. Thus, people would ask the currency board to exchange Hong Kong dollars for U.S. dollars, which would have more purchasing power. In response, however, the supply of Hong Kong dollars would shrink, which would put a brake on inflation in Hong Kong.

In contrast, if inflation in the United States were greater than in Hong Kong, just the opposite would happen. People would exchange U.S. dollars (which would have less purchasing power) for Hong Kong dollars. In turn, the supply of Hong Kong dollars would increase and bring prices in Hong Kong back into line with prices in the United States. Thus, the purchasing power of the Hong Kong dollar is closely tied to the U.S. dollar (7.2 Hong Kong dollars is essentially the same thing as a U.S. dollar), and recognition of this fact increases its acceptability around the world.

In contrast with countries like Hong Kong that give up their monetary independence in order to tie the exchange rate value of their currency to another that is widely accepted, several countries try to both fix the exchange rate value of their currency and maintain monetary independence, which is often used to follow a highly inflationary monetary policy. This strategy generally results in the exchange rate value of the country's currency being fixed above the market level.

When a country fixes the exchange rate value of its currency above the market level, however, it is simultaneously fixing the price of foreign currencies below market level. This policy will make it extremely difficult for domestic residents to convert their domestic currency to foreign exchange. Since domestic citizens are less able to acquire foreign currencies, they will be less able to trade with foreigners. As a result, the volume of the country's international trade will decline.

Using the Dominican Republic as an example, Exhibit 19.6 illustrates the impact of exchange rate controls. When the Dominican Republic fixes the price of foreign exchange (in terms of the Dominican peso) below equilibrium, the quantity of foreign exchange demanded by Dominicans (so they can buy from foreigners) will exceed the quantity generated by Dominican exports. Under a flexible rate system, this excess demand for foreign currency would be eliminated by a depreciation of the Dominican peso in the exchange rate market. The price of foreign exchange would rise from $P_f$ to $P_e$. With a fixed rate, however, this cannot happen. Instead, Dominican citizens will confront a shortage ($Q_d - Q_s$) of foreign exchange. Since they are able to obtain only $Q_s$ units of foreign exchange, the volume of their trade with foreigners will decline (from $Q_e$ to $Q_s$). In other words, since Dominicans cannot, at least not legally, convert as much of their currency to foreign exchange as they would like, they will not be able to buy as much from foreigners as they would like.

Of course, when price controls lead to shortages, as they inevitably do, black markets develop. Currency markets are not an exception to this rule. If

**EXHIBIT 19.6**

**Fixing the Price of Foreign Currencies below Equilibrium**

When the price of foreign currency in terms of a country's domestic currency is fixed below equilibrium, a shortage of foreign currency will emerge. Illegal black markets will develop as the citizens of the country seek more foreign currency so they can trade with people in other countries.

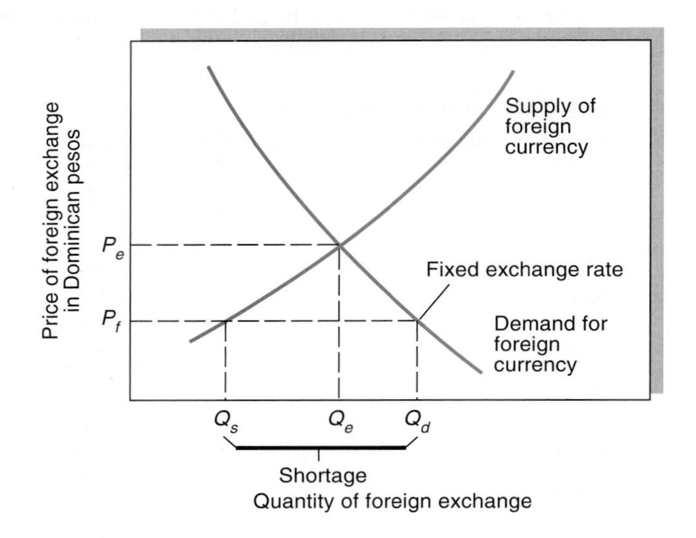


you have ever traveled in a country that imposes exchange rate controls and been approached by someone offering to trade local currency at a premium for your foreign currency, you have observed the black market in foreign exchange. The greater the black-market premium, the more the fixed price of the country's currency is out of line with market conditions, and is thereby restricting the volume of trade with foreigners.

Our analysis illustrates that fixing exchange rates and limiting the convertibility of one's currency will retard international trade and reduce the ability of people to realize gains from specialization and adoption of mass-production methods. Like other trade restrictions, this limitation on exchange will reduce both productivity and living standards.

Exhibit 19.7 presents data on the growth rate of countries where the black-market exchange rate premium was more than 25 percent in 1990. In most cases, these 19 countries imposed tight exchange rate controls during the 1980s. Thirteen of the 19 countries experienced declines in per capita GDP during the 1980s. Only three (Czechoslovakia, Egypt, and Bangladesh) were able to achieve an annual growth rate in excess of 0.3 percent during the 1980s. On average, the per capita GDP of these 19 countries *declined* at an annual rate of 1 percent during the 1980–1990 period. Given the negative impact of exchange rate controls on trade and prosperity, the poor economic performance of these countries is an expected result.

**EXHIBIT 19.7**

**Growth Record of Countries with a Significant Black-Market Exchange Rate Premium, 1980–1990**

| Country/Region | Black-Market Exchange Rate Premium | | | Annual Growth Rate of per Capita GDP |
|---|---|---|---|---|
| | 1980 | 1985 | 1990 | 1980–1990 |
| **North and South America** | | | | |
| Dominican Republic | 37 | 14 | 66 | –0.1 |
| Jamaica | 61 | 19 | 27 | 0.3 |
| Paraguay | 7 | 213 | 26 | –0.7 |
| Trinidad/Tobago | 49 | 39 | 40 | –6.0 |
| **Middle East, Europe, Asia** | | | | |
| Czechoslovakia | 387 | 423 | 61 | 1.1 |
| Egypt | 9 | 146 | 56 | 2.6 |
| Iran | 164 | 533 | 2197 | –1.1 |
| Syria | 35 | 251 | 301 | –1.5 |
| Bangladesh | 111 | 168 | 165 | 2.0 |
| **Africa** | | | | |
| Algeria | 263 | 335 | 140 | 0.1 |
| Ethiopia | 39 | 122 | 202 | –1.3 |
| Mauritania | 41 | 136 | 170 | –1.0 |
| Mozambique | 142 | 4107 | 117 | –3.3 |
| Rwanda | 67 | 49 | 28 | –2.3 |
| Sierra Leone | 62 | 206 | 165 | –0.9 |
| Somalia | 41 | 147 | 200 | –0.7 |
| Tanzania | 224 | 259 | 78 | –0.3 |
| Uganda | 360 | 25 | 40 | 0.3 |
| Zambia | 70 | 38 | 212 | –2.9 |
| **Average growth rate** | | | | **–1.0** |

**Source:** The black-market exchange rate data are from International Currency Analysis, *World Currency Yearbook* (various issues). The data on growth of per capita GDP are from the World Bank, *World Development Report, 1992.* All countries with a population of more than 1 million and a black-market exchange rate premium of more than 25 percent in 1990, for which the data were available, are included.

## LOOKING AHEAD

As we have proceeded, we have from time to time considered the impact of various government policies on economic prosperity. We have not, however, attempted to analyze comprehensively the operation of government and its importance as a source of economic prosperity. Neither have we considered how governments, including democratic governments, can be structured in a manner that will increase the likelihood that they will be a force promoting economic prosperity. The following chapter will focus on these topics.

## CHAPTER SUMMARY

1. The foreign exchange market is a highly organized market in which currencies of different countries are bought and sold. The exchange rate is

the price of one national currency in terms of another. The exchange rate permits consumers in one country to translate the prices of foreign goods into units of their own currency.

2. When international trade takes place, it is usually necessary for one party to convert its currency to the currency of its trading partner. Imports of goods, services, and assets (both real and financial) by the United States generate a demand for foreign currency with which to pay for these items. On the other hand, exports of goods, services, and assets supply foreign currency to the exchange market because foreigners exchange their currency for the dollars needed to purchase the export items.
3. The value of a nation's currency on the exchange market is in equilibrium when the supply of the currency (generated by imports—broadly conceived to include all purchases of goods, services, and assets from foreigners) is just equal to the demand for the currency (generated by exports—broadly conceived to include the sale of goods, services, and assets to foreigners).
4. Under a flexible rate system, if there is an excess supply of dollars (excess demand for foreign currencies) on the foreign exchange market, the value of the dollar will depreciate relative to other currencies. A depreciation will make foreign goods and assets more expensive to U.S. buyers and U.S. goods and assets cheaper for foreign purchasers, reducing the value of our imports and increasing the value of our exports until equilibrium is restored. On the other hand, an excess demand for dollars (excess supply of foreign currencies) will cause the dollar to appreciate, stimulating imports and discouraging exports until equilibrium is restored.
5. With flexible exchange rates, a nation's currency tends to appreciate when (a) rapid economic growth *abroad* (and slow growth at home) stimulates exports relative to imports, (b) the rate of domestic inflation is below that of the nation's trading partners, and (c) domestic real interest rates increase relative to one's trading partners. The reverse of these conditions will cause a nation's currency to depreciate.
6. The balance-of-payments accounts record the flow of payments accompanying exchanges of the citizens, businesses, and governments of a country with foreigners. The entries into the balance-of-payments accounts are closely related to the forces underpinning supply and demand in the foreign exchange market. All transactions (for example, exports) that generate a demand for the nation's currency in the foreign exchange market are recorded as credit items in the balance-of-payment accounts. All transactions (for example, imports) that supply a nation's currency to the foreign exchange markets are recorded as debits.
7. In aggregate, the balance-of-payments accounts must balance. Thus, (a) the current-account balance plus (b) the capital-account balance plus (c) the official reserve–account balance must equal zero. However, the individual components of the accounts need not be in balance. A deficit in one area implies an offsetting surplus in other areas.
8. Under a purely flexible rate system, there will not be any official reserve-account transactions. Under these circumstances, a current-account deficit implies a capital-account surplus (and vice versa).
9. A country's current account (and trade balance) position reflects the voluntary choices of businesses and individuals. In contrast with a budget

deficit of an individual, business, or government, there is no legal entity that is responsible for a current-account (or trade) deficit. Whether a country runs a current-account deficit or surplus is dependent upon the attractiveness of domestic investment opportunities relative to the nation's saving rate. Countries with more attractive investment opportunities and a low saving rate will tend to run capital-account surpluses (capital inflow) and current-account deficits. On the other hand, countries with less attractive investment opportunities and a high saving rate will tend to experience capital account deficits and current-account surpluses under a flexible rate system.

10. When a country fixes the exchange rate value of its currency above the market level (and that of foreign currencies below the market level), a shortage of foreign exchange will result. Since residents of the country are less able to acquire foreign exchange, they are less able to engage in international trade. The decline in the volume of trade accompanying such exchange rate controls will reduce the productivity and income level of the country.

# Study Guide

CHAPTER

19

## Developing the Economic Way of Thinking

## CRITICAL-ANALYSIS QUESTIONS

*1. If the dollar depreciates relative to the German mark, how will your ability to purchase the BMW you have longed for be affected? How will this change influence the quantity of BMWs purchased by Americans? How will it affect the dollar expenditures of Americans on BMWs?

*2. The chart below indicates the actual newspaper quotation of the exchange rate of various currencies:

| | U.S. Dollar Equivalent | |
|---|---|---|
| | Feb. 1 | Feb. 2 |
| British pound | 1.755 | 1.746 |
| French franc | .1565 | .1575 |

On February 2, did the dollar appreciate or depreciate against the British pound? How did it fare against the French franc?

3. "If a current-account deficit means that we are getting more items from abroad than we are sending to foreigners, why is it considered a bad thing?" Comment.

*4. Suppose the exchange rate between the United States and Mexico freely fluctuated in the open market. Indicate which of the following would cause the dollar to appreciate (or depreciate) relative to the peso.
   a. An increase in the quantity of drilling equipment purchased in the United States by Pemex, the Mexican oil company, as a result of a Mexican oil discovery.
   b. An increase in the U.S. purchase of crude oil from Mexico as a result of the development of Mexican oil fields.
   c. Higher real interest rates in Mexico, inducing U.S. citizens to move their financial investments from U.S. to Mexican banks.
   d. Lower real interest rates in the United States, inducing Mexican investors to borrow dollars and then exchange them for pesos.
   e. Inflation in the United States and stable prices in Mexico.
   f. Ten percent inflation in both the United States and Mexico.
   g. An economic boom in Mexico, inducing Mexicans to buy more U.S.-made automobiles, trucks, electric appliances, and television sets.
   h. Attractive investment opportunities, inducing U.S. investors to buy stock in Mexican firms.

5. How do flexible exchange rates bring about balance in the exchange rate market? Do flexible exchange rates lead to a balance between merchandise exports and imports? Explain.

*6. Suppose that the United States were running a current-account deficit. How would each of the following changes influence the size of the deficit?
   a. A recession in the United States.
   b. A decline in the attractiveness of investment opportunities in the United States.
   c. An improvement in investment opportunities abroad.

*Asterisk denotes critical-analysis questions for which the answers are given in Appendix A.

7. "A nation cannot continue to run a deficit on current account. A healthy, growing economy will not persistently expand its indebtedness to foreigners. Eventually, the trade deficits will lead to national bankruptcy." Evaluate this view.
8. In recent years, a substantial share of the domestic capital formation in the United States has been financed by foreign investors. Is this inflow of capital from abroad indicative that the U.S. economy is in poor health? If not, what does it indicate?
9. Is a trade surplus indicative of a strong, healthy economy? Why or why not?
10. "Foreigners are flooding our markets with goods and using the proceeds to buy up America. Unless we do something to protect ourselves, the Japanese, Europeans, and Arabs are going to own America." Evaluate this recent statement of an American political figure.

*11. If foreigners have confidence in the U.S. economy and therefore move to expand their investments in the United States, how will the U.S. current-account balance be affected? How will the exchange rate value of the dollar be affected?

## MULTIPLE-CHOICE SELF-TEST

1. Suppose that the dollar rises in value from 125 to 150 yen. As a result,
   a. Exports to Japan are likely to increase.
   b. Japanese tourists will be more likely to visit the United States.
   c. U.S. businesses will be less likely to use Japanese shipping lines to transport their products.
   d. U.S. consumers will be more likely to purchase Japanese-made automobiles.
2. Suppose that a group of students at your university decides to spend the summer touring the United Kingdom. This action
   a. Creates a demand for dollars and a supply of English pounds in the foreign currency market.
   b. Creates a demand for English pounds and a supply of dollars in the foreign currency market.
   c. Causes the U.S. dollar to appreciate.
   d. Causes the English pound to depreciate.
3. If the exchange rate between the U.S. dollar and the French franc were 0.15 (15 cents = one franc), what would be the price in dollars of a bottle of French wine selling for 400 francs?
   a. $26.66.
   b. $60.00.
   c. $150.00.
   d. $600.00.
4. If the exchange rate value of the English pound goes from $1.75 to $1.50, then the pound has
   a. Appreciated, and the English will find U.S. goods cheaper.
   b. Appreciated, and the English will find U.S. goods more expensive.
   c. Depreciated, and the English will find U.S. goods cheaper.
   d. Depreciated, and the English will find U.S. goods more expensive.

5. Which of the following would be most likely to cause a nation's currency to depreciate?
   a. An increase in domestic real interest rates.
   b. An increase in exports coupled with a decline in imports.
   c. An increase in the nation's rate of inflation.
   d. A balance of trade surplus.
6. Under a purely flexible exchange rate system, the exchange rate that equates demand and supply in the exchange rate market will also lead to a balance of
   a. Merchandise exports and merchandise imports.
   b. Current-account transactions.
   c. Capital-account transactions.
   d. Current- and capital-account transactions.
7. Which of the following is true?
   a. Items that supply the nation's currency to the foreign exchange market are recorded as credits in the nation's balance-of-payments accounts.
   b. Items that create a demand for the nation's currency in the foreign exchange market are recorded as debits in the nation's balance-of-payments accounts.
   c. The purchase of the BMW from a German automaker by a U.S. college student would be recorded as a debit in the U.S. balance-of-payments accounts.
   d. Parts a and b are both true.
8. What is the difference between the balance of merchandise trade and the balance of payments?
   a. Only the value of goods imported and exported are included in the balance of merchandise trade, while the balance of payments includes the value of all payments to and receipts from foreigners.
   b. The value of goods imported and exported is included in the balance of merchandise trade, while the balance of payments includes only capital-account transactions.
   c. The value of all goods, services, and unilateral transfer is included in the balance of merchandise trade, while the balance of payments includes both current account and capital account transactions.
   d. Balance of merchandise trade and balance of payments are different terms used to describe the same international exchange transactions.
9. Under a true flexible exchange rate system, if a nation is experiencing a deficit on its current account transactions,
   a. The nation's currency must appreciate.
   b. The nation's currency must depreciate.
   c. The nation must experience an offsetting surplus on its capital-account transactions.
   d. The nation must also experience a deficit on its capital-account transactions.
10. Which of the following is a true statement?
    a. The U.S. current-account deficit is a financial obligation of the federal government.
    b. A nation cannot run a current-account deficit over a long period of time.

c. A country with relatively poor (compared with other countries) domestic investment opportunities and a high saving rate will tend to run a current-account deficit.

d. A country with highly attractive (compared with other countries) domestic investment opportunities and a low saving rate will tend to run a current-account deficit.

## PROBLEMS

1. The accompanying table presents the balance-of-payments data of the United States in 1989.

| Debits | Billions of Dollars | Credits | Billions of Dollars |
|---|---|---|---|
| **Current account** | | | |
| Merchandise imports | 490 | Merchandise exports | 369 |
| Service imports | 80 | Service exports | 107 |
| Net investment income | 1 | | |
| Unilateral transfers | 15 | | |
| **Capital account** | | | |
| Capital outflow | 49 | Capital inflow | 151 |

a. Calculate the following for 1989:
   i. Balance of merchandise trade.
   ii. Balance on goods and services.
   iii. Balance on current account.
   iv. Balance on capital account.
   v. Balance on current and capital account.

b. Comparable data for 1991 are presented in Exhibit 19.5. What happened to the U.S. balance of merchandise trade and balance on current account between 1989 and 1991?

2. Each of the diagrams below represents the U.S. demand for and supply of foreign exchange (English pounds). For each of the events described below, diagram how the demand and/or supply of pounds changes (use a +, −, or 0 to show no change); and then fill in the blanks to the right of the diagram, indicating in the last blank whether the dollar has appreciated, depreciated, or undergone an indeterminate change as a result of the event(s). (The first question has been partially answered as an example). (Hint: $P$ = dollars per pound.)

| Events | Diagrams | D | S | Change in Value of Dollar |
|---|---|---|---|---|
| a. As a result of recovering from a depression, U.S. incomes rise significantly. | 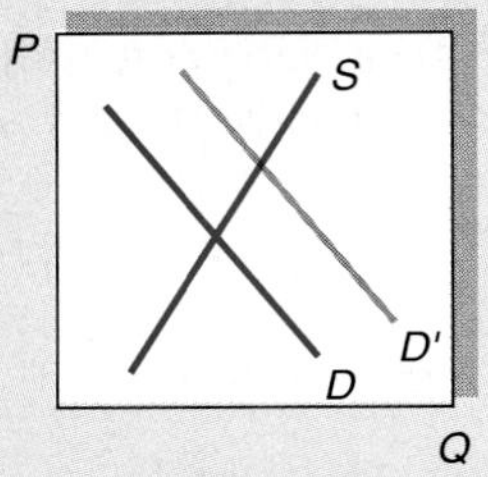 | + | 0 | |
| b. The United Kingdom experiences a serious recession, causing a decline in income. | 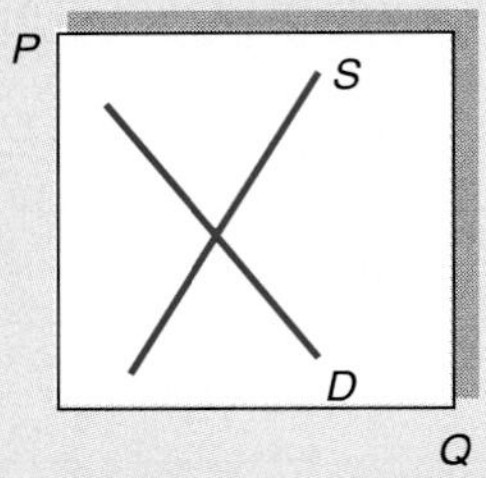 | | | |
| c. Restrictive monetary policy in the United States causes U.S. interest rates to rise relative to U.K. rates. | 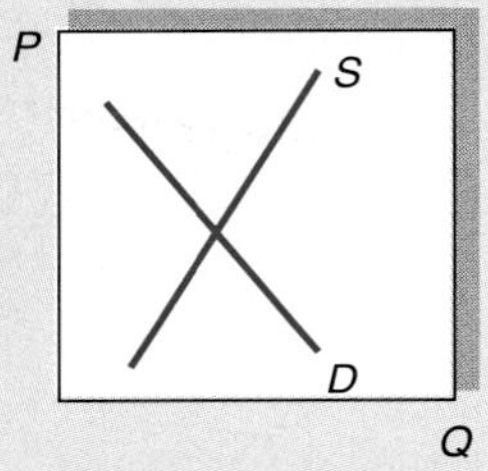 | | | |
| d. Both the United States and the United Kingdom experience inflation rates of 20 percent. | 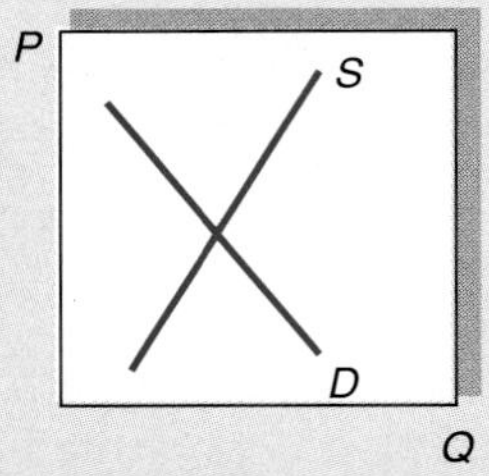 | | | |
| e. While the United States experiences stable prices, prices in the United Kingdom rise by 15 percent. | 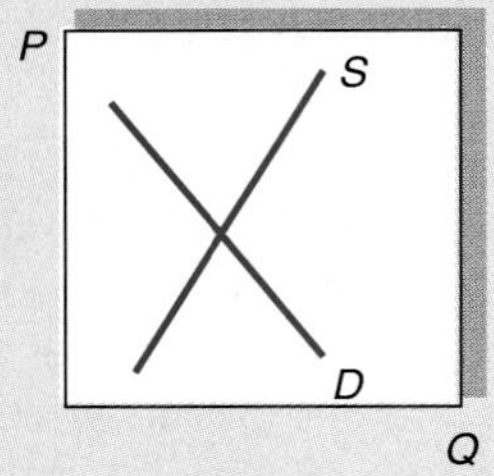 | | | |

# PART V

## THE WEALTH AND POVERTY OF NATIONS

CHAPTER

# 20

# ECONOMIC PROGRESS AND THE ROLE OF GOVERNMENT

The principal justification for public policy intervention lies in the frequent and numerous shortcomings of market outcomes.

*Charles Wolf*[1]

It does not follow that whenever laissez faire falls short, government interference is expedient; since the inevitable drawbacks of the latter may, in any particular case, be worse than the shortcomings of private enterprise.

*Harry Sidgwick* (1887)[2]

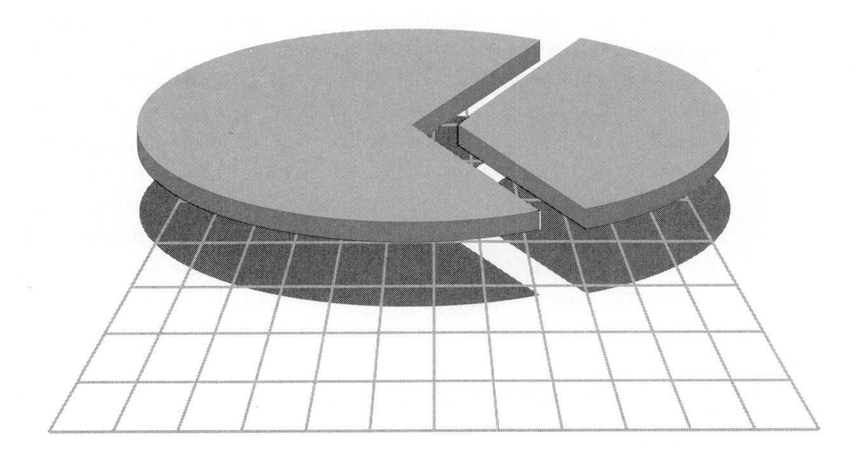

## CHAPTER FOCUS

- What is government? What can government do to promote economic progress?
- How does the democratic political process work? How do voters decide whom to support? How do politicians decide what policies to favor?
- Under what conditions do voting and representative government work quite well?
- Will democratic representative government generally result in economic efficiency? Why or why not?
- What can be done to improve the results of government?

In most industrial countries, between one-quarter and one-half of the nation's income is channeled through various government departments and agencies. Governments also establish the "rules of the game" for the market sector and impose various regulations on both personal and business activity. Because of its broad economic role, it is vital that we understand what government can do to promote economic progress, how it works, the type of activities that it does well, and things that it does not do so well. This chapter will focus on these issues.

## WHAT IS GOVERNMENT?

At the simplest level, the distinguishing characteristic of government is its monopoly on the use of coercive force to modify the actions of adults. Most societies allow parents to use force to influence the actions of their children. But with regard to adults, governments possess the exclusive right to use force. No individual has a right to use violence in order to take your wealth. Neither can a business firm, no matter how large or powerful, levy a "tax" on your income or force you to buy its product. The legitimate use of force to control the behavior of adults is reserved for government.

Most of us do not care much for coercion. We would prefer to "do our own thing." There are cases, however, when coercion can clearly expand our freedom of action. For example, governments throughout the world mandate the side of the road on which vehicles can be driven. If you do not drive on the side mandated by government, you will be stopped and arrested (assuming you do not have an accident first). Clearly, this type of coercion makes it easier for people to get where they want to go. Government's ability to coerce can sometimes help individuals accomplish objectives that would be impossible or costly to achieve by other means.

[1]Charles Wolf, Jr., *Markets or Government* (Cambridge: MIT Press, 1988), p. 17.
[2]Ibid.

# IMPORTANT SOURCE OF PROSPERITY: PROTECTIVE AND PRODUCTIVE FUNCTIONS OF GOVERNMENT

From an economic viewpoint, what are the proper functions of government? Philosophers, economists, and other scholars have disputed these issues for centuries. General agreement exists, however, that there are two legitimate economic functions of government: (1) protection against invasions by others and (2) provision of goods that cannot easily be provided through markets. These two functions correspond to what Nobel laureate James Buchanan conceptualizes as the *protective* and *productive* functions of government.

## Protective Function

People can gain from the assignment of the exclusive use of violence to the government for the purpose of protecting citizens and their property from other citizens and from outsiders. As philosopher John Locke wrote more than three centuries ago, individuals are constantly threatened by "the invasions of others." Therefore, each individual "is willing to join in society with others, who are already united, or have a mind to unite, for the mutual preservation of their lives, liberties, and estates."[3]

The protective function encompasses the government's maintenance of a framework of security and order, an infrastructure of rules within which people can interact peacefully with one another. It entails the enforcement of rules against theft, fraud, and the like. It also involves provision of national defense designed to protect domestic residents against invasions from a foreign power.

It is easy to see the economic importance of this function. Without the assurance that the wealth they create will not be taken from them by others, individuals will have little incentive to produce. Simply put, this protection provides citizens with assurance that if they sow (produce), they will be permitted to reap. When individuals are protected in this way, their resources will be directed toward productive activities that benefit the nation as a whole.

If private property rights are not clearly defined and strictly enforced, some parties will engage in actions that impose harm on nonconsenting secondary parties. Economists call such spillover effects **external costs**. A paper pulp mill that belches smoke and other waste products into the air imposes an external cost on surrounding residents who prefer clean air. Similarly, a manufacturer that releases large quantities of pollutants into a river imposes an external cost on downstream residents.

**external costs** Costs imposed on nonconsenting secondary parties whose property rights are violated by the actions of another.

When property rights are poorly defined and external costs are present, markets will send decision-makers inaccurate signals, and economic inefficiency will generally result. Exhibit 20.1 illustrates this point. Suppose that a business firm is permitted to discharge smoke into the air or sewage into a river. Valuable resources, clean air and pure water, are used essentially to provide garbage-removal services. When they are not held accountable for the damages done, neither firms nor the consumers of their products will pay for these

[3]John Locke, *Treatise of Civil Government* (1690), Charles Sherman, ed., (New York: Appleton-Century-Crofts, 1937), p. 82.

**EXHIBIT 20.1**

**Impact of External Costs**

When a producer is permitted to invade the property of others without their permission, markets will not register the external costs imposed on the secondary parties. Therefore, the supply curve ($S_1$) will understate the true cost of production. Compared to the ideal, too much of the good is produced ($Q_1$ rather than $Q_2$), and the market price is too low ($P_1$ rather than $P_2$).

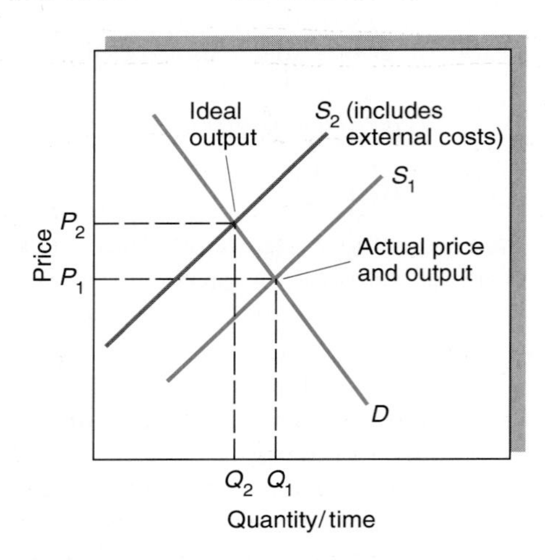


costs. As a result, the firm's costs will understate the true costs—including the costs imposed on the secondary parties—of producing the good. Since the producer only has to consider the cost to the firm and can ignore the cost imposed on secondary parties, supply curve $S_1$ will result. If the producers had to pay all costs, supply would be $S_2$. The actual supply curve, $S_1$, does not reflect the full opportunity cost of producing the good. For the producer, the opportunity cost paid is low enough to merit the larger supply. Output is expanded beyond $Q_2$ (to $Q_1$), even though the buyers' valuation of the additional units is less than their full opportunity cost. Some units will be produced (the units between $Q_2$ and $Q_1$) that are valued less than the costs to society for their production. Excessive air and water pollution are side effects. The harm caused by this added pollution outweighs the net gains the additional production generates for buyers and sellers of the good.

To summarize, when a producer is permitted to invade the property rights of others without compensation, the costs imposed on the secondary parties will not be registered through markets. As a result, the producer will supply too much of the good and charge less for it than would be best from the viewpoint of economic efficiency.

The English common-law system provides owners with a right to compensation for harm done by invasions from others. If this right is to be meaningful, however, owners must be able to prove that their rights were actually violated by another party. If John runs into Mary's car, the case is often fairly simple, and the parties may not even have to go to court. When John knows that Mary can prove him at fault and quantify the damages, he (or his insurance company) will simply compensate Mary for the damage done. (If John was insured, his rates will likely rise.) But, consider the case of Jim, the factory owner whose smoke fouls the air at Mary's home. Mary may have a right to clean air, which is violated by Jim's factory's smoke. To receive compensation, however, she must be able to demonstrate the extent of the damage inflicted by the pollution, and that the pollutant causing the damage came from Jim's plant. This burden of proof is similar to the case of damage to a car, but in the case of pollution, proving the contention will be much more difficult. If Mary is unable to prove her case, then her property rights, although defined, will not be enforceable. A judge who hears allegations will be naturally reluctant to force compensation unless the weight of evidence supports her claim. Cases of this type, especially when they involve a large number of parties and uncertainty of information about violators and magnitude of damages, are particularly troublesome cases for a legal system to handle efficiently. As a result, government often steps in to protect individuals against possible damage, using pollution-control rules.

## Productive Function

Governments may also enhance the wealth of people by undertaking productive activities that cannot easily be organized through market transactions. When a good is jointly consumed by a large number of people, and it is costly to prevent nonpaying customers from consuming the good, market allocation does not work well. Such goods are called **public goods** by economists. There are two distinguishing characteristics of public goods: (1) jointness in consumption—supplying the good to one person also makes it available to others and (2) nonexcludability—it is difficult, if not impossible, to withhold consumption of the good from people who do not pay for it.

**public goods** Jointly consumed goods. When consumed by one person, they are also made available to others. National defense, clear air, and scientific theories are all public goods.

Examples of pure public goods are rare. National defense is a classic example. The national defense that protects you from foreign invaders also protects others, independent of the amount they pay. The actions of a central monetary authority provide another example of a public good. The monetary system that influences the prices of things you buy and sell also influences the prices and incomes of others. The system of legal justice, flood-control projects, and insect-abatement programs provide other examples of public goods. In each of these cases, provision of the good to one person simultaneously makes the good available to others.

It is easy to see why markets have difficulty supplying public goods. In the normal marketplace, if you do not pay, you cannot consume. If you want to consume a good, you have to pay the purchase price. In turn, the payments of consumers provide producers with the incentive to supply the good. With public goods, however, nonpaying consumers cannot be excluded, at least not at a reasonable cost. Producers cannot establish a one-to-one link between payment for and receipt of the good. Since the nature of the good makes it difficult to exclude those who do not pay, each individual has an incentive to become a **free rider,** one who receives benefits without paying toward the costs.

**free rider** One who receives benefits without paying toward the costs.

Why contribute to the cost of supplying national defense or a mosquito-abatement program? Why would a self-interested individual help pay for these and other public goods? The amount you contribute will exert little impact on the availability of a public good. If others contribute a large amount, the public good will be provided regardless of what you do. Simultaneously, if others do not pay, your actions will not make much difference anyway. Each person thus has an incentive to opt out—to become a free rider. But when numerous individuals opt out, little if any of the public good is produced. Predictably, therefore, the market will undersupply public goods. Therefore, government provision of such goods may create wealth and thereby enhance the general standard of living.

While pure public goods are rare, several generate spillover benefits that accrue to persons other than the primary consumer. Consider the example of education. Clearly education is not a pure public good. As the presence of private schools illustrates, consumption of schooling can be linked to payment by the consumer. Nonetheless, many believe that consumption of schooling promotes better citizenship, reduces crime, and in many other ways generates spillover benefits for persons other than the students going to school. When such spillover benefits are present, market allocation may produce less than the ideal quantity of such goods. Some government provision or subsidy of private provision may be productive.

For still other near-public goods, it may be costly to administer a market collection system linking consumption and payment. Consider the case of streets and highways. It would be costly to set up a tollbooth to charge for the use of streets in heavily congested urban areas. New technology shows some promise of lowering these costs dramatically. Up to now however, given the resources required to establish the payment-consumption link, it has been generally more efficient to have the government supply highways and streets for the use of all. When these roads are financed with gasoline taxes, the system may even approximate the outcome that would result if people were required to pay directly for their use of the roads.

Finally, a productive government will also promote competitive markets. In this area, the first guideline should be borrowed from the medical profession: make sure that you do no harm. A productive government will refrain from the imposition of licenses, discriminatory taxes, price controls, tariffs, quotas, and other entry and trade restraints that lessen the intensity of competition. When there are only a few firms in an industry and competition from new firms (including rival foreign firms) can be restricted, market participants may collude in an effort to rig the market. Government legislation prohibiting collusion and price-fixing agreements can help promote competition in such markets.

## Government Is Not an Automatic Corrective Device

Some people have a tendency to think of government, particularly a democratically elected government, as a corrective device. Whenever a problem arises, they expect government to follow sound policies to solve the problem. This view is false. Government cannot be counted on to always make decisions in the "public interest," however that nebulous term might be defined. Neither is it an automatic corrective device available for use when market organization fails to achieve a desired outcome.

Government is merely a method of social organization—an institutional process through which individuals collectively make choices and carry out activities. No matter how lofty the rhetoric, the actions of governments reflect the choices of ordinary mortals, people with ethical standards and personal motivations very much like those who are in the private sector. The elements of competition and exchange are present in government also, as individuals and groups seek what they want from government, just as in the private sector. To gain support for their own issues, they are willing to work with others in the political and bureaucratic arenas, exchanging political support in order to achieve their major goals.

Recognition that government is not a god-like mechanism that will automatically do what is right challenges us to think seriously about how the political process works and how it might be redesigned to yield more desirable outcomes.

## ECONOMICS OF COLLECTIVE ACTION

In a democratic setting, the choices of individuals affect collective outcomes. Voters elect representatives to direct the actions of governments. In turn, the representatives establish agencies and hire bureaucrats to conduct the day-to-day government affairs. Voters, politicians, and bureaucrats are the major players in the democratic political process. Under representative democracy, government action is the result of a complex set of interrelationships among the members of these three groups. Like consumers in the market, voters use their electoral support, money, and other political resources to express their demand for legislation. Like business entrepreneurs, politicians are suppliers: they design and shape legislation. Finally, just as managers and employees are assigned the details of the production process in the market, bureaucrats perform this task in the public sector.[4]

In recent years, the tools of economics have been used to analyze the political process—how it works and when it is likely to encourage the efficient use of resources. Since this approach focuses on collective decisions, it is referred to as **public-choice analysis.**

**public-choice analysis**
The study of decision-making as it affects the formation and operation of collective organizations, such as governments. This discipline bridges the gap between economics and political science. In effect, it applies the principles and methodology of economics to political science topics.

Public-choice analysis is based on the idea that people making political choices will be motivated by the same factors that influence their market choices. Just as personal self-interest—things like wealth, power, and prestige—influence market choices, so too will they influence decisions in the political arena. Therefore, we can expect that political choices, like market choices, will be influenced by the structure of personal benefits relative to costs.

### Voter-Consumer

How do voters decide whom to support? No doubt, many factors influence their decisions. Which candidate is the most persuasive, and which presents the best television image? Who appears to be honest, sincere, and competent? However, the self-interest postulate of public-choice analysis suggests that one prime question voters will ask is: "What can you do for me, and how much will it cost me?" The greater the voter's perceived net personal gain from a particular candidate's platform, the more likely it is that the voter will favor that candidate. In contrast, the greater the perceived net economic

[4]For a more comprehensive view of public choice theory and the operation of democratic governments, see James Gwartney and Richard Wagner (eds.), *Public Choice and Constitutional Economics* (Greenwich: JAI Press, 1988). Our analysis borrows from this work.

cost imposed on the voter by the positions of a candidate, the less inclined the voter will be to support the candidate. Other things equal, voters will tend to support candidates whom they believe will provide them the most political goods, services, and transfer benefits, net of personal costs.

When decisions are made collectively, the direct link between the individual voter's choice and the outcome of the issue is broken. Most voters recognize that their individual vote is not going to decide the election, particularly when the size of the decision-making group is large. In fact, in state and national elections, it is more likely that the citizen will be killed in an auto accident on the way to vote than it is that his or her vote will determine the outcome of the election. Since their vote is highly unlikely to resolve the issue at hand, citizens have little incentive to spend much effort to seek the information needed to cast an informed ballot. Economists refer to this lack of incentive as the **rational ignorance effect.**

**rational ignorance effect**
Voter ignorance that is present because people perceive their individual votes as unlikely to be decisive. Voters rationally have little incentive to spend much effort informing themselves in order to cast an informed vote.

The rationally uninformed voter is merely exercising good judgment. It makes no sense to invest the time and effort required to understand most of the issues and cast a highly informed vote when your vote is not going to affect the outcome of the issue. It is not surprising, then, that most voters are uninformed on where candidates stand on issues and how tariffs, agricultural price supports, or spending on various government programs will affect their lives. Rather than carefully analyzing a wide range of issues, most voters will simply rely on information acquired from friends, newspapers, television news, or political advertisements.

## Politician-Supplier

Public-choice theory postulates that pursuit of votes is the primary stimulus shaping the behavior of political suppliers. In varying degrees, such factors as pursuit of the public interest, compassion for the poor, and the achievement of fame, wealth, and power may also influence the behavior of politicians. But regardless of ultimate motivation, the ability of politicians to achieve their objectives is sorely dependent upon their ability to get elected and reelected. Just as profits are the lifeblood of the market entrepreneur, votes are the lifeblood of the politician.

The goal of the political supplier is to put together a majority coalition—to win the election. Vote-seeking politicians, like profit-seeking business decision-makers, will have a strong incentive to cater to the views of politically active constituents. The easiest way to win votes, both politically and financially, is to give these constituents, or at least appear to give them, what they want. A politician who pays no heed to the views of his or her constituents is as rare as a businessperson selling bikinis in the Arctic.

Voters are likely to be more interested in their work and market decisions (where their choices are decisive) or local sport teams (which are probably more entertaining) than they are in learning the details of political issues. Therefore, successful politicians must figure out how to convey their support for popular positions to rationally uninformed voters. An expert staff, polls to ferret out which issues and which positions will be favored by voters, and high-quality advertising to project the candidate's image to voters are of great value in politics. Money can help politicians achieve these objectives.

This is not to deny that factors other than electoral gain also will influence political suppliers. If they feel strongly about an issue, some politicians may even take positions that will damage their electoral prospects. Political competition, however, limits their ability to do so. Politicians who fail to support policies that are vote-getters, perhaps because they consider them counterproductive or morally wrong, run a high risk of being replaced by competitors. Just as neglect of economic profit is the route to market oblivion, neglect of potential votes is the route to political oblivion.

---

Clearly, government action can improve the economic well-being of citizens. When government protects lives and property against intruders, it promotes the realization of gains from specialization and trade and enhances the incentive of individuals to produce. In addition, government provision of public goods like national defense and a stable currency can generally provide citizens with net benefits. Production suffers when people and their property are not safe. Government actions that promote competition and protect consumers against monopoly are also a source of economic progress. Thus, people gain when the protective and productive functions of government are performed properly.

Will voting and representative government provide support for productive projects while rejecting unproductive projects? People have a tendency to believe that support by a majority makes a political action productive or legitimate. Perhaps surprising to some, if a government project is really productive, it will always be possible to allocate the project's cost so that *all* voters will gain. Exhibit 20.2 illustrates this point. Column 1 presents hypothetical data on the distribution of benefits from a government road construction project. These benefits sum to $40, which exceeds the $25 cost of road. Since voter benefits exceed costs, the project is indeed productive. If the project's $25 cost were allocated equally among the voters (Plan A), Adams and Brown gain

**EXHIBIT 20.2**

**Benefits Derived by Voters from Hypothetical Road Construction Project**

| Voter | Benefits Received (1) | Tax Payment Plan A (2) | Tax Payment Plan B (3) |
|---|---|---|---|
| Adams | $20 | $5 | $12.50 |
| Brown | 12 | 5 | 7.50 |
| Green | 4 | 5 | 2.50 |
| Jones | 2 | 5 | 1.25 |
| Smith | 2 | 5 | 1.25 |
| **Total** | $40 | $25 | $25.00 |

substantially, but Green, Jones, and Smith will lose. The value of the project to the latter three voters is less than their $5 cost. If the fate of the project were decided by majority vote, the project would be defeated by the "no" votes of Green, Jones, and Smith.

In contrast, look what happens if the cost of the project is allocated among voters in proportion to the benefits that they receive (Plan B). Under this arrangement, Adams would pay half ($12.50) of the $25 cost, since he receives half ($20) of the total benefits ($40). The other voters would all pay in proportion to their benefits received. Under this finance plan, all voters would gain from the proposal. Even though the proposal could not muster a majority when the costs were allocated equally among voters, it would be favored by all five voters when they are taxed in proportion to the benefits that they receive (Plan B).

This simple illustration highlights an extremely important point about voting and productive projects. *When voters pay in proportion to benefits received,* all voters will gain if the government action is productive (and all will lose if it is unproductive).[5] When the benefits and costs of voters are directly related, productive government actions will be favored by all, or most all voters. Correspondingly, if a project is counterproductive—if the costs exceed the benefits generated for voters—it would tend to be opposed by almost all voters. Therefore, when voters pay in proportion to benefits received, there is a harmony between good politics and sound economics.

With public-sector action, however, the link between receipt of and payment for a good can be broken—the beneficiaries of a proposal may not bear its cost. Public-choice theory indicates that the pattern of benefits and costs among voters will influence the workings of the political process. The benefits derived from a government action may be either widespread among the general populace or concentrated among a small subgroup (for example, farmers, students, business interests, or members of a labor union). Similarly, the costs may be either widespread or highly concentrated among voters. As Exhibit 20.3 illustrates, there are four possible patterns of voter benefits and costs: (1) widespread benefits and widespread costs, (2) concentrated benefits and widespread costs, (3) concentrated benefits and concentrated costs, and (4) widespread benefits and concentrated costs.

When both the benefits and costs are widespread among voters (Type 1), essentially everyone benefits and everyone pays. While the costs of Type 1 measures may not be precisely proportional to benefits, there will be a rough relationship. When Type 1 measures are productive, almost everyone gains more than they pay. There will be little opposition, and political representatives have a strong incentive to support such proposals. In contrast, when Type 1 proposals generate costs in excess of benefits, almost everyone loses, and representatives will confront pressure to oppose such issues. Thus, for Type 1 projects, the political process tends to be consistent with economic efficiency.

Interestingly, the provision of traditional public goods—like provision of national defense, a legal system for the protection of persons and property

[5] The principle that productive projects generate the potential for political unanimity was initially articulated by Swedish economist Knut Wicksell in 1896. See Wicksell, "A New Principle of Just Taxation," in James Gwartney and Richard Wagner (eds.), *Public Choice and Constitutional Economics* (Greenwich: JAI Press, Inc., 1988). Nobel laureate James Buchanan has stated that Wicksell's work provided him with the insights that led to his large role in the development of modern public-choice theory.

**EXHIBIT 20.3**

**Distribution of Benefits and Costs among Voters**

It is useful to visualize four possible combinations for the distribution of benefits and costs among voters and to consider how the alternative distributions affect the operation of representative government. When the distribution of benefits and costs are widespread among voters (1) or concentrated among voters (3), representative government will tend to undertake projects that are productive and reject those that are unproductive. In contrast, when the benefits are concentrated and the costs are widespread (2), representative government is biased toward adoption of counterproductive activity. Finally, when benefits are widespread but the costs concentrated (4), the political process may reject projects that are productive.

| Distribution of Costs among Voters | Distribution of Benefits among Voters: Widespread | Concentrated |
|---|---|---|
| Widespread | (1) | (2) |
| Concentrated | (4) | (3) |

and enforcement of contracts, and a monetary system to oil the wheels of exchange—best fits Type 1. Nearly everyone pays and nearly everyone benefits from public-sector action of this type.

Similarly, there is reason to believe that the political process will work pretty well for Type 3 measures—those for which both benefits and costs are concentrated on one or more small subgroups. In some cases, the concentrated beneficiaries may pay for the government to provide services. This would be the case when user charges finance public services (for example, air safety or garbage collection) benefiting subgroups of the populace. Under these circumstances, voter support will provide politicians with an incentive to provide public services that generate value in excess of cost.

Of course, the subgroup of beneficiaries might differ from the subgroup footing the bill. But even in this case, if the benefits exceed the costs, the concentrated group of beneficiaries will have an incentive to expend more resources supportive of the measure than those harmed by it will expend opposing it. Thus, productive measures will tend to be adopted. Similarly, unproductive measures will tend to be rejected when both the benefits and costs are concentrated.

## WHEN VOTING CONFLICTS WITH ECONOMIC EFFICIENCY

While the political process works well when there is close relationship between receipt of benefits and payment of cost, the harmony between good politics and sound economics sometimes breaks down. There are four major reasons why unrestrained majority-rule voting may conflict with economic prosperity.

### Special Interest Effect

Public-choice analysis indicates that problems will arise when an issue generates substantial personal benefits for a small number of constituents while imposing a small individual cost on a large number of other voters (Type 2 in Exhibit 20.3). Economists refer to measures of this type as **special interest issues.**

**special interest issue** An issue that generates substantial individual benefits to a small minority while imposing a small individual cost on many other voters. In total, the net cost to the majority might either exceed or fall short of the net benefits to the special interest group.

It is easy to see how politicians can improve their election prospects by catering to the views of special interests. Since their personal stake is large, members of the interest group (and lobbyists representing their interests) have a strong incentive to inform themselves and their allies and to let legislators know how strongly they feel about an issue of special importance. Many of them will vote for or against candidates strictly on the basis of whether they support their interests. In addition, such interest groups are generally an attractive source of campaign resources, including financial contributions. In

### THE POWER OF SPECIAL INTERESTS

#### The Case of Rice Farmers

There are roughly 33,000 rice farmers in the United States. In essence, the government guarantees them an above-market price for rice by paying them to grow less rice so the artificially high price can be maintained. The program reduces output, pushes up the price of rice, and requires higher taxes. As a nation, we are worse off as a result.

Nonetheless, Congress continues to support the program. The rice farmers gain more than $800 million in gross income, approximately $25,000 per rice farm. More than 60 percent of these subsidies go to rice farmers receiving payments of $50,000 or more. Given the sizable impact on their personal wealth, it is perfectly sensible for rice farmers to inform themselves and use their votes, contributions and political influence to help politicians who support their interests. In contrast, it makes no sense for the average voter to investigate this issue or give it any significant weight when deciding for whom to vote. In fact, most Americans are unaware that they pay approximately $4 more per year to help rice growers, most of which goes to wealthy farmers. As a result, politicians can generally gain more by continuing to support the rice farmers, even though the subsidy program wastes resources and reduces the wealth of the nation.

contrast, most other voters will care little about a special interest issue. For the non-special interest voter, opportunity cost of the time and energy necessary to examine the issue will generally exceed any possible personal gain from a preferred resolution. Thus, most non-special interest voters will simply ignore such issues.

If you were a vote-seeking politician, what would you do? Clearly, little gain would be derived from supporting the interest of the largely uninformed and disinterested majority. In contrast, support for the interests of easily identifiable, well-organized groups would generate vocal supporters, campaign workers, and most importantly, campaign contributors. Predictably, politicians will be led as if by an invisible hand to support legislation that provides concentrated benefits to interest groups at the expense of disorganized groups (such as taxpayers and consumers), even if such policies waste resources.

The rational-ignorance effect strengthens the power of special interests. Since the cost imposed on individual voters is small, and since the individual is unable to avoid the cost even by becoming informed, voters bearing the cost of special interest legislation tend to be uninformed. This will be particularly true if the complexity of the issue makes it difficult for voters to figure how an issue affects their personal welfare. Thus, politicians often make special interest legislation complex in order to hide the cost imposed on the typical voter.

In addition, the interests of bureaucrats are often complementary with those of interest groups. The bureaucrats who staff an agency usually want to see their department's goals furthered, whether the goals are to protect more wilderness, build more roads, or provide additional subsidized irrigation projects. To accomplish these things requires larger budgets, which—not so incidentally—are likely to provide the bureaucrats with expanded career opportunities while helping to satisfy their professional aspirations as well. Bureaus, therefore, are usually happy to work to expand their programs to deliver benefits to special interest groups, who, in turn, work with politicians to expand their bureau budgets and programs.

The bottom line is clear: public-choice analysis indicates that majority voting and representative democracy does not work so well when concentrated interests benefit at the expense of widely dispersed interests. This special interest bias of the political process helps to explain the presence of many programs that reduce the size of the economic pie. For example, the agriculture price support programs of the United States and Western Europe promote inefficient methods of production (for example, the use of too much fertilizer relative to land), protect high-cost producers, and result in higher food prices. Approximately 1 percent of the populace (primarily large farmers) individually gain a lot at the expense of consumers and taxpayers, each of whom pay somewhat higher food prices and taxes than they otherwise would. Given their substantial personal gain, the agricultural interests feel strongly about the price-support programs, while most others are uninformed and largely uninterested in the issue. Therefore, politicians find it advantageous to support the programs even though they waste resources and reduce the general standard of living.

Numerous other examples abound. Tariffs and quotas retard the gains from specialization and trade. But they also benefit concentrated industrial interests (manufacturers and workers in steel, automobiles, and textiles, for example) at the expense of consumers. Economic studies have shown that government support for subsidized water and irrigation projects in the western United States, for example, generate substantially smaller benefits than costs. Legislation mandating that Alaskan oil be transported by the high-cost American maritime industry promotes inefficiency. These programs and numerous others like them demonstrate the conflict between economic efficiency and good politics when the benefits are highly concentrated and the costs widely dispersed.

The analysis is symmetrical. When the benefits of a government action are widespread and the costs highly concentrated (Type 4 of Exhibit 20.3), the concentrated interests will strongly oppose the proposal. Most others will be largely uninterested. Once again, politicians will have an incentive to respond to the views of the concentrated interests. Projects of this type will tend to be rejected even when they are productive—that is, when they would generate larger benefits than costs.

## Shortsightedness Effect

The complexity of many issues makes it difficult for voters to identify their effects over time. Thus, voters will tend to rely primarily on current economic conditions when evaluating the performance of political incumbents. Unfortunately, policies that look good around election day may have substantial negative side effects after the election. On the other hand, policies that generate pre-election costs in order to provide long-term gains that emerge only after the next election reduce the re-election prospects of incumbents. As a result, the political process is biased toward the adoption of shortsighted policies and against the selection of sound long-range policies that involve observable costs prior to the next election. Economists refer to this bias inherent in the collective decision-making process as the **shortsightedness effect.**

**shortsightedness effect**
Misallocation of resources that results because public-sector action is biased (1) in favor of proposals yielding clearly defined current benefits in exchange for difficult-to-identify future costs and (2) against proposals with clearly identifiable current costs yielding less concrete and less obvious future benefits.

The nature of democratic institutions restricts the planning horizon of elected officials. Positive results must be observable by the next election, or the incumbent is likely to be replaced by someone who promises more rapid results. Policies that will eventually pay off in the future (after the next election) will have little attractiveness to vote-seeking politicians if those policies do not exert a beneficial impact by election day. This shortsighted nature of the political process, even when decisions are made democratically, will tend to result in some economic inefficiency.

It is easy to think of instances where positive short-term effects have increased the political attractiveness of policies that exert a long-term detrimental impact. For example, budget deficits allow politicians to finance current projects with future taxes. This strategy has political attractiveness even though it may result in higher interest rates and less capital formation than otherwise would be the case. Rent controls that reduce the current price of rental housing provide another example. The short-term results will be far more positive than the effects in the long run (housing shortages, black markets, and deterioration in the quality of housing).

## Rent-Seeking

There are two ways individuals can acquire wealth: production and plunder. People can get ahead by producing things (or services) and exchanging them for income. This method of acquiring income both helps the individual and enhances the wealth of the society. Sometimes the rules also allow people to get ahead by plundering what others have produced. This method fails to generate additional income—the gain of one is a loss to another—and it consumes resources and thereby reduces the wealth of the society.

**rent-seeking** Actions by individuals and interest groups designed to restructure public policy in a manner that will either directly or indirectly redistribute more income to themselves.

**Rent-seeking** is a term used by economists to describe actions taken by individuals and groups seeking to use the political process to plunder the wealth of others. The incentive to engage in rent-seeking activities is directly proportional to the ease with which the political process can be used for personal (or interest group) gain at the expense of others. When the effective law of the land makes it difficult to take the property of others or force others to pay for projects favored by you and your interest group, rent-seeking is unattractive. Under such circumstance, its benefits are relatively low, and few resources flow into rent-seeking activities. In contrast, when government fails to levy user fees or similar forms of financing to allocate the cost of its projects to the primary beneficiaries, or when it becomes heavily involved in tax-transfer activities, the payoff to rent-seeking expands.

Rent-seeking will also increase when governments, including democratic governments, become more heavily involved in erecting trade barriers, mandating employment benefits, prohibiting various types of agreements, providing subsidies, fixing prices, levying discriminatory taxes (taxes unrelated to the provision of public services to the taxpayer), and redistributing income.

When a government, rather than acting as a neutral force protecting property rights and enforcing contracts, attempts to favor some at the expense of others, counterproductive activities will expand while positive-sum productive activities will shrink. People will spend more time organizing and lobbying politicians and less time producing goods and services. Since fewer resources will be utilized to create wealth (and more utilized in rent-seeking activities), economic progress will be retarded.

## Inefficiency of Government Operations

The incentive for government bureaus and enterprises to operate efficiently is weak. In the private sector, there is a strong incentive to produce efficiently because lower costs mean higher profits. Public-sector enterprises confront an incentive structure that is less conducive to operational efficiency. Direct competition in the form of other firms trying to take an agency's customers is rare in the public sector. Since there is no easily identifiable index of performance analogous to profit rate in the private sector, public-sector managers can often gloss over economic inefficiency. While bankruptcy weeds out inefficiency in the private sector, there is no parallel mechanism to eliminate inefficiency in the public sector. In fact, poor performance and failure to achieve objectives are often used as an argument for *increased* funding in the public sector. Furthermore, public-sector managers are seldom in a position to gain personally from measures that reduce costs. The opposite is often true. If an agency fails to spend this year's allocation, its case for a larger budget next year is weakened. Agencies typically go on a spending spree at the end of the budget period if they discover that they have failed to spend all of this year's appropriation.

It is important to note that the argument of internal inefficiency is not based on the assumption that employees of a bureaucratic government are necessarily lazy or incapable. Rather, the emphasis is on the structure of information and incentives under which managers and other workers toil. No individual or relatively small group of individuals has much incentive to ensure efficiency. Their performances cannot readily be judged, and without private ownership, their personal wealth cannot be significantly altered by changes in the level of efficiency. Since public officials and bureau managers spend other people's money, they are likely to be less conscious of cost than they would be with their own resources. Without a need to compare sales revenues to costs there is no test with which to define economic inefficiency or measure it accurately, much less eliminate it. The perverse incentive structure of a bureaucracy is bound to have an impact on its internal efficiency.

The empirical evidence is consistent with this view. Economies dominated by government control, like those of Eastern Europe, the former Soviet Union, and Latin America, have fashioned a poor economic record. Similarly, when private firms are compared with government agencies providing the same goods or services, the private firms generally have been shown to provide them more economically.

## CONSTITUTIONAL ECONOMICS

The role of government is central to the achievement of economic progress. When government performs its protective function well, it will improve the efficiency of markets. Similarly, government's production of public goods can create wealth and help promote prosperity. Public-choice analysis, however, indicates that unconstrained democratic governments will often enact programs that waste resources and impair the general standard of living of citizens. How can we reap the benefits available from government while minimizing its unwanted, counterproductive activities?

An efficient political organization does not emerge naturally. It must be shaped by the legal environment. The "founding fathers" of the United States recognized this point. They sought to establish a constitutional order that would limit the misuse of the ordinary political process, while allowing government to undertake activities important to the welfare of citizens. With time, many of the safeguards embodied in the U.S. Constitution have either eroded or been modified. Nonetheless, the general idea was a sound one.

What would a constitutional structure consistent with economic efficiency look like? Interestingly, public-choice analysis indicates that it would incorporate a number of the ideas emanating from the Philadelphia convention 200 years ago. First, it would seek to constrain government from taking the rights and wealth from some in order to bestow them on others. The U.S. Constitution contains provisions designed to prevent such takings. The Fifth Amendment states, "nor shall private property be taken for public use without just compensation."[6] Article I, Section 10, mandates, "No state shall . . . pass any . . . law impairing the obligations of contracts." These provisions might be strengthened and supplemented with prohibitions against the use of government to fix prices and to bar entry into the production of otherwise legal goods, both of which restrain trade and are indirect forms of taking property without compensation. With regard to income transfer programs, federal transfer activities might be restricted to those directed toward the poor (means-tested programs).

[6]For a detailed analysis of the importance of this clause from a law and economics viewpoint, see Richard A. Epstein, *Takings: Private Property and the Power of Eminent Domain* (Cambridge: Harvard University Press, 1985).

Second, the efficiency of the political process would be enhanced if the primary beneficiaries of government activities were required to foot the bill for their cost. Again, there is evidence that this is what the founding fathers had in mind. The U.S. Constitution, Article I, Section 8, states: "The Congress shall have power to lay and collect taxes, duties, imports and excises to . . . provide for the common defense and general welfare of the United States, but all duties, imports and excises shall be uniform throughout the United States." This constitutional provision indicates that it was the intent of the Founders that, at the federal level, uniformly levied taxes would be used only for the finance of expenditures yielding general benefits—the common defense and general welfare (Type I issues in Exhibit 20.3). In order to strengthen this substantive provision, tax and spending proposals at the federal level could be required to secure the approval of a supra-majority (for example, three-fourths) of the legislative members. Such a provision would reduce the power of interest groups and the viability of pork-barrel spending projects.

Finally, if we want efficiency in government, the constitutional structure could strengthen independent state and local governments. One reason to expand the role of lower levels of government, is that higher levels, such as the federal government, have a greater ability to spread costs for projects that provide benefits to only a few. Another reason is to promote competition. In *The Federalist Papers,* James Madison argues that competition among state and local governments will help check abusive and counterproductive government action.[7] Public choice analysis indicates that Madison's perception was correct.

How might the constitutional order promote competition among governments? One way would be to require more inclusive majorities in the higher levels of government. For example, local legislative bodies (city commissions, county commissions, regional authorities, and so on) might continue to act with the approval of only a simple majority, while a three-fifths majority might be required for legislative action at the state level, and a three-fourths majority at the federal level. The increasing majorities required for legislative action at higher levels of government would help remedy a deficiency of the current system—the tendency of federal and state governments to get involved with issues that are best dealt with at lower levels of governments. Decentralization in government would permit states and localities to adopt different government environments. Those that people like best—the ones that supply public-sector goods highly valued relative to their tax cost—would grow and prosper relative to those that people appreciate less. This structure would allow individuals and businesses to "vote with their feet" as well as with their ballots.

Of course, public-choice theorists are continuing to investigate the operation of alternative forms of political organization. The challenge is to develop political institutions capable of bringing, to the fullest extent possible, the self-interest of politicians, bureaucrats, and voters into harmony with the general welfare of a society.

[7]See Charles Tiebout, "A Pure Theory of Local Expenditures," *Journal of Political Economy* (October 1956); Vincent Ostrom, *The Political Theory of a Compound Republic* (Fairfax: Center for Study of Public Choice, George Mason University, 1971); and Robert Bish, "Federalism: A Market-Economics Perspective" in James Gwartney and Richard Wagner (eds.), *Public Choice and Constitutional Economics* (Greenwich: JAI Press, 1988) for additional information on the importance of competition among government units.

## LOOKING AHEAD

Democratic governments are a creation of the interactions of human beings. Public-choice analysis helps us better understand these interactions and think more clearly about constitutional rules capable of improving the results achieved from government. The next two chapters will focus on the relationship between economic organization and prosperity. Our analysis of the role of government and the operation of the political process will enrich our consideration of this issue.

## CHAPTER SUMMARY

1. The distinguishing characteristic of government is its monopoly on the use of force to modify the actions of adults.
2. The functions of government might be divided into two broad categories: the protective function and the productive function. The protective function encompasses the protection of the lives and property of citizens against the potential intrusions of both domestic and foreign invaders. The productive function involves the production of public goods and near-public goods that would be difficult to produce and sell through markets.
3. External costs arise when property rights are not firmly established and strictly enforced. When the actions of a producer generate external costs, the producer's costs will understate the true opportunity cost of supplying the good. When external costs are present, competitive markets will lead to a larger output and lower price than what would be best from the viewpoint of economic efficiency.
4. When it is costly or impossible to withhold a public good from persons who do not or will not help pay for it, the market system breaks down, because everyone has an incentive to become a free rider. With enough free riders, production of the public good will be lower than the socially ideal level. When this is the case, government provision of public goods and near-public goods can enhance economic prosperity.
5. Government, even if it is democratic, is not a corrective device that can always be counted on to provide sound policies. Government policies reflect the choices of ordinary mortals and the incentive structure that emanates from the political arrangements of a country. Public-choice analysis applies the principles and methodology of economics to group decision-making in order to help us better understand how the political process works.
6. Voters cast ballots, make political contributions, lobby, and adopt other political strategies to demand public-sector action. Other things constant, voters have a strong incentive to support the candidate who offers them the greatest personal gain relative to personal costs. Since group decision-making breaks the link between the choice of the individual and the outcome of the issue, voters have little incentive to invest time and energy informing themselves on issues. Predictably, voters will be uninformed on many issues, particularly those that exert only a small impact on their personal welfare.

7. In a democratic system, politicians have a strong incentive to follow a strategy that will enhance their chances of getting elected (and reelected). Political competition more or less forces politicians to focus on how their actions influence their support among voters and on their ability to raise contributions that will help them project a positive image to voters.
8. The distribution of the benefits and costs among voters influences how the political process works. When voters pay in proportion to the benefits they receive from a public-sector project, democratic representative government works quite well. Productive projects tend to be approved and counterproductive ones rejected.
9. Democratic representative government does not work very well when an issue generates substantial personal gain for a small group of people at the expense of widely dispersed costs that are imposed on others. For issues of this type, the special interest will have a strong incentive to provide both votes and political contributions to politicians who support their interests, while most other voters will tend to ignore the issue. As the result, politicians have a strong incentive to support the special interests even when it results in counterproductive public policy.
10. The shortsightedness effect is another potential source of conflict between good politics and sound economics. Both voters and politicians tend to support projects that promise substantial current benefits at the expense of difficult-to-identify future costs. There is a bias against legislation that involves immediate and easily identifiable costs but complex future benefits.
11. When government acts as a neutral force, protecting property rights, enforcing contracts, and providing public goods, rent-seeking activities will be unattractive. However, when a government becomes heavily involved in tax and regulatory activities that benefit some at the expense of others, counterproductive rent-seeking activities will expand while productive activities will shrink. As resources are moved from wealth-creating to wealth-reducing activities, the size of the economic pie will decline.
12. The incentive for public-sector agencies and enterprises to operate efficiently is weak. In the public sector, no individual or relatively small group of individuals can capture the gains derived from lower costs and improvements in operational efficiency. It is often difficult to evaluate the efficiency of public sector enterprises since there usually is not an easily identifiable index of performance, like profit. Neither is there a force analogous to the threat of bankruptcy in the private sector that will systematically bring inefficient behavior to a halt. Competition, which would generally help keep a firm on its toes, is often weak in the public sector. As the result of this incentive structure, public-sector operations are generally less efficient than private-sector firms producing similar outputs.
13. Keeping government from engaging in counterproductive activities while encouraging it to undertake things that it does well is difficult. Properly designed constitutional rules and restraints can help achieve that objective.

# Study Guide

**CHAPTER**

# 20

## DEVELOPING THE ECONOMIC WAY OF THINKING

## CRITICAL-ANALYSIS QUESTIONS

1. English philosopher John Locke argued that the protection of each individual's person and property was the primary function of government. Why is the secure protection of each individual's person and property acquired without the use of violence, theft, or fraud important to the efficient operation of an economy?

*2. If producers are to be provided with an incentive to produce a good, why is it important for them to be able to prevent nonpaying customers from receiving the good?

3. Suppose that Abel builds a factory next to Baker's farm, and air pollution from the factory harms Baker's crops. Is Baker's property right to her land being violated? Is an external cost present? What if the pollution invades Baker's home and harms her health. Are her property rights violated? Is an external cost present? Explain.

4. "A democratic government is a corrective device used to remedy inefficiencies that arise when market allocation is not working well." True or false? Explain.

*5. How can you determine if a market action is efficient? How can you determine if a government action is efficient? If the majority of the citizens favor a project, does this indicate it is productive?

6. Do you think special interest groups exert much influence on local government? Why or why not? As a test, check the composition of the local zoning board in your community. How many real-estate agents, contractors, developers, and landlords are on the board? Are there any citizens without real-estate interests on the board?

*7. "Government can afford to take a long view when it needs to, while a private firm has a short-term outlook. Corporate officers, for example, typically care about the next 3 to 6 months, not the next 50 to 100 years. Government, not private firms, should own things like forests, where centuries, rather than the next few months, are at stake." Evaluate.

8. Are shoppers making decisions in the local supermarket likely to make better informed choices than voters making choices in political races? Why or why not?

9. One explanation for the shortsightedness effect in the public sector is that future voters cannot vote now to represent their future interests. Are the interests of future generations represented in market decisions? For example, if the price of chromium were expected to rise rapidly over the next 30 years due to increased scarcity, how could speculators grow rich while providing the next generation with more chromium at the expense of current consumers?

10. Many countries in Eastern Europe and the former Soviet Union are moving toward democratic decision-making. Will democracy make these countries prosperous? Why or why not? Should these countries establish constitutional restraints limiting the economic role of government? If so, indicate what constitutional provisions you would recommend. Be specific.

*Asterisk denotes critical-analysis questions for which answers are given in Appendix A.

11. "Public policy is necessary to protect the average citizen from the power of vested interest groups. In the absence of government intervention, regulated industries, such as airlines, railroads, and trucking, would charge excessive prices, products would be unsafe, and the rich would oppress the poor. Government curbs the power of interest groups." Evaluate this view.

## MULTIPLE-CHOICE SELF-TEST

1. The primary reason why allocation of a good that generates external costs creates problems for a market-directed economy is that
   a. Less of the good is produced than is ideal to society.
   b. There will be some units of the good for which benefits will exceed costs that will not be produced.
   c. Fewer individuals will be employed in this industry than is ideal to society.
   d. There are some costs associated with the production of the good that the producer need not take into consideration.
2. In terms of economic efficiency, which of the following is the most compelling justification for government rather than private enterprise providing certain goods and services?
   a. Government provision of goods eliminates the misallocation that results from the special interest effect.
   b. It is important that political goods and services be provided free of charge.
   c. There is often no way to sell "public goods" in a private market, since their benefits cannot be withheld from those who are unwilling to pay for them.
   d. It would be unethical and unreasonable for individuals to profit from provision of education, police protection, and similar services.
3. In economic theory, a "free rider" is
   a. A consumer who obtains a good without payment for its cost because it is difficult to exclude nonpaying customers from the receipt of the good.
   b. A consumer who obtains a good without paying a middleman a fee for arranging the purchase of the good.
   c. A consumer who is well informed on the quality of a good purchased because he or she purchases the good often.
   d. A person who consumes any commodity supplied and paid for by the government.
4. People who spend more resources investigating the advantages and disadvantages of automobiles before buying, than of presidential candidates before voting are, in effect, saying that
   a. A good car is more important to their well-being than a good president.
   b. They expect to use the information on the merits of alternative cars to greater personal advantage than they could expect to use information on the merits of alternative presidential candidates.
   c. They are irrational, because the choice of a president is obviously far more important than the choice of a car.
   d. They do not think it matters who is elected president.

5. Public-choice theory indicates that competitive forces provide a politician with a strong incentive to offer voters a bundle of political goods that the politician feels
   a. Is best for the economic and political situations that the country faces.
   b. Is most likely to pass through the legislative process.
   c. Will increase the welfare of society in general.
   d. Will increase his or her chances of winning elections.
6. Which of the following is true of government activities under a system of representative democracy?
   a. If a majority favors an activity, it must be productive.
   b. If a majority is opposed to an activity, it must be counterproductive.
   c. When voters pay in proportion to benefits received, a productive activity of government will be favored by an overwhelming majority of the voters.
   d. Economic activities undertaken by government are like a zero-sum game; if one party gains, others must lose an equal amount.
7. The interests of producers tend to be better represented in lobbying efforts and other elements of the political process than the interests of consumers because
   a. The profits of producers are greater than the income of consumers.
   b. The political process generally leads to larger gains for producers than losses for consumers.
   c. *Individual* producers generally have a much larger stake in the outcome of a specific issue than do *individual* consumers.
   d. The number of producers affected by the outcome of a particular political issue is usually greater than the number of consumers affected.
8. Democratic representative government tends to be biased in favor of actions that generate
   a. Current costs that are readily observable and future benefits that are readily observable.
   b. Future costs that are difficult to identify and current benefits that are readily observable.
   c. Future costs that are difficult to identify and future benefits that are difficult to identify.
   d. Current costs that are readily observable and current benefits that are difficult to identify.
9. As both the budget and regulatory powers grow, public-choice analysis indicates that individuals will find it in their interest to
   a. Increase their efforts devoted to production activities.
   b. Spend more time looking for gains through government.
   c. Spend less time looking for gains through government, since the majority of these opportunities will have already been granted.
   d. Ignore the political process since it will be beyond their control.
10. Public-choice analysis indicates that
   a. Politicians under representative democracy are led as if by an invisible hand to adopt legislation that enhances the wealth of a nation.
   b. Political structures consistent with economic efficiency tend to emerge naturally from the ordinary political process.

c. Constitutional rules establishing procedures and limiting the authority of the ordinary political process can improve the economic efficiency of government.
d. All of the above.

## PROBLEMS

1. The accompanying table shows the supply and demand schedules for pulp paper in Academia, a hypothetical country.

| Price (per ton) | Quantity (tons/year) | |
|---|---|---|
| | Demanded | Supplied |
| $150 | 1,000 | 7,000 |
| 140 | 2,000 | 6,000 |
| 130 | 3,000 | 5,000 |
| 120 | 4,000 | 4,000 |
| 110 | 5,000 | 3,000 |
| 100 | 6,000 | 2,000 |

a. Plot the demand and supply curves on graph paper and show the equilibrium price and quantity for pulp paper in Academia.
b. Suppose that the production of pulp paper results in external pollution costs of $20 per ton produced. In your diagram, show a supply curve that would include these external costs. What are the "ideal" (efficient) price and output for pulp paper? Show these in your diagram.

2. The accompanying table presents data on the voter benefits derived from a flood-control project undertaken by a seven-person local government.

| Voter | Benefits Received | Tax Payment | |
|---|---|---|---|
| | | Plan A | Plan B |
| Adams | $50,000 | _____ | _____ |
| Brown | 35,000 | _____ | _____ |
| Carlson | 35,000 | _____ | _____ |
| Dunn | 35,000 | _____ | _____ |
| Emerson | 35,000 | _____ | _____ |
| Frank | 5,000 | _____ | _____ |
| Green | 5,000 | _____ | _____ |
| **Total** | _____ | _____ | _____ |

a. If the flood-control project cost $140,000, would wealth be created if it were undertaken?

b. Under Plan A, the $140,000 cost would be allocated equally among the seven voters. Indicate the amount each voter would pay in the space provided. If the seven individuals voted on the project, what would be the outcome?
c. Devise a finance plan that would lead to gain for all seven voters, and indicate the allocation of the cost to each person in the space under plan B.
d. Suppose that the project cost $224,000. If the costs are shared equally among the seven persons, would the project pass? Would it create wealth?
e. Will majority rule always lead to the acceptance of productive projects and the rejection of counterproductive ones? Why or why not?

CHAPTER

# 21

# THE ENVIRONMENT, NATURAL RESOURCES, AND THE FUTURE

The essence of economic activity is the removal of materials from the environment, their transformation by production and consumption, and their eventual return to the environment.

*Edwin Mills*[1]

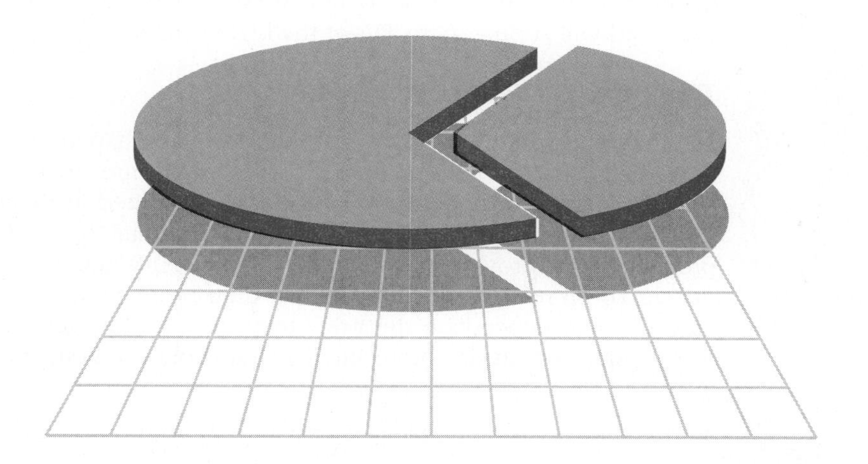

## CHAPTER FOCUS

- What does the economic way of thinking have to say about resource markets and environmental decision-making?
- Are we in danger of running out of vital natural resources in the future?
- Is economic growth harmful to the environment?
- How do private ownership and competitive markets affect the quality of the environment?
- Can government regulation help protect the quality of the environment?

Natural-resource and environmental issues have become increasingly important, especially over the past 30 years. Will there be enough minerals, water, and other natural resources for future generations? Will pollution increase as capital formation and technological improvements lead to greater production of goods and services? What does economics have to say about protecting the environment and using natural resources wisely? This chapter will focus on these questions and related topics.

# RESOURCE MARKETS AND THE ENVIRONMENT

For most goods and services, as we saw in earlier chapters, both suppliers and demanders are influenced by price and by the availability of substitutes. A higher price for one good makes others more attractive as substitutes. If, for example, movie tickets rise in price, then a host of substitutes, such as cable TV subscriptions, books, and live concerts, become more attractive options for entertainment. The price increase causes fewer movie tickets to be purchased. Similar forces are at work on the supply side, since investors and workers have options as well. For example, if the price of TV sets increases, those manufacturers will be able to bid more capital and labor away from other uses, and will supply more TVs at the higher price.

## The Case of Resource Markets

Are the demand and supply of natural resources shaped by similar influences? For something so basic as water, for example, are good substitutes readily available? The use of water by industry, as illustrated in Exhibit 21.1, provides a good example of the extent to which capital, or different production processes, can provide substitution possibilities. When automakers, steel producers, or oil refineries need water for their production processes, the amount they use will depend on the price they must pay to get the water. A higher water price will justify more efficient radiators, or perhaps filtration devices

[1]Edwin Mills, *Economic Analysis of Environmental Problems* (New York: Columbia University Press, 1975), p. 1.

EXHIBIT 21.1

**How Water "Requirements" Can Vary**

When the use of water is expensive, people find ways to use less of it. These numbers, all from actual industrial plants, demonstrate the wide variations possible, even within specific industrial use. How much water is needed to generate a unit of electricity? That depends very much on how costly water is, as the table shows. The "need" can vary from 1.32 gallons to 170 gallons. With time, technology can further expand this range of options.

| | Draft (in gallons) | | |
|---|---|---|---|
| **Product or User and Unit** | **Maximum** | **Typical** | **Minimum** |
| Steam-electric power (kw-h) | 170 | 80 | 1.32 |
| Petroleum refining (gallon of crude oil) | 44.5 | 18.3 | 1.73 |
| Steel (finished ton) | 65,000 | 40,000 | 1,400 |
| Soaps, edible oils (pound) | 7.5 | — | 1.57 |
| Carbon black (pound) | 14 | 4 | 0.25 |
| Natural rubber (pound) | 6 | — | 2.54 |
| Butadiene (pound) | 305 | 160 | 13 |
| Glass containers (ton) | 667 | — | 118 |
| Automobiles (per car) | 16,000 | — | 12,000 |
| Trucks, buses (per unit) | 20,000 | — | 15,000 |

**Source:** H. E. Hudson and Janet Abu-Lughod, "Water Requirements," *Water for Industry,* Jack B. Graham and Meredith F. Burrill, eds. Publication no. 45 (Washington, D.C.: American Association for the Advancement of Science, 1956), pp. 19–21.

providing for the reuse of water. Some processes use much more water than others, so when water costs are high, producers will tend to use processes requiring less water.

When economists examine markets for water, petroleum products, minerals, and other natural resources, they find that the sensitivity of decision-makers to price and cost is similar to that found for other goods and services. Substitutes, it seems, are everywhere. For example when the price of gasoline rises, users find many ways to use less of it: smaller cars, less distant vacation destinations, fewer shopping trips, and the use of public transportation, to name just a few. When the price of any resource rises, users will respond in the same way, as they find new and better ways to keep down the cost to themselves of achieving their goals.

Higher prices will also induce resource suppliers to search for more of the resource and recover more of the known deposits. For example, when oil prices increase, wildcatters will search new territories, drillers will dig deeper, and water flooding and other techniques will be used to recover more oil from existing wells. Thus, the quantity supplied of oil—or any other resources—is positively related to price.

As in other markets, the responsiveness of producers and users will vary with time. The longer a sharp rise or fall in price persists, the stronger the

## MYTHS OF ECONOMICS

*We are running out of energy, minerals, timber, and other nonrenewable natural resources. Doomsday is just around the corner.*

For centuries, various social commentators have argued that the world is about to run out of trees, vital minerals, or various sources of energy. In sixteenth-century England, fear arose that the supply of wood would soon be exhausted as that resource was widely used as a source of energy. As Clayburn LaForce notes, however; the price of wood "gradually rose as forest around urban centers receded. In response to higher prices, people gradually began to substitute coal for charcoal, a wood derivative, in both personal and commercial uses. England entered its greatest period of economic growth and that 'sceptered isle' still has forests."

In the middle of the nineteenth century, dire predictions arose that the United States was about to run out of whale oil, at the time the primary fuel for artificial lighting. As the demand for whale oil increased, many predicted that all of the whales would soon be gone and that Americans would face long nights without light. Whale-oil prices rose sharply from 23 cents per gallon in 1820 to $1.42 per gallon in 1850. As LaForce explains, higher prices again motivated consumers and entrepreneurs to seek alternatives, including distilled vegetable oils, lard oil, and coal gas. By the early 1850s, coal oil (kerosene) had won out. And very soon thereafter, a new substitute for whale oil appeared: Petroleum replaced coal oil as the source of kerosene. As for whale oil, by 1896, its price had fallen to 40 cents per gallon, and even at that price few people used it. The whale-oil crisis had passed.

As people switched to petroleum, doomsday predictions about its exhaustion arose almost as soon as the resource was developed. In 1914 the Bureau of Mines reported that the total U.S. supply of oil was 6 million barrels, an amount less than the United States now produces approximately every 20 months. In 1926 the Federal Oil Conservation Board informed people that the U.S. supply of oil would last only seven years. A couple of decades later the secretary of interior forecast that the United States would run out of oil in just a few more years.

Dire predictions about our natural-resource future became a fad during the 1970s. The "year of exhaustion" of important natural resources, especially crude oil, was a popular news item. The arithmetic of the doomsday calculations was unassailable. One simply found the current annual consumption rate (averaged over, say, the last two decades) and divided that number into the quantity of proved reserves of the resource. That provided the years of the resource remaining. Add that number to the current date, and you had the "year of exhaustion."

So why have such projections proved to be so wrong? There are two major reasons for their inaccuracy. First, "proved reserves" of a mineral resource are the verified quantity of the resource that producers have discovered that they believe can be produce *at current prices*

response will be to the change in price. It takes time for both users and suppliers to adjust fully to new market prices by changing the equipment they use, their consumption patterns, and the capital and labor used to produce items whose prices have changed. Product innovation and technological change are among the additional factors that have greater impact over time, both on quantities demanded and on those supplied, in response to a price change.

Resource markets are quite similar to other markets. The quantity of a natural resource demanded will fall and the quantity supplied will rise when its price increases (other things constant). Higher resource prices will increase the *and levels of technology.* Contrary to popular belief, they reveal little or nothing about the sufficiency of a mineral reserve for the future. Instead, proved reserves are quite similar to inventories in manufacturing industries. Just as it is costly to produce and hold inventories of a manufactured good—for example, automobiles—so, too, it is costly to find and verify reserves of a mineral resource. Just as automobile dealers choose to hold only a two- or three-month inventory of cars, mineral producers commonly hold only a ten- to fifteen-year supply of mineral resources. And, just as the current inventory of automobiles reveals little about their future availability, the size of current proved reserves reveals little about the absolute quantity of a mineral resource that can be supplied in the future.

Second, doomsday predictions have generally failed to consider the role of price changes. When a resource becomes more scarce, its price rises. This provides additional incentive for (1) resource users to cut back on their consumption, (2) suppliers to develop new methods of discovering and recovering larger quantities of the resource, and (3) both users and producers to search for and develop substitutes. To date, these forces have pushed doomsday farther and farther into the future.

In fact, the empirical evidence indicates that the relative scarcity of most resources is declining, and as a result, the relative price of most resources is falling. The classic study of Harold Barnett and Chandler Morse illustrates this point. Using data from 1870 to 1963, Barnett and Morse found that the real price of resources declined during that long period. Updates and extensions of this work indicate that resource prices are continuing to decline. In 1980 economist Julian Simon bet doomsday environmentalist Paul Ehrlich that the inflation-adjusted price of any five natural resources of Ehrlich's choosing would decline during the 1980s. In fact, the prices of all five of the resources chosen by Ehrlich declined, and Simon won the highly publicized bet. A recent study found that of 38 major natural resources, only two (manganese and zinc) increased in price (after adjustment for inflation) during the 1980s.

Far from suggesting that doomsday is just around the corner, the price data paint a much more optimistic picture. Historical data on relative prices of key resources indicate that technology and the ever-increasing availability of substitutes tend to outrun our use of scarce natural resources. When price changes are allowed to reflect changing scarcities, constructive human responses to specific scarcities are a predictable occurrence. Just as they have been wrong in the past, future doomsday forecasts that fail to incorporate human response to relative price changes will likely prove to be wrong in the future.

Sources: J. Clayburn LaForce, "The Energy Crisis: The Moral Equivalent of Bamboozle," International Institute for Economic Research, Original Paper 11 (Los Angeles, April 1978); Harold Barnett and Chandler Morse, *Scarcity of Growth: The Economics of Natural Resource Availability* (Baltimore: The Johns Hopkins University Press for Resources for the Future, 1963); Manuel H. Johnson, Fredrick W. Bell, and J. T. Bennett, "Natural Resource Scarcity: Empirical Evidence and Public Policy," *Journal of Environmental Economics and Management* 7 (September 1980), pp. 258–269; and Stephen Moore, "So Much for 'Scarce Resources,' "*Public Interest* (Winter 1992).

incentive of users to conserve on their use of a resource and to find substitutes for it. The higher price also brings forth extra production, providing additional supplies. Lower prices have the opposite effects, reducing the quantity supplied of the resource, and increasing the quantity demanded.

## The Case of Environmental Decisions

Markets coordinate the choices of people with regard to natural-resource use. But what about environmental decisions, which often are made outside the markets, and thus without the benefit of fully priced goods and services? There are relatively few markets for clean air, water purity, and endangered species. As we have previously discussed, the absence of clearly defined and securely enforced property rights and the resulting lack of markets and decision-maker accountability are at the heart of pollution and other externality problems. Can we nevertheless use the economic way of thinking to enhance our understanding of decisions that affect the environment?

One economics professor demonstrated the importance of incentives in environmental decisions by walking into class with a lighted cigarette, taking a puff, then dropping the cigarette on the floor, and grinding it out with his shoe. Then he pointed out that he would never do such a thing in his own living room, where he personally would bear the cost of having to clean up the mess. In fact, he said, he probably would not do it if the building's janitor were watching and likely to voice strong disapproval of the behavior. Further, he said that he would be less likely to grind out the cigarette on a classroom floor if an ashtray were handy—in other words, if he were not required to go to the trouble of finding one. The professor's actions regarding the environment around him thus depended on the incentives given him.

Do incentives matter in the preservation of wildlife? Consider the case of African elephants, which are valuable for their meat and ivory, among other factors. Poachers like to kill the wild elephants illegally, to take the most valuable parts. Poaching is illegal, but the animals in central African nations are not owned by the local residents, who might most easily help prevent poaching. The residents gain nothing from the presence of the elephants. The control of poaching is consequently weak, and the herds in Central Africa have been declining—almost to the point of extinction.[2] In southern African nations, however, many elephants are owned privately. Even when the elephants are not owned privately, the residents of the villages near each herd are allowed to share the gains from the human use of elephants, whether from hunting or tourism. These partial, private ownership rights provide local residents with an incentive to help control poaching, and they have been quite effective in doing so. As a result, elephant herds thrive in southern African nations.

As these simple examples demonstrate, when people make decisions affecting the environment, their actions will be guided by expected benefits and opportunity costs, just as they are for other decisions.

The fact that values are subjective also bears on environmental decisions. How valuable is a tract of unroaded wilderness land, relative to the same land with roads and campgrounds added to enhance recreation, or the same land developed for high-quality residential use? Individuals will differ dramatically in their evaluations of those alternatives. Some believe that wilderness is the highest and best use for such a tract of land. Others view more intensive recreational use or tastefully planned residential development, where people can be in close contact with the beauty of nature, to be a better use of such land.

Consider another, similar question: Will persons living near a river be willing to vote for sewage plant improvements to help clean up a half-mile stretch of the river, even though that will add an extra $12 per month to their water

[2]See Randy Simmons and Urs Kreuter, "Herd Mentality: Banning Ivory Sales Is No Way to Save the Elephant," *Policy Review,* Fall 1989, pp. 46–49.

bill? Again, we can expect people to differ in how much value they place on making a stretch of river a little cleaner. Some will be quite happy to pay the fee, while others will probably object. Environmental values, like all others, are subjective. Individuals will differ substantially in the value they place on various options for environmental management.

As in other areas of human action, the secondary effects of environmental actions must be considered. For example, when citrus growers use chemical pesticides to protect their fruit against certain insects, the pesticides may impose some danger to consumers if they are not washed completely from the fruit. To avoid such danger to consumers, government agencies have banned the use of certain pesticides. That was the case for DDT, which was banned by the U.S. Environmental Protection Agency in 1972 because it was believed to be a source of human health risk and damage to wild birds. Unfortunately, the ban had unwanted secondary effects. In place of DDT, some other pesticides were used that were more risky to the workers who applied them in the fields.

In other nations, the results were even more tragic when DDT was banned. In Sri Lanka, for example, where mosquitoes had been controlled by DDT, the incidence of malaria had declined from 2.8 million cases in 1946 to only 110 cases in 1961. After the government of Sri Lanka banned the use of DDT in the early 1960s, however, the number of malaria cases jumped back up to 2.5 million in 1968–1969. So banning DDT has eliminated certain risks, but the unwanted secondary effects in some countries have been worse than the original risks.

It is important that environmental decision-makers, like those in other policy areas, be alert for secondary effects. This basic economic principle is just as important for environmental decision-making as it is in other areas of human action.

We have seen that economic principles apply to decisions people make regarding natural resources and the environment, just as they do to other areas of human action. But since markets and easily defended property rights are not always present, especially for air and water quality and other environmental services, observers often worry that as an economy grows, more resources will be used and additional waste will be imposed on the environment. Clearly, this is an extremely important concern. What can economists say about the effects of economic growth on environmental quality? We turn now to examine this important question.

## IS ECONOMIC GROWTH HARMFUL TO THE ENVIRONMENT?

The choice between economic growth and environmental quality may seem obvious when economic activities affect the quality of our air or water. In the United States, the federal government has been asked to constrain polluters, and, historically, courts have protected the rights of those harmed by pollution, requiring polluters to pay damages and sometimes ordering them to stop the polluting activities. More recently, government regulations have required polluters to clean up their emissions or even to cease the polluting activity. As a result, certain economic activities are made more costly and specific economic outputs are reduced in order to maintain environmental quality. It is not surprising then that many people believe that a choice must be made between economic growth on the one hand and environmental protection on the other. Yet data from around the world suggest otherwise.

As we will see, many of the same forces that encourage economic growth, such as market institutions and the acceptance of technological advance, also help to reduce pressures on the environment by an economy. In addition, rising incomes foster the willingness and the ability to pay for a cleaner, more pleasant environment. While environmental protection often imposes some cost on economic activities, growth can still proceed when the controls are intelligently applied. And growth itself, properly controlled to avoid environmental harms, has some important beneficial effects on environmental protection.

Once people have enough income so that they are not struggling to put food on the table, they become more willing and able to take actions to reduce (or avoid) environmental damage and improve the quality of environment. For example, as incomes have risen in North America, Europe, and other parts of the world, private actions to maintain nature preserves have proliferated. Individuals, firms, and nonprofit groups have established areas for the protection of plant and animal habitats.[3] Profit-seeking firms such as Big Sky of Montana, find it profitable to buy large tracts of mountainous land, far more than they plan to develop, then sell tracts with environmentally protective restrictions. By guaranteeing the pristine quality of the resort with legal restrictions on what the new owners can do, they increase the value of the property they sell.

Economic growth generally leads to environmental improvements because people with higher incomes are willing to pay more for environmental quality. Economist Donald Coursey has studied this topic extensively. He finds that in the United States and in other industrial nations, citizens' support for measures to improve environmental quality is highly sensitive to income changes.[4] In economic terms, willingness to pay for environmental measures, such as costly environmental regulations, is highly elastic with respect to income. He estimates that in industrial nations the income elasticity of demand for environmental quality is 2.5. Thus, a 10 percent increase in income leads to a 25 percent increase in citizens' willingness to pay for environmental measures. Similarly, a 10 percent decline in a community's income leads to a 25 percent decline in that community's support for costly environmental measures. According to Coursey, the demand for environmental quality has approximately the same income elasticity as the demand for luxury automobiles like the BMW and Mercedes-Benz.

Technological change is another factor that generally improves the environment. Economic growth and technological change generally accompany each other. The same market processes that encourage growth also encourage technological advances. In the United States, advancing technology was itself cleaning the environment well before major environmental laws were passed.

In a market system, producers using advanced technology can profit by getting a given performance from a smaller amount of a costly resource.

[3]Chapter 9 of *Environmental Quality, 1984,* the annual report of the President's Council on Environmental Quality, describes a representative sample of these private projects, some of which date back to the last century, to benefit the environment.

[4]Donald Coursey discussed this topic in "The Demand for Environmental Quality," a paper presented January 1993 at the annual meeting of the American Economic Association in Anaheim, California.

**EXHIBIT 21.2**

**Required per 1000 Cans**

By improving their engineering techniques and switching to a thinner can made of light-weight aluminum, producers reduced their use of metal per can by almost 80 percent between 1965 and 1990.

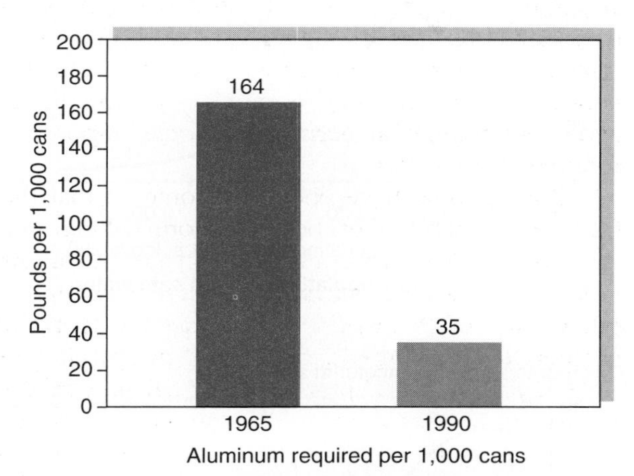


**Source:** Lynn Scarlett, "Make Your Environment Dirtier—Recycle," *The Wall Street Journal,* January 14, 1991.

Exhibit 21.2 illustrates this process for producers and users of soft-drink and beer cans. As they sought greater profits, producers found ways to reduce the amount of metal they used per can, and switched to lightweight, recyclable aluminum. As a result, less ore was dug and processed, and less energy was needed to transport both the raw materials and the filled cans, reducing the pollution resulting from the use of the cans. Because this search for lower-cost means of producing each marketed service is going on constantly in a market economy, the result is a continuing series of reductions in the emissions of polluting wastes. Partially offsetting this, of course, is the increased quantity of goods and services produced.

Economic growth does tend to make some kinds of environmental problems worse rather than better. Certain potential environmental problems seem to grow worse with increases in income, up to a point, then improve with still higher levels of economic development. Exhibit 21.3 illustrates the general relationship between levels of certain pollutants and per capita income.

Some pollution problems, such as a lack of safe drinking water (Exhibit 21.3a), are steadily reduced as income rises. As people become richer, they are more able to reduce waterborne diseases by installing sewers to handle human waste, and by reducing water contamination by animals. Other pollutants, such as particulates in the air (Exhibit 21.3b), tend initially to become worse as incomes rise from extremely low levels. But as income levels rise further, heavily used roads are paved and industrial processes become more efficient and emit smaller amounts of waste. As a result, particulate pollution in the air declines with additional income increases.

**EXHIBIT 21.3** **Pollution Problems as National Income Rises**

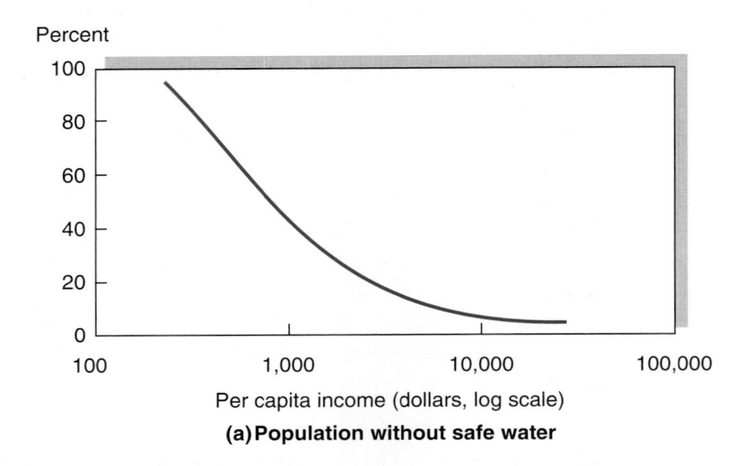


**(a) Population without safe water**

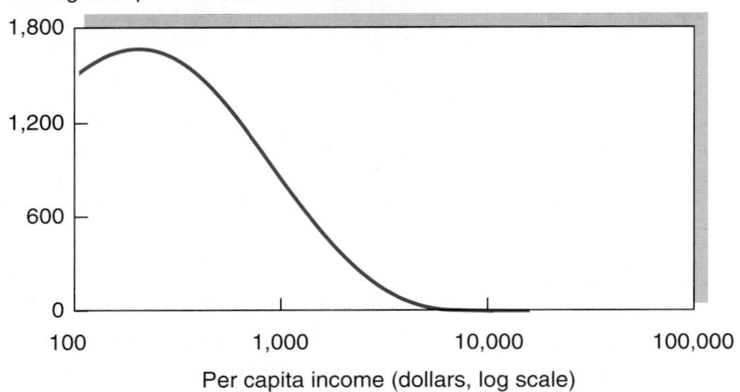


**(b) Urban concentration of particulate matter**

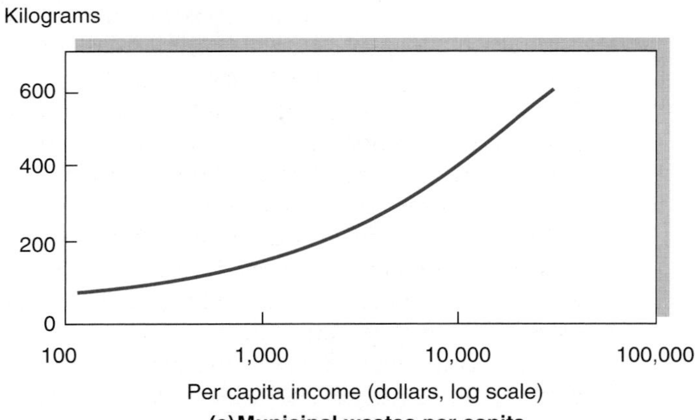


**(c) Municipal wastes per capita**

*Note:* Estimates are based on cross-country regression analysis of data from the 1980s.

**Source:** World Bank, *World Development Report, 1992,* p. 11.

Especially among developed countries, economic growth most often brings cleaner air and water, along with improvements in several other aspects of environmental quality.

Not every element of environmental quality improves with economic development. The amount of solid waste generated normally increases steadily (Exhibit 21.3c), for example. But proper disposal facilities can minimize the negative effects of that problem also. On balance, richer seems to be environmentally better.[5] Why is a cleaner environment generally associated with economic development? What causes richer nations to be generally cleaner? One answer seems to be the establishment of property rights to land and other natural resources.

We turn now to an examination of the several roles played by property rights in encouraging both economic growth and environmental improvement.

## PROPERTY RIGHTS AND THE ENVIRONMENT

> *When people have open access to forests, pastureland, or fishing grounds, they tend to overuse them. Providing land titles to farmers in Thailand has helped to reduce damage to forests. The assignment of property titles to slum dwellers in Bandung, Indonesia, has tripled household investment in sanitation facilities. Providing security of tenure to hill farmers in Kenya has reduced soil erosion. Formalizing community rights to land in Burkina Faso is sharply improving land management. And allocating transferable rights to fishery resources has checked the tendency to overfish in New Zealand.*
>
> World Bank[6]

Income growth helps to increase the demand for environmental quality, while technological advance helps to lower the cost of reducing resource use. Yet incomes above the poverty level and an understanding of technology are not enough to protect the environment. The recent opening up of Eastern European nations and the Soviet Union exposed widespread environmental disasters. These occurred despite good technical capabilities in those nations and per capita incomes that were well above the world average.

Why have these advanced nations not taken better care of their environments? The answer appears to lie in the fact that property rights and market exchange were largely missing. As indicated in the preceding quote from a World Bank report on economic development and the environment, property rights are an important factor influencing environmental quality. The former Soviet Union and the Eastern European nations, in the decades during which they were controlled by socialist governments, refused to allow most resources to be privately owned and declared that most market exchanges were criminal acts. Entrepreneurship of most kinds was declared to be criminal behavior. Production instead was centrally planned. Land and other resources were owned by the state, rather than by individuals.

In a competitive market, the profit motive provides clear incentives to reduce resource usage and waste products. When a firm is privately owned, the personal wealth of the owners is enhanced by effective economizing behavior. For government-operated enterprises, however, this is much less true.

[5]The *World Development Report, 1992,* published by the World Bank, especially Chapters 2 and 3, provides a detailed look at the connection between economic development and environmental quality.

[6]The quoted passage is from *World Development Report, 1992* (New York: World Bank, 1992), p. 12.

There is no owner (or group of owners) whose wealth is directly affected by economizing behavior (or the lack of it) on the part of the managers of government enterprises. Thus, government-owned firms are less likely than their market counterparts to minimize cost and thus resource use.

Decisions in socialist economies show substantially less movement toward the adoption of resource-saving techniques and technologies. One index of resource conservation is energy use per unit of output. In modern economies, energy constitutes more than half of all the resources utilized. Mikhail Bernstam has compiled data to compare the energy use in the largest 12 industrialized market economies with its use in the Eastern European socialist countries (plus North Korea). The market-based economies used only 37 percent as much energy per $1,000 worth of output as the socialist nations in 1986. The figure had fallen from 44 percent in 1980. The same sort of comparison applies to the use of steel. Socialist economies used more than three times as much steel per unit of output as market economies did.[7]

The data gathered by Bernstam show that across a variety of socialist economies, resource use is far greater per unit of output than across a variety of market-oriented economies. All of these nations have the capability of using advanced technologies, but without a market process in which producers and consumers individually choose among competing options, and individually pay for what they choose, these countries fail to conserve resources effectively. A less efficient economy tends to be a less clean economy.

After the fall of rigidly socialist regimes in the Soviet Union and Eastern Europe, new leaders sought ways to increase the role of markets in their economies. This meant that the role of private ownership received much more favorable attention. What, exactly, is important about private ownership of resources? Four functions of property rights are especially important to the economy and to the environment. Private ownership provides

1. Resource owners with the right to sell access to others, but the accompanying resource prices also provide users with an incentive to minimize their use of resources.
2. A reason for owners to exercise good stewardship.
3. The support for owners to prevent others from damaging their resources by polluting or other invasive activities.
4. The necessary ingredient for capital markets to operate, giving future market participants a voice in today's market decisions.

Let us look more closely at each of these four functions of privately held property rights.

1. *Private property rights provide owners with the incentive to share (sell to others) resource access, while resource prices provide users with the incentive to conserve.* As we learned in earlier chapters, markets cannot function unless sellers own rights that they can, if they wish, sell to buyers in the marketplace. If a resource is utilized in highly productive ways, its owner can receive high levels of payment from the resource users. Lower valued uses will pay less in competitive markets. When resources are privately owned, producers will have a strong incentive to conserve on their use of the costly resources. In

[7]The facts in this paragraph are from Mikhail Bernstam, *The Wealth of Nations and the Environment* (London: Institute of Economic Affairs, 1991), pp. 1–28.

essence, private ownership encourages less resource usage per unit of output. In addition, pursuit of profits provides business firms with a strong incentive to implement new technologies that conserve on the use of resources. Thus, it should not be surprising that resource-saving changes tend to occur earlier in a market setting than under socialism. The experience of Eastern Europe and the former Soviet Union under socialism is consistent with the view.

2. *A resource owner has a strong incentive to exercise good stewardship.* Private ownership of property provides an incentive for good care that is lacking under government control. If the resource is well cared for, it will be more valuable and add more to the wealth of its owner. If the owner allows the resource to deteriorate, he or she personally bears the cost of that negligence in the form of a decline in the value of the resource. The value of the property right to the resource is, in a very real sense, a hostage to good care of that resource.

3. *A resource owner has legal rights against anyone seeking to harm the resource.* A private owner of a resource has more than just the incentive to preserve the value of that resource. Private property rights also provide to the legal owner rights in law against anyone (usually including a government agency) who invades and harms the resource. Much environmental damage is prevented this way. The private owner of a forest or a farm will not sit idly by if someone is cutting down trees or invading the property with hazardous pollutants. Lawsuits can be used to protect those rights. For example, owners of copper and lead smelters in the United States have been forced to compensate owners of land and homes for damage from sulfur dioxide emissions. Once such a company has been successfully sued, the decision sets a legal precedent that effectively discourages further such action.

Before they closed it down, the owners of a smelter near Tacoma, Washington, had been sued in such a manner. After they were found to be liable, they took measures to reduce pollution damages. Moreover, whenever unusual weather conditions nonetheless caused sulfur dioxide from its smokestack to damage the foliage or the homes of downwind households, the company routinely made payments of compensation to avoid further lawsuits.

When resources are not privately owned, no individual will receive large personal rewards for bringing suit against polluters, even when the source of the pollution is clear. In the United States, fish in a river might be damaged by pollution, but they are not owned by anyone whose personal wealth depends on their safety. Political and bureaucratic authorities must be counted on to protect the resource. In England, by contrast, where fishing rights on a stream are privately owned, the owners guard jealously the quality of the water. Long before Earth Day 1970, fishing rights owners took polluters to court and stopped them, setting precedents that deter other potential polluters to this day. Of course if damages are small compared to the cost of eliminating pollution, polluters may be able to buy out the rights of those downstream, or downwind.

4. *Changes in the value of a privately owned resource bring all of the anticipated future benefits and costs of today's resource decisions immediately to bear on the resource owner.* An additional benefit of private property rights is their ability to bring expected future effects of current decisions to bear now. Property rights provide long-term incentives for maximizing the value of a resource, even for owners whose personal outlook is short term. If using a tract of land for the construction of a toxic waste dump reduces its future productivity, its value *today* falls, and the decline in the land's value reduces the

owner's wealth. That happens because land's current worth reflects the net value of its future services—the revenue from production or services received directly from the land, minus the costs (including amounts that must be paid to anyone harmed by escaping wastes) required to generate the revenues.

Thus, fewer services from a privately owned resource, or greater costs associated with it in the future, mean lower value (and less wealth for the owner) now. In fact, as soon as an appraiser or potential buyer can see future problems, the wealth of the owner declines by the amount of the reduction in potential buyers' willingness to pay for the resource. Not only does using land to store hazardous waste reduce future options for the land's productivity, but the value also may be reduced by the risk of future lawsuits if the wastes leak and cause damage to other people or property.

This is true even if the owner of the resource is a corporation, and the corporate officers, rather than the owner-stockholders, are in control. Corporate officers may be concerned mainly about the short term, not expecting to be present when future problems arise. However, property rights hold such decision-makers accountable. If a current action is expected to cause future problems, or if current expenditures are seen to promise future benefits, those who buy and sell stock will push the stock price up or down accordingly, capturing the reduction or the increase in future net benefits.

Of course, the average owner of stock is not a pollution expert, but anyone can gain the necessary knowledge by reading the published reports of stock analysts, who are tuned in to all phases of the industry they cover. Watchdog environmental groups also spread the word about suspected problems. It is in the stockholder's interest to keep an "ear to the ground" because correctly anticipating how the market will react can allow the discerning investor to buy before good news is fully captured in the stock price, or to sell before bad news is fully reflected in a falling stock price. Such self-interested scrutiny and the resultant decisions of investors provide a continual assessment of corporate strategies, and thus an influence on them as stock prices rise or fall accordingly.

Property rights are an important factor in preserving and enhancing environmental quality. Another, alternative way to seek environmental quality is through government regulation. It, too, has important effects on both the economy and the environment.

## GOVERNMENT REGULATION AND THE ENVIRONMENT

Environmental quality is an economic good. People are willing to pay for it, and as their incomes rise, they demand more of it. Substantial contributions to environmental quality are made through the normal operation of property rights and a market system. However, certain kinds of environmental problems cannot be solved merely by the enforcement of individual property rights. Only when pollution is local, affecting strongly a few people who can enforce their rights in court, can property rights deal effectively with the problem. Most pollutants capable of doing proven and serious damage are of this sort. But others of potentially great harm are not. If the effects of an emitted substance are both serious and very widespread, or if the substance has many sources, making it impossible to assign individual responsibility, then the protective role of government may require it to step in with regulation.

Regulation, however, can be enormously expensive. In the early 1990s estimates of the cost of environmental regulation in the United States were about $120 billion per year. Regulation is seldom based on market signals, and so it is subject to all the problems caused by lack of information and lack of incentives that have plagued the socialist nations. It can be very wasteful.[8] Scientific uncertainty is often great, in cases where regulation is demanded, and the stakes can be very high.

Consider the issue of global warming. Emissions of carbon dioxide, from the efficient burning of all fuels, cause no harm where they are emitted. No one's rights are being violated by the invasion of a harmful pollutant. Yet these emissions may in the future require regulation if, as some scientists claim, carbon dioxide builds up in the atmosphere to the point where it acts as an invisible blanket, causing the earth to warm. Such warming could change weather patterns, making hurricanes and other storms more intense, and might even result in rising sea levels around the globe. If the "worst-case scenarios" suggested by scientists were to materialize, some communities would face the flooding of their lands, serious ecological disruptions, and other problems.

Some scientists and many environmental groups argue that the threat of global warming is so serious that despite high costs, the nations of the world must impose strong regulations quickly. Government limits of some sort, they point out, are the only way that carbon dioxide emissions can be controlled. Other scientists, and many policy analysts, believe that imposing strong regulation at this time would be a mistake. They point out that the science of global warming is filled with uncertainties. For example:

1. We do not know whether changes in the Earth's cloud cover will enhance the warming effects of carbon dioxide or offset them. Water vapor and clouds in the atmosphere account for more than 98 percent of the total warming we now experience, so even small changes in where that water is, in the atmosphere, and the form it takes, could easily overcome the impact of the buildup in carbon dioxide. All scientists agree that the atmospheric models used to predict global warming do not accurately incorporate the effects of atmospheric water vapor.
2. It is true that in the past several thousand years, added carbon dioxide has been associated with warming, but the warming seems to have come first. Did carbon dioxide buildups cause the warming, or did warming cause the buildups?
3. If warming does occur, will sea levels rise or fall? Warming would cause the polar ice caps to melt and shrink at the edges, but warmer air carries more moisture, and the added precipitation would build up snow and ice in their still-frigid centers, increasing their thickness. The net effect on sea level is unknown.

These questions and many more are in dispute.

[8]For a more thorough explanation of why environmental regulation is often inefficient, and some quantitative estimates of how costly it is, see Robert Crandall, *Why Is the Cost of Environmental Regulation So High?* Policy Study No. 110 (St. Louis: Center for the Study of American Business, February 1992).

We cannot even be sure whether the buildup and a warmer world would, on balance, be better or worse. Some people would gain from a warmer, wetter world. Also, the direct effects of carbon dioxide are helpful to plants. Owners of greenhouses routinely purchase carbon dioxide to enrich the enclosed atmosphere. These facts and the many scientific uncertainties combine to make many economists unwilling to endorse strong regulations to force reductions in the emissions of carbon dioxide. The cost of such policies is another consideration. One large study estimates that in the United States alone, the cost of merely stabilizing emissions at their current levels, with no net reduction, would be $95 billion in the first year, with larger costs after that. Economist William Nordhaus, in an article about global warming, suggests, "The best investment today may be in learning about climatic change, rather than in preventing it."[9]

In sum, environmental regulation is a powerful tool, capable of providing important improvements in environmental quality, but it tends to be very costly, and its unintended consequences can be serious also. Regulations banning DDT illustrated that point, as we described earlier, especially in the tragic case of Sri Lanka.

Policymakers and analysts considering environmental regulations should recognize that environmental quality is an economic good. Like food, clothing, and shelter, it is something that people are willing to pay for, though not in unlimited amounts. In addition, policymakers should recognize that the linkage between environmental quality and economic prosperity is important. Environmental regulations can exert a powerful influence on both, for good or for ill. Finally, they should not forget that property rights were for many years our main form of environmental policy, and that overall, they continue to play a positive role in the preservation of a quality environment.

## Looking Ahead

In this chapter, we noted the linkage between economic prosperity and environmental quality. The following chapter investigates income differences across countries and analyzes the key ingredients of economic growth and prosperity.

## Chapter Summary

1. In resource markets, as in other markets, incentives matter. Both the quantity demanded of a resource and the quantity supplied depend on the resource price. Substitutes can be found everywhere. Both the demand and the supply curves will be more elastic when buyers and sellers have more time in which to respond to a price change.
2. Even though environmental decisions are often made outside a market context, the basic principles of economics still apply. Purposeful choices, guided by opportunity costs, are made without full knowledge. Values are subjective, and the secondary effects of decisions are often important.

[9]William Nordhaus, "Global Warming: Slowing the Greenhouse Express," in Henry J. Aaron, ed., *Setting National Priorities: Policies for the Nineties* (Washington: The Brookings Institution, 1990), p. 207.

3. Environmental quality and economic growth tend to go together. People living in poverty are hard on the environment. Technological improvements enhance economic growth and reduce resource waste. The demand for environmental quality is positively and strongly linked to income levels.
4. Resources are better protected and more efficiently allocated, producing less waste and pollution, when property rights are protected and markets are utilized to allocate resources. The stronger economic and environmental performance of market economies, relative to socialist economies, confirm this point.
5. Private resource ownership is important to environmental quality and resource conservation because it (a) is necessary for the wide, but controlled access encouraged by the market process, (b) provides an incentive for resource stewardship, (c) gives owners legal standing against those who would overuse or harm the resource, and (d) through asset value, gives future users a voice in today's markets.
6. Environmental policy is implicit in property rights and a market system. Enforceable property rights cannot always be put into place, so government's protective role may require government regulation to protect citizens from environmental harms. Since regulatory choices are not based on information and incentives from market prices, however, regulation has the same potential for inefficiency and ineffectiveness faced by the socialist governments whose citizens have suffered many environmental harms. Environmental regulations cost the U.S. economy about $120 billion per year. Benefits are mostly unmeasured, but potentially large.
7. Neither economic analysis nor empirical evidence is supportive of the view that the world is about to run out of key natural resources. When private property rights are present, increased scarcity (relative to demand) of a natural resource will increase the price of the resource and thereby encourage (a) conservation, (b) the use of substitutes, and (c) the development of new technologies capable of both enhancing the supply of the resource and reducing our reliance on it. The fact that the real prices of most natural resources have declined during the last century is inconsistent with the doomsday view of resource scarcity.

# *Study Guide*

## CHAPTER 21

# DEVELOPING THE ECONOMIC WAY OF THINKING

# Critical-Analysis Questions

*1. Does a resource that is not owned, and therefore is not priced, have a zero opportunity cost? Might it be treated as if it did? Explain.

2. Why is the price elasticity of demand for resources, such as water and natural gas, greater in the long run than the short run? What examples of responses to price changes can you think of that are more complete after one year than after one week?

*3. "Steel production typically requires 40,000 gallons of water per finished ton of steel. Steel is important to U.S. industry and our national defense. As water becomes more scarce in the nation, it is imperative that the required amounts of water be reserved for the steel industry." Evaluate.

4. "The federal government should do a complete survey of mineral availability in the nation. It is inexcusable that we do not know how much oil, for example, the country can ultimately produce." Evaluate.

*5. Why will more oil in total be produced from an oil well when the price of crude oil is higher?

6. "Unlike a market, where pollution is profitable, government control of resources and pollution can take into account the desires of all the people." What does economic thinking have to say about this statement?

*7. "Private ownership of a natural resource, such as a lake in the woods, is tantamount to setting aside that resource for the personal, selfish enjoyment of one owner. Society will be better off if it is recognized that such a resource was provided by Nature, for all to enjoy." Evaluate.

8. Will the world ever run out of any mineral resource? In your answer, be sure to consider the role played by rising extraction costs and by the existence of property rights to minerals. Does a negative answer to the question imply that increasing resource scarcity will never be a problem?

*9. "Corporations should not be allowed to own forests. Corporate managers are just too shortsighted. Their philosophy is to make a profit now, regardless of the future consequences. For example, trees may be cut after growing 30 years to get revenue now, even though another 20 years' growth would yield a very high rate of return. The long-run health of our forests is too important to entrust them to this sort of management." Evaluate.

10. "Since our national forests are owned by all the people, their resources will be conserved for the benefit of all, rather than exploited in a shortsighted way, to produce benefits only for the owners." Evaluate.

# Multiple-Choice Self-Test

1. Which of the following is true?
   a. A price change usually has a greater effect on the quantity demanded of a resource in the long run than in the short run.
   b. The demand curve for a commodity as basic as energy is vertical.

*Asterisk denotes critical-analysis questions for which answers are given in Appendix A.

   c. The impact of a price change on the quantity demanded of a resource will usually be greater in the short run than in the long run.
   d. In response to a price change, producers will increase the quantity supplied of a resource by a larger amount in the short run than will be possible in the long run.

2. Predictions of resource exhaustion and the ensuing doom
   a. Were first made during the 1970s.
   b. Usually assume that a higher market price will induce consumers to conserve on the use of the resource, while simultaneously providing the incentive for suppliers to find more of the resource as long as it is available.
   c. Fail to consider the fact that proved reserves are usually greater than absolute reserves.
   d. Have often proved incorrect because they have failed to consider completely the crucial role of prices and technological developments.

3. The classic study of Barnett and Morse found that
   a. During the last century, the real price of resources has been doubling approximately every 10 years.
   b. The supply of most minerals will be exhausted within 50 years.
   c. Resource prices declined between 1870 and 1920, but since 1920 the *relative* price of natural resources has been increasing at an annual rate of approximately 3.5 percent.
   d. Technology and the development of substitutes have outrun our use of scarce natural resources during the last century. Thus, relative resource prices have declined.

4. When industrial engineers plan a vegetable processing plant, and are deciding on the daily intake of water for the plant, the daily requirement they settle on will be higher when
   a. The newest available technology uses more water.
   b. More water is physically available to the plant.
   c. The expected price of water delivered to the plant is lower.
   d. The governor of the state in which the plant is located has requested that all water users conserve water.

5. Suppose that new demands reduce the proved reserves of titanium to an unexpectedly low level, and it appears that the new demands will continue. If the market price is unregulated, we should expect that titanium prices will increase,
   a. Encouraging additional exploration and more effective (and more costly) recovery methods that will provide additional new supplies of titanium.
   b. Providing manufacturers with an additional incentive to conserve titanium and to find substitutes for it.
   c. And that at the higher price, proved reserves will gradually be built back up, since price is one determinant of proved reserves.
   d. All of the above.

6. New York City does not meter the flow of water to most users, but instead charges each user a flat fee for water delivery. Economic analysis suggests that
   a. The mayor of the city will have to ask people each year to conserve water in order to achieve effective water conservation.

b. Conservation efforts are unlikely to be taken seriously by many users, since their personal marginal cost of using more water is approximately zero.
c. Users will be very cooperative with conservation programs, since any extra water they use will be free of extra charge, and they will be grateful.
d. If the flat fee is high, water will be conserved, but a low flat fee will encourage greater water use.

7. If a forest or a farm is privately owned, any damage done to it is likely to lower its market value. If the owner does not sell the resource,
   a. There is no effect on the owner's *current* wealth from damage done now.
   b. The market value of the resource will be unaffected.
   c. The owner will not be harmed by the damage done now.
   d. The market value of the resource will nonetheless decline, and the owner's wealth will be immediately reduced.
8. The research of Mikhail Bernstam indicates that with regard to the use of steel *per unit of output,* market economies used
   a. Less than half as much as socialist economies.
   b. More than twice as much as socialist economies.
   c. About the same as socialist economies.
   d. The minimum required, by scientific standards.
9. Under a system of private ownership, if a factory owned by Tom Jones is the source of pollution that harms others who are downstream or downwind, Jones
   a. Is the one who has the ability to stop the pollution.
   b. Is liable for damages done to the resources of others by the pollution.
   c. Will save on inputs if he can find a more efficient process that converts more of the raw materials to output and emits less polluting waste products.
   d. All of the above are true.
10. Property rights and legal liability are at their best in protecting resources when
    a. There are many sources of pollution and many resources harmed, as in the Los Angeles area air pollution basin.
    b. There is a single pollution source and it is relatively easy for resource owners to prove that the emissions from the specific source damaged their property.
    c. Pollution damage is large, but it is widespread among many resource owners.
    d. Pollution damage is small and it is widespread among many resource users.

# Problems

1. Each of the following statements ignores one of the four functions of private property rights pertaining to environmental quality. In each case identify the function and explain how it has been ignored.
   a. "The National Park Service uses the market mechanism. Visitors at many parks are charged a fee, which goes to the U.S. Treasury, from which the Park Service gets its budget appropriations."

b. "Unlike a private corporation, whose only duty is to make a current profit, the Environmental Protection Agency looks to the future. That is why it writes regulations to protect streams against future pollution."
c. "The State Fish and Game Commission will surely be more careful to protect deer and elk in the forest, than would owners of the forest, even if those forest owners also owned the deer and elk."
d. "A system of private ownership is a sham. An ordinary person, such as a homeowner, has no chance in a market system against a large, well-financed corporation that is polluting the downwind homeowners. Only an Environmental Protection Agency can protect the citizen against large corporate polluters who refuse to sacrifice profits in order to avoid damaging people with industrial pollution."

2. Robert Balling, in *The Heated Debate* (San Francisco: Pacific Research Institute, 1992) presents evidence used by those on both sides of the global warming scientific debate, and provides hundreds of references. Using that book, along with what you have learned in this and earlier chapters of the text, and any other references you wish, write an essay on one side or the other of the following debate issue. "Resolved: Global warming due to emissions of carbon dioxide from the burning of fossil fuels will cause problems so serious that the U.S. government should immediately establish a program to substantially reduce carbon dioxide emissions."

CHAPTER

# 22

# THE POLITICAL ECONOMY OF PROSPERITY

The great object of the political economy of every country is to increase the riches and power of that country.

*Adam Smith*[1]

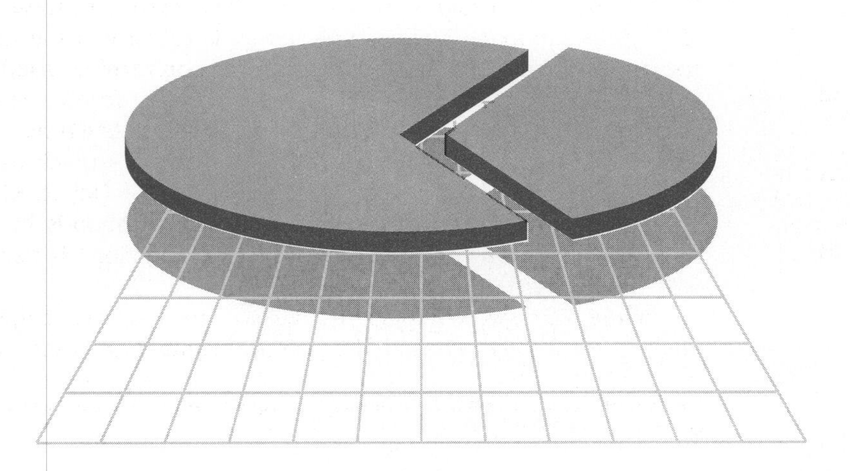

## CHAPTER FOCUS

- How is income measured across countries?
- How does per capita income vary among nations?
- What are the major sources of economic growth?
- What can governments do to promote economic growth?
- How do the policies of prosperous growing economies differ from those that are stagnating?

Throughout history, periods of economic growth and income levels substantially greater than those required for survival have been rare. As recently as 250 years ago, people around the world struggled 50, 60, and 70 hours per week just to obtain the basic necessities of life—food, clothing, and shelter. Sustained economic growth has changed that situation for most people in North America, Europe, Oceania, Japan, and a few other countries. Nonetheless, low incomes and poverty are still the norm in most countries—particularly those of South and Central America, Africa, and Southern Asia. Are these low-income countries showing any growth? Why have some countries prospered while others have stagnated? What can governments do to promote economic prosperity? These questions and related issues have been the focal point of this book. In this concluding chapter, we will pull together the lessons of basic economics and consider these questions in a more comprehensive manner.

## MEASURING INCOMES ACROSS COUNTRIES

**exchange rate conversion method**
Method that uses the foreign exchange rate value of a nation's currency to convert that nation's GDP to another monetary unit, such as the U.S. dollar.

The gross domestic product (GDP) of each country is measured in units of the country's domestic currency. Mexico's GDP is measured in pesos, Japan's in yen, Germany's in marks, and so on. How, then, can these various measures of GDP be compared? The simplest way is to convert the income figures to a common currency by the **exchange rate conversion method.** This method uses the value of each nation's currency in the foreign exchange market to convert the nation's GDP to a common currency, such as the U.S. dollar. For example, if the British pound is worth 1.5 times as much as the U.S. dollar in the foreign exchange market, then the GDP of the United Kingdom is converted to dollars by multiplying the British GDP in pounds by 1.5. Similarly, the exchange rate value of the currency of other nations is used to convert their GDP to dollars.

While income comparisons based on the exchange rate conversion method are widely reported, they are sometimes highly misleading. The foreign

[1]Adam Smith, *An Inquiry into the Nature and Causes of the Wealth of Nations* (Cannon's ed., Chicago: University of Chicago Press, 1976), p. 394.

exchange value of a currency is influenced by only a limited number of goods and services that are traded internationally. It is also influenced by the purchase and sale of assets—particularly financial assets—across countries. Thus, the exchange rate value of a currency may not be a reliable indicator of the currency's purchasing power over the typical bundle of goods and services purchased by households in the domestic market. For example, merely because a British pound purchases 1.5 dollars in the foreign exchange market, it does not follow that it will purchase 1.5 times as much housing, recreation, child-care service, and similar items in the United Kingdom as a dollar will purchase in the United States. Thus, income comparisons based on the exchange rate conversion method are not highly regarded among professional economists.

**purchasing power parity method** The relative purchasing power of different currencies is determined by calculating the amount of each currency required to purchase a typical bundle of goods and services in domestic markets. This information is then used to convert the GDP of each nation to a common monetary unit.

Economists favor the use of the **purchasing power parity method** to make income comparisons across nations. This method compares the cost of purchasing the typical bundle of goods and services consumed by households in the domestic market of various nations. Each category in the bundle is weighted according to its contribution to GDP. The cost of purchasing the typical bundle in each nation is then compared to the dollar cost of purchasing the same bundle in the United States. Once the purchasing power of each nation's currency (in terms of the typical bundle) is determined, this information can be used to convert the GDP of each country to a common monetary unit (for example, the U.S. dollar).

## PER CAPITA INCOME OF NATIONS

Per capita GDP is a measurement of how much output (and income) is generated by the people of a nation. Since it measures output *per person,* it is a broad indicator of the standard of living experienced by the citizens of a nation.

In recent years, Robert Summers and Alan Heston of the University of Pennsylvania have spearheaded a project of the United Nations Statistical Office which has used the purchasing power parity method to develop measures of output for 138 countries.[2] Exhibit 22.1 presents the 1990 per capita GDP data (measured in 1985 U.S. dollars) from this project for 80 of the largest countries. These data illustrate that there is wide variation in per capita GDP among countries. In 1990 there were 21 countries with a population of 7 million or more with a per capita GDP of less than $1,000. In Ethiopia, the poorest of these countries, the estimated annual per capita GDP was only $305. At the other end of the spectrum, there were 18 countries with a population of 5 million or more that had per capita incomes of more than $8,000. The estimated per capita annual GDP of the United States in 1990 was $18,715, the highest in the world. In fact, the U.S. figure was nearly $2,000 more than Switzerland, the country with the next highest level of annual output in 1990.

Most of the poorest countries (annual GDP less than $1,000) were in Africa, with a few from Asia (Burma, Afghanistan, Nepal, and India). On the other hand, with the exception of Saudi Arabia, Australia, Japan, and Hong Kong, the high-income countries were either European or North American.

[2]Robert Summers and Alan Heston, "The Penn World Table (Mark 5): An Expanded Set of International Comparisons, 1950–1988," *Quarterly Journal of Economics,* May 1991, pp. 327–368.

**EXHIBIT 22.1** **Annual per Capita Output of Nations by Purchasing Power Parity Method, 1990 (in 1985 dollars)**

| Poorest Countries[a] (annual output less than $1,000) | | Low-Income Countries[b] (annual output $1,000 to $3,000) | | Middle-Income Countries[b] (annual output $3,000 to $8,000) | | High-Income Countries[b] (annual output more than $8,000) | |
|---|---|---|---|---|---|---|---|
| **Country** | **Per Capita GDP, 1990** | **Country** | **Per Capita GDP, 1990** | **Country** | **Per Capita GDP, 1990** | **Country** | **Per Capita GDP, 1990** |
| Ethiopia | $305 | Nigeria | $1,061 | Tunisia | $3,134 | Spain | $ 8,008 |
| Zaire | 321 | Senegal | 1,089 | Thailand | 3,486 | Saudi Arabia | 9,771 |
| Uganda | 449 | Côte d'Ivoire | 1,151 | Iraq | 3,508[c] | Austria | 12,016 |
| Mali | 500 | Honduras | 1,284 | Poland | 3,632 | Italy | 12,223 |
| Tanzania | 501 | Zimbabwe | 1,299 | Colombia | 3,696 | Netherlands | 12,245 |
| Malawi | 562 | Bolivia | 1,374 | Iran | 3,742 | Unit. Kingdom | 12,286 |
| Niger | 565 | Yemen | 1,562[c] | Argentina | 3,763 | Belgium | 12,288 |
| Rwanda | 578 | Pakistan | 1,627 | Turkey | 3,828 | Denmark | 12,418 |
| Madagascar | 615 | Cameroon | 1,431 | S. Africa | 4,105 | France | 12,814 |
| Zambia | 650 | El Salvador | 1,705 | Syria | 4,177 | Finland | 12,829 |
| Burma | 659[c] | Indonesia | 1,911 | Brazil | 4,225 | Sweden | 13,072 |
| Afghanistan | 714[c] | Egypt | 1,738 | Chile | 4,460 | Australia | 13,161 |
| Somalia | 732 | Philippines | 2,017 | Mexico | 5,146 | Japan | 13,395 |
| Bangladesh | 733 | Morocco | 2,054 | Venezuela | 5,284 | Germany | 13,444 |
| Nepal | 747 | Sri Lanka | 2,077 | Malaysia | 5,366 | Hong Kong | 13,629 |
| Sudan | 828 | Dominican Rep. | 2,079 | Hungary | 5,348 | Canada | 16,304 |
| India | 830 | Guatemala | 2,253 | Portugal | 5,800 | Switzerland | 16,782 |
| Angola | 840[c] | Peru | 2,338 | S. Korea | 5,891 | United States | 18,715 |
| Ghana | 888 | China | 2,427 | Greece | 6,003 | | |
| Kenya | 926 | Algeria | 2,634 | Taiwan | 6,050 | | |
| Mozambique | 937 | Ecuador | 2,683 | | | | |

[a]Includes countries with a population of 7 million or more in 1990.
[b]Includes countries with a population of 5 million or more in 1990.
[c]Data are for 1988.

**Source:** Robert Summers and Alan Heston, "The Penn World Table (Mark 5): An Expanded Set of International Comparisons, 1950–1988," *Quarterly Journal of Economics,* May 1991. The estimates of Summers and Heston were for 1988. The growth rate data for 1989 and 1990 from the World Bank, *World Tables, 1992* were used to update the Summers-Heston data to 1990.

South and Central American countries generally fell into the middle categories with annual per capita incomes in the $1,000 to $6,000 range.

If the output of a nation is increasing more rapidly than its population, the nation's per capita GDP will grow. When per capita GDP increases, on average, the economic wellbeing of people tends to improve. Conversely, a reduction in per capita GDP indicates that average incomes and living standards of people are declining.

With the passage of time, economic growth—increases in per capita GDP—can exert a substantial impact on incomes. Nations that experience sustained periods of rapid economic growth will move up the income ladder and eventually achieve high-income status. On the other hand, nations that grow slowly or experience declines in real GDP per capita will slide down the economic ladder.

Exhibit 22.2 illustrates how sustained economic growth can change income levels over the span of a few decades. Measured in 1985 dollars, the per capita GDP of Hong Kong in 1960 was only $2,307, about two-thirds the comparable figure ($3,440) for Argentina. Three decades later, the situation was dramatically different. The per capita GDP of Hong Kong was $13,629 in 1990, compared to only $3,763 for Argentina. During 1960–1990, the income of Hong Kong expanded at an average annual rate of 6.1 percent, compared to a growth rate of 0.3 percent annually for Argentina. As a result, Hong Kong is now a wealthy country, while Argentina is relatively poor. The figures for Japan compared to Venezuela and Mexico are similar. The per capita GDP in

**EXHIBIT 22.2**

**Impact of Economic Growth on Four Countries**

In 1960 the per capita GDP of Hong Kong was only two-thirds that of Argentina. By 1990, however, the per capita GDP of Hong Kong was 3.5 times that of Argentina. Similarly, the per capita output of Japan was less than that of Venezuela and Mexico in 1960, but well above the latter countries in 1990.

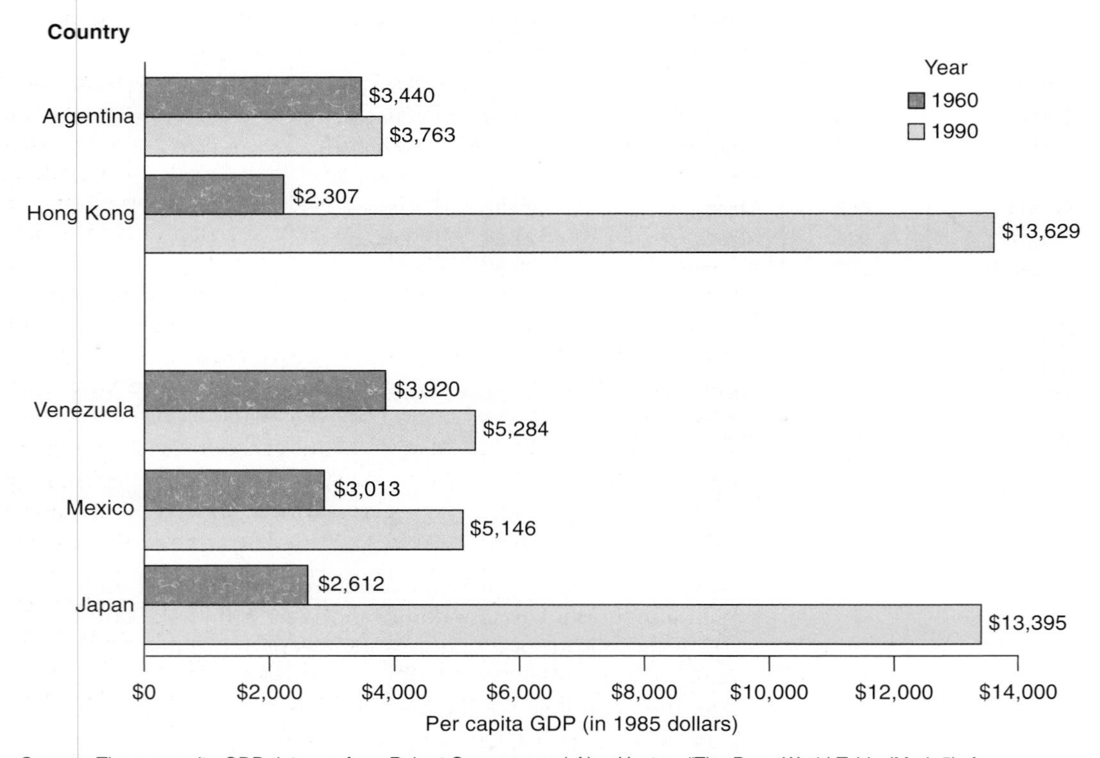


**Source:** The per capita GDP data are from Robert Summers and Alan Heston, "The Penn World Table (Mark 5): An Expanded Set of International Comparisons, 1950–1988," *Quarterly Journal of Economics,* May 1991. The data were updated by the authors.

Japan was less than that of both Venezuela and Mexico in 1960. By 1990, however, the per capita income of Japan was more than two and a half times that of Venezuela and Mexico.

## IMPORTANT SOURCES OF ECONOMIC GROWTH AND PROSPERITY: A COMPREHENSIVE VIEW

Why have some countries like Hong Kong and Japan prospered, while others like Argentina, Venezuela, and Mexico experienced economic stagnation? Laypersons often argue that natural resources are the key ingredient of economic growth. Of course, other things constant, countries with abundant natural resources do have an advantage. It is clear, though, that natural resources are neither a necessary nor sufficient condition for economic growth. Hong Kong has practically no natural resources (other than its harbor), very little fertile soil, and no domestic sources of energy. Japan likewise has few natural resources, and it imports almost all of its industrial energy supply. Nonetheless, both Hong Kong and Japan have grown rapidly and are prosperous. In contrast, the poorer country of Argentina has a great deal of fertile land and several other natural resources. Venezuela and Mexico are among the most oil-rich countries in the world. Yet, these countries along with other resource-rich countries like Ghana, Kenya, and Bolivia are poor—they have been growing slowly, if at all. Natural resources can help promote economic prosperity, but clearly they are not the primary determinant of growth.

Other observers have stressed the importance of technological improvements as a source of economic growth. Clearly, improvements in technology enhance our production possibilities. During the last 250 years, the substitution of power-driven machines for human labor, the development of miracle grains, fertilizer, new sources of energy, and improvements in transportation and communication have vastly improved living standards around the world. Technological improvements continue to change our lives. Consider the impact of compact disk players, microcomputers, word processors, microwave ovens, video cameras and cassette players, fax machines, and automobile air conditioners. Development and improvement of these products during just the last couple of decades has vastly changed the way many people work and play.

However, as in the case of natural resources, it is important to keep the contribution of technology in perspective. Modern technology is available to all nations—rich and poor alike. Poor nations do not have to invest in research and development—they can emulate or import the proven technologies of the developed countries. Thus, the opportunity to grow by adopting improved technology is greater for poor developing countries than it is in high-income developed nations. If technology were the primary factor limiting the creation of wealth, low-income developing countries would be growing more rapidly than developed nations. And indeed this sometimes occurs; but in most cases it does not.

### Ten Key Sources of Growth

If neither natural resources nor the availability of technology are the key to why some countries grow and prosper while other stagnate, what is? The answer is multifaceted. Economic growth is a complex process, and the factors contributing to it are often interdependent. Much as the performance of an athletic team reflects the joint output of the team members, economic growth is jointly determined by several factors. And just as one or two weak players can substantially reduce overall team performance, a counterproductive policy in one or two key areas can substantially harm the overall performance of an economy.

As we have proceeded, we have highlighted key sources of economic growth and sought to explain why they are important. Let us briefly reconsider ten of these key ingredients (see accompanying "Thumbnail Sketch").

**GAINS FROM TRADE** Exchange is mutually advantageous to trading partners. Policies like price controls, high taxes, and licensing requirements that restrict entry into businesses and occupations reduce the gains from trade and retard economic prosperity.

## THUMBNAIL SKETCH

### Ten Key Factors That Influence the Growth and Prosperity of Nations

1. **Gains from trade** *Policies that reduce the volume of exchange retard economic progress.*
2. **Private ownership** *When property is privately owned, people take better care of things, develop resources with less waste, and use them in ways that are more beneficial to society.*
3. **Market prices** *Markets direct the actions of buyers and sellers and bring them into harmony with each other and the general welfare.*
4. **Competition among firms** *Competition more or less forces business firms to operate efficiently, cater to the preferences of consumers, improve products, and discover lower-cost production methods.*
5. **Investment and efficient use of capital** *Nations that invest more and channel more of their investments into wealth-creating projects tend to grow more rapidly.*
6. **Tax rates** *High marginal tax rates reduce the incentive of people to earn and use resources efficiently.*
7. **Stable money and prices** *Inflationary monetary policies distort price signals, generate uncertainty, and undermine confidence in government.*
8. **Open economy** *International competition and trade help keep domestic producers on their toes and permit even small nations to gain by specializing in areas where they have a comparative advantage.*
9. **Convertibility of domestic currency** *Exchange rate controls and other policies that limit the convertibility of a domestic currency into foreign exchange (other currencies) tend to reduce gains from international trade.*
10. **Protective and productive functions of government** *Governments that clearly define and protect property rights while providing public goods at a low cost help promote economic progress.*

**PRIVATE OWNERSHIP** As a general rule, people will take better care of things and use them in ways that are more beneficial to others when they personally own them. Decentralization and independent resource owners increase the rate of innovation, since entrepreneurs do not need to sell a new idea to a majority of decision-makers before the idea is tried. Similarly, the more secure present and future property rights are, the more capital formation there will be. In contrast, government ownership generally results in poor maintenance and insecurely defined property rights that repel private investment. Furthermore, political instability, excessive regulation, and high taxes can undermine the security of owners even when the legal remanents of private ownership are maintained.

**MARKET PRICES** Markets direct producers toward the production of goods and services that are valued most highly relative to their opportunity costs. The substitution of price controls, subsidies, and political directives for markets will undermine this process. Remember, government is not a corrective device. Predictably, subsidies and tax breaks doled out by even a democratic government will be influenced by political considerations. Legislators will tend to favor those with political clout. Substitution of politics for markets will tend to favor older firms, even if they are economically weaker than growth-oriented, newer firms. Compared to the newer firms, older established businesses have a stronger record of political contributions, better knowledge of lobbying techniques, and a closer relationship with powerful political figures.

**COMPETITION AMONG FIRMS** In a competitive environment, business firms have an incentive to serve the interests of consumers since they need to woo them away from other firms. Competitive firms have to produce efficiently, discover better ways of doing things, and provide consumers what they want in order to make a profit. In the process, of course, they promote the economic prosperity of the country in which they operate. In contrast, when competition is weakened, business firms have more leeway to raise prices and pursue their own objectives. Business subsidies, price floors, entry restraints, and other policies that protect producers from the process of competition therefore conflict with economic prosperity.

**INVESTMENT AND EFFICIENT USE OF CAPITAL** Investment in both physical capital (machines) and human capital (knowledge and skill) can help people produce and earn more. Nations that invest more tend to grow more. This will be true, however, only when investment funds are directed toward productive projects. Policies such as interest rate ceilings and exchange rate controls will limit the ability of a capital market to perform this function—and will lead instead to the political allocation of a limited supply of investment funds. In general, such policies reduce the level and efficiency of investment.

**HIGH TAX RATES** High tax rates seriously distort market signals and reduce the incentive of individuals to work and undertake business projects. High tax rates may even drive highly productive citizens and businesses to other countries where taxes are lower. They may also discourage foreigners from financing domestic investment projects. In short, economic theory indicates that high marginal tax rates will retard productive activity, capital formation, and economic growth.

**STABLE MONEY AND PRICES** A stable monetary environment provides the foundation for the efficient operation of a market economy. In contrast, monetary and price instability make both the price level and relative prices unpredictable, generating uncertainty and undermining the security of contractual property rights. When prices increase 20 percent this year, 50 percent the next year, 15 percent the year after that, and so on, individuals and businesses are unable to develop sensible long-term plans. The uncertainty will reduce the attractiveness of time-dimension exchanges, particularly investment decisions. Rather than dealing with the uncertainties that accompany double- and triple-digit inflation rates, citizens will save less, while many investors and business decision-makers will move their activities to countries with a more stable environment. Foreigners will invest elsewhere, and citizens will often go to great lengths to get their savings (potential funds for investment) out of the country. As a result, potential gains from capital formation and business activities will be lost.

**INTERNATIONAL TRADE AND AN OPEN ECONOMY** In the absence of trade barriers, producers in various countries will be directed toward those areas where they have a comparative advantage, and the competition from abroad will help keep domestic producers on their toes. Tariffs, quotas, exchange rate controls, and other trade barriers undermine this highly productive process.

**CONVERTIBILITY OF DOMESTIC CURRENCY** Domestic residents are unable to buy from foreigners unless they have access to foreign currencies. Similarly, if a nation fixes the exchange rate value of its currency above the market level, the country's export products will be too expensive for foreigners to buy. Thus, exchange rate controls and limitations on the convertibility of the domestic currency stifle potential gains from international trade and thereby retard economic growth.

**PROTECTIVE AND PRODUCTIVE FUNCTIONS OF GOVERNMENT** Government is assigned a monopoly on the use of force in order to protect people from each other and from outsiders. When a government performs its protective function well, individuals can have confidence that the wealth they create will not be taken from them. In contrast, if a government fails to perform its protective function well, uncertainty and insecurity will result. In addition to its protective function, government may have a productive function—that is, it may promote progress by providing public goods, a class of goods difficult for markets to allocate efficiently.

## Political Economy and Prosperity

*Policy can influence growth, either for good or ill, in many ways. The task is thus to try to exploit as many as possible of these avenues for good.*

Arnold C. Harberger[3]

What can governments do to promote economic progress? Basic economics indicates that they are bound to have an influence—for good or for ill, as

[3]Arnold C. Harberger, *Economic Policy and Economic Growth* (San Francisco: International Center for Economic Growth, 1985), p. 8.

Harberger said. Certain types of economic organization are more beneficial to economic progress than others. The ten key elements just discussed are central to sound economic organization. Other factors may also be important—remember, we do not have a complete theory of economic growth. Some countries may be able to grow while following policies that conflict with some of the ten key elements. In other cases, perhaps even sound policies will fail. There is no single recipe that will work in all instances.

We can nevertheless state with confidence that countries that consistently follow policies that conflict with several of the key ingredients of economic prosperity are unlikely to prosper. Conversely, those whose policies harmonize with these key elements greatly enhance the likelihood of prosperity. We turn now to an examination of the data for nations that have grown rapidly versus those that have not.

## POLICIES OF HIGH-GROWTH VERSUS STAGNATING ECONOMIES

Exhibit 22.3 presents data on population and per capita GDP in 1990 for the 11 countries that grew most rapidly during 1980–1990. Both the World Bank and the estimates developed for the United Nations by Summers and Heston

**EXHIBIT 22.3** **Countries with Best Growth Record, 1980–1990**

| | | | Annual Growth of per Capita GDP, 1980–1990 | |
|---|---|---|---|---|
| **Country** | **Population (in millions)** | **Per Capita GDP, 1990** | **World Bank** | **Summers-Heston** |
| *Asia* | | | | |
| China | 1133.7 | 2,427 | 8.1 | 6.8 |
| Hong Kong | 5.8 | 13,629 | 5.7 | 5.1 |
| Japan | 123.5 | 13,395 | 3.5 | 3.2 |
| Pakistan | 112.4 | 1,627 | 3.2 | 3.6 |
| Singapore | 3.0 | 12,068 | 4.2 | 5.4 |
| S. Korea | 42.8 | 5,891 | 8.6 | 6.9 |
| Thailand | 55.8 | 3,486 | 5.8 | 4.9 |
| Taiwan | 20.0 | 6,290 | — | 5.4 |
| *Africa* | | | | |
| Botswana | 1.3 | 2,645 | 8.0 | 4.1 |
| Mauritius | 1.1 | 5,025 | 5.0 | 3.8 |
| *Europe* | | | | |
| Malta | 0.4 | 7,750 | 3.7 | 4.5 |
| **Average Growth Rate** | | | **5.6** | **4.9** |

**Source:** The data on population are from the World Bank, *World Development Report, 1992.* The per capita GDP data are from Robert Summers and Alan Heston, "The Penn World Table (Mark 5): An Expanded Set of International Comparisons, 1950–1988," *Quarterly Journal of Economics,* May 1991. The data were updated by the authors. Growth rate data from both sources are presented. All countries with an annual growth rate of per capita GDP of 3 percent or more as measured by both sources are included.

indicate that the per capita GDP of these countries grew at an annual rate of 3 percent or more during the 1980s. In many ways these countries are quite diverse. Only three (Hong Kong, Japan, and Singapore) are high-income countries. The per capita income in China, Pakistan, and Botswana is still less than $3,000 despite rapid economic growth. In terms of population, several (Hong Kong, Singapore, Botswana, Mauritius, and Malta) of the high-growth countries are quite small. Others (China, Japan, and Pakistan) are large. Eight are Asian countries, while only one—the small island nation of Malta—is European.

Exhibit 22.4 presents similar data for the 17 countries with the poorest growth record during 1980–1990. Both the World Bank and Summers-Heston estimate that the per capita GDP of these countries *declined* by 1 percent or more annually during 1980–1990. While none are high-income countries at this point, several had relatively high incomes at one time. Even after a decade of declining income, the per capita GDP of two—Mexico and Venezuela—exceeded $5,000 in 1990. As in the case of the high-growth countries, both large countries (such as Nigeria and Mexico) and small countries are included among the stagnating economies.

**EXHIBIT 22.4** **Countries with Poorest Growth Record, 1980–1990**

| Country | Population (in millions) | Per Capita GDP, 1990 | Annual Growth of per Capita GDP, 1980–1990 | |
|---|---|---|---|---|
| | | | World Bank | Summers-Heston |
| *Africa* | | | | |
| Cote d'Ivoire | 11.9 | 1151 | –3.3 | –4.4 |
| Ethiopia | 51.2 | 305 | –1.3 | –1.3 |
| Madagascar | 11.7 | 615 | –1.9 | –3.4 |
| Mozambique | 15.7 | 937 | –3.3 | –4.9 |
| Niger | 7.7 | 574 | –4.6 | –3.3 |
| Nigeria | 115.5 | 1061 | –1.8 | –3.8 |
| Rwanda | 7.1 | 574 | –2.3 | –1.8 |
| Zaire | 37.3 | 321 | –1.4 | –1.1 |
| Zambia | 8.1 | 650 | –2.9 | –3.2 |
| *Latin America* | | | | |
| Argentina | 32.3 | 3763 | –1.7 | –2.0 |
| Bolivia | 7.2 | 1374 | –2.6 | –2.9 |
| Guatemala | 9.2 | 2253 | –2.1 | –1.6 |
| Haiti | 6.5 | 815 | –2.5 | –2.2 |
| Mexico | 86.2 | 5146 | –1.0 | –1.2 |
| Peru | 21.7 | 2338 | –2.6 | –3.0 |
| Venezuela | 19.7 | 5284 | –1.7 | –3.0 |
| *Other* | | | | |
| Syria | 12.4 | 4177 | –1.5 | –2.2 |
| **Average Growth Rate** | | | **–2.3** | **–2.7** |

**Source:** The data on population are from the World Bank, *World Development Report, 1992.* The per capita GDP data are from Robert Summers and Alan Heston, "The Penn World Table (Mark 5): An Expanded Set of International Comparisons, 1950–1988," *Quarterly Journal of Economics,* May 1991. The data were updated by the authors. Growth rate data from both sources are presented. All countries for which both sources indicate a negative annual growth rate of per capita GDP of 1 percent or more during the period are included.

On average, the per capita income of the high-income economies increased by approximately 5 percent annually, while that of the stagnating economies declined by 2 percent annually during the 1980–1990 period. Over the entire 11 years, the per capita income of the high-growth economies rose by approximately 70 percent while that of the stagnating economies fell by more than 30 percent.

If the factors presented in the "Thumbnail Sketch" are really important, we should find that the high-growth countries followed the policies listed as promoting growth and prosperity more closely than the low-growth countries did. Unfortunately, some of the factors are difficult to quantify. For example, we do not have a precise measure of how competitive markets are across nations, or how well various governments perform their protective and productive functions.

In some cases, however, it is possible to quantify important policy variables and determine their consistency with economic prosperity. Exhibit 22.5 provides data on several policy indicators for both the high-growth and low-growth countries during the 1980s. First, look at the inflation rate data. As we have previously shown, inflation is closely linked with monetary expansion (see Exhibit 16.9). Countries experience high inflation rates because they finance government expenditures with "printing press" money. Except for Botswana, which had an inflation rate of 12.1 percent, the average annual inflation rate during the 1980s was less than 10 percent in each of the high-growth countries. The *median* (meaning the middle, the point where 50 percent are higher and 50 percent are lower) annual inflation rate in the high-growth countries was 5.3 percent, compared to 18.2 percent for the low-growth countries. Five of the 17 low-growth countries (Cote d'Ivoire, Ethiopia, Niger, Rwanda, and Haiti) also experienced single-digit inflation rates during the 1980s. The other 12 low-growth countries, however, followed policies of monetary expansion that lead to inflation. In seven of the low-growth countries, excessive monetary expansion caused severe inflation during the 1980s. The annual inflation rates of Mozambique, Zaire, Zambia, and Mexico ranged from 36.5 percent to 70.4 percent. Three of the low-growth countries (Argentina, Bolivia, and Peru) experienced triple-digit average annual rates of inflation during the 1980s. Clearly, inflation rates at this level generate enormous uncertainty and undermine the usefulness of information provided by the pricing system.

How open were the economies of the high- and low-growth countries during the 1980s? Exhibit 22.5 also presents data on tariff rates and exchange rate controls (the black-market exchange rate premium) that shed light on this question. Of course, high tariffs tend to discriminate against foreign producers and reduce the volume of international trade. Similarly, exchange rate controls restrict trade because they make it more difficult for domestic citizens to get their hands on the foreign currencies that are generally required for trade with foreigners. In turn, the controls lead to black markets. The more restrictive the exchange rate controls, the larger the black-market premium that must be paid to obtain foreign currencies, and the greater the negative impact on the volume of international trade.

Compared to the low-growth countries, both the tariff rates and the black-market exchange rate premiums were substantially lower in the high-growth countries. The tariff rates of Hong Kong, Japan, and Singapore were exceedingly small, less than 1 percent of the volume of trade during the 1980s.

**EXHIBIT 22.5** **The Record of the High- and Low-Growth Countries with Regard to Inflation, Tariffs, Exchange Rates, Interest Rates, and Investment during the 1980s.**

| | Average Annual Inflation Rate | Average Tariff Rate | | Black-Market Exchange Rate Premium | | Average Real Interest Rate | | Investment as a Share of GDP |
|---|---|---|---|---|---|---|---|---|
| | 1980–1990 | 1985 | 1989 | 1985 | 1988 | 1983–1985 | 1988–1990 | 1980–1990 |
| *High-Growth Countries* | | | | | | | | |
| China | 5.8 | — | — | 9 | 168 | — | — | 35.5 |
| Hong Kong | 7.2 | 0.00 | 0.00 | 0 | 0 | 2.2 | –1.3 | 26.5 |
| Japan | 1.5 | 0.72 | 0.71 | 0 | 0 | 2.5 | 1.1 | 30.2 |
| Pakistan | 6.9 | 15.11 | 16.07 | 4 | 10 | 1.9 | –1.6 | 18.7 |
| Singapore | 1.7 | 0.36 | 0.18 | 0 | 0 | 4.1 | 0.1 | 41.5 |
| S. Korea | 5.3 | 3.55 | 2.96 | 11 | 10 | 4.9 | 3.4 | 29.9 |
| Thailand | 4.2 | 6.48 | 5.24 | 3 | 1 | 11.5 | 4.8 | 26.4 |
| Taiwan | 3.1 | 2.80 | 2.16 | 3 | 1 | 5.5 | 4.2 | 21.0 |
| Botswana | 12.1 | 7.60 | 6.21 | 22 | 53 | 0.9 | –14.0 | 27.1 |
| Mauritius | 8.8 | 9.64 | 8.18 | 1 | 3 | 2.5 | 1.5 | 24.2 |
| Malta | 6.2 | 4.46 | 5.30 | 7 | 3 | 4.6 | 1.7 | 28.2 |
| **Median** | **5.3** | **4.00** | **4.13** | **3** | **3** | **3.3** | **1.3** | **27.1** |
| *Low-Growth Countries* | | | | | | | | |
| Cote d'Ivoire | 2.7 | 9.70 | 9.70 | 1 | 2 | 0.2 | 4.6 | 16.5 |
| Ethiopia | 2.1 | 13.27 | 13.72 | 122 | 226 | — | 2.2 | 12.0 |
| Madagascar | 17.1 | 8.50 | 12.46 | 9 | 16 | — | — | 11.2 |
| Mozambique | 36.5 | — | — | 4108 | 104 | — | — | 20.5 |
| Niger | 3.3 | 8.40 | — | 1 | 2 | 0.2 | 4.0 | 13.8 |
| Nigeria | 18.2 | 5.09 | 4.00 | 270 | 87 | –3.1 | –15.0 | 17.1 |
| Rwanda | 3.8 | 13.30 | — | 49 | 30 | –1.8 | 3.4 | 15.4 |
| Zaire | 60.9 | 8.51 | 9.81 | 6 | 15 | — | — | 15.7 |
| Zambia | 42.3 | 6.69 | 4.20 | 38 | 900 | –16.2 | –77.2 | 15.3 |
| Argentina | 395.1 | 12.46 | 7.00 | 40 | 50 | –163.6 | –1178.9 | 13.5 |
| Bolivia | 318.4 | 5.24 | 2.74 | 9 | 6 | –4240.6 | — | 12.2 |
| Guatemala | 14.6 | 7.47 | 8.01 | 89 | 28 | –0.8 | –5.9 | 13.3 |
| Haiti | 7.2 | 8.03 | 6.70 | 60 | 151 | — | — | 13.2 |
| Mexico | 70.4 | 2.56 | 3.03 | 25 | 15 | –14.6 | –6.5 | 21.8 |
| Peru | 233.7 | 8.82 | 4.95 | 51 | 240 | –101.1 | — | 21.0 |
| Venezuela | 19.3 | 8.97 | 2.75 | 25 | 0 | –2.6 | –28.3 | 19.6 |
| Syria | 14.7 | 5.63 | 3.40 | 251 | 354 | — | — | 20.7 |
| **Median** | **18.2** | **8.45** | **5.83** | **40** | **30** | **–3.1** | **–1.8** | **15.4** |

**Source:** Derived from World Bank, *World Development Report: 1992* (and various earlier issues) and the *World Tables, 1992;* The International Monetary Fund, *Government Finance Statistics Yearbook, 1992;* and International Currency Analysis, *The World Currency Yearbook, 1989–90.*

Among the high-growth countries, only Pakistan had an average tariff rate of more than 10 percent. In contrast, only Mexico among the 17 low-growth countries, had an average tariff rate less than the median for the high-growth countries during both 1985 and 1989.

The differences in the black-market exchange rate premiums are even more dramatic. For 6 of the low-growth countries (Ethiopia, Mozambique, Zambia, Haiti, Peru, and Syria) the black market exchange rate premium exceeded 100 percent in 1988; it was between 15 percent and 87 percent in 7 other low-growth countries (Madagascar, Nigeria, Rwanda, Zaire, Argentina, Guatemala, and Mexico). Among the high-growth countries, only China and Botswana imposed exchange controls resulting in black-market premiums in this range. The premium was consistently less than 10 percent in 7 of the 11 high-growth countries, but only 3 (Cote d'Ivoire, Niger, and Bolivia) of the 17 low-growth countries.

Taken together, the data on tariffs and black-market exchange rates indicate that the economies of the high-growth countries were considerably more open than those of the low-growth countries. Since trade restrictions reduce gains from trade and retard growth, these results are not surprising.

Finally, Exhibit 22.5 also presents data on capital markets—interest rates and investment as a share of GDP—for each country. If a country's capital market is well integrated with the world capital market, its real interest rate will be near the world rate—approximately 1 percent to 5 percent throughout most of the 1980s. On the other hand, if the country imposes interest-rate controls and follows inflationary policies, its real interest rate may differ substantially from the world rate. With the exception of Botswana during 1988–1990, the real interest rate of the high-growth countries did not differ much from the world rate. In contrast, 7 of the 12 low-growth countries (Nigeria, Zambia, Argentina, Bolivia, Mexico, Peru, and Venezuela) for which the data were available, had double-digit *negative* real interest rates at various times throughout the 1980s. This indicates that these countries were following policies that disrupted their capital markets and restricted the flow of funds between savers and investors.

Perhaps the most dramatic difference between the high- and low-growth countries involves the rate of investment. The average investment rate as a share of GDP in the high-growth countries was 27.1 percent, compared to 15.4 percent in the low-growth countries. Eight of the 11 high-growth countries invested more than 26 percent of their GDP during the 1980s. Only one of the high-growth countries (Pakistan) had an investment rate of less than 21 percent of its GDP. In contrast, 16 of the 17 low-growth countries invested less than 21 percent of their GDP during the 1980s.

With regard to capital markets and investment, the data of Exhibit 22.5 are clear. Countries that grow rapidly tend to (1) utilize capital markets to allocate saving and investment and (2) invest a large share of their GDP. Conversely, countries with negative real interest rates and/or low investment rates tend to experience low or negative rates of economic growth.

The data of Exhibit 22.5 shed light on the process of economic growth. The high-growth countries have not done everything right. Neither have the low-growth countries—at least not all of them—done everything wrong. A pattern, however, is present. Compared to the low-growth countries, the high-growth countries have tended to follow monetary policies more consistent with price stability, and they have imposed lower tariff rates, maintained the convertibility of their currency, and allowed capital markets to attract savings and allocate investment. Economic analysis indicates that these are key elements of growth and prosperity. Political decision-makers seeking to promote prosperity should take heed.

Exhibit 22.5 also provides an answer to our previous question of why Hong Kong and Japan have prospered while Argentina, Mexico, and Venezuela have stagnated. We can see from the exhibit that Hong Kong and Japan have generally followed policies consistent with prosperity and growth.

## GROWTH RATE OF CHINA

Some may be surprised to find China among the high-growth countries of Exhibit 22.3. After all, isn't China a centrally planned socialist economy that has generally followed policies inconsistent with growth and prosperity?

When considering the recent growth of China, it is important to keep two points in mind. First, China has taken several important steps toward liberalization in recent years. The initial reforms adopted in the late 1970s focused on agriculture, a sector of the economy encompassing nearly three-fourths of the Chinese work force. The collective farms were dismantled and replaced with what the Chinese refer to as a "contract responsibility system." Under this organizational form, individual families are permitted to lease land for up to 15 years in exchange for supplying the state with a fixed amount of production at a designated price (which is generally below the market price). Amounts produced over and above the required quota belong to the individual farmer. The output in excess of the production quota may either be consumed or sold at a free market price. In effect, this system of long-term land leases provides farmers with something akin to a private property right. Legal ownership remains with the state, but individual farmers are permitted to lease the land for long periods of time in exchange for a fixed quantity of output. In turn, the farmer gets to keep everything over and above the fixed quota. Thus, at high rates of productivity the farmer's marginal tax rate is zero. Clearly, this system provides farmers with a strong incentive to increase output.

Other reforms were adopted that enhanced the development of markets in agricultural products. Restrictions on individual stock breeding, household sideline occupations, transport of agricultural goods, and trade fairs (marketplaces) were removed. Farmers were permitted to own tractors and trucks, and even hire laborers to work in their "leased" fields. By the late 1980s, less than 15 percent of the grain (rice, wheat, and barley) produced in China was turned over to the state. The rest was marketed privately.

The success in agriculture encouraged reforms in other sectors. Restrictions on the operation of small-scale service and retail businesses were relaxed. Private restaurants, stores, and repair shops sprang up and began to compete with state-operated enterprises.

Restraints on both trade and joint ventures with foreigners have also been relaxed. By the mid-1980s, Chinese cities were teeming with sidewalk vendors, restaurants, small retail businesses, and hundreds of thousands of individuals providing personal services. After losing their monopoly position, even state enterprises began to stay open longer and pay more attention to serving their customers. In the late 1980s China began to take steps toward greater reliance on markets in the production and distribution of industrial products and allow far greater freedom for private firms to compete in these areas. No doubt, these moves toward liberalization have contributed substantially to the recent growth of the Chinese economy.

In interpreting the data, however, it is also important to keep a second point in mind. Since centrally planned economies do not rely on product prices to allocate goods and services, output is measured by the quantity of inputs. Yet, with central planning, inputs may be a highly unreliable indicator of the value of what is actually being produced. Clearly, this was the case in Eastern Europe and the former Soviet Union during the 1970s and 1980s. The use of inputs to measure economic growth substantially overstated the growth rate of these economies. Some economists suspect that similar forces are at work in China—that the output of the centrally planned sector is exaggerated in China just as it was in Eastern Europe and the former Soviet Union. Accordingly, the income estimates for China should be interpreted with caution.

In contrast, Argentina, Mexico, and Venezuela have (1) followed policies of monetary expansion that have fueled inflation, (2) imposed high tariffs and exchange controls that have restricted trade and fueled black markets, and (3) fixed interest rates at levels that have led to negative real interest rates and low rates of capital investment. In short, these three countries have adopted policies that conflict with economic prosperity.

## WINDS OF CHANGE

As Adam Smith noted long ago, the wealth of nations is crucially dependent upon gains from (1) specialization and trade, (2) expansion in the size of the market, and (3) the discovery of better ways of doing things. Governments that respect property rights and freedom of exchange while following monetary (and fiscal) policies consistent with relatively stable prices establish the foundation for economic growth. This is the strategy that resulted in the "economic miracles" of West Germany and Japan following World War II. It is also the strategy followed by the growth economies of the 1980s.

In contrast with this approach, governments around the world have often used price controls, trade restraints, regulations, industrial subsidies, and government planning in an effort to promote growth. In addition, governments have often followed expansionary monetary policies that have generated double- and even triple-digit inflation rates. Many governments have also levied high marginal tax rates, which, in turn, discourage production and drive both capital and productive citizens elsewhere. In varying degrees, these types of policies plague almost all poor countries. They constitute a strategy that doesn't work. And countries that follow this course will continue to experience poverty and economic stagnation.

The winds of change are now beginning to blow; there is evidence of significant policy changes in several less developed countries. Among Latin American countries, Chile began shifting away from policies of monetary expansion, price controls, and trade restrictions in the 1980s. The annual inflation rate in Chile during the 1980s was approximately 20 percent, down from 130 percent during the 1970s. Tariff rates were cut; the top marginal tax rate was reduced from 80 percent to 50 percent; interest rates and exchange rate controls were eliminated; and several state enterprises were privatized during the 1980s. The result? In recent years, Chile has become the growth economy of Latin America. While most Latin American economies stagnated, the real GDP of Chile expanded at an average annual rate of 6.5 percent during the 1984–1992 period.

Beginning in the late 1980s, both Mexico and Argentina began emulating the course followed by Chile. Both shifted toward substantially more restrictive monetary policies that decelerated their inflation rates. Both reduced tariffs sharply, relaxed exchange rate controls, sliced high marginal tax rates, and began privatizing various government enterprises. While it is too early to fully assess the results of these changes, the early returns are encouraging. In contrast with the 1980s, the economies of both Mexico and Argentina were growing in the early 1990s.

Several less developed countries now appear more receptive to sound policies than at any other time in the recent past. In addition, the formerly communist countries of Eastern Europe and Asia are instituting changes and searching for forms of economic organization consistent with growth and prosperity. The dynamic forces of economic change will make the 1990s an exciting time to study economics and apply its basic principles.

## CHAPTER SUMMARY

1. Most income comparisons across countries are derived by the exchange rate conversion method. Since this method reflects the exchange rate value of a currency rather than its purchasing power over a broad range of goods and services, income comparisons derived by this method are often unreliable.
2. The purchasing power parity method uses data on the cost of purchasing a typical bundle of consumer goods and services to determine the relative purchasing power of each currency and estimate the GDP of each nation in terms of a common currency. In recent years, income comparisons derived by this method have provided more accurate estimates of incomes and living standards across countries.
3. Most of the poorest countries—those with a per capita annual GDP of less than $1,000—are located in Africa and Southern Asia (Burma, Afghanistan, Nepal, and India). Most of the high-income countries are located in North America, Europe, Oceania, and East Asia (Japan and Hong Kong).
4. The availability of domestic natural resources is not the major determinant of growth. Countries such as Japan and Hong Kong have impressive growth rates without such resources, while many resource-rich nations continue to stagnate.
5. Improvements in technology contribute substantially to economic prosperity. Less developed countries, however, can emulate and import proven technologies from developed countries. Thus, technology is a lesser restraint for low-income countries than it is for high-income industrial countries.
6. Economic growth is a complex process, and we do not have a complete theory of growth. Basic principles, however, indicate several elements of economic organization that contribute to growth and prosperity: private ownership, competitive markets, investment, monetary stability, avoidance of high taxes, and an open economy.
7. Countries that have grown rapidly during the 1980s generally followed a stable monetary policy, imposed few restrictions on international trade, relied on markets to determine exchange and interest rates, and invested a large portion of their GDP. In contrast, stagnating economies were characterized by rapid monetary expansion, high inflation rates, high tariffs, exchange and interest rate controls, and low rates of investment.
8. Growth and development are influenced by the ability of people to realize gains from (a) specialization and trade, (b) capital formation, (c) the discovery of better (more productive) ways of doing things. Governments that respect property rights, protect the freedom of exchange, and follow monetary and fiscal policies consistent with a stable price level help provide the framework for the creation of wealth. In contrast, governments retard economic progress when policies are adopted that restrict trade, generate uncertainty, undermine property rights, and reduce competition.

# *Study Guide*

## CHAPTER 22

# Developing the Economic Way of Thinking

# CRITICAL-ANALYSIS QUESTIONS

1. How do the exchange rate conversion and purchasing power parity methods differ as tools for comparing relative incomes among countries? Which is the most widely cited in the popular news media? Why? Which is the most reliable? Why?

*2. It is often argued that the rich nations are getting richer and the poor are getting poorer. Is this view correct? Is it an oversimplification? Explain.

*3. "Without aid from the industrial nations, poor countries are caught in the poverty trap. Because they are poor, they are unable to save and invest; and lacking investment, they remain poor." Evaluate this view.

4. Imagine you are an economic adviser to the president of Mexico. You have been asked to suggest policies to promote economic growth and a higher standard of living for the citizens of Mexico. Outline your suggestions, and discuss why you believe they would be helpful.

5. Evaluate each of the following policies in terms of their impact on the growth and prosperity of a nation?
   a. Adoption of a regulation that would limit foreign ownership of domestic businesses.
   b. Imposition of a surtax on the corporate profits of foreign firms operating in the country.
   c. A 50 percent increase in tariff rates.
   d. Adoption of a minimum wage equal to 50 percent of the country's average hourly wage.
   e. Legislation requiring employers to provide health care for all of their employees.
   f. Legislation requiring employers to provide one year of severance pay to any employee who is dismissed from employment.

6. Discuss the importance of the following as determinants of economic growth: (a) natural resources; (b) physical capital; (c) human capital; (d) technical knowledge; (e) attitudes of the work force; (f) size of the domestic market; and (g) economic policy.

*7. Do you think that the absence of international trade barriers would be more important for a small country like Costa Rica than for a larger country like Mexico? Explain.

8. "Since government-operated firms do not have to make a profit, they can usually produce at a lower cost and charge a lower price than privately-owned enterprises." Evaluate this view.

9. "Governments can promote economic growth by using taxes and subsidies to direct investment funds toward high-tech, heavy manufacturing, and other growth industries that will enhance the future income of the nation." Evaluate this view.

10. If the investment funds of a country are going to promote prosperity, they must be directed toward the production of goods that are valued more highly than the resources used in their production. Why is this important? Will additional investment always increase the wealth of a nation? Explain.

*Asterisk denotes questions for which answers are given in Appendix A.

11. Suppose you were hired as a consultant to develop a comprehensive economic reform plan that would improve the standard of living in Russia. What *specific* reforms would you suggest? Indicate why you think they would be effective.

## MULTIPLE-CHOICE SELF-TEST

1. Of the following, which uses the value of a nation's currency in the foreign exchange market to convert the GDP of each nation to a common monetary unit when making income comparisons across countries?
   a. Purchasing power parity method.
   b. Import-substitution method.
   c. Exchange rate conversion method.
   d. GDP deflator method.
2. "This method calculates the purchasing power of each nation's currency in terms of the typical bundle of goods and services that is included in GDP. Once the purchasing power of each nation's currency is determined, this information is used to convert the GDP of each country to a common monetary unit such as the U.S. dollar." This statement describes the
   a. Purchasing power parity method of converting GDP to a common monetary unit.
   b. Exchange rate conversion method of converting GDP to a common monetary unit.
   c. Vicious cycle of poverty of less developed nations.
   d. Trickle-down theory of measuring economic development.
3. Which one of the following would be most likely to improve the standard of living of a less developed country?
   a. Development of strong labor unions.
   b. A sharp increase in the legal minimum wage.
   c. An increase in expenditures on education and capital investment.
   d. Rapid growth of the money supply.
4. The recent growth records of Japan and Hong Kong indicate that a nation can grow rapidly without
   a. Securely defined property rights.
   b. The adoption of modern technology.
   c. Significant amounts of capital formation.
   d. Abundant domestic natural resources.
5. Which of the following most accurately states the importance of technological advancements as a source of economic growth for less developed countries?
   a. Restraints imposed by the slow advancements in modern technology have severely constrained the growth of less developed countries.
   b. If modern technology were the only requirement for economic growth, less developed countries would be growing rapidly.
   c. Most less developed nations have the necessary complementary factors of production to make good use of modern technology if they could just afford the complex machines.
   d. The rate of return on the adoption of modern technology is high in less developed countries, but nonetheless capital investors are unwilling to channel investment funds to these countries.

6. During the 1980s several countries fixed nominal interest rates and financed their government operations with "printing press" money. As a result, the countries experienced negative real interest rates. The evidence indicates that this policy combination leads to a
   a. High rate of investment and rapid economic growth.
   b. High rate of savings and a lower cost of investment capital.
   c. High rate of business profit.
   d. Low rate of investment and a slow rate of economic growth.
7. How do high tariffs and other restraints on international trade affect the prosperity of a nation?
   a. They increase employment and thereby promote the growth of real GDP.
   b. They prevent the nation from realizing fully the potential gains from specialization, exchange, and competition.
   c. They protect domestic producers and thereby promote economic growth.
   d. Both a and c are correct.
8. Which of the following countries experienced the most rapid growth of GDP during 1980–1990?
   a. Argentina, Mexico, and Venezuela.
   b. South Korea, Thailand, and Taiwan.
   c. France, Germany, and Sweden.
   d. Nigeria, Zaire, and Syria.
9. Which of the following was generally true of the countries that experienced declines in per capita GDP during the 1980s?
   a. They were small countries.
   b. Their investment rates as a share of GDP were low.
   c. Their tariff rates were low.
   d. They were mostly high-income countries.
10. If the political leaders of a country wanted to promote economic growth, which of the following policy alternatives would be most effective?
   a. Price controls on agricultural products in order to keep the price of food low.
   b. Expansionary monetary policies designed to keep interest rates low.
   c. Regulations prohibiting foreigners from owning domestic business and withdrawing profits from domestic investments.
   d. Elimination of price controls and trade restraints and establishment of a monetary policy consistent with long-run price stability (or a low rate of inflation).

## PROBLEMS

1. One handy device to help get a good feel for what various growth rates mean is the "Simple 70" rule. The rule is just a formula for closely approximating how long it takes a growing value to double in size:

$$\text{Doubling time} = 70/\text{percentage growth rate}$$

a. The Simple 70 rule works quite well. Try it with the following hypothetical GDP growth rates:

| Annual Growth Rate of GDP | Years Required for GDP to Double | |
|---|---|---|
| | Actual | Simple 70 Rule Estimate |
| 2.0 | 35.0 | ____ |
| 3.5 | 20.1 | ____ |
| 7.0 | 10.2 | ____ |

b. Use the Simple 70 rule to contrast the estimated per capita GDP doubling times for each of the following countries:

| | Annual Growth of GDP per Capita, 1960–1990 | Years Required for GDP per Capita to Double |
|---|---|---|
| Argentina | 0.3 | ________ |
| Venezuela | 1.0 | ________ |
| United States | 2.1 | ________ |
| Canada | 2.6 | ________ |
| Malaysia | 3.7 | ________ |
| Thailand | 4.4 | ________ |
| Singapore | 6.0 | ________ |

2. *Special project* Choose one of the high-growth countries of Exhibit 22.3 and one of the low-growth countries of Exhibit 22.4. Do a detailed study of the economy of each. Be sure to address the following:
   a. How did the economic policies of the two countries differ?
   b. Why do you think the one country grew rapidly during the 1980s, while the other regressed?
   c. What changes in economic policy would you recommend for each of the countries?

# APPENDIX A

## ANSWERS TO STUDY GUIDE QUESTIONS

# CHAPTER 1

## Critical-Analysis Questions

2. Production of scarce goods always involves a cost; there are no free lunches. When the government provides goods without charge to consumers, other citizens (taxpayers) will bear the cost of their provision. Thus, provision by the government affects *how* the costs will be covered, not whether they are incurred.
3. Money has nothing to do with whether an individual is economizing. Any time a person makes a choice, in an attempt to achieve a goal, he or she is economizing.
4. a. Increase your study time.
   b. Decrease your study time.
   c. Decrease your study time.
   d. Decrease your study time.
5. The legislation would increase the cost of traveling by air with a small child. Given the higher cost, some parents might choose to drive rather than fly. Since auto travel is more dangerous than air travel, an increase in injuries and fatalities due to the additional automobile travel—a secondary effect—must also be considered.
6. False. The key to sound policy is not the intentions of the advocate, but rather the ability of the policy to bring individual self-interest and the general welfare into harmony. People are not like pieces on a chess board. They have self-will and personal interests. As Adam Smith pointed out in the *The Theory of Moral Sentiments* (1759), "In the great chess board of human society, every single piece [individual] has a principle of motion of its own, altogether different from that which the legislature might choose to impress on it. If the two coincide [the self-interest of individuals and the objectives of a policy], the game of human society will go on easily and harmoniously, and is very likely to be happy and successful. If they are opposite or different, the game will go on miserably, and the society must be at all times in the highest degree of disorder."

## Multiple-Choice Self-Test

1. c. 2. c. 3. d. 4. d. 5. a. 6. a. 7. c. 8. b. 9. c. 10. d.

# CHAPTER 2

## Critical-Analysis Questions

2. The statement reflects the "exchange is a zero sum game" view. The view is false. No private business can force customers to buy. Neither can a customer force a business to sell. Unless both buyer and seller believe the exchange is in their interest, they will not enter into the exchange. Mutual gain provides the foundation for voluntary exchange.
4. In general, it sanctions all forms of competition except for the use of violence (or the threat of violence), theft, or fraud.

6. When used to generate *personal* services for the owner, *private property rights* permit owners to satisfy their own preferences while ignoring the wishes of others, if they so choose. However, when property is used for investment purposes or put up for sale, owners must cater to the preferences of others if they want to maximize the return on sale value of the property. Finally, private property rights do provide legal protection against selfish persons who would use violence or theft to take the property of another.

9. Since individuals could keep all of the output from a private plot but only a small fraction of that produced on a collectively owned farm, economics indicates that the private plots will be cultivated and used more intensely than the collective farms. Thus, one would expect the value of the output per acre on the private plots to exceed that for the collectively owned farms. Indeed, this was the case. Even though the private plots constituted only 1 percent of the farmland, they produced approximately 25 percent of the total agricultural output of the former Soviet Union.

### Multiple-Choice Self-Test

1. d. 2. c. 3. d. 4. c. 5. d. 6. d. 7. c. 8. d. 9. a. 10. c.

# CHAPTER 3

### Critical-Analysis Questions

1. Water is usually cheaper than oil because its *marginal utility* at current consumption levels is less than that of oil. Since water is so abundant relative to oil, the benefit derived from an *additional* quart of water is less than the benefit from an additional quart of oil, even though the *total utility* from all units of water is far greater than the total utility from all units of oil. However, the price of a product will reflect marginal utility, not total utility.

4. a. Profitable production increases the value of resources owned by people and leads to mutual gain for resource suppliers, consumers, and entrepreneurs.
   b. Losses reduce the value of resources, which reduces the well-being of at least some people.
   c. No.

### Multiple-Choice Self-Test

1. c. 2. b. 3. c. 4. d. 5. d. 6. a. 7. b. 8. c. 9. c. 10. a.

### Problems

1. b. $1.00.
   c. Consumers would demand 110,000 pounds, which is 70,000 more than would be supplied. As a result of this, the price of tomatoes would rise until the equilibrium price was achieved.
   d. There would be 100,000 more pounds supplied than demanded, causing the price to fall until equilibrium was achieved.

2. a. Yes. It is her opportunity cost of the time she spends making dresses.
   b. $14,200 is the total cost; $28.40 is the cost per dress.
   c. $15,000 is her total monthly sales revenue.
   d. Susan is making an $800 economic profit; since the value of the dresses is higher than the value of the resources used to produce them, the dressmaking is a productive activity.

# CHAPTER 4

## Critical-Analysis Questions

1. a. Increase demand.
   b. Decrease demand.
   c. Increase demand.
   d. Decrease incentive to develop nongasoline-powered car.
   e. Leave *demand* unchanged; *quantity demanded* declines.
3. a. Reductions in the supply of feed gains and hay led to sharply higher prices.
   b. The higher feed grain and hay prices increased the cost of *maintaining* a cattle herd and thereby caused many producers to sell (an increase in *current* supply), depressing cattle prices in 1988.
   c. The reduction in the size of cattle herds led to a smaller future supply and higher cattle prices in 1989.
7. a. True.
   b. True.
   c. False.
10. True. "Somebody" must decide who will be the business winners and losers. Neither markets nor the political process leave the determination of winners and losers to chance. Under market organization, business winners and losers are determined by the decentralized choices of millions of consumers who use their dollar votes to reward firms (and industries) that provide preferred goods at a low cost and penalize others who fail to do so. Under political decision-making, the winners and losers are determined by political figures and planning boards who use taxes, subsidies, regulations, and mandates to favor some businesses (and industries) and penalize others.
13. Allocation by price encourages future output; waiting in a line does not. Like a higher price, a longer wait in line allocates the *current* supply by increasing the consumer's opportunity cost. However, the consumer's cost of waiting in line is wasted. It generates nothing for suppliers. In contrast, while a higher price also increases the consumer's opportunity cost, this cost transfers resources to suppliers, increases their returns, and thereby encourages them to expand the future availability of the good.

## Multiple-Choice Self-Test

1. c. 2. b. 3. b. 4. c. 5. c. 6. b. 7. c. 8. b. 9. b. 10. d.

## Problems

1. a. Total expenditures (in millions): $187.5, $176, $170, $169.2, $171, $172, $174.3; elastic, inelastic, inelastic.
   b. Minus 1.02, elastic; minus 0.77, inelastic; minus 0.84, inelastic; yes. (Note: Your numeric answers will be slightly different if you used the arc elasticity formula presented in footnote 2.)
2. a. Inelastic, elastic.
   b. No; yes. As the price of gasoline rises, tire consumption falls and air travel rises.
3. a. $3.75; 155,000 bushels.
   b. 180,000; 110,000. The price ceiling causes fewer apples to be produced and traded. $4.50; yes, both consumers and producers would gain.
   c. 210,000; 130,000; 130,000. Purchase the surplus of 80,000 bushels of apples.

# CHAPTER 5

## Critical-Analysis Questions

1. The economic profit of a firm is its total revenues minus the opportunity cost of all resources used in the production process. Accounting profit often excludes the opportunity cost of certain resources—particularly the equity capital of the firm and any labor services provided by an owner-manager. Zero economic profit means that the resources owned by the firm are earning their opportunity cost—that is, the rate of return is as high as the highest valued alternative forgone. Thus, the firm would not gain by pursuing other lines of business.
2. None of them reflect sound analysis for the following reasons: (a) sunk costs are irrelevant; (b) there is an opportunity cost of owning a house; (c) sunk costs should not affect one's current decision; (d) there is an opportunity cost of public education even if it is provided free to the consumer.
4. Since owners receive profits, clearly profit maximization is in their interest. Managers, if they are not owners, have no property right to profit and therefore no *direct* interest in profit maximization. Since a solid record of profitability tends to increase the market value (salary) of corporate managers, they do have an indirect incentive to pursue profits. However, corporate managers may also be interested in power, nice offices, hiring friends, expansion of sales and other activities, which may conflict with profitability. Thus, the potential for conflict between the interests of owners and managers is present.
8. $2,500—the $2,000 decline in market value during the year plus $500 of potential interest on funds that could be obtained if the machine were sold now. Costs associated with the decline in the value of the machine last year are sunk costs.
9. Because they believe they will be able to restructure the firm and provide better management so that the firm will have positive net earnings in the future. If the firm is purchased at a low enough price, this will allow the

new owners to cover the opportunity cost of their investment and still earn an economic profit. Alternatively, they may expect to sell off the firm's assets, receiving more net revenue than the cost of purchasing the firm.

10. The crew would be more productive with the monitoring of the man with the whip. Shirking would fall, because any crewmember who shirked risked the immediate sting of the whip, and because no crewmember would be distracted by having to watch others to prevent their shirking. Their productivity, and therefore their hourly reward, would rise—apparently by more than enough to offset what they paid the man with the whip.

### Multiple-Choice Self-Test

1. a. 2. b. 3. a. 4. d. 5. c. 6. d. 7. c. 8. b. 9. d. 10. d.

### Problems

2. a. $29,000.
   b. Owner's labor services and interest income forgone on Sam's equity capital.
   c. $68,000 + 0.10(100,000) + 30,000 = $108,000.
   d. $11,000 loss.
3. a. TVC: 50, 90, 127, 166, 215, 274, 349, 446.
   ATC: 100, 70, 59, 54, 53, 54, 57, 62.
   AVC: 50, 45, 42.3, 41.5, 43, 45.7, 49.9, 55.75.
   MC: 100, 40, 37, 39, 49, 59, 75, 97.
   b. 5.
4. a. Auto A = 32 cents per mile; Auto B = 31 cents per mile. Auto B is cheaper.
   b. Auto A = 25 cents per mile; Auto B = 25.5 cents per mile. Auto A is cheaper.
   c. They decline primarily because average fixed cost is falling as the miles driven increase from 10,000 to 20,000.
5. a. 4.
   b. 5.
   c. Because *AFC* was so high; because diminishing marginal returns resulted in high marginal cost.
   d. It continues to fall.

## CHAPTER 6

### Critical-Analysis Questions

1. In a highly competitive industry such as agriculture, lower resource prices might improve the rate of profit in the short run, but in the long run, competition will drive prices down until economic profit is eliminated. Thus, lower resource prices will do little to improve the long-run profitability in such industries.

2. New firms will enter the industry and the existing firms will expand output; market supply will expand, causing the market price to fall until economic profit is eliminated.

5. a. Increase.
   b. Increase.
   c. Increase; firms will earn economic profit.
   d. Rise (compared with its initial level) for an increasing cost industry, but return to initial price for a constant cost industry.
   e. Increase even more than it did in the short run.
   f. Economic profit will return to zero.

6. a. Decline.
   b. Increase.
   c. Decline.
   d. Decline.

## Multiple-Choice Self-Test

1. d. 2. a. 3. b. 4. d. 5. c. 6. d. 7. c. 8. c. 9. d. 10. b.

## Problems

1. a. MC: 200, 150, 200, 350, 400, 450, 500, 550, 600, 750.
   AVC: 200, 175, 183.3, 225, 260, 291.7, 321.4, 350, 377.8, 415.
   ATC: 1200, 675, 516.7, 475, 460, 458.3, 464.3, 475, 488.9, 515.
   Profits: −700, −350, −50, 100, 200, 250, 200, 100, −150.
   b. Either 6 or 7 tons yield $250 in profits.
   c. Either 7 or 8 tons yield $600 in profits.
   d. Either 5 or 6 tons yield $50 in losses; they should produce in the short-run because price is still greater than AVC.

2. a. ATC and AVC: 25, 25, 23, 21, 20, 19.8, 20, 21.
   b. MC: 25, 25, 19, 15, 16, 19, 21, 28.
   c. 6; $1.00 per month.
   d. 7; $35.00 per month.

3. a. FC: 40,000.
   VC: 0, 20,000, 40,000, 60,000, 80,000, 102,000, 128,000, 158,000, 192,000, 230,000, 275,000.
   ATC: –, 60,000, 40,000, 33,333, 30,000, 28,400, 28,000, 28,286, 29,000, 30,000, 31,500.
   AFC: –, 40,000, 20,000, 13,333, 10,000, 8,000, 6,667, 5,714, 5,000, 4,444, 4,000.
   AVC: –, 20,000, 20,000, 20,000, 20,000, 20,400, 21,333, 22,571, 24,000, 25,556, 27,500.
   MC: –, 20,000, 20,000, 20,000, 20,000, 22,000, 26,000, 30,000, 34,000, 38,000, 45,000.
   b. 6; $9,000 per month.
   c. 7; $26,000 per month.
   d. 5; $17,000 per month loss; 4; $36,000 per month loss; yes, in the short run, but not in the long run.

# Chapter 7

## Critical-Analysis Questions

2. Building the new resort is more risky (and less attractive) because if the market analysis is incorrect, and demand is insufficient, it probably will be difficult to find other uses for the newly built resort. If the airline proves unprofitable, however, the capital (airplanes) should be extremely mobile. The resort would have one offsetting advantage: If demand were stronger than expected, and profits larger, it would take competitors longer to enter the market (build a new resort), and they would be more reluctant to make the more permanent investment.
3. The amount of variety is determined by the willingness of consumers to pay for variety relative to the cost of providing it. If consumers value variety highly and the added costs of producing different styles, designs, and sizes is low, there will be a lot of variety. Alternatively, if consumers desire similar products or if variation can be produced only at a high cost, little variety will be present. Apparently, consumers place a substantial value (relative to cost) on variety in napkins, but not in toothpicks.
4. The tax would increase the price of lower-quality (and lower-priced) automobiles by a larger percentage than higher-quality automobiles. Consumers would substitute away from the lower-quality autos since their relative price would have increased. This substitution would increase the average quality of automobiles sold. Since the funds from the tax are rebated back to citizens through the lottery, one would expect this substitution effect to dominate any possible income effect.
7. No. A firm that maximizes *total* revenue would expand output as long as *marginal* revenue is positive. When marginal costs are positive, the revenue-maximizing price would be lower (and the output greater) than the price that would maximize the firm's profit.
11. In a competitive setting, only the big firms will survive if economies of scale are important. When economies of scale are unimportant, small firms will be able to compete effectively.

## Multiple-Choice Self-Test

1. d. 2. b. 3. a. 4. a. 5. c. 6. d. 7. a. 8. d. 9. b. 10. b.

## Problems

1. a. 30.
   b. 14.
   c. 420; 270; 150.
   d. Firms will enter the market until all firms earn only a normal rate of return (zero economic profit).
2. a. His plan will work if demand for the firm's tricycles is elastic and if other firms don't follow his move.
   b. By 5,000 units to a total of 25,000 tricycles.
   [TR − TC = profits → \$9 (Q) − (120,000 + \$4 (Q)) = 5000 → Q = 25,000].

c. Price elasticity = (5,000/20,000)/(1/10) = minus 2.5.
(Note: if the arc elasticity formula is used, the price elasticity coefficient will be minus 2.11.)

# CHAPTER 8

## Critical-Analysis Questions

1. Profits cannot exist in the long run without barriers to entry, because without them new entrants seeking the profits would increase supply, drive down price, and eliminate the profits. But as the chapter shows, barriers to entry are no guarantee of profits. Sufficient demand is also a necessary condition.
3. No; no; no.
7. Since this would increase competition from foreign sources, the effect should be to reduce the fears of market power being held by domestic firms. The need for antitrust action should decline.
8. Product variation provides each firm in the oligopoly a chance to "cheat" by raising the quality of its product in order to entice customers from rivals. This raises cost and helps to defeat the purpose, for the oligopolistic group, of controlling price. But if collusion has raised price much above marginal cost, there will be a powerful incentive for each firm to compete in a hidden way to get more customers.
11. Reductions in the cost of transportation generally increase competition because they force firms to compete with distant rivals and permit consumers to choose among a wider range of suppliers. As a result, the U.S. economy today is generally more competitive, in the rivalry sense, than it was 100 years ago.

## Multiple-Choice Self-Test

1. d. 2. a. 3. d. 4. c. 5. a. 6. c. 7. d. 8. a. 9. d. 10. a.

## Problems

1. a. See the table below.

| Total Revenues | Marginal Revenues | Fixed Cost | Total Cost |
|---|---|---|---|
| $ 60 | $60 | $40 | $ 90 |
| 110 | 50 | 40 | 110 |
| 150 | 40 | 40 | 134 |
| 180 | 30 | 40 | 163 |
| 200 | 20 | 40 | 198 |
| 210 | 10 | 40 | 243 |

b. Reduce price so you can increase quantity sold.
c. $45; 4; $17.

2. a. Since the *LRATC* curve decreases over the range of quantities that are demanded, a single firm would be the lowest-cost producer.
   e. Probably not; new competitors would have very high production costs if they started out small and thus it is unlikely that they would be profitable.

3. a. Demand when industry price varies:
      TR: 270, 280, 250, 180, 70, 0, 0.
      MR: 50, 10, –30, –70, –110, –70, 0.
   Demand when only SC's price varies:
      TR: 240, 280, 300, 300, 280, 240, 180, 100.
      MR: 60, 40, 20, 0, –20, –40, –60, –80.
   b. $70; $240.
   c. 5; $60; $250; profit has increased.
   d. No.

4. a. TR (market): 750,000; 1,000,000; 1,350,000; 1,600,000; 2,400,000; 3,000,000; 3,200,000; 3,500,000; 3,600,000; 3,500,000; 3,200,000.
   TR (firm): 187,500; 250,000; 337,500; 400,000; 600,000; 750,000; 800,000; 875,000; 900,000; 875,000; 800,000.
   b. $150; 24,000; 6,000.
   c. $400; $300; $250.
   d. $250 or $300. In both cases the industry price will be $1.2 million.
   e. A certain amount of collusion is likely since there are only four firms with equal cost conditions and equal output.

# CHAPTER 9

## Critical-Analysis Questions

3. Other things constant, a lengthy training requirement to perform in an occupation reduces supply and places upward pressure on the earnings level. However, resource prices, including those for labor services, are determined by *both* demand and supply. When demand is weak, earnings will be low, even though a considerable amount of education may be necessary to perform in the occupation. For example, the earnings of people with degrees in English literature and world history are generally low, even though most people in these fields have a great deal of education.
6. U.S. workers are more productive. By investing in human capital, the laborers contribute substantially, but the superior tools and physical capital that are available to U.S. workers also contribute to their higher wages.
8. The opportunity cost of leisure (nonwork) for higher-wage workers is greater than for lower-wage workers.
10. False. Several additional factors including differences in preferences (which would influence time worked, the trade-off between money wage and working conditions, and evaluation of alternative jobs), differences in jobs, and imperfect labor mobility would result in variations in earnings.
11. Yes. General increases in the productivity of the labor force will cause a general increase in wages. The higher general wage rates will increase the opportunity cost of barbering and cause the supply of barbers to decline.

The reduction in the supply of barbers will place upward pressure on the wages of barbers, even if technological change and worker productivity have changed little in barbering.

12. a, b, e, and f will generally increase hourly earnings; c and d will generally reduce hourly earnings.
13. While this statement often made by politicians sounds true, in fact, it is false. Output of goods and services valued by consumers, not jobs, is the key to economic progress and a high standard of living. Real income cannot be high unless real output is high. If job creation were the key to economic progress, it would be easy to create millions of jobs. For example, we could prohibit the use of farm machinery. Such a prohibition would create millions of jobs in agriculture. However, it would also reduce output and our standard of living.
14. Hourly wages will be highest in B because the higher wages will be necessary to compensate workers in B for the uncertainty and loss of income during layoffs. Annual earnings will be higher in A in order to compensate workers in A for the additional hours they will work during the year.

## Multiple-Choice Self-Test

1. c. 2. a. 3. a. 4. d. 5. d. 6. d. 7. b. 8. b. 9. c. 10. a.

## Problems

1. a. Q = 3,000; P = $300.
   b. Q = 4,000; P = $200.
   c. Employment rises from 12,000 to 12,800.
   d. See "Myths of Economics," pp. 218.
2. a. Two times as high; ten times as high; five times as high.
   b. Brazil; Canada; no difference.
   c. False. Canadian workers can still compete because of their greater productivity.
3. a. B1.
   b. B2.
   c. A3.
   d. A2 and B2.
   e. A2 and B2.
   f. B2.

# CHAPTER 10

## Critical-Analysis Questions

1. All of the changes would increase interest rates in the United States.
4. No. The *average* outstanding balance during the year is only about half of $1,000. Therefore, the $200 interest charge translates to almost a 40 percent annual rate of interest.
7. *Hints:* Which is more risky? Purchasing a bond or a stock? How does risk influence the expected rate of return?

9. 6 percent.

12. a. Mike.
    b. Yes, people who save a lot are able to get a higher interest rate on their savings as the result of people with a high rate of time preference.
    c. Yes, people who want to borrow money will be able to do so at a lower rate when there are more people (like Alicia) who want to save a lot.

13. Helped. This question is a lot like prior questions involving Alicia and Mike. Potential gains from trade are present. If obstacles do not restrain trade, the low-income countries will be able to attract savings (from country's with a high saving rate) at a lower interest rate than would exist in the absence of trade. Similarly, people in the high-income countries will be able to earn a higher return than would otherwise be possible. Both can gain because of the existence of the other.

### Multiple-Choice Self-Test

1. c. 2. b. 3. a. 4. d. 5. b. 6. d. 7. d. 8. a. 9. d. 10. d.

### Problems

1. The project is profitable at 8 percent but not at 12 percent. Use Exhibit 10.3 to calculate the present value of $400 received at the end of each of the next three years at the two interest rates.
2. a. Approximately $1.277 million.
   b. Yes.
   c. The lottery earnings are less liquid. Since there is not a well-organized market transforming lottery earnings into present income, the transaction costs of finding a "buyer" (at a price equal to the present value of the earnings) for the lottery earnings "rights" may be higher than for the bond, if one wants to sell in the future.
3. Buy the new refrigerator. The present value of the savings on your electric bill plus the $200 market value five years from now is approximately $735, more than the cost of the refrigerator.
4. No. The present value of the $500 annual additions to earnings during the next ten years is less than the cost of the schooling.

## CHAPTER 11

### Critical-Analysis Questions

2. Differences in family size, age of potential workers, nonmoney "income," taxes, and cost-of-living among areas reduce the effectiveness of annual money income as a measure of economic status. In general, high-income families are larger, more likely to be headed by a prime-age worker, have less nonmoney income (including leisure), pay more taxes, and reside in higher cost-of-living areas (particularly large cities). Thus, money-income comparisons between high- and low-income groups often overstate the economic status of the former relative to the latter.

4. If there were no intergenerational mobility, the diagonal numbers would all be 100 percent. If there were complete equality of opportunity and outcomes, the numbers in each column and row would be 20 percent.
6. No. The increase in marginal tax rates will reduce the incentive of the poor to *earn* income. Therefore, their income will rise by $1,000 minus the reduction in their personal earnings due to the disincentive effects of the higher marginal tax rates.
7. 67 percent.
9. Here, as in other areas, it is important to remember that government is merely an alternative form of social organization, rather than a corrective device. The structure of income transfers reflects political clout. The elderly, farmers, and business and labor interests are easily identifiable, politically potent interest groups. In contrast, the poor have a low voter participation rate and offer little in the way of financial support to politicians. Given these factors, it is not surprising that most income transfers go to the nonpoor.

### Multiple-Choice Self-Test

1. a. 2. b. 3. d. 4. b. 5. c. 6. c. 7. c. 8. a. 9. b. 10. b.

### Problems

1. a. 200 hours.
   b. 1,143 hours.
   c. 571 hours.
   d. 667 hours.
   g. Probably not. Presumably, Hillary could drop out of the transfer program if she wished.
2. a. Yes. His productivity on the job would add $200 per week to national income.
   b. No. He will lose $18 a week by taking the job.
   c. Marginal tax rate = 109%.
   d. Yes. His net income from the job would be greater than his net unemployment compensation.
3. a. Falling from the top.
   b.

| | | |
|---|---|---|
| 100 | 0 | 0 |
| 0 | 100 | 0 |
| 0 | 0 | 100 |

   c.

| | | |
|---|---|---|
| 20 | 60 | 20 |
| 20 | 60 | 20 |
| 20 | 60 | 20 |

## CHAPTER 12

### Critical-Analysis Questions

2. a. $1,000.
   b. $600.
   c. $200.

d. 0.
e. $10,000.

5. a. 0.
b. $300.
c. $300.
d. 0.
e. 0.

6. One of the most harmful side effects of inflation is the uncertainty it creates with regard to time-dimension contracts. As the statement indicates, it tends to undermine the ability of markets to allocate goods and resources to those who value them the most. In effect, it encourages speculation rather than production. The "well known" economist who made the statement referred to in the question was John Maynard Keynes, perhaps the best known economist of the twentieth century. See *The Economic Consequences of Peace* (New York: Harcourt Brace, 1920, pages 235–236).

7. a. Unemployed.
b. Unemployed.
c. Unemployed.
d. Not in labor force.
e. Employed.
f. Employed.

8. No. When cyclical unemployment is zero, the actual and natural rates of unemployment will be equal. When cyclical unemployment is positive (negative), the actual rate of unemployment will exceed (be less than) the natural rate of unemployment.

9. Job seekers do not know which employers will offer them the more attractive jobs. They find out by searching. Job search is "profitable" and consistent with economic efficiency as long as the marginal gain from search exceeds the marginal cost of searching.

## Multiple-Choice Self-Test

1. d. 2. b. 3. c. 4. b. 5. b. 6. c. 7. a. 8. d. 9. b. 10. d.

## Problems

1. a. $80 billion.
b. −20 percent.
c. 50 percent.

2. a. 60 percent.
b. 8.3 percent.

3. a. $1,974.6.
b. $2,879.5.
c. 49.2 (percent).
d. $2,707.6.
e. 94.4 (percent).
f. $4,883.8.

4. a. 124.67 million; 13.71 million; 63.74 million.
b. 66.3; 67.2; 62.6; 55.0; 55.4; 64.0; 47.4; Canada; Italy.
c. 5.5; 8.1; 2.1; 5.1; 9.1; 6.9; 9.9; Italy, Japan.

5. a. See Exhibit 12.2, $5,678 billion.
   b. See Exhibit 12.2, $5,678 billion.

# CHAPTER 13

## Critical-Analysis Questions

3. The key things held constant when constructing the demand and supply schedules for a specific good are demand (consumer income, prices of related goods, consumer preferences, expected future price of the good, and number of consumers) and supply (resource prices, technology, and expected future price of the good). Changes in these factors shift the relevant schedule.

   The key things held constant when constructing the *aggregate* schedules are *AD* (money supply, the government's tax and spending policies, real wealth, business optimism, real income of one's trading partners, and the expected future price level); *LRAS* (size of resource base, technology, and institutional structure of the economy); and *SRAS* (factors held constant in the *LR* plus resource prices and the expected price level). Again, change in these factors will shift the schedules indicated.

4. If the inflation rate unexpectedly falls from 3 percent to zero, the real wages of union members will rise. If other unions have similar contracts, the unemployment rate will increase because employment costs have risen relative to product prices. Profit margins will be cut, and producers will respond by reducing output and laying off workers. In contrast, if the inflation rate rises to 8 percent, profit margins will improve, producers will expand their output, and the unemployment rate will decline.

7. a. Would decrease *AD*.
   b., c., and d. Would increase *AD*.
   e. Would leave *AD* unchanged.

   For the "why" part of the question, see the section, "Unanticipated Changes in Aggregate Demand."

8. a, b, c, and d will reduce *SRAS;* e will increase it.

12. In the short run, the unanticipated expansion in demand will tend to increase output and employment, while exerting modest upward pressure on the price level. In the long run, the primary impact will be a higher price level, with no change in output and employment.

14. In the short run, the decline in spending (aggregate demand) may reduce output. However, changes in the interest rate will help redirect the economy back to full employment. When consumers spend less of their income, an increase in saving is implied. Similarly, a reduction in investment spending will reduce the demand for loanable funds. These actions will increase the supply of loanable funds relative to the demand. Predictably, real interest rates will fall. In turn, the lower real interest rates will stimulate additional current spending and help reverse the decline in demand stemming from the business pessimism.

## Multiple-Choice Self-Test

1. b. 2. d. 3. b. 4. a. 5. b. 6. c. 7. c. 8. a. 9. b. 10. d.

## Problems

2. a. Real GDP = 300; P = 130.
   b. 390.
   d. Recession; output is below full employment level.
   e. 150; overestimated.
   f. Resource costs are too high relative to product prices.
3. a. T. b. T. c. F. d. F. e. F. f. T. g. F. h. F.
4. a. +, 0, 0, +, +
   b. 0, +, +, −, +
   c. −, 0, 0, −, −
   d. 0, +, +, −, +

# CHAPTER 14

## Critical-Analysis Questions

4. Automatic stabilizers (for example, unemployment compensation, corporate profit tax, and progressive income tax) are built-in features that tend automatically to promote a budget deficit during a recession and a budget surplus (or smaller deficit) during an inflationary boom. Automatic stabilizers have the major advantage of providing needed restraint, or stimuli, without congressional approval which, in turn, minimizes the problem of proper timing.
5. The crowding-out effect is the theory that budget deficits will lead to higher real interest rates, which retard private spending. The crowding-out effect indicates that fiscal policy would not be nearly so potent as the simple Keynesian model implies. The new classical theory indicates that anticipation of higher future taxes (rather than higher interest rates) will crowd out private spending when government expenditures are financed by debt.
6. There is a major defect in this view. If the budget deficits stimulated demand and thereby output and employment, we would expect the inflation rate to accelerate. In fact, the inflation rate declined. The failure of the inflation rate to accelerate during the expansion of the 1980s strongly suggests that factors other than demand stimulus were at work.
8. This statement depicts the views of many economists two decades ago. Today, most economists recognize that it is naive. Given our limited ability to accurately forecast future economic conditions, timing of fiscal policy is more difficult than it was previously thought. Political considerations—remember, the government is merely an alternative form of social organization, not a corrective device—reduce the likelihood that fiscal policy will be used as a stabilization tool. Changes in interest rates and private spending may offset fiscal actions and thereby reduce the potency of fiscal policy. All factors considered, it is clear that the use of fiscal policy to stabilize the economy is both difficult and complex.
9. High marginal tax rates make tax-deductible expenditures (for example, business entertainment, elegant office, or luxury automobile for business use) cheap *to the purchaser* (but not to society). A reduction in marginal tax rates will increase the purchaser's cost of deductible expenditures,

since the lower rates reduce the tax savings accompanying deductible expenditures. Thus, lower marginal rates will tend to reduce expenditures on deductible items and other forms of tax avoidance.

### Multiple-Choice Self-Test

1. d. 2. b. 3. b. 4. d. 5. b. 6. d. 7. a. 8. c. 9. a. 10. c.

### Problems

1. a. K. b. C. c. NC. d. K. e. C. f. SS. g. NC.
2. b. 2.2 percent.
   c. 180 percent.
   d. For those making less than $10,000, the rate reduction will reduce revenues by approximately 20 percent. For those making more than 70,000, the revenue reduction will generally be substantially less than 20 percent; revenues might even increase. As the answers to a and b indicate, the impact on the incentive to earn will be substantially greater in the upper income bracket.
3. a. $686.
   b. 450.
   c. 152 percent.
   d. It would have increased.

## CHAPTER 15

### Critical-Analysis Questions

1. Money is valuable because of its scarcity relative to the availability of goods and services. The use of money facilitates (reduces the cost of) exchange transactions. Money also serves as a store of value and a unit of account. Doubling the supply of money, holding output constant, would simply cause its purchasing power to fall without enhancing the services that it performs. In fact, *fluctuations* in the money supply would create uncertainty as to its future value and reduce the ability of money to serve as a store of value, accurate unit of account, and medium of exchange for time-dimension contracting.

3. a. False. Statements of this type often use money when they are really speaking about wealth (or income).
   b. False. The checking deposit also counts as money. In addition, the deposit increases the reserves of the receiving bank, and thereby places it in a position to extend additional loans which would increase the money supply.
   c. False. Only an increase in the availability of goods and services valued by people will improve our standard of living. Without an additional supply of goods and services, more money will simply lead to a higher price level.

6. a. No change. Currency held by the public increases, but checking deposits decrease by an equal amount.
   b. Bank reserves decrease by $100.

c. Excess reserves decrease by $100 minus the required reserve ratio multiplied by $100.

8. Options b, e, and f will reduce the money supply; a and c will increase it; if the Treasury's deposits (or the deposits of persons who receive portions of the Treasury's spending) are considered part of the money supply, then d will leave the money supply unchanged.

### Multiple-Choice Self-Test

1. a. 2. b. 3. a. 4. b. 5. c. 6. c. 7. d. 8. b. 9. a. 10. d.

### Problems

1. a. + 0
   b. 0 +
   c. + +
   d. – 0

2. a. Increase the money supply by $100,000.
   b. See table below.

| | Change in Checking Deposits | Required Reserves | Additional Loans | Amount of Loans Held as Currency outside Banks |
|---|---|---|---|---|
| Round 1 | 90,000 | 9,000 | 81,000 | 8,100 |
| Round 2 | 72,900 | 7,290 | 65,610 | 6,561 |
| Round 3 | 59,049 | 5,905 | 53,144 | 5,314 |
| Round 4 | 47,830 | 4,783 | 43,047 | 4,305 |
| Round 5 | 38,742 | 3,874 | 34,868 | 3,487 |
| Total (5 rounds) | 308,521 | 30,852 | 277,669 | 27,767 |

c. $10,000 (additional currency initially held by Midas) + $308,521 (additional checking deposits) + $27,767 (additional currency held outside of bank by people who took out the loans) = $346,288.

## CHAPTER 16

### Critical-Analysis Questions

2. a. The cost of *obtaining* the house is $100,000.
   b. The cost of *holding* it is the interest forgone on the $100,000 plus any expected change in the value of the house during the next year.
   c. The cost of *obtaining* a dollar is the amount of goods one must give up in order to acquire a dollar. For example, if a pound of sugar sells for 50 cents, the cost of obtaining a dollar in terms of sugar is two pounds.
   d. As in the case of the house, the cost of *holding* a dollar is the interest forgone. The nominal interest rate will tend to reflect any expected

change in the value of the dollar (that is, the expected rate of inflation) during the new year.

4. Aggregate demand will decline as individuals and businesses reduce spending in an effort to build up their money balances.

8. Association does not reveal causation. Decision-makers—including borrowers and lenders—will eventually anticipate a high rate of inflation and adjust their choices accordingly. As the expected rate of inflation increases, the demand for loanable funds will increase and the supply will decrease. This will lead to higher nominal interest rates. Thus, economic theory indicates that the causation tends to run the opposite direction from that indicated by the statement.

12. The wages people earn are also prices (prices for labor services) and like other prices they usually rise as the general level of prices increases. The statement ignores this factor. It implicitly assumes that money wages are unaffected by inflation; that they would have increased by the same amount (6 percent) even if prices would have been stable. Generally, this will not be the case.

## Multiple-Choice Self-Test

1. a. 2. b. 3. b. 4. d. 5. a. 6. c. 7. b. 8. b. 9. d. 10. d.

## Problems

1. a. Higher real GDP and a higher price level.
   b. No.
   c. Continued price level increases (sustained inflation).

2. a. See table below.

| | | | Rate of Change | |
|---|---|---|---|---|
| | | Real GDP | Money Supply | Price Level |
| United States | 1986 | 4405.2 | — | — |
| | 1987 | 4539.9 | 3.5 | 3.2 |
| | 1988 | 4716.5 | 5.5 | 3.9 |
| | 1989 | 4839.4 | 5.1 | 4.4 |
| Turkey | 1986 | 52724 | — | — |
| | 1987 | 56763 | 45.6 | 38.1 |
| | 1988 | 58746 | 55.0 | 66.7 |
| | 1989 | 59843 | 72.0 | 64.3 |
| Argentina | 1986 | 159.7 | — | — |
| | 1987 | 163.5 | 171.9 | 127.8 |
| | 1988 | 159.2 | 437.0 | 387.9 |
| | 1989 | 147.9 | 2192.5 | 3073.4 |

   b. Argentina.
   c. Argentina.
   d. Turkey.

# CHAPTER 17

## Critical-Analysis Questions

1. Economists in the mid-1970s thought inflation would reduce unemployment; they failed to recognize that decision-makers would eventually come to anticipate the inflation. The modern view of the Phillips curve incorporates expectations into the analysis.

4. a. and b; Actual and natural rates of unemployment will be equal.
   c. Actual rate will be less than the natural rate.
   d. Actual rate will be greater than the natural rate.

5. Nonactivists think that a monetary rule would result in less instability from monetary sources. The changing nature of money may reduce the stabilizing effects of a monetary rule.

9. No. Both private corporations and governments can, and often do, have continual debt outstanding. Borrowers can continue to finance and refinance debt as long as lenders have confidence in their ability to pay. This will generally be the case as long as the borrower's interest liability is small relative to income (or the potential tax base).

11. A failure to anticipate fully the future taxes accompanying debt implies an underestimation of the true cost of government. Since politicians will want to exaggerate the benefits and conceal the cost of their actions, the ability of debt to hide the true cost of government increases its attractiveness with vote-seeking politicians.

12. Rather than defaulting, the federal government could, as a last resort, meet its debt obligations by borrowing from the Fed. In essence, this means the government is paying its debt with printing-press money. It would lead to inflation.

## Multiple-Choice Self-Test

1. a. 2. d. 3. b. 4. d. 5. a. 6. b. 7. b. 8. b. 9. d. 10. b.

## Problems

1. a. Go down in the short run; return to 5 percent in the long run.
   b. Follow a policy that would result in more than a 5 percent rate of inflation. The lower rate of unemployment could not be maintained.
   c. Unemployment would rise. No
   d. If expectations are rational, the impact of the policy shifts would be unpredictable, even in the short run. If this were true, a shift to a more expansionary policy would not be as attractive as is the case under adaptive expectations.

1. a. See table below.

| | Budget Deficit | National Debt | GDP | Budget Deficit as a Share of GDP | National Debt as a Share of GDP |
|---|---|---|---|---|---|
| 1992 | X | X | X | 2.42% | 70.0% |
| 1993 | $150 | $4350 | $6360 | 2.36 | 68.4 |

b. Because the budget deficit as a share of GDP was less than the growth rate of real GDP.

# CHAPTER 18

## Critical-Analysis Questions

1. Availability of goods and services, not jobs, is the source of economic prosperity. When a good can be purchased more cheaply abroad than it can be produced at home, a nation can expand the quantity of goods and services available for consumption by (a) specializing in the production of those goods for which it is a low-cost producer and (b) trading them for the cheap (relative to domestic costs) foreign goods. Trade restrictions limiting the ability of Americans to purchase low-cost goods from foreigners stifles this process and thereby *reduces* the living standard of Americans.
3. Answers a and b are not in conflict. Since trade restrictions are typically a special interest issue, political entrepreneurs can often gain by supporting them even when they promote economic inefficiency.
7. True. If country A imposes a tariff, other countries will sell less to A and therefore acquire less purchasing power in terms of A's currency. Thus, they will have to reduce their purchases of A's export goods.
8. a. No. Americans would be poorer if we used more of our resources to produce things for which we are a high opportunity-cost producer and less of our resources to produce things for which we are low opportunity-cost producer. Employment might either increase or decrease, but the key point is that it is the value of goods produced, not employment, which generates income and provides for the wealth of a nation. The answer to b is the same as a.
9. In thinking about this issue, consider the following points. Suppose the Japanese were willing to give products such as automobiles, electronic goods, and clothing to us free of charge. Would we be worse off if we accepted the gifts? Should we try to keep the free goods out? What is the source of real income—jobs or goods and services? If the gifts make us better off, doesn't it follow that partial gifts would also make us better off?

## Multiple-Choice Self-Test

1. c. 2. d. 3. d. 4. b. 5. a. 6. a. 7. c. 8. b. 9. b. 10. c.

## Problems

1. a. U.S.; U.S.; South Korea; U.S.
   b. South Korea.
   c. +10 −50
   + 2 +30
   +16 −32
   −10 +50
   + 6 +18
2. a. $4,000; 900.
   b. $3,000; 1,300; 700; 600; 200.

c. \$3,500; 100; 200; 300.
d. Rise to \$3,500; 100.
e. The only difference is that with a tariff the government gets the \$500 per motorcycle, and with the quota the motorcycle importers receive the \$500 difference (per imported motorcycle) between the import price of \$3,000 and the domestic motorcycle price of \$3,500.

# CHAPTER 19

## Critical-Analysis Questions

1. The depreciation will make the dollar price of BMWs more expensive, which will reduce the *quantity purchased* by Americans. If the American demand for BMWs is inelastic (elastic), then the dollar expenditures on BMWs will rise (fall).
2. On February 2, the dollar appreciated against the pound and depreciated against the franc.
4. Answers a and g would cause the dollar to appreciate; b, c, d, e, and h would cause the dollar to depreciate, f would leave the exchange rate unchanged.
6. Each of the changes would reduce the size of the current-account deficit.
11. The current-account balance will move toward a larger deficit (or smaller surplus), and the dollar will appreciate.

## Multiple-Choice Self-Test

1\. d. 2. b. 3. b. 4. d. 5. c. 6. d. 7. c. 8. a. 9. c. 10. d.

## Problems

1. a. i. −121. ii. −94. iii. −110. iv. 102. v. −8.
   b. There was a substantial reduction in the size of the balance-of-merchandise-trade deficit and the current-account deficit between 1989 and 1991.
2. a. +; 0; depreciate.
   b. 0; −; depreciate.
   c. −; +; appreciate.
   d. 0; 0; no change.
   e. −; +; appreciate.

# CHAPTER 20

## Critical-Analysis Questions

2. When payment is not demanded for services, potential customers have a strong incentive to attempt a "free ride." However, when the number of nonpaying customers becomes such that the sales revenues of sellers are diminished (and in some cases eliminated), the sellers' incentive to supply the good is thereby reduced (or eliminated).

5. In both markets and government, mutual consent is the only conclusive test of whether an action is productive. If all parties affected by an activity agree to it, then it is productive. Projects favored by a majority are not necessarily productive because the cost imposed on the nonconsenting minority may exceed the net gain to the majority.
7. Corporate officers, while they surely care about the next few months and the profits during that time, care also about the value of the firm and its stock price. If the stock price rises sufficiently in the next few months—as it will if investors believe that current investments in future-oriented projects (planting new trees, for example) are sound—then the officers will find their jobs secure even if current profits do not look good. Rights to the profits from those (future) trees are saleable now in the form of the corporation's stock. There is no such mechanism to make the distant fruits of today's investments available to the political entrepreneurs who might otherwise fight for the future-oriented project. Only if the project appeals to today's voters, and they are willing to pay today for tomorrow's benefits, will the program be a political success. In any case, the wealth of the political entrepreneur is not directly enhanced by his or her successful fight for the project.

### Multiple-Choice Self-Test

1. d. 2. c. 3. a. 4. b. 5. d. 6. c. 7. c. 8. b. 9. b. 10. c.

### Problems

1. a. P = $120, Q = 4,000 tons/year.
   b. P = $130, Q = 3,000 tons/year (*Hint:* Add $20 to each price and graph new supply curve with the old quantity supplied and the new prices. Find the new equilibrium point.)
2. a. Yes.
   b. Each would pay $20,000. The plan would pass because five of the seven voters value the flood-control project more than $20,000.
   c. There are many alternatives that would provide net benefits for all seven voters. One example: $35,000 for Adams, $24,500 for Brown, Carlson, Dunn, and Emerson, and $3,500 for Frank and Green. Any option that allocates the costs to voters in approximately the same proportion as the share of the total benefits that they receive will generate a net benefit for all voters.
   d. The project would still pass with five of seven votes because the individual tax is $32,000. The project will, however, reduce the wealth of the group because the total benefits are only $200,000.
   e. No. Projects favored by a majority are not necessarily productive, because the cost imposed on the nonconsenting minority may exceed the net gain to the majority.

## CHAPTER 21

### Critical-Analysis Questions

1. The use of an unowned, unpriced resource might have a high opportunity cost. Yet if there is no owner to protect it, or to allocate it to its highest-

valued use, then it might indeed be treated as if it had no opportunity cost. If it is valuable, however, then it might pay an entrepreneur to find a way to establish ownership. That, in fact, is the history of many natural resources in the United States. Ownership of land, for example, was often not established until it became economically attractive enough to reward the initial claimants who established ownership.

3. The "requirement" of water for the steel industry depends on the value placed on water, as well as on the value placed on steel. The same amount of steel can be produced with vastly differing amounts of water, as illustrated in Exhibit 21.1 of this chapter. Also, steel itself is not indispensable in all its uses, including national defense uses. There are many substitutes, not only for water in the making of steel, but also for steel in the making of tanks, and for tanks in providing national defense. So a given amount of water for steel is not really a requirement.
5. Wells are abandoned by producers when the cost of extracting and delivering additional oil exceeds its value. When the value of crude oil rises, additional oil can be produced, since water flooding, steam, and chemical measures—all of which are costly—can be paid for by the higher prices gained from the extra oil.
7. The owner who enjoys the resource selfishly also pays the opportunity cost by failing to receive revenue from renting or leasing access, or selling the resource to someone else. Without such ownership, the incentive to preserve or conserve the resource is diminished.
9. If an investment, such as leaving the trees to grow another 20 years, yields a higher return than other investments, then the stock price will fall if the trees are cut too soon, or will go higher if a new, more profitable investment path (leaving the trees to grow) is announced. Either way, the stock price immediately rewards good long-term decisions and penalizes bad ones.

## Multiple-Choice Self-Test

1. a. 2. d. 3. d. 4. c. 5. d. 6. b. 7. d. 8. a. 9. d. 10. b.

## Problems

1. a. The function ignored is, "Private property rights provide owners with the incentive to share (sell to others) resource access, and resource prices provide users with the incentive to conserve." The Park Service is not selling the right to use the parks in return for revenue it can keep. The money goes to the Treasury, and thus provides no incentive to the Park Service to give visitors what they want. Nor is the price a market-clearing price, because the Park Service has no right to change the fees. Thus neither the incentives nor the information produced by market prices is being generated here, because the Park Service does not have a true property right to the parks. Its discipline and incentives are politically determined.

   b. The function ignored is, "Changes in the value of the privately held ownership right to a resource bring all anticipated future benefits and costs of today's resource decisions immediately to bear on the resource owner." When rights to a stream, or to fish in it, are held privately, then a corporation that is a potential polluter of the stream must consider its future liability for polluting activities. Dumping pollution reduces the present value of the corporation (and the value of its stock) to the extent that future liability is anticipated.

c. The function ignored is, "A resource owner has a strong incentive to exercise good stewardship." If the deer and elk are valuable for hunting, or photography, or to add a valued characteristic to the land, then the landowner's personal wealth is at stake, providing a stewardship incentive.

d. The function ignored is, "A resource owner has legal rights against anyone seeking to harm the resource." Corporations have in fact been successfully sued by homeowners and others for pollution damage.

# CHAPTER 22

## Critical-Analysis Questions

2. There is considerable diversity among the poor nations. The real GDP of several poor countries has declined during recent decades (see Exhibit 22.4). Others have stagnated or experienced only slow growth. Still others have experienced rapid growth. In fact, most all of the high-growth nations (Exhibit 22.3) were relatively poor countries in 1960s. On the encouraging side, the average growth rates of per capita GNP in China and India (the two most populous less developed countries) were 6.8 percent and 2.8 percent during the 1980–1990 period. If these two giants are able to follow the path of Japan, and more recently Hong Kong, South Korea, Singapore, and Indonesia, perhaps two-thirds of the world's population will have incomes well above subsistence levels early in the next century.

3. Many believe that this view is essentially true. However, there are reasons for doubting it. Foreign aid has not played a significant role in the progress of most of the high growth, less developed countries. Often, financial aid disrupts markets and retards the incentive of producers in less developed countries. Finally, attractive investment alternatives will draw investment from abroad even if domestic saving is inadequate. Thus, the efficacy of aid as a tool to promote economic growth is highly questionable.

7. Yes. Trade barriers limit the ability of both businesses and consumers to benefit from economies associated with an expansion in the size of the market. This limitation will be more restrictive for small countries (like Costa Rica) than for larger countries (like Mexico) because the latter will often have sizable domestic markets.

## Multiple-Choice Self-Test

1. c. 2. a. 3. c. 4. d. 5. b. 6. d. 7. b. 8. b. 9. b. 10. d.

## Problems

a. 35; 20; 10.
b. 233; 70; 33.3; 26.9; 18.9; 15.9; 11.7.

APPENDIX

# B

# Economic Indicators for the United States (1929–1992) and 58 Other Countries

## SECTION 1

**National Income and Product Accounts**

| | The Sum of These Expenditures | | | | Equals |
|---|---|---|---|---|---|
| | Personal Consumption Expenditures | Gross Private Domestic Investment | Government Purchases of Goods and Services | Net Exports of Goods and Services | Gross Domestic Product (GDP) |
| 1929 | 77.3 | 16.7 | 8.9 | 1.1 | 103.1 |
| 1930 | 69.9 | 10.3 | 9.2 | 1.0 | 90.4 |
| 1931 | 60.5 | 5.6 | 9.2 | 0.5 | 75.8 |
| 1932 | 48.6 | 1.0 | 8.1 | 0.4 | 58.0 |
| 1933 | 45.8 | 1.4 | 8.3 | 0.4 | 55.6 |
| 1934 | 51.3 | 3.3 | 9.8 | 0.6 | 65.1 |
| 1935 | 55.7 | 6.4 | 10.0 | 0.1 | 72.2 |
| 1936 | 61.9 | 8.5 | 12.0 | 0.1 | 82.7 |
| 1937 | 66.5 | 11.8 | 11.9 | 0.3 | 90.4 |
| 1938 | 63.9 | 6.5 | 13.0 | 1.3 | 84.9 |
| 1939 | 67.0 | 9.5 | 13.6 | 1.2 | 90.8 |
| 1940 | 71.0 | 13.4 | 14.2 | 1.8 | 100.0 |
| 1941 | 80.8 | 18.3 | 25.0 | 1.5 | 125.0 |
| 1942 | 88.6 | 10.3 | 59.9 | 0.2 | 158.5 |
| 1943 | 99.5 | 6.2 | 88.9 | –1.9 | 192.4 |
| 1944 | 108.2 | 7.7 | 97.1 | –1.7 | 211.0 |
| 1945 | 119.6 | 11.3 | 83.0 | –0.5 | 213.1 |
| 1946 | 143.9 | 31.5 | 29.1 | 7.8 | 211.9 |
| 1947 | 161.9 | 35.0 | 26.4 | 11.9 | 234.3 |
| 1948 | 174.9 | 47.1 | 32.6 | 7.0 | 260.3 |
| 1949 | 178.3 | 36.5 | 39.0 | 6.5 | 259.3 |
| 1950 | 192.1 | 55.1 | 38.8 | 2.2 | 287.0 |
| 1951 | 208.1 | 60.5 | 60.4 | 4.5 | 331.6 |
| 1952 | 219.1 | 53.5 | 75.8 | 3.2 | 349.7 |
| 1953 | 232.6 | 54.9 | 82.8 | 1.3 | 370.0 |
| 1954 | 239.8 | 54.1 | 76.0 | 2.6 | 370.9 |
| 1955 | 257.9 | 69.7 | 75.3 | 3.0 | 404.3 |
| 1956 | 270.6 | 72.7 | 79.7 | 5.3 | 426.2 |
| 1957 | 285.3 | 71.1 | 87.3 | 7.3 | 448.6 |
| 1958 | 294.6 | 63.6 | 95.4 | 3.3 | 454.7 |
| 1959 | 318.1 | 78.8 | 99.0 | –1.7 | 494.2 |

| | The Sum of These Expenditures | | | | Equals |
|---|---|---|---|---|---|
| | Personal Consumption Expenditures | Gross Private Domestic Investment | Government Purchases of Goods and Services | Net Exports of Goods and Services | Gross Domestic Product (GDP) |
| 1960 | 332.4 | 78.7 | 99.8 | 2.4 | 513.4 |
| 1961 | 343.5 | 77.9 | 107.0 | 3.4 | 531.8 |
| 1962 | 364.4 | 87.9 | 116.8 | 2.4 | 571.6 |
| 1963 | 384.2 | 93.4 | 122.3 | 3.3 | 603.1 |
| 1964 | 412.5 | 101.7 | 128.3 | 5.5 | 648.0 |
| 1965 | 444.6 | 118.0 | 136.3 | 3.9 | 702.7 |
| 1966 | 481.6 | 130.4 | 155.9 | 1.9 | 769.8 |
| 1967 | 509.3 | 128.0 | 175.6 | 1.4 | 814.3 |
| 1968 | 559.1 | 139.9 | 191.5 | −1.3 | 889.3 |
| 1969 | 603.7 | 155.2 | 201.8 | −1.2 | 959.5 |
| 1970 | 646.5 | 150.3 | 212.7 | 1.2 | 1010.7 |
| 1971 | 700.3 | 175.5 | 224.3 | −3.0 | 1097.2 |
| 1972 | 767.8 | 205.6 | 241.5 | −8.0 | 1207.0 |
| 1973 | 848.1 | 243.1 | 257.7 | 0.6 | 1349.6 |
| 1974 | 927.7 | 245.8 | 288.3 | −3.1 | 1458.6 |
| 1975 | 1024.9 | 226.0 | 321.4 | 13.6 | 1585.9 |
| 1976 | 1143.1 | 286.4 | 341.3 | −2.3 | 1768.4 |
| 1977 | 1271.5 | 358.3 | 368.0 | −23.7 | 1974.1 |
| 1978 | 1421.2 | 434.0 | 403.6 | −26.1 | 2232.7 |
| 1979 | 1583.7 | 480.2 | 448.5 | −23.8 | 2488.6 |
| 1980 | 1748.1 | 467.6 | 507.1 | −14.7 | 2708.0 |
| 1981 | 1926.2 | 558.0 | 561.1 | −14.7 | 3030.6 |
| 1982 | 2059.2 | 503.4 | 607.6 | −20.6 | 3149.6 |
| 1983 | 2257.5 | 546.7 | 652.3 | −51.4 | 3405.0 |
| 1984 | 2460.3 | 718.9 | 700.8 | −102.7 | 3777.2 |
| 1985 | 3667.4 | 714.5 | 772.3 | −115.6 | 4038.7 |
| 1986 | 2850.6 | 717.6 | 833.0 | −132.5 | 4268.6 |
| 1987 | 3052.2 | 749.3 | 881.5 | −143.1 | 4539.9 |
| 1988 | 3296.1 | 793.6 | 918.7 | −108.0 | 4900.4 |
| 1989 | 3523.1 | 832.3 | 975.2 | −79.7 | 5250.8 |
| 1990 | 3748.4 | 799.5 | 1043.2 | −68.9 | 5522.2 |
| 1991 | 3887.7 | 721.1 | 1090.5 | −21.8 | 5677.5 |
| 1992 | 4093.9 | 769.7 | 1114.8 | −32.7 | 5945.7 |

## SECTION 2 Real Output and Prices

| | Gross Domestic Product (GDP) | | | GDP Deflator | | Consumer Price Index | |
|---|---|---|---|---|---|---|---|
| | 1987 Prices (billions) | Annual Real Rate of Growth | Real GDP per Capita (1987 dollars) | Index (1987 = 100) | Annual Percentage Change | Index (1982–1984 = 100) | Annual Percentage Change[a] |
| 1929 | 821.8 | — | 6743 | 12.5 | — | 17.1 | 0.0 |
| 1930 | 748.9 | –8.9 | 6079 | 12.1 | –9.1 | 16.7 | –2.5 |
| 1931 | 691.3 | –7.7 | 5568 | 11.0 | –9.1 | 15.2 | –8.8 |
| 1932 | 599.7 | –13.3 | 4800 | 9.7 | –11.8 | 13.6 | –10.3 |
| 1933 | 587.1 | –2.1 | 4671 | 9.5 | –2.1 | 12.9 | –5.1 |
| 1934 | 632.6 | 7.7 | 5001 | 10.3 | 8.4 | 13.4 | 3.4 |
| 1935 | 681.3 | 7.7 | 5349 | 10.6 | 2.9 | 13.7 | 2.5 |
| 1936 | 777.9 | 14.2 | 6069 | 10.7 | 0.0 | 13.8 | 1.0 |
| 1937 | 811.4 | 4.3 | 6292 | 11.2 | 5.7 | 14.3 | 3.4 |
| 1938 | 778.9 | –4.0 | 5993 | 10.9 | –2.7 | 14.1 | –1.9 |
| 1939 | 840.7 | 7.9 | 6416 | 10.8 | –0.9 | 13.9 | 1.4 |
| 1940 | 906.0 | 7.8 | 6857 | 11.0 | 1.9 | 14.0 | 1.0 |
| 1941 | 1070.6 | 18.2 | 8025 | 11.7 | 6.4 | 14.7 | 5.0 |
| 1942 | 1284.9 | 20.0 | 9528 | 12.3 | 5.1 | 16.3 | 10.7 |
| 1943 | 1540.5 | 19.9 | 11266 | 12.5 | 1.6 | 17.3 | 6.1 |
| 1944 | 1670.0 | 8.4 | 12067 | 12.6 | 0.8 | 17.6 | 1.7 |
| 1945 | 1602.6 | –4.0 | 11453 | 13.3 | 5.6 | 18.0 | 2.3 |
| 1946 | 1272.1 | –20.6 | 8997 | 16.7 | 25.6 | 19.5 | 8.7 |
| 1947 | 1252.8 | –1.5 | 8692 | 18.7 | 12.0 | 22.3 | 14.4 |
| 1948 | 1300.0 | 3.8 | 8866 | 20.0 | 7.0 | 24.1 | 2.7 |
| 1949 | 1305.5 | 0.4 | 8751 | 19.9 | –0.5 | 23.8 | –1.8 |
| 1950 | 1418.5 | 8.7 | 9352 | 20.2 | 1.5 | 24.1 | 5.8 |
| 1951 | 1558.4 | 9.9 | 10101 | 21.3 | 5.4 | 26.0 | 5.9 |
| 1952 | 1624.9 | 4.3 | 10353 | 21.5 | 0.9 | 26.5 | 0.9 |
| 1953 | 1685.5 | 3.7 | 10563 | 22.0 | 2.3 | 26.7 | 0.6 |
| 1954 | 1673.8 | –0.7 | 10307 | 22.2 | 0.9 | 26.9 | –0.5 |
| 1955 | 1768.3 | 5.6 | 10699 | 22.9 | 3.2 | 26.8 | 0.4 |
| 1956 | 1803.6 | 2.0 | 10722 | 23.6 | 3.1 | 27.2 | 2.9 |
| 1957 | 1838.2 | 1.9 | 10733 | 24.4 | 3.4 | 28.1 | 3.0 |
| 1958 | 1829.1 | –0.5 | 10504 | 24.9 | 2.0 | 28.9 | 1.8 |

[a]From December of the prior year to December of the current year.

| | Gross Domestic Product (GDP) | | | GDP Deflator | | Consumer Price Index | |
|---|---|---|---|---|---|---|---|
| | 1987 Prices (billions) | Annual Real Rate of Growth | Real GDP per Capita (1987 dollars) | Index (1987 = 100) | Annual Percentage Change | Index (1982–1984 = 100) | Annual Percentage Change[a] |
| 1959 | 1928.8 | 5.5 | 10892 | 25.6 | 2.8 | 29.1 | 1.7 |
| 1960 | 1970.8 | 2.2 | 10903 | 26.0 | 1.6 | 29.6 | 1.4 |
| 1961 | 2023.8 | 2.7 | 11014 | 26.3 | 1.2 | 29.9 | 0.7 |
| 1962 | 2128.1 | 5.2 | 11405 | 26.9 | 2.3 | 30.2 | 1.3 |
| 1963 | 2215.6 | 4.1 | 11704 | 27.2 | 1.1 | 30.6 | 1.6 |
| 1964 | 2340.6 | 5.6 | 12195 | 27.7 | 1.8 | 31.0 | 1.0 |
| 1965 | 2470.5 | 5.5 | 12712 | 28.4 | 2.5 | 31.5 | 1.9 |
| 1966 | 2616.2 | 5.9 | 13307 | 29.4 | 3.5 | 32.4 | 3.5 |
| 1967 | 2685.2 | 2.6 | 13510 | 30.3 | 3.1 | 33.4 | 3.0 |
| 1968 | 2796.9 | 4.2 | 13932 | 31.8 | 5.0 | 34.8 | 4.7 |
| 1969 | 2873.0 | 2.7 | 14171 | 33.4 | 5.0 | 36.7 | 6.2 |
| 1970 | 2873.9 | 0.0 | 14013 | 35.2 | 5.4 | 38.8 | 5.6 |
| 1971 | 2955.9 | 2.9 | 14232 | 37.1 | 5.4 | 40.5 | 3.3 |
| 1972 | 3107.1 | 5.1 | 14801 | 38.8 | 4.6 | 41.8 | 3.4 |
| 1973 | 3268.6 | 5.2 | 15422 | 41.3 | 6.4 | 44.4 | 8.7 |
| 1974 | 3248.1 | −0.6 | 15185 | 44.9 | 8.7 | 49.3 | 12.3 |
| 1975 | 3221.7 | −0.8 | 14917 | 49.2 | 9.6 | 53.8 | 6.9 |
| 1976 | 3380.8 | 4.9 | 15502 | 52.3 | 6.3 | 56.9 | 4.9 |
| 1977 | 3533.3 | 4.5 | 16039 | 55.9 | 6.9 | 60.6 | 6.7 |
| 1978 | 3703.5 | 4.8 | 16635 | 60.3 | 7.9 | 65.2 | 9.0 |
| 1979 | 3796.8 | 2.5 | 16867 | 65.5 | 8.6 | 72.6 | 13.3 |
| 1980 | 3776.3 | −0.5 | 16584 | 71.7 | 9.5 | 82.4 | 12.5 |
| 1981 | 3843.1 | 1.8 | 16710 | 78.9 | 10.0 | 90.9 | 8.9 |
| 1982 | 3760.3 | −2.2 | 16194 | 83.8 | 6.2 | 96.5 | 3.8 |
| 1983 | 3906.6 | 3.9 | 16672 | 87.2 | 4.1 | 99.6 | 3.8 |
| 1984 | 4148.5 | 6.2 | 17549 | 91.0 | 4.4 | 103.9 | 3.9 |
| 1985 | 4279.8 | 3.2 | 17944 | 94.4 | 3.7 | 107.6 | 3.8 |
| 1986 | 4404.5 | 2.9 | 18299 | 96.9 | 2.6 | 109.6 | 1.1 |
| 1987 | 4539.9 | 3.1 | 18694 | 100.0 | 3.2 | 113.6 | 4.4 |
| 1988 | 4718.6 | 3.9 | 19252 | 103.9 | 3.9 | 118.3 | 4.4 |
| 1989 | 4838.0 | 2.5 | 19556 | 108.5 | 4.4 | 124.0 | 4.6 |
| 1990 | 4877.5 | 0.8 | 19513 | 113.2 | 4.3 | 130.7 | 6.1 |
| 1991 | 4821.0 | −1.2 | 19077 | 117.8 | 4.1 | 136.2 | 3.1 |

[a]From December of the prior year to December of the current year.

## SECTION 3

### Population and Employment

| | Population and Labor Force | | | | |
|---|---|---|---|---|---|
| | Civilian Noninstitutional Population Age 16 and Over | Civilian Labor Force (millions) | Civilian Labor Force Participation Rate | Employment Population Ratio | Unemployment Rate |
| 1929 | 85.6 | 49.2 | 57.5 | 55.9 | 3.2 |
| 1930 | 87.1 | 49.8 | 57.2 | 52.5 | 8.7 |
| 1931 | 88.2 | 50.4 | 57.1 | 48.4 | 15.9 |
| 1932 | 89.3 | 51.0 | 57.1 | 43.8 | 23.6 |
| 1933 | 90.5 | 51.6 | 57.0 | 43.1 | 24.9 |
| 1934 | 91.7 | 52.2 | 56.9 | 44.9 | 21.7 |
| 1935 | 92.9 | 52.9 | 56.9 | 45.8 | 20.1 |
| 1936 | 94.1 | 53.4 | 56.7 | 47.5 | 16.9 |
| 1937 | 95.2 | 54.0 | 56.7 | 49.0 | 14.3 |
| 1938 | 96.5 | 54.6 | 56.6 | 46.2 | 19.0 |
| 1939 | 97.8 | 55.2 | 56.4 | 47.2 | 17.2 |
| 1940 | 100.4 | 55.6 | 55.4 | 47.8 | 14.6 |
| 1941 | 101.5 | 55.9 | 55.0 | 51.2 | 9.9 |
| 1942 | 102.6 | 56.4 | 55.0 | 56.3 | 4.7 |
| 1943 | 103.7 | 55.5 | 53.5 | 61.2 | 1.9 |
| 1944 | 104.6 | 54.6 | 52.2 | 62.5 | 1.2 |
| 1945 | 105.6 | 53.9 | 51.0 | 60.9 | 1.9 |
| 1946 | 106.5 | 57.5 | 54.0 | 55.1 | 3.8 |
| 1947 | 101.8 | 59.4 | 58.3 | 56.7 | 3.9 |
| 1948 | 103.1 | 60.6 | 58.8 | 57.2 | 3.8 |
| 1949 | 104.0 | 61.3 | 58.9 | 56.1 | 5.9 |
| 1950 | 105.0 | 62.2 | 59.2 | 57.2 | 5.2 |
| 1951 | 104.6 | 62.0 | 59.3 | 59.4 | 3.2 |
| 1952 | 105.2 | 62.1 | 59.0 | 59.5 | 2.9 |
| 1953 | 107.1 | 63.0 | 58.8 | 59.2 | 2.8 |
| 1954 | 108.3 | 63.6 | 58.7 | 57.5 | 5.4 |
| 1955 | 109.7 | 65.0 | 59.3 | 58.6 | 4.3 |
| 1956 | 111.0 | 66.6 | 60.0 | 59.3 | 4.0 |
| 1957 | 112.3 | 66.9 | 59.6 | 58.8 | 4.2 |
| 1958 | 113.7 | 67.6 | 59.5 | 57.1 | 6.6 |
| 1959 | 115.3 | 68.4 | 59.3 | 57.6 | 5.3 |

## Population and Labor Force

| | Civilian Noninstitutional Population Age 16 and Over | Civilian Labor Force (millions) | Civilian Labor Force Participation Rate | Employment Population Ratio | Unemployment Rate |
|---|---|---|---|---|---|
| 1960 | 117.2 | 69.6 | 59.4 | 57.7 | 5.4 |
| 1961 | 118.8 | 70.5 | 59.3 | 57.0 | 6.5 |
| 1962 | 120.1 | 70.6 | 58.8 | 57.2 | 5.4 |
| 1963 | 122.4 | 71.8 | 58.7 | 57.0 | 5.5 |
| 1964 | 124.5 | 73.0 | 58.6 | 57.3 | 5.0 |
| 1965 | 126.5 | 74.5 | 58.9 | 57.7 | 4.4 |
| 1966 | 128.1 | 75.8 | 59.2 | 58.6 | 3.7 |
| 1967 | 130.0 | 77.3 | 59.5 | 59.0 | 3.7 |
| 1968 | 132.0 | 78.7 | 59.6 | 59.2 | 3.5 |
| 1969 | 134.3 | 80.7 | 60.1 | 59.7 | 3.4 |
| 1970 | 137.1 | 82.8 | 60.4 | 58.9 | 4.8 |
| 1971 | 140.2 | 84.4 | 60.2 | 58.0 | 5.8 |
| 1972 | 144.1 | 87.0 | 60.4 | 58.3 | 5.5 |
| 1973 | 147.1 | 89.4 | 60.8 | 59.0 | 4.8 |
| 1974 | 150.1 | 91.9 | 61.2 | 59.0 | 5.5 |
| 1975 | 153.2 | 93.8 | 61.2 | 57.1 | 8.3 |
| 1976 | 156.2 | 96.2 | 61.6 | 57.9 | 7.6 |
| 1977 | 159.0 | 99.0 | 62.3 | 58.9 | 6.9 |
| 1978 | 161.9 | 102.3 | 63.2 | 60.3 | 6.0 |
| 1979 | 164.9 | 105.0 | 63.7 | 60.9 | 5.8 |
| 1980 | 167.7 | 106.9 | 63.8 | 60.1 | 7.0 |
| 1981 | 170.1 | 108.7 | 63.9 | 60.0 | 7.5 |
| 1982 | 172.3 | 110.2 | 64.0 | 58.7 | 9.5 |
| 1983 | 174.2 | 111.6 | 64.0 | 58.8 | 9.5 |
| 1984 | 176.4 | 113.5 | 64.4 | 60.5 | 7.4 |
| 1985 | 178.2 | 115.5 | 64.8 | 61.1 | 7.1 |
| 1986 | 180.6 | 117.8 | 65.3 | 61.6 | 6.9 |
| 1987 | 182.8 | 120.0 | 65.6 | 62.5 | 6.1 |
| 1988 | 184.6 | 121.7 | 65.9 | 63.2 | 5.4 |
| 1989 | 186.4 | 123.9 | 66.5 | 63.9 | 5.2 |
| 1990 | 188.0 | 124.7 | 66.3 | 63.6 | 5.4 |
| 1991 | 189.8 | 125.3 | 66.0 | 62.4 | 6.6 |
| 1992 | 191.6 | 127.3 | 66.4 | 62.2 | 7.3 |

## Section 4 Money Supply, Interest Rates, and Federal Finances

| | Money Supply Data | | | | Interest Rate | Federal Budget Totals (billions of dollars) | | | National Debt | |
|---|---|---|---|---|---|---|---|---|---|---|
| | Money Supply, M1 (billions) | Annual Change in M1 | Money Supply, M2 (billions) | Annual Change in M2 | Corporate Bonds | Fiscal Year Outlays | Fiscal Year Receipts | Surplus or Deficit | Billions of Dollars | As a Percent of GDP |
| 1929 | 26.5 | — | | | 4.73 | 3.1 | 3.9 | 0.7 | 16.9 | 16.4 |
| 1930 | 25.4 | −4.2 | | | 4.56 | 3.3 | 4.1 | 0.8 | 16.1 | 17.8 |
| 1931 | 23.6 | −7.1 | | | 4.58 | 3.6 | 3.1 | −0.5 | 16.8 | 22.2 |
| 1932 | 20.7 | −12.3 | | | 5.01 | 4.7 | 1.9 | −2.7 | 19.5 | 33.6 |
| 1933 | 19.5 | −5.8 | Data not available prior to 1958. | | 4.49 | 4.6 | 2.0 | −2.6 | 22.5 | 40.5 |
| 1934 | 21.5 | 0.3 | | | 4.60 | 6.6 | 3.0 | −3.6 | 27.7 | 42.5 |
| 1935 | 25.6 | 19.1 | | | 3.60 | 6.5 | 3.7 | −2.8 | 28.7 | 39.8 |
| 1936 | 29.1 | 13.7 | | | 3.24 | 8.4 | 4.0 | −4.4 | 38.5 | 46.6 |
| 1937 | 30.3 | 4.1 | | | 3.26 | 7.7 | 5.0 | −2.8 | 41.3 | 45.7 |
| 1938 | 30.1 | −0.7 | | | 3.19 | 6.8 | 5.6 | −1.2 | 42.0 | 49.5 |
| 1939 | 33.6 | 11.6 | | | 3.01 | 9.1 | 6.3 | −3.9 | 45.0 | 49.6 |
| 1940 | 39.0 | 16.1 | | | 2.84 | 9.5 | 6.5 | −2.9 | 48.5 | 48.5 |
| 1941 | 45.4 | 16.4 | | | 2.77 | 13.7 | 8.7 | −4.9 | 55.3 | 44.2 |
| 1942 | 55.2 | 21.6 | | | 2.83 | 35.1 | 14.6 | −20.5 | 77.0 | 48.6 |
| 1943 | 72.3 | 31 | | | 2.73 | 78.6 | 24.0 | −54.6 | 140.8 | 73.2 |
| 1944 | 86.0 | 18.9 | | | 2.72 | 91.3 | 43.7 | −47.6 | 202.6 | 96.0 |
| 1945 | 99.2 | 15.3 | | | 2.62 | 92.7 | 45.2 | −47.6 | 259.1 | 121.6 |
| 1946 | 106.0 | 6.9 | | | 2.53 | 55.2 | 39.3 | −15.9 | 269.9 | 127.4 |
| 1947 | 113.1 | 6.7 | | | 2.61 | 34.5 | 38.5 | 4.0 | 258.4 | 110.3 |
| 1948 | 111.5 | −1.4 | | | 2.82 | 29.8 | 41.6 | 11.8 | 252.4 | 97.0 |
| 1949 | 111.2 | −0.3 | | | 2.66 | 38.8 | 39.4 | 0.6 | 252.8 | 97.5 |
| 1950 | 116.2 | 4.5 | | | 2.62 | 42.6 | 39.4 | −3.1 | 257.4 | 90.0 |
| 1951 | 122.7 | 5.6 | | | 2.86 | 45.5 | 51.6 | 6.1 | 255.3 | 77.0 |
| 1952 | 127.4 | 3.8 | | | 2.96 | 67.7 | 66.2 | −1.5 | 259.2 | 74.1 |
| 1953 | 128.8 | 1.1 | | | 3.20 | 76.1 | 69.6 | −6.5 | 266.1 | 71.9 |
| 1954 | 132.3 | 2.7 | | | 2.90 | 70.9 | 69.7 | −1.2 | 271.3 | 73.1 |
| 1955 | 135.2 | 2.2 | | | 3.06 | 68.4 | 65.5 | −3.0 | 274.4 | 67.9 |
| 1956 | 136.9 | 1.3 | | | 3.36 | 70.6 | 74.6 | 3.9 | 272.8 | 64.0 |
| 1957 | 135.9 | −0.7 | | | 3.89 | 76.6 | 80.0 | 3.4 | 270.6 | 60.3 |
| 1958 | 141.1 | 3.8 | | | 3.79 | 82.4 | 79.6 | −2.8 | 276.4 | 60.8 |
| 1959 | 140.0 | 0.1 | 297.8 | — | 4.38 | 92.1 | 79.2 | −12.8 | 284.8 | 57.6 |

| | Money Supply Data | | | | Interest Rate | Federal Budget Totals (billions of dollars) | | | National Debt | |
|---|---|---|---|---|---|---|---|---|---|---|
| | Money Supply, M1 (billions) | Annual Change in M1 | Money Supply, M2 (billions) | Annual Change in M2 | Corporate Bonds | Fiscal Year Outlays | Fiscal Year Receipts | Surplus or Deficit | Billions of Dollars | As a Percent of GDP |
| 1960 | 140.7 | 0.5 | 312.4 | 4.9 | 4.41 | 92.2 | 92.5 | –0.3 | 286.5 | 55.8 |
| 1961 | 145.2 | 3.2 | 335.5 | 7.4 | 4.35 | 97.7 | 94.4 | –3.3 | 289.2 | 54.4 |
| 1962 | 147.9 | 1.9 | 362.7 | 8.1 | 4.33 | 106.8 | 99.7 | –7.1 | 298.6 | 52.2 |
| 1963 | 153.4 | 3.7 | 393.3 | 8.4 | 4.26 | 111.3 | 106.6 | –4.8 | 306.5 | 50.8 |
| 1964 | 160.4 | 4.6 | 424.8 | 8.0 | 4.40 | 118.5 | 112.6 | –5.9 | 312.5 | 48.2 |
| 1965 | 167.9 | 4.7 | 459.4 | 8.1 | 4.49 | 118.2 | 116.9 | –1.4 | 317.9 | 45.2 |
| 1966 | 172.1 | 2.5 | 480.0 | 4.5 | 5.13 | 134.5 | 130.8 | –3.7 | 320.0 | 41.6 |
| 1967 | 183.3 | 6.5 | 524.4 | 9.2 | 5.51 | 157.5 | 148.8 | –8.6 | 322.3 | 39.6 |
| 1968 | 197.5 | 7.7 | 566.4 | 8.0 | 6.18 | 178.1 | 153.0 | –25.2 | 344.4 | 38.7 |
| 1969 | 204.0 | 3.3 | 589.6 | 4.1 | 7.03 | 183.6 | 186.9 | 3.2 | 351.7 | 36.7 |
| 1970 | 214.5 | 5.1 | 628.1 | 6.5 | 8.04 | 195.6 | 192.8 | –2.8 | 369.0 | 36.5 |
| 1971 | 228.4 | 6.5 | 712.7 | 13.5 | 7.39 | 210.2 | 187.1 | –23.0 | 396.3 | 36.1 |
| 1972 | 249.3 | 9.2 | 805.2 | 13.0 | 7.21 | 230.7 | 207.3 | –23.4 | 425.4 | 35.2 |
| 1973 | 262.9 | 5.5 | 861.0 | 6.9 | 7.44 | 245.7 | 230.8 | –14.9 | 456.4 | 33.8 |
| 1974 | 274.4 | 4.4 | 908.6 | 5.5 | 8.57 | 269.4 | 263.2 | –6.1 | 473.2 | 32.4 |
| 1975 | 287.6 | 4.8 | 1023.3 | 12.6 | 8.83 | 332.3 | 279.1 | –53.2 | 532.1 | 33.6 |
| 1976 | 306.4 | 6.5 | 1163.7 | 13.7 | 8.43 | 371.8 | 298.1 | –73.7 | 619.2 | 35.0 |
| 1977 | 331.3 | 8.1 | 1286.6 | 10.6 | 8.02 | 409.2 | 355.6 | –53.6 | 697.6 | 35.3 |
| 1978 | 358.4 | 8.2 | 1388.7 | 7.9 | 8.73 | 458.7 | 399.7 | –59.0 | 767.0 | 34.3 |
| 1979 | 382.7 | 6.8 | 1496.7 | 7.8 | 9.63 | 503.5 | 463.3 | –40.2 | 819.0 | 32.9 |
| 1980 | 408.8 | 6.8 | 1629.5 | 8.9 | 11.94 | 590.9 | 517.1 | –73.8 | 906.4 | 33.5 |
| 1981 | 436.5 | 6.8 | 1792.9 | 10.0 | 14.17 | 678.2 | 599.3 | –78.9 | 996.5 | 32.9 |
| 1982 | 474.6 | 8.7 | 1951.9 | 8.9 | 13.79 | 745.7 | 617.8 | –127.9 | 1140.9 | 36.2 |
| 1983 | 521.4 | 9.9 | 2186.1 | 12.0 | 12.04 | 808.3 | 600.6 | –207.8 | 1375.8 | 40.4 |
| 1984 | 552.5 | 6.0 | 2374.3 | 8.6 | 12.71 | 851.8 | 666.5 | –185.3 | 1559.6 | 41.3 |
| 1985 | 620.2 | 12.3 | 2569.4 | 8.2 | 11.37 | 946.3 | 734.1 | –212.3 | 1821.0 | 45.1 |
| 1986 | 724.6 | 16.8 | 2811.1 | 9.4 | 9.02 | 990.3 | 769.1 | –221.2 | 2122.7 | 49.7 |
| 1987 | 750.0 | 3.5 | 2910.8 | 3.5 | 9.38 | 1003.8 | 854.1 | –149.7 | 2347.8 | 51.7 |
| 1988 | 786.9 | 4.9 | 3071.1 | 5.5 | 9.71 | 1064.1 | 909.0 | –155.1 | 2599.9 | 53.1 |
| 1989 | 794.1 | 0.9 | 3227.3 | 5.1 | 9.26 | 1144.1 | 990.7 | –153.4 | 2836.3 | 54.0 |
| 1990 | 826.1 | 4.0 | 3339.0 | 3.5 | 9.32 | 1251.7 | 1031.3 | –220.4 | 3210.9 | 58.1 |
| 1991 | 899.3 | 8.9 | 3445.8 | 3.2 | 8.77 | 1323.8 | 1054.3 | –269.5 | 3662.8 | 64.5 |
| 1992 | 1026.6 | 14.2 | 3503.5 | 1.7 | 8.14 | 1381.4 | 1091.2 | –290.2 | 4061.8 | 68.3 |

SECTION 5

## Size of Government as a Share of GDP, 1929–1992

| | Federal, State, and Local Government | | | | |
|---|---|---|---|---|---|
| | Expenditures (percent of GDP) | Revenues (percent of GDP) | Purchase of Goods and Services (percent of GDP) | Non–Defense Purchase of Goods and Services (percent of GDP) | Transfer Payments to Persons (percent of GDP) |
| 1929 | 10.1 | 12.0 | 8.3 | — | 0.9 |
| 1933 | 22.3 | 19.4 | 16.7 | — | 3.8 |
| 1937 | 19.9 | 20.4 | 15.9 | — | 2.7 |
| 1939 | 33.6 | 29.4 | 25.9 | 23.2 | 2.8 |
| 1940 | 35.3 | 34.0 | 27.1 | 22.6 | 2.7 |
| 1941 | 38.6 | 33.5 | 33.5 | 14.8 | 2.1 |
| 1942 | 54.1 | 27.6 | 50.5 | 8.7 | 1.7 |
| 1943 | 53.3 | 28.1 | 50.8 | 5.1 | 1.2 |
| 1944 | 54.3 | 26.9 | 51.1 | 4.8 | 1.4 |
| 1945 | 53.3 | 30.6 | 47.7 | 5.1 | 2.8 |
| 1946 | 27.2 | 30.4 | 16.8 | 7.2 | 6.2 |
| 1947 | 22.7 | 30.2 | 13.7 | 8.6 | 5.6 |
| 1948 | 24.9 | 29.1 | 15.9 | 10.3 | 5.5 |
| 1949 | 31.1 | 29.3 | 20.3 | 13.0 | 6.5 |
| 1950 | 27.5 | 31.1 | 17.4 | 10.8 | 6.2 |
| 1951 | 26.6 | 28.7 | 20.2 | 8.7 | 4.4 |
| 1952 | 30.9 | 29.7 | 24.9 | 9.6 | 4.1 |
| 1953 | 31.6 | 29.5 | 25.7 | 10.5 | 4.1 |
| 1954 | 31.7 | 29.4 | 24.7 | 11.1 | 4.6 |
| 1955 | 29.8 | 28.1 | 20.9 | 10.0 | 4.6 |
| 1956 | 28.4 | 29.8 | 21.5 | 10.5 | 4.3 |
| 1957 | 29.4 | 29.6 | 22.2 | 10.9 | 4.9 |
| 1958 | 28.2 | 25.4 | 21.0 | 10.9 | 5.8 |
| 1959 | 25.8 | 25.5 | 19.1 | 10.2 | 5.5 |
| 1960 | 25.8 | 26.4 | 18.9 | 10.6 | 5.6 |
| 1961 | 26.3 | 25.6 | 19.0 | 9.1 | 6.2 |
| 1962 | 26.8 | 26.3 | 19.7 | 11.2 | 6.0 |
| 1963 | 26.2 | 26.3 | 19.1 | 11.3 | 6.0 |
| 1964 | 25.5 | 25.1 | 18.6 | 11.3 | 5.8 |

| | Federal, State, and Local Government | | | | |
|---|---|---|---|---|---|
| | **Expenditures (percent of GDP)** | **Revenues (percent of GDP)** | **Purchase of Goods and Services (percent of GDP)** | **Non–Defense Purchase of Goods and Services (percent of GDP)** | **Transfer Payments to Persons (percent of GDP)** |
| 1965 | 24.7 | 24.8 | 18.1 | 11.4 | 5.8 |
| 1966 | 26.6 | 26.5 | 19.5 | 11.9 | 5.9 |
| 1967 | 27.7 | 26.1 | 20.3 | 12.0 | 6.7 |
| 1968 | 28.5 | 27.8 | 20.6 | 12.4 | 7.1 |
| 1969 | 28.8 | 29.7 | 20.5 | 12.7 | 7.3 |
| 1970 | 29.0 | 28.0 | 19.9 | 12.9 | 8.4 |
| 1971 | 28.8 | 27.2 | 19.3 | 13.2 | 9.1 |
| 1972 | 28.0 | 27.7 | 18.6 | 12.8 | 9.3 |
| 1973 | 28.3 | 28.9 | 18.3 | 13.0 | 9.5 |
| 1974 | 29.5 | 29.2 | 18.9 | 13.7 | 10.4 |
| 1975 | 30.8 | 27.1 | 19.0 | 13.9 | 12.0 |
| 1976 | 30.8 | 27.9 | 18.1 | 13.4 | 11.8 |
| 1977 | 28.5 | 27.7 | 17.4 | 12.9 | 11.3 |
| 1978 | 28.0 | 28.0 | 17.1 | 12.8 | 10.8 |
| 1979 | 28.5 | 29.0 | 17.4 | 12.8 | 10.9 |
| 1980 | 29.5 | 28.3 | 17.6 | 12.8 | 11.9 |
| 1981 | 32.1 | 31.1 | 18.8 | 13.4 | 12.1 |
| 1982 | 32.8 | 29.5 | 19.0 | 13.2 | 13.0 |
| 1983 | 31.8 | 28.4 | 18.1 | 12.3 | 12.9 |
| 1984 | 31.9 | 29.2 | 18.4 | 12.4 | 12.0 |
| 1985 | 33.3 | 30.0 | 19.4 | 13.1 | 12.0 |
| 1986 | 33.1 | 29.9 | 19.4 | 13.3 | 12.1 |
| 1987 | 32.3 | 30.1 | 18.9 | 13.0 | 11.9 |
| 1988 | 31.7 | 29.9 | 18.4 | 12.9 | 11.8 |
| 1989 | 32.5 | 30.9 | 18.8 | 13.3 | 11.9 |
| 1990 | 34.1 | 31.8 | 19.6 | 14.1 | 12.4 |
| 1991 | 34.2 | 30.8 | 19.2 | 13.5 | 13.6 |
| 1992 | — | — | 18.7 | 13.7 | 14.6 |

## SECTION 6

### Basic Economic Data for 58 Countries

| | Real GDP per Capita (1985 dollars) | | | Average Annual Growth Rate of Real GDP | | |
|---|---|---|---|---|---|---|
| | 1960 | 1980 | 1990 | 1960–1973 | 1973–1980 | 1980–1990 |
| **High Income Countries** | | | | | | |
| United States | 9954 | 15203 | 18715 | 2.7 | 1.1 | 2.1 |
| Switzerland | 9283 | 14040 | 16782 | 3.0 | 0.4 | 1.8 |
| Canada | 7663 | 13640 | 16304 | 3.1 | 2.6 | 1.8 |
| Hong Kong | 2302 | 8288 | 13629 | 7.0 | 5.9 | 5.1 |
| Germany | 6053 | 11029 | 13444 | 3.5 | 2.2 | 2.0 |
| Japan | 2723 | 9776 | 13395 | 8.7 | 2.7 | 3.2 |
| Australia | 7170 | 11681 | 13161 | 3.1 | 1.3 | 1.2 |
| Sweden | 6437 | 10829 | 13072 | 3.3 | 1.4 | 1.9 |
| Finland | 4689 | 9829 | 12829 | 4.4 | 2.6 | 2.7 |
| France | 5313 | 11041 | 12814 | 4.6 | 2.1 | 1.5 |
| Denmark | 5853 | 10287 | 12418 | 3.7 | 1.3 | 1.9 |
| Belgium | 5203 | 10484 | 12288 | 4.3 | 2.2 | 1.6 |
| United Kingdom | 6346 | 9692 | 12286 | 2.7 | 1.1 | 2.4 |
| Netherlands | 5544 | 10551 | 12245 | 3.9 | 2.1 | 1.5 |
| Italy | 4369 | 9929 | 12223 | 4.4 | 3.8 | 2.1 |
| Austria | 4519 | 9666 | 12016 | 4.4 | 2.9 | 2.2 |
| Singapore | 2074 | 7031 | 11896 | 6.4 | 6.1 | 5.4 |
| Saudi Arabia | 9909 | 23132 | 9771 | 5.8 | 1.6 | –9.0 |
| Spain | 2679 | 6505 | 8008 | 6.6 | 0.7 | 2.1 |
| **Africa** | | | | | | |
| Botswana | 444 | 1770 | 2645 | 7.3 | 6.9 | 4.1 |
| Cameroon | 740 | 1513 | 1439 | 2.8 | 5.2 | –0.5 |
| Cote d'Ivoire | 1000 | 1770 | 1151 | 3.7 | 1.4 | –4.4 |
| Ethiopia | 264 | 347 | 305 | 1.7 | 0.8 | –1.3 |
| Ghana | 962 | 1001 | 888 | 0.2 | –1.0 | –1.2 |
| Kenya | 637 | 964 | 926 | 3.0 | 0.4 | –0.4 |
| Mauritius | 2092 | 3459 | 5022 | 0.9 | 5.6 | 3.8 |
| Mozambique | 1410 | 1497 | 937 | 2.9 | –6.2 | –4.9 |
| Nigeria | 1132 | 1541 | 1061 | 1.8 | 1.1 | –3.8 |
| S. Africa | 2964 | 4580 | 4105 | 2.9 | 0.9 | –1.1 |
| Tanzania | 273 | 506 | 501 | 3.2 | 3.0 | –0.1 |
| Uganda | 381 | 501 | 449 | 0.9 | –8.1 | 1.5 |
| Zaire | 337 | 358 | 321 | 3.2 | –6.8 | –1.1 |
| **Asia and Pacific** | | | | | | |
| Bangladesh | 602 | 657 | 733 | –1.0 | 3.1 | 1.1 |
| China | 725 | 1257 | 2427 | 2.3 | 3.7 | 6.8 |
| India | 614 | 630 | 830 | 0.2 | 0.0 | 2.8 |
| Indonesia | 957 | 1522 | 1911 | 0.0 | 6.7 | 2.3 |
| Korea (South) | 912 | 3023 | 5891 | 6.7 | 5.2 | 6.9 |
| Malaysia | 1779 | 4402 | 5366 | 3.9 | 6.0 | 2.0 |
| Pakisan | 732 | 1142 | 1627 | 2.6 | 1.6 | 3.6 |
| Philippines | 1174 | 2017 | 2017 | 2.5 | 3.2 | 0.0 |
| Taiwan | 910 | 3576 | 6050 | 7.5 | 6.3 | 5.4 |
| Thailand | 998 | 2161 | 3486 | 3.8 | 4.2 | 4.9 |
| **South/Central America** | | | | | | |
| Argentina | 3386 | 4587 | 3763 | 2.3 | 0.1 | –2.0 |
| Brazil | 1381 | 4441 | 4225 | 7.1 | 4.0 | –0.5 |
| Chile | 3086 | 4201 | 4460 | 1.8 | 1.1 | 0.6 |
| Colombia | 1859 | 3313 | 3696 | 3.0 | 2.8 | 1.1 |
| Dominican Rep. | 1215 | 2251 | 2079 | 3.9 | 1.7 | –0.8 |
| Guatemala | 1674 | 2641 | 2253 | 2.2 | 2.5 | –1.6 |
| Haiti | 912 | 1048 | 819 | –0.6 | 3.1 | –2.5 |

| | Real GDP per Capita (1985 dollars) | | | Average Annual Growth Rate of Real GDP | | |
|---|---|---|---|---|---|---|
| | 1960 | 1980 | 1990 | 1960–1973 | 1973–1980 | 1980–1990 |
| Mexico | 2913 | 5801 | 5149 | 3.4 | 3.7 | –1.2 |
| Peru | 2104 | 3142 | 2338 | 2.9 | 0.4 | –3.0 |
| Venezuela | 3974 | 7101 | 5284 | 2.7 | 3.4 | –3.0 |
| **Middle East/Mediterranean** | | | | | | |
| Egypt | 552 | 1527 | 1738 | 3.5 | 8.4 | 1.3 |
| Greece | 1888 | 5489 | 6003 | 7.3 | 2.1 | 0.9 |
| Iran | 2808 | 3705 | 3742 | 4.3 | –4.0 | 0.1 |
| Israel | 3938 | 8496 | 9478 | 5.6 | 0.8 | 1.1 |
| Syria | 1781 | 5192 | 4177 | 3.5 | 9.2 | –2.2 |
| Turkey | 1664 | 2990 | 3828 | 3.5 | 2.0 | 2.5 |

| | Population (millions) | Annual Growth Rate of Money Supply | Average Annual Inflation Rate | Gross Investment as Share of GDP | Central Government Expenditures as Share of GDP |
|---|---|---|---|---|---|
| | 1990 | 1980–1990 | 1980–1990 | 1990 | 1990 |
| **High Income Countries** | | | | | |
| United States | 250.0 | 8.4 | 3.7 | 16 | 24 |
| Switzerland | 6.7 | 7.3 | 3.7 | 29 | — |
| Canada | 26.5 | 8.6 | 4.4 | 21 | 23 |
| Hong Kong | 5.8 | 19.6 | 7.2 | 28 | 15 |
| Germany | 79.5 | 6.1 | 2.7 | 22 | 29 |
| Japan | 123.5 | 9.0 | 1.5 | 33 | 17 |
| Australia | 17.1 | 12.8 | 7.4 | 21 | 26 |
| Sweden | 8.6 | 9.8 | 7.4 | 21 | 42 |
| Finland | 5.0 | 13.8 | 6.8 | 27 | 31 |
| France | 56.4 | 9.9 | 6.1 | 22 | 43 |
| Denmark | 5.1 | 12.0 | 5.6 | 17 | 41 |
| Belgium | 10.0 | 7.1 | 4.4 | 21 | 49 |
| United Kingdom | 57.4 | 16.5 | 5.8 | 19 | 35 |
| Netherlands | 14.9 | 4.8 | 1.9 | 21 | 53 |
| Italy | 57.7 | 12.0 | 9.9 | 21 | 48 |
| Austria | 7.7 | 7.3 | 3.6 | 25 | 39 |
| Singapore | 3.0 | 13.3 | 1.7 | 39 | 23 |
| Saudi Arabia | 14.9 | 8.4 | –5.2 | 16 | — |
| Spain | 39.0 | 10.4 | 9.2 | 26 | 33 |
| **Africa** | | | | | |
| Botswana | 1.3 | 25.9 | 12.1 | 27 | 42 |
| Cameroon | 11.7 | 7.9 | 5.6 | 17 | 21 |
| Cote d'Ivoire | 11.9 | 4.6 | 2.7 | 10 | — |
| Ethiopia | 51.2 | 12.2 | 2.1 | 13 | — |
| Ghana | 14.9 | 44.8 | 42.7 | 15 | 14 |
| Kenya | 24.2 | 14.9 | 9.2 | 24 | 31 |
| Mauritius | 1.1 | 21.9 | 8.8 | 30 | 24 |
| Mozambique | 15.7 | — | 36.5 | 37 | — |
| Nigeria | 115.5 | 14.1 | 18.2 | 15 | 24 |
| South Africa | 35.9 | 16.6 | 14.4 | 19 | 35 |
| Tanzania | 24.5 | 21.5 | 25.7 | 25 | — |
| Uganda | 16.3 | 88.0[a] | 107.0 | 12 | — |
| Zaire | 37.3 | 69.1 | 60.9 | 11 | 13 |

[a]1980–1986

(Continued on next page)

(Continued from previous page)

| | Population (millions) | Annual Growth Rate of Money Supply | Average Annual Inflation Rate | Gross Investment as Share of GDP | Central Government Expenditures as Share of GDP |
|---|---|---|---|---|---|
| | 1990 | 1980–1990 | 1980–1990 | 1990 | 1990 |
| **Asia and Pacific** | | | | | |
| Bangladesh | 106.7 | 21.6 | 9.6 | 12 | 15 |
| China | 1,133.7 | 25.4 | 5.8 | 39 | — |
| India | 849.5 | 16.7 | 7.9 | 23 | 18 |
| Indonesia | 178.2 | 25.8 | 8.4 | 36 | 20 |
| Korea (South) | 42.8 | 21.0 | 5.1 | 37 | 16 |
| Malaysia | 17.9 | 12.6 | 1.6 | 34 | 31 |
| Pakistan | 112.4 | 13.3 | 6.7 | 19 | 24 |
| Philippines | 61.5 | 16.1 | 14.9 | 22 | 20 |
| Taiwan | 20.0 | 18.8 | 3.1 | | 21 |
| Thailand | 55.8 | 18.8 | 3.3 | 37 | 15 |
| **South/Central American** | | | | | |
| Argentina | 32.3 | 368.5 | 395.1 | 9 | 16 |
| Brazil | 150.4 | 178.3[b] | 284.4 | 22 | 36 |
| Chile | 13.2 | 30.3 | 20.5 | 20 | 33 |
| Colombia | 32.3 | 22.0[c] | 24.8 | 19 | 15 |
| Dominican Rep. | 7.1 | 26.9 | 21.8 | 15 | 15 |
| Guatemala | 9.2 | 15.7 | 14.6 | 12 | 12 |
| Haiti | 6.5 | 8.6 | 7.2 | 11 | — |
| Mexico | 86.2 | 62.4 | 70.4 | 20 | 18 |
| Peru | 21.7 | 157.0 | 233.7 | 23 | 10 |
| Venezuela | 17.7 | 17.8 | 19.3 | 9 | 23 |
| **Middle East/Mediterranean** | | | | | |
| Egypt | 52.1 | 21.9 | 11.9 | 23 | 40 |
| Greece | 10.1 | 27.5 | 18.0 | 19 | 38[d] |
| Iran | 55.8 | 16.7 | 13.8 | 21 | 17 |
| Israel | 4.7 | 101.8 | 101.4 | 18 | 51 |
| Syria | 12.4 | 19.4 | 14.7 | 14 | 28 |
| Turkey | 56.1 | 51.9 | 43.2 | 23 | 25 |

[b] 1980–1985
[c] 1980–1988
[d] 1989

**Sources:** The data for the United States are from the following tables of the *Economic Report of the President, 1993:*

Section 1: Tables B–1 and B–111.

Section 2: Tables B–2, B–3, B–5, and B–56.

Section 3: Tables B–29 and B–30.

Section 4: Tables B–65, B–69, B–74, and B–82.

Section 5: Tables B–1, B–23, B–77 and B–78.

In many cases, data for years prior to 1959 are from earlier issues of the *Economic Report of the President.*

The data for various countries presented in Section 6 are from Robert Summers and Alan Heston, "The Penn World Tables (Mark 5): An Expanded Set of International Comparisons, 1950–1988," *Quarterly Journal of Economics,* May 1991 (GDP and growth rate data), and the World Bank, *World Tables, 1992* and *World Development Report, 1992.* The GDP estimates of Summers and Heston were derived by the purchasing power parity method. The 1989 and 1990 data from *The World Tables, 1992* were used to update the 1988 data from Summers and Heston.

# GLOSSARY

**accounting profits** The sales revenues minus the expenses of a firm over a designated time period, usually one year. Accounting profits typically make allowances for changes in the firm's inventories and depreciation of its assets. No allowance is made, however, for the opportunity cost of the equity capital of the firm's owners, or other implicit costs.

**activist strategy** The view that deliberate changes in monetary and fiscal policy can be used to inject demand stimulus during a recession and apply restraint during an inflationary boom, thereby minimizing economic instability.

**adaptive expectations hypothesis** The hypothesis that economic decision-makers base their expectations of the future on actual outcomes observed during recent periods. For example, according to this view, the rate of inflation actually experienced during the last two or three years would be the major determinant of the rate of inflation expected for next year.

**aggregate demand curve** A downward-sloping curve indicating an inverse relationship between the price level and the quantity of goods and services that households, business firms, governments, and foreigners (net exports) are willing to purchase during a period.

**aggregate supply curve** A curve indicating the relationship between the nation's price level and quantity of goods supplied by its producers. In the short run, it is probably an upward-sloping curve, but in the long run most economists believe the aggregate supply curve is vertical (or nearly so).

**anticipated change** A change that is foreseen by decision-makers in time for them to adjust.

**anticipated inflation** An increase in the general level of prices that is expected by economic decision-makers based on their evaluation of past experience and current conditions.

**appreciation** An increase in the value of a domestic currency relative to foreign currencies. An appreciation increases the purchasing power of the domestic currency over foreign goods.

**automatic stabilizers** Built-in features that tend automatically to promote a budget deficit during a recession and a budget surplus during an inflationary boom, even without a change in policy.

**automation** A production technique that reduces the amount of labor required to produce a good or service. It is beneficial to adopt the new labor-saving technology only if it reduces the cost of production.

**average fixed cost** Fixed cost divided by the number of units produced. It always declines as output increases.

**average total cost** Total cost divided by the number of units produced. It is sometimes called per unit cost.

**average variable cost** The total variable cost divided by the number of units produced.

**balance of merchandise trade** The difference between the value of merchandise exports and the value of merchandise imports for a nation. The balance of trade is only one component of a nation's total balance of payments.

**balance of payments** A summary of all economic transactions between a country and all other countries for a specific time period usually a year. The balance-of-payments account reflects all payments and liabilities to foreigners (debits) and all payments and obligations (credits) received from foreigners.

**balance on current account** The import-export balance of goods and services plus net investment income and net unilateral transfers. If the figure is positive (negative), a current account surplus (deficit) is present.

**balance on goods and services** The exports of goods (merchandise) and services of a nation minus its imports of goods and services.

**balanced budget** A situation in which current government revenue from taxes, fees, and other sources is just equal to current expenditures.

**bank reserves** Vault cash plus deposits of the bank with Federal Reserve Banks.

**budget deficit** A situation in which total government spending exceeds total government revenue during a specific time period, usually one year.

**budget surplus** A situation in which total government spending is less than total government revenue during a time period, usually a year.

**business cycle** Fluctuations in the general level of economic activity as measured by such variables as the rate of unemployment and changes in real GDP.

**capital formation** The production of buildings, machinery, tools, and other equipment that will enhance the ability of future economic participants to produce. The term can also be applied to efforts to upgrade the knowledge and skill of workers and thereby increase their ability to produce in the future.

**capital** Man-made resources that enhance our ability to produce output in the future.

**capital assets** Long-lasting assets like buildings, machinery, and durable resources that are used to produce goods and services.

**cartel** An organization of sellers designed to coordinate supply decisions so that the joint profits of the members will be maximized. A cartel will seek to create a monopoly in the market.

**choice** The act of selecting among alternatives.

**collective decision-making** The method of organization that relies on public-sector decision-making (voting, political bargaining, lobbying, and so on). It can be used to resolve basic economic problems.

**collusion** Agreement among firms to avoid various competitive practices, particularly price reductions. It may involve either formal agreements or merely tacit recognition that competitive practices will be self-defeating in the long run. Tacit collusion is difficult to detect. In the United States, antitrust laws prohibit collusion and conspiracies to restrain trade.

**comparative advantage** The ability to produce a good at a lower opportunity cost than others can produce it. Relative costs determine comparative advantage. A nation will have a comparative advantage in the production of a good when its production costs for the good are low relative to its production costs for other goods.

**compensating wage differentials** Wage differences that compensate workers for risk, unpleasant working conditions, and other undesirable nonpecuniary aspects of a job.

**competition as a dynamic process** A term that denotes rivalry or competitiveness between or among parties (for example, producers or input suppliers), each of which seeks to deliver a better deal to buyers when quality, price, and product information are all considered. Competing implies a lack of collusion among sellers.

**competitive price-searcher market** A market where the firms have a downward-sloping demand curve and it is relatively easy for them to enter into and exit from the market.

**complements** Products that are usually consumed jointly (for example, lamps and light bulbs). An increase in the price of one will cause the demand for the other to fall.

**constant returns to scale** Unit costs are constant as the scale of the firm is altered. Neither economies nor diseconomies of scale are present.

**consumer price index (CPI)** An indicator of the general level of prices. It attempts to compare the cost of purchasing the market basket bought by a typical consumer during a specific period with the cost of purchasing the same market basket during an earlier period.

**consumer surplus** The difference between the maximum amount a consumer would be willing to pay for a unit of a good and the payment that is actually made.

**consumption** Household spending on consumer goods and services during the current period. Consumption is a flow concept.

**contestable market** A market in which the costs of entry and exit are low, so a firm risks little by entering. Efficient production and zero economic profits should prevail in a contestable market. A market can be contestable even if capital requirements are high.

**corporation** A business firm owned by shareholders who possess ownership rights to the firm's profits, but whose liability is limited to the amount of their investment in the firm.

**countercyclical policy** A policy that tends to move the economy in an opposite direction from the forces of the business cycle. Such a policy would stimulate demand during the contraction phase of the business cycle and restrain demand during the expansionary phase.

**crowding-out effect** A reduction in private spending as a result of higher interest rates generated by budget deficits that are financed by borrowing in the private loanable funds market.

**current account** The record of all transactions with foreign nations that involve the exchange of merchandise goods and services or unilateral gifts.

**cyclical unemployment** Unemployment due to recessionary business conditions and inadequate aggregate demand for labor.

**demand deposits** Non-interest-earning deposits from a bank that either can be withdrawn or made payable on demand to a third party via check. In essence, they are "checkbook money" because they permit transactions to be paid for by check rather than by currency.

**demand for money** At any given interest rate, the amount of wealth that people desire to hold in the form of money balances; that is, cash and checking account deposits. The quantity demanded is inversely related to the interest rate.

**depreciation** A reduction in the value of a domestic currency relative to foreign currencies. A depreciation reduces the purchasing power of the domestic currency over foreign goods.

**depression** A prolonged and very severe recession.

**differentiated products** Products distinguished from similar products by such characteristics as quality, design, location, and method of promotion.

**discounting** The procedure used to calculate the present value of future income. The present value of future income is inversely related to both the interest rate and the amount of time that passes before the funds are received.

**discount rate** The interest rate the Federal Reserve charges banking institutions for borrowing funds.

**economic profit** The difference between the firm's total revenues and total costs.

**economic theory** A set of definitions, postulates, and principles assembled in a manner that makes clear the "cause-and-effect" relationships of economic data.

**economies of scale** Reductions in the firm's per unit costs that are associated with the use of large plants to produce a large volume of output.

**economizing behavior** Decisions that are based on the objective of gaining a specific benefit at the least possible cost. A corollary of economizing behavior implies that when choosing among items of equal cost, individuals will choose the option that yields the greatest benefit.

**employment discrimination** Unequal treatment of persons on the basis of their race, gender, or religion, which restricts their employment and earnings opportunities compared to others of similar productivity. Employment discrimination may stem from the prejudices of employers, consumers, or fellow employees.

**entrepreneur** A profit-seeking decision-maker who decides which projects to undertake and how they should be undertaken. A successful entrepreneur's actions will increase the value of resources.

**equilibrium** A state of balance between the conflicting market forces of supply and demand; a balance of forces permitting the simultaneous fulfillment of plans by buyers and sellers.

**Eurodollar deposits** Deposits denominated in U.S. dollars at banks and other financial institutions outside the United States. Although this name originated because of the large amounts of such deposits held at banks in Western Europe, similar deposits in other parts of the world are also called Eurodollars.

**excess reserves** Actual reserves that exceed the legal requirement.

**excess supply of money** Situation in which the actual money balances of individuals and business firms are in excess of their desired level. Thus, decision-makers will increase their spending on other assets and goods until they reduce their actual balances to the desired level.

**exchange rate** The domestic price of one unit of foreign currency. For example, if it takes $1.50 to purchase one English pound, the dollar-pound exchange rate is 1.50.

**exchange rate conversion method** Method that uses the foreign exchange rate value of a nation's currency to convert that nation's GDP to another monetary unit, such as the U.S. dollar.

**expansionary fiscal policy** An increase in government expenditures and/or a reduction in tax rates such that the expected size of the budget deficit expands.

**expansionary monetary policy** An acceleration in the growth rate of the money supply.

**explicit costs** Money paid by a firm to purchase the services of productive resources.

**exports** Goods and services produced domestically but sold to foreigners.

**external costs** Costs imposed on nonconsenting secondary parties whose property rights are violated by the actions of another.

**external debt** The portion of the national debt owed to foreign investors.

**Federal Reserve System** The central bank of the United States; it carries out banking regulatory policies and is responsible for the conduct of monetary policy.

**final goods and services** Goods and services purchased by their ultimate users.

**fiscal policy** The use of government taxation and expenditure policies for the purpose of achieving macroeconomic goals.

**fixed costs** Costs that do not vary with output. However, fixed costs will be incurred as long as a firm continues in business and the assets have alternative uses.

**flexible exchange rates** Exchange rates that are determined by the market forces of supply and demand. They are sometimes called floating exchange rates.

**foreign exchange market** The market in which the currencies of different countries are bought and sold.

**fractional reserve banking** A system that enables banks to keep less than 100 percent reserves against their deposits. Required reserves are a fraction of deposits.

**full employment** The level of employment that results from the efficient use of the civilian labor force after allowance is made for the normal (natural) rate of unemployment due to information cost, dynamic changes, and the structural conditions of the economy. For the United States, full employment is thought to exist when between 94 and 95 percent of the labor force is employed.

**GDP deflator** The price index that measures changes in the cost of all goods included in GDP.

**going out of business** The sale of a firm's assets and its permanent exit from the market. By going out of business, a firm is able to avoid fixed cost, which would continue during a shutdown.

**good** Anything that people find desirable and therefore would like to have or consume.

**government purchases** Current expenditures on goods and services provided by federal, state, and local governments; they exclude transfer payments.

**gross domestic product (GDP)** The total market value of all final goods and services produced domestically during a specific period, usually a year.

**human resources** The abilities, skills, and health of human beings that can contribute to the production of both current and future output. Investment in training and education can increase the supply of human resources.

**implicit costs** The opportunity costs associated with a firm's use of resources that it owns. These costs do not involve a direct money payment. Examples include wage income and interest forgone by the owner of a firm who also provides labor services and equity capital to the firm.

**import quota** A specific quantity (or value) of a good permitted to be imported into a country during a given year.

**imports** Goods and services produced by foreigners but purchased by domestic consumers, investors, and governments.

**income mobility** Movement of individuals and families either up or down income distribution rankings when comparisons are made at two different points in time. When substantial income mobility is present, one's current position will not be a very good indicator as to what one's position will be a few years in the future.

**index of leading indicators** An index of economic variables that historically has tended to turn down prior to the beginning of a recession and turn up prior to the beginning of a business expansion.

**indirect business taxes** Taxes that increase the business firm's costs of production and therefore the prices charged to consumers . Examples would include sales, excise, and property taxes.

**inflation** A general increase in the level of prices and therefore a decline in the purchasing power of the money.

**inflationary premium** A component of the money interest rate that reflects compensation to the lender for the expected decrease, due to inflation, in the purchasing power of the principal and interest during the course of the loan. It is determined by the expected rate of future inflation.

**innovation** The successful introduction and adoption of a new product or process; the economic application of inventions and marketing techniques.

**interest-earning checkable deposits** Deposits that earn interest and are also available for checking.

**intermediate goods** Goods purchased for resale or for use in producing another good or service.

**invention** The discovery of a new product or process, often facilitated by the knowledge of engineering and scientific relationships.

**investment** The flow of expenditures on durable assets (fixed investment) plus the addition to inventories (inventory investment) during a period. These expenditures enhance our ability to provide consumer benefits in the future.

**investment in human capital** Expenditures on training, education, and skill development designed to increase the productivity of an individual.

**invisible hand principle** The tendency of market prices to direct individuals pursuing their own interests into productive activities that also promote the economic well-being of the society.

**labor force** The portion of the population 16 years of age and over who are either employed or unemployed.

**Laffer curve** A curve illustrating the relationship between tax rates and tax revenues. It suggests that tax revenues are low for both very high and very low tax rates.

**law of comparative advantage** A principle that states that individuals, firms, regions, or nations can gain by specializing in the production of goods that they produce cheaply (that is, at a low opportunity cost) and exchanging those goods for other desired goods for which they are high opportunity-cost producers.

**law of demand** The principle that there is an inverse relationship between the price of a good and the amount of it buyers are willing to purchase.

**law of diminishing marginal utility** The principle that as the rate of consumption increases, the utility derived from consumption of additional units of a good will decline.

**law of diminishing marginal utility** The principle that as the rate of consumption increases, the utility derived from consumption of additional units of a good will decline.

**law of diminishing returns** The postulate that as more and more units of a variable resource are combined with a fixed amount of other resources, employment of additional units of the variable resource will eventually increase output only at a decreasing rate. Once diminishing returns are reached, it will take successively larger amounts of the variable factor to expand output by one unit.

**law of supply** The principle that there is a direct relationship between the price of a good and the amount of it offered for sale.

**long run** A time period of sufficient length to enable decision-makers to adjust fully to a market change. For example, in the long run, producers will have time to alter their utilization of all productive factors, including the heavy equipment and physical structure of their plants.

**loss** Deficit of sales revenue relative to the cost of production, considering the opportunity costs of resources used. Losses are a penalty imposed on those who use resources in lower rather than higher valued uses as judged by buyers in the market.

**marginal** Term used to describe the effects of a change, given the current situation. For example, the marginal cost is the cost of producing an additional unit of a product, given the producer's current facility and production rate.

**marginal cost** The change in total cost required to produce an additional unit of output.

**marginal product** The change in total output that results from the employment of one additional unit of a factor of production, one workday of skilled labor, for example.

**marginal revenue** The incremental change in total revenue derived from the sale of one additional unit of a product.

**marginal tax rate** The amount of one's additional (marginal) earnings that must be paid explicitly in taxes or implicitly in the form of a reduction in the level of one's income supplement. Since it establishes the fraction of an additional dollar earned that an individual is permitted to keep, it is an important determinant of the incentive to work.

**market** An abstract concept that encompasses the trading arrangements of buyers and sellers that underlie the forces of supply and demand.

**market mechanism** A method of organization that allows unregulated prices and the decentralized decisions of private property owners to resolve the basic economic problems of consumption, production, and distribution.

**market power** The ability of a firm that is not a pure monopolist to earn unusually large profits, indicating that it has some monopoly power. Because the firm has a few (or weak) competitors, it has a degree of freedom from the discipline of vigorous competition.

**means-tested income transfers** Transfers that are limited to persons or families with an income below a certain cutoff point. Eligibility is thus dependent on low-income status.

**medium of exchange** An asset that allows the buying and selling of goods and services.

**minimum-wage legislation** Legislation requiring that all workers in specified industries be paid at least the stated minimum hourly rate of pay.

**monetary policy** The deliberate control of the money supply, and in some cases credit conditions, for the purpose of achieving macroeconomic goals.

**money rate of interest** The rate of interest in monetary terms that borrowers pay for borrowed funds. During periods when borrowers and lenders expect inflation, the money rate of interest exceeds the real rate of interest.

**money supply** Defined two ways: M1 is the sum of (1) currency in circulation (including coins), (2) demand deposits, (3) other (interest-earning) checkable deposits of depository institutions, and (4) traveler's checks. M2 is the combined amount of M1 plus (1) savings and time deposits (accounts of less than $100,000) of all depository institutions, (2) money market mutual fund shares, (3) money market deposit accounts, (4) overnight loans from customers to commercial banks, and (5) overnight Eurodollar deposits held by U.S. residents.

**monopoly** A market structure characterized by (1) a single seller of a well-defined product for which there are no good substitutes and (2) high barriers to the entry of any other firms into the market for that product.

**national debt** The sum of the indebtedness of the federal government in the form of outstanding interest-earning bonds. It reflects the cumulative impact of budget deficits and surpluses.

**natural monopoly** A market situation in which the average costs of production continually decline with increased output. Therefore, average costs of production will be lowest when a single large firm produces the entire output demanded.

**natural rate of unemployment** The long-run average unemployment rate due to frictional and structural conditions of labor markets. This rate is affected both by dynamic change and by public policy. It is sustainable in the future.

**net exports** Exports minus imports.

**net federal debt** The portion of the national debt owed to domestic and foreign investors. It does not include bonds held by agencies of the federal government or the Federal Reserve.

**new classical economists** Modern economists who believe there are strong forces pushing a market economy toward full-employment equilibrium and that macroeconomic policy is an ineffective tool with which to reduce economic instability.

**nominal values** Values expressed in current dollars. Also called money values.

**nonactivist strategy** The view that the economy would be more stable if macroeconomic policymakers followed stable monetary and fiscal policies rather than modifying these policies in response to changing economic indicators.

**nonhuman resources** The durable, nonhuman inputs that can be used to produce both current and future output. Machines, buildings, land, and raw materials are examples. Investment can increase the supply of nonhuman resources. Economists often use the term physical capital when referring to nonhuman resources.

**nonpecuniary job characteristics** Working conditions, prestige, variety, location, employee freedom and responsibilities, and other nonwage characteristics of a job that influence how employees evaluate the job.

**oligopoly** A market situation in which a small number of sellers comprise the entire industry. It is competition among the few.

**open market operations** The buying and selling of U.S. government securities (national debt) by the Federal Reserve.

**opportunity cost** The highest valued benefit that must be sacrificed (forgone) as the result of choosing an alternative.

**partnership** A business firm owned by two or more individuals who possess ownership rights to the firm's profits and are personally liable for the debts of the firm.

**Phillips curve** A curve that illustrates the relationship between the rate of change in prices (or money wages) and the rate of unemployment.

**positive rate of time preference** The desire of consumers for goods now rather than in the future.

**poverty threshold income level** The level of money income below which a family is considered to be poor. It differs according to family characteristics (for example, number of family members) and is adjusted when consumer prices change.

**present value** The current worth of future income after it is discounted to reflect the fact that revenues in the future are valued less highly than revenues now.

**price ceiling** A legally established maximum price that sellers may charge.

**price discrimination** A practice whereby a seller charges different consumers different prices for the same product or service.

**price elasticity of demand** The percent change in the quantity of a product demanded divided by the percent change in the price causing the change in quantity. Price elasticity of demand indicates the degree of consumer response to variation in price.

**price elasticity of supply** The percent change in quantity supplied, divided by the percent change in price that causes that change in quantity supplied.

**price equalization principle** The tendency for markets, when trade restrictions are absent, to establish a uniform price for each good throughout the world (except for price differences due to transport costs and differential tax treatment of the good).

**price floor** A legally established minimum price that buyers must pay for a good or resource.

**price index** Measures the cost of purchasing a given bundle of goods at a point in time relative to the cost of the same goods during a prior base year, which is assigned a value of 100.

**price searcher** A firm that faces a downward-sloping demand curve for its product. The amount that the firm is able to sell is inversely related to the price that it charges.

**price takers** Sellers who must take the market price in order to sell their product. Because each price taker's output is small relative to the total market, price takers can sell all of their output at the market price, but are unable to sell any of their output at a price higher than the market price. Thus, they face a horizontal demand curve.

**principal-agent problem** The incentive problem arising when the purchaser of services (the principal) lacks full information about the circumstances faced by the seller (the agent) and thus cannot know how well the agent performs the purchased services. The agent may to some extent work toward objectives other than those sought by the principal paying for the service.

**private property rights** Property rights that are exclusively held by an owner, and that can be transferred to others at the owner's discretion.

**producer surplus** The difference between the price producers receive for a good and the amount that would be necessary to induce producers (including resource owners) to supply each unit of the good.

**production possibilities curve** The maximum amount of two products that can be produced from a fixed set of resources, given the current technology and legal institutions.

**progressive income tax** A tax that requires those with higher taxable incomes to pay a larger percentage of their incomes to the government than those with lower taxable incomes. Under this type of system the marginal tax rate of taxpayers will increase as their income rises.

**proprietorship** A business firm owned by an individual who possesses the ownership right to the firm's profits and is personally liable for the firm's debts.

**public-choice analysis** The study of decision-making as it affects the formation and operation of collective organizations, such as governments. This discipline bridges the gap between economics and political science. In effect, it applies the principles and methodology of economics to political science topics.

**public goods** Jointly consumed goods. When consumed by one person, they are also made available to others. National defense, poetry, and scientific theories are all public goods.

**purchasing power parity method** Method for determining the relative purchasing power of different currencies by comparing the amount of each currency required to purchase a typical bundle of goods and services in domestic markets. This information is then used to convert the GDP of each nation to a common monetary unit.

**required reserve ratio** A percentage of a specified liability category (for example, transaction accounts) that banking institutions are required to hold as reserves against that type of liability.

**required reserves** The minimum amount of reserves that a bank is required by law to keep on hand to back up its deposits. Thus, if reserve requirements were 15 percent, banks would be required to keep $150,000 in reserves against each $1 million of deposits.

**rate of labor force participation** The number of persons 16 years of age or over who are either employed or actively seeking employment as a percentage of the total noninstitutional population 16 years of age and over.

**rate of unemployment** The percent of persons in the civilian labor force who are not employed. Mathematically, it is equal to (number of persons unemployed/number in civilian labor force) ×100.

**rate-of-return equalization principle** The tendency for capital investment in each market to move toward a uniform, or normal, rate of return. An abnormally high return in a market will attract additional investment, which will drive returns down. Conversely, an abnormally low return will result in investment flight from the market, which will eventually lead to the restoration of normal returns.

**rational expectations hypothesis** The hypothesis that economic decision-makers base their expectations of the future on all available evidence, including information concerning the probable effects of current and future economic policy, not just on observed actual outcomes in recent periods.

**rational ignorance effect** Voter ignorance that is present because people perceive their individual votes as unlikely to be decisive. Voters rationally have little incentive to inform themselves so as to cast an informed vote.

**real rate of interest** The money rate of interest minus the expected rate of inflation. The real rate of interest indicates the interest premium, in terms of real goods and services, that one must pay for earlier availability.

**real values** Values that have been adjusted for the effects of inflation.

**recession** A downturn in economic activity characterized by declining real GDP and rising unemployment. In an effort to be more precise, many economists define a recession as two consecutive quarters in which there is a decline in real GDP.

**rent-seeking** Actions by individuals and interest groups designed to restructure public policy in a manner that will either directly or indirectly redistribute more income to themselves.

**residual claimant** Individual who personally receives the excess, if any, of revenues over costs. Residual claimants gain if the firm's costs are reduced and if revenues are increased.

**resource** An input used to produce economic goods. land, labor, skills, natural resources, and capital are examples.

**resource market** A highly aggregate market encompassing all resources (labor, physical capital, land, and entrepreneurship) that contribute to the production of current output. The labor market forms the largest component of this market. Resource markets are also sometimes called factor markets.

**restrictive fiscal policy** A reduction in government expenditures and/or an increase in tax rates such that the expected size of the budget deficit declines (or the budget surplus increases).

**restrictive monetary policy** A deceleration in the growth rate of the money supply.

**saving** Current income that is not spent on consumption goods.

**scarcity** Fundamental concept of economics which indicates that less of a good is freely available than consumers would like.

**secondary effects** Economic consequences of an initial economic change, even though they are not immediately identifiable. Secondary effects will be felt only with the passage of time.

**shirking** Working at less than a normal rate of productivity, thus reducing output. Shirking is more likely when workers are not monitored and the cost of their lower output falls on others.

**short run (in production)** A time period so short that a firm is unable to vary some of its factors of production. The firm's plant size typically cannot be altered in the short run.

**short run** A time period of insufficient length to permit decision-makers to adjust fully to a change in market conditions. For example, in the short run, producers will have time to increase output by using more labor and raw materials, but they will not have time to expand the size of their plants or to install additional heavy equipment.

**shortage** A condition in which the amount of a good offered by sellers is less than the amount demanded by buyers at the existing price. An increase in price will eliminate the shortage.

**shortsightedness effect** Misallocation of resources that results because public-sector action is biased (1) in favor of proposals yielding clearly defined current benefits in exchange for difficult-to-identify future costs and in (2) against proposals with clearly identifiable current costs yielding less concrete and less obvious future benefits.

**shutdown** A temporary halt in the operation of a business. The firm does not sell its assets. Its variable cost will be eliminated , but fixed costs will continue. The shutdown firm anticipates a return to operation in the future.

**socialism** A system of economic organization in which (a) the ownership and control of the basic means of production rest with the state and (b) resource allocation is determined by centralized planning rather than by market forces.

**special drawing rights** Supplementary reserves, in the form of accounting entries, established by the International Monetary Fund (also called paper gold). Like gold and foreign currency reserves, they can be used to make payments on international accounts.

**substitutes** Products that are related such that an increase in the price of one will cause an increase in demand for the other (for example, butter and margarine, or Chevrolets and Fords).

**sunk costs** Costs that have already been incurred as a result of past decisions. They are sometimes referred to as historical costs.

**supply of money** The amount of cash and checking account deposits present. It is determined by the policies of the central monetary authority, the Fed in the case of the United States. For some purposes, the quantity of various savings accounts that can easily be converted to cash or checking deposits may also be included in the supply of money.

**supply-side economists** Modern economists who believe that changes in marginal tax rates exert important effects on aggregate supply.

**surplus** A condition in which the amount of a good that sellers are willing to offer is greater than the amount that buyers will purchase at the existing price. A sufficient decline in price will eliminate the surplus.

**tariff** A tax levied on goods imported into a country.

**tax base** The level of the activity that is taxed. For example, if an excise tax is levied on each gallon of gasoline, the tax base is the number of gallons of gasoline sold. Since higher tax rates generally make the taxed activity less attractive, the size of the tax base is inversely related to the rate at which the activity is taxed.

**team production** Employees hired by a firm to work together under the supervision of the owner or the owner's representative.

**technology** The body of skills and technological knowledge available at any given time. The level of technology establishes the relationship between inputs and the maximum output they can generate.

**total cost** The costs, both explicit and implicit, of all the resources used by the firm. Total cost includes an imputed normal rate of return for the firm's equity capital.

**transaction costs** The time, effort, and other resources needed to search out, negotiate, and consummate an exchange.

**transfer payments** Payments to individuals or institutions that are not linked to the current supply of a good or service by the recipient.

**unanticipated change** A change that decision-makers could not reasonably foresee. Thus, choices made prior to the event did not take the event into account.

**unanticipated inflation** An increase in the general level of prices that was not expected by most decision-makers.

**unemployed** The term used to describe a person, not currently employed, who is either (1) actively seeking employment or (2) waiting to begin or return to a job.

**utility** The benefit or satisfaction expected from a choice or course of action.

**variable costs** Costs that vary with the rate of output. Examples include wages paid to workers and payments for raw materials

**velocity of money** The average number of times a dollar is used to purchase final goods and services during a year. It is equal to GDP divided by the stock of money.

# INDEX

## N

## R



## S



## T